PENGUIN BOOKS

Interpreting Dreams

Sigmund Freud was born in 1856 in Moravia; between the ages of four and eighty-two his home was in Vienna: in 1938 Hitler's invasion of Austria forced him to seek asylum in London, where he died in the following year. His career began with several years of brilliant work on the anatomy and physiology of the nervous system. He was almost thirty when, after a period of study under Charcot in Paris, his interests first turned to psychology; and after ten years of clinical work in Vienna (at first in collaboration with Breuer, an older colleague) he invented what was to become psychoanalysis. This began simply as a method of treating neurotic patients through talking, but it quickly grew into an accumulation of knoweldge about the workings of the mind in general. Freud was thus able to demonstrate the development of the sexual instinct in childhood and, largely on the basis of an examination of dreams, arrived at his fundamental discovery of the unconscious forces that influence our everyday thoughts and actions. Freud's life was uneventful, but his ideas have shaped not only many specialist disciplines, but also the whole intellectual climate of the twentieth century.

J. A. Underwood was born in London in 1940 and educated at Trinity Hall, Cambridge. He has worked as a freelance translator (from French as well as German) since 1969, translating texts by a wide variety of modern authors including Elias Canetti, Jean-Paul Sartre, Julien Green, and Alain Robbe-Grillet. But it is for his Kafka translations that he is best known; his new translation of *The Castle* (also available in Penguin Books) was joint winner of the 1998 Schlegel-Tieck prize for translation from the German.

John Forrester is Professor of History and Philosophy of the Sciences at the University of Cambridge. He is the author of *Language and the Origins of Psychoanalysis* (1980), *The Seductions of Psychoanalysis* (1990), (with Lisa Appignanesi) *Freud's Women* (1992, 3rd edition

2005), *Dispatches from the Freud Wars* (1997) and *Truth Games* (1997). With Laura Cameron he is completing *Freud in Cambridge*, to be published by C.U.P. in 2007.

SIGMUND FREUD

Interpreting Dreams

Translated by J. A. Underwood
with an Introduction by John Forrester

PENGUIN BOOKS

PENGUIN BOOKS

Published by the Penguin Group
Penguin Books Ltd, 80 Strand, London WC2R 0RL, England
Penguin Group (USA) Inc., 375 Hudson Street, New York, New York 10014, USA
Penguin Group (Canada), 90 Eglinton Avenue East, Suite 700, Toronto, Ontario, Canada M4P 2Y3
(a division of Pearson Penguin Canada Inc.)
Penguin Ireland, 25 St Stephen's Green, Dublin 2, Ireland
(a division of Penguin Books Ltd)
Penguin Group (Australia), 250 Camberwell Road,
Camberwell, Victoria 3124, Australia (a division of Pearson Australia Group Pty Ltd)
Penguin Books India Pvt Ltd, 11 Community Centre,
Panchsheel Park, New Delhi – 110 017, India
Penguin Group (NZ), cnr Airborne and Rosedale Roads, Albany,
Auckland 1310, New Zealand (a division of Pearson New Zealand Ltd)
Penguin Books (South Africa) (Pty) Ltd, 24 Sturdee Avenue,
Rosebank, Johannesburg 2196, South Africa

Penguin Books Ltd, Registered Offices: 80 Strand, London WC2R 0RL, England

www.penguin.com

Die Traumdeutung first published in 1899 (Leipzig and Vienna)
This translation first published in Penguin Classics 2006

015

Sigmund Freud's German texts collected in *Gesammelte Werke* (1940–52)
copyright © Imago Publishing Co., Ltd, London, 1941, 1948, 1950
Translation and editorial matter copyright © J. A. Underwood, 2006
Introduction copyright © John Forrester, 2006
All rights reserved

The moral right of the translator and of the author of the Introduction has been asserted

Set in 10/12.5 pt PostScript Adobe New Caledonia
Typeset by Rowland Phototypesetting Ltd, Bury St Edmunds, Suffolk
Printed and bound in Great Britain by Clays Ltd, Elcograf S.p.A.

ISBN-13: 978-0-141-18708-2

www.greenpenguin.co.uk

MIX
Paper from
responsible sources
FSC
www.fsc.org   FSC™ C018179

Penguin Books is committed to a sustainable
future for our business, our readers and our planet.
This book is made from Forest Stewardship
Council™ certified paper.

Contents

Contents

Introduction

When Freud published this book, he was a forty-three-year-old doctor with an established if occasionally erratic medical practice in his home town, Vienna – a respected neurologist, a leader in the field, with a reputation for risky, speculative conjectures in the theory and treatment of the neuroses. His passionate love for Martha Bernays when they met in 1882 was the principal, if not the only reason for his giving up the career he had been set on up until his mid-twenties, the rocky and unpredictable path of the research scientist within the German-speaking universities. He had resigned himself to giving up the academic world in order to earn more money in the hurly-burly of a general medical practice. By 1896, he had six children and a considerable ménage to support. However, although Freud was absorbed in his clinical work, this did not mean he had given up his scientific ambitions. Far from it; he hoped to contribute epoch-making discoveries in the causation and treatment of nervous diseases. As he put it in a letter to his one intimate friend and colleague, Wilhelm Fliess, in May 1895: 'a man like me cannot live without a hobby-horse, without a consuming passion, without . . . a tyrant. I have found one . . . It is psychology, which has always been my distant, beckoning goal, and which now, since I have come upon the problem of neuroses, has drawn so much nearer.'[1] Having in 1895 published a well-regarded book with Josef Breuer, *Studies in Hysteria*, Freud aimed 'to examine what shape the theory of mental functioning takes if one introduces quantitative considerations, a sort of economics of nerve forces' and to discover what psychopathology could offer the study of ordinary psychology. In short, he intended to found a scientific psychology.

The methods he employed derived, naturally and sensibly enough, from his daily work: the treatment of neurotic patients by means of the new methods of psychotherapy, as these developed out of the craze for medical hypnotism that swept Europe in the 1880s and early 1890s. The project for a scientific psychology was on the agenda of many researchers at the end of the century, employing radically different methods. In many German-speaking university departments of philosophy, experimental psychology was emerging as a distinct and ambitious programme, studying the reactions of the normal mind in laboratory experiments, often by and on the researchers themselves. In Britain, there emerged a project for the study of statistical variation in large populations of subjects, begun by Francis Galton and associated with 'psychometry' and the eugenic improvement of the race. Freud, like Pierre Janet in France, deployed the intensive clinical study of the individual abnormal mind. Of the three 'subjects' of psychology – the experimental, the statistical and the clinical – only the third was of interest to Freud. The dream-book was the extension of the clinical investigation of the 'abnormal' mind to a new domain to provide the base for an ambitious and truly scientific psychology. Dreams were the ideal vehicle for this project: universal experiences with a history of fascination expressed in popular and esoteric literature, but with clear links to the extreme states of insanity and everyday abnormality.

Although Freud had had a documentable interest in dreams for years, it was the combination of two events in his life and work that led to the writing of a full-length book on the topic. The centre of his work had been, since the late 1880s, the theory and therapy of the neuroses and he had developed clinical and grand speculative theories in that domain, not least the theory of abreaction, the part played by traumatic memories in the production of symptoms – increasingly focusing on memories of childhood sexual experiences. At the same time, he had refined his methods of psychological exploration, introducing 'free association' to replace catharsis under hypnosis or in a specially induced abnormal state of mind; and it was as part of the flood of material produced by free association that he increasingly came upon dreams, fantasies and other detritus of everyday mental life. How traumatic experiences – in particular sexual ones – became elaborated through the 'mechanisms of defence' to produce symptoms became the focus of his work in the mid-1890s; the same processes were at work, he thought, in dreams. Yet in the autumn of 1897, all this work seemed to run aground: he was forced to discard his theory of the neuroses when he realized that he had no way of distinguishing fantasy or dream-states from reality, and therefore no clear-cut causal conditions for the production of symptoms. As he reflected in a letter to his close friend in Berlin, Wilhelm Fliess: 'In this collapse of everything valuable, the psychological alone has remained untouched. The dream stands entirely secure and my beginnings of a metapsychological work have only grown in my estimation. It is a pity that one cannot make a living, for instance, by interpreting dreams!'[2]

Freud did find a way of living off dream-interpretation. He put the dream and the metapsychology together in the book published in late 1899. But there was another crucial ingredient. The failure of his theory of the neuroses may have spurred him to take the sidetrack of the dream, but the crucial material used in that book came not from his therapeutic practice but from his 'self-analysis'. In October 1896 Freud's father died; just like his own patients, Freud found himself beset with strange states of mind, enormous unaccountable shifts of mood, neurotic symptoms. Over the next months, extending throughout the time of writing the book, he plunged into analysis of his own dreams as a reaction to that bereavement. He had had many of the basic ingredients of the book ready to hand by the end of 1897 and had started work on a draft. But he encountered setbacks, not least the problem of indiscretion and the censorship Fliess was imposing on his material: 'I myself have lost the feeling of shame required of an author . . . [I] confess that I regret [the exclusion of the dream] and that I have no hopes of finding a better one as a substitute. As you know, a beautiful dream and no indiscretion – do not coincide.'[3] The book lay fallow for another year until Freud determined to find a way around the censorship; in a frenzy of writing over the summer of 1899, he completed the book, early chapters being set in print even while he wrote the later ones.[4]

'This book . . . contains, even according to my present-day judgement, the most valuable of all the discoveries it has been my good fortune to make. Insight such as this falls to one's lot but once in a lifetime.' So Freud wrote in 1931 in the preface to the third English edition of A. A. Brill's translation of *Die Traumdeutung*. It is unquestionably Freud's masterpiece. Yet it is an ungainly elephant of a book. Impressive in the overall control of argument over hundreds of pages, it is also occasionally ponderous, crammed full of subtle argument about dreams, about sleep, about mental life in general. A page-turner in places, in others it is a cluttered cull of snippets from the sleep of patients and colleagues. What kind of a book is this, we find ourselves asking fretfully as we read? And does that problem stem from a larger background question: what kind of an author is Freud?

The most obvious book to compare Freud's with is *On the Origin of Species*. The gentleman naturalist and the Jewish physician may seem to have little in common, beyond the crucial fact[5] that neither ever worked for a salary in an institution. Even in 1859 it was unusual for a major scientific theory to be advanced in a book aimed at a general public; by 1900 it was positively anomalous.[6] After 1900, one would have thought, no major work of science could be published in a book, let alone by a professional outsider. Turn the argument around: Freud published his book just when the tide of public science, mounting so powerfully throughout the nineteenth century, was turning. The chief markers of science in the twentieth century would be size (measured in manpower, in capital investment) necessitating linkage to established and wealthy institutions (industry, universities, government) and its closed and esoteric character (publication in professional journals, specialized monographs, patents, research-group memos). No modern science could hope to speak principally in the open language of a book and be taken seriously by the insiders who counted. No science could be established without the intense competitiveness and sceptical scrutiny associated with the policing functions of closed, hegemonic institutions and the intense pressure towards anonymous, depersonalized, inert prose – a characteristic singularly lacking throughout Freud's work.

There is no doubt of the authority in the tone of the author of *Interpreting Dreams*. Yet it is always a personal and a playful authority. Freud's voice is incisive and certain, even when he is speaking in a casual conversational style, even when he is humbly, and with due nods towards provisionality, advancing challengingly novel theoretical views. It is a curious and unsettling feature of his style that the most avowedly speculative constructions about a patient's early childhood can sound as certain as the fact that today is Tuesday. Incredulity at his presumption turns to confusion when one re-examines the sentences and usually finds that all the requisite disclaimers and qualifications are in place. One encounters the voice of a unique stylist pronouncing the universal truths of a science.[7] The inimitable voice – particularly clear in the analysis of his own dreams – reminds us that this 'new science' is a science of the singular individual and bears the mark of one very specific individual, its founder.

Freud was aware that his strange new discipline of interpreting dreams raised profound problems of authority. One of the solutions he found was to open the book with a virtuoso display of mastering the 'scientific' literature on dreams – 'the authorities'. He regarded this as a thankless task but he performed it so well that he extracted seemingly clear positions from that literature on which to build his own theory. His exposition of it – and continual reference to it throughout the dream-book – allowed him to hand out compliments and criticisms, brickbats and flowers. At times he deploys these authorities as allies; at other times as unfortunately blinkered enemies, in order to demonstrate the mastery and sufficiency of his own theories.

Dealing with the authorities in Chapter 1 was only a preamble: the whole thing is planned on the model of an imaginary walk. At the beginning, the dark forest of authors (who do not see the trees), hopelessly lost on wrong tracks. Then a concealed pass through which I lead the reader – my specimen dream with its peculiarities, details, indiscretions, bad jokes – and then suddenly the high ground and the view and the question: which way do you wish to go now?[8]

But the metaphor of the walk does not tell us through what territory the concealed pass takes the reader; nor does the metaphor of the view specify the landscape one sees. What journey does Freud take us on?

The 'concealed pass' is Chapter 2 – the birth canal of psychoanalysis, one might say. Freud describes the method he has discovered for interpreting dreams: breaking dreams up into elements and then applying the technique of free association to each of them in turn. He applies this method to the specimen dream, his own dream of Irma's injection, dreamed in July 1895, the moment when he crystallized this method and its 'solution'. What Freud achieves with his specimen dream is twofold. He exposes his own inner life as the material on which a method of dream-interpretation can be built. He also offers a bold and original discovery about the essential nature of dreams as the first result of this method: the dream is a fulfilment of a wish.

It is here that the questions start. How can Freud claim *all* dreams are fulfilments of wishes based only on one dream and that one his own? The counterclaims are so obvious: are anxiety-dreams, let alone nightmares,[9] fulfilments of wishes? Finding an adequate answer to the question, 'Why does Freud advance the thesis of the universality of wish-fulfilment in dreams with such conviction, despite so much evidence to the contrary? goes a long way to the heart of this book. I think there are four very different answers to this question. I will call them the 'traditional' answer, the 'theoretical' answer, the 'world-view' answer and the 'dialectical' answer. I will take these in turn.

The 'traditional' answer

The strategy of Chapter 2 is to contrast to its advantage his method with that of the 'scientific' writers he had just so carefully reviewed and in addition to give support to the 'lay view' (*Laienmeinung*) of dreams. Allying himself with lay views, 'popular' views, 'old wives' tales' against official, respectable science was a frequent move on Freud's part. He advances a brash and bold theory of dreams which is simply an intrepid extension of that sense of the word 'dream', so tenacious and, in the age of advertising and populist politics, so ubiquitous. In the dictionary, a dream is defined as 'an ideal or aspiration' – as in 'I have a dream', 'the American Dream' or the immortal song from *Pinocchio*: 'When you wish upon a star / Your dreams come true.' Responding to Freud with the question: 'Surely not *everything* that happens in sleep is a dream in the sense of the fulfilment of an "an ideal or aspiration"?' can be met with an immediate counter-statement: 'Ordinary people know as well as scientists that not all dreams are pleasant portrayals of vast dinners and constantly available sex partners, but they still mean exactly what they say when they talk about "making their dreams come true". Fly in the face of this ancient wisdom at your peril!'

This call upon the force and cogency of traditional, 'popular' views would be a crucial part of the attraction of psychoanalysis in later years. Freud was not replacing the traditional language of human life with a new esoteric, scientific language. There is no secret language of psychoanalysis, from which ordinary human beings are in principle closed off, since they can find no equivalent in their own experience – no neurons, no chemical messengers, no subcortical processes. This eschewal would be the object of much scorn and criticism: the so-called anthropomorphism of Freud's theories – censor, super-ego, id, the patient's resistances – was an extension, in the face of mechanistic scientific disapproval, of the ordinary language of everyday life. Most importantly, it allowed the objects of Freud's science – the patients, the dreamers, the jokers, the religious enthusiasts – to talk the same language as the analyst and the Freudian scientist. Proclaiming the centrality of the 'wish' at the heart of human psychology was the first step in this process of elaborating a modern psychology which was an extension of 'folk psychology', not its replacement.

The 'wish' as theoretical psychology

The second answer is relatively invisible until Section C of Chapter 7, 'On the Psychology of Dream-Processes', which approaches the topic of wish-fulfilment from a theoretical point of view. Freud opens the section by even-handedly treating the possible contribution of a variety of kinds of wishes: wishes left over from the previous day, wishes rejected by the waking mind, wishes, such as for liquid or sex, derived from bodily sensations during the night, and the deeper wishes repressed in the unconscious, derived from childhood. But he soon dismisses this even-handed approach to assert that *'the wish represented in a dream must be an infantile wish'*. From then on, his argument takes the form of a deduction. Ordinary preconscious mental activity is closed down or severely restricted under conditions of sleep. Therefore, 'nocturnal arousal in the *prec* has no alternative but to use the route taken by wish-triggers from the *unc*; it must seek reinforcement from the *unc* and follow the detours of unconscious arousals'.[10] Mental activity which is not principally a wish has to take a ride on the back of the unconscious wishes that are allowed such freedom at night precisely because the way is barred to motility, to action. It is because of the closing down of the body's physical activity that the unconscious, which deals only in wishes, comes to dominate the mental activity of sleep, i.e. dreams.

And why does the unconscious deal only in wishes? Freud says he will give an answer derived not from a study of dreams, but with the help of the diagram of the psychical apparatus he had developed some pages earlier. This gives a linear schema of the process, modelled on the reflex, by which perceptions pass through, via the mnemic systems, to the motor output. Yet the account he now elaborates does not owe much to that diagram. Rather, it is the first outing for the fundamental 'metapsychological' hypotheses on which the psychoanalytic theory of the mind rests. Freud tells us a story of the origin of mind.

Under the pressure of internal needs (e.g. hunger), a helpless, hungry baby finds its way to an 'experience of satisfaction':

> An essential component of that experience is the appearance of a certain perception (in our example: being fed), recollection of which henceforth remains associated with the memory-trace of arousal of the need. As soon as that need reappears, thanks to the association a psychical stirring will arise that seeks to recharge the memory of that perception and recall the perception itself – in fact, to put it another way, it aims to restore the situation of the first satisfaction. Such a stirring we call a wish; reappearance of the perception is the fulfilment of that wish, and when arousal of the need invests such a perception with a full charge, that is the shortest way to such wish-fulfilment. There is nothing to prevent us from positing a primitive state of the psychical apparatus in which this path is actually followed – in other words, wishing turns into hallucination. So this initial psychical activity aims at an *identity of perception*, namely at repeating the perception associated with satisfaction of the need. (p. 582)

However, bitter experience teaches that hallucination of the wished-for object does not lead to sustained satisfaction. A secondary system inhibits the investing of the memory and turning it into a perception, in other words inhibits fulfilling the wish until perceptions which are received from the external world (and how the system is assured that these are from the external world and are not residues of memories is a delicate matter) match the cluster of traces associated with the experience of satisfaction. This secondary system, running in accordance with the 'secondary process' of thinking, is the guarantee that satisfaction can now be achieved in reality. 'All thinking is simply a roundabout way of getting from the satisfaction-memory adopted as purposive idea to the identical charging of the same memory, which is to be regained by way of motor experiences.' (p. 618)

This deductive argument leads to a straightforward conclusion concerning the ontology of wishing:

> Thinking, after all, is simply a substitute for hallucinatory wishing, and if dream is wish-fulfilment, this in fact becomes self-evident, since nothing but a wish is capable of prompting our mental apparatus into action. Dream, which fulfils its wishes along short, regredient paths, has simply preserved for us a sample of the primary mode of operating (since abandoned as inefficient) of the psychical apparatus. What once dominated the waking state, at a time when psychical life was still young and inept, is now, it seems, exiled to the life of night – rather as we rediscover in the nursery the bow and arrow, the primitive weapons of adult mankind, since laid aside. *Dreaming is a piece of the mental life of childhood, which has now been superseded.* (p. 583)

The argument is supremely powerful and direct. The primary mode of operation of the mind is wishing: only wishing drives the engine we call thought. If it seems plausible to argue that dreaming is driven by the domain of the mind still dominated by that ancient mode of mental operation, then it is obvious that dreams will be driven by wishes. The force of the argument depends on the plainly plausible assumption that the other part of the mind, the part active in waking life, in 'voluntary motility', is shut down during the night, leaving the field open to the unconscious. In this unconscious, there is no fear, no hope, no guilt, no shame; there is only wishing and aversion.

Freud was allying this theoretical argument with another shift, one that would have momentous long-term effects. To a nineteenth-century philosophical psychologist, and to many alienists and psychiatrists, the mind had three main functions and modes of operation: there was reasoning (what we would now call 'cognition'); there was feeling (into which Freud would introduce the language of 'affects') and there was the will. This threefold division of mental functions mapped easily on to that characteristic Victorian emphasis on the will as the centre of moral life: taking responsibility for one's actions was acknowledging that one had 'willed' them and moral improvement centred overwhelmingly on the exercise, trained or untrained, educated or not, improved or native, of the will. The language of the will disappears entirely from Freud's psychology; with it goes the inseparable moral dimension of 'improvement' to which physicians, educators, philosophers were so devoted at the turn of the century. The new psychology would be a psychology that put the moral at arm's length, particularly after the sea-change of the Great War; Freud's psychoanalysis would be a leader in this fundamental shift away from a moral conception of the human mind. The language of 'wishing' allowed this shift to take place invisibly. As Freud developed psychoanalysis, the 'wish' would become incorporated into the language of the drives or instincts. Drives and wishes replaced the will as the 'driving force'. We can catch symptoms of this shift in early English-language expositions of Freudian thought; in 1912, the psychologist T. H. Pear, analysing his own dreams in accordance with Freud's method, refers to the 'conative' dimension of the mind as found in Freud's theory of wish-fulfilment, drawing on William Hamilton's philosophical psychology to attempt to encompass Freud's metapsychology.[11] 'Conative' derives from the Latin *conatus*, endeavour or striving. Thus Freud's language of 'wishing' leading to action was developed to encompass and then replace an older and ideologically loaded language of will and responsibility.

Freud's entire argument concerning the experience of satisfaction and the mechanics of thinking had been written out on a train in autumn 1895, but in the language of neurones and nerve-excitations. Freud subsequently discarded this manuscript but it was later published as the 'Project for a Scientific Psychology' (*Standard Edition*, vol. I). This may temper a little our astonishment that Freud wrote the final hundred-page theoretical chapter of the dream-book in eleven days, sending it direct to the printer for setting. The argument had already been written four years earlier and had been considered and criticized by its author, who was supremely confident that he could turn a neurological model into a psychological theory and knew how to justify his theoretical daring

– 'we may give free rein to conjecture, provided only that in the process we keep a cool head and do not mistake the scaffolding for the building'.

This argument, sophisticated in its appreciation of the relationship of theory to phenomena, allowed Freud to regard his earlier speculative brain-mythology – putative neurones, putative laws of facilitation and conduction, or inhibition and lateral feedback systems – as expedient 'scaffolding' for the building, 'the psyche' itself. Freud would never again be tempted to identify the laws of the brain with the workings of the mind; instead, he had found the path for maximal exploitation of the conceptual resources available to him. A few pages before he had modelled the primal experience of satisfaction and the origin of wishing, he deployed another metaphorical register, mapping the economy of wishing with the multiple relations of entrepreneurs and capitalists. In one model, the driving force of the mind is a bodily need, transmitted as nervous quantity to the mind, the fruit of his raid on the resources of brain-science; in the other model, the driving force of the mind is money.

> It is entirely possible for a daytime thought to play the part of *entrepreneur* for a dream; however, the entrepreneur, the person who is said to have the idea and the impetus to put it into action, can do nothing without capital; he needs a *capitalist* to cover the expense, and that capitalist, who contributes the psychical expenditure for the relevant dream, is always, without exception, *a wish from the unconscious*. (p. 578)

An entrepreneur may have ideas, contacts, skills and savoir-faire; without capital, without money, he goes nowhere, nothing happens. The metaphor of capital introduces three features: the blind universality so characteristic of money, eroding all differences between particulars; the driving force involved in production; and the element Freud focused upon, 'The *tertium comparationis* of the metaphors employed here, the quantity made freely available in a measured amount'. But hidden within the metaphor is another claim as to why 'wishing' is the privileged mode of operation of the mind. The entrepreneur, the actor in the present, may hold and use money, but money always comes from elsewhere – the capitalist and further down the line, a network of past accumulation, of structures and relationships of trust sedimented as the foundation for the institution of money itself. These structures of trust are comparable to the foundational 'experiences of satisfaction' in Freud's account of early development.

There is, then, a long and closely argued chain of reasoning which takes Freud from an anthropological argument concerning the nature of human beings, from the first functioning of the psychical apparatus, via the elaboration of adult thinking, to the claim that, under the conditions of sleep, only a wish can be sufficiently power-ful to drive the mind, and thus to produce dreams. It is a theoretical argument deeply embedded in the models of the brain, yet detached so freely from those models that Freud makes it patently clear that other models – from economics or from Homeric mythology or from all those other spheres in which his nimble metaphorical wit delighted – will be as serviceable as brain physiology. Freud was never to be confined to a speciality. He had the luck to make his way outside of the academic world with its disciplinary boundaries and restrictions. He turned this good fortune into conceptual capital by drawing freely on all registers of metaphor for the development of his model of the mind.

The wish as world-view

At the time of the publication of *Interpreting Dreams*, Freud was as private a citizen as one could wish for. His collegial activities had diminished virtually to zero; the one Society he attended regularly was the B'nai B'rith. His disappointment at the quiet reception for his book manifested itself in this report to Fliess in early 1900 concerning his everyday existence:

> The reception of the book and the ensuing silence have again destroyed any budding relationship with my milieu . . . I found a way

` out [of the impasse in my work] by renouncing all conscious mental activity so as to grope blindly among my riddles . . . In my spare time I take care not to reflect on it. I give myself over to my fantasies, play chess, read English novels; everything serious is banished. For two months I have not written a single line of what I have learned or surmised. As soon as I am free of my trade, I live like a pleasure-seeking philistine. You know how limited my pleasures are. I am not allowed to smoke anything decent; alcohol does nothing for me; I am done begetting children; and I am cut off from contact with people. So I vegetate harmlessly, carefully keeping my attention diverted from the subject on which I work during the day. Under this regimen I am cheerful and equal to my eight victims and tormentors.[12]

Yet the books and papers would soon start to flow from his pen. Starting with the dream, the appropriately private and unreal object for a man in retreat from the world, Freud would reach out to a series of previously unconsidered objects and phenomena, shining the light of his psychoanalytic method on them and recruiting them as bridges, allowing him to bring under his control the ever-widening and more public world. As he reflected in 1932, with *Interpreting Dreams*, 'analysis took the step from being a psycho-therapeutic procedure to being a depth-psychology'.[13]

The second such object was the 'Freudian slip'. As Paul Keegan observes in his brilliant Introduction to the new Penguin translation of *The Psychopathology of Everyday Life*, the scene of this book is not, as with dreams, the guarded privacy of night-time life, but the teeming metropolis, where we stumble and fall, forget names and places, where 'our days are full of farcical detour and unscripted subplots . . . a makeshift city comedy . . . : a café theatrical about our improvisations, the contingencies by which we live'.[14] In *Psycho-pathology*, psychoanalysis comes out of the bedroom into the street: 'parapraxes occur where our unconscious gangs up with circum-stance, and gets to ridicule us merely for getting up in the morning and agreeing to appear on the stage of day'. Its explanatory schema is the extended version of the dream-book's: a conflict between two psychical systems or trends, in which a wish normally kept on a tightly civilized leash momentarily is on the loose, biting its owner and his interlocutors with callous lack of discrimination. But the extended formula is still not entirely social: the slip may be the revenge of the unconscious on the ego, but the culprit and the victim are still both 'me', although the cruelty of a successful slip should not be underestimated.[15]

With the *The Joke and Its Relation to the Unconscious* of 1905, psychoanalysis became irremediably social. It takes two to joke and Freud's account distributes the roles accordingly: the joker performs the joke-work on behalf of the hearer, whose unconscious wishes are released from repression momentarily by the joke; their fulfilment is expressed in the explosion of laughter, that orgasmic spasm of the diaphragm, just as the dream's driving force finds expression in the streaming of charge into the perceptual system. But alongside the joke and the slip, Freud retraced his steps from the dream in another direction, taking his starting-point from the day-dream, which he had already discussed in the dream-book:

> Like dreams, they are wish-fulfilments; like dreams, they are largely based on the impressions of childhood experiences; like dreams, they enjoy a certain relaxation of censorship as regards their creations. Looking closely at how they are put together, one becomes aware of how the wish-motive that operates in their production, seizing the material of which they are constructed, has jumbled that material up, rearranged it and assembled it to form a fresh whole. To the childhood recollections to which they hark back, they stand in something like the same relationship as some of Rome's baroque palaces stand to the classical ruins whose columns and dressed stones provided the materials for their reconstruction in modern forms. (pp. 508–509)

But day-dreams face not only backwards into the night, but forwards into the public world of creative literature. The ubiquitous everyday activities of the slip and the joke are matched by the specialized craft of rendering phantasy into the public form of art. And there is another public realm Freud opened up to the wish-model of the dream: the universal obsessional symptom known as religious ritual. The wish-series is now extensive: dream – day-dream – phantasying – play[16] – creative writing – art – religious ritual. Freud's professional work was still focused on the symptom, also structured as the result of the fulfilment of wishes, specifically a repressed unconscious wish and one stemming from the repressing agency, but the symptom was only one member of this extensive series, if a privileged member. It too could have its purview extended: through the analogy of the obsessional compulsion and religious ritual, and then through the analogy of the phobic object with the totem animal of 'primitive' societies. Freud's wish-theory thus carries him from the privacy of the Viennese consulting-room to the *raison d'être* of primitive social structure. And further to the origin of belief in magic.

> It is easy to perceive the motives which lead men to practise magic: they are human wishes. All we need to suppose is that primitive man had an immense belief in the power of his wishes. The basic reason why what he sets about by magical means comes to pass is, after all, simply that he wills it. To begin with, therefore, the emphasis is only upon his wish.[17]

In contrast with the infant who hallucinates the object of satisfaction, primitive man engages in an analogue of the child's play, what Freud piquantly calls 'motor hallucinations'.[18]

> If children and primitive men find play and imitative representation enough for them, that is not a sign of their being unassuming in our sense or of their resignedly accepting their actual impotence. It is the easily understandable result of the paramount virtue they ascribe to their wishes, of the will that is associated with those wishes and of the methods by which those wishes operate.[19]

In general, the system of magic demonstrates the excessive value humans come to confer on wishes and the thoughts derived from them; it reveals the 'omnipotence of thoughts' which governs primitive animism and obsessional thinking alike.

By developing the wish-model of the dream to encompass religion, magic and the totemic object, psychoanalysis had thus become an anthropology, a theory of the process of human mental evolution itself. As it did so, it became an increasingly influential presence as a cultural force in its own right; Freud's voice came to have cultural authority. Hence the late works which deal directly with social and cultural matters: *The Future of an Illusion* and *Civilization and its Discontents*. In these works, Freud's attack on religion has often been taken to be weak and somewhat out of character or, at the very least, lacking in his customary subtlety: what is the great advocate of the power of the irrational in human affairs doing when he is so downright rude and contemptuous of a great achievement of mankind?

Freud's main concern in these later works was to demonstrate the sources of religious feeling and belief in the development of infant to adult. What this development leads to is the peculiar vulnerability of humans to dependence on authority. It is this dependence that then makes them sufficiently gullible to believe the nonsense that religions teach, both in the moral and epistemic spheres. For Freud, religions are 'mass delusions'[20] or, more frequently, simply illusions whose strength derives from the wishes of childhood as reflected in the childhood of human history:

> [religious ideas] are illusions, fulfilments of the oldest, strongest and most urgent wishes of mankind. The secret of their strength lies in the strength of those wishes . . . What is characteristic of illusions is that they are derived from human wishes. In this respect they come near to psychiatric delusions. But they differ from them, too, apart from the more complicated structure of delusions. In the case of delusions, we emphasize as essential their being in contradiction with reality. Illusions need not necessarily be false – that is to say, unrealizable or in contradiction to reality.[21]

Seeking the truth of religion in mystical perception – as in the 'oceanic feeling' examined in *Civilization and its Discontents* – is no antidote to the conviction that *all* religious feelings are regressive states induced by confrontation with hard reality. Religion is the citadel of childishness, a socially sanctioned mass regression, fleeing from hard reality – the truths of science, of death, the fundamental inhospitality of the universe – into consolations in which, at bottom, Freud will not distinguish between Santa Claus and Jesus Christ.

Although the nineteenth-century critique of religion supplies Freud with much of his ammunition – biblical criticism's treatment of religious documents, Feuerbach's account of religion as projection, the evolutionary anthropological project (Darwin, Tylor, Robertson Smith, Frazer) that revealed 'the fatal resemblance between the religious ideas which we revere and the mental products of primitive peoples and times' – the fundamental denunciatory attitude derives from the Enlightenment critique of religion. There is nothing more in tune with Freud's account of the childishness of religion than Kant's famous declaration: 'Enlightenment is man's emergence from his self-incurred immaturity. Immaturity is the inability to use one's own understanding without the guidance of another.' When Freud turns to the three types of arguments for religion – divine tradition, miracles and the mystery of faith expressed in the prohibition against asking for evidence – he is continuing a familiar attack on the grounding of religion as dependent on the ungrounded authority of others.[22] This 'animus of the Enlightenment', as Philip Rieff accurately names it, denounces religion as childish, its proponents situated somewhere between the scheming priests of Voltaire's tirades and the patronizing cynicism of Dostoevsky's Grand Inquisitor. The crucial addition to this denunciatory mode is the shift to a psychological account of religion. The mercilessness of nature is personified; just as in a dream-wish's fulfilment, 'a man makes the forces of nature not simply into persons with whom he can associate as he would with his equals – that would not do justice to the overpowering impression which those forces make on him – but he gives them the character of a father'.[23] The awareness of intentionality at work in nature – animism – eventually leads to the creation of gods, who, even in the higher 'religious' stage, when nature is deprived once again of its animating spirits, are still required to perform tasks which answer to the deepest wishes of mankind: 'they must exorcize the terrors of nature, they must reconcile men to the cruelty of Fate, particularly as it is shown in death, and they must compensate them for the sufferings and privations which a civilized life in common has imposed on them'. Freud's critique of religion has its counterpoise and its foil: 'scientific work is the only road which can lead us to a knowledge of reality outside ourselves'.[24] It is as if the old Freud was led back to the enthusiasms of his youth – for positivism, for *Darwinismus*, for Feuerbach, and for his faith and pride in science. But these had never really gone away: on his long detour, they had simply been underpinned by psychology.

The key doctrine which ruled this whole development of the wish-theory was first announced in the 1890s: 'Reality – wish-fulfilment – it is from these opposites that our mental life springs.'[25] It was fully developed in the distinction between the pleasure and reality principles and its consequences are plain to see in the unnerving certainty of Freud's views on religion and the aim of human life. Its discovery, or its fixing as the foundation of his thought, took place very early. Throughout the period from 1894 to 1899, Freud had continually rediscovered – and then forgotten – the importance of this contrast, this fundamental opposition and irreconcilable conflict at the heart of mental life, between wish and reality. The early hints of the wish-fulfilment theory were in the domain of the psychoses. Freud's clinical examples seem to cry out for the concept: 'the mother who has fallen ill from the loss of her baby, and now rocks a piece of wood unceasingly in her arms, or the jilted bride who, arrayed in her wedding-dress, has for years been waiting for her bridegroom'.[26] Alongside these examples, Freud's sharp eye was caught by convenience dreams: the medical student who can grab another few minutes' sleep while he dreams he is a patient asleep in the hospital with a hospital chart in his name hanging over his head.

So if there is a doctrine that can be regarded as the heart of Freud's thought, it is the contrast between human wishes and the unbending nature of reality. For Freud, this is a simple statement of the facts as brought to light by science. It is a world-view derived, in his eyes, from the progress of science. The inexhaustible force of our wishes is met by the immovability of reality, so that humans are riven by the unceasing conflict that then develops from the attempt to alter, to dress up, to ignore reality or the neurotic attempt to refuse, to ignore, to distort the individual's fundamental wishes. This contrast, reality versus wish-fulfilment, is a refrain that sounds throughout the development of psychoanalysis. *Interpreting Dreams* was an extended overture, announcing many of the themes, to that dimension of psychoanalysis, which, beyond the clinical and professional, would sound out as a cultural critique, as a crusade against religion and the higher morality, as an ideology for the faithless moderns. No wonder that Freud defended with such tenacity and self-confidence the thesis that all dreams are wish-fulfilments.

The dialectical answer

The simple statement 'all dreams are wish-fulfilments' invites contradiction. Why give such a hostage to fortune? Why not be more circumspect? Freud's most original and revolutionary move is his invitation to the reader to contradict him. So the strategy of the book is to engage immediately with the reader in energetic argument. He places the reader in the position of being an aggressive critic, and finds himself on the defensive, confronted with an incredulous interlocutor. And this is actually how Freud likes it. This is not a personal preference of his, a temperamental quirk: it is at the heart of the process of 'interpreting', which is the key element of his approach to dreams.

Chapter 3, entitled 'Dream is Wish-Fulfilment', opens with all the excitement of the new vistas opened up by the discovery that dreams have a meaning, bubbling with a host of questions. Freud raises the key question in his reader's mind:

> Our first dream was an act of wish-fulfilment; another may turn out to be a fear fulfilled; a third may embody a reflection; a fourth may simply reproduce a memory. So are there other wish-dreams, or is there perhaps nothing but wish-dreams? (p. 137)

But he doesn't address this question at all in what follows. Instead, he recounts a series of utterly charming, transparently wish-fulfilling dreams, closely followed by an equally charming series of children's wish-dreams. The sceptic will certainly feel cheated by this approach. Yet the busy chatter of the Freud circle's dream-life gives us an early indication of how things are going to go with the bold thesis:

> A friend who is familiar with my dream-theory and has told his wife about it said to me one day, 'I'm to tell you that my wife dreamed yesterday that her period had arrived. You'll know what that means.' I certainly do: if the young woman dreamed that her period had come, it meant that she had missed it. I can well imagine she would have liked to enjoy her freedom for a while longer before the problems of motherhood set in. This was a clever way of announcing her first pregnancy. (p. 139)

The friend's wife is an early example of a key figure in Freud's dream-book: a clever dreamer in dialogue with his method; the dissemination, even prior to publication, of Freud's theories brings useful examples out of the woodwork. More to the point, these are knowing examples, examples in the spirit of, or contesting, his theory. But the dynamics are peculiar: the husband, usually impli-cated in the first pregnancy of a wife, is here simply the messenger carrying news back and forth between his wife and Freud. And Freud takes the dream to be a semi-public communication: 'a clever way of announcing her first pregnancy', as if it were the equivalent of having a formal card printed and circulated. Note that the dreamer did not dream of a still-born baby, as if the best way of fulfilling her desire not to be pregnant would be to kill her embryo; she dreamed of her period, of a restoration of the *status quo ante*. The reason why it was a clever way of announcing the pregnancy was that she could only have a wish to have a period if she knew that she was *not* going to have a period: wishes only arise from the soil of a lack of the thing wished for (we do not wish for that which we have). Combined in this dream is the fundamental negativity out of which wishes arise and the positive denial, a fulfilment of that negativity, together with a communicational function of the dream: announcing the pregnancy, first and foremost to the man who was making dreams his professional preoccupation.

Of course at this point in the book we want to say: this dream is already 'contaminated' as data. Freud's theories are known to this woman; she goes to sleep in full knowledge of the expectations derived from that theory and she then dutifully dreams according to the Freudian formula. Most of the dreams in Chapter 3 come into the category Freud calls *'Bequemlichkeitsträume'*, 'comfort dreams', or 'dreams of convenience' (Strachey). In this instance, we can certainly stretch the term 'comfort' to include dreams dreamed to please Dr Freud. The dreamer somehow fulfils a night-time need, like thirst or sexual desire, by dreaming a fulfilment of that need; in this instance the need is either to please Dr Freud or to reassure oneself that his theories are correct.

If all dreamers were as enthusiastic to feed Freud's collection of wishful dreams as the newly pregnant friend's wife, there would be no problem with confirming his thesis. But not all dreams are as neatly corroborating and not all dreamers are as credulous. The willing wish-fulfillers are equally matched by the resistant sceptics. So Chapter 4, 'Dream-Distortion', is centrally preoccupied with these nay-dreamers. Again, Freud picks up these examples from those in his circle – the old schoolfriend, now a barrister, who had seen Freud come top of the class year after year, and was now presenting the bold wish-fulfilment theory of dreams; the dream he reported of losing all his legal cases was a way, Freud concluded, of seeing Freud fall flat on his face after all these years. We, in a post-Freudian spirit, might see this dream as disporting its masochism in the spirit of Samson, bringing down his own house just so long as he can defeat his enemy. Indeed, in the 1909 edition, Freud recognized this style of dream as not only performing a refutation of his theory but also as stemming from an ' "ideational" masochism'. But such 'counter-wish' dreams are for Freud principally about attempts at refuting his theories of dreams or of psychopathology.

It is this immediate and close engagement of the dreamer with

Freud that I want to highlight. Dreams appear to be the most solipsistic and inwardly directed of all our mental experiences. Yet as soon as he has exposed his own inner life with Chapter 2's Irma dream and put forward his bold thesis, Freud's pages become populated with dreamers eager to corroborate or refute his theories. Freud enters into a dialectical relationship with his friends and patients, and by extension, with the reader. 'Indeed, I can expect many a reader to react in the same way: to be quite prepared to sacrifice a wish in a dream simply in order to have the wish that I might be wrong fulfilled.'

Given the bait Freud offers, and given the toes he may well have trodden on in the circle of his nearest and dearest through the merciless treatment he hands out to them in his dreams, it is apt that one of the very first to respond to the book was Freud's brother, Alexander. On New Year's Eve, 31 December 1899, Alexander presented a manuscript entitled *'The Interpretation of Dreams* by Prof. A. Freud' to his older brother Sigmund. It is a spoof, a fraternal dig in the ribs and a piece of holiday hilarity. Its tone is serious enough, mirroring Sigmund's phrasing and deploying some of the same cast of characters who had peopled his brother's dreams and their interpretations: Count Thun, a lawyer friend of the family, a friend called Emma from 'the best society', Dr Königstein, and, as the *pièce de résistance*, a dream of Alexander's which culminates in a Latin tag – *mundus vult decipi*, 'the world wants to be deceived' – in which the childhood memory surfacing through the dream is of older brother Sigmund's childhood name, 'Mundi'. The Latin tag can be loosely retranslated as 'Sigmund wants to be deceived' – as he has been, in his theory of dreams; because Alexander's thesis, as proved by his own and his circle's dreams, is that 'dreams bring the fulfilment of only those wishes that *are not fulfilled in waking life*'.[27] Exactly how Alexander is contradicting his brother's theory is not entirely clear, but the disputatious intent is in no doubt. He certainly lands a palpable hit: in noting the failures of the psychoanalytic method, which prompted him to take 'the opposite tack: I first constructed the dream-interpretation, which made the dreams themselves significantly simpler and transparent'. His best joke is, as so often, one of timing: the third dream he analyses, 'Emma's dream', takes place 'during the night of 31/12/1899–1/1/ 1900'. In other words, the interpretation in the manuscript handed over as a New Year's Eve gift preceded the dream. The very first dream Alexander analysed featured a very 'Freudian' play on words around the honorific 'HOFRATH' (Court Councillor) by which professors were addressed and a neologism 'HOFUNRATH' ('court-rubbish/excrement'). Salt in the wounds is what one expects from a professorial brother at holiday-time, one might reflect, especially on reading the book in which the ambition to be a professor figures so prominently and is so lightly tossed aside.

Alexander Freud was not the first nor was he to be the last to react to the wish-fulfilment thesis in the fashion of the bull and the red rag; Sigmund the matador is more than content to make this confrontation explicit. Indeed, the bold thesis is tailored to this aim. Freud's wish-fulfilment hypothesis is designed to bring out in the open the *relationship* that dreamers have to – Freud. There are two important aspects to this dynamic relationship that Freud encourages. The first is what he deals with in the fourth chapter of the book. Having expounded the wish-fulfilment hypothesis, brought on board confirmations from 'comfort-dreams', the dreams of children and the dreams of those eager to dream in accordance with his theories, he turns to the outright opponents.

> If at this point I advance the claim that wish-fulfilment is the meaning of *every* dream – in other words, that there can be no other dreams but wish-dreams – I can be sure of the flattest contradiction in advance ... Nevertheless, these apparently cogent objections are not too hard to overcome. Notice, if you will, that our theory is not based on an appreciation of the manifest content of the dream in question but relates to the thought-content that the work of interpretation shows to underlie that dream. Let us compare the two: *manifest dream-content* and *latent dream-content*. (pp. 148–9.)

In outline, the dialectic Freud's wish-dream theory promotes is between manifest and latent, between dreamer and Freud, between dreamer and interpreter. The dreamer is, by definition, master of the manifest content; following Freud's method, the interpreter uncovers beneath the manifest content another meaning, the latent content, which, Freud now asserts, is antipathetic to the dreamer. The path to this latent content is beset with barriers, obstacles, diversions, red herrings. So that, as Freud will assert later in the book, 'whatever interferes with continuation of the work constitutes resistance'.[28] This resistance is attributable to the dreamer, although it is clearly inherent in the very notion of the dream being a complex structure produced by 'work'; the means by which one overcomes the resistance is to be found on the axis along which the interpreter performs *his* labour: the task of the interpreter is to help the dreamer overcome these resistances. But this very means of dividing up the labour, this dialectics as I am calling it, places the interpreter in the field of the 'latent', beyond the manifest content and the resistances that prevent the dreamer going much beyond that content. There is a force that prevents the dreamer understanding his own dreams and the interpreter bears witness to that force.

This function of the interpreter points to the second important aspect of this dynamic relationship between dreamer and interpreter which Freud's framing of his argument incites and promotes: the transference. In his later psychoanalytic work, transference became the central idea around which the process of therapy was conceptualized: the analyst and the analytic situation became the focus of all the patient's ideas, fantasies, fears and hopes, sucking up into themselves the entire structure and symptomatic panoply of neurosis. This transference-structure was, Freud asserted, the repetition, in increasingly ill-disguised form, of the primary relationships and significant scenes from childhood, in particular the idiosyncratic character of the patient's relationships to his parents, siblings and other key figures from childhood. This conceptualization of transference is pretty well absent from *Interpreting Dreams*, save for a few allusions. None the less, Freud was well aware of the importance of such 'transferences' in the therapeutic process, having brought his account of therapy in the final pages of *Studies in Hysteria* (1895) to a climax by concluding that:

no great increase in effort was demanded by this kind of transference. The patient's work remained the same, that is, overcoming the painful affect that she could harbour a wish of this kind even momentarily, and whether she made this psychical repulsion the theme of her work in the historic instance or in the recent one connected with me seemed to make no difference to its success. The patients, too, gradually learnt to see that these kinds of transference to the person of the doctor were a matter of a compulsion and an illusion that would melt away when the analysis was brought to a close.[29]

These early remarks concerning transference indicate how important the phenomenon was to Freud's earliest conception of the psychotherapeutic process; and they reveal that his earliest formulation of the transference was of transference-*wishes*. This framework of transference-wishes would be transferred over into the dream-theory. From 1895 onwards, not without deviation and back-tracking, Freud would deploy a model which gives primacy to wishes both in dreams and in the construction of neurotic symptoms. For a period this wish-model was in tension with his claim about the aetiology of neuroses, the seduction theory: the claim that the necessary and sufficient condition for the production of neurotic symptoms in adulthood was a 'pre-sexual sexual shock', a traumatic seduction or sexual assault in childhood. But the seduction theory also easily translated into the language of 'wishing' which Freud was developing. Why does a sexual assault in childhood cause neurosis in adulthood? Because the memory of the assault comes to 'infect' or create a template for sexual desires later, desires which the adult subject feels are repulsive and incompatible with her or his sense of self (ego). It is these distorted wishes, as transfigured by the primeval memories, that are thus repudiated, repressed, defended against and form the starting point for secondary formations – fantasies, day-dreams, defensive mental structures – which form the bedrock of the neurotic symptoms.

So one sees a number of strands from Freud's work feeding into his concept of 'wish'. Take the transference scene: a patient reports a scene of Freud sexually assaulting her. Freud does not castigate the patient or repudiate the scene as an unjustified vilification of his medical reputation, nor does he search his soul too long wondering if he 'led her on' or had talked so much about sexuality that she was simply complying with his expectations. Instead, he asks what scenes in the past – at first conceived of as actual events, then as either real or fantasized – this 'wish' in the present is modelled upon. He demands first and foremost that the patient comes to recognize her own desires, her own 'wishes', no matter how foreign and alien these wishes feel to her. Transference leads to wishes.

It is no accident that at a crucial moment in his argument in the dream-book, Freud evokes transference. Apologizing to his reader for having to go into all the private detail of his own life in order to show how dreams do have a meaning, he makes the following request:

> Now, however, I must ask the reader to make my interests his or her own for a time, plunging with me into the tiniest details of my life, because that kind of transference is very much demanded by an interest in the hidden meaning of dreams. (pp. 117–18)

This is the moment in the book when the reader will become involved not only with Freud's contentious arguments, but with his complex inner life. So under the 'dialectical' argument we must include 'transference' on to Freud's world, which is the only path, the 'concealed pass', which leads to true understanding of dreams.

The 'dialectical' sense of wish-fulfilment is closely tied to the fundamental innovation of the dream-book: the introduction of the distinction between the manifest and latent contents of the dream. Much of Freud's account of the structure of dreams follows from this distinction, which leads him, at the end of Chapter 4, to announce the completed version of his general formula: '*Dream is the (disguised) fulfilment of a (suppressed [*unterdrückten]* or repressed) wish.*' Much of the rest of the book, in particular Chapter 6, a book in itself, is devoted to the principal mechanisms deployed by 'dream-work', the process by which dream-thoughts are converted into images which come to consciousness in sleep; the descriptions of these mechanisms, of compression, displacement, symbolism, concern for representability, lay the foundation for knowledge of unconscious processes. The distinction between 'latent' and 'manifest' is even more bitterly contested by Freud's critics than the claim that all dreams are wish-fulfilments. In light of my argument, one can see why: the distinction is at the core of the dialectical relation one develops to Freud and to the function of the interpreter in general. It is this distinction that opens the way to the unending task of interpretation, layer upon layer, and to the threat or fear that the interpreter has an unchallengeable power over the person whose dream is being interpreted. The latent content of the dream opens the way to the inner secrets of the dreamer, to the certainty that he is the keeper of inner secrets, past, present and future, of which even he is unaware. Paul Ricoeur used the winning phrase 'the hermeneutics of suspicion' to describe Freud's stance towards the dream and the dreamer. He also supplied an incisive insight into why the Freudian account of human nature as founded on wishes or desires goes hand in hand with the necessity for interpretation: 'As a man of desires I go forth in disguise.'[30]

With the distinction between latent and manifest content goes the introduction of an internal censorship, patrolling the borders between the acceptable and unacceptable parts of the mind. Without forbidden desires – wishes – there would be no need to dissemble; precisely because we Freudians know that our fellow dreamers desire what they do not wish to desire. We know they dissemble and that understanding their dreams requires a struggle with the censorship, a struggle to overcome their unwillingness to recognize their own desires.

Without the distinction between latent and manifest, there is no call for interpretation – there is nothing to interpret, no depth beneath the surface (and therefore no surface above the depth). Human mental life is transparent by definition. Freud's scorn for the philosophers centred on this point: he accused them of asserting the a priori identity of the mental and the conscious. Affirming that there is an unconscious psyche, that there is 'the latent' as well as 'the manifest' is the sole means, Freud asserts, for establishing a science of the mind. But there are many other grounds for objecting to the latent/manifest distinction; Susan Sontag's famous essay 'Against Interpretation' (1963) repudiates the distinction on the grounds of its cowardly over-intellectualization of the world:

> [For Freud], to understand is to interpret. And to interpret is to restate the phenomenon, in effect to find an equivalent for it . . . In some cultural contexts, interpretation is a liberating act. It is a means of revising, of transvaluing, of escaping the dead past. In other cultural contexts, it is reactionary, impertinent, cowardly, stifling . . . It is the revenge of the intellect upon the world. To interpret is to impoverish, to deplete the world – in order to set up a shadow world of 'meanings'.

The protest against interpretation is a defence of the perfection of this world against the violation of the intellect. It is as much a protest against the stance of the interpreter, the project of mastery of the world through its meanings, as it is a refusal of the language of those meanings (sexuality, childhood, the egoism of the repressed).

Sontag's uneasiness with the shadowy world of meanings is more forthrightly and more aggressively displayed in another group of critics, those closely associated with the neurophysiological study of sleep and dreams, that attempted from the early 1950s on to 'make Freud history' by displacing his theory of dreams. Through the discovery of the association of REM sleep with specific brain-wave patterns during sleep, through the attempts to show how specific parts of the brain, which have known and specific functions – some of them entirely sub-cognitive, part of the autonomic nervous system – are active in REM sleep and others entirely quiescent, the site of the scientific study of dreaming shifted entirely away from the associations and interpretations of dreamer and analyst towards the sleep laboratory, where the sleep of brain-doctored cats was as informative as the faintly perceived childhood memories of a human dreamer. The assault by some neuroscientists – though not all, but certainly those most imperialistically committed to their disciplinary projects – on Freud recognized that the practice of dream-interpretation was the purest form of a project of understanding the human mind that was inimical to neuroscientific visions. If the dimension of depth, the dimension of thought behind the thinker, is permitted, not only would the interpretative practices for understanding other humans be permissible, they would be essential. Hence the neuroscientists launched a full-frontal assault not only on the notion that dreams have meaning, but particularly that they have a hidden (latent) meaning that can be discovered by another person in collaboration with the dreamer. Such hidden meaning entails, interestingly enough, that the meaning is potentially shareable, that the dream is potentially a public act of revelation and communication, or can properly be rendered so. The realization that a dream is a form of language, with its own peculiar syntax – to which Freud had devoted so many intricate pages of *Interpreting Dreams* – would spell out a definitive limitation on the interest or comprehensiveness of the neurophysiological account of dreams. Establishing whether or not dreams are such a 'language' is an empirical matter, seemingly established beyond doubt by the many thousands of dream-interpretations offered and published since Freud. But if one could establish that dreams have no depth, are perfectly transparent, as Allan Hobson attempted to do by publishing his own dreams in a forlornly impoverished attempt to compete with Freud, then the very project of dream-interpretation could be consigned to oblivion.[31] Similarly for the ambitious speculations of Crick and Mitchison[32] that dreams are the result of a reverse-learning mechanism made necessary by the assumed properties of the brain as a parallel distributed processing system – and are therefore simply the dim echoes of a 'cleaning-up mechanism, to remove potentially parasitic nodes'. These speculations lead to the recommendation that one should not try to remember one's dreams, since this effort may undo the beneficial cleansing effects of sleep. There is no hidden meaning of dreams for Crick and Mitchison; dreams are mental sewage, pungent and copious, but certainly not the royal road to the unconscious.

Dream-interpretation and the telling of a life

The dream-book is a how-to book for interpreting dreams; it is the details of these interpretations that show the reader how to go about it. Yet that is not even half the story. True, many of the dreams Freud analyses are touching, sobering, delightful and revealing of gaucheness or sad predicaments. But the conviction that this project of dream-interpretation is worthwhile comes principally from the central protagonist, Freud himself. The most fully analysed dreams in the book are all Freud's. If Freud's name has become a byword for a certain kind of portrait of the mind, then that picture was first drawn in his own interpretations of his own dreams: 'what is untamed and indestructible in the human mind, the *demonic* element that furnishes the dream-wish and that we find again in our unconscious'. (p. 629)

Ever since the dream-book's publication, the logic of exhibition and dissimulation, as it applies to all human beings and as it is manifest in Freud's own case, has preoccupied ordinary readers and scholars, disciples and adversaries alike. Freud himself recognized only later that the dream-book was a fundamentally personal document. In the Foreword to the second edition, he wrote:

> The fact is, for me this book has a further subjective significance that I was not able to understand until I had finished writing it. It turned out to be part of my own self-analysis, as my reaction to the death of my father – in other words, to the most important event, the most drastic loss, in a man's life. Having once recognized this, I felt unable to erase the traces of such an effect. For the reader, however, it may be a matter of indifference by means of what material he or she learns to appreciate and interpret dreams. (pp. 5–6)

Note how there is a repeated rhythm to this admission: first Freud recognizes that this work was a part of his self-analysis, as the reaction to his father's death, and then he asserts the universal truth that the death of the father has this effect on everyone; secondly he accepts his reluctance to efface this overly personal history, and defends himself by implying that in this book it is perfectly proper for Freud himself to stand in for Everyman. Freud's life will, it turns out, be Everyman's life.

To give some sense of how Freud's analyses of his own dreams open up this novel and revolutionary way of telling the story of a life, I am going to consider one dream in some detail: the dream of Freud's uncle with a yellow beard. As with each of the dreams discussed, Freud is making a didactic point. This dream is introduced to illustrate first a general process, whereby distortion in dreams is 'deliberate' and 'a means of dissimulation', and secondly a particular example of that process, whereby the affect is reversed into its opposite.[33] Later in the book Freud returns to this dream, dissatisfied with the account he had given earlier, to demonstrate the connection of dreams with a childhood wish and to address more directly the misplaced affection he felt in the dream for an uncle he hardly knew.

The background to the dream was Freud's having received the recognition from his seniors of being put forward for Affiliated Professorship at the University of Vienna.[34] The day before the dream, a friend of Freud's, R., who had also had his name put forward to the Minister, told Freud a story of a recent encounter with the Minister in which he had pressed him to reveal whether or not his professorial candidacy was being blocked because of denominational considerations – a polite reference to anti-Semitism. 'In reply he had been informed that, in point of fact, given the present climate, His Excellency was not in a position . . . and so on and so forth. "Now at least I know where I stand," my friend told me, winding up a story that told me nothing new but had the inevitable effect of fortifying my resignation.' That night Freud had a short and rather minimal dream:[35]

> I. *My friend R. is my uncle. – I feel very tender towards him.*
>
> II. *I see his face before me somewhat changed. It is as if drawn-out lengthways, while the yellow beard framing it is emphasized with especial clarity.* (p. 151)

His response to the dream on recalling it the next day tells us much about the 'dialectical' relation that the dreamer has with his own dreams: 'I burst out laughing and said, "The dream is nonsense." However, it would not let go and stayed with me all day until eventually, that evening, I told myself reproachfully, "If one of your patients had nothing to say about a dream-interpretation other than 'It's nonsense', you'd admonish him and assume that some unpleasant story lay hidden behind the dream, a story he wished to spare himself the trouble of thinking about. Treat yourself no differently."' Freud here is halfway down that path, captured so well by a very Freudian poet, W. H. Auden:

> Bound to ourselves for life,
> we must learn how to
> put up with each other.[36]

Rather than being the compliant dreamer, eager to corroborate his theories, Freud finds himself in the position of the sceptical dreamer. He buckles down to the work of overcoming his resistance. Because this is a brief dream – a thought followed by an image – Freud does not follow the method of free association very strictly: he does not 'associate' to each element one by one. He starts with the thought of R. as his uncle. The face is that of Uncle Josef, who had got involved in a criminal money-making scheme – literally, as recent scholarship has shown, since the scheme was counterfeiting roubles – and was apprehended by the authorities. 'My father, who at the time went grey from worry in the course of a few days, used always to say that Uncle Josef had never been a bad man but he had certainly been a dimwit [*Schwachkopf*]. That was the word he used.' The dream seems to be saying: my friend R. is a dimwit. It is this conclusion that Freud finds acutely embarrassing; the rest of his account of the dream is an attempt to make sense of this, as if to explain it away: why is his dream so uncomplimentary about his dear friend?

Observe that this question presupposes that one take dreams seriously as mental acts, as part of one's inner world. Freud has already dispensed with the attitude 'it's only a dream'. There is no 'only' in his version of mental life. So he pursues another association: his friend R. also has a criminal record, since he was once convicted of knocking over an apprentice with his bicycle. This comparison is also an unworthy treatment of his friend – 'That would be to take the comparison to ridiculous extremes.' Freud then recalled a conversation of a few days earlier with N., another, more pessimistic colleague, whose dossier is also sitting on the Minister's desk:

> 'Don't you remember – someone once threatened to take me to court? I needn't tell you that the investigation was discontinued; it was a wretched attempt at blackmail; I had my work cut out, saving the accuser herself from prosecution. But it's possible they're holding this matter against me at the Ministry in order to block my appointment.' So, there I have the criminal, but at the same time I also have the interpretation and the intention of my dream. In it, Uncle Josef represents both colleagues who had not been appointed to professorships: one as a dimwit, the other as a criminal. (pp. 152–3)

The logic of the dream is now clear: the background wish is to be appointed as a Professor. To clear the way for this wish, Freud must depict, in an alternative dream-Vienna, the Minister as entirely free from anti-Semitism; to do so, his dream asserts: 'My two colleagues are not being blocked for being Jewish, but one for being a dimwit, the other for being a criminal.'

Freud's method of interpreting dreams, like his investigations into the aetiology of neurotic symptoms, seeks out scenes, described with vivacity, humour, irony, pathos, sly intelligence: the scene of the conversation with R. the day before the dream, with its vivid picture of him button-holing the Minister and the diplomatic response which by saying nothing reveals all; the conversation with N. a few days earlier, featuring Freud's curious refusal to accept his congratulations; and the scene from Freud's childhood of Uncle Josef's arrest. Each of these scenes is transparent and clear, yet they have twists and turns within them which call out for further commentary that Freud does not necessarily offer.[37] What troubles Freud, despite having made sense of the dream, despite having discovered the wish fulfilled in it – his wish to be a Professor, his wish that anti-Semitism disappear – is the tender affection he feels for R. in the dream, which strikes him as 'untrue and exaggerated'. It is this affection that Freud now argues is the principal vehicle of the resistance – his dismissing the dream as nonsense, his reluctance to interpret it.

> I am reluctant to interpret it because the interpretation will contain something I am resisting. The dream-interpretation once complete, I learn what it was that I was resisting; it was the assertion that R. is a dimwit. I cannot trace the tenderness that I feel towards R. to any latent dream-thoughts, but I can trace it back to this resistance of mine. If in comparison with its latent content my dream distorts at this point (is in fact distorted into its opposite), the tenderness manifest in the dream serves that distortion; in other words, the *distortion* here turns out to be intentional, as an instrument of *disguise*. (p. 154)

This is the point in the book where Freud introduces the fundamental idea that the distortion of dreams, which makes them difficult to make sense of and therefore necessitates the labour of interpretation, is a *motivated* distortion: there is an agency, the censorship, which deliberately distorts.

But Freud is still not satisfied with his account of the dream; like a patient in deep resistance, he baulks at another element in the dream-analysis, the discovery of such a strong wish for a professorship, which suggests 'a morbid ambition that I fail to recognize in myself – to which, in fact, I believe I am a complete stranger'. So he again sets himself to work on the dream, now discovering the childhood sources of this pathological ambition. He pooh-poohs his first association, that the old woman who told his mother at his birth that she had brought a great man into the world could be the source of such ambition – 'there are so many expectant mothers and so many aged peasants or other old women who, having lost all their power on earth, have turned to the future'. But he then turns to a second prophecy, when he was eleven or twelve, at a family outing to the entertainment park of Vienna, the Prater, from a prophesying poet doing the rounds of the tables, that he would one day be a government minister.

> This was at the time of the *Bürgerministerium* ['cabinet of citizens'], and my father had recently brought home pictures of 'Citizen' Drs Herbst, Giskra, Unger, Berger, etc., in whose honour we had made a kind of illuminated shrine. Some of them were even Jews, so that every hard-working Jewish boy carried a ministerial portfolio in his school-bag. In fact, it must have had to do with the impressions of that period that, until shortly before matriculating at university, I intended to study law, and only at the last moment did I change my mind. A ministerial career, you see, is closed to a medic. And now my dream! For the first time I notice that it transplants me from the dreary present back to the optimistic years of the *Bürgerministerium* and does its best to fulfil what was my wish at the time. In treating my two learned and estimable colleagues so badly because they are Jews – one as if he were a dimwit, the other as if he were a criminal – in doing this I am behaving as if I were the minister, I have put myself in the minister's place. What radical revenge on His Excellency! He refuses to make me a *professor extraordinarius*, so in return I take his place in the dream!

Here is another scene: the scene of prophecy in the Prater from which Freud's pathological ambition – to be a Minister, it now turns out, a Minister in whose gift is the making and breaking of professors – can be derived. Yet cleverly embedded in the narrative of the scene of prophecy are two other scenes: the first of the boy-Freud swept up by his father's celebration of the unlooked-for fulfilment of his political dreams, deciding then and there, in front of the candle-lit array of portraits of successful middle-class politicians, to become a lawyer. And then, when he was seventeen, in October 1873, he registered at the University not as a law student but as a medical student. Thus this account of Freud's temporary ambition to be a Minister reveals, for those who have eyes to detect it, his adoption and then discarding of his father's political ideals. Woven into the revenge Freud takes on the Minister are his shifting relations to his father: at age eleven, he takes on the ideal of the professional Jewish statesman, only to discard it at age seventeen, when he chooses love of nature, of truth, rather than power, as his path.[37] One might say that embedded in this story of the aberrant ambition to be a Minister are foreshadowed many of Freud's later choices: at age seventeen, he chose the erotics of nature over those of justice and power; at age twenty-six, in falling in love with his fiancée, he chose love over the ascetic path of academic research. In the elaboration of his theory of the instincts, especially as contrasted with Adler and Jung, Freud would always place sex – Eros – over the Nietzschean alternative of power.

The scene of Freud's father decorating the family home with the portraits of admired politicians is not the only paternal scene in the dream. Freud's analysis had opened with another: 'My father, who at the time went grey from worry in the course of a few days, used always to say that Uncle Josef had never been a bad man but he had certainly been a dimwit [*Schwachkopf*]. That was the word he used.' The trial of Uncle Josef took place in February 1866, when Freud was nearly ten; the Austro-Prussian War of summer 1866 was followed by the momentous constitutional events that brought the *Bürgerministerium* to power in December 1867, with the debates on educational reforms giving non-Catholics equal civil rights taking place in May 1868. So when Freud recalls that 'every hard-working Jewish boy carried a ministerial portfolio in his school-bag' we can recognize that the path of law that leads to government might have been even more inviting to a boy whose uncle had recently been sentenced to ten years in prison.

The actual dream-image is of his uncle with a yellow beard. This image progressively loses its importance as the analysis progresses, taking Freud back to other memories. But there is much packed into the image:

> But there is the face, which I see in my dream, with its elongated features and yellow beard. My uncle really did have a face like that: elongated, and framed by a fine yellow beard. My friend R. had

jet-black hair, though when black-haired men start to go grey, they pay for the splendour of their younger years. Hair by hair, their black beards undergo an unpleasant colour-change, becoming first reddish-brown, then yellowish-brown, and only then properly grey. My friend's beard is currently going through this stage (so is mine, by the way, as I note to my displeasure). The face I see in the dream is simultaneously that of my friend R. and that of my uncle. It is like one of the composite photographs that Galton made when, studying family resemblances, he photographed a number of faces on the same plate. So there can be no doubt about it: I really do mean that my friend R. is a dimwit – like Uncle Josef. (p. 152)

So there are a number of faces condensed together: there is Uncle Josef with his fine beard, R. with a beard turning from black to yellowish-brown, Freud himself who is unfortunately undergoing the same transformation, but not as rapidly as his father, who went grey in a few days – a remarkable transformation for a nine-year-old boy to witness, one would have thought. To set against these unfortunate signs of decline and decay is the series of portraits of the middle-class Ministers, a pantheon for the Freud family to admire. All condensed into one face. Here Freud is again showing the general mechanisms by which dream-images are composed. Yet in doing so, he shows us a veritable family portrait.

The dream of the uncle with a yellow beard introduced a number of new elements in the unfolding of the book's argument. First, it placed Freud as a Jew in the complex professional politics of Vienna; indeed, there are only a few dreams in the book that do this and this dream is perhaps the most direct. Freud named himself as a Jew in the course of his analysis of this dream. Secondly, and perhaps linked to this, it was the first of Freud's dreams to reveal the importance of childhood experiences for the interpretation of dreams.[39] But these are not any old childhood experiences: these are memories of his father, whose dictum that 'Uncle Josef had never been a bad man but he had certainly been a dimwit' gave the dream-thoughts expressed in the dream their terms of reference, and whose admiration of the *Bürgerministerium* infected Freud, amid the general political enthusiasm of 1868, with the long-standing boyhood ambition of studying the law and becoming a Cabinet Minister. The wish that is fulfilled in the dream appears to be Freud's wish to be a professor; the dream achieves this end by demonstrating that any ministerial opposition to this appointment would arise not from his Jewishness; true, his Jewish friends were unsuccessful, but that was not because they were Jewish but because they were criminals, dimwits or both.

One might speculate that a deeper wish of Freud's is the wish not to be Jewish; but in order to implement such a wish, he would have to have a different father. The 'infantile moment' changes one's view of the dream entirely: through the recounting of the political excitement of the Freud household in the heady days of liberal reform in the late 1860s, Freud reveals an entirely new version of himself: the ambitious young politician who was determined to become a Minister and thus bring joy and pride to his father. It is this ambition, his *father's* ambition, that places him in the position of Minister, deciding who is a criminal, who is a dimwit and who is obviously thoroughly deserving of his professorship, whether or not he is Jewish. By identifying with the Minister, Freud indicates the location within his psychic universe occupied by his father's ideals – a political ambition. This revelation is achieved in a masterpiece of writing, in which the reader commences with an indefinite sense of the arbitrary and distant power of the Minister subjecting the Freud circle to ill-defined political forces and prejudices, only to find that the journey via Freud's childhood has brought him to a triumphant mastery through his becoming the Minister.

The dream-analysis conforms to the classic prototype of psychic structure, as Freud developed it during the 1890s, now most clearly seen in the structure of the dream: recent events (day residues, transferential elements) are linked to memories from the past, including temporary – or, sometimes, more permanent – 'screen fantasies or memories' (in this instance, the prophecy at Freud's birth that he would be a 'great man'). But the structure does not conform to the conventional chronology of a life; there is no beginning at the beginning, no narrative climax or ending. Freud's past is not a glorious past to be celebrated, nor is it a past without consequence. It is certainly not a past that contains the seeds of the present let alone the future within it; nor is the present so urgent in its call on the past as to iron out its incontrovertible difference.

It is not just knowing who Freud became that prompts one to see the question of the father confronted in this dream. To start with, there is the father's brother's face, with a beard, the sharp image in the dream; we learn that – somehow connected with the dream – the father's hair turned grey overnight with worry over the uncle's stupidity. Also that Freud has reached the age when his hair is turning grey. In the dream he sees a dim reflection of himself. So the dream-image points to a more uncanny experience: standing in front of a mirror and seeing his father's face staring back. Freud does not state these implications, not exactly; but they are lurking, as resonant notes, as if the dream were a sounding board. The other childhood memory is equally freighted: the father's heroic politicians' portraits, no doubt each with an impressive beard, lit by candles, firing up the young Freud with a barely understood enthusiasm, his father's enthusiasm communicated in the vigorous act of homage, to become a lawyer, a statesman, a Jew in power. The dream reconnects the mature Freud once again with his early enthusiasm, and thus with his father's enthusiasm; once again he can feel the imperative desire to be a Jew in power, a Minister with honours and riches to confer, and the dream represents this as a fact – he is the Minister! He has lived an alternative life, not the life of the struggling Jewish doctor beset by prejudice, but the life his recently dead father would have admired him for living, would even have envied him for living. Yet the very fact of the dream – predicated on Freud not being a powerful Minister, but being a searcher after scientific truths at the mercy of political and cultural forces beyond his control – also shows that Freud turned away from his father's ideals. His desire to take revenge on the Minister by becoming him is only an echo of his father's ideals which were once his but which he long ago relinquished.

Beyond its crucial place in the dream-book, opening up the most important conceptual distinction Freud was to make, between latent and manifest content, and its function in clarifying how affects in dreams are also at the mercy of processes of distortion and disguise, the dream of the uncle with a yellow beard points towards two later major Freudian themes: the fundamental conflictual relationship a man has with his father (a major axis of the Oedipus complex) and the distinctively psychoanalytic conception of the relationship of past, present and future. Day residues become saturated with references to the past; conflict in the present awakens memories of childhood and the wishes sustaining them, 'recalling the legendary Titans on whom since ancient times the great mountain masses had rested that had once been rolled down on them by the victorious gods and that still, from time to time, quaked from the twitching of their limbs'. We could redescribe the theme of the dream as 'the place of the father in the development of the individual', but this would be to nullify the revolutionary implications of the way in which past and present are linked in the unpacking of the dream: past is awakened through its connection with present, present comes alive through its connection with the past. Freud's dream-analysis eschews entirely conventional chronological narrative in favour of a perpetually dynamic relationship of past, present and future – both the past and the future are always there, sometimes latent, sometimes foreboding, sometimes enticing, in the very idea of a 'fulfilment' (the future) of a (prehistoric) wish. As Philip Rieff notes, 'Smashing up the past, denying any meaningful future and yet leaving that question reasonably open, Freud concentrated entirely on the present. Posterity will revere him as the first prophet of a time that is simply each man's own.'[40] Freud closed the book with exactly this formula: 'By showing us a wish as having been fulfilled, the dream does in fact lead us into the future; however, the future that the dreamer takes as present is moulded by the indestructible wish into a mirror of that past.'

The most important achievement of Freud's recounting of a life in dreams – his own life – is to provide an example, a model, for making an extraordinary life out of the ordinariness of the everyday. The heroic and the bestial are both simultaneously deprived of their magic and made the property of all; each of us, through following our dreams as Freud did, can discover the 'excitement of the wholly interesting life'.[41] Freud presages the possibility of a democracy of the inner life to follow on the heels of the democracies of suffrage and education. Sixty years on, the most Freudian of comedians would open his night-club act with the breathtaking – and clairvoyant – announcement: 'A lot of significant things have occurred in my private life that I thought we could go over.'[42] Everyone has an inner life and the right, if not always the chutzpah, to share it with the first comer, just as Freud declared in the dream-book that he was making use of 'my own dreams as offering a plentiful, convenient source of material stemming from an approximately normal person and relating to a wide variety of everyday occasions'. This process of analysis, conducted with the interpreter – even Freud had his Fliess, and knew that self-analysis is impossible – opened up a new form of conversation, beyond art, beyond friendship, beyond communion and community:

> You gave me an ideal
> Of conversation – entirely about me
> But including almost everything else in the world.
> But this wasn't poetry it was something else.[43]

What exactly this 'something else' is that Freud invented and promulgated – a science of the singular, an everyday art for everyone, a moral quest beyond any obligation, hope or promise, living solely in accordance with what appears to be the merely technical rule of honesty – is still not resolved. We still do not know whether to class this book with *On the Origin of Species* and the *Opticks*, with the *Confessions* and *Thus Spake Zarathustra*, or with *In Search of Lost Time* and *Finnegans Wake*. Whichever it belongs with, it will also have to be recognized as a Baedeker of the mind, a very personal travel guide to an undiscovered country that is Freud's own.

Book as collage

Interpreting Dreams was the one book Freud kept revising and updating, changing its structure considerably. The 1930 edition may have been Freud's last word on his masterpiece, but by then it was clearly a collage of revisions and developments subsequent to the first edition of thirty years earlier. It already had something of a patchwork structure on first publication and this aspect became only more prominent the more Freud added material, whether in the form of new examples, largely from his growing band of psychoanalytic colleagues – in particular substantial sections by Otto Rank and those concerning Herbert Silberer's work, an entirely reworked and enormously expanded section concerning dream-symbolism, under the influence of Wilhelm Stekel, Carl Jung and others.[44]

Its first translation, of the third edition by the Austro-American A. A. Brill in 1913 (with help from, among others, the young liberal journalist Walter Lippmann), did much to disseminate Freud's ideas in the English-speaking world and familiarize ordinary readers as well as doctors and the clergy with the psychoanalytic mode. Since the 1950s, it has been most familiar in the quasi-variorum edition prepared by James Strachey for the *Standard Edition of the Complete Psychological Works of Sigmund Freud*, which was adapted for the Pelican Freud Library of the 1970s and then the Penguin Freud Library of the 1980s. Strachey's edition, with its annotations and careful noting of when passages were added, changed or deleted, is indispensable for detailed study of the book. In addition, in 2000 a new translation by Joyce Crick of the first edition of *Die Traumdeutung* was published by Oxford World's Classics. But this is the only English translation of the final edition Freud prepared in his lifetime, the eighth edition of 1930; this is the book as he left it, now in a bold and entirely new translation.

John Forrester, 2006

Notes

1. Sigmund Freud, *The Complete Letters of Sigmund Freud to Wilhelm Fliess, 1887–1904*, edited by J. M. Masson, Cambridge, Mass., 1984, letter of 25 May 1895, p. 129.
2. Ibid. Letter of 21 September 1897, pp. 264–6. Translation modified.
3. Ibid. Letter of 9 June 1898, p. 315.
4. For a detailed discussion of the writing of the book, see J. Forrester, 'Dream readers' in *Dispatches from the Freud Wars*, Cambridge, Mass., 1997, pp. 138–83; Ilse Grubrich-Simitis, 'Metamorphoses of the Interpretation of Dreams', *Int. J. Psycho-Anal.*, 81 (2000), pp. 1155–83; Lydia Marinelli and Andreas Mayer, *Dreaming by the Book. Freud's The Interpretation of Dreams and the History of the Psychoanalytic Movement*, translated by Susan Fairfield, New York 2003; Didier Anzieu, *Freud's Self-analysis*, translated by Peter Graham, London 1986; Alexander Grinstein, *Sigmund Freud's Dreams*, New York 1980.
5. Shared with Nietzsche after his brief period as a Professor of Philology and with Marx earlier in the century.
6. I. B. Cohen regards *Die Traumdeutung* as the last revolutionary work of science to be published in book form; see his *Revolutions in Science*, Cambridge, Mass., 1985, p. 356.
7. Compare Einstein's often-voiced admiration for Freud's style with his scepticism about his scientific conclusions: 'I quite specially admire your achievement [in 'Moses the Man and Monotheistic Religion'], as I do with all your writings, from a literary point of view. I do not know any contemporary who has presented his subject in the German language in such a masterly fashion. I have always regretted that for a non-expert, who has no experience with patients, it is hardly possible to form a judgement about the finality of the conclusions in your writings' (Letter, 4 May 1939 in Ernest Jones, *Sigmund Freud. Life and Work*, vol. III, London 1957, p. 259).
8. Freud, *Complete Letters of Sigmund Freud to Wilhelm Fliess*, 6 Aug 1899, p. 365.
9. The nightmare was traditionally distinguished from anxiety-dreams; the '*Alptraum*', '*cauchemar*' or nightmare involved heavy pressure on the chest and an overwhelming feeling of suffocation. Freud only uses the term '*Alptraum*' twice in this work, both times in Chapter 1 when discussing previous writers: once in a quoted passage from another author and the second time when noting that the 'well-known nightmare' is especially

frequent in those with lung diseases and can also be experimentally induced by restricting the breathing. Freud clearly adheres to the traditional view of the 'nightmare' as a restricted class of nocturnal phenomena; his theory of dreams does not deal with this class in any specific manner. Note that the usage of 'nightmare' towards the end of Chapter 7, Section B 'Regression' of this translation is of a term, *'Schreckgespenst'*, which would be classically linked to the *Alptraum* – 'incubus' or, literally, 'frightful spectre'. For further details, I am indebted to Lisa Downing, 'Narrating the Nightmare: Literary and Scientific Accounts of Night Terrors in Nineteenth-Century France', paper given to Psy Studies Seminar, University of Cambridge, 17 November 2004. See also Ernest Jones, *On the Nightmare*, London 1931.

10. These passages are quoted from this new translation, *Interpreting Dreams*.

11. T. H. Pear, 'The analysis of some personal dreams with reference to Freud's theory of dream interpretation', *British Journal of Psychology*, 6 (1913–14), pp. 281–303.

12. Freud, *Complete Letters*, 11 March 1900, p. 404.

13. Sigmund Freud, *New Introductory Lectures on Psycho-Analysis, Standard Edition*, vol. XXII, p. 7; *An Outline of Psychoanalysis*, translated by Helena Ragg-Kirkby, London 2003.

14. Sigmund Freud, *The Psychopathology of Everyday Life*, Introduction by Paul Keegan, translated by Anthea Bell, London 2002, pp. viii–ix.

15. And Freud had already noted such moments in the dream-book: 'A young woman who has become accustomed to receiving a bunch of flowers from her husband for her birthday misses this token of affection on one such occasion and bursts into tears over the omission. Her husband arrives and is unable to account for her tears until she tells him, "It's my birthday today." Whereupon he slaps his forehead, exclaims, "I'm so sorry, I'd quite forgotten!" and is about to go out and get her some. She, however, is inconsolable, seeing her husband's forgetfulness as proof that she no longer occupies the place in his thoughts that she once enjoyed' (p. 182).

16. Distinguished from phantasy by awareness of the link to objects in the real world.

17. Sigmund Freud, *Totem and Taboo, Standard Edition*, vol. XIII, p. 83; *On Murder, Mourning and Melancholia*, translated by Shaun Whiteside, London 2005.

18. Freud, *Totem and Taboo, Standard Edition*, vol. XIII, p. 84. Although Freud only uses this phrase once in his work, it is clear that it is tailor-made to apply to certain religious as opposed to magical rituals as well.

19. Ibid.

20. Sigmund Freud, *Civilization and its Discontents* (1930), *Standard Edition*, vol. XXI, pp. 64–145; *Civilization and Its Discontents*, translated by David McLintock, London 2002.

21. Sigmund Freud, *The Future of an Illusion* (1927), *Standard Edition*, vol. XXI, pp. 30–31; and in *Mass Psychology and Other Writings*, translated by J. A. Underwood, London 2004.

22. Ibid., pp. 25–9.

23. Ibid., p. 17.

24. Ibid., p. 31.

25. Freud, *Complete Letters*, 19 February 1899, p. 345.

26. Sigmund Freud, 'The neuro-psychoses of defence (I)' (1894), *Standard Edition*, vol. III, p. 60.

27. The seven-page manuscript is printed in translation in Lydia Marinelli and Andreas Mayer, *Dreaming by the Book. Freud's The Interpretation of Dreams and the History of the Psychoanalytic Movement*, translated by Susan Fairfield, New York 2003, pp. 151–8.

28. 'The work' refers here to the labour of analysis (interpretation) palpably experienced, or undergone, by both analyst and patient.

29. Freud, 'On the Psychotherapy of Hysteria' in Sigmund Freud and Josef Breuer, *Studies in Hysteria*, translated by Nicola Luckhurst, Introduction by Rachel Bowlby, London 2004, p. 305.

30. Paul Ricoeur, *Freud and Philosophy. An Essay on Interpretation*, translated by Denis Savage, New York 1970, p. 7.

31. J. Allan Hobson, *The Dreaming Brain. How the Brain Creates both the Sense and the Nonsense of Dreams*, New York 1988, pp. 134–222.

32. Francis Crick and Graeme Mitchison, 'The function of dream sleep', *Nature*, 304, 14 July 1983, pp. 111–14.

33. Anzieu, *Freud's Self-Analysis*, translated by Peter Graham, London 1986, p. 214.

34. 'Affiliated Professor' seems to me to be the best translation of *professor extraordinarius*, which position has the rank of full Professor, but without payment by the University. A *professor extraordinarius* is not an employee of the University, but is attached to it. Having been appointed as (unpaid) *Privatdozent* at the University in 1886, Freud already had the right to deliver lectures, for which his audience paid a fee – he had done so every year since 1886, when he lectured to five students on the Anatomy of Spinal Cord and Medulla oblongata; being appointed *professor extraordinarius* would not alter his position – there were no duties attached to the position – but would be a mark of recognition and prestige, thus also helping in attracting patients.

35. This dream was followed by a similarly structured second dream, a thought followed by an image, which Freud decided not to include in the book.

36. W. H. Auden, *Collected Poems*, ed. Edward Mendelson, London 1991, p. 885.

37. Just as the dream of Irma's injection implicitly evoked Freud's sexual desires for his women patients, without addressing in any way the sexual wish underpinning the dream. See Lisa Appignanesi and John Forrester, *Freud's Women*, 3rd edition, London 2005, pp. 120–45.

38. In *An Autobiographical Study* (1925), Freud writes: 'Under the powerful influence of a school friendship with a boy rather my senior who grew up to be a well-known politician, I developed a wish to study law like him and to engage in social activities. At the same time, the theories of Darwin, which were then of topical interest, strongly attracted me, for they held out hopes of an extraordinary advance in our understanding of the world; and it was hearing Goethe's beautiful essay on Nature read aloud at a popular lecture by Professor Carl Brühl just before I left school that decided me to become a medical student' (*Standard Edition*, vol. XX, p. 8).

39. In the first edition of *Die Traumdeutung*, the right-hand pages displayed running heads which changed not for each chapter or section, but for each page; this was an unusual feature for German-language publishing at the time. These heads were added by Freud. For the first discussion of the 'dream of Uncle with a yellow beard', the running heads were *'Der Onkeltraum'* (p. 95), *'Die Deutung des Onkeltraumes'* (p. 97) and *'Die psychische Censur'* (p. 99); when the interpretation was taken up again the heading was *'Das infantile Moment zum Onkeltraum'* ('The infantile moment of the uncle dream') (p. 131). In the *Gesammelte Werke* edition, edited after Freud's death, where some of these running heads were retained, this is changed to: *'Der infantile Ehrgeiz im Onkeltraum'* – 'The infantile ambition in the uncle dream' (*Gesammelte Werke*, vols II and III, p. 199).

40. Philip Rieff, *Freud. The Mind of the Moralist*, Chicago 1979, Preface to the first edition (1959), pp. x–xi.

41. Ibid., p. 304.

42. Woody Allen, *Standup Comic* (recorded in Chicago, 1964) CD, Rhino 75721.

43. Kenneth Koch, 'To Psychoanalysis', in *New Addresses*, New York 2000.

44. For these revisions, and the way in which the dream-book in consequence became something of a 'central bureau' for collective psychoanalytic work on dreams, see Marinelli and Mayer, *Dreaming by the Book*; for Jung's influence see, in particular, John Forrester, *Language and the Origins of Psychoanalysis*, London 1980, Chapter 3.

Translator's Preface

I make no apology for calling a new English translation of this famous book *Interpreting Dreams*. It's what the first English version (the Austrian/American A. A. Brill's 1913 translation of the third edition) should have been called; it's what the phrase *'die Traumdeutung'* naturally suggests in English. That said, the present edition does not presume to replace the edition previously published by Penguin Books (the one translated and meticulously edited by James Strachey and widely accepted as 'canonical'); it simply seeks to 'carry [Freud's text] across' into the English language as authentically as possible – which in a small way involves questioning certain 'traditional' assumptions.

For example, to regard the form of words *'The Interpretation of Dreams'* as an English equivalent of *'Die Traumdeutung'* is to accept the widespread but totally erroneous idea that translation is simply a matter of finding superficial equivalents and stringing them together in accordance with the syntactical rules of the target language. (Actually, the German and English definite articles are nowhere near equivalent. Only the English one is really definite; there are even occasions when the German *der/die/das* is most naturally rendered by the English 'a'.)

Seen in this very simplified, ideal way, translation is in fact impossible. Effective, useful translation is for the most part a very messy process of compromise – the result buffed up a bit, one hopes, in order to spare those unable to read the original the sight of the unlovely residue of forcing that original into a foreign mould. Languages – in this instance, German and English – are very different.

As just one illustration of that difference, take the German phrase *'der Traum'* (literally, 'the dream'; remember that all nouns in German are written with initial capitals), which covers two linguistically distinct English concepts: the uncountable, undefined, general phenomenon 'dream' (roughly, 'conscious mental activity during sleep') and the countable, defined, specific instance of such activity that is, say, 'the dream I had last night'. This is not a distinction that the German language draws. For Freud, generating and writing German, the two concepts existed along a single line, as it were (in fact there are occasions – there is one in Chapter 1, section E – where the lack of distinction allows Freud to move back and forth along the line, bridging the gap, so to speak, between the general and the particular, evoking both with the words *'der Traum'*); for the English reader the two concepts are, I repeat, distinct (related, yes, but not identical, as things lying along a continuum are in some sense identical). 'Ah,' one might say, pointing to a particular use of the phrase, 'but here Freud *obviously* means the uncountable "dream".' To which I should reply, 'Linguistically, it isn't obvious at all.'

However, since studiously avoiding the convenient English uncountable 'dream' in this translation would have led to a lot of awkward paraphrasing ('dreams', 'dreaming', 'the dream-state', and other glosses; paraphrasing has no more place in authentic translation than invention – of which more later), and since it would also have impaired legibility, I have not made the attempt. May I, in return, ask the reader to remember that what Freud understood by *'der Traum'* as a general phenomenon (rendered here as 'dream' without an article) cannot, strictly speaking, be made wholly clear in English?

Another problem is that of linguistic usage in the professional medical world that Freud inhabited. German medical usage tends to be quite direct, whereas English medical usage is often 'removed' and deliberately unfamiliar. For instance, where an English physician intones 'gastroenteritis' (possibly thinking, '*I* know what I'm talking about but I don't necessarily want *them* to'), his or her German counterpart will refer to (literally translated) a 'stomach-gut flare-up'. (There is no value-judgement implicit here; doubtless the

German medical world has other ways of fortifying its boundaries.)
In the context of the New Penguin Freud, which aims among other
things to 'despecialize' Freud (to 'return Freud to the ordinary
reader, showing us how much we still need him', as Hanif Kureishi
put it in the *Guardian Review* of 4 December 2004), let me take
just one example: it has become common practice, in psychology,
to talk about the 'excitation' of a sense organ as part of the process
of perception, but to my ear the word 'excitation' has a tinny,
remote, specialized sound; I choose 'arousal' (no, it isn't 'just about
sex'; nor, of course, is Freud) as echoing more of the associative
resonance of '*Erregung*'. Other departures from 'accepted'
Freudian usage are explained in notes where they occur.

By and large, Freud has not been well served by his English
translators. Most commentators seem puzzled by this, since Freud
knew English well, as did his daughter Anna, and the two of them
are said to have approved the English editions of his works as they
appeared. Part of the blame (as well as much of the credit for
disseminating the great man's writing) must be laid at the door of
James Strachey, who translated many of Freud's works himself and
also edited the English *Standard Edition of the Complete Psychological Works of Sigmund Freud* (twenty-four volumes), which began
to appear in 1953 – performing the latter task to such 'good' effect
that many German scholars prefer his edition to their own.

Indeed, for scholarly purposes the Strachey edition of this book
can scarcely be bettered in terms of its historical analysis of the text
and its invaluable notes, although much of the additional explanatory material provided in it is now available on the internet. However, new readers may appreciate a fresh approach to Freud's lively
prose. And I hope they will not mind my insisting that, for example,
James Strachey earned infamy in certain translating circles by
inventing renditions ('cathexis', 'parapraxis') of quite ordinary German words or simple neologisms used by Freud in admittedly
specialized senses. Writers invent; translators translate the outcome.
This is *a* translation of a very important book that English readers
have traditionally been misled into thinking Freud claimed was
definitive – which he didn't at all.

*

My source text was the eleventh corrected impression (of the final, eighth edition) published by Fischer Taschenbuch Verlag in August 2003. Square brackets in the text and notes (except where it is stated that they are Freud's own brackets or where they clearly serve some other purpose) enclose material added by myself. Translations of source material are also mine unless indicated otherwise. Finally, while accepting full responsibility for this translation, I am extremely grateful to Professors Gerhard Fichtner and John Forrester and to my friends Anna Ketterl, Nino Lazzaretti and Dr Kathryn Vale for their generous help.

Flectere si nequeo superos, acheronta movebo

['If I can't bend those above, I'll stir the lower regions'
(Virgil, *Aeneid*, VII, 312)]

Preface

In making this attempt to describe the process of dream-interpretation, I believe I have not stepped outside the circle of neuropathological concerns. This is because, under psychological examination, dreaming proves to be the first link in the chain of abnormal psychical patterns, other links in which (hysterical phobia, compulsive and delusive ideas) inevitably occupy the physician for practical reasons. Dreams (as we shall see) cannot lay claim to the same kind of practical significance; however, that makes the theoretical value of the phenomenon as a paradigm all the greater, and anyone who cannot explain how dream-images come into being will strive in vain to understand phobias, obsessions and delusions and possibly how to influence them therapeutically.

However, the same connection as lends our topic its importance is also to blame for the shortcomings of the present study. The breaks that will be found in such quantity in this account correspond to as many points of contact at which the problem of dream-formation impinges on wider problems of psychopathology that it has not been possible to deal with here; to these, if time and strength suffice and further material presents itself, subsequent revisions will need to be addressed.

Certain peculiarities of the material that I employ to explain dream-interpretation have also made this publication difficult for me. It will emerge from the study itself why all the dreams recounted in literature or to be gathered from persons unknown were inevitably unusable for my purposes; my choice had to be between my own dreams and those of my patients currently undergoing psychoanalytical treatment. I was barred from using the latter material by the fact that in this case the dream-processes were subject to an undesirable complication as a result of the admixture of neurotic features. But communicating my own dreams turned out to be inseparably bound up with my exposing more of the intimacies of my psychical life to other people's inspection than could possibly be welcome to me and than an author who is not a poet but a natural scientist would usually be required to do. This was embarrassing but inevitable; I therefore bowed to it, in order not to have to dispense altogether with presenting the case for my psychological outcomes. Even so, I have of course been unable to resist the temptation to make certain omissions and substitutions in order to take the sting out of many an indiscretion; wherever this occurred, it crucially impaired the value of the examples I have used. I can only voice the twin hope that the reader of this study will place himself or herself in my difficult situation in order to exercise clemency towards me and also that anyone who feels in any way involved in the dreams recounted will not wish to deny freedom of expression to dream-life at least.

Foreword to the second edition

The fact that this book, which is not an easy one to read, requires a second edition even before the first decade is up, is not one I owe to the interest of the professional circles to which I had addressed these words. My colleagues in psychiatry do not appear to have bothered to reach beyond the initial sense of unease that my new approach to the phenomenon of dream may have aroused, and the professional philosophers who have got into the habit of discussing the problems of dream-life in a few (usually the same) sentences as a supplement to states of consciousness have clearly not noticed that at this very point all kinds of things can be drawn out that will inevitably lead to a radical reorganization of our psychological theories. The reaction of scientific book reviewers could but justify the expectation that the fate of this work of mine was inevitably to be passed over in complete silence; not even the little band of bold supporters who follow my lead in the medical implementation of psychoanalysis and who interpret dreams as I do myself in order to make use of such interpretations in the treatment of neurotics – not even they would have exhausted the first edition of the book. So I feel under some obligation to that wider circle of educated people with a thirst for knowledge whose interest and sympathy challenge me to take another look, after nine years, at this difficult and in so many ways fundamental study.

I am pleased to be able to say that I found little to alter. Here and there I have added fresh material, I have inserted individual insights from my greater experience, and in a few places I have attempted revisions. However, everything essential concerning dreams and their interpretation as well as concerning the psychological theories to be deduced therefrom remains unchanged. Subjectively, at least, the book has stood the test of time. Anyone familiar with my other studies (concerning the aetiology and mechanics of psychoneuroses) will know that I never present incomplete work as complete and have always sought to amend what I say in accordance with my advancing knowledge; in the field of dream-interpretation I have been able to stand by my original remarks. In the long years of my work on the problems of neurosis I have wavered repeatedly and in some instances gone astray; at such times, over and over again, it was *Interpreting Dreams* that restored my confidence. In other words, my many scientific opponents demonstrate a sure instinct in not wishing to follow me in the particular field of dream-research.

Even the material of this book, by means of which I had illustrated the rules of dream-interpretation (my own dreams, largely rendered invalid by or overtaken by events), evinced, when it came to revision, an inertia that resisted intrusive amendment. The fact is, for me this book has a further subjective significance that I was not able to understand until I had finished writing it. It turned out to be part of my own self-analysis, as my reaction to the death of my father – in other words, to the most important event, the most drastic loss, in a man's life. Having once recognized this, I felt unable to erase the traces of such an effect. For the reader, however, it may be a matter of indifference by means of what material he or she learns to appreciate and interpret dreams.

Where I was unable to fit an irrefutable remark into the existing context, I have indicated its origin as being from the second edition by means of square brackets.[1]

Berchtesgaden, summer 1908

Foreword to the third edition

Whereas between the first and second editions of this book a period of nine years elapsed, the need for a third edition made itself felt after little more than a year. I may take some delight at this turn of events; however, having previously refused to allow the neglect of my work on the part of readers to count as evidence of its lack of merit, I cannot now take this revival of interest as evidence of its worth.

The advance of scientific knowledge has affected everything, including *Interpreting Dreams*. When I wrote it in 1899, *Sexual Theory* did not yet exist, and analysis of the more complicated forms of psychoneuroses was just beginning. The interpretation of dreams was to be an aid, making the psychological analysis of neuroses possible; since then, a deeper understanding of neuroses has reacted on the way we see dreams. The theory of dream-interpretation has itself developed further in a direction on which the first edition of this book had placed insufficient emphasis. As a result of my own experience, as well as through the studies of Wilhelm Stekel and others, I have since reached a juster assessment of the scope and importance of symbolism in dreams (or rather in unconscious thought). Much, then, has accumulated in recent years that demanded to be taken into account. I have tried to allow for these innovations by making numerous interpolations in the text and by inserting extra notes. If in places these additions have threatened to overstretch the account or if it has not been possible, at all points, to bring the earlier text up to the level of our present understanding, I crave indulgence for these shortcomings of the book on the grounds that they are simply consequences and indications of the now accelerated growth of our knowledge. I also make so bold as to predict in what other directions subsequent editions of *Interpreting Dreams* (should the need for such arise) will diverge from this one. They would need firstly to seek a closer connection with the wealth of material represented by poetry, myth, linguistic usage and folklore; secondly, they would need to discuss more thoroughly than has been possible here the links between dream on the one hand and neurosis and mental disturbance on the other.

Otto Rank gave me valuable assistance in choosing what to add, and he did all the proof-reading. I am obliged to him and to many others for their contributions and corrections.

Vienna, spring 1911

Foreword to the fourth edition

Last year (1913) Dr A. A. Brill completed an English translation of this book in New York. [*The Interpretation of Dreams*, G. Allen & Co., London]

This time Dr Otto Rank not only took care of the proof-reading; he has also expanded the text by two independent contributions (appendix to chapter 6 [but see below]).

Vienna, June 1914

Foreword to the fifth edition

Interest in *Interpreting Dreams* continued during the [First] World War, making a new edition necessary even before it came to an end. However, in the new edition it has not been possible to take full account of the new literature that has appeared since 1914; where this was in other languages, it wholly escaped my and Dr Rank's attention.

A Hungarian translation of *Interpreting Dreams* by Dr Hollós and Dr Ferenczi is close to publication. In my *Vorlesungen zur Einführung in die Psychoanalyse* [*Introductory Lectures on Psycho-Analysis*, 1916–17, *Standard Edition*, vols XV–XVI], published by H. Heller of Vienna, the middle section, comprising eleven lectures, is devoted to an account of dream that seeks to be more elementary and sets out to establish a closer link with the theory of neurosis. Altogether, it has the character of an abstract of *Interpreting Dreams*, although in places it supplies greater detail.

A radical revision of this book, which would bring it up to the level of our present way of thinking in matters of psychology but would also destroy its historical uniqueness, was more than I felt like undertaking. However, I do think that in almost twenty years of existence it has done its job.

Budapest-Steinbruch, July 1918

Foreword to the sixth edition

The difficulties currently facing the book trade have meant that this new edition has come out much later than would have been appropriate in the light of the demand, and also that, for the first time, it appears as an unchanged reprint of the previous edition. Only the Bibliography at the end of the book has been completed and continued by Dr Otto Rank.

In other words, my assumption that in almost twenty years of existence this book had done its job has not received corroboration. I might say instead, in fact, that it has a fresh task to perform. Before, it was a question of furnishing a certain amount of information about the nature of dream; now it has become equally important to counter the stubborn misunderstandings with which that information has met.

Vienna, April 1921

Foreword to the eighth edition

The period between the last, seventh edition of this book (1922) and the present replacement has seen the publication of my *Collected Writings*[2] by the Internationale Psychoanalytische Verlag in Vienna, of which the restored text of the first edition constitutes the second volume (all subsequent additional material being assembled in the third volume). The translations that have appeared in the same intervening period are from the separate version of the book; they include I. Meyerson's French translation, entitled *La Science des rêves* and published by the Bibliothèque de Philosophie contemporaine in 1926, the 1927 Swedish rendition by John Landquist (*Drömtydning*), and the Spanish one by Luis López Ballesteros y de Torres, which takes up the sixth and seventh volumes of the *Obras Completas*. The Hungarian translation that I thought imminent back in 1918 is not out even now.

I have again, in the present revised edition of *Interpreting Dreams*, treated the study essentially as a historical document and made only such changes to it as were suggested to me by the clarification and consolidation of my own views. As part of this approach, I have finally given up listing in this book the literature on dream problems since the first appearance of *Interpreting Dreams* and have omitted the relevant sections contained in previous editions. Similarly, the two essays 'Dream and poetry' and

9

'Dream and myth' that Dr Otto Rank had contributed to previous editions have also been dropped.

Vienna, December 1929

Notes

1. In subsequent editions these were dropped.
2. [The first edition of Freud's *Gesammelte Schriften* began to appear in 1924.]

1

The Scientific Literature on Dream-Problems

I shall show in the following pages that there is a psychological technique making it possible to interpret dreams and that, if this procedure is applied, every dream turns out to be a meaningful psychical construct that should be allotted a specific place in the mental whirl of waking life. I shall further attempt to explain the processes that lie at the origin of the strangeness and indecipherability of dream[1] and from them draw a conclusion regarding the nature of the psychical forces from the combination or collision of which dream springs. Having achieved this, my account will break off, for it will have reached the point at which the problem of dreaming touches upon broader problems that will need to be tackled using different material.

I start with a survey of the works of previous authors and the current status of dream-problems in science, since in the course of discussion I shall not often have occasion to return to them. The fact is, despite several thousand years of effort, the scientific understanding of dream has made very little progress. This is so generally conceded by writers that it seems superfluous to cite individual voices. In the writings that I list at the end of my study there are many stimulating comments and a great deal of interesting material on our subject, yet there is little or nothing that penetrates to the heart of dream or provides a definitive answer to any of its riddles. Even less, of course, has passed into the knowledge of the educated layman.

The view of dream that primitive peoples may have taken in the early years of the human race, and how it may have affected their understanding of the world and of the mind,[2] are subjects of such enormous interest that it is with reluctance that I exclude them from discussion in this context. I refer to the well-known works of Sir John Lubbock, Herbert Spencer, E. B. Tylor and others, and simply add that the scope of these problems and speculations will become clear to us only when we have completed the task before us, namely that of 'interpreting dreams'.

An echo of the primeval view of dream obviously underlies the estimates of the phenomenon formed by the peoples of classical antiquity.[3] They assumed that dreams were connected with the world of superhuman beings in which they believed, bringing revelations imparted by the gods and demons. Moreover, they could not help suspecting that dreams served an important purpose for the dreamer – usually that of telling him the future. However, the extraordinary variety in the content and impression of dreams made it difficult to construct a uniform view of them and necessitated a multiplicity of distinctions and groupings of dreams, depending on their value and reliability. Among individual philosophers of antiquity, their assessment of dream was of course not unconnected with the status that they were prepared to accord to *divination* in general.

In both of Aristotle's books that deal with dream, the phenomenon has already become an object of psychology. We are told that dream is not sent by the gods, nor is it divine in nature but more likely demonic, since nature itself is demonic rather than divine; in other words, dream does not spring from any supernatural revelation but is a product of the laws of the human spirit (which is of course related to the divine). Dream is defined as the mental activity of the sleeper in as much as he is asleep.

Aristotle is familiar with certain characteristics of dream-life, e.g. that dream reinterprets small stimuli occurring during sleep as large ones ('a person thinks he is walking through fire and becoming hot when all that is happening is a very slight increase in temperature affecting one or another limb'), and he infers from this behaviour that dreams may very well give the physician the first indications (unnoticed by day) that a change is beginning in the body.[4]

Before Aristotle, the ancients did not, as we know, regard dream as a product of the dreaming mind but as inspiration provided by the gods, and the two opposing tendencies in the appraisal of dream-life that we shall find to have been present at all times were already apparent among them. A distinction was drawn between true and worthy dreams, which were sent to the sleeper to warn him or tell him the future, and vain, delusive, trivial dreams, intended to lead the sleeper astray or bring disaster upon him.

Gruppe (*Griechische Mythologie und Religionsgeschichte* ['History of Greek mythology and religion'], p. 390) describes this kind of classification of dreams, as found in Macrobius and Artemidorus: 'Dreams were divided into two classes. One was said to be influenced only by the present (or past) but to have no significance for the future; it comprised ἐνύπνια, *insomnia*, which immediately reflects the given image or its opposite, e.g. hunger or its satisfaction, and φαντάσματα, which expand the given image in a fantastic manner, as for example the nightmare, *ephialtes*. The other class is different, being seen as determining the future; it includes: 1) direct prophecy received in dream (χρηματισμός, *oraculum*); 2) prediction of an imminent occurrence (ὅραμα, *visio*); 3) the symbolic dream, requiring explanation (ὄνειρος, *somnium*). This theory survived for many centuries.'

The task of 'interpreting' dreams was connected with this changing evaluation. Since dreams in general were expected to supply important information, though not all dreams were immediately comprehensible and there was no way of knowing whether a particular incomprehensible dream did in fact proclaim something significant, the impetus was there to seek to replace the incomprehensible content of the dream by a clear and at the same time meaningful one. In later antiquity the greatest authority in dream-interpretation was held to be Artemidorus Daldianus, for whose detailed work we must be grateful as a substitute for the writings on the subject that have not survived.[5]

The ancients' pre-scientific conception of dream was undoubtedly consonant with their entire worldview, which was in the habit of projecting as reality in the outside world that which had reality only in the life of the mind. Moreover, it took account of the chief impression that the waking mind receives from the memory of a dream that is left behind in the morning, because in recollection dream appears as something alien, something that, as it were, stems from another world, running counter to the remaining content of the mind. Incidentally, it would be a mistake to think that the theory of the supernatural origin of dreams lacks disciples in our own day; apart from all the pietistic, mystical writers (who quite rightly, let it be said, keep what remains of the once extensive area of the supernatural under occupation, where it has not yet been conquered by scientific explanation), one finds even astute men with no taste for the adventurous seeking to base their religious belief in the existence and intervention of supernatural spiritual forces precisely on the inexplicability of dream-phenomena (Haffner).[6] The evaluation of dream-life reached by certain schools of philosophy (the followers of Schelling, for example) is a clear echo of the divinity of dream (unchallenged in antiquity). Nor is the debate yet closed regarding the prognosticatory, future-proclaiming power of dream. The fact is, psychological attempts at explanation are not equal to dealing with the accumulated material, no matter how unambiguously the sympathies of anyone who has devoted himself to the scientific approach may mind him to refute such a claim.

What makes writing a history of our scientific understanding of dream-problems so difficult is that in it, however valuable it may have been in some respects, progress in specific directions is not in evidence. No foundation of solid results has been laid on which the next researcher might have continued to build; on the contrary, each new author takes up the same problems anew and, as it were, from scratch. If I wished to stick to the chronological sequence of authors and extract from each a summary of his views on the problems of dream, I should have to abandon the idea of sketching a clear overall picture of the current state of knowledge of the subject; I have therefore decided instead to organize my account by topics rather than by authors, and under each problem I shall say what material for the solution of that problem is set down in the literature.

However, since I have not managed to tackle all the relevant literature, which is so diffuse and strays into other areas, I must ask my reader to be content only that no fundamental fact and no important viewpoint has been passed over in this account.

Until recently, most authors felt compelled to deal with sleep and dream in the same context, usually also including an appreciation of similar states that extend into psychopathology as well as dream-like occurrences (hallucinations, visions and so on). By contrast, the latest studies show a concern to keep the subject within limits – for example, by focusing on a single question from the field of dream-life. I should like to see the change as expressing a conviction that, in such obscure matters, enlightenment and agreement can probably only be reached through a series of detailed investigations. Just such a detailed investigation (in the event, one of a specifically psychological nature) is all I can offer here. I have had little occasion to deal with the problem of sleep, since that is an essentially physiological problem, although the description of the sleeping state must include the alteration of the operating conditions for the machinery of the mind.[7] So the literature of sleep is also left out of account in these pages.

Scientific interest in dream-phenomena as such prompts the following pattern of investigation, parts of which flow into one another.

A *How dream relates to waking life*

The naïve verdict of the person who has just woken up assumes that his or her dream, if it does not in fact come from another world, did actually carry the sleeper off into another world. The old physiologist [Karl Friedrich] Burdach [1838], to whom we owe a careful and sensitive description of dream-phenomena, expressed this conviction in a passage that has been much commented on: '. . . the life of the day is never rehearsed with its exertions and pleasures, its joys and griefs; instead, dream sets out to release us from them. Even when our whole mind had been preoccupied with something, when deep pain had rent our inner being, or when a particular task had commanded our entire intellectual attention, our dreams either give us something wholly strange, or they extract mere individual elements from reality for their combinations, or they simply take up the key of our mood and symbolize reality' (p. 474). I. H. Fichte ([1864] I, 541) talks in the same sense directly about *complementary dreams*, calling them one of the mind's secret 'good deeds' of a self-healing nature. Strümpell [1877] expresses himself in similar terms in his study (quite rightly held in universally high esteem) of the nature and origin of dreams: 'A person who dreams has turned his back on the world of waking consciousness . . .' (p. 16); 'In dream, memory of the ordered substance of waking consciousness and its normal behaviour is almost wholly lost . . .' (p. 17); 'The virtually memory-free seclusion of the dreaming mind, cut off from the regular contents and course of waking life . . .' (p. 19).

However, the overwhelming majority of writers took the opposite view as regards how dream relates to the waking life. Haffner, for instance, writes ([1887] p. 245): 'Initially, dreaming is an extension of waking life. Our dreams are always linked to the ideas[8] that occupied consciousness shortly beforehand. Close observation will almost always find a thread linking dream to the events of the past day.' Weygandt ([1893] p. 6) directly contradicts Burdach's frequently cited claim: '. . . because it can often be observed (in the vast majority of dreams, apparently) that these lead us straight back to everyday life rather than releasing us from it'. Maury (*Le sommeil et les rêves* ['Sleep and dreams', 1878], p. 51) puts it pithily: '*nous rêvons de ce que nous avons vu, dit, désiré ou fait*' ['we dream of what we have seen, said, wanted, or done'];[9] Jessen, in his 1855 *Psychologie* (p. 530), is more detailed: 'To a greater or lesser extent the content of dreams is always determined by the individual personality, by his age, sex, class, level of education, usual way of life, and by the events and experiences of his entire life hitherto.'

The most explicit answer to this question is provided by the philosopher J. G. E. Maass (*Über die Leidenschaften* ['Concerning the passions'], 1805): 'Experience confirms our claim that we most frequently dream of the things at which our warmest passions are directed. From this it may be seen that our passions must influence the generation of our dreams. The ambitious man dreams of (perhaps purely imaginary) laurels attained or yet to be attained, while the lover concerns himself in his dreams with the object of his tender hopes . . . All sensual desires and loathings that lurk in the heart may, if for any reason they are aroused, bring it about that from the ideas associated with them a dream is engendered or that those ideas become involved in an already existing dream' (cited by Winterstein in *Zbl. für Psychoanalyse*).

This was no different from the way in which the ancients believed dream-content depended on life. Radestock ([1879] p. 134) recounts how, when on the eve of his campaign against Greece Xerxes was deterred from his decision by good advice but was repeatedly encouraged in it by dreams, the Persians' old rational dream-interpreter, Artabanos, promptly and aptly told him that dream-images usually contained what the person thought when awake.

The didactic poem *De rerum natura*, written by Lucretius, includes the passage:

> *Et quo quisque fere studio devinctus adhaeret,*
> *aut quibus in rebus multum sumus ante morati*
> *atque in ea ratione fuit contenta magis mens,*
> *in somnis eadem plerumque videmur obire;*
> *causidici causas agere et componere leges,*
> *induperatores pugnare ac proelia obire,*
> *. . . etc., etc.* (IV, v, 959)

> [And to whate'er pursuit
> A man most clings absorbed, or what the affairs
> On which we theretofore have tarried much,
> And mind hath strained upon the more, we seem
> In sleep not rarely to go at the same.
> The lawyers seem to plead and cite decrees,
> Commanders they to fight and go at frays . . . etc. etc.
> (translated by William Ellery Leonard, 1921)]

Cicero (*De Divinatione*, II, lxvii, 140) says something very similar, as does Maury much later: '*Maximeque reliquiae rerum earum moventur in animis et agiantur, de quibus vigilantes aut cogitavimus aut egimus.*' ['Then especially do the remnants of our waking thoughts and deeds move and stir within the soul' (translated by W. A. Falconer, 1923).]

The contradiction between these two views of the relationship between dream-life and waking life does indeed seem insoluble. So it is appropriate to recall the account written by F. W. Hildebrandt [1875], who feels that the peculiarities of dream simply cannot be described otherwise than by means of a 'series of antitheses, which seem to intensify to the point of becoming contradictions' (p. 8). 'The *first* of these antitheses are on the one hand the *strict seclusion or isolation* of dream from real, true life, and on the other hand the constant *reaching across* from one to the other, the constant dependence of the one upon the other. – Dream is something quite separate from reality as experienced in the waking state; one might almost say it represents a hermetically sealed existence, divided from real life by an unbridgeable gulf. It detaches us from reality, erases normal recall of the same in us, and places us in a different world and in a quite different life-story, which deep down has nothing to do with the real one . . .' Hildebrandt goes on to explain how when we fall asleep our whole being with its forms of existence disappears 'as if behind an invisible shutter'. One may then (in a dream, say) voyage to St Helena to serve something exquisite in the way of Moselle wines to Napoleon, imprisoned there. One is most charmingly received by the ex-emperor and is almost sorry to see the interesting illusion shattered on waking. But then one compares the dream-situation with reality. One was never a wine merchant, nor had one ever wished to become one. One has never made a sea voyage, and if one did St Helena would be one's least likely choice of destination. One's attitude to Napoleon is far from sympathetic; in fact, it is one of fierce patriotic hatred. And to cap it all, the dreamer was not yet among the living when Napoleon died on the island; forming a personal relationship with him lay outside the realm of possibility. The dream-experience thus appears as something alien inserted between two sections of life, the one perfectly consonant with and continuing the other.

'And yet,' Hildebrandt goes on, 'the apparent *opposite* is equally true and correct. I believe that, with this seclusion and isolation, the most profound relationship and connectedness in fact go hand in hand. We can almost say: whatever a dream presents, it draws the material for it from reality and from the intellectual life that unfolds against the background of that reality . . . However wonderfully dream carries on, actually it can never get away from the real world and both its most sublime and its most farcical images must always borrow their basic material from what has either come before our eyes in the sensory world or already found some place in our waking thoughts – in other words, from what, outwardly or inwardly, we have already experienced.'

Notes

1. [This is the first use, in Freud's text, of *der Traum* as a general phenomenon. See the Translator's Preface.]

2. [I have chosen to render Freud's *Seele* as 'mind', which I see as a vast (and perhaps peculiarly English) concept embracing the whole range of human response from the most trivial perception to the most 'soulful' experience. 'Soul', despite what Bruno Bettelheim says in *Freud and Man's Soul* (1982), is to me simply an aspect of mind.]

3. What follows is taken from Büchsenschütz's careful account (*Traum und Traumdeutung im Altertum* ['Dream and dream-interpretation in the ancient world'], Berlin 1868).

4. The Greek physician Hippocrates deals with how dream relates to disease in a chapter of his famous book.

5. For what happened to dream-interpretation later, in the Middle Ages, see Diepgen and the special investigations of M. Förster, Gotthard, and others. Dream-interpretation among the Jews is discussed by Almoli, Amram, Löwinger, and, most recently, taking the psychoanalytic standpoint into account, by Lauer. Knowledge of Arab dream-interpretation is provided by Drexl, F. Schwarz, and the missionary Tfinkdji, of Japanese by Miura and Iwaya, of Chinese by Secker, and of Indian by Negelein.

6. [For further bibliographical details on this and other authors referred to, see Other Literature at the end of this volume.]

7. [In the specifically neurological context of Chapter 7, it will be appropriate to render Freud's *seelische Apparat* with the somewhat technical 'mental apparatus', but not here.]

8. [*Vorstellungen*; again a very ordinary, very concrete German word (literally: 'placings in front') but in this context something of a technical term. In their *The Language of Psychoanalysis* (1973), translated by Donald Nicholson-Smith, Jean Laplanche and Jean-Bertrand Pontalis, quoting Lalande, define *Vorstellung* ('idea') as being a 'classical term in philosophy and psychology for "that which represents to oneself, that which forms the concrete content of an act of thought", and "in particular the reproduction of an earlier perception". Freud contrasts the idea with the affect; these two elements suffer distinct fates in psychical processes.']

9. [Freud, confident of his readers' linguistic skills, gave many French,

Italian, English and Latin quotations in the original, without a translation. Here the reader will find an English translation substituted or appended as appropriate.]

B *Dream-material – memory in dream*

That all the material that makes up dream-content stems in some way from experience, in that it is reproduced in dream, *remembered* in dream – that much at least we may deem an undisputed finding. Yet it would be a mistake to assume that this kind of connection between dream-content and waking life must emerge without effort as the self-evident outcome of the comparison we have just made. Rather, it must be looked for attentively and will in a whole series of cases contrive to remain long hidden. The reason for this lies in a number of peculiarities that the faculty of recall evinces in dream and that, though widely remarked upon, have thus far eluded explanation. It will be worth appraising those characteristics in detail.

One thing that happens is that material will figure in dream-content that a person does not, in his waking life, recognize as forming part of his knowledge and experience. He recalls dreaming the material concerned well enough but cannot recall experiencing it or when he experienced it. That leaves him unclear as to what sources dream has drawn on, and he may well be tempted to believe in an autonomously productive activity on the part of dream until (often a long while later) a fresh experience, by bringing back the recollection of the earlier experience that had been given up for lost, lays the dream-source bare. The person is then obliged to admit to having known and recalled something in a dream that had eluded his faculty of recall in the waking state.[1]

A particularly impressive example of this kind is recounted by Delboeuf from his own dream-experience. He once dreamed that he saw the garden of his house covered in snow and found two tiny lizards half frozen and buried beneath the snow, which, being an animal-lover, he rescued, warmed up and returned to the little holes in the wall where they belonged. He also gave them a few leaves from a small fern that grew on the wall and of which he knew they were very fond. In the dream he knew the name of the plant: *Asplenium ruta muralis*. The dream then continued, coming back to the lizards after an interpolation and revealing to an astonished Delboeuf two further animals tucking in to the rest of the fern. Looking away, he saw a fifth and then a sixth lizard making for the hole in the wall, and in the end the whole street was covered with a procession of lizards, all travelling in the same direction – and so on.

In the waking state, Delboeuf's knowledge included only a few Latin names of plants, and an *Asplenium* was not among them. To his great astonishment, he was forced to concede that there really was a fern of that name. Its correct description was *Asplenium ruta muraria*, which the dream had distorted slightly. A chance coincidence could presumably not be contemplated; but for Delboeuf it was a puzzle where his dream had drawn this knowledge of the name *Asplenium* from.

The dream occurred in 1862; sixteen years later, visiting a friend, the philosopher spotted a small album of dried flowers of the kind that in many parts of Switzerland are sold to foreigners as gifts. A recollection rose up in him, he opened the herbarium, found in it the *Asplenium* of his dream, and recognized his own handwriting in the accompanying Latin name. Now the connection could be made. In 1860 (two years before the lizard dream), a sister of this friend had visited Delboeuf while honeymooning. On that occasion she had had the album (which was destined for her brother) on her, and Delboeuf had taken the trouble to inscribe in it, at the dictation of a botanist, the Latin names of each of the dried flowers.

The happy accident that makes this example so much worth recounting enabled Delboeuf to trace another part of the content of the dream back to its forgotten source. One day in 1877 he came across an old volume of an illustrated magazine in which he saw a picture of the whole procession of lizards as he had dreamed it in

1862. The volume was dated 1861, and Delboeuf was able to recall that he had been one of the magazine's subscribers from its first appearance.

That dream has access to memories unavailable to the waking person is so noteworthy and theoretically significant a fact that I now wish, by recounting other 'hypermnesic' dreams, to direct more attention to them. Maury tells how, for a while, the word *Mussidan* had a habit of coming into his mind during the day. He knew it as the name of a French town, but that was all. One night he dreamed[2] of a conversation with a certain person, who told him that she came from Mussidan, and to his question as to where the town was, she replied that Mussidan is a district capital in the Département de la Dordogne. On waking, Maury placed no faith in the information contained in the dream; however, the geographical lexicon informed him that it was perfectly correct. In this case the greater knowledge of dream is confirmed but the forgotten source of that knowledge left untraced.

Jessen ([1855] p. 551) recounts a very similar dream-occurrence from an earlier period: 'One of these is a dream by the elder Scaliger (Hennings [1784], p. 300), who wrote a poem in praise of the famous men of Verona and to whom a person named *Brugnolus* appeared in a dream, complaining that he had been overlooked. Although Scaliger could not remember ever having heard of him, he made up some lines about him all the same, and his son later learned in Verona that a man called *Brugnolus* had once enjoyed fame in the city as a critic.'

A hypermnesic dream with the particular characteristic that in a subsequent dream the initially unrecognized memory is identified is recounted by the Marquis d'Hervey de St Denys (quoted in Vaschide [1911], p. 232): 'I once dreamed about a young woman with golden-blonde hair whom I saw chatting with my sister as she showed her a piece of embroidery. In the dream, she struck me as very familiar; I had seen her, I believed, on numerous occasions. After waking, I still have the face vividly before me but am quite unable to recognize it. I go back to sleep, and the dream-image recurs. In this new dream, I address the blonde lady and ask her whether I have had the pleasure of meeting her before somewhere. "Oh, yes," the lady replies, "just think back to the seaside resort of Pornic." I instantly woke up again, now able to recall with complete certainty the details with which this lovely dream-face was once associated.'

The same author (in Vaschide, p. 233) reports: A musician of his acquaintance once heard in a dream a tune that seemed wholly new to him. Not until several years later did he come across the tune in an old anthology of pieces that even then he was unable to recollect ever having had in his hand before.

In a publication to which I unfortunately have no access (*Proceedings of the Society for Psychical Research*), apparently Myers reproduced a whole collection of such hypermnesic dreams. It is my belief that anyone dealing with dreams must accept as an entirely normal phenomenon that dream bears witness to items of knowledge and experience that the waking person does not think he or she possessed. In psychoanalytical work with neurotics, which I shall be reporting on later, I find myself in the situation, several times a week, of proving to patients from their dreams that they do in fact know certain quotations, obscene words and the like perfectly well and make use of them in dream, despite the fact that in their waking lives they have forgotten them.

Let me tell you about an innocuous case of dream-hypermnesia here, because in it the source of the knowledge accessible only to the dreaming mind can be found very easily. A patient dreamed in a more extended context that he had ordered a *Kontuszówka* in a coffee-house, but after telling me this he asked what such a thing might be; he had never heard the name. I was able to reply that *Kontuszówka* was a Polish schnapps that he could not possibly have invented in the dream since the name had long been familiar to me from posters. The man refused to believe me at first. Some days later, having in the mean time allowed his dream in the coffee-house to become reality, the man spotted the name on a poster – on a street corner that he must have passed at least twice a day for months.

I have myself learned from dreams of my own how much we remain reliant on chance as regards discovering the origins of individual dream-elements. For example, I used to be haunted for years before writing this book by the image of a very simply shaped church tower that I could not remember having seen. Then suddenly I recognized it, with utter certainty, at a stop on the railway between Salzburg and Reichenhall. That was in the late 1890s, and I had first travelled the stretch in 1886. In later years, when I was already deeply involved in the study of dreams, the often recurring dream-image of a certain curious location became almost a burden to me. I saw, in a specific topographical relationship to my person, on my left, a dark space out of which several grotesque sandstone figures shone forth. A glimmer of memory to which I was unwilling to give credence told me that this was the entrance to a beer cellar; however, I could explain neither what this dream-image was trying to tell me nor where it came from. In 1907, chance brought me to Padua, which to my regret I had not been able to revisit since 1895. My first visit to that beautiful university city had remained unsatisfactory: I had not been able to see Giotto's frescoes in the Madonna dell'Arena; in fact, I had turned back halfway along the street leading to the chapel on being told that it was closed that day. On my second visit, twelve years later, I thought to make up for this, and the first thing I did was seek out the Madonna dell'Arena. In the street leading to it, on my left, probably at the place where I had turned back in 1895, I discovered the locality I had seen so often in dreams, complete with its sandstone figures. It was indeed the entrance to a tavern garden.

One of the sources from which dream draws material for reproduction (some of it material unremembered by and unused in the mental activity of waking life) is the life of childhood. I shall cite only a few of the authors who have noticed and laid emphasis on this:

Hildebrandt ([1875] p. 23): 'It has been explicitly conceded that dream will sometimes, with marvellous reproductive power, faithfully bring back before our mind's eye quite remote and even forgotten occurrences from the most distant past.'

Strümpell ([1877] p. 40): 'Matters intensify even further if we observe how sometimes dream draws out, as it were from beneath the deepest and most solid deposits with which later life has overlaid the earliest youthful experiences, images of individual places, objects and persons fully intact and with all their original freshness. This is not merely confined to impressions that on coming into existence attained vivid awareness or became associated with powerful psychical values and that subsequently, in dream, return as actual memories in which the adult consciousness delights. It is rather that the depths of dream-memory also include images of persons, objects, places and experiences from the earliest years that had either attained only slight awareness or possessed no psychical value or had lost both the one and the other long ago and that therefore also appear both in dreams and after waking as wholly strange and unfamiliar – until such time as their early origin is discovered.'

Volkelt ([1875] p. 119): 'It is particularly remarkable how readily memories of childhood and youth enter into dream. Things we have not thought about for ages, that lost all importance for us ages ago – these things dream tirelessly remind us of.'

The way dream holds sway over childhood material (most of which notoriously falls through the gaps of our conscious ability to remember) prompts the emergence of some interesting hypermnesic dreams, of which again I want to give you a few examples.

Maury ([1878] p. 92) recounts how, as a child, he frequently travelled from his home town of Meaux to nearby Trilport, where his father was supervising the construction of a bridge. One night, dream transports him to Trilport and again has him playing in the streets of the town. A man comes up to him, wearing a sort of uniform. Maury asks him his name; the man introduces himself as C. and says he is the bridge watchman. After waking, still doubting the reality of the memory, Maury asks an old servant who has been with him since childhood whether she can remember a man of that name. 'Oh, yes,' comes the answer. 'He was the watchman of the bridge your father was building at the time.'

An equally neatly confirmed example of the reliability of the childhood memory that crops up in dream is one Maury records about a Mr F., who as a child had grown up in Montbrison. Twenty-five years after leaving the place, this man decided to go back to his home town and revisit old family friends whom he had not seen since. The night before his departure, he dreams that he has reached his destination and that near Montbrison he meets a gentleman whom he does not know by sight; the gentleman tells him he is Mr T., a friend of his father. The dreamer was aware that as a child he had known a gentleman of that name, but in waking life he could no longer remember what he looked like. A few days later, having really arrived in Montbrison, he identifies the site of the dream (which he had thought he did not know) and meets a man whom he immediately recognizes as the T. of the dream. The only difference was that the real person had aged very much more than the dream-image had shown him.

Here I can recount a dream of my own in which the impression to be recalled is replaced by a relationship. In a dream I saw a person concerning whom I was aware in the dream that he was the doctor in my home town. His face was not clear but was mixed up with the way I remember one of my secondary-school teachers, whom I still see occasionally. Awake, I was unable to work out the connection between these two persons. But when I asked my mother about the doctor who had overseen my earliest childhood years, I learned that he had had only one eye – as had the secondary-school teacher whose person had overlaid that of the doctor in the dream. Thirty-eight years had passed since I had last seen the doctor, and to the best of my knowledge I had never, in my waking life, given him a thought.

It sounds like an attempt to create a counterweight to the immense role of childhood impressions in dream-life when a number of writers claim that, in most dreams, elements from the immediate past can be proven. Robert ([1886] p. 46) even says that, generally speaking, the normal dream is concerned only with the impressions of the last few days. We shall learn, though, that the dream-theory developed by Robert absolutely requires such a pushing back of the earliest experiences and a moving forward of the most recent. However, the fact to which Robert gives expression does in fact hold, as I can confirm from my own investigations. An

American writer, Nelson, suggests that the impressions used most often in dreams are those of the day prior to the day of the dream or of the day before that, as if the impressions of the day immediately preceding the dream-day were not sufficiently softened, were not remote enough.

Several writers who would not wish to cast doubt on the close connection between dream-content and waking life have been struck by the fact that impressions that intensively preoccupy the waking mind do not occur in dream until the everyday work of thought has pushed them to one side, so to speak. For instance, people do not usually dream about a departed loved one in the time immediately following that loved one's death, while the survivors are still wholly taken up with mourning (Delage [1891]). However, one of the most recent observers, Hallam [1896], has also collected examples of the opposite behaviour, championing the cause of psychological individuality with regard to this point.

The third, most remarkable and least understandable characteristic of dream-memory comes out in the selection of the material reproduced. It is not, as in waking life, only the most significant things that are regarded as worth remembering but on the contrary also the most trivial and unprepossessing. On this subject, let us listen to the words of those writers who have voiced their surprise at this in the most powerful terms.

Hildebrandt ([1875] p. 11): 'Because what is most remarkable is that dream does not usually draw its elements from the great, far-reaching events, not from the powerful, driving interests of the day gone by, but from the most peripheral details, the worthless bits and pieces, so to speak, of the past most recently experienced or lying further back in time. The shattering death in the family, the oppressive weight of which kept us from sleep until the early hours, remains erased from our memory until the first instant of waking brings it back with crushing force. By contrast, the wart on the brow of a stranger in the street to whom we do not give a moment's thought after passing him by – that will play a part in our dream [. . .].'

Strümpell ([1877]) p. 39): '[. . .] such cases where dissecting a dream uncovers components of the same that, while they stem from the experience of the previous day or the day before that, were of such small importance and value to the waking consciousness that shortly after being experienced they sank into oblivion. Experiences of this kind may be remarks overheard by chance or another's actions superficially observed, rapid and transient perceptions of things or persons, individual fragments of things read – that sort of thing.'

Havelock Ellis ([1899] p. 727): 'The profound emotions of waking life, the questions and problems on which we spread our chief voluntary mental energy, are not those which usually present themselves at once to dream consciousness. It is, so far as the immediate past is concerned, mostly the trifling, the incidental, the "forgotten" impressions of daily life which reappear in our dreams. The psychic activities that are awake most intensely are those that sleep most profoundly.'[3]

Binz ([1878] p. 45) takes the very characteristics of dream-memory as an opportunity to express his dissatisfaction with the explanations of dream that he backs himself: 'And the natural dream confronts us with similar questions. Why do we not always dream the memory-impressions of the days last experienced but often immerse ourselves, for no apparent reason, in past times that lie far behind us and are almost extinct? Why does consciousness, in dream, so often receive the impression of *trivial* memory-images, while the brain cells, in places where they carry within them the most sensitive records of experience, usually lie mute and rigid – except where an urgent renewal during waking has excited them shortly before?'

It is easy to see how dream-memory's extraordinary predilection for the trivial and hence unheeded among the day's experiences usually led inexorably to our simply failing to spot how dependent dream is on everyday existence, which then made it more difficult at least to prove the same in each individual instance. It was possible, for instance, for Mary Whiton Calkins [1893], when processing her (and her partner's) dreams statistically, to be left with eleven per cent of the total in which no relationship to everyday life could be seen. Hildebrandt was undoubtedly right to say that all dream-images would be explicable to us genetically if on each occasion we spent sufficient time and concentration on tracing their origins. He admittedly calls this 'an extremely laborious and thankless task. Because it would mostly come down to flushing out all manner of psychically quite worthless things in the remotest corners of memory, disinterring all manner of entirely indifferent moments from times long forgotten that the very next hour may have buried, and returning them to the light of day.' However, I have to say how sorry I am that this astute writer allows himself to be prevented from pursuing an avenue that starts so unprepossessingly; it would have led him straight to the heart of explaining dreams.

The behaviour of dream-memory is undoubtedly of great significance as regards any theory of memory generally. It teaches us (according to Scholz [1887], p. 34) that 'nothing that our minds once possessed can ever be wholly lost'. Or, as Delboeuf puts it, *'que toute impression, même la plus insignifiante, laisse une trace inaltérable, indéfiniment susceptible de reparaître au jour'* ['that every impression, even the least significant, leaves a permanent trace, forever liable to come back to light'] – a conclusion towards which so many other pathological manifestations of the inner life likewise press. Let us bear in mind this extraordinary efficiency of memory in dream in order that we may experience more vividly the contradiction that certain dream-theories (we shall be coming to these later) are obliged to posit in seeking to explain the absurdity and incoherence of dreams by means of a partial forgetting of our daytime knowledge.

It might, for example, occur to one to reduce the whole phenomenon of dream to one of remembering, seeing dreams as the expression of a reproductive activity that does not cease even at night and is an end in itself. Contributions such as the one made by Pilcz [1899] would agree; according to this author, fixed connections between the time of dreaming and the content of dreams can be proved, with impressions from the earliest times being reproduced during deep sleep, whereas towards morning more recent impressions crop up. However, such a view is rendered unlikely from the outset by the way in which dreams deal with the material to be recalled. Strümpell rightly points out that repetitions of experiences do not occur in dream. A dream may well start out in that direction, but the follow-up fails to materialize; the experience appears in an altered form, or something quite different appears instead. Dream brings only fragments of reproductions. This is undoubtedly so often the case as to permit a theoretical assessment. There are exceptions, however, in which a dream repeats an experience as completely as our memory is able to do when we are awake. Delboeuf tells how a university colleague of his re-experienced in dream, with all the details, a dangerous carriage journey in which he had escaped accident only as if by a miracle. Mary Whiton Calkins mentions two dreams consisting of precise reproductions of an experience of the preceding day, and I shall myself take the opportunity later on to recount an example that has come to my attention of a childhood experience recurring in dream unchanged.[4]

Notes

1. Vaschide [1899] also claims that it has often been remarked that in dream a person is able to speak foreign languages with greater fluency and correctness than when awake.
2. [*Eines Nachts traümte ihm* . . . The reader should be aware that German has this impersonal structure ('One night there dreamed to him . . .'), which presumably reflects the very question Freud is here discussing: is dream an *activity* of the mind or is it *experienced by* the mind?]
3. [Here Freud quotes the original English.]
4. I would add from subsequent experience that it is by no means infrequent for innocuous and unimportant concerns of the day to be repeated by dream: it might be packing suitcases, preparing food in the kitchen, etc. However, in connection with such dreams, the dreamer does not personally stress the nature of memory but that of 'reality'. 'I really did do all that on the day.'

C *Dream-stimuli and sources of dream*

What should be understood by 'dream-stimuli and sources of dream' can be clarified by reference to the [German] popular saying: *'Träume kommen vom Magen'* ['Dreams come from the stomach']. Underlying this concept is a theory that sees dream as resulting from a disturbance of sleep. One would not have dreamed unless something had occurred to disturb one's sleep, and one's dream is the reaction to that disturbance.

Discussion about what prompts dreams takes up the largest amount of space in the various accounts. Self-evidently, the problem could only arise once dream had become an object of biological research. The ancients, for whom dream was a divine missive of some kind, had no need to seek a stimulus for it; dream flowed from the will of the divine or demonic power, its content from what that power knew or intended. For science, the question immediately arose as to whether the incentive for dreaming is always the same or whether it can be a number of things, and this led to people weighing up whether the causal explanation of dream lies in the realm of psychology or that of physiology. Most writers seem to assume that the causes of sleep disturbance (the sources of dream, in other words) may be of many different sorts, and that physical urges as well as states of mental arousal play a part in prompting dream. When it comes to preferring one source of dream over the other, placing them in order of precedence according to their significance in terms of engendering the phenomenon, opinions differ widely.

Where the enumeration of sources of dream is complete, the

eventual result is four types, which are also used for classifying dreams themselves:

1. external (objective) sensory arousal
2. internal (subjective) sensory arousal
3. internal (organic) physical stimulus
4. purely psychical stimuli.

1 *External sensory stimuli*

As we know, the younger Strümpell,[1] son of the philosopher whose work on the subject of dream we have already used several times as a guide to dream-problems, reported his observation of a patient afflicted with general anaesthesia of the integument and paralysis of several of the higher sense organs. When this man was deprived experimentally of the few sensory gateways to the outside world still open to him, he fell asleep. If we wish to go to sleep, we generally seek to put ourselves in a situation similar to that in Strümpell's experiment. We close the principal sensory gateways, namely the eyes, and try to prevent the other senses from receiving any stimuli or any alteration of the stimuli already operating on them. We then fall asleep, although our efforts are never wholly successful. We can neither keep stimuli away from our sense organs entirely nor wholly rid those organs of their susceptibility. The fact that we can be woken at any time by more powerful stimuli is our proof 'that even in sleep the mind [has remained] in constant contact with the world beyond the body'. The sensory stimuli that reach us during sleep may very well become sources of dream.

Such stimuli exist in great numbers, of course, ranging from those that the sleeping state inevitably involves or need only occasionally countenance to the chance waking stimulus that is likely or intended to bring an end to sleep. A brighter light may shine into the eyes, a noise make itself heard, some odorous material stimulate the mucous membrane of the nose. We may, in sleep, make involuntary movements that expose individual parts of the body, causing them to feel cold, or by changing our position ourselves generate feelings of pressure and contact. A fly may bite us, or a minor nocturnal accident may bombard a number of senses simultaneously. The keen attention of observers has collected a whole series of dreams in which the stimulus noted on waking and a portion of the dream-content coincide so closely that it was possible to identify the stimulus as a dream-source.

Here is a collection of such dreams going back to objective (more or less accidental) sensory stimulation, as cited by Jessen ([1855] p. 527): Any vaguely perceived sound arouses corresponding dream-images, the rumble of thunder transports us to the heart of a battle, the crowing of a cockerel may turn into a human cry of fear, a creaking door may evoke dreams of thieves breaking in.

If we lose our bedclothes at night, we may dream that we are walking around naked or that we have fallen into some water. If we are lying diagonally in bed and our feet project beyond the edge, our dream may be that we are standing on the edge of a fearful abyss or that we are falling down a steep slope. Should our head accidentally find its way beneath the pillow, an immense rock is hanging over us, about to bury us beneath its weight. Accumulations of semen generate lascivious dreams, localized pains produce the idea of our suffering mistreatment, hostile assaults, or actual physical injury . . .

'Meier (*Versuch einer Erklärung des Nachtwandels* ['An attempt to explain sleep-walking'], Halle, 1758, p. 33) once dreamed that he was being attacked by several persons, who had laid him full-length on the ground, on his back, and were driving a stake into the earth between his big toe and second toe. Imagining this in his dream, he woke up to feel that a piece of straw was poking between his toes. The same man, according to Hennings (*Von den Träumen und Nachtwandlern* ['Of dreams and sleep-walkers'], Weimar, 1784, p. 258), dreamed on another occasion, having bunched his shirt up rather hard around his neck, that he was being hanged. Hoffbauer [1796] dreamed in his youth of falling from a high wall and noticed on waking that the bed had come apart and that he really had fallen . . . Gregory reports that he had once, on going to bed, placed a bottle filled with hot water at his feet and that he had then, in the dream, climbed to the summit of Etna, where he had found the earth he stood on almost intolerably hot. Someone else, having laid a poultice on his head, dreamed that he was being scalped by a troop of Red Indians; a third person, who was sleeping in a damp shirt, believed that he was being dragged through a stream. An attack of gout occurring during sleep caused one patient to believe that he had fallen into the hands of the Inquisition and was being tortured' (Macnish [1835]).

The argument based on the similarity between stimulus and dream-content receives some reinforcement when a successful attempt is made, by deliberately applying sensory stimuli to a sleeping person, to engender the dream corresponding to the particular stimulus. According to Macnish, such experiments were carried out by Girou de Buzareingues. 'He left his knees uncovered and dreamed that he was travelling on a post-coach at night. He remarked in this connection that travellers would no doubt know that, in a carriage, the knees get cold at night. Another time he left the back of his head uncovered and dreamed that he was attending a religious ceremony in the open. It was the custom, you see, in the country he lived in, to keep the head covered at all times, except on such occasions as the one just mentioned.'

Maury tells of fresh observations of self-engendered dreams. (A series of other experiments was unsuccessful.)

1) He is tickled with a feather on the lips and the tip of his nose. – He dreams of a frightful torture; a pitch-mask is placed on his face, then torn away, taking the skin with it.

2) A pair of shears is sharpened. – He hears bells ringing, then sounds of a storm, and is transported back to the June of 1848.

3) He is made to smell *eau de Cologne*. – He is in Cairo, in the shop of Johann Maria Farina. Marvellous adventures follow, which he is unable to reproduce.

4) He is given a light tap on the back of the neck. – He dreams that he is having a poultice applied, and thinks of a doctor who treated him when he was a child.

5) A hot iron is brought close to his face. – He dreams about *chauffeurs*;[2] some have slipped into the house and are forcing the inmates to surrender their money by sticking their feet in the fire. Then the Duchess of Abrantès appears, whose secretary he dreams he is.

8) A little water is poured on his forehead. – He is in Italy, sweating profusely and drinking Orvieto white wine.

9) The light of a candle is repeatedly allowed to shine on him through a sheet of red paper. – He dreams about weather, about heat, and is back in a storm at sea that he once experienced in the English Channel.

Other attempts to generate dreams experimentally stem from d'Hervey and Weygandt, among others.

Numerous writers have remarked on the 'striking skill with which dream [...] weaves sudden impressions from the world of the senses into its fabric in such a way that they form in it a gradually pre-prepared, induced catastrophe' (Hildebrandt [1875]). 'In recent years,' the same writer tells us, 'I have sometimes made use, in order to get up regularly at a specific time in the morning, of the alarm that, notoriously, is usually attached to clocks. There have probably been hundreds of occasions when I found that the sound of this instrument fitted so neatly into an apparently very lengthy and coherent dream as to suggest that the whole dream had in fact been based on it alone and found therein its truly essential logical point, its naturally indicated final objective.'

I cite three of these alarm-clock dreams below, for a different purpose.

Volkelt ([1875] pp. 108f.) writes: 'A composer once dreamed that he was teaching a class and was just trying to explain something to his pupils. As soon as he had finished, he turned to a boy and asked him, "Did you understand what I was saying?" The boy yelled back like one possessed, "Oh, yes!" Indignantly, he pointed out that the boy was yelling. But by then the whole class was yelling, "Or-ya." Then, "Ire-yo." And finally, "Fire-yo."[3] And at this point he was woken up by real shouts from the street – about an actual fire.'

Garnier (*Traité des facultés de l'âme* ['Treatise on the powers of the mind'], 1865 [1872 2nd edn]), cited by Radestock [1878], reports that Napoleon I was woken by the exploding time bomb from a dream that he had while sleeping in his carriage and that brought back to him the experience of crossing the Tagliamento and of the Austrian bombardment, so that he started up shouting, 'We are undermined.'

A dream that Maury once had ([1878] p. 161) has become famous. He was sick and lying in bed in his room; his mother sat beside him. He had a dream about the Reign of Terror at the time of the Revolution, witnessed ghastly scenes of murder, and was eventually himself indicted. In the court he saw Robespierre, Marat, Fouquier-Tinville, and all the sorry heroes of that dreadful time, justified himself before them, and after a variety of incidents that did not fix themselves in his memory was condemned and subsequently, accompanied by vast crowds, taken to the place of execution. He climbed the scaffold, and the executioner attached him to the board; the board turned over; the blade of the guillotine descended; he felt his head being separated from his body and woke in the most appalling fear – to find that part of the bed had come down and hit him on the back of the neck, just like a guillotine blade.

This dream gave rise to an interesting discussion, launched by Le Lorrain and Egger in the pages of the *Revue philosophique*, about whether and how it was possible for the dreamer, in the brief time between perceiving the waking stimulus and actually waking up, to cram in such an apparent wealth of dream-content.

Instances such as these make objective sensory stimuli during sleep appear to be the best-guaranteed sources of dream. Moreover, in the minds of laymen, this is the only kind of dream of which there is any question. Ask an educated man (who otherwise has no knowledge of the literature of dream) how dreams happen and he will undoubtedly reply by referring to a case that he has heard about where a dream was explained in terms of an objective sense perception identified after waking. The scientific approach cannot stop there; it is prompted to ask further questions by observing that the stimulus operating on the senses during sleep does not, in dream, appear in its true guise but is represented by some other conceit that is in some way related to it. However, the relation between the dream-stimulus and the dream-outcome is, in Maury's words ([1853] p. 72), *'une affinité quelconque, mais qui n'est pas unique et exclusive'* ['some kind of affinity, but one that is not unique and exclusive']. Listening to three of Hildebrandt's alarm-clock dreams, for example, one needs to ask why the same stimulus evoked such different dream-outcomes, and why those precisely ([1875] p. 37):

Out walking one spring morning, I stroll through green fields to a neighbouring village, where I see the inhabitants in their best clothes, hymnbooks tucked under their arms, proceeding in large numbers to church. Of course! It's Sunday, is it not, and early service is about to start. I decide to attend, but beforehand, since I am feeling rather warm, to cool off in the graveyard surrounding the church. As I am reading various gravestones, I hear the bellringer climbing the tower and see, at the top, the little village bell that will give the sign for worship to begin. For quite a while it continues to hang there motionless, then it starts to swing. And suddenly its strokes ring out, high and piercing – so high and so piercing as to terminate my sleep. However, the ringing is from my alarm clock.

A second combination. It is a bright winter's day; the streets are piled high with snow. I have agreed to go on a sleigh ride, but I have to wait a long time before hearing that the sleigh is at the door. There follow the preparations for getting in – the fur is put in place, the foot bag pulled out – and at length I am sitting in my seat. But still the departure is delayed until the reins give the waiting horses the sign they can feel. They begin to pull; the powerfully agitated bells start up their well-known Turkish music, playing with such force as instantly to shred the delicate web of dream. Again, it is simply the shrill sound of the alarm clock.

Now for the third example! I see a kitchen maid striding along the passage to the dining-room with several dozen plates stacked high. The pile of china in her arms seems to me to be in danger of toppling. 'Look out!' I warn. 'The whole lot will come crashing down.' Naturally, I get the inevitable contradiction: we do this sort of thing all the time, etc., whilst I, meanwhile, continue to follow the maid's progress with anxious glances. Sure enough, on the threshold she stumbles on the sill – and the fragile dishes fall and shatter into hundreds of shards on the floor all around. Except that the sound, which goes on and on, is not, as I soon become aware, one of shattering at all but a real ringing – for which, as the waker now realizes, the alarm clock bears sole responsibility.

The question as to why, in dream, the mind fails to recognize the nature of the objective sensory stimulus is answered by Strümpell (and in almost the same terms by Wundt) to the effect that it finds itself, vis-à-vis such stimuli arising in sleep, meeting the conditions of illusion formation. A sense impression is *recognized* by us and *correctly interpreted*, i.e. classified in the memory group to which, according to all previous experience, it belongs, if the impression is powerful, clear, lasts for long enough, and if we have the required time at our disposal for such reflection. If those conditions are not fulfilled, we fail to recognize the object from which the impression stems; on the basis of that object, we form an illusion. 'If someone goes for a walk in open country and dimly perceives a distant object, it may happen that he thinks at first it is a horse.' As he draws closer, the interpretation of a cow lying down may impose itself, and eventually the picture may resolve itself with certainty into that of a group of seated people. Well, the impressions that the mind receives in sleep as a result of external stimuli are of a similarly indistinct nature; on that basis, it forms illusions in that the impression evokes a larger or smaller number of memory pictures that give the impression its psychical value. From which of the many possible memory groups the relevant images are aroused and what potential associative links are activated in this connection – these are things that Strümpell himself believes cannot be determined, being at the whim of the inner life, so to speak.

At this point, we face a choice. We can concede that the laws of dream-formation really cannot be pursued any further, thus neglecting to enquire whether interpreting the illusion evoked by the sense impression is not subject to different conditions. Or we can surmise that the objective sensory stimulus operating in sleep plays only a minor role as a source of dream and that other factors determine the selection of the memory-images to be evoked. The fact is, examining Maury's experimentally induced dreams (which I have recounted at such length with this in mind), one is tempted to say that the experiment he set up actually covers only one of the elements of dream so far as its origin is concerned. The remaining dream-content seems too autonomous, too set in its details, to be explicable in terms of the one requirement that it should be consistent with the element introduced experimentally. Indeed, one begins to question the illusion theory oneself and to doubt the power of the objective impression to shape dream when one learns that there are occasions when that impression receives, in dream, the most unlikely and far-fetched interpretation. Simon [1888], for example, recounts a dream in which he saw gigantic people seated at table and clearly heard the appalling clatter made by their jaws smiting together as they chewed. He woke to hear the hoofbeats of a horse galloping by outside his window. If in this instance the noise of a horse's hooves evokes images from *Gulliver's Travels*, of his sojourn with the giants of Brobdingnag, and of the horses endowed with reason (which is the interpretation that, without any help from the author, I want to advance), then surely the selection of what, given the stimulus, is so unusual a memory group can be explained more easily with the addition of other motives as well?[4]

2 *Internal (subjective) sensory arousal*

All objections notwithstanding, it must be conceded that the role of objective sensory arousals during sleep as a source of dream indubitably exists, and if such stimuli perhaps seem inadequate in terms of their nature and frequency to explain all dream-images, the suggestion is that we look for different sources of dream, but ones having a similar effect. I do not know where the idea first cropped up of enlisting not only external sensory stimuli but also internal (subjective) arousals in the sense organs; the fact is, however, that in all recent accounts of the aetiology of dreams this happens in a more or less explicit manner. 'A key role is also, as I believe,' writes Wundt ([1880] p. 363), 'played in connection with dream-illusions by the subjective visual and aural sensations known to us from the waking state as the luminous chaos of the dark field of vision, as ringing or buzzing in the ears, and so on. Such sensations particularly include subjective retinal arousals. Hence the curious inclination of dream to conjure up before the eye similar or wholly identical objects in the plural. We see vast numbers of birds, butterflies, fish, coloured beads, flowers and the like spread out before us. Here the luminous dust of the dark field of vision has taken on fantastic form, and the countless points of light that make it up are embodied by dream into as many individual images, which because of the mobility of luminous chaos are viewed as objects *in motion*. This is no doubt also the root of dream's marked inclination towards the most multifarious animal shapes, the great variety of which marries easily with the distinctive shape of subjective luminous images.'

As sources of dream-images, subjective sensory arousals have the clear advantage that they are not, like objective stimuli, dependent on external chance. They are (one might say) open to explanation as often as they require it. However, they take second place to objective sensory stimuli in that it is only with difficulty (if at all) that they are susceptible of the kind of confirmation of their role as dream-triggers that observation and experiment grant to the latter. The main evidence for the power of subjective sensory arousals to trigger dreams is provided by what are called 'hypnagogic hallucinations', which Johannes Müller described as 'fantastical visual manifestations'. These are often extremely vivid and varied images that during the period of falling asleep appear very regularly in the case of many people and may remain in existence for some time even after they open their eyes. Maury, who was subject to them to a high degree, devoted a thorough appreciation to them, claiming that they are connected with – indeed, actually identical to – dream-images (as had Müller before him). According to Maury, a certain emotional passivity, a slackening of attention, is necessary for them to emerge (pp. 59f.).[5] All it takes, however, is for a person to lapse into that kind of lethargy for a second in order, in such a mood, to see a hypnagogic hallucination; subsequently he or she may wake up again, until after several repetitions the game ends with the person falling asleep. If, after not too long a time, that person then wakes up again, it often happens, according to Maury, that the same images can be shown to have appeared in dream as those he or she glimpsed fleetingly as hypnagogic illusions before falling asleep (p. 134). This happened to Maury on one occasion with a series of grotesque figures with contorted faces and odd hairstyles that pestered him with incredible insistence in the period of falling asleep and about which he remembered, after waking, that he had dreamed. Another time, when suffering from hunger pangs because he had imposed a meagre diet on himself, he saw, hypnagogically, a dish together with a hand brandishing a fork that helped itself to some of the food in the dish. In the dream, he was seated at a richly decked table and could hear the sound that the diners were making with their forks. Another time, going to sleep with irritated, painful eyes, he had the hypnagogic illusion of microscopically tiny characters that it cost him a great deal of effort to decipher; waking up an hour later, he recalled a dream featuring an open book with very small print that he had been required very laboriously to read.

Much like such images, auditory illusions of words, names and so on may also appear hypnagogically and then recur in dream, almost as an overture heralds the themes of the opera it is introducing.

The same paths as are traced by Müller and Maury are followed by a recent observer of hypnagogic illusions, G. Trumbull Ladd [1892]. He trained himself to the point where, between two and five minutes after gradually falling asleep, he could wrench himself out of sleep without opening his eyes, giving himself the opportunity to compare the retinal sensations then in the process of disappearing with the dream-images that survived in his memory. He assures us that, on each occasion, a close relationship could be recognized between the two in that the luminous points and lines of the spontaneous light of the retina as it were provided the outline for the dream-figures that he perceived psychically. For instance, a dream in which he clearly saw lines of print that he read and studied reproduced an arrangement of points of light on the retina forming parallel lines. To put it his way: the clearly printed page that he read in dream dissolved into an object that to his waking perception resembled a piece of an actual printed page being looked at (from too far away to make anything out distinctly) through a tiny hole in a sheet of paper. Ladd's view (incidentally, without underestimating the central importance of the phenomenon) is that scarcely a single visual dream unfolds within us that does not depend on the material of the inner states of arousal of the retina. This is particularly true [he says] of the dreams that come shortly after the dreamer falls asleep in a darkened room, whereas with regard to the dreams that come in the morning, shortly before waking, the objective light forcing its way into the eye in the brightened room provides the stimulus. The varied, endlessly variable character of spontaneous luminous arousal corresponds precisely to the restless, fleeting sequence of images with which our dreams present us. If we attach importance to Ladd's observations, we cannot dismiss the fertility of this subjective dream-trigger lightly, since visual images, as we know, constitute the major component of our dreams. The contribution of other areas of sensory perception, including hearing, is of lesser importance and inconstant.

3 *The internal, organic physical stimulus*

While we are in the process of looking for sources of dream not outside but inside the organism, we must bear in mind that almost all our internal organs, which in the healthy state draw little attention to their continued existence, become, in states of stimulation (as we call them) or during illness, a source of what are usually painful sensations for us that must be placed on an equal footing, so to speak, with the causes of pain and sensory stimuli coming from outside. The experiences are very old ones that prompt Strümpell

([1877] p. 107), for example, to say: 'In sleep, the mind reaches a very much deeper and broader awareness of its physicality than in the waking state, and is obliged to receive and be subject to the effects of certain sensory impressions stemming from parts of the body and changes in the body of which, in the waking state, it knew nothing.' Aristotle stated that it could well be that, in dream, we have our attention drawn to incipient states of ill-health of which we had noticed nothing as yet when awake (by virtue of the magnification that dream permits impressions to undergo; see p. 12 above), and medical writers whose way of looking at things certainly did not include crediting dream with a prophetic gift were, at least so far as heralding sickness was concerned, prepared to grant dream this significance (see Simon [1888], p. 31, and many earlier writers).[6]

There seems to be no shortage of authenticated examples of such diagnoses provided by dream in recent times as well. For instance, Tissié (cited in Artigues [1884]), tells of a thirty-four-year-old woman who, through several years of apparently perfect health, was visited by anxiety dreams and whom subsequent medical examination showed to have incipient heart disease, from which she promptly died.

Pronounced disturbances of the internal organs clearly act as dream-triggers in a whole series of people. Generally, it is the frequency of anxiety dreams among sufferers from heart and lung disorders that is talked about; in fact, many writers thrust this aspect of dream-life so much into the foreground that all I need do here is simply refer to the literature: Radestock, Spitta, Maury, Simon and Tissié. Tissié goes so far as to assert that the diseased organs give the dream-content its characteristic shape. The dreams of heart patients are usually very short and end with a sudden, frightened awakening; death in hideous circumstances almost always features in the content of such dreams. Tubercular patients dream of suffocating, being crowded, taking flight, and a striking number of them have the familiar nightmare that, incidentally, Börner [1855] was able to provoke experimentally by laying subjects face-down and covering their breathing orifices. In people with digestive disorders, dream contains ideas from the realms of eating and nausea. Lastly, the influence of sexual arousal on the content of dreams is pretty concrete so far as every individual's experience is concerned and gives the whole theory of dream-triggering by organic stimulation its most cogent support.

Another thing that is quite unmistakable from a perusal of the literature of dream is that some writers (Maury, Weygandt) were led to a preoccupation with dream-problems by the influence of their own state of health on the content of their dreams.

Actually, the increase in dream-sources from these indubitably established facts is not as great as one might think. Dream, after all, is a phenomenon that occurs with healthy people (possibly with everyone, possibly every night), and clearly organ disorder is not among its indispensable conditions. Our concern, though, is not with where exceptional dreams spring from but what things may trigger the ordinary dreams of normal people.

However, from here it is only a step to finding a dream-source that flows more plentifully than any we have yet encountered and in fact promises in no instance to run dry. If it is established that the interior of the body becomes a source of dream-stimuli when sick, and if we concede that the mind, during sleep, is turned away from the outside world and able to devote greater attention to the interior of the body, it is natural to suppose that the organs do not have to be sick before allowing states of arousal that somehow turn into dream-images to reach the sleeping mind. The thing that in the waking state we dimly perceive as common sensation only in terms of its quality, and to which in the opinion of doctors all organic systems contribute, would at night, having achieved great influence and operating with all its components, provide the most powerful and at same time most customary source for the awakening of dream-conceits. It would then become superfluous to study the laws whereby organic stimuli turned into dream-conceits.

Here we have touched on the theory of dream-genesis that became the one most favoured by all medical writers. The darkness in which the core of our being (what Tissié calls the *moi splanchnique*) is shrouded so far as our cognition is concerned and the darkness of dream-genesis make too good a match not to be brought into relationship with each other. Moreover, the imaginative process that turns the autonomic organic impression into a dream-creator holds, for the doctor, the further attraction that it also provides an aetiological link between dream and mental disturbance, which show so much correspondence in their manifestations, since changes in common sensation and stimuli proceeding from internal organs are also held to possess far-reaching importance as regards the emergence of psychoses. So it is not surprising if the physical-stimulus theory can be traced back to more than one cause that has given rise to it independently.

For a series of writers, the train of thought developed by the philosopher Schopenhauer in 1851 became decisive. Our image of the world stems from the fact that our intellect, receiving the impressions that reach us from outside, recasts them in the form of time, space and causality. Stimuli from the interior of the organism, produced by the sympathetic nervous system, exercise at most an unconscious influence on our mood during the day. At night, however, when the deadening influence of daytime impressions has ceased, the impressions forcing their way up from the interior are able to gain attention – much as at night we hear the bubbling of the spring that the day's din made imperceptible. But how else is the intellect to react to those stimuli than by performing its own peculiar function? In other words, it moulds the stimuli into figures that occupy space and time and dance to the strings of causality – and this gives rise to dream. Scherner [1861] and after him Volkelt [1875] sought to explore the closer relationship between physical stimuli and dream-images; our assessment thereof will be found in the section on theories of dream. [See section G below.]

In an investigation performed with particular rigour, the psychiatrist A. Krauss derived the genesis of dream, like that of deliriums and delusions, from the same element: *organically determined sensation*. Scarcely any point in the organism could be thought of, he said, that could not become the starting-point of a dream or delusion. 'However, [organically determined sensation] can be divided into two series: 1) that of total determinations (common sensation); 2) the specific sensations inherent in the principal systems of the autonomic organism, of which we distinguish five groups: a) muscular sensations, b) pneumatic sensations, c) gastric sensations, d) sexual sensations, and e) peripheral sensations' (p. 33 of the second article).

What happens in the case of dream-image formation on the basis of physical stimuli is something Krauss pictures like this. The sensation aroused, operating through some law of association, evokes a related idea and combines with it to form an organic structure towards which, however, consciousness behaves in a way that is different than normal, paying no attention to the sensation itself but concentrating entirely on the accompanying ideas, which is also the reason why this state of affairs remained unappreciated for so long (pp. 11f.). Krauss also finds a special expression for the process: the *transubstantiation* of sensations into dream-images (p. 24).

While the influence of organic physical stimuli on dream-formation is almost universally accepted today, the question of the law governing the relationship between the two is answered in very different ways, often with obscure information. Given the physical stimulus theory, a special task of dream-interpretation is tracing the content of a dream back to the organic stimuli that occasioned it, and unless the rules of interpretation uncovered by Scherner [1861] are acknowledged, one will frequently come up against the unfortunate circumstance that the only thing that reveals the organic source stimulus is in fact the content of the dream.

However, there is a fair degree of agreement about interpreting various forms of dream that have been labelled 'typical' because for so many people they occur repeatedly with very similar content. These are the well-known dreams of falling from a great height, of one's teeth dropping out, of flying, and of embarrassment at being naked or poorly clothed. The latter form, we are told, rests purely on the perception, made during sleep, that one has thrown off the covers and is lying there exposed. The dream about one's teeth falling out is traced back to the so-called 'tooth stimulus', which does not necessarily refer to a pathological state of arousal affecting the teeth. The flying dream, according to Strümpell, is what the mind employs as a suitable image by which to interpret the stimulus quantum emanating from the inflation and deflation of the lungs, if at the same time the skin sensitivity of the thorax has already sunk to the level of unconsciousness. The latter state conveys the sensation associated with the imaginative form of floating. The sense of dropping from a great height apparently has its origin in the period after the sensation of skin pressure has become unconscious and is brought on by either an arm sliding off the body or a drawn-up knee suddenly being stretched out flat, as a result of which the sensation of skin pressure becomes conscious once more but the transition to consciousness finds psychical embodiment in a dream of falling (Strümpell [1877], p. 118). Obviously, the weakness of these plausible attempts at explanation lies in the fact that, without further justification, they cause this or that group of organic sensations to disappear from mental perception or impose themselves upon it until the situation favouring the explanation is produced. I shall have occasion later on to return to typical dreams and what triggers them. [See Chapter 5, section D.]

Simon [1888] tried by comparing a series of similar dreams to derive a few rules for the influence of organic stimuli on determining their dream-outcomes. He writes (p. 34): If during sleep some organ system that in the normal course of events is involved in the expression of an affect finds itself thrown by some other cause into the state of arousal in which it is usually placed by that affect, the resultant dream will contain ideas suited to the affect.

Another rule (p. 35) runs like this: If during sleep an organ system finds itself in a state of activity, arousal, or disturbance, the resultant dream will bring forth ideas that relate to the organic function performed by that system.

J. Mourly Vold [1896] set out to prove experimentally, so far as a single area was concerned, the influence on dream-generation posited by the physical stimulus theory. He carried out experiments that changed the position of a sleeper's limbs and compared the dream-outcomes with his changes. He claims to have identified the following principles:

1) The position of a limb in dream corresponds approximately to its position in reality; in other words, a person dreams of a static state of the limb that corresponds to its true state.

2) If a person dreams of the movement of a limb, it is always the case that one of the positions occurring during the execution of that movement corresponds to the true one.

3) A person may also attribute the position of his or her limb in dream to another person.

4) A person may also dream that the movement in question is impeded.

5) The limb in the position in question may, in dream, appear as an animal or monster, with a certain analogy being created between them.

6) The position of a limb may, in dream, provoke thoughts that relate to that limb in some way, e.g. a person whose fingers are busy will dream of numbers.

I would conclude from such findings that not even the physical stimulus theory can wholly eradicate the apparent freedom in determining the dream-images to be awakened.[7]

4 *Psychical stimuli*

When we were discussing the relations between dream and waking life and the origin of dream-material, we learned that the earliest and the most recent students of dream all agree that people dream about what they do during the day and what interests them in waking life. That interest, arising in waking life and continuing in dream, is not [they say] merely a psychical bond connecting dream and life; it also points us to a dream-source that ought not to be underestimated, one that, in addition to what has become interesting in the sleeping state (the stimuli operating during sleep), should be sufficient to explain the origin of all dream-images. However, we have also heard the opposite, namely that dream draws the sleeper away from the day's interests and that (usually) we do not dream about the things that most affected us during the day until, so far as waking life is concerned, they have lost the attraction of current relevance. In our analysis of dream-life, therefore, we get the impression at every step that it is inadmissible to draw up universal rules without allowing for reservations in the form of an 'often' or 'in the main' or 'usually', and without being prepared for exceptions to have validity.

If waking interest, in addition to internal and external sleep stimuli, were sufficient to cover the aetiology of dream, that would put us in a position to give an adequate account of the origin of every element in a dream; the riddle of the sources of dream would be solved, and all that would remain to be done would be to demarcate the relative shares of psychical and somatic dream-stimuli in individual dreams. In reality, this kind of total resolution of a dream has never yet succeeded, and everyone who has tried it has been left with dream-components (usually a large number of them) about whose origin nothing can be said. Clearly, the interest of the day as psychical dream-source is not as productive as one might expect, given the confident claims that everyone, in dream, continues to go about his business.

No other psychical sources of dream are known. In other words, all the explanations of dream put forward in the literature (with the exception of the work of Scherner [1861], to which we shall return later) leave a gaping hole as regards deducing dream's most characteristic material for image-forming. Thus embarrassed, most writers have developed a tendency to keep the psychical contribution to dream-triggering (so difficult to pin down) as small as possible. They may, as their principal classification, distinguish the nerve stimulus dream and the associative dream, of which the latter finds its source exclusively in reproduction (Wundt [1880], p. 365), but they can never shake off the doubt as to 'whether they appear without a physical stimulus giving rise to them' (Volkelt [1875], p. 127). The description of the purely associative dream also falls short: 'In true associative dreams there can no longer be any question of this kind of solid core. Here this loose grouping penetrates to the very heart of the dream. The life of the imagination, in any case liberated from responsibility and rationality, is here no longer lent coherence even by those weightier physical and mental stimuli but is left free to follow its own colourful toing and froing, its own relaxed somersaulting around' (Volkelt, p. 118). Wundt seeks to reduce the psychical contribution to dream-generation by arguing that 'the phantasms of dream are no doubt wrongly regarded as pure hallucinations. In reality, most dream-conceits are probably illusions in that they proceed from the muted sense-impressions that never disappear in sleep' (pp. 359f.). Weygandt [1893] adopted this view and generalized from it, claiming in respect of all dream-conceits that 'their immediate cause are sensory stimuli to which reproductive associations attach themselves only subsequently' (p. 17). Tissié takes the suppression of psychical stimuli further, maintaining that *'Les rêves d'origine absolument psychique n'existent pas'* ['Dreams of entirely psychical origin do not exist'; p. 183] and stating elsewhere that *'Les pensées de nos rêves nous viennent du dehors'* ['The thoughts that we dream come to us from the outside world'; p. 6].

Those writers who, like the influential philosopher Wundt, take up a middle position, do not neglect to remark that in most dreams somatic stimuli and the psychical dream-triggers that are unknown or are acknowledged as a daytime interest work together.

We shall learn later that the riddle of dream-formation can be solved by the discovery of an unsuspected psychical source of stimuli. For the time being, let us not be surprised at what, so far as dream-formation is concerned, is the excessive importance attached to stimuli not proceeding from the inner life. Not only are these easy to spot and even susceptible of experimental confirmation; the somatic view of how dreams come about is also very much in line with the prevalent intellectual trend in psychiatry today. Although it is stressed most emphatically that the brain controls the organism, anything that might suggest that the inner life is independent of verifiable organic changes or provide evidence of spontaneity in the ways in which the inner life finds expression quite terrifies the modern psychiatrist, as if taking it on board would inevitably bring back the days of the philosophy of nature and the metaphysical soul. The mistrust of psychiatrists has placed the psyche under wardship, as it were, and now demands that none of the ward's movements shall give away the fact that it possesses means of its own. Yet what such behaviour indicates is nothing less than a lack of trust in the strength of the chain of cause and effect between the physical and mental spheres. Even where the psychical is acknowledged by research to constitute the prime cause of a phenomenon, closer examination will eventually find its way through to the organic ground of the inner life. However, where, given our current state of knowledge, the psychical must inevitably indicate the end of the line, that is no reason to deny it.

Notes

1. The physician Adolf von Strümpell (1853–1925). His philosopher father, L. Strümpell, was the author of *Die Natur und Entstehung der Träume* ['The nature and origin of dreams'], Leipzig 1877.
2. *Chauffeurs* were robber bands in the Vendée, who employed this method of torture.
3. *Feuerjo* (as it were, 'Fire ahoy!') was a traditional cry in German-speaking countries to attract the attention of the authorities to a fire.
4. Gigantic people in dream suggests that what we have here is a scene from the dreamer's childhood. Incidentally, the foregoing interpretation, suggesting a similarity with *Gulliver's Travels*, is a good example of how interpretation should not operate. The person interpreting a dream ought not to allow his or her own wit to come into play at the expense of following up the ideas occurring to the dreamer. [On the subject of 'ideas occurring to the dreamer', I want to draw the reader's attention to a pleasing directness in the German language that, as in this case, it is often difficult to reproduce in English. An important technique in psychoanalysis is known as 'free association', when the analysand is asked to say what springs to mind in a particular connection. German calls such an idea an *Einfall* – literally a 'fall-in', which perhaps gives a better impression of the precipitate, often startling nature of such a phenomenon than 'the first thing that occurs to you'.]
5. [The source references in the German edition are not always very precise. Three Maury sources are given in the German bibliography (here

called Other Literature), but the German text does not tell us to which of them this page reference relates.]

6. Apart from this diagnostic use of dreams (by Hippocrates, for example), we must not forget their therapeutic importance in antiquity. The Greeks had dream oracles, who were usually frequented by sick persons in search of recovery. The patient went into the temple of Apollo or Asclepius, where he underwent various ceremonial acts; he was bathed, rubbed down, perfumed with incense, and in the resultant state of exaltation laid, inside the temple, on the skin of a sacrificed ram. He fell asleep and dreamed of remedies, which were shown to him in their natural form or in symbols and images that the priests subsequently interpreted.

For more on the healing dreams of the Greeks, see Lehmann [1908], I, p. 74, Bouché-Leclercq [1879], Hermann, *Gottesd. Altert. d. Gr.*, §41, *Privataltert.*, §38, p. 16, Böttinger, in Sprengels, *Beitr. z. Gesch. d. Med.*, II, pp. 163ff., W. Lloyd, *Magnetism and Mesmerism in Antiquity*, London 1877, Döllinger, *Heidentum und Judentum* ['Heathendom and Jewry'], Regensburg 1857, p. 130.

7. For more details of the dream records of this researcher, which have since been published in two volumes, see Other Literature.

D Why are dreams forgotten after waking?

Proverbially, dreams 'fade' in the morning. They are, of course, capable of being remembered. The fact is, all we know about dreams is from their being remembered after waking; however, we very often think we remember a dream only imperfectly, whereas in the night there was more of it present; we are able to observe how a dream that we still remembered vividly in the morning dissipates during the course of the day, leaving only fragments; we are often aware of having dreamed but not of what we dreamed about, and we are so used to the experience of dream being in thrall to oblivion that we do not reject as absurd the possibility that a person may have dreamed during the night even if that person does not, in the morning, have any recollection of either the dream-content or the fact of having dreamed. On the other hand, dreams sometimes show extraordinary durability in memory. I have analysed dreams for my patients that they had had twenty-five or more years previously, and I can recall one of my own dreams that occurred at least thirty-seven years ago, yet has lost none of its freshness in memory. All this is very remarkable and at first incomprehensible.

The subject of forgetting dreams is dealt with most thoroughly by Strümpell [1877]. This kind of forgetting is clearly a complex phenomenon, since Strümpell traces it back not to one but to a whole series of reasons.

To start with, all the same reasons are operative with regard to forgetting dreams as induce forgetting in waking life. We tend, in the waking state, to forget countless sensations and perceptions immediately because they were too faint, because the emotional

55

arousal associated with them was too weak. The same applies in respect of many dream-images; they are forgotten because they were too weak, whereas more powerful images in their vicinity are remembered. Incidentally, the intensity factor is not solely responsible as regards retention of dream-images; Strümpell, together with other writers (Calkins [1893], concedes that one rapidly forgets numerous dream-images that one knows to have been extremely vivid, while those retained in memory include a great many shadowy, sensorily feeble images. Moreover, in the waking state one tends to forget quickly things that happened only once and to take better notice of what one was able to perceive repeatedly. Most dream-images, however, are unique experiences;[1] this peculiarity will likewise contribute towards all dreams being forgotten. But far more important is a third reason for such forgetting. If sensations, ideas, thoughts and so on are to achieve a certain magnitude for the purposes of memory, they must lose their isolation and form suitable connections and associations with one another. If a line of poetry is broken down into individual words and these are then shuffled, the line will become very hard to spot. 'Properly arranged and in the correct sequence, one word will help the next and the whole thing, making sense, easily finds a lasting place in memory. Things that make no sense we usually find as hard to retain, and do so as infrequently, as that which is confused and disordered.' Dreams, in most instances, lack comprehensibility and order. Dream-compositions, inherently incapable of being remembered, are forgotten for the reason that they usually fall apart in the next few moments. These remarks do not of course entirely chime with something Radestock ([1878] p. 168) claims to have noticed: that it is precisely the most exceptional dreams that we best remember.

Strümpell [1877] sees other factors as even more influential in the matter of dreams being forgotten, factors that stem from the relationship between dream and waking life. Plainly, the forgettability of dreams so far as the waking consciousness is concerned is simply the counterpart of a circumstance we mentioned earlier, which is that dream (almost) never borrows orderly memories from waking life but only details of the same, stripping them of their customary psychical associations – that is to say, of the context in which they are recalled in waking life. Dream-composition thus does not belong in the company of the psychical sequences that fill the mind. It employs no memory aids. 'In this manner the dream-figment rises, so to speak, from the ground of our inner life and floats in psychical space like a cloud in the sky, which the reactivated breath swiftly dispels' (p. 87). A similar effect is produced by the fact that, when a person wakes up, the sensory world immediately crowds in, monopolizing his attention in such a way that very few dream-images manage to survive the onslaught. They fall back before the advance of the new day as the brightness of the moon and stars gives way to the light of the sun.

Finally, the forgetting of dreams is favoured by the fact that most people have little interest in their dreams anyway. Someone who does take an interest in dream for a time (as a researcher, for instance) will also dream more than usual during that period, which presumably means that he will remember his dreams more easily and more often.

Two further reasons for forgetting dreams, which Bonatelli (in Benini [1898]) adds to those cited by Strümpell (in which they are probably already contained), are these: 1) that the change in common sensation between sleeping and waking does not favour reciprocal reproduction, and 2) that the different arrangement of imaginative material in dream makes the latter untranslatable, as it were, so far as the waking consciousness is concerned.

Given all these reasons for forgetting, what is really remarkable (as Strümpell himself insists) is that so much of what has been dreamed is in fact retained in memory. The continuing efforts of writers to capture in rules the remembering of dreams rather add up to an admission that here too something mysterious and unresolved remains. Quite rightly, individual peculiarities of the process of remembering dream have recently received special attention – for instance, that a dream one had thought forgotten in the morning may, as the day wears on, be remembered because of a perception that happens to touch on the (forgotten) contents of the dream

(Radestock, Tissié). Yet all recall of dream is subject to an objection that is likely to diminish its value very greatly in the eyes of critics. It is questionable whether our memory, which leaves so much of the dream out, does not in fact falsify what it has retained.

Such doubts as to the accuracy with which dream is reproduced are also voiced by Strümpell [1877]: 'The fact is, it easily occurs in such a case that the waking consciousness involuntarily inserts a good deal into the memory of the dream: one imagines one dreamed all sorts of things that the actual dream did not contain.'

Jessen (p. 547) expresses himself with particular force: 'In addition, though, when investigating and interpreting cohesive and logically consistent dreams, much heed must be paid to the (apparently) hitherto largely overlooked fact that the truth, in this connection, almost always comes off badly. The reason is that, in recalling a dream of ours we will tend, without being aware of or willing such action, to fill in and complement the gaps in the dream-images. Rarely if ever was a coherent dream as coherent as it appears to us in memory. Even the most truth-loving individual is scarcely able to narrate a curious dream he has had without a lot of fill-ins and embroidering: so determinedly does the human mind endeavour to see everything as a coherent whole that when it recalls a partially incoherent dream it involuntarily makes up for any lack of coherence.'

The comments of Egger, though without a doubt independently conceived, read almost like a translation of Jessen's remarks: '[. . .] there are special problems attached to observing dreams, and the only way of avoiding error in such a matter is to commit to paper without a moment's delay what one has just experienced and remarked; otherwise, one quickly forgets – either completely or in part; forgetting completely is not serious; but partial forgetting is treacherous; because if one then proceeds to recount what one has not forgotten, one risks completing imaginatively the incoherent, disjointed fragments that memory supplies [. . .]; one becomes an unwitting artist, and the account, repeated at intervals, comes to monopolize its author's credence, and its author, acting in good faith, presents it as authentic fact, properly established in accordance with the right methods [. . .].'2

Spitta ([1892, 2nd edn] p. 338) says something very similar, appearing to assume that it is only when we try to reproduce dream that we introduce order into the loose assemblage of associated dream-elements – 'make a juxtaposition into a sequence of separate parts, ourselves contributing the process of logical association that dream lacks'.

However, since we have no alternative to an objective means of checking the fidelity of our memory, but since in connection with dream, which is our own experience and for which we know no other source than memory, such is not possible, how much is our memory of dream still worth?

Notes

1. Periodically recurring dreams have been noted on many occasions. See the anthology compiled by Chabaneix [1897].
2. [Freud, able to assume in his reader a working knowledge of French, quotes Egger's original words.]

E *Psychological distinguishing characteristics of dream*

In our scientific examination of dream we take as our starting-point that dream is a product of our own mental activity; yet we see the finished product as something alien and feel so little urge to claim authorship of it that we are as likely to say 'It dreamed to me'[1] as 'I dreamed'. Where does it stem from, this sense that dream originates outside the mind? What we have been saying about dream-sources would incline us to think that it is not determined by the material that finds its way into dream-content; after all, this is largely common to both dream-life and waking life. Is it possible that alterations in psychical processes in dream evoke this impression, and can we perhaps attempt a psychological description of dream on this basis?

No one has placed greater emphasis on the essential difference between dream and waking life and used it for further-reaching conclusions than G. T. Fechner in his *Elemente der Psychophysik* [1889]. In it he says (vol. II, p. 520) that 'neither simply pushing the conscious inner life below the main threshold' nor abstracting attention from the influences of the outside world is sufficient to account for the peculiarities of dream-life as compared to waking life. Instead, he suggests that *the very arena of dreams is different from that of the waking life of the imagination.* 'Were the arena of psychophysical activity during sleep and in the waking state identical, then in my view dream could be no more than a continuation of the waking life of the imagination at a lower level of intensity, and must incidentally share the latter's form and substance. However, the situation is quite different.'

Fechner did not clarify what he meant by such a relocation of mental activity; nor, so far as I am aware, has anyone else continued down the avenue he signposts in that remark. An anatomical interpretation in terms of physiological localization within the brain or even with reference to the histological stratification of the cerebral cortex must presumably be excluded. Possibly, however, the idea will turn out to be meaningful and fruitful when applied to a mental apparatus made up of a number of agencies installed in sequence.

Other writers have been content to highlight one or another of the tangible psychological peculiarities of dream-life and, for example, to take this as the starting-point for further-reaching attempts at explanation.

It has rightly been pointed out that one of the chief peculiarities of dream-life lies in the very condition of falling asleep and should be described as the phenomenon that induces sleep. According to Schleiermacher ([1862] p. 351), the distinguishing feature of the waking state is that cognitive activity takes place in *concepts* rather than in *images*. Dream, however, thinks mainly in images, and it is possible to observe that, in a person approaching sleep, as the [mental] activities that that person wishes to perform become more difficult, so (and to the same extent) *involuntary ideas* emerge that all belong in the category of images. The inability to perform such imaginative work as we feel to be deliberately willed and the emergence of images that is regularly associated with this *state of distraction* are two characteristics that remain attached to dream and that, when subjecting the same to psychological analysis, we must acknowledge to be essential characteristics of dream-life. Of such images (hypnagogic hallucinations) we have learned that even in terms of content they are identical with dream-images.[2]

Dream, then, thinks predominantly in visual images. But not exclusively: it also operates with aural images and to a lesser extent with impressions received from the other senses. In dream, too, many things are simply thought or imagined (that is to say, they are probably represented by residues of verbal ideas), just as in the waking state. However, the only elements of content typical of dream are those that behave like images (in other words, that resemble perceptions more than memories). Disregarding all the debates so familiar to the psychiatrist about the nature of hallucinations, we can state in company with all informed writers that dream *hallucinates*, that it replaces thoughts by hallucinations. In this respect there is no difference between visual and acoustic ideas; it has been remarked that the memory of a sequence of musical notes with which a person dozes off is transformed, as that person sinks into sleep, into the hallucination of the same melody – to give way once again, as the person comes to (which he may do several times, alternating with dozing off), to the quieter, qualitatively different activity of remembering.

The transformation of idea into hallucination is not the only way in which dream diverges from a waking thought that may correspond to it. Out of such images dream moulds a situation; it depicts something as present; it *dramatizes* an idea, as Spitta ([1892] p. 145) says. However, the description of this aspect of dream-life is not complete until it is also accepted that when dreaming (exceptions generally require a separate explanation) one feels one is not thinking but having an experience; in other words, one gives the hallucinations complete credence. The criticism that one has not experienced anything but only thought in a peculiar way (that is to say, dreamed) does not arise until one wakes up. This characteristic distinguishes the true sleeping dream from day-dreaming, which is never mistaken for reality.

Burdach ([1838] p. 476) summarized the nature of dream-life, as considered hitherto, in the following sentences: 'The key features of dream include *a)* that the subjective activity of our mind is seen as objective in that the faculty of perception interprets the products of fantasy as if they were sensory arousals; [. . .] *b)* sleep is a removal of autonomy. Falling asleep therefore implies a certain passivity [. . .]. Sleep-images are dictated by the relaxing of autonomy.'

We are dealing here with an attempt to explain the trust placed by the mind in dream-hallucinations that can emerge only after a certain autonomy of action has ceased. Strümpell [1877] argues that the mind, when it does this, is behaving correctly and being true to its mechanism. Dream-elements are not simply ideas – not at all. They are *true and actual experiences of the mind*, like those that in the waking state appear through the medium of the senses (p. 34). Whereas in the waking state the mind imagines and thinks in word-images and language, in dream it imagines and thinks in actual sense-images (p. 35). Furthermore, in dream there is an additional spatial awareness in that, as in the waking state, sensations and images are placed in an external structure (p. 36). It must be admitted, then, that the mind is in the same position with regard to its images and perceptions in dream as in the waking state (p. 43). If it nevertheless makes a mistake in this connection, the reason is that, while asleep, it lacks the criterion that is alone capable of distinguishing between sense perceptions coming from outside and sense perceptions coming from inside. It cannot subject its images to the tests that will alone demonstrate their objective reality. *Furthermore*, it also ignores the difference between *arbitrarily* interchangeable images and others where this arbitrary element is not present. It makes a mistake because it cannot apply the law of causality to the content of its dream (pp. 50f.). In short, its turning-away from the outside world also contains the reason for its belief in the subjective dream-world.

The same conclusion, after in part divergent psychological developments, is reached by Delboeuf [1885]. We accept dream-images as reality because in sleep we have no other impressions to compare them with, being detached from the external world. However, the reason why we believe in the truth of our hallucinations is not that we have no opportunity, in sleep, to put them to the test. Dream is capable of feigning all such tests for our benefit – of showing us, for example, that we are touching the rose we can see, yet at the same time dreaming. According to Delboeuf, there is no valid criterion as to whether something is a dream or waking reality except (and this simply as a practical generality) the fact of waking up. I declare everything experienced between going to sleep and waking up to be illusory when I wake up to find I am undressed and lying in my bed (p. 84). While asleep, I took the dream-images to be true because of the indestructible thought habit of assuming an external world to which I oppose my 'I'.[3]

If such a turning-away from the external world is elevated to the status of one of the determining factors behind the striking nature of dream-life, it is worth citing some of the subtle observations of old Burdach [1838], which throw light on the relationship between the sleeping mind and the external world and may possibly prevent us from rating the above deductions too highly. 'Sleep,' says Burdach (p. 457), 'ensues only on condition that the mind is not excited by sensory stimuli, [. . .] but at the same time it is not the lack of sense impressions that is the prerequisite for sleep but rather the lack of interest in them;[4] a certain amount of sense impression is in fact necessary, provided that it helps to calm the mind, as when the miller cannot sleep unless he can hear the clacking of his mill, and a person who finds it necessary, as a precaution, to leave a nightlight burning is incapable of falling asleep in the dark.'

'The mind, in sleep, cuts itself off from the external world and [. . .] draws back from the edge. [. . .] However, the link is not entirely broken; were one unable to hear or feel in sleep itself but only after waking, one could in fact never be roused. An even stronger indication of the continuance of sensation is that one is not always roused by the purely sensory strength of an impression so much as by the psychical relevance of that impression; a word of no significance will not rouse a sleeper, but if his name is called he will wake up [. . .] in other words, the mind, in sleep, distinguishes between sensations. [. . .] It follows that a person can also be awakened by the absence of a sensory stimulus, where this relates to something that is important for ideation; he may wake up if the nightlight goes out, for instance, as the miller may wake up if his mill stops turning (that is to say, when sensory activity ceases), and this presupposes that the thing had been perceived, but as something of no importance, or rather as something reassuring that did not disturb the mind' (pp. 46off.).

Even disregarding these not inconsiderable objections, we have to admit that the properties of dream-life evaluated hitherto (properties derived from turning away from the external world) cannot fully account for the exotic quality of that life. Otherwise, it would need to be possible to transform the hallucinations of dream[5] back into ideas and the situations of dream back into thoughts, solving the task of dream-interpretation in this way. In fact, we do just that when, after waking, we reproduce a dream from memory, and whether this re-translation is wholly or only partially successful, the dream retains its mysterious quality undiminished.

The writers also all assume without reservation that, in dream, other, more extensive changes have occurred with the ideational material of waking life. Strümpell ([1877] p. 27) seeks to single out one of those changes in the following discussion: 'The mind, when its view of the world through the senses and normal consciousness cease, also loses the ground in which its feelings, desires, interests and actions have their roots. Likewise those intellectual conditions, feelings, interests and value-assessments that attach to memory-images in waking life undergo [. . .] an obscure pressure, as a result of which their link to the images disappears; the perceived images of things, people, places, events and actions are individually reproduced in enormous numbers, but none of them brings its *psychical value* with it. This is detached from them, so that they float around in the mind under their own power, as it were [. . .].'

This stripping of images of their psychical value, which is again traced back to the turning away from the external world, is, according to Strümpell, a major contributor to the impression of strangeness that dream possesses in memory, as compared with life.

We have heard that falling asleep already involves a renunciation of one of the activities of the mind, namely the voluntary management of the unrolling of the imagination. Consequently, the (in any case obvious) supposition imposes itself that the sleeping state may also extend itself over mental functions. One or another of those functions is entirely arrested; whether the rest are able to continue to operate undisturbed, whether in such circumstances they can do normal work, now becomes questionable. The view emerges that the peculiarities of dream might be explained by the reduced psychical performance that characterizes the sleeping state, yet the impression that dream makes on our waking judgement opposes such a conception. Dream is incoherent; it unhesitatingly combines the most blatant contradictions and contemplates utter impossibilities, disregarding the knowledge that so influences us by day and portraying us as ethically and morally stupid persons. If anyone behaved in the waking state as dream with its situations suggests, we should judge him mad; if in the waking state a person spoke or sought to communicate such things as occur in dream-content, that person would strike us as confused or feeble-minded. In other words, we believe we are only expressing the way things are when we rate psychical activity in dream as being at a very low level and in particular when we say that the higher intellectual functions are suspended in dream or at least seriously impaired.

With surprising unanimity (we shall talk about the exceptions elsewhere), writers in the past have passed such judgements on dream as also point immediately to a specific theory or account of dream-life. It is time for me to substitute for the summary I have just given a collection of statements by various writers (philosophers and physicians) about the psychological nature of dream:

Lemoine [1855] contends that the *incoherence* of dream-images is the only essential characteristic of dream.

Maury agrees, saying ([1878] p. 163), 'There are no wholly reasonable dreams or ones that do not contain some incoherence, some anachronism, some absurdity.'[6]

According to Hegel, as cited in Spitta [1892], dream lacks any objective, sensible coherence.

Dugas [1897] says, 'Dream is psychical, affective, mental anarchy; it is the interplay of functions given over to themselves and operating without control and aimlessly; in dream, the mind is a spiritual automaton.'

Even Volkelt [1875], according to whose theory psychical activity during sleep does not by any means appear pointless, talks about 'the relaxation, dissolution, and jumbling up of what in the waking state is lent coherence by the logical force of the central "I"'.

The absurdity of imaginative associations occurring in dream could scarcely be condemned in stronger terms than in those employed by Cicero (see *De divinatione*, II): 'There is nothing thinkable, no matter how preposterous, confused, or monstrous, that we cannot dream.'

Fechner ([1889] p. 522) says, 'It is as if psychological activity crossed over from the brain of a sensible person to that of a fool.'

Radestock ([1879] p. 145): 'It does indeed appear impossible to spot any fixed laws in this mad hustle and bustle. Giving the slip to the strict police of the sensible will and attentiveness that guide the waking imagination, dream whirls everything around like a kaleidoscope in crazy play.'

Hildebrandt ([1875] p. 45): 'The magnificent leaps the dreamer permits himself, e.g. in the deductions he makes! With what nonchalance does he see the most familiar empirical principles actually stood on their heads! What ridiculous contradictions in the orderly arrangements of nature and society he will tolerate before, as we say, things become too hot to handle and the overstretching of absurdity wakes him up! We sometimes multiply quite innocently: three threes are twenty; we feel no surprise when a dog recites a poem for us, a corpse climbs into its own grave, a rock floats in water; we travel in all seriousness, following high orders, to the Duchy of Bernburg or the Principality of Liechtenstein to inspect the national fleet; or we sign up with Charles XII as a volunteer, shortly before the battle of Poltava.'

Binz ([1878] p. 33) refers to the theory of dream that springs from these impressions: 'At least nine out of ten dreams are absurd in terms of their content. In them, we bring people and things together that do not bear the slightest relationship to each other. Next moment, as in a kaleidoscope, the grouping has changed, if possible becoming more absurd and crazy than it was before; and so it goes on, this shifting game played by the imperfectly sleeping brain, until we wake up, cup our brow, and wonder whether we are in fact still in possession of the faculty of rational thought and imagination.'

Maury ([1878] p. 50) finds what to the physician is a very striking simile for the relationship between dream-images and waking thoughts: 'Production of such images, which in the waking man usually gives rise to intention, is the mental equivalent of what, so far as motility is concerned, is represented by certain movements familiar to us from Huntingdon's chorea and from paralytic ailments [. . .].' He sees dream, in fact, as 'a whole series of erosions of the faculty of thought and reason' (p. 27).

It is scarcely necessary to cite the comments made by authors who echo Maury's proposition regarding the individual higher mental functions.

According to Strümpell ([1877] p. 26), all logical operations of the mind based on circumstances and relationships are diminished in dream – even, of course, in dreams where the nonsense element is not immediately apparent. In the opinion of Spitta ([1892] p. 148), ideas, in dream, appear wholly removed from the law of causality. Radestock [1879] joins other authors in highlighting the weakness of judgement and deduction that peculiarly characterizes dream. According to Jodl ([1896] p. 123), there is no criticism in dream, no adjustment of a set of perceptions in the light of the picture presented by overall consciousness. The same author writes, 'All types of consciousness activity occur in dream, but incompletely, inhibitedly, in isolation from one another.' The positions that dream takes up in contrast to our waking knowledge are something that Stricker (along with many other writers) explains in terms of facts in dream being forgotten or logical relationships between ideas going astray, and so on and so forth.

The writers who in general judge psychical performance in dream so unfavourably do nevertheless concede that a certain residue of mental activity remains in dream. Wundt [1880], whose theories have become standard for so many other students of dream-problems, admits this explicitly. To a query about the nature and constitution of the residue of normal mental activity finding expression in dream, it would be almost universally conceded that the reproductive faculty, namely memory, appears to have suffered least in dream – is able, in fact, to demonstrate a certain superiority over the same function in waking life (see also above, p. 22), although some of the absurdities of dream are to be explained by the very forgetfulness of dream-life. According to Spitta, it is the emotional life (*Gemütsleben*) of the mind that is not affected by sleep and that then directs dream. He defines 'emotion' as 'the constant collation of feelings as the innermost subjective essence of a person' (p. 84).

Scholz ([1887] p. 37) sees one of the mental activities that find expression in dream as being the *allegorizing re-interpretation* to which dream-material is subjected. Siebeck ([1877] p. 11) notes the presence in dream, too, of the mind's *supplementary interpretive faculty*, which the mind exercises on everything perceived and conceived. In respect of dream it is particularly difficult to judge what is said to be the highest psychical function, namely consciousness. Since it is only through consciousness that we know anything of dream, its preservation can be in no doubt; however, Spitta contends that, in dream, only consciousness is preserved, not *self*-consciousness as well. Delboeuf [1885] admits that the distinction is not one that means anything to him.

The laws of association by which ideas knit together apply to dream-images, too; indeed, in dream their dominance finds purer and more powerful expression. Strümpell ([1877] p. 70): 'Dream unfolds either purely (as appears to be the case) in accordance with the laws of naked ideas or [in accordance with the laws of] organic stimuli accompanied by such ideas – in other words, without reflection and reason, aesthetic taste and moral judgement being able to do anything about it.' The writers whose views I reproduce here see dreams as being formed more or less in the following manner. The sum total of the sensory stimuli operating in sleep, having arisen from the various sources listed elsewhere, initially evoke in the mind a number of imaginings that present themselves as hallucinations (proper illusions, according to Wundt, since they arise from external and internal stimuli). These form links among themselves in accordance with the familiar laws of association and in turn, following the same laws, evoke a fresh series of ideas (images). All this material is then processed (so far as possible) by what remains of the ordering and thinking mental faculty still active (compare, say, Wundt and Weygandt). Only no one has yet succeeded in understanding the motives determining whether the evocation of images not stemming from external sources proceeds in accordance with this or that law of association.

However, it has been repeatedly pointed out that the associations binding dream-ideas together are of a very special kind and differ from those that operate in waking thought. Thus Volkelt ([1875] p. 15) writes, 'In dream, ideas chase one another around, fishing for chance similarities and barely perceptible connections. All dreams are criss-crossed with such casual, careless associations.' Maury ([1878] p. 126) attaches the greatest value to this characteristic of association of ideas, which enables him to draw a close analogy between dream-life and certain mental disturbances. He recognizes two chief characteristics of what he calls *'délire'*: '1) spontaneous and as it were automatic mental action; 2) a perverted and irregular association of ideas.' Maury himself gives two excellent examples of dreams where the mere fact that two words have similar sounds provides the link between dream-ideas. He once dreamed that he was on a pilgrimage (*pèlerinage* in French) to Jerusalem or Mecca. He then, after many vicissitudes, found himself in the company of the chemist Pelletier,[7] who following a conversation gave him a shovel (*pelle* in French) made of zinc, which in a subsequent dream-fragment became his great war-sword (p. 137). On another occasion, he was walking (in dream) along a country road, reading off the *kilo*metres on the marker stones; afterwards, he was with a grocer who owned a huge pair of scales, and a man was placing *kilo* weights in the pan to measure Maury's weight; thereupon the grocer told him, 'You're not in Paris; you're on the island of *Gilolo*.' There followed several scenes featuring the flower *lobelia*, then General *Lopez*, of whose death he had recently read; he eventually woke up – playing a game of *lotto*.[8]

However, we are quite prepared to acknowledge that this disparagement of psychical performance in dream did not go uncontradicted. Contradiction, admittedly, seems difficult here. Nor does it mean very much that one of the disparagers of dream-life (Spitta [1892] p. 118) should affirm that the same psychological laws as govern the waking life also rule dream, or that another (Dugas [1897]) should proclaim that 'dream is not insanity, nor is it pure unreason'; the fact is, neither writer makes any attempt to bring his estimate into line with what both describe as the psychical anarchy and dissolution of all functions that characterize dream. Others, however, appear to have glimpsed the possibility that the madness of dream is perhaps not altogether without method and may be a mere disguise, as in the case of the Prince of Denmark (to whose madness the very reasonable verdict cited here refers). These writers must have avoided judging by appearances – or else the appearance that dream presented to them was a different one.

Havelock Ellis, for example, pays tribute to dream, showing no desire to linger over its apparent absurdity, as 'an archaic world of vast emotions and imperfect thoughts', studying which could teach us lessons about primitive stages in the development of the psychical life. J. Sully ([1893] p. 362) upholds the same view of dream in a way that goes even further and penetrates even more deeply. His comments deserve even greater attention when we remember that he, perhaps more than any other psychologist, was convinced of the hidden significance of dream. *'Now our dreams are a means of conserving these successive personalities. When asleep we go back to the old ways of looking at things and of feeling about them, to impulses and activities which long ago dominated us.'* A thinker such as Delboeuf ([1885] p. 222) asserts (albeit without adducing proof against the contradictory material and hence in fact wrongly): 'In sleep, apart from perception, all the mental faculties (intelligence, imagination, memory, will, morality) remain essentially intact; the only thing is, they apply to imaginary, inconstant objects. The dreamer is an actor who plays any part he likes: fools and wise men, executioners and victims, dwarves and giants, devils and angels.' Disparagement of psychical performance in dream seems to have been most vigorously contested by the Marquis d'Hervey, against whom Maury inveighs energetically and a copy of whose essay I have been unable, despite every effort, to obtain. Maury says of him ([1878] p. 19):

> The Marquis d'Hervey credits the intelligence during sleep with its full freedom of action and attention and seems to have sleep consist solely in the occlusion of the senses as being closed to the external world; such that a person who is asleep scarcely differs, in terms of

the way he sees things, from a person who stops up his senses and allows his mind to wander; the entire difference that then separates ordinary thinking from that of the sleeper is that, in the latter, ideas take visible, objective form and bear a deceptive resemblance to the sensation occasioned by external objects; memory takes on the appearance of present fact.

Maury does, however, add 'that there is a further, crucial difference, which is that the intellectual faculties of the person asleep do not afford the balance that they retain in the case of the person who is awake'.

In Vaschide, who gives us a better account of d'Hervey's book, we find this author expressing himself in the following terms about the apparent incoherence of dream: 'The dream image is a copy of the idea. First comes the idea; what is pictured is secondary. That said, one must be able to follow the march of ideas; one must know how to analyse the tissue of dreams; the incoherence then becomes comprehensible and the most fantastic conceptions become simple, perfectly logical facts' ([1899] p. 146). And on the following page he adds: 'The strangest dreams even find a quite logical explanation when one knows how to analyse them.'

Johann Stärcke [1913] points out that a similar view of the incoherence of dream was defended by an earlier author, Wolf Davidson (new to me), writing towards the end of the eighteenth century ([1799] p. 136): 'The extraordinary leaps that our ideas take in dream all have their basis in the law of association; it is simply that the link sometimes occurs very obscurely in the mind, with the result that we often think we are looking at a leap of the imagination where none is present.'

The range of appreciation of dream as psychical product has enormous breadth in the literature, extending from the deepest disparagement (an expression of which we have seen) through suspecting an as yet unfathomed value, all the way to overestimation, which rates dream far above what waking life can produce. Hildebrandt, who as we know outlined a psychological description of dream-life in three antitheses, summed up the end of the series in the third of those contrasts ([1875] p. 19):

> It is that [contrast] between *an increase, an enhancement* often to the point of *virtuosity*, and on the other hand a *disparagement* and *enfeeblement* of the inner life, often leading to a point below the human level.
>
> With regard to the former, who is not able to confirm from personal experience that the workings and weavings of the genius of dream occasionally bring to light a depth and intensity of emotion, a delicacy of feeling, a clarity of vision, a subtlety of observation, and a sharpness of wit of which we would modestly decline to claim constant ownership during waking life? Dream possesses wonderful poetry, a fine sense of allegory, incomparable humour, exquisite irony. It sees the world in a uniquely idealizing light and often enhances the influence of the world's manifestations through the most apt appreciations of the essence underlying them. It represents earthly beauty to us in truly heavenly radiance, the sublime in the greatest majesty, things experienced as fearsome in the most atrocious guise, things that appear ridiculous with an indescribably graphic sense of comedy; and occasionally, after waking, we are still so full of one of these impressions as to feel, inevitably, that the real world has never before given us anything comparable.

One wonders whether it is really the same object that provokes such disparagement and prompts such enthusiastic admiration. Have some people forgotten the superficial dreams, others the more profound, penetrating ones? And if both kinds of dream occur, some that merit the former assessment and others that merit the latter, does it not seem pointless to look for a single psychological description of dream; is it not sufficient to say that in dream everything is possible, from the deepest disparagement of the inner life to what, in the waking state, is a rare heightening of the same? Convenient though this solution would be, it has against it the fact that the efforts of all students of dream appear to rest on the premise that there is such a single description of dream, universally valid in all its essential features, and that this should help to overcome the contradictions.

Unquestionably, psychical performance in dream found readier, warmer recognition in intellectual periods that now lie behind us, periods when philosophy rather than the precise natural sciences ruled men's minds. Statements such as that made by G. H. Schubert [1814] to the effect that dream is a liberation of the spirit from the power of external nature, a release of the mind from the bonds of sensuality, and similar verdicts from the young Fichte [1864] and others,[9] who all depict dream as an ascent by the inner life to a higher level, strike us today as barely comprehensible; nowadays they are echoed only by mystics and sanctimonious hypocrites.[10] As scientific thinking became more prevalent, there was a reaction in the appraisal of dream. In fact, medical writers show the greatest tendency to disparage psychical activity in dream and brand it as worthless, while philosophers and lay observers (amateur psychologists), whose contributions to this field in particular ought not to be overlooked, show themselves more in sympathy with public opinion by holding, for the most part, to the psychical value of dreams. Anyone tending to belittle psychical functioning in dream understandably gives priority, as regards the aetiology of dream, to somatic stimuli; the person for whom the dreaming mind retains most of the faculties it enjoys in the waking state naturally has no reason to refuse it autonomous dream-triggers as well.

Among the super-attainments that, even when drawing a sober comparison, one may be tempted to ascribe to dream-life, the most striking is that of memory; we have dealt at length with the by no means infrequent experiences attesting it. Another superiority of dream-life often praised by the earlier writers, namely that it shows a supreme disregard for distance, whether of time or space, is easily recognizable as an illusion. As Hildebrandt [1875] points out, this is in fact an illusory superiority; dreaming does not disregard time and space any differently than does waking thought – precisely because it is simply a form of thought. Dream ought, in relation to temporality, to enjoy a further superiority, namely that of being in a different sense independent of the march of time. Dreams such as the one Maury recounted (cited above on p. 38) about being executed by guillotine appear to show that dream can cram into an extremely short span of time very much more perceptual content than, in the waking state, our psychical activity is able to process thought-content. This conclusion, however, has been contested with a broad range of arguments; since the essays of Le Lorrain and Egger [both 1895] 'on the apparent duration of dreams', an interesting discussion has been in progress in which the last word has probably not yet been said on this difficult and deeply significant subject.[11]

That dream is able to resume the intellectual labours of the day and bring them to a conclusion that the day failed to reach, that it is capable of solving doubts and problems and of providing writers and composers with a source of fresh inspiration – these things, by a wide variety of accounts and after the anthology put together by Chabaneix [1897], appear beyond dispute. However, if the facts are beyond dispute, the way in which they are received is subject to many doubts touching on matters of principle.[12]

Lastly, the alleged divinatory power of dream constitutes an object of dispute in which misgivings that are hard to overcome meet assurances that are obstinately repeated. People avoid (no doubt rightly) denying that there is anything real about this subject because in a series of instances the possibility of a natural psychological explanation is perhaps imminent.

Notes

1. [If, of course, our first language is German, which has many such non-personal constructions (though English has a few, an example being 'It came to me that [. . .]'). John Reddick (translator of *Beyond the Pleasure Principle*, London 2003) has suggested that the prevalence of these constructions in German may help us to understand what Freud called *'das Es'* – 'the Id' or 'the It'.]

2. Herbert Silberer has shown with some fine examples how even abstract

thoughts become transformed, in the state of drowsiness, into vivid plastic images that seek to express the same thing (*Jahrbuch von Bleuler-Freud*, vol. I, 1909). I shall be returning to these findings in a different context.

3. A similar attempt to Delboeuf's at explaining dream-activity by the change that an abnormally induced condition must inevitably produce in the otherwise correct functioning of the intact mental apparatus was undertaken by Haffner [1887], although the latter describes that condition in slightly different terms. According to Haffner, the first characteristic of dream is its timelessness and placelessness – that is to say, the emancipation of the imagination from the particular slot accorded to the individual in the temporal and spatial order. Connected with this is the second basic feature of dream, namely its confusion of hallucinations, imaginings and fantasy conjectures with external perceptions. 'Since the totality of the higher mental faculties (notably concept-formation, judgement and logical thought) on the one hand and free self-determination on the other attach themselves to sensory fantasy-images and have these as their permanent background, such activities also participate in the random nature of dream-ideas. We say that they participate because when all is said and done our power of judgement, like our will-power, undergoes no alteration in sleep. In terms of what we can do, we are as sharp-witted and as free as when we are awake. Even in dream, a person cannot violate the laws of thought as such, he cannot call himself identical to what represents itself as standing opposite him – that sort of thing. Even in dream, he can only desire what he perceives to be something good (*sub ratione boni*). However, in this application of the laws of thought and desire the human mind is led astray, in dream, by mistaking one idea for another. This is why, in dream, we are able to posit and commit the greatest contradictions, while on the other hand reaching the most acute judgements, drawing the most logical conclusions, and forming the most virtuous, most devout resolutions. *Lack of orientation* is the whole secret of the flight with which, in dream, our imagination moves about, and *lack of critical reflection*, together with communication with others, is the chief source of the boundless extravagance of our judgements and of our hopes and desires in dream' (p. 243).

4. Compare this with the *désintérêt* that Claparède (1905) sees as the mechanism of falling asleep.

5. [Here is an example (see the Translator's Preface) of the German language being able to imply the whole spectrum from general to particular where English feels obliged to decide between the two.]

6. [As on many occasions when it is a question of French, Italian, English

or Latin sources, Freud gives the original; where appropriate I give a translation.]

7. [Pierre-Joseph Pelletier (1788–1842).]

8. Later on, the meaning of such dreams, which are full of words having the same initial letter and similar initial sounds, will become clear to us. [In this connection, the English reader is reminded that in both French and German the game of chance referred to is pronounced with two long Os.]

9. See also Haffner [1887] and Spitta [1892].

10. The intellectually stimulating mystic Du Prel, one of the few authors for whose omission from earlier editions of this book I offer apologies, states that it is not waking life but dream that constitutes the gateway to metaphysics, so far as human beings are concerned (*Philosophie der Mystik* ['Philosophy of mysticism'], p. 59).

11. Further literature on and critical discussion of these problems may be found in the Parisian dissertation submitted by Tobowolska (1900).

12. See also the criticism voiced by Havelock Ellis in *The World of Dreams* ([1911] p. 268).

F *Ethical feelings in dream*

For reasons that can only be understood after perusal of my own investigations into dream, I have separated off from the subject of the psychology of dream the sub-problem of whether and to what extent the moral susceptibilities and sensitivities of the waking state also extend into dream-life. Here, too, the same contradictory accounts in the literature as we must have found disconcerting with regard to all other mental operations once again fill us with consternation. Some authors assert with as much conviction that dream knows nothing of moral requirements as do others that a person's moral nature persists in dream-life as well.

Reference to the nightly experience of dream would appear to place the first contention beyond doubt. Jessen ([1855] p. 553) writes, 'Nor does a person become better and more virtuous in sleep. In fact, conscience seems to fall silent in dreams in that one feels no sympathy and is able to commit the most appalling crimes such as robbery, murder and manslaughter with complete indifference and with no regrets.'

Radestock ([1879] p. 146): 'It should be noted that, in dream, associations take place and ideas come together without thought and understanding, aesthetic taste and moral judgement being able to do anything about it; judgement is at its most feeble, and an atmosphere of *ethical indifference* reigns.'

Volkelt ([1875] p. 23): 'But the goings-on in dream, as everyone knows, are particularly unrestrained in the matter of sex. Just as the dreamer is himself utterly shameless and abandons all moral sensibility and judgement, so too he sees everyone else, even highly esteemed persons, involved in activities with which, in the waking state, he would shrink from even thinking of associating them.'

In the sharpest contrast to this are comments such as those of Schopenhauer [1851] to the effect that everyone, in dream, acts and speaks in complete conformity with his character. K. P. Fischer [cited by Spitta, 1892] contends that subjective feelings and endeavours or affects and passions reveal themselves in the arbitrariness of dream-life and that people's moral characteristics are reflected in their dreams.[1]

Haffner ([1887] p. 251): 'With few exceptions [. . .] a virtuous person will also be virtuous in dream; he will resist the temptation to close his eyes to hatred, envy, anger and all vices; the man of sin, however, will usually find in his dreams, too, the images he had before him while awake.'

Scholz ([1887] p. 36): 'In dream there is truth; notwithstanding all disguise in elevation or degradation, we recognize our own self [. . .]. The honourable man cannot, even in dream, commit a dishonourable crime, or if he does so none the less, he is horrified by it as by something alien to his nature. The Roman emperor who had one of his subjects executed because that subject had dreamed that he had ordered the emperor's head to be chopped off was therefore not so wrong to justify his action on the grounds that a man who dreams thus must have similar thoughts in his waking life. That is why we say, significantly, of something that can have no place in our inmost being: I would not dream of it.'

Conversely, Plato holds those to be the best to whom things that others do awake occur only in dream.

Pfaff (as cited in Spitta [1892] p. 192), adapting a well-known proverb, says, 'Recount your dreams to me for a while, and I will tell you what state your inner being is in.'

Hildebrandt's short essay [*Der Traum und seiner Verwertung fürs Leben* ('Dream and using it for life'); Leipzig 1875], from which I have already quoted so extensively, is the most perfectly wrought and thoughtful contribution to exploring dream-problems that I have found in the literature. It concentrates precisely on the problem of morality in dream. For Hildebrandt, too, the rule is: the purer the life, the purer the dream; the less pure the former, the less pure will be the latter.

A person's moral nature survives in dream:

> But while no miscalculation, however blatant, no turning-away from science, however Romantic, no anachronism, however playful, offends or is even suspected by us, we never lose sight of the difference between good and evil, between right and wrong, between virtue and vice. And however much of what accompanies us by day leaves us during the hours of slumber – Kant's categorical imperative has attached itself to our heels as an inseparable companion, one that not even in sleep are we able to shake off [. . .]. But the only explanation [of this fact] is precisely that the very basis of human nature, namely its moral essence, is too firmly embedded to partici-pate in the effect of kaleidoscopic upheaval to which imagination, reason, memory, and other faculties of like rank are subject (Hilde-brandt [1875], pp. 45ff.).

Further discussion of the matter in hand produces, so far as both groups of writers are concerned, some remarkable shifts and inconsistencies. Strictly speaking, for all who believe that a person's moral personality disintegrates in dream, any interest in immoral dreams will terminate with that statement. They might dismiss any attempt to make the dreamer responsible for his dreams, to deduce from the badness of his dreams some wicked dictate in his nature – they might dismiss any such attempt with as little compunction as the apparently equivalent attempt to use the absurdity of his dreams to prove the worthlessness of his intellectual performance in the waking state. The rest, for whom the 'categorical imperative' also extends to dream, would have to accept full responsibility for immoral dreams; all they might hope for is that dreams of their own of so reprehensible a kind did not inevitably confuse them with regard to their normally firm appreciation of their own morality.

However, it seems no one is quite sure, in his own eyes, of how good or evil he is, and no one can deny having some personal memory of immoral dreams. Because, quite apart from this clash of views in the assessment of dream-morality, both groups of writers appear keen to explain the origin of immoral dreams, and a fresh antithesis is emerging, depending on whether that origin is sought in the functions of psychical life or in somatically determined disturbances of that life. The compelling force of actuality then causes champions of the responsibility and champions of the irresponsibility of dream-life to come together in acknowledging a separate psychical source for the immorality of dreams.

All those who think morality persists in dream are careful not to accept full responsibility for their dreams. Haffner ([1887] p. 250) says: 'We are not responsible for dreams because our thinking and willing have been deprived of the sole basis on which our life possesses truth and reality [. . .]. For that very reason, no dream-willing and no dream-action can constitute virtue or sin.' Yet a person is responsible for the sinful dream in so far as he is the indirect cause of it. It is therefore incumbent upon him, not merely in the waking state but also (and most particularly) before going to sleep, to purify his mind morally.

A far more profound analysis of this mixture of rejection and acceptance of responsibility for the moral content of dreams is found in Hildebrandt [1875]. Having explained that the dramatic manner of presentation found in dream, the squeezing of the most complicated thought-processes into the tiniest time-span, as well as what even he concedes are the devaluation and confusion of ideational elements in dream – having explained that these must be deducted, as it were, from the immoral appearance of dreams, he admits to having the gravest misgivings about simply repudiating all responsibility for dream-transgression and guilt.

On page 49 Hildebrandt writes:

> If we wish to reject some unjust accusation (particularly one that relates to our intentions and basic convictions) quite categorically, we may well employ the saying: We never dreamed of [doing/believing] that. In so reacting, we are of course on the one hand saying that we regard the world of dream as the furthest, most remote place where we might be required to answer for our thoughts, the reason

being that, in that place, our thoughts are so loosely attached to our true being that they can scarcely be deemed to be still ours; however, precisely because we feel prompted expressly to deny the presence of such thoughts even in such a 'world', we are at the same time conceding, indirectly, that our justification would not be complete unless it extended there too. And it is my belief that we are here, albeit unwittingly, speaking the language of truth.

He goes on to add the further point: 'The fact is, no dream-deed can be thought of whose prime motive had not, in some form or another (as a wish, as a desire, or as a stirring), previously passed through the mind of the waking person.' Of this initial stirring we have [in Hildebrandt's view] to say that dream did not invent it; dream merely reproduced it, span it out; dream simply processed, in dramatic form, a scrap of historical material that it found within us; it stages the words of the apostle: Anyone who hates his brother is a murderer.[2] And while one may smile, after waking, aware of one's moral strength, at the whole extended figment of the depraved dream, the original material from which the dream sprang refuses to yield a funny side. One feels responsible for the aberrations of the way the dream ends, not for the whole thing but certainly for a percentage. 'In short, if it is in this barely disputable sense that we understand Christ's words: "Out of the heart of man come evil thoughts",[3] then we can likewise scarcely fend off the conviction that every sin committed in dream carries with it an obscure minimum (at least) of guilt.'

So it is in the seeds and suggestions of evil impulses, which as tempting thoughts pass through our minds by day, that Hildebrandt locates the source of the immorality of dreams, and he does not hesitate to include these immoral elements in his moral assessment of the personality. Just such thoughts and this selfsame assessment of them, as we know, are what have throughout history caused god-fearing persons and saints to bewail the fact that they are inveterate sinners.[4]

The universal incidence of these *contrasting* ideas (in the case of most people and also in areas other than the ethical) is presumably beyond doubt. How they are judged has sometimes been a less serious affair. Spitta ([1892] p. 144) cites the following comment by A. Zeller, which is relevant in this connection (from the article '*Irre*' in Ersch and Gruber's *Allgemeine Enzyklopädie der Wissenschaften* ['General encyclopedia of the sciences']): 'Rarely is a mind so successfully organized that it is in full possession of its powers at all times and does not have the steady, lucid progression of its thoughts repeatedly interrupted by ideas that are not merely unimportant but utterly grotesque and nonsensical; indeed, the greatest thinkers have had occasion to complain about this dreamlike, teasing, embarrassing riff-raff of ideas since it disturbs their profoundest meditations and their most solemn and serious thoughts.'

More light is shed on the psychological standing of these contrasting thoughts by something else that Hildebrandt ([1875] p. 55) says about dream allowing us the occasional glimpse into the depths and folds of our being, which in the waking state usually remain closed to us. The same insight is shown by Kant in a passage in the *Anthropologie* [1798], where he writes that the purpose of dream, presumably, is to uncover hidden tendencies and reveal to us not what we are but what we might have become had we had a different upbringing; and by Radestock ([1878] p. 84) when he says that, often, dream reveals to us only what we refuse to admit to ourselves, and that we are therefore wrong to brand it a liar and a cheat. J. E. Erdmann writes: 'Never has a dream shown me how a person should be thought of, only what I think of him and how I feel towards him; I have learned that from a dream – much to my surprise – on several occasions.' And I. H. Fichte [1864] says something similar: 'The nature of our dreams remains a very much more faithful mirror of our overall mood than what we learn of this from self-observation in the waking state.' Our attention is drawn to the fact that the emergence of these impulses from beyond our moral consciousness is simply analogous to what we already know about dream's ability to use different imaginative material (material not present in the waking state or playing a minor role in it) from comments made by Benini ([1898] p. 149): 'Inclinations we believed long since dead and gone come back to life; ancient, buried emotions reawaken; people and things who never normally cross our minds are suddenly standing there before us', and by Volkelt ([1875] p. 105): 'Ideas, too, that entered waking consciousness almost unobserved and that such consciousness might never have retrieved from oblivion tend very often to apprise dream of their presence in the mind.' Lastly, this is the place to remind ourselves that, according to Schleiermacher [1862], falling asleep was already accompanied by the emergence of *involuntary* ideas (images).

'*Involuntary ideas*' is perhaps a good heading under which to gather all the ideational material that so disconcerts us when it occurs in either immoral or absurd dreams. The only difference that matters is that, in the moral sphere, such involuntary ideas are recognizably opposed to our normal sensibility, whereas the others we simply find strange. Nothing has yet been undertaken that would enable us to remove that distinction as a result of some deeper understanding.

So, what is the significance of the fact that involuntary ideas emerge in dream; what conclusions for the psychology of the waking and the dreaming mind can be drawn from this nocturnal appearance of contrasting ethical impulses? Here we must point to a fresh difference of opinion in the literature, once again placing writers in different camps. The train of thought followed by Hildebrandt and other champions of his basic approach can only lead to the view that immoral impulses also possess a certain power in the waking state, though there it is inhibited from finding expression in action, and that in sleep something falls away that, operating in the manner of a scruple, had prevented us from realizing that such an impulse existed. In this way dream [according to Hildebrandt] reveals the true essence of a person, even if not his entire essence, and is one of the means by which we can obtain knowledge of the hidden inner life of the mind. Only on the basis of such premises can Hildebrandt allocate to dream a *warning* role, whereby it draws our attention to hidden moral damage to the mind, just as, by the admission of doctors, it is also able to notify consciousness of physical disorders that have avoided detection hitherto. And Spitta, too, can be guided by no other belief when he points to the sources of arousal pouring into the psyche at the time of puberty, for instance, and consoles the dreamer by saying that he, the dreamer, has done everything in his power if, in the waking state, he has negotiated a strictly virtuous life-change and tried hard to suppress sinful thoughts whenever they arise and not allow them to mature and become deed. According to this view we might describe such *'invol-untary'* ideas as ones that had been *'suppressed'* during the day and would have to see their appearance as a genuine psychical phenomenon.

According to other writers, we are not entitled to draw the latter conclusion. For Jessen ([1855] p. 360), in both dream and waking as well as in feverish and other deliriums, involuntary ideas possess 'the character of a deactivated voluntary activity and an *almost mechanical* process of images and ideas through internal agitation'. All an immoral dream proves so far as the dreamer's inner life is concerned [Jessen further informs us] is that the dreamer has somehow obtained knowledge of the ideas therein contained; it is certainly not evidence of a stirring of the dreamer's own emotions. In the case of another author, Maury, one might question whether he too does not credit the dream-state with the ability to break down the activity of the mind into its individual components rather than unthinkingly destroy it. Discussing the dreams in which a person transgresses the bounds of morality, Maury ([1878] p. 113) writes:

> It is our inclinations that speak and make us act, without conscience holding us back, though it does occasionally warn us. I have my faults and my perverted inclinations, I struggle against them while awake, and quite often I manage not to succumb to them. But in my dreams I invariably do succumb to them, or rather I act under their impulse, without fear and without remorse [. . .]. Clearly, the visions that unfold before my mind's eye and that constitute my dream have been suggested to me by the stimuli that I feel and that my will, being absent, does not seek to suppress.

If one believed in the ability of dream to uncover an immoral disposition of the dreamer's that was actually present but had been suppressed or concealed, one could not voice the view more strongly than Maury did when he wrote ([1878] p. 165), 'In dream, then, a person reveals himself to himself in all his innate nakedness and wretchedness. As soon as he suspends the exercise of will, he becomes the plaything of all the passions against which, in the waking, conscious state, our sense of honour and fear defend us.' Elsewhere ([1878] p. 462), he really hits the nail on the head: 'In dream, it is above all the instinctive person that is revealed [. . .]. Man, so to speak, returns to the state of nature when he dreams; but the less the extent to which acquired ideas have penetrated his mind, the greater the extent to which *inclinations in conflict* with these will continue to affect him in dream.' He then cites as an example the fact that quite often his dreams depict him as a victim of the very superstition that his writings so vehemently attack.

In Maury's case, however, the value of all these penetrating comments for a psychological understanding of dream-life is influenced by the fact that in the phenomena that he so correctly observes he insists on seeing only evidence of the 'psychological automatism' that, according to him, dominates dream-life. That automatism he understands as forming a complete contrast to psychical activity.

A passage in Stricker's *Studien über das Bewusstsein* ['Studies in consciousness'; 1879] runs: 'Dream does not consist simply and solely of illusions; for instance, if in dream a person is afraid of robbers, the robbers may be imaginary but the fear is real.' This draws our attention to the fact that affect-development in dream cannot be judged in the same way as the rest of dream-content, and we are then faced with the problem of what can be real about psychical processes in dream and as such can claim a place among the psychical processes of the waking state.

Notes

1. K. P. Fischer, *Grundzüge des Systems der Anthropologie* ['Rudiments of the system of anthropology'], Erlangen 1850.
2. [I John 3:15. This and other quotations from the Bible are from the Revised Standard Version (RSV).]
3. [Mark 7:21.]
4. It is not without interest to discover how the Holy Inquisition viewed our problem. Thomas Careña's *Tractatus de Officio sanctissimae Inquisitionis*, Lyons edition, 1659, contains the following passage: 'If a person utters heresies in dream, the inquisitors shall take this as a reason to look into his way of life, because what has occupied a man during the day tends to recur in sleep' (Dr Ehniger, S. Urban, Switzerland).

G Dream-theories and function of dream

A statement about dream that seeks to account for as many of its observed characteristics as possible from a single viewpoint and at the same time determines its position in relation to a wider phenomenological field may be called a dream-theory. Individual dream-theories will be distinguished from one another by the fact that they regard this or that characteristic of dream as essential and take it as their starting-point for explanations and connections. A function (which is to say, a use or other thing that dream provides) will not necessarily be derivable from the theory, but our expectations, which are habitually oriented towards teleology, will certainly tend to be met by theories that are associated with an understanding of a function of dream.

We have already come across several views of dream that to a greater or lesser extent merit the title of dream-theories in this sense. The ancients' belief that dream was a message from the gods by which they might direct the actions of men was a complete theory of dream, giving information about everything in dream that was worth knowing. Since dream became an object of biological research, we have seen a great number of theories of dream – some of which, however, are anything but complete.

If we agree not to cover all of them, we can perhaps venture the following loose grouping of dream-theories, according to the assumption underlying them with regard to the extent and type of psychical activity in dream:

1) Theories such as the one formulated by Delboeuf [1885] that have the full psychical activity of the waking state continue in dream. Here the mind does not go to sleep, its apparatus remains intact, but when subjected to the conditions of sleep, which are different from those of the waking state, it inevitably, while functioning normally, produces different results than in the waking state. In connection with these theories, one wonders whether they are able to derive the entire difference between dream and waking thought from the conditions that obtain in the sleeping state. Furthermore, they lack any possibility of gaining access to a function of dream; there is no understanding of the purpose for which a person dreams, why the intricate mechanism of the mental apparatus continues to operate, even when placed in circumstances for which it seems ill-suited. Dreamless sleep or, if disturbing stimuli occur, waking up remain the only expedient reactions rather than the third, that of dreaming.

2) Theories that, on the contrary, assume for dream a lower level of psychical activity, a loosening of coherence, an impoverishment of material that may be called upon. According to such theories, a very different psychological description of sleep must be furnished than, say, Delboeuf provides. Sleep extends over much of the mind; it does not consist simply in blocking the mind off from the outside world but actually penetrates the machinery of the mind, rendering it temporarily unusable. If I may be permitted a comparison with psychiatric material, I should be inclined to say that the former theories construe dream as paranoia while the latter see it as a kind of mental deficiency or amentia.

The theory that in dream-life only a fraction of the mental activity paralysed by sleep finds expression is the favourite one by a long way among medical writers and in the scientific world generally. In fact, in so far as a wider interest in explaining dreams may be assumed, this can be described as the *prevalent* theory of dream. It should be stressed how easily this theory in particular negotiates the worst obstacle of any attempt to explain dream, namely running on to the rocks of one of the antitheses embodied in dream. Seeing dream as the outcome of a partial waking ('a gradual, partial and at the same time very strange sort of waking', as Herbart puts it in his *Psychologie über den Traum*), it is able through a series of states from progressive awakening to full waking to cover the whole spectrum from the underperformance of dream, which comes out in absurdity, to fully concentrated thinking.

Anyone to whom the physiological mode of representation has become indispensable or who thinks scientifically will find this theory of dream expressed in the description provided by Binz ([1878] p. 43):

> However, this state (of paralysis) only gradually comes to an end in the early hours of the morning. The fatigue substances accumulated in the brain protein become fewer and fewer and they are increasingly broken down or swept away by the ceaselessly moving bloodstream. Here and there individual bundles of cells already shine forth awake, while around them everything still lies paralysed. The *isolated work of individual groups* now appears before our misty consciousness, and it lacks the control of other parts of the brain that are in charge of association. That is why the images created, which usually correspond to the material impressions of the recent past, ally together in a wild and disorderly fashion. More and more brain cells become free, the irrationality of dream becomes less and less.

The view of dreaming as an incomplete, partial waking, or traces of its influence, will undoubtedly be found in the writings of all modern physiologists and philosophers. It is represented in the greatest detail in the work of Maury, where it often looks as if the author thought that being awake and being asleep could be located in anatomical regions, in which connection an anatomical province did in fact seem to him to be associated with a specific psychical function. Here, however, I simply wish to suggest that, were the theory of partial waking to be corroborated, a great deal would need to be discussed regarding the finer details thereof.

Of course, a function of dream cannot emerge in connection with this view of dream-life. Rather, the status and significance of dream are more consistently assessed by what Binz ([1878] p. 35) says: 'All the facts, as we see, urge us to label dream a *physical* process that is in every instance useless and in many instances almost morbid. [. . .]'

The term 'physical' as applied to dream (and emphasized by the author himself) has more than one connotation. Initially, it relates to the aetiology of dream, which was of course a matter of particular importance to Binz when he looked into generating dreams experimentally by administering poisons. There is a particular connection, in fact, between this type of dream-theory and having the stimulus to dream proceed as purely as possible from the somatic side. Put in its most extreme form, this says: once by removing stimuli, we have placed ourselves in a sleeping state, there would be neither need nor occasion for dreaming until the morning, when our gradual awakening as a result of freshly arriving stimuli might be reflected in the phenomenon of dreaming. However, sleep can never be kept stimulus-free; like Mephisto[pheles] complaining of the seeds of life, the sleeper is visited by stimuli from everywhere – from outside, from inside, even from all those parts of the body that he had never thought about while awake. Consequently, his sleep is disturbed, and his mind, shaken awake now by this, now by that extremity, functions for a while with the woken part, happy to go back to sleep. Dream is the reaction to the sleep disturbance caused by the stimulus – an entirely superfluous reaction, incidentally.

However, describing dream as a physical process when after all it is a product of the mind has a further connotation. The intention is to deny dream the *dignity* of a psychical process. The hoary simile (as applied to dream) of the 'ten fingers of a person who knows nothing of music running up and down the keyboard of the instrument' perhaps best illustrates the kind of appreciation usually accorded to what it is that dream achieves by representatives of exact science. Dream, in this view, becomes something that utterly and completely defies interpretation; for how could the unmusical player's ten fingers produce a piece of music?

The theory of partial waking ran into plenty of objections early on. Burdach ([1830] p. 483) wrote: 'When people say that dream is partial waking, in the first place this does not explain either waking or sleeping; in the second place, they are simply saying that certain mental forces are active in dream while others are at rest. However, the same inequality occurs throughout life [. . .].'

The prevailing theory of dream that sees dream as a 'physical' process lends support to a very interesting view of dream first put forward by Robert in 1886. This has the attraction of suggesting a possible function for dreaming in terms of a useful result. Robert bases his theory on two observed facts that we have already looked at when evaluating dream-material (see above, p. 29): that one so often dreams about the most peripheral impressions of the day, and that one so seldom carries the day's major preoccupations over into sleep. Robert claims (p. 10) that the sole correct position is: things that a person has thought out in full never trigger dreams, only ever things that linger in memory incomplete or that touch the mind briefly in passing. 'That is why one cannot, as a rule, explain a dream to oneself, because it was occasioned precisely by *those sense impressions of the bygone day that the dreamer had inadequately apprehended*.' In other words, the condition of an impression entering a dream is either that its processing was interrupted or that it was too insignificant to merit such processing.

Dream, says Robert, is 'a physical process of excretion that reaches knowledge in terms of mind's response to it'. *Dreams are excretions of thoughts that have failed to germinate.* 'If a person were deprived of the ability to dream, in time that person would inevitably become mentally disturbed, because a huge mass of unfinished, unresolved thoughts and shallow impressions would accumulate in his brain, the sheer weight of which would certainly stifle what should have been incorporated into memory as a finished whole.' Dream provides the overburdened brain with a safety valve. *Dreams possess healing, relieving power* (p. 32).

It would be a misunderstanding to ask Robert to explain how, as a result of something being dreamed about, the mind can find relief. Clearly, this author concludes from the aforesaid two characteristics of dream-material that, in sleep, such an elimination of worthless impressions takes place *somehow* as a somatic sequence of events and that dreaming is not a particular kind of psychical process but simply the notification we receive that that secretion is taking place. Incidentally, evacuation is not the only thing that goes on in the mind at night. Robert himself adds that the day's stimuli are also worked through and that 'what cannot be eliminated of the ideas that lie undigested in the mind is *joined together to form a rounded whole by trains of thought borrowed from the imagination* and thus classified in memory as harmless fantasy pictures' (p. 23).

However, Robert clashes with prevailing theory most sharply when it comes to assessing the sources of dream. Whereas in the prevailing view there would be no dreaming at all if the mind's external and internal stimuli were not repeatedly aroused, according to Robert's theory the driving force behind dream is located in the mind itself, in its cluttered state, which clamours for relief, and Robert is entirely consistent in saying that the causes of dream lying in a person's physical condition occupy a subordinate place and could never induce dream in a mind that had no material for dream-formation taken from waking consciousness. His only concession is that the fantasy images that emerge from the depths of the mind in dream may be influenced by nervous stimuli (p. 48). According to Robert, then, dream is not in fact entirely independent of the somatic sphere. Granted, it is not a psychical process and has no place among the psychical processes of waking life; rather, it is a nightly somatic process affecting the apparatus of mental activity, and it has a function to perform, namely to protect that apparatus against overload or, if I may switch metaphors, to muck out the mind.

It is on the identical characteristics of dream, which come out clearly in the selection of dream-material, that another author, Yves Delage [1891], bases his own theory, and it is instructive to observe how a slight change of direction in the apprehension of the same things can lead to an end-result with a very different scope.

Delage had had personal experience, after someone dear to him had died, of the way in which a person does *not* dream about the thing that has thoroughly preoccupied him during the day – or does so only when that thing is starting, during the day, to give way to other interests. Enquiries among other persons confirmed his belief that such a state of affairs was universal. Delage made a fine observation along these lines (should it turn out to be generally true) regarding the dreams of a young married couple: 'Although they were deeply in love, almost never did they dream of each other before their wedding or during the honeymoon; and if they did dream of love it was in order to commit an infidelity with some indifferent or obnoxious person.' But then what does a person dream about? Delage recognized the material occurring in our dreams as consisting of fragments and leftovers of impressions of recent days and former times. Everything that appears in our dreams, everything that we may at first be inclined to regard as having been created by dream-life, turns out on closer inspection to be unacknowledged reproduction – what Delage calls *'souvenir inconscient'* ['unconscious memory']. However, that ideational material does have one common characteristic: it is derived from impressions that probably affected our senses more than our mind, or from which attention was diverted very soon after their appearance. The less conscious and yet the stronger an impression was, the better its chances of playing a part in the next dream.

In essence, these are the same two categories of impression (the peripheral and the unresolved) as Robert highlights, but Delage steers the connection in a different direction by saying that the reason why these impressions do not form potential dream-material is not that they are unimportant but that they are unresolved. Peripheral impressions, too, are not fully resolved, so to speak; they too are by their nature (as new impressions) 'so many stretched springs' that will discharge their tension during sleep. An even greater claim to a role in dream than the weak, almost unnoticed impression will attach to a powerful stimulus that had accidentally been blocked as it was being processed or had deliberately been repudiated. The psychical energy stored up during the day as a result of inhibition or suppression becomes, at night, the trigger of dream. In dream, what the psyche had suppressed comes to light.[1]

Unfortunately, Delage's train of thought breaks off at this point;

he is able to assign only a very minor role to any autonomous mental activity in dream, as a result of which he and his dream-theory unexpectedly side with the prevailing doctrine of the brain [in dream] being partly asleep: 'To sum up, dream is the product of errant, aimless, directionless thought, successively fixing on memories that have retained sufficient intensity to place themselves in its path and interrupt its passage, establishing between those memories a link that is now weak and indecisive, now strong and more closely woven, depending on whether the current activity of the brain is to a greater or lesser extent done away with by sleep.'

3) A third group of dream-theories may be said to comprise those that attribute to the dreaming mind the ability and inclination to perform particular psychical operations that it can either not perform at all in the waking state or can perform only imperfectly. Usually, activating such abilities gives rise to a useful function for dream. Most estimates of dream in the works of earlier psychological writers belong in this group. However, I shall content myself with quoting in their place Burdach's comment ([1838] p. 486) that dream 'is the natural activity of the mind; it is not constrained by the power of individuality, not disturbed by self-consciousness, and not steered by self-determination, but is the liveliness (enjoying free rein, so to speak) of the sensitive key points'.

This indulgence in the free use of the mind's own forces is something that Burdach and others clearly see as a condition in which the mind finds recreation and gathers fresh strength for the day's work – a kind of holiday, as it were. That is why Burdach cites with acceptance the delightful passage in which the writer Novalis praises the dominion of dream: 'Dream is a bulwark against the regularity and ordinariness of life, a period of free rest and recreation for the chained imagination in which it tosses all the images of life into confusion and interrupts the steady seriousness of the waking person with a joyous childhood game; without dreams we should certainly age faster, so dream, even if not directly bestowed from above, may still be seen as a precious duty, a congenial companion on our pilgrimage to the grave.'

The refreshing, healing activity of dream is described even more vividly by Purkinje ([1846] p. 456):

> In particular, productive dreams would perform such functions. These are lightweight games of the imagination that have nothing to do with the events of the day. The mind does not wish to continue the tensions of waking life but to dissolve them, get over them. It generates, first and foremost, the circumstances opposite to those of the waking state. It heals sadness with joy, worry with hopes and happy, diverting images, hatred with love and affection, fear with courage and confidence; it calms doubts with conviction and firm belief, vain expectations with fulfilment. Many wounds in the heart, which day would perpetually keep open, dream heals by shielding and preserving them from fresh upset. Hence, to some extent, the way in which time soothes pain.

We all have experience of how sleep brings relief to the life of the mind, and the vague suspicion of popular awareness is clearly reluctant to part with its presumption that dream is one of the ways in which sleep dispenses such relief.

The most original and ambitious attempt to explain dream in terms of a separate activity of the mind that can unfold freely only in the sleeping state was made by Scherner in 1861. Scherner's book, which is written in an overheated, overblown style and propelled by an almost drunken enthusiasm for its subject that is bound to put off anyone whom it does not carry along with it, places such difficulties in the way of analysis that we eagerly reach for the clearer, briefer account that the philosopher Volkelt [1875] gives of Scherner's teachings. 'No doubt there gleams and flashes forth from his mystical accumulations, from all that glorious surging, some prescient glimpse of meaning, but it scarcely lights the philosopher's steps.' Even Scherner's supporters deliver similar verdicts.

Scherner is not one of those writers who let the mind carry its faculties over into dream-life undiminished. He himself sets out how, in dream, the centrality and spontaneous energy of the 'I' are enervated, how in consequence of that decentralization the faculties of cognition, feeling, will and ideation become different, and how what is left of those mental forces is no longer truly spiritual in character but is simply in the nature of a mechanism. But at the same time, in dream, the mental activity to be termed 'imagination', freed from control by reason and hence from any kind of strict moderation, attains absolute dominance. Taking the last-remaining building-blocks from the memory of the waking state, it uses them to fashion constructions that are worlds apart from those of the waking state; in dream, it shows itself to be not only reproductive but also *productive*. Its peculiarities are what give dream-life its particular character. It demonstrates a preference for everything *immoderate, exaggerated, outrageous*. At the same time, however, being relieved of the hindrance of thought-categories gives it greater flexibility and nimbleness and a positive delight in changing direction; it is exquisitely sensitive to the delicate stimuli of mood, to emotional upheaval, and it instantly incorporates the inner life in graphic, external, three-dimensional form. Dream-imagination *lacks conceptual language*; what it wants to say, it has to portray graphically, and since there is no concept here to have an enfeebling effect, it does so in the fullness and with the strength and dimensions of visual form. As a result its language, no matter how clear, becomes long-winded, cumbersome, clumsy. The clarity of its language is particularly impeded by its tendency to give expression to an object by means of its actual image and by its preferring to choose a *borrowed image*, provided that this is capable of expressing, through itself, only that element of the object that it is concerned to represent. This is the *symbolizing activity* of imagination . . . Another very important thing is that dream-imagination does not portray objects in their entirety but only in outline – and that in the freest fashion. Its pictures appear to have been painted with the lightest of touches, brilliantly. But dream-imagination goes further than simple depiction of the object: it is under an inner compulsion to involve the dream-'I' to a greater or lesser extent and thus to generate action. The visual-stimulus dream, for instance, depicts gold coins in the street; the dreamer collects these, is delighted, carries them off.

According to Scherner, the material on which dream-imagination performs its artistic activity is primarily that of organic bodily stimuli (see above, p. 44), material that by day is so obscure. Consequently, in their assumptions regarding the sources and triggers of dream the over-imaginative theory of Scherner and the perhaps excessively restrained teachings of Wundt [1880] and other physiologists, which are otherwise poles apart, here coincide completely. However, whereas according to the physiological theory the reaction of the mind to internal bodily stimuli goes no further than to arouse certain appropriate ideas, which then seek the support of other ideas through the channel of association, and that stage seems to mark the end of the pursuit of the psychical processes of dream, according to Scherner's theory bodily stimuli simply supply the mind with material that it can then use for its imaginative purposes. For Scherner, dream-formation begins at the point where others believe it dries up.

It is pointless, of course, trying to discover what dream-imagination does with bodily stimuli. It plays a teasing game with them, seeing the organic sources from which the stimuli in the relevant dream proceed in some sort of three-dimensional symbolism. In fact, Scherner thinks (and here Volkelt and others do not follow him) that dream-imagination has a certain favourite way of representing the entire organism – as a *house*. Fortunately, it does not appear to be confined to this material for its representations; it may also, conversely, use whole rows of houses to portray a single organ, an example being very long terraces for the intestinal stimulus. At other times, individual parts of the house really do stand for individual parts of the body – as for example in the headache dream, where the ceiling of a room (which the dreamer sees as being covered with revolting toad-like spiders) represents the head.

Quite apart from house symbolism, any number of other objects are used to represent the parts of the body emitting the dream-stimulus. 'Thus the breathing lungs find their symbol in the flame-filled oven with its air-like roar, the heart in hollow boxes and baskets, the bladder in round, pouch-shaped or simply hollowed-out objects. The male sexual-stimulus dream causes the dreamer to find the upper part of a clarinet or the same part of a tobacco pipe or it may be a fur lying in the street, clarinets and tobacco pipes representing the approximate shape of the male member, the fur the pubic hair. In the female sex-dream the place where the thighs join may be symbolized by a narrow courtyard surrounded by houses, the vagina by a soft, slippery and extremely narrow footpath across the middle of the courtyard that the dreamer must negotiate, perhaps in order to bring a letter to a gentleman' (Volkelt [1875], p. 34). It is particularly important that, at the end of such a bodily-stimulus dream, dream-imagination unmasks itself, as it were, by presenting the organ that produced the arousal or presenting its function without disguise. The 'tooth-stimulus dream', for instance, usually concludes with the dreamer taking a tooth out of his or her mouth.

However, dream-imagination may pay heed not only to the shape of the organ causing arousal; it may equally take the substance contained in it as the object of symbolization. The intestinal-stimulus dream, for instance, leads through filthy streets, the bladder-stimulus dream to foaming water. Or the stimulus itself, the manner of its arousal, the object of its desire are represented symbolically, or the dream-'I' enters into actual contact with the symbolizations of its own condition – when, for instance, in connection with pain stimuli we wrestle desperately with snapping dogs or maddened bulls, or when a woman having a sex dream sees herself being pursued by a naked man. All the potential variety of execution notwithstanding, a symbol-forming imaginative operation remains the key force behind every dream. Finding out more about the nature of that imagination, giving the psychical activity thus acknowledged its proper place in a system of philosophical thought – these are things that Volkelt [1875] then tried to do, though his fine, warmly written book remains extremely difficult for anyone to understand who lacks prior training in the mysterious business of understanding philosophical language.

The activation of Scherner's symbolizing imagination in dreams is not coupled with a useful function. The mind, in dream, plays with the stimuli presented to it. One might suppose that it does so mischievously. But one might also enquire of us whether our detailed preoccupation with Scherner's theory of dream can ever lead to anything useful, given that its arbitrariness and detachment from all the rules of academic research are all too strikingly apparent. There would be a case, in fact, for vetoing any rejection of Scherner's theory before any kind of examination as being excessively arrogant. That theory is based on someone's impression of his dreams, someone who paid a great deal of attention to those dreams and who seems to have had a deep personal inclination to explore obscure matters of the mind. It further deals with an object that for thousands of years has appeared puzzling, certainly, but at the same time rich in content and associations and towards the elucidation of which strict science has, by its own admission, contributed little apart from seeking, in complete contrast to popular experience, to deny it all substance and significance. Finally, let us frankly admit to ourselves that it looks very much as if, in our attempts to shed light on dream, we cannot easily escape the world of fantasy. There is ganglion-cell fantasy, too; the passage quoted above (see p. 90) by the very sober, precise scientist Binz, in which he describes how the aurora of awakening moves steadily over the cell masses of the sleeping cerebral cortex, is no less fantastic and (let's face it) improbable than Scherner's attempts at interpretation. I hope to be able to show that behind the latter there is something real, though it has been only hazily acknowledged and does not possess the characteristic of universality to which a theory of dream may lay claim. For the time being, Scherner's theory of dream (in contrast to the medical theory, for instance) may serve to remind us between what extremes the explanation of dream-life still uncertainly hovers.

Note

1. The writer Anatole France (in *Le Lys rouge* [1894]) says something very similar: 'What we see at night are the wretched remains of what we had ignored the previous day. Dream is often the revenge of things scorned or the reproach of people abandoned.'

H *Links between dream and mental illnesses*

Anyone talking about how dream relates to mental disorders may mean one of three things: 1) aetiological and clinical relationships – say, when a dream represents a psychotic state, or heralds such a state, or (afterwards) renders it superfluous; 2) changes that dream-life undergoes in the event of mental illness; 3) internal relationships between dream and psychoses, analogies suggesting an essential kinship.

In an earlier medical era (and again in the present day), such manifold relationships between the two sets of phenomena constituted a favourite theme for medical writers, as demonstrated by the literature on the subject gathered in the works of Spitta, Radestock, Maury and Tissié. Recently, Sante de Sanctis has turned his attention to this question.[1] For the purposes of our account, it will be enough merely to touch on this important subject.

Regarding the clinical and aetiological relationships between dream and psychoses, let me offer the following observations as paradigms. Hohnbaum (in Kraus [1858–9]) reports that the initial outbreak of insanity sometimes originated in an anxious, rather alarming dream and that the dominant idea bore a connection to that dream. Sante de Sanctis contributes similar observations of the paranoid state and in certain of those observations states that dream is 'the true determinant of madness'. A psychosis may spring to life suddenly, along with the operative dream containing the delusionary enlightenment, or it may develop gradually, through further dreams that must still wrestle with doubt. In one case reported by de Sanctis the engulfing dream was followed by mild attacks of hysteria and subsequently by a state of anxious melancholy. Féré (in Tissié) tells of a dream that resulted in a hysterical paralysis. Here dream is presented to us as aetiology of mental disorder, although we are also allowing for this state of affairs if we say that the mental disorder first expressed itself in dream-life, first broke through in dream. In other examples, dream-life contains the morbid symptoms, or the psychosis remains confined to dream-life. Thus Thomayer [1897] draws attention to *anxiety dreams* that must be understood as equivalent to epileptic fits. According to Radestock [1879], Allison described instances of what he called 'nocturnal insanity' in which the individuals concerned seemed in perfect health during the day, whereas at night, hallucinations, attacks of maniacal rage and so on appeared regularly. Similar observations are reported by de Sanctis (paranoiac dream-equivalent in the case of an alcoholic, voices accusing the wife of infidelity) and by Tissié; Tissié contributes a large number of recent observations in which actions of a pathological nature (based on delusional premises, obsessive impulses) proceed from dreams. Guislain describes a case in which sleep was replaced by intermittent insanity.

There can be no doubt that, one day, alongside the psychology of dream, doctors will be preoccupied by a psychopathology of dream.

It is particularly clear, often in cases of recovery following mental illness, that while a person functions healthily by day his dream-life may still be in thrall to psychosis. Gregory (according to Krauss [1858–9]) is said to have been the first to have drawn attention to this state of affairs. Macario is quoted by Tissié as telling of one maniac who, a week after his complete restoration to health, reexperienced in dreams the rapid flow of ideas and impassioned drives of his illness.

Regarding the changes that dream-life undergoes in long-term psychotics, very few investigations have yet been mounted. By contrast, the inner relationship between dream and mental disturbance, which finds expression in the very extensive correspondence between the manifestations of both, received attention early on. According to Maury, the first reference to it was by Cabanis in his

Rapports du physique et du moral; he was followed by Lélut [1853], J. Moreau [1855] and above all the philosopher Maine de Biran [1792]. Undoubtedly, the comparison is even older. Radestock heads the chapter in which he discusses it with a collection of comments drawing an analogy between dream and madness. Kant says at one point: 'The madman is a dreamer awake.' Krauss: 'Madness is a dream within sensory awakeness.' Schopenhauer calls dream a brief madness and madness a long dream. Hagen describes delirium as dream-life induced not by sleep but by illness. Wundt in his *Rudiments of Physiological Psychology* writes: 'Indeed, in dream we are able to experience personally nearly all the phenomena we come across in lunatic asylums.'

The individual correspondences on the basis of which such a comparison asks to be drawn are placed by Spitta (very like Maury, incidentally) in the following order: 1) abolition or at least retardation of self-awareness, hence ignorance of one's state as such, i.e. impossibility of surprise, lack of moral awareness; 2) altered perception of the sense organs – reduced in dream, greatly increased all round in madness; 3) interconnectedness of ideas purely in accordance with the laws of association and reproduction – in other words, automatic sequencing, hence disproportionality of relations between ideas (exaggerations, fantasms) and everything flowing therefrom; 4) change or reversal of personality and occasionally of peculiarities of character (perversities).

Radestock adds one or two features in terms of similarities of material: 'It is in the areas of sight, hearing and common sensation that one comes across most hallucinations and illusions. As in dream, fewest elements are provided by the senses of smell and taste. The patient with a high temperature will be visited in his deliriums, as will the dreamer, by memories from the distant past; what the person in the waking state and the healthy person appear to have forgotten, the sleeper and the invalid recall.' But what gives the analogy between dream and psychosis its full value is the fact that, like a family resemblance, it extends to subtle mimicry and even to individual peculiarities of facial expression.

Dream provides the patient suffering from physical or mental disorders with what reality has withheld: well-being and bliss; the bright images of happiness, greatness, superiority and wealth are received by the mental patient, too. The supposed possession of assets and the imagined fulfilment of desires, the refusal or destruction of which provided a psychical reason for a person's madness, often furnish the principal content of the associated delirium. The woman who has lost a dear child experiences in her delirium the joys of motherhood, the man who has lost property regards himself as exceptionally rich, the girl who has been betrayed sees herself as an object of tender affection.

(This passage from Radestock is an abbreviated version of a sensitive argument by Griesinger [(1871) p. 111], who very clearly shows *wish-fulfilment* to be a type of ideation common to both dream and psychosis. My own investigations have taught me that this is where the key to a psychological theory of dream and psychoses is to be found.)

'Bizarre associations of ideas and weakness of judgement are the things that chiefly characterize dream and madness.' The kind of *overrating* of one's own intellectual performance that rational judgement deems nonsensical occurs in the one as in the other; the *briskness of dream ideation* corresponds to the *rapid flow of ideas* typical of psychosis. Both lack any *sense of time*. The *splitting of the personality in dream* (which, for example, distributes what one person knows between two persons, with the stranger correcting, in dream, the first person's 'I') is entirely equivalent to the familiar dividing of the personality that takes place in hallucinatory paranoia; the dreamer, too, hears his own thoughts spoken by other voices. There is even an analogy for constant delusions in stereotypically recurring pathological dreams (the *'rêve obsédant'*). Following recovery from a delirium, patients not infrequently say that throughout the entire period their illness seemed to them to be an often not uncomfortable dream; indeed, they tell us that even while ill they had the occasional inkling that they were simply caught up in a dream – just as often happens in a sleeping dream.

After all this it comes as no surprise to find Radestock summing up his opinion (shared by many) in the words: 'Madness, which is an abnormal, morbid phenomenon, should be seen as an intensification of the regularly recurring, normal state of dream' ([1878] p. 228).

Perhaps more profoundly than is possible through this analogy of the phenomena manifesting themselves, Krauss [1858–9] sought to account for the relationship between dream and madness in terms of aetiology (or rather: in the sources of arousal). As we have heard, according to him the basic element common to both is the *organically determined feeling*, the physical stimulus, the common sensation brought about as a result of contributions from all the organs (see also Peisse, as cited by Maury [1878], p. 52).

The indisputable correspondence between dream and mental illness, which extends into characteristic details, is one of the strongest pillars of the medical theory of dream-life, which says that dream represents itself as a pointless, disruptive process and as the expression of a sinking level of mental activity. However, one cannot expect the final elucidation of dream to come from the direction of mental disorders when everyone knows how unsatisfactory is the state of our knowledge regarding the course taken by the latter. It is, however, probable that an altered view of dream will inevitably help to influence the way we think about the internal mechanism of mental disturbance, so we are entitled to say we are working on elucidating psychoses in endeavouring to shed light on the mystery of dream.

Added in 1909:

Some justification is required for the fact that I have not continued the literature dealing with dream-problems over the period between the first publication of this book and its second edition. That literature may strike the reader as somewhat unsatisfactory; it has been my guide none the less. The motives that had prompted me to take the original step of setting out how dream had been dealt with in the literature were covered exhaustively in the foregoing introduction; continuing the work would have cost me a huge effort and – well, it would have served very little purpose and imparted very little new knowledge. The reason is that the nine-year period in question has contributed nothing innovative or valuable as regards the understanding of dream either in terms of actual material or in terms of viewpoints. My book receives no mention and is left entirely out of account in most of the publications that have appeared in the interim; it has received least attention, of course, from so-called 'dream-researchers' – who have thus provided a splendid example of the disinclination, peculiar among scientific people, to learning anything new. 'Scholars are incurious folk,' said the wit Anatole France. If there is a right of reply in science, I too should no doubt be justified in doing the same thing and in ignoring all the literature since this book appeared. The few reviews that have been published in scientific journals are so full of silliness and misunderstandings that I can only answer the critics by saying: read the book again. Perhaps I should just say: read the book.

In the works of those physicians who have decided to implement psychoanalytical treatment, and in other works too, a great many dreams have been published and interpreted in accordance with my instructions. Where such works go beyond simply confirming my ideas, I have incorporated their findings in the context of my account. A second bibliography at the end presents a selection of the most important publications since this book first appeared. The comprehensive book on dreams written by Sante de Sanctis, which received a German translation shortly after its publication, appeared around the same time as my *Interpreting Dreams*, with the result that I was no more able to take note of him than the Italian author was of me. I then, unfortunately, had to pronounce his painstaking work to be exceptionally poor in ideas – so poor that one gained no glimpse, in its pages, of the mere possibility of the problems with which I deal.

I need mention only two publications that touch closely on my own treatment of dream-problems. A young philosopher, H. Swoboda, adopting the discovery of biological periodicity (in groups of 23 and 28 days) first put forward by Wilhelm Fliess, set out to extend it to psychical events; he sought in an imaginative essay[2] to use this key to unlock (among other things) the riddle of dreams. This, I feel, does rather less than justice to the significance of dreams, dream-content being explained in terms of the coming-together of all the recollections that on that particular night happened to complete one of those biological periods for the first time or for the *n*th time. A private communication from the author initially led me to assume that he was himself no longer serious about wishing to champion this theory. Evidently I was mistaken; I shall be publishing certain observations regarding Swoboda's thesis elsewhere, although those observations have not, so far as I am concerned, delivered a convincing outcome. Much more satisfactory was my chance encounter, in an unexpected location, with a view of dream that fully matches the core of my own. Temporal circumstances rule out the possibility that this offering was influenced by reading my book; I must therefore hail it as the only verifiable instance, in the literature, of an independent thinker agreeing with the essence of my theory of dream. The book containing the passage about dreaming that I have in mind is called *Phantasien eines Realisten* ['Fantasies of a realist']; the author is Lynkeus, and the second edition was published in 1900.[3]

Added in 1914:

The above justification was penned in 1909. In the mean time, of course, the situation has changed; my contribution to the subject of interpreting dreams is no longer overlooked in the literature. However, the new situation makes it quite impossible for me to extend the present account. *Interpreting Dreams* threw up a whole series of new propositions and problems that the authors of the literature have now discussed in a wide variety of ways. I can hardly describe such studies before unfolding my own views – the views to which those authors refer. For that reason, what seems to me to be of value in this new literature I acknowledge in the context of what now follows.

Notes

1. Subsequent authors dealing with such relationships include Féré, Ideler, Lasègue, Pichon, Régis, Vespa, Giessler, Kazodowsky and Pachantoni.
2. H. Swoboda, *Die Perioden des menschlichen Organismus* ['Periods of the human organism'], 1904.
3. See also 'Josef Popper-Lynkeus und die Theorie des Traumes' (1923) in vol. XI of my *Gesammelte Schriften*. [*Standard Edition*, vol. XIX, p. 261].

2

Method of Dream-Interpretation: Analysis of a Specimen Dream

The title I have given my book shows which tradition in the perception of dreams I wish to take as my starting-point. I propose to show that dreams are capable of interpretation, and so far as I am concerned contributions towards clarifying the dream-problems that we have just been discussing will provide only a kind of incidental benefit as I perform my true task. Predicating that dreams can be interpreted immediately places me in conflict with prevailing dream-doctrine – indeed, with all theories of dream except for the one advanced by Scherner [1861]. The reason is that to 'interpret' a dream is to indicate its 'meaning', substituting for it something that forms a link in the chain of our mental actions, a link possessing the same importance and the same value as any other. However, as we have seen, the scientific theories of dream leave no room for a problem of interpreting dreams, since for them dream is not a mental act at all but a somatic process that manifests its presence in the mental apparatus through signs. Yet the lay view has always been otherwise. Asserting its perfect right to proceed illogically, and conceding that dream is incomprehensible and absurd, the lay view is nevertheless unable, ultimately, to deny dream all significance. Guided by a dim suspicion, it apparently assumes that dream has some meaning (albeit a hidden meaning), that dream serves as substitute for a different mental process, and that it is simply a question of exposing that substitution in the correct fashion in order to reach the hidden significance of a particular dream.

The lay world has therefore, since time began, sought to 'interpret' dream, and in the process it has experimented with two radically different methods. The first looks at the content of a particular dream as a whole and tries to substitute for it a different, comprehensible and in certain respects similar content. This is *symbolic* dream-interpretation, and of course it fails from the outset with those dreams that appear not only incomprehensible but also confused. An example of how it proceeds is the explanation that the biblical Joseph furnishes for the pharaoh's dream. Seven fat cows followed by seven thin ones that eat up the former are a symbolic substitute for the prediction of seven years of famine in the land of Egypt that consume the entire surplus created by seven fertile years. Most of the artificial dreams created by writers are intended for this kind of symbolic interpretation, since they reflect the writer's thoughts in a guise that is found to suit what we know from experience to be the characteristics of our dreaming activity.[1] The view that dream concerns itself mainly with the future, the shape of which it knows in advance (a residue of the prophetic importance once attributed to dream), then becomes the motive for taking the meaning of a particular dream, discovered by symbolic interpretation, and shifting it into the future tense by means of an 'it will'.

How to find one's way to this kind of symbolic interpretation is not of course something that instruction can teach. Success remains a matter of brilliant insight, of sudden intuition, so that the method of interpreting dreams using symbolism came to be elevated to the status of an art, which seemed to be coupled with a special gift.[2] This is not something to which the second of the popular methods of dream-interpretation remotely lays claim. The second method might be called the 'decoding method'; it treats dream as a kind of secret writing in which, following a fixed key, each character is translated into a different character whose meaning is known. I dream about a letter, say, but also about a funeral – that sort of thing. I consult a 'dream-book' and find that 'letter' is to be translated as 'frustration' and 'funeral' is to be translated as 'betrothal'. It is then up to me to create a context from the headwords that I have decoded and to accept that context as lying in the future. An interesting amendment of the 'decoding method', as a result of which its character as purely mechanical translation is to some extent corrected, may be found in the essay on dream-interpretation written by Artemidorus of Daldis.[3] He takes account not only of dream-content but also of the person and circumstances of the dreamer, with the result that the same dream-element has a different meaning for the rich man, the married man or the orator than for the poor man, the bachelor and (say) the businessman. The essential thing about this method is that the work of interpretation is directed not at the dream as a whole but at each piece of the dream-content independently, as if dream[4] were a conglomerate in which each fragment of stone demanded its own special purpose. It is undoubtedly from incoherent, confused dreams that the impulse to create the deciphering method proceeded.[5]

As regards the scientific treatment of the subject, the uselessness of both popular dream-interpretation methods cannot be in doubt for a moment. The symbolic method is limited in its application and not susceptible of general exposition. As for the decoding method, everything would depend on the 'key' (the codebook) being reliable, and of that there is no guarantee. One is tempted to say that the philosophers and psychiatrists are right and, with them, rule out the problem of interpreting dreams as something one simply imagines needs doing.[6]

However, I now know better. I have been forced to accept that, here again, we have one of those not unusual instances of an age-old popular belief, obstinately clung to, having apparently come closer to the truth of the matter than the verdict of modern scholarship. I must assert that dream really does have meaning and that a scientific method of dream-interpretation is possible. I became aware of that method in the following manner:

For years I have been concerned with resolving certain psycho-pathological figments, hysterical phobias, obsessions and the like with a view to healing them – ever since, in fact, I learned from an important contribution by Josef Breuer that, so far as these formations (experienced as symptoms of illness) are concerned, resolution and dissolution are one and the same thing.[7] When one has succeeded in tracing such a pathological idea back to the elements in the mental life of the patient from which it sprang, it disintegrates and decays; the patient is set free. Given the impotence of our other therapeutic endeavours and in view of the mysterious nature of such conditions, it struck me as tempting, all the difficulties notwithstanding, to press on along the path taken by Breuer until everything became clear. How the technical aspects of the procedure eventually emerged and what findings such efforts produced – these are things I shall have to report on in detail another time. In the course of these psychoanalytical studies, I came to the business of dream-interpretation. The patients whom I had placed under an obligation to tell me all the ideas and thoughts that sprang to mind in connection with a certain subject recounted their dreams to me, teaching me in the process that a dream can be fitted into the psychical chain of events that, starting from a pathological idea, can be traced back in memory. The obvious next step was to treat dream itself as a symptom, applying to the former methods of interpretation that had been developed for the latter.

For this, a certain psychical preparation of the patient is required. Here two things are aimed at: a heightening of the patient's attention so far as his[8] psychical perceptions are concerned and a switching-off of the critical faculty with which he is otherwise in the habit of inspecting the thoughts that occur to him. For the purposes of self-examination with undivided attention, it is an advantage to have the patient adopt a restful position with his eyes closed; renunciation of criticism of the mental images that occur to him is something that must be expressly imposed. In other words, the patient is told that the success of psychoanalysis depends upon his observing and communicating whatever occurs to him and not allowing himself to be tempted into suppressing, say, this idea[9] because it seems to him unimportant or of no relevance to the subject or the other because it strikes him as making no sense. He needs to behave with complete impartiality towards what comes into his mind because (he must be told) it will be precisely the fault of criticism if he otherwise fails to find the desired resolution of the dream, the obsession, or whatever it is.

In my psychoanalytical work I have noticed that the psychical state of a man who is thinking is quite different from that of a man who is observing his own psychical processes. In the case of the thinker, more psychical action is involved than in the case of the most attentive self-observation, as evinced partly by the drawn features and furrowed brow of the thoughtful person in contrast to the mimic calm of the self-observer. In both instances a gathering of attentiveness must be present, but the thinking man will also be exercising criticism, in consequence of which he will reject some of the ideas that pop into his head, once he has become aware of them; others he will break off abruptly, with the result that he does not follow the trains of thought they would place before him; as regards yet other ideas, he knows how to prevent them from even entering consciousness, so that they are suppressed even before they are perceived. All the self-observer has to do, on the other hand, is to suppress his critical faculty, and if he is successful in this a host of ideas will enter his consciousness that would otherwise have remained beyond his grasp. With the aid of this newly acquired material (so far as self-perception is concerned), pathological ideas can be interpreted and so can dream-figments. As we see, it is a question of creating a psychical state that shares with that immediately preceding sleep (and certainly with that of the hypnotized subject) a certain similarity in the distribution of psychical energy (flexible attentiveness). As a person enters sleep, his 'involuntary ideas' come to the fore as a result of the slackening of a certain arbitrary (and undoubtedly also critical) action that we allow to influence the course of our ideas; the reason we usually give for such slackening is 'being tired'; the involuntary ideas that then occur transform themselves into visual and acoustic images. (See also, among other sources, the remarks of Schleiermacher [1862], pp. 64f.)[10] In the state that is used for the analysis of dreams and pathological ideas, a person deliberately and arbitrarily renounces all activity and uses the psychical energy thus saved (or part of it) for following attentively the involuntary thoughts that now occur to him and that retain their character as 'ideas' (this is what distinguishes this state from that of falling asleep). *In this way he turns his 'involuntary' ideas into 'voluntary' ones.*

The attitude I am calling for here (one of focusing on apparently 'free-rising' notions while forgoing the criticism normally directed against them) is for some people evidently not an easy one. The 'involuntary' thoughts usually provoke the liveliest resistance, which seeks to prevent them from showing themselves. But if we are to believe our great poet-philosopher Friedrich Schiller, a very similar attitude must also constitute the condition for poetic production. At one point in his correspondence with Körner (for tracing which we owe Otto Rank a debt of gratitude), Schiller replies to his friend's complaint of insufficient productivity:

> The ground for your accusation lies, it seems to me, in the constraints that your reason places on your imagination. Here I must set down an idea and flesh it out with the help of an allegory. It seems to be not a good thing and detrimental to the creative work of the mind when reason, taking up a position at the gates, as it were, subjects the incoming stream of ideas to excessive scrutiny. Considered in isolation, an idea may be quite inconsiderable and highly bizarre, but an idea coming along after it may make it important; maybe, combined in a certain way with others that perhaps seem equally outrageous, it will furnish a very useful link. None of this can reason judge unless it holds on to the idea for long enough to have sight of it in conjunction with those others. In a creative mind, on the other hand, it seems to me that reason has pulled back its sentry from the gates, ideas pour in pell-mell, and only afterwards does it take stock and examine the whole great crowd. So, then, you critics or whatever you call yourselves, be ashamed or in awe of the brief, fleeting madness that is found in all proper creators and the longer or shorter duration of which separates the thinking artist from the dreamer. Hence your complaints of unfruitfulness, because you discard too soon and filter out too rigorously (letter of 1 December 1788).

Yet this 'pulling back of the sentry from the gates of reason', as Schiller expresses it, this sort of putting oneself in a state of uncritical self-observation, is not at all difficult.

Most of my patients manage it after the first instruction; I myself can manage it perfectly if I aid myself in the process by writing down the things that occur to me. The amount of psychical energy by which one reduces critical activity in this way and with which one can increase intensity of self-observation fluctuates considerably, depending on the topic on which such attention was meant to focus.

Now, the first step in the application of this procedure teaches that one may not make the whole dream the object of attention but only individual bits of its content. If I ask the as yet unpractised patient, 'What does this dream make you think of?' he is not as a rule able to register anything in his intellectual field of vision. I have to lay the dream before him in pieces, then he will give me, for each piece, a series of notions that occur to him and that can be described as the 'ulterior motives' behind that segment of the dream. So in this initial important condition the method of dream-interpretation that I use already diverges from the popular method, the method famed in history and legend, of interpretation by symbolism; it is closer to the second, so-called 'decoding' method. Like the latter, it proceeds *en détail* rather than *en masse*; it also treats dream as something put together, a conglomerate of psychical formations.

In the course of my psychoanalyses among neurotics I have probably already brought over a thousand dreams to interpretation, but I do not wish to use this material here to introduce the technique and theory of dream-interpretation. Quite apart from the fact that I should be exposing myself to the objection that these are of course the dreams of neuropaths and do not admit of a conclusion regarding the dreams of healthy people, there is another reason why I am compelled to reject them. The theme on which such dreams focus is of course always the medical history underlying the particular neurosis. Consequently, for each dream it would be necessary to provide a very lengthy prefatory account and to penetrate the essence and aetiological conditions of psychoneuroses – things that are for the most part new and in the highest degree disconcerting and as such would divert attention away from the problem of dream. It is much more my intention to create, through dream-resolution, a piece of preliminary work towards tackling the more difficult problems of neurosis psychology. However, if I decline to use the dreams of neurotics, which are my main source of material, I can hardly be too choosy with regard to the rest. All I am left with are the dreams that have occasionally been recounted to me by healthy persons of my acquaintance or that I find described by way of examples in the literature on dream-life. Unfortunately, in connection with all these dreams I lack the analysis without which I am incapable of finding the meaning of the particular dream concerned. You see, my procedure is not as convenient as that of the decoding method, which translates a given dream-content in accordance with a fixed key; I am quite prepared to find that the same dream-content may, with different persons and in another context, conceal different meanings. So I am thrown back on to my own dreams as offering a plentiful, convenient source of material stemming from an approximately normal person and relating to a wide variety of everyday occasions. Doubts are bound to be voiced regarding the reliability of such 'self-analyses'. Some arbitrariness, people will say, cannot be ruled out. In my judgement, circumstances are more favourable in connection with self-observation than in connection with observing others. The attempt can be made, at any rate; let us see how far self-analysis brings us in terms of dream-interpretation. There are other difficulties, too, that I must overcome in my inner self. One is understandably reluctant to reveal so much private material from one's own mental life, knowing that there is no guarantee against being misinterpreted by others. However, one must be able to stand outside all that. 'Every psychologist,' writes Delboeuf [1885], 'is obliged to own up to his very weaknesses if he believes that, by so doing, he can shed light on some obscure problem.' In the reader, too, no doubt, an initial interest in the indiscretions I shall be obliged to commit will very soon give way to unalloyed concentration on the psychological problems thus illuminated.[11]

So I shall look out one of my own dreams and use it to explain my method of interpretation. Each such dream needs to be prefaced. Now, however, I must ask the reader to make my interests his or her own for a time, plunging with me into the tiniest details of my life, because that kind of transference is very much demanded by an interest in the hidden meaning of dreams.

Prefatory remarks

In the summer of 1895 I had been treating a young woman psycho-analytically who, as a friend, was very close to me and my circle. Of course, such mixing of relationships can become the source of all kinds of stimuli for the physician, especially for the psychotherapist. The physician's personal interest is greater, his authority less. Failure will threaten to loosen the old ties of friendship with the patient's relations. The treatment resulted in partial success in that the patient lost her hysterical fear but not all her somatic symptoms. At the time I was not yet quite sure of the criteria indicating that a medical history of hysteria is definitively terminated, and I put to the patient a solution that she found unacceptable. In this state of disunity, we broke off treatment for the summer season.

One day I received a visit from a junior colleague, one of my closest friends, who had recently visited the patient (Irma) and her family at their country retreat. I asked him how he had found her, and his answer was: Better, but not entirely well. I know that my friend Otto's words or the tone in which he had uttered them irritated me. I felt I detected a note of reproach, perhaps that I had promised the patient too much, and whether rightly or wrongly I attributed what I took to be Otto's hostility towards me to the influence of the patient's relatives, who had never, I assumed, looked kindly on my treatment of her case. Incidentally, my feelings of embarrassment were not clear to me and I did not mention them. That same evening I wrote up Irma's medical history, meaning (as if in an attempt at self-justification) to give it to Dr M., a mutual friend and the person who at the time set the tone in our group. In the night that came after that evening (probably towards morning, in fact) I had the following dream, which was recorded immediately upon waking.[12]

Dream of 23/24 July 1895

A large hall – many guests, whom we are receiving. – Among them is Irma, whom I immediately take on one side in order, as it were, to answer her letter and to rebuke her for not yet accepting the 'solution'. I tell her, 'If you still get pains, you really have only yourself to blame.' She replies, 'If you knew how much pain I am in now. My throat hurts, my stomach hurts, my abdomen hurts, I feel as if I'm being tied in knots.' Alarmed, I examine her appearance. She has a pale, bloated look; the thought occurs to me that, when all's said and done, I must be overlooking something organic. I take her over to the window and look down her throat. At this, she shows some reluctance, like women who wear a denture. I think to myself, she has no need. Her mouth then does open all right, and I find a large white patch on the right, and on the other side, on curious crinkly formations obviously patterned on turbinates, I see extensive greyish-white scabs. I quickly call in Dr M., who repeats and confirms my examination . . . Dr M. looks quite different from usual: he is very pale, limps, and has no beard . . . My friend Otto is now also standing beside her, and another friend, Leopold, is listening to her chest, saying, 'There is a change of resonance at the left base.' He also points to an infiltrated area of skin on the left shoulder (of which, like him, I am aware in spite of the dress) . . . M. says, 'No doubt about it, it's an infection, but never mind, she'll get dysentery as well and the poison will be eliminated . . .' We also know immediately where the infection stems from. My friend Otto recently gave her an injection, when she was not feeling well, using a propyl preparation . . . propylene . . . propionic acid . . . trimethylamine (the formula of which I see before me in bold type) . . . Such injections are not administered lightly . . . Probably the syringe was not clean, either.

This dream has one advantage over many others. One knows instantly which events of the past day it relates to and what topic it is dealing with. The prefatory remarks tell us those. The news I had received from Otto regarding Irma's condition, the medical history I had stayed up late writing – these things also preoccupied my mental activity in sleep. Even so, probably no one who had taken note of the prefatory remarks and of the content of the dream could possibly guess what the dream means. I do not know myself. I am surprised at the symptoms about which Irma complains to me in the dream because they are not the same as those for which I had been treating her. I smile at the preposterous idea of an injection with propionic acid and the words of reassurance spoken by Dr M. The dream seems to me to be darker and more compressed towards the end than it is at the beginning. To learn what all this means, I have to make up my mind to embark on a thorough analysis.

Analysis

The hall – many guests, whom we are receiving. We were living up at Bellevue that summer, a detached house in the foothills of the Kahlenberg. The house had been designed as a place of entertainment, whence the unusually high-ceilinged, hall-like rooms. The dream also occurred at Bellevue, a few days before my wife's birthday. That day my wife had expressed the wish that on her birthday we should entertain a number of friends, including Irma. So my dream anticipates this situation: it is my wife's birthday, and many people, including Irma, are being welcomed by us as guests in the great hall of Bellevue.

I rebuke Irma for not having accepted the solution. I tell her, 'If you still get pains, it's your own fault. I could have said that to her when awake, or did say it. At the time I was of the opinion (subsequently acknowledged to be incorrect) that my job went no further than to tell patients the hidden meaning of their symptoms; whether or not they then accept the solution on which success depends is no longer, I thought, my responsibility. I have this error (now fortunately behind me) to thank for making my life easier at a time when, in all my inevitable ignorance, I was expected to produce therapeutic results. However, I notice from the words that

I address to Irma in the dream that I am anxious above all not to be to blame for the pain she is still experiencing. If Irma is herself to blame, then it cannot be my fault. Is this the direction in which the intention of the dream should be sought?

Irma's complaints: pains in the throat, abdomen and stomach, as if she were being tied in knots. Stomach pains were one of my patient's complex of symptoms, but they were not particularly serious; she complained more of feelings of nausea and disgust. Pains in the throat and abdomen and a feeling of constriction hardly came into the picture. I am surprised as to why I decided to include this selection of symptoms in the dream, and for the moment I cannot think of a reason.

She has a pale, bloated look. My patient was always rosy-cheeked. I suspect that someone else is creeping in behind her here.

I am alarmed at the thought that I have overlooked some organic condition. No one will be surprised to hear that this is a permanent anxiety with the specialist who sees almost exclusively neurotics and who is accustomed to ascribing to hysteria so many manifestations that other doctors treat as organic. On the other hand, a tiny doubt creeps in here (where from, I do not know) as to whether my alarm is wholly honest. If Irma's pains have an organic basis, it is not in fact my responsibility to heal them. My treatment only does away with hysterical pain. So it sounds to me as if I was hoping for a mistaken diagnosis; in that case the reproach of failure would also be removed.

I take her over to the window to examine her throat. She shows some slight resistance, like women who wear false teeth. I think to myself, she really has no need. With Irma, I never had occasion to inspect her oral cavity. When this happens in the dream, I am reminded of when, some time earlier, I had examined a governess, who had given an initial impression of youthful beauty but on opening her mouth adopted certain contrivances to hide her teeth. This case brings with it other memories of medical examinations and of little secrets being revealed – likewise unwillingly. *She has no need* is at first no doubt a compliment to Irma; however, I suspect another meaning. The attentive analyst senses whether all the ulterior motives to be expected have been cited or not. The way in which Irma stands at the window abruptly puts me in mind of another experience. Irma has a close friend, a woman whom I hold in very high regard. Visiting this friend one evening, I found her standing by a window in the same posture as the dream reproduced, and her doctor, the same Dr M., explained that she had a diphtheritic membrane. The person of Dr M. and the membrane in fact appear as the dream continues. Now it occurs to me that I have had every reason in recent months to assume that this other woman is also hysterical. Indeed, Irma herself has told me so. But what do I know of her condition? Precisely one thing: that she suffers from a hysterical choking feeling like my Irma in the dream. So what I have done in the dream is to replace my patient with her friend. I now recall that I often toyed with the supposition that this woman too might ask me to free her from her symptoms. However, I myself thought this unlikely, since she is of a very retiring nature. *She shows some reluctance*, as the dream indicates. Another explanation would be *that she has no need*; hitherto she really has shown herself strong enough to master her condition without outside help. This leaves just a few features that I am unable to accommodate either with Irma or with her friend: *pale, bloated, false teeth*. The false teeth brought me back to that governess; I now feel inclined to be content with bad teeth. Then another person occurs to me to whom those features may allude. She is also not a patient of mine, and I should not like to have her as a patient, because I have noticed that she is shy in my presence and I do not believe she would do as I say. She is usually pale, and once when she was having a particularly good time she was bloated.[13] So I have compared my patient Irma with two other people who would also resist treatment. What can be the meaning of my having, in dream, exchanged her for her friend? Is it that I wish to exchange her, either because the other woman arouses greater sympathy in me or because I have a higher opinion of her intelligence? The fact is, I think Irma is unwise not to accept my solution. The other woman would be cleverer, therefore more likely to obey. *Her mouth then does open all right*; she would be more forthcoming than Irma.[14]

What I see in the throat: a white patch and encrusted turbinates.
The white patch is reminiscent of diphtheritis and thus of Irma's
friend, but it also puts me in mind of the serious illness suffered by
my eldest daughter almost two years ago and of all the alarms of
that terrible time. The scabs on the turbinates remind me of a worry
about my own health. I was making frequent use of cocaine at the
time to suppress some tiresome nasal swellings, and I had heard a
few days before that a woman patient who was doing the same
as me had given herself extensive necrosis of the nasal mucous
membrane. The cocaine recommendation, which I had given in
1885, had earned me some serious reproaches. A dear friend of
mine who had died in 1895 had hastened his end by abusing this
substance.

I quickly call in Dr M., who repeats the examination. This would
simply reflect the standing that M. had among us. But the 'quickly'
is striking enough to require special explanation. It reminds me of
a sad medical experience. Once, by continuing to prescribe a drug
that was regarded as harmless at the time (sulphonal), I had induced
a severe case of poisoning in one of my patients, and I had then
very swiftly turned for support to older, experienced colleagues. An
incidental circumstance confirms that I really am thinking of this
case. The patient who suffered the intoxication had the same name
as my eldest daughter. I had never thought of this before; now it
comes to me almost as an instance of fate taking its revenge. As if
the replacement of persons should continue in a different sense:
this Mathilde for that Mathilde; an eye for an eye, a tooth for a
tooth. As if I was looking for every opportunity to blame myself for
lacking professional conscientiousness.

Dr M. is pale, beardless and limps. The first is right; in fact,
his wretched appearance has often prompted concern among his
friends. The other two characteristics must belong to someone else.
My elder brother, who lives abroad, occurs to me here. He shaves
his chin, and if I remember rightly he did on the whole look like
M. in the dream. We had had news of him a few days earlier that
he now has an arthritic hip and limps. There must be a reason why
in the dream I had blended the two persons into one. I do actually

recall that I was in a bad mood with both for similar reasons. Both had rejected a certain suggestion that I had recently put to them.

My friend Otto is now standing beside the patient, and another friend, Leopold, examining her, refers to a change of resonance at the left base. My friend Leopold is also a doctor, a relative of Otto. Since they both practise the same speciality, fate has made them competitors who are constantly compared with each other. They both worked as my assistants for years when I managed a public surgery for children with nervous illnesses. Scenes like that reproduced in the dream often took place there. While Otto and I were discussing the diagnosis of a case, Leopold, having re-examined the child, made a surprising contribution to the decision. Between the two of them there was a difference in character similar to that between [popular fictional characters] Inspector Bräsig and his friend Karl. One was noted for his 'speed'; the other was slow and deliberate but thorough. If in dream I compare Otto and the cautious Leopold, this is clearly in order to draw attention to Leopold. It is a similar comparison to the one described above between the disobedient patient Irma and her friend, whom I thought cleverer. I now also become aware of one of the rails along which my train of thought in the dream is moving: from sick child to hospital for sick children. *The attenuation at lower left* strikes me as a detailed match of an individual case in which Leopold had made a deep impression on me with his thoroughness. I further have in mind some sort of metastatic condition, but it may also relate to the patient whom I should like to have instead of Irma. The fact is, that woman (so far as I can judge) is faking tuberculosis.

An infiltrated area of skin on the left shoulder. I know instantly that this is my own shoulder rheumatism, which I regularly feel whenever I stay up late. Also the wording of the dream sounds so ambiguous: 'of which, like him, I am *aware*'. What I mean is: 'am aware on my own body'. Incidentally, I am struck by how odd the expression 'infiltrated area of skin' sounds. We are accustomed to 'infiltration at upper back left'; that refers to the lungs and hence again to tuberculosis.

In spite of the dress. This, by the way, is merely an interpolation.

At the children's hospital, we naturally examined patients with their clothes off – which is in some contrast to the way in which adult female patients must be examined. It used to be said of one famous physician that he had invariably examined his female patients through their clothes. The rest is obscure to me, and quite frankly I have no inclination to get more deeply involved here.

Dr M. says, it's an infection, but never mind, she'll get dysentery as well and the poison will be eliminated. Initially, this strikes me as absurd, but like everything else it needs to be carefully dissected. On closer examination, a sort of sense does emerge. What I found on the patient was a local area of diphtheritis. I remember the debate about diphtheritis and diphtheria from the time of my daughter's illness. The latter is the general infection that proceeds from local diphtheritis. Leopold detects such a general infection from the attenuation, which therefore suggests metastatic foci. I believe that, particularly with diphtheria, no such metastases occur. They remind me more of pyaemia.

Never mind is a consolation. I think this is how it fits in: The content of the last section of the dream is to the effect that the patient's pain derives from a severe organic disorder. I have a suspicion that this is another attempt on my part simply to shift the blame away from myself. My psychical treatment cannot be made responsible for the continuance of diphtheritic affliction. All the same, I feel awkward about imputing such a serious disease to Irma, simply and solely in order to exonerate myself. It looks so cruel. So I need some reassurance that all will be well in the end, and it strikes me as rather a good choice that I should have put the words of comfort into the mouth of no less a person than Dr M. But here I am rising above the dream that needs explaining.

Why, though, is the reassurance so nonsensical?

Dysentery. Some sort of tenuous theoretical notion that pathogenic matter can be got rid of through the gut. Is this an attempt on my part to poke fun at Dr M.'s many far-fetched explanations for peculiar pathological links? Regarding dysentery, something else occurs to me. A few months before, I had taken on a young man with remarkable bowel problems, whom other colleagues had treated as a case of 'anaemia coupled with under-nourishment'. I recognized it as hysteria but was unwilling to try my psychotherapy on him, sending him on a sea voyage instead. But then a few days earlier I had received a desperate letter from him from Egypt, saying that there he had had a fresh attack that the doctor had diagnosed as dysentery. While assuming that the diagnosis was simply an error on the part of the unwitting colleague, who had been fooled by the hysteria, I could not spare myself the reproach of having placed the patient in a situation in which, on top of a hysterical bowel disorder, he now had an organic one as well. Also, 'dysentery' sounds rather like 'diphtheria', which name ††† is not specified in the dream.

Yes, it must be the case that, with the reassuring prognosis about dysentery and so on, I must be poking fun at Dr M. because I remember him once, some years ago, laughingly saying something very similar about a colleague. Called in with the colleague for advice regarding a severely ill patient, he had felt obliged to rebuke the other for excessive optimism, on the grounds that he, Dr M., had found protein in the patient's urine. Not at all put out, his fellow doctor answered calmly, '*Never mind*, colleague, the protein will be eliminated!' So there is no further doubt in my mind: this bit of the dream contains a 'dig' at the colleague who knows nothing about hysteria. As if corroborating this, it now occurs to me to wonder: Does Dr M. know that the symptoms displayed by his patient (Irma's friend), which cause one to fear tuberculosis, also have a hysterical basis? Has he spotted the hysteria, or has he been taken in by it?

But what can be my motive for treating this friend so badly? Very simple: Dr M. has as little time for my 'solution' to Irma's problem as Irma herself. In this dream, therefore, I take revenge on two people: on Irma with the words 'If you're still in pain, it's your own fault', and on Dr M. with the wording of the nonsensical reassurance that I place in his mouth.

We know immediately where the infection stems from. This instant knowledge in dream is remarkable. The fact is, previously we did not yet know, the infection only having been established by Leopold.

My friend Otto gave her an injection when she was not feeling well. Otto really had told me that in the brief period when he was present with Irma's family he had been summoned to the next-door hotel to give an injection to someone who had suddenly felt unwell. The injections once again remind me of the unfortunate friend who had poisoned himself with cocaine. I had recommended the drug to him for oral use only while coming off morphine; however, he promptly gave himself injections of cocaine.

Using a propyl preparation ... propylene ... propionic acid. However did I get here? On that same evening when I wrote out the medical history and subsequently dreamed about it, my wife opened a bottle of liqueur on which *Ananas* [pineapple][15] could be read and that had been given to us by our friend Otto. Otto was in the habit of presenting one with gifts on every conceivable occasion; with luck, some day a wife will cure him of it. The liqueur smelled so strongly of rotgut that I declined to have any. My wife said, 'We'll give this bottle to the servants', and I, exercising greater caution, forbade it with the benevolent remark, 'We don't want them poisoning themselves, either.' The rotgut smell (amyl . . .) clearly reminded me of the whole series: propyl, methyl, etc., supplying the 'propyl preparation' for the dream. Except that I made a substitution here, smelling amyl but then dreaming propyl – but perhaps such substitutions are allowed, particularly in organic chemistry.

Trimethylamine. I see the chemical formula of this one in my dream, which certainly testifies to a tremendous effort of memory on my part, and it is even printed in bold type, as if to make it stand out from its context as something particularly important. And where does it take me, this trimethylamine that is being thus brought to my attention? To a conversation with another friend, who for years has known about all my nascent works, as I have about his. He once told me about certain ideas he had concerning a chemistry of sexuality, mentioning among other things that he believed one of the products of sexual metabolism to be trimethylamine. So this substance takes me to sexuality, the factor to which I ascribe the greatest importance as regards the origin of the nervous disorders that I seek to heal. My patient, Irma, is a young widow; if I am at pains to excuse the failure of my treatment in her case, I shall probably do best to refer to this circumstance, which her friends would like to see altered. How curiously such a dream is ordained, by the way! The other woman, whom, in the dream, I should like to have as a patient in Irma's stead, is also a young widow.

I have a suspicion as to why the trimethylamine formula featured so prominently in the dream. So much of importance comes together in this one word, 'trimethylamine'. It is not simply an allusion to the all-powerful sexuality factor; it also alludes to a person whose approval I recall with pleasure when I feel abandoned and alone with my views. Should this friend, who plays such a major role in my life, not reappear in the thought context of this dream? Indeed he should; he is an exceptional expert on the effects that proceed from disorders of the nose and sinuses and has revealed to science some exceedingly curious relationships between the turbinates and the female sex organs. (The three crinkly formations in Irma's throat.) I had him examine Irma to see whether her stomach aches might possibly be of nasal origin. But he suffers from nasal suppuration himself, which concerns me, and this is no doubt what is alluded to by the pyaemia that occurs to me in connection with the metastases of the dream.

No one gives such injections lightly. Here the charge of acting without due thought is hurled directly at my friend Otto. I believe some such thought had passed through my mind that afternoon when what he said and the way he looked at me appeared to indicate that he had taken sides against me. It was something like: 'How easily he lets himself be swayed'; 'How lightly he delivers his opinion'. Also, the above sentence once again points me in the direction of my dead friend, who so rashly decided to inject cocaine. As I have said, I had certainly not meant him to inject the drug. In connection with the accusation I am levelling at Otto (of treating this chemical substance 'lightly'), I notice that I am once again touching on the story of that unfortunate Mathilde from which the identical accusation against myself proceeds. Clearly, I am here collecting instances of my conscientiousness – but also of the contrary.

Probably the syringe was not clean, either. A further accusation against Otto, though this one stems from a different source. Yesterday I happened to bump into the son of an eighty-two-year-old lady to whom I have to administer two morphine injections daily. She is currently out of town, and I heard that she is suffering from phlebitis. I immediately thought that what we had here was a case of infiltration resulting from a dirty needle. It is my proud boast that in two years I have not given her a single infiltrate; of course, I always worry about whether the syringe is clean or not. I am conscientious. This phlebitis brings me back to my wife, who suffered from the condition during one of her pregnancies, and now three similar situations have floated to the surface of memory (with my wife, with Irma and with the late Mathilde), the identity of which evidently gave me the right to interchange the three people in dream.

*

I have now completed the task of interpreting the dream.[16] During it, I had difficulty in fending off all the associated ideas inevitably prompted by my comparing the content of the dream with the dream-thoughts concealed behind it. In the process, I also worked out what the dream 'meant'. I noticed an intention that is realized by the dream and must have been the motive for my dreaming it. The dream fulfils a number of wishes that the events of the previous evening (Otto's news, writing down the medical history) had awakened in me. The outcome of the dream, do you see, is that I am not to blame for Irma's continuing pain and that Otto is to blame. The fact is, with his comment about Irma's incomplete cure Otto annoyed me. The dream avenges me by throwing the reproach back against himself; it absolves me of responsibility for Irma's condition by tracing it back to other factors (like a whole series of justifications). The dream represents a certain state of affairs in the way I would wish it to be. *Its content, in other words, is wish-fulfilment, its motive a wish.*

That much is self-evident. But regarding the details of the dream, too, many things become clear to me from the standpoint of wish-fulfilment. Not only do I have my revenge against Otto for his over-hasty partisanship against me by blaming an over-hasty medical procedure (the injection) on him; I also take revenge on him for the poor liqueur that smells of fusel oil, and in the dream I find an instrument of expression that combines both reproaches: injection with a propylene preparation. Still not satisfied, I continue my revenge by comparing him with his more reliable competitors. In so doing, I seem to be saying: 'I prefer him to you.' But Otto is not the only one to feel the strength of my anger. I also take my revenge on the disobedient patient by exchanging her for a cleverer, more submissive one. I also do not let Dr M. get away with his contradiction but in an unambiguous allusion tell him what I think, namely that he does not know what he is talking about here ('She'll get dysentery as well', etc.). Indeed, it seems to me that I am appealing, away from him, to another, more knowledgeable party (my friend, the one who told me about trimethylamine), just as I turned away from Irma towards her friend and from Otto towards Leopold. Get rid of these people for me, replace them with three others of my own choosing, and I am acquitted of charges that I do not feel I merit. The fact that those charges are in fact groundless is made clear to me in the dream at enormous length. Irma's pain does not weigh upon me; she is to blame for it herself because she refuses to accept my solution. Irma's pain has nothing to do with me because it is organic in nature and quite incurable by psychical treatment. Irma's pain is adequately explained by her widowhood (trimethylamine!), and I can do nothing about that. Irma's illness was induced by an incautious injection administered by Otto, using an unsuitable substance – an injection I would never have given her. Irma's illness stems from an injection with a dirty needle like my old lady's phlebitis, whereas when I give an injection I never start anything. I notice, in fact, that these explanations for Irma's illness, while they agree in exonerating myself, are not mutually consistent; indeed, they rule one another out. This whole 'address to the jury' (for that is what the dream is) is powerfully reminiscent of the defence of a man accused by his neighbour of having returned a bucket in a damaged state. First, he had returned it intact; secondly, the bucket already had holes in it when he borrowed it; thirdly, he had never borrowed a bucket from his neighbour. But so much the better: if only one of these three types of defence is found to be conclusive, the man must be acquitted.

Other themes play a part in the dream whose relevance to my exoneration from Irma's illness is not so clear: the illness of my daughter and that of a patient of the same name, the damaging effects of cocaine, the disorder suffered by the patient of mine who travelled to Egypt, concern about the health of my wife, of my brother and of Dr M., my own physical complaints, and my concern about the absent friend who suffers from nasal suppuration. Yet when I consider all these things, they fit into a single group of ideas that one might label 'etiquette': concerns about health (my own and others'), medical conscientiousness. I recall an obscure feeling of embarrassment when Otto brought me the news of Irma's condition. From the group of ideas playing a part in the dream, I should like (belatedly) to use the expression for this momentary feeling. It is as if he had said to me: 'You do not take your medical duties seriously enough, you aren't conscientious, you don't keep your promises.' Whereupon this group of ideas had made itself available to enable me to show how very conscientious I am, how deeply concerned I am about the health of my family, my friends and my patients. Interestingly, these thoughts also include embarrassing memories that lend more support to the accusation ascribed to my friend Otto than to my own exoneration. The material is non-partisan, as it were, but the connection between this wider material upon which the dream rests and the narrower subject of the dream from which the wish to be innocent of Irma's illness proceeds – that is surely unmistakable.

I do not claim to have uncovered the meaning of this dream in its entirety or that my interpretation of it is complete.

I could dwell on it a lot longer, teasing out further explanations and discussing new riddles that the dream seems to pose. I am myself aware of the junction-points from which other trains of thought ask to be pursued; but considerations that enter the picture with regard to any dream of one's own hold me back from the work of interpretation. If anyone cannot wait to criticize such reserve, let that person try to be more honest than I have been. For the moment, I am content with a single, freshly mined discovery: if the method of dream-interpretation set out here is followed, it will be found that dream really does have a point to it and is by no means the expression of fragmented cerebral activity, as the literature maintains. *When the task of interpretation is complete, dream can be seen to constitute wish-fulfilment.*

Notes

1. In a novella by W[ilhelm] Jensen entitled *Gradiva* I chanced to come across a number of artificial dreams that were represented with perfect correctness and could be interpreted as if they had not been made up but had been dreamed by real people. I asked the author, and he confirmed that he had known nothing about my dream-theory. I took this agreement between my research and the creative work of this writer as evidence that my dream-analysis is right ('Der Wahn und die Träume in W. Jensens *Gradiva*' ['Delusion and dreams in W. Jensen's *Gradiva*'] in the first issue of *Schriften zur angewandten Seelenjunde* [*Essays in applied psychology*], edited by myself, 1906, third edition 1924 (*Gesammelte Schriften*, vol. IX [*Standard Edition*, vol. IX, p. 3]).

2. Aristotle said something to the effect that the best interpreter of dreams was the person who best apprehended similarities: because dream-images, like images in water, are distorted by movement, and the person who, looking at the distorted images, is able to recognize what is true will have the surest aim (Büchsenschütz [1868], p. 65).

3. Artemidorus of Daldis [now more commonly referred to as Artemidorus Daldianus; 'The author's surname, Daldianus, derives either from his mother's home, Daldis in Lydia, now in Turkey, or because he was an initiated votary of Apollo Daldiaios' (*Encyclopaedia Britannica*, fifteenth edition)], who was probably born early in the second century CE, left us the most complete and most meticulous work [the *Oneirocritica*] on dream-interpretation in the Graeco-Roman world. As T. Gomperz [1866] stressed, he attached value to basing the interpretation of dreams on observation and experience and drew a sharp distinction between his art

and other, deceitful arts. In Gomperz's account, the principle of his interpretive art was the same as that of magic, namely the principle of association. A dream-thing means what it brings to mind. That is, of course, to
the mind of the person interpreting the dream! An uncontrollable source
of arbitrariness and uncertainty flows from the fact that the dream-element
may put the interpreter in mind of various things and everyone else of
something different. The technique I discuss in the following pages differs
from that practised in antiquity in one essential point, namely that it
imposes the work of interpretation on the dreamer him/herself. It takes
account not of what the interpreter is reminded of by the dream-element
concerned but of what the dreamer is reminded of.

However, according to recent reports by the missionary Abbé Tfinkdji
(1913), dream-interpreters of the present-day East also draw extensively
on the co-operation of the dreamer. Talking about dream-interpreters
among the Arabs of Mesopotamia, this source writes [Freud, as usual, gives
the quotation in the original French]: 'In order to interpret a dream
precisely, the most skilful oneiromancers ask those who consult them about
all the circumstances that they deem necessary for a proper explanation.
[. . .] In a word, our oneiromancers let no circumstance escape them and
will not provide the interpretation they have been asked for until they have
fully understood and received answers to all desirable interrogations.' The
questions regularly include some about precise details of the closest family
members (parents, wife, children) in addition to the typical form of words
[which Freud cites in Latin]: *habuistine in hac nocte copulam conjugalem
ante vel post somnium?* ['That night, did you have conjugal relations either
before or after sleep?'].

'The prevailing notion in the interpretation of dreams consists in explaining the dream by its opposite.'

4. [Going back to what I said in my Translator's Preface, may I repeat my
warning to the reader that throughout this chapter (and indeed throughout
the book) I have had to distinguish between general and particular in a
way that Freud, writing in German, was not obliged to do.]

5. Dr Alfred Robitsek [1910] draws my attention to the fact that Eastern
dream-books (of which ours are pale imitations) usually interpret dream-
elements in terms of harmony of sound and similarity between words. Such
relationships are inevitably lost in translation, hence the incomprehensibility of the substitutions made in our popular dream-books.

On the subject of the exceptional importance of pun and word-play in
the cultures of the ancient East, the reader will find the works of Hugo
Winkler instructive. The finest example of dream-interpretation that has

come down to us from the ancient world is based on a pun. Here is Artemidorus: 'However, it seems to me that Aristandros too gave a most fortunate interpretation to Alexander of Macedon [Alexander the Great], when the latter had cut off and laid siege to Tyros [Tyre] and, angry and depressed at the huge loss of time, felt he could see a 'satyros' dancing on his shield. Aristandros happened to find himself in the vicinity of Tyre and in the retinue of the king who was waging war on the Syrians. By breaking the word down into σά and τύρος, he managed to persuade the king to reinforce his siege effort until he eventually became master of the city' (Σα Τύρος = Tyros is yours).

In fact dream is so closely dependent on its linguistic expression that Ferenczi can rightly remark that every language has its own dream-language. A dream is usually untranslatable, and I used to think a book such as this one must be so too. Nevertheless, first Dr A. A. Brill of New York and subsequently others as well have managed to make translations of my *Traumdeutung*.

6. After I had completed my manuscript and sent it off, a book by Stumpf arrived on my desk that, in its intention to prove that dream is meaningful and can be interpreted, coincides with my own work. However, interpretation occurs by means of an allegorizing symbolism with no guarantee that the process is universally valid.

7. J[osef] Breuer and S[igmund] Freud, *Studien über Hysterie* ['Studies on hysteria'], Vienna 1895 (fourth edition, 1922; *Gesammelte Schriften*, vol. I [*Standard Edition*, vol. II; *Studies in Hysteria*, a new translation by Nicola Luckhurst in the New Penguin Freud series, London 2004]).

8. [Or, of course, 'her'. German is a gendered language; the noun *Patient* is masculine (there is a feminine/female form *Patientin* for specific usage but in general the masculine is used), so its associated pronouns are also masculine. For Freud, writing German, there will have been no social gender connotation here.]

9. [This 'fall-in'. See note 4, p. 53.]

10. H[erbert] Silberer gained important findings about dream-interpretation from first-hand observation of this transformation of ideas into visual images (*Jahrbuch für psychoanalytischen Forschungen*, I and II, pp. 1909ff.).

11. Nevertheless, by way of qualifying what I have said above, I am keen to add that in almost no instance have I communicated the full interpretation of one of my own dreams as this was available to me. I was probably right not to place too much faith in the reader's discretion.

12. This is the first dream that I subjected to thorough interpretation.

13. The as yet unexplained complaints about abdominal pain can also be traced back to this third person. I am of course talking about my own wife; the abdominal pain reminds me of one of the occasions when I saw clearly how shy she is. I have to admit that, in this dream, I do not treat Irma and my wife particularly kindly; but let it be said in my own defence that I am measuring both against the ideal of the good, submissive patient.

14. I suspect that the interpretation of this fragment has not been taken far enough to trace all its hidden meaning. If I wished to continue the comparison of the three women, that would take me a long way off course. Every dream has at least one point where it eludes explanation – a sort of umbilicus linking it to the unknown.

15. The word '*Ananas*', by the way, contains a quite remarkable echo of the surname of my patient, Irma.

16. Although I have not, understandably, disclosed everything that occurred to me in connection with my work of interpretation.

3

Dream is Wish-Fulfilment

When, having negotiated a narrow defile, one suddenly comes out
on to a piece of high ground where the paths divide and there are
huge views in various directions, one may be excused for lingering
briefly to reflect on which way to go next. Something similar has
happened to us, now that this first dream-interpretation is behind
us. We have emerged into the clarity of a sudden realization. Dream
cannot be likened to the irregular sounding of a musical instrument
that, rather than being struck by the hand of the player, responds
to the impact of some other force; it is not meaningless, it is not
absurd, it does not presuppose that part of our treasury of ideas is
asleep while another part is beginning to stir. It is an entirely valid
psychical phenomenon, namely an act of wish-fulfilment; it has its
place among what we find to be the wholly comprehensible mental
operations of the waking state; a highly complicated piece of intellectual activity put it together. However, a host of questions assails
us just as we want to celebrate this discovery. If, as our interpretation suggests, dream represents a wish fulfilled, why does that act
of wish-fulfilment find expression in so conspicuous and disconcerting a form – where does that come from? What change have
the dream-thoughts undergone before the manifest dream as we
recall it on waking is able to develop from them? Along what lines
did that change proceed? What is the origin of the material from
which dream is wrought? What about many of the peculiarities we
have noticed in connection with dream-thoughts – for instance, that
they may contradict one another (see the analogy with the bucket
on pp. 130–31); where do they come from? Can dream teach us

something new about our internal psychical processes? Is dream-content able to correct opinions in which we placed faith during the day? I suggest that we leave all these questions aside for the moment and follow a single path. We have learned that dream represents a wish fulfilled. Let our next concern be to explore whether this is a general characteristic of dream or simply the fortuitous content of the particular dream ('Irma's injection') with which our analysis began. Because, even if we are prepared for every dream to be meaningful and to possess psychical value, we must still leave open the possibility that that meaning will not be the same in every dream. Our first dream was an act of wish-fulfilment; another may turn out to be a fear fulfilled; a third may embody a reflection; a fourth may simply reproduce a memory. So are there other wish-dreams, or is there perhaps nothing but wish-dreams?

It is easy to show that dreams often reveal their nature as wish-fulfilment quite openly, so that one wonders why the language of dreams was not understood long ago. There is one dream, for example, that I am able to generate at will – experimentally, so to speak. If I have had anchovies, olives or other very salty foods for supper, I feel thirsty during the night, which wakes me up. Waking, however, is preceded by a dream of which the content is always the same, namely that I am drinking. I am slurping water in great gulps, and to me it tastes as exquisite as only a cold drink can taste when one is parched, and then I wake up and really have to drink something. This simple dream is prompted by thirst – the thirst I feel on waking. From this sensation proceeds the desire to drink, and dream shows me this desire fulfilled. In so doing, it serves a function – which I soon detect. I am a sound sleeper, not accustomed to being woken by a need. If I succeed in quelling my thirst by dreaming that I am drinking, I do not have to wake up in order to satisfy it. In other words, it is a comfort-dream.[1] Dreaming takes the place of action, as it does elsewhere in life. Unfortunately, the need for water to slake my thirst cannot be satisfied by dreaming about it, as can my thirst for vengeance against my friend Otto and Dr M., but the excellent intention is the same. Recently, the same dream underwent slight modification. This time I felt thirsty before falling asleep, and I drank the whole glass of water that stood on the little cupboard by my bed. Some hours later, during the night, I had a fresh attack of thirst – with awkward results. To obtain water I should have had to get out of bed and go and fetch the glass that stood on my wife's bedside table. So I dreamed (appropriately enough) that my wife was giving me a drink from a particular vessel; this was an Etruscan cinerary urn that I had brought back from a trip to Italy and since given away. However, the water in it tasted so salty (obviously from the ashes) that I had to wake up. Notice how conveniently dream manages to arrange things; wish-fulfilment being its sole purpose, it can be totally selfish. Love of comfort and of one's own convenience really is incompatible with consideration for others. Bringing in the cinerary urn is probably another piece of wish-fulfilment; I regret no longer having the urn in my possession – as, incidentally, the glass of water on my wife's side is also beyond my reach. The cinerary urn also fits in with the now stronger feeling of the salty taste, which I know will force me awake.[2]

I used to have such comfort-dreams very frequently in my younger years. Having always worked until very late at night, I invariably found it hard to rise early. So I formed the habit of dreaming that I had already got out of bed and was at the washstand. After a time, I could no longer resist the notion that I was not yet up but had in fact slept on for some while. The same lethargy-dream was recounted to me in a particularly amusing form by a young colleague who evidently shares my proneness to sleep. The landlady of the house near the hospital where he lodged had strict instructions to wake him up every morning at the right time – but also real problems in carrying out those instructions. One morning, sleep was particularly sweet. The woman called out, 'Time to get up, Mr Pepi; you must be off to the hospital.' Whereupon the sleeper dreamed of a room in the hospital, a bed in which he lay asleep and a nameplate above it that read: 'Pepi H. . . . *cand. med.*, age 22'. Still dreaming, he said to himself, 'Right, if I'm at the hospital already, I don't need to go there.' And he turned over and went on sleeping. In the process, he had quite openly admitted the motive behind his dreaming.

Here is another dream where the stimulus likewise took effect during sleep itself. A patient of mine who had had to undergo a dental operation that had gone wrong was asked by her doctors to wear a cooling appliance on the affected cheek day and night. However, she had developed the habit of making it slide off as soon as she had gone to sleep. One day I was asked to rebuke her on the subject, since she had once again thrown the appliance to the floor. The patient justified herself: 'This time I really can't do anything about it. It was because of a dream I had in the night. In the dream, I was in a box at the opera, deeply involved in the production. In the hospital, however, lay Mr Karl Meyer, complaining fearfully of toothache. I said that I am in no pain so do not need the appliance; that's why I threw it off.' This dream by my poor long-suffering patient sounds like a version of a popular saying that we find automatically passing our lips in difficult situations: 'I can think of things I'd rather be doing . . .' The dream shows one of the things my patient would rather be doing. The 'Mr Karl Meyer' on to whom the dreamer shifted her pain was the least distinctive young man she could think of from her circle of acquaintances.

It is equally easy to uncover the wish-fulfilment in a number of other dreams that I have garnered from healthy people. A friend who is familiar with my dream-theory and has told his wife about it said to me one day, 'I'm to tell you that my wife dreamed yesterday that her period had arrived. You'll know what that means.' I certainly do: if the young woman dreamed that her period had come, it meant that she had missed it. I can well imagine she would have liked to enjoy her freedom for a while longer before the problems of motherhood set in. This was a clever way of announcing her first pregnancy. Another friend writes that his wife recently dreamed of noticing milk stains on the front of her blouse. This also announces a pregnancy, though not a first pregnancy this time; the young mother's wish is that she will be able to feed the second child more generously than she could the first.

A young woman who had been cut off from society for weeks, nursing her infectiously ill child, dreams after the illness is fortunately past of a party attended by A. Daudet, Bourget and

M. Prévost,[3] among others, who are all extremely charming to her and provide excellent entertainment. Even in the dream, the writers concerned have the features given them by their portraits; M. Prévost, whose portrait she has never seen, looks like – the man who disinfected the sickroom the day before and who was her first visitor for a long time. The dream would seem to be perfectly translatable: 'High time [the young woman thought] I had more fun than doing this everlasting sick-nursing.'

Possibly this selection will suffice to show that one very often, and in the most varied conditions, comes across dreams that can be understood purely as wish-fulfilment and that display their content undisguised. They are mostly short, simple dreams, agreeably different from the intricate, over-elaborate dream-compositions that attract so much attention in the literature. However, it is worth dwelling on these simple dreams a little longer. The very simplest forms of dreaming can presumably be expected in children, whose psychical output is surely going to be less complicated than that of adults. The vocation of child psychology, in my view, is to perform a similar service for adult psychology as the study of the structure and development of the lower animals performs for the investigation of the structure of the highest animal classes. Hitherto, few positive steps have been taken towards using child psychology for this purpose.

The dreams of small children are often simple acts of wish-fulfilment and, as such, unlike the dreams of adults, of no particular interest. They pose no riddle to be solved, but of course they are of inestimable importance as regards proving that dream is essentially wish-fulfilment. From material gathered from my own children, I have been able to extract a number of examples of such dreams.

An excursion from [Bad] Aussee to the lovely town of Hallstatt in the summer of 1896 furnished me with two dreams, one by my daughter, then aged eight and a half, the other by a boy aged five and a quarter. I must preface my account by explaining that we were spending that summer in a house on a hill near [Bad] Aussee, from which in fine weather we had a marvellous view of [the mountain called] the Dachstein. Using a telescope, we could easily make out the Simony Lodge. The children tried time after time to see it through the telescope; I do not know with what success. Before the trip, I had told the children that Hallstatt lay at the foot of the Dachstein. They were very much looking forward to the day. From Hallstatt, we entered [the valley called] the Echerntal, which delighted the children with its ever-changing views. Only one of them, the five-year-old boy, became steadily more morose. Each time a fresh peak came into view, he asked, 'Is that the Dachstein?' to which I had to reply, 'No, just a foothill.' After several repetitions of this question, he fell completely silent; the steps up to the waterfall did not attract him at all and he stayed behind. I thought he must be tired. Next morning, however, he came up to me all smiles and said, 'Last night I dreamed we were in the Simony Lodge.' Now I understood: when I had mentioned the Dachstein, he expected that on the Hallstatt trip he would get to climb the mountain and see for himself the building of which we had made so much in connection with the telescope. Then, realizing that he was being fobbed off with foothills and a waterfall, he felt let down and became disgruntled. The dream was his compensation. I tried to find out details of the dream, but they were sparse. 'You climb steps for six hours,' he had been told.

The trip also awakened wishes in the eight-and-a-half-year-old girl that dream had to satisfy. We had taken our neighbours' twelve-year-old boy with us to Hallstatt, a perfect little cavalier who had already, it seemed to me, aroused every sympathetic feeling in my daughter's young heart. Well, the next morning she recounted the following dream: 'Guess what – in my dream Emil is one of us, calls you Daddy and Mummy, and sleeps with us all in the big room like our boys. Then Mummy comes into the room and throws a handful of big chocolate bars in blue and green wrappers under our beds.' Her brothers, whose dream-interpreting skills owe nothing to heredity, said (just like our writers), 'This dream makes no sense.' The girl spoke up for at least part of the dream, and it is important for neurosis theory to find out which part it was: Emil being entirely 'one of us' clearly makes no sense, but the business with the chocolate bars does. It was precisely this latter detail that was obscure to me. Mother supplied the explanation. On the way back from the station to the house, the children had stopped at a vending machine and asked for just such chocolate bars in shiny metallic paper, which they knew from experience the vending machine dispensed. Mummy had rightly said she thought the day had brought sufficient wish-fulfilment, and she had left this wish for dream to fulfil. I had missed this little scene. The segment of the dream my daughter had related first I readily understood. I had heard with my own ears how on the footpath our charming guest had told the children to wait for Daddy or Mummy to catch up. The girl's dream had turned this temporary affiliation into a permanent adoption. Her tender young mind was as yet unaware of other forms of togetherness than those mentioned in the dream (and taken from her brothers). Why the chocolate bars were thrown under the beds could of course not be explained without interrogating the children.

A very similar dream to my boy's was told me by a friend. It concerns an eight-year-old girl. The father had set out with several children to walk to Dornbach with the intention of visiting the Rohrer Lodge,[4] but had turned back because it was getting too late, promising the children to take them there another time. On the way back they came to the sign indicating the way to the Hameau.[5] The children now asked if they might be taken to the Hameau, too, but for the same reason they had to make do with a similar promise. Next morning, the eight-year-old girl came up to him, all delighted: 'Daddy, last night I dreamed that you were with us at the Rohrer Lodge and on the Hameau.' In other words, her impatience had anticipated the fulfilment of the promise Daddy had made.

Equally sincere is another dream that the rustic beauty of [the lake at Bad] Aussee inspired in my little daughter, who was then aged three years and three months. It was the first time she had crossed the lake by boat, and the trip was over too quickly for her. At the landing-stage she refused to leave the boat and wept bitterly. Next morning she said, 'In the night I was going across the lake.' Let us hope the duration of the dream-crossing was more to her liking.

My eldest boy, currently aged eight, already, in dream, makes his fantasies come true. He has ridden with Achilles in a chariot driven by Diomedes. The previous day, of course, he had been reading with great enthusiasm a book about the legends of Ancient Greece, which his elder sister had given him as a present.

If the reader will allow that children's sleep-talking also belongs to the realm of dreaming, the following counts as one of the youngest dreams in my collection. My little girl, who was nineteen months old at the time, had been sick one morning so had been made to fast all day. During the following night, she was heard to call out excitedly in her sleep: '*Anna F. . .eud, Erdbeer, Hochbeer, sc(r)ambled egg, pap.*' At that time she used her name to express the idea of possession; the menu presumably comprised everything that at the time must have seemed to her to constitute a desirable meal; the fact that it included two kinds of strawberry was a demonstration against the domestic health police and had its origin in the circumstance, of which she had doubtless taken note, that Nanny had attributed her indisposition to excessive consumption of that fruit; for this opinion, which was not to her liking, her dream took revenge.[6]

If we value childhood as a time of happiness as yet innocent of sexual desire,[7] we must not forget what a rich source of disappointment, renunciation and hence dream-arousal life's other major business can become. Here is a second example. My twenty-two-month-old nephew is given the job of congratulating me on my birthday and presenting me with a little basket of cherries, which at that time of year[8] are very much an early-season product. This he evidently finds hard to do, repeating over and over again, 'Che(rr)ies in it!' and refusing steadfastly to let go of the basket. But he knows a way of compensating. He was in the habit of telling his mother each morning that he had dreamed about the 'white soldier', a becloaked Guards officer whom he had once admired in the street. On the morning after the birthday sacrifice, he wakes up happy, announcing something that can only have come from a dream: '*He'mann eat up all che'ies!*'[9]

What animals dream about, I do not know. An Austrian proverb, for which I have one of my listeners to thank, does claim to know, for to the question, 'What does the goose dream of?' it replies, '*Kukuruz* [maize].'[10] The entire theory that dream is wish-fulfilment lies encapsulated in that brief exchange.[11]

We note at this stage that we might also have reached our theory of the hidden significance of dream by the shortest route by simply examining linguistic usage. It does occasionally speak of dream with some scorn (almost as if it sought to prove science right in its verdict: *Träume sind Schäume* ['Dreams are froth']). Nevertheless, for linguistic usage dream is first and foremost the great wish-fulfiller. 'I'd never have imagined it in my wildest dreams,' is the delighted reaction of everyone who finds reality exceeding his or her expectations.

Notes

1. [*Bequemlichkeitstraum*. But the German word *Bequemlichkeit* covers a slightly larger area of meaning than 'comfort', overflowing into 'convenience' as well. I have tried to indicate this a few lines further on.]

2. The reality of thirst dreams was also known to Weygandt [1893], who on p. 41 has this to say about them: 'The feeling of thirst especially is conceived of in the most precise terms of all and invariably generates an idea of thirst being quenched. The ways in which dream represents this thirst-quenching are very diverse; the particular method will be specified in line with a memory that suggests itself. Here, too, a general phenomenon is that, immediately after the picturing of the thirst-quenching, disappointment sets in with regard to the unsatisfactory effect of the supposed refreshment.' However, he overlooks the universally valid nature of dream's reaction to the stimulus.

If other people assailed by nocturnal thirst wake up without dreaming first, this does not imply an objection to my experiment; it merely marks them out as lighter sleepers. See also Isaiah 29:8: 'And it shall be as when an hungry man dreameth, and, behold, he eateth; but he awaketh, and his soul is empty [*so ist seine Seele noch leer*]; or as when a thirsty man dreameth, and, behold, he drinketh; but he awaketh, and, behold, he is faint, and his soul hath appetite.' [This time I cite the Revised Version of 1884 as being closer to what Freud himself will have read.]

3. [The young woman's imaginary guests included the then very fashionable

French writers Alphonse Daudet (1840–97), Paul Bourget (1852–1935) and Marcel Prévost (1862–1940).]

4. [*Die Rohrer-Hütte*; a popular place of refreshment for Vienna's walkers.]

5. [A small hill on the outskirts of Vienna, offering a fine view of the city.]

6. Not long afterwards dream performed the same function for the grandmother, who was some seventy years older than this, her youngest grandchild. A troublesome floating kidney having obliged her to fast for a day, she subsequently dreamed (in an obvious reversion to the happy days of her blooming girlhood) that she was warmly invited to both main meals of the day and on each occasion had the daintiest morsels placed before her.

7. Of course, a more thorough study of the mental life of children shows us that, in an infantile form, sexual drives play a quite large, too long overlooked part in the child's psychical activity. Indeed, such a study casts some doubt on the happiness of childhood as adults subsequently construe it. (See the author's *Drei Abhandlungen zur Sexualtheorie* [*Three Essays on the Theory of Sexuality*], 1905 [*Standard Edition*, vol. VII; new translation by Shaun Whiteside in *The Psychology of Love* (New Penguin Freud), London 2006].

8. [Freud's birthday was 6 May.]

9. Note, too, that it is not long, with small children, before more complicated, less transparent dreams normally start to appear, and that conversely, in certain circumstances, dreams of this kind of simple, childish nature often occur among adults. Just how rich in unsuspected content the dreams of children between the ages of four and five can be is shown by the examples in my 'Analyse der Phobie eines fünfjährigen Knaben' ['Analysis of the phobia of a five-year-old boy'] in *Jahrbuch von Bleuler-Freud*, I, 1909 [*Standard Edition*, vol. X, p. 3] and in [Carl Gustav] Jung's 'Über Konflikte der kindlichen Seele' ['Concerning conflicts in the infant mind'], ibid., II, 1910. For child dreams interpreted analytically, see also the works of Hug-Hellmuth, Putnam, Raalte, Spielrein and Tausk; others may be found in Bianchieri, Busemann, Doglia and particularly in Wiggam, who stresses the wish-fulfilment tendencies of the same [see Other Literature, pp. 638–57 of the present volume]. On the other hand, dreams of the infantile type seem to reappear in adulthood with particular frequency when the adults concerned are subjected to unusual conditions. Thus Otto Nordenskjöld, in his 1904 book *Antarctic*, says of the team over-wintering with him:

Very indicative of the direction of our innermost thoughts were our dreams, which had never been more vivid and more numerous than they were now.

Even those of our comrades who normally dreamed only on exceptional occasions now had long tales to tell when, in the morning, we exchanged our latest experiences of this fantasy world. All the tales concerned that outside world that was now so far away, but often they were adapted to suit our current circumstances. A particularly characteristic dream consisted in one of us thinking that he was back on the school bench and had been set the task of skinning tiny miniature seals that had been made especially for lesson purposes. Incidentally, eating and drinking were the foci around which our dreams most often revolved. One of our number, whose nocturnal speciality was attending large lunch parties, was blissfully happy when he was able, one morning, to report that he had 'eaten a three-course dinner'; another dreamed of tobacco, whole mountains of tobacco; yet others of the ship skimming over the open ocean under full sail. One further dream deserves mention: the postman arrives with the post, giving a lengthy explanation as to why it has been so long delayed: he had delivered it all wrong, he says, and only after great efforts had he managed to get it back. There were of course other more obscure things that preoccupied our sleep, but the lack of imagination in nearly all the dreams that I had myself or heard others recount was very striking. It would undoubtedly be of great psychological interest if all these dreams had been recorded. But it will be readily appreciated how longed-for sleep was, since it was able to furnish all the things that each one of us desired most ardently (loc. cit., vol. I, p. 336).

Another quotation from Du Prel: 'Mungo Park, close to dying of thirst on a journey in Africa, dreamed incessantly of the lush valleys and meadows of his homeland. Trenck, too, tormented by hunger, saw himself in the *Sternschanze* restaurant in Magdeburg, surrounded by sumptuous meals. And George Back, a member of Franklin's first expedition, when after appalling privations he was close to starvation, dreamed regularly and uniformly of rich dishes of food' (p. 231).

10. A Hungarian proverb cited by Ferenczi claims more comprehensively that 'the pig dreams of acorns, the goose of maize'. A Jewish proverb asks, 'What does the chicken dream of?' and answers, 'Millet seed' (*Sammlung jüdischer Sprichwörte und Redensarten* ['Anthology of Jewish proverbs and sayings'], ed. Bernstein, second edition, p. 116).

11. Far be it from me to claim that no author before me thought of tracing a dream to a wish (see also the first few sentences of the next chapter). Anyone setting store by such suggestions might go back to the ancient world, to the physician Herophilus, who lived under the first of the Ptolemies. According to Büchsenschütz ([1868] p. 33), Herophilus distinguished

three types of dreams: god-sent, natural (which arise through the mind picturing to itself what is beneficial to it and what is going to happen) and mixed (which arise spontaneously as a result of convergence of images when we see what we want). From the anthology of examples collected by Scherner [1861], Johann Stärcke [1913] picks out a dream that the author himself describes as wish-fulfilment. Scherner writes, 'The dreamer's waking wish was immediately fulfilled by her imagination simply because it existed vividly in her mind' ([1861] p. 239). This dream is listed among 'Mood dreams'; near it are dreams for 'male and female love-pining' and for 'moroseness'. Clearly, there is no question of Scherner ascribing a different importance (so far as dream is concerned) to wishing than to any other mental condition of the waking state – let alone of his associating wish with the essence of dream.

4

Dream-Distortion

If at this point I advance the claim that wish-fulfilment is the meaning of *every* dream – in other words, that there can be no other dreams but wish-dreams – I can be sure of the flattest contradiction in advance. I shall be told: 'The fact that some dreams should be seen as wish-fulfilments is not new, experts have been saying this for years.[1] But to say there can be nothing but wish-fulfilment dreams is another unjustified generalization, which fortunately can be rebutted without difficulty. After all, plenty of dreams occur that clearly have the most painful [because embarrassing] content but in which there is no trace of wish-fulfilment. The pessimist philosopher Eduard von Hartmann is probably the writer furthest removed from the wish-fulfilment theory. In the second part of his *Philosophy of the Unconscious* he says at one point: "As regards dream, with it all the grind of waking life is taken over into sleep except for one thing, namely that which is to some extent capable of reconciling the educated man to life: enjoyment of science and art . . ."[2] But less dissatisfied observers[3] have likewise stressed that, in dream, pain and aversion occur more frequently than pleasure. Indeed, two female writers, Sarah Weed and Florence Hallam, were able, after processing their dreams, to give numerical expression to the prevalence of aversion in dreams, describing 57.2 per cent of dreams as painful and only 28.6 per cent as positively pleasurable. In addition to dreams that continue the many different painful feelings of waking life in sleep, there are also anxiety-dreams[4] in which this most terrible of aversion sensations grips us until we wake, and such anxiety-dreams readily assail those children in particular[5] among whom you (my critics will remind me) found wish-dreams undisguised.'

The fact is, anxiety-dreams especially would seem to make it impossible to give general validity to the principle that we distilled from the examples of the previous chapter – namely, that dream is wish-fulfilment. Indeed, they appear to brand that principle an absurdity.

Nevertheless, these apparently cogent objections are not too hard to overcome. Notice, if you will, that our theory is not based on an appreciation of the manifest content of the dream in question but relates to the thought-content that the work of interpretation shows to underlie that dream. Let us compare the two: *manifest dream-content* and *latent dream-content*. It is true that there are dreams whose manifest content is of an extremely painful nature. But has anyone tried to interpret such dreams and discover the latent thought-content behind them? If not, the two objections no longer apply, and it is possible, after all, that even painful dreams and anxiety-dreams may, after interpretation, turn out to constitute wish-fulfilment.[6]

In the context of scientific work it is often an advantage, if the solution of one problem proves difficult, to bring in a second – much as it is easier to crack two nuts together than one on its own. Doing this, we are not only faced with the question of how painful dreams and anxiety-dreams can be acts of wish-fulfilment; we can also, arising out of our discussions of dream hitherto, ask a second question: Why do dreams of indifferent content that turn out to be wish-fulfilments not show plainly that this is their significance? Take the dream of Irma's injection, which we have dealt with at length; it is not at all painful, and interpretation shows it to be flagrant wish-fulfilment. But why does it need interpreting in the first place? Why does dream not say directly what it means? The fact is, the dream of Irma's injection also fails, initially, to give the impression that it represents a wish of the dreamer's as having been fulfilled. The reader will not have received that impression, nor was I aware of it myself before conducting my analysis. If we call this behaviour of dream as requiring explanation *the fact of dream-distortion*, a further question arises: Where does such dream-distortion come from?

Interrogating the first ideas to occur to one on this subject, one might come up with various possible solutions – for instance, that there is an inability during sleep to give appropriate expression to dream-thoughts. However, analysis of certain dreams forces us to admit a different explanation for dream-distortion. I want to illustrate this with another dream of mine, which again calls for a great many indiscretions, but by way of compensating for this personal sacrifice sheds a great deal of light on the problem.

Preface: In the spring of 1897 I learned that two professors at our university had put my name forward for appointment as *professor extraordinarius*.[7] The news came as a surprise to me and caused me keen delight as expressing a recognition on the part of two outstanding men that could not be explained by personal relations. However, I told myself immediately that I must pin no hopes on this happening. The Ministry had taken no account of such proposals for the last several years, and a number of colleagues who were senior to me and at least equally deserving had been waiting in vain all that time for an appointment. I had no reason to assume that I should fare any better. So I decided privately to forget all about it. I am not ambitious, so far as I am aware, and I practise my profession as a physician to gratifyingly successful effect even without having a title to recommend me. And anyway there was no question of my calling the grapes either sweet or sour; the plain truth was, they hung beyond my reach.

One evening I received a visit from a friend and colleague, one of those whose fate I had taken as a warning. For some time he had been a candidate for promotion to a professorship, which in our society raises a doctor to the status of a demigod in his patients' eyes, and being less resigned than I, he still, from time to time, presented himself at the offices of the exalted Ministry to press his case. It was after one such visit that he called on me. This time, he told me, he had trapped the high-up in a corner and asked him straight out whether the postponement of his appointment really was due to – religious considerations. In reply he had been informed that, in point of fact, given the present climate, His Excellency was not in a position . . . and so on and so forth. 'Now at least I know where I stand,' my friend told me, winding up a story that told me nothing new but had the inevitable effect of fortifying my resignation. The fact was, the same religious considerations applied in my case, too.

The morning after this visit, I had the following dream, which was partly noteworthy because of its form. It comprised two thoughts and two images, with the second thought and the second image replacing the first. Here, however, I shall give only the first half of the dream, the other half having nothing to do with the purpose that my recounting the dream is intended to serve.

I. *My friend R. is my uncle. – I feel very tender towards him.*

II. *I see his face before me somewhat changed. It is as if drawn-out lengthways, while the yellow beard framing it is emphasized with especial clarity.*

Then come the other two fragments: once again, a thought and an image, which I pass over.

The interpretation of this dream went as follows:

When the dream occurred to me during the morning, I burst out laughing and said, 'The dream is nonsense.' However, it would not let go and stayed with me all day, until eventually, that evening, I told myself reproachfully, 'If one of your patients had nothing to say about a dream-interpretation other than "It's nonsense", you'd admonish him and assume that some unpleasant story lay hidden behind the dream, a story he wished to spare himself the trouble of thinking about. Treat yourself no differently. Your dismissing the dream as nonsense simply indicates an inner reluctance to interpret it. Don't let it stop you.' So I proceeded to interpret it.

R. is my uncle. What can that mean? I had only one uncle, Uncle Josef.[8] However, something sad happened to him. Once upon a time, over thirty years ago, hoping to make some money, he allowed himself to be persuaded to commit a crime for which the law prescribes a heavy penalty, and he was subsequently punished. My father, who at the time went grey from worry in the course of a few days, used always to say that Uncle Josef had never been a bad man but he had certainly been a dimwit [*Schwachkopf*]. That was the word he used.[9] So if my friend R. is my Uncle Josef, what I am trying to say is that R. is a dimwit. Scarcely credible and highly embarrassing! But there is the face, which I see in my dream, with its elongated features and yellow beard. My uncle really did have a face like that: elongated, and framed by a fine yellow beard. My friend R. had jet-black hair, though when black-haired men start to go grey, they pay for the splendour of their younger years. Hair by hair, their black beards undergo an unpleasant colour-change, becoming first reddish-brown, then yellowish-brown, and only then properly grey. My friend's beard is currently going through this stage (so is mine, by the way, as I note to my displeasure). The face I see in the dream is simultaneously that of my friend R. and that of my uncle. It is like one of the composite photographs that Galton made when, studying family resemblances, he photographed a number of faces on the same plate. So there can be no doubt about it: I really do mean that my friend R. is a dimwit – like Uncle Josef.

As yet, I have no idea to what end I have established this relationship, which I must strive all the time to resist. It does not go very deep, because my uncle was a criminal whereas my friend R. has a clean record. Except for that time when he knocked over an apprentice with his bicycle. Am I alluding to that misdemeanour? That would be to take the comparison to ridiculous extremes. Then I recall another conversation that I had had a few days earlier with another colleague, N. – on the same topic, in fact. I met N. in the street; his name had also been put forward for a professorship, and knowing of my honour he offered me his congratulations. I would have none of it. 'You of all people ought not to make such jokes, because you have personal experience of the value of such a recommendation.' To which he retorted, probably not seriously, 'You never know. There's something specific against me. Don't you remember – someone once threatened to take me to court? I needn't tell you that the investigation was discontinued; it was a wretched attempt at blackmail; I had my work cut out, saving the accuser herself from prosecution. But it's possible they're holding this matter against me at the Ministry in order to block my appointment. You, on the other hand, have a completely clean record.' So, there I have the criminal, but at the same time I also have the interpretation and the intention of my dream. In it, Uncle Josef represents both colleagues who had not been appointed to professorships: one as a dimwit, the other as a criminal. Now I also know what I use that representation for. If the delay in appointing my two friends R. and N. is dictated by 'religious' considerations, my own appointment is also in question; if, however, I can shift the rejection of both on to other reasons that have nothing to do with me, I can still hope. And that is what my dream does: it makes one of them, R., a dimwit, and the other, N., a criminal; I, however, am neither one nor the other; with any link between us now abolished, I can look forward to my appointment as *professor extraordinarius*, and I have escaped the painful task (which I would otherwise have had to perform) of applying to my own person the information that R. had been given by that important gentleman at the Ministry.

I need to pursue the interpretation of this dream further. To my mind, it is not yet satisfactorily completed; I am still unsettled by the frivolous ease with which I demote two esteemed colleagues in order to keep the way free for myself to be appointed *professor extraordinarius*. Mind you, my dissatisfaction with my own action is already less, now that I know how to assess the value of things said in dream. I would argue with anyone who said that I really regard R. as a dimwit and that I do not believe N.'s account of that blackmail business. Nor do I believe that Irma fell dangerously ill as a result of Otto's infecting her with a propylene preparation; in both cases, what my dream expresses is simply my *wish that things might be so*. The assertion in which my wish is realized seems less absurd in the second dream than in the first; here it is formed of clever use of actual clues – a bit like a corrected slander where there is 'something in it', because my friend R. had at that time had the vote of a specialist professor against him, and my friend N. had unwittingly provided me with the material for his denigration himself. Nevertheless, I repeat, the dream seems to me to require further explanation.

I now remember that the dream contained another bit that the interpretation has hitherto left out of account. After it has occurred to me that R. is my uncle, I experience, in the dream, a warm tenderness towards him. Where does that sensation come in? I never, of course, had tender feelings for Uncle Josef. R. has been a dear and cherished friend for years; yet were I to come to him and express my affection for him in words corresponding approximately to the degree of my tenderness in the dream, he would indubitably get a shock. My tenderness towards him strikes me as untrue and exaggerated, like my verdict on his intellectual qualities, to which I give expression by merging his personality with that of my uncle; exaggerated, however, in the opposite sense. But I now glimpse a fresh state of affairs. The tenderness of the dream is not part of its latent content; it does not belong to the thoughts underlying the dream. It contrasts with that content, being such as to keep me from knowing how the dream should be interpreted. Probably, in fact, that is its purpose. I recall how reluctantly I set about interpreting this dream and how long I tried to put it off, saying the dream was arrant nonsense. I know from my psychoanalytical practice how such a rejection verdict needs to be interpreted. It has no cognitive value; the only value it has is that of the expression of an affect. If my small daughter does not want an apple she has been offered, she will claim that the apple tastes bitter without even trying it. If my patients behave in the same way, I know that what is present in their case is an idea that they wish to *repress*. The same applies with regard to my dream. I am reluctant to interpret it because the interpretation will contain something I am resisting. The dream-interpretation once complete, I learn what it was that I was resisting; it was the assertion that R. is a dimwit. I cannot trace the tenderness that I feel towards R. to any latent dream-thoughts, but I can trace it back to this resistance of mine. If in comparison with its latent content my dream distorts at this point (is in fact distorted into its opposite), the tenderness manifest in the dream serves that distortion; in other words, the *distortion* here turns out to be intentional, as an instrument of *disguise*.[10] My dream-thoughts contain an insult against R.; to keep me from noticing this, dream includes the opposite – namely, feelings of tenderness towards him.

This discovery could have universal validity. As the examples in Chapter 3 showed, there are in fact dreams that are naked instances of wish-fulfilment. Where the wish-fulfilment is unrecognizable, dressed up as something else, there must have been some intention of putting up a defence against the wish, and as a result of that defence the wish could not help but find expression in a distorted form. I want to find the counterpart in social life of this occurrence in the interior life of the mind. Where in social life do we find a similar distortion of a psychical act? Only in relations between two people, one of whom possesses a certain power while the other, because of that power, has to exercise discretion. The second person then distorts his or her psychical acts or, as we might also say, adopts a *disguise*. The politeness that I exercise every day is in large part such a disguise; if I interpret my dreams for the reader, I am obliged to make such distortions. The poet, too, laments being forced to distort:

> The best things you can know
> You still mayn't tell to boys.[11]

The political writer finds himself in a similar position when he has unpleasant truths to tell to those in power. If he speaks plainly, the ruler will suppress what he says – after the event, where oral utterance is concerned; preventively, where such truths are to be proclaimed in print. The writer lives in fear of censorship, so he moderates what he says and distorts his meaning. Depending on the strength and sensitivity of that censorship, he finds himself compelled either to cease certain forms of assault entirely or to speak in innuendoes rather than in direct terms, or he must hide his offensive statement behind a seemingly innocuous mask – for instance, by narrating incidents between two mandarins in the Middle Kingdom when what he really has in mind are civil servants in his own country. The stricter the censorship, the more detailed the mask and often the more amusing the means by which the reader is nevertheless set on the trail of the true meaning.[12]

The close correspondence (it could be traced in detail) between the phenomena of censorship and those of dream-distortion justifies us in predicating similar conditions for both. We can assume, in other words, that dream-formation stems from two psychical forces (tendencies, systems) in the individual, one of which shapes the wish expressed in dream while the other exercises censorship over that dream-wish, thereby imposing distortion on the way in which it is expressed. The only question is: what is the authority of this second, quasi-judicial instance, permitting it to practise its censorship? If we recall that latent dream-thoughts are not conscious prior to analysis but that the manifest dream-content proceeding therefrom is remembered as conscious, the obvious assumption is that the prerogative of the second agency is in fact admission to consciousness. According to this assumption, no part of the first system is able to attain consciousness that has not previously passed the second agency, and the second agency lets nothing past without exercising its rights and imposing on the candidate for consciousness whatever changes it cares to impose. Here we reveal a very specific view of the 'essence' of consciousness; for us, becoming conscious is a special kind of psychical act, different from and independent of the process of becoming fixed or represented as an idea, and consciousness seems to us to be a sense organ that perceives a substance that is present elsewhere. Psychopathology (it can be shown) simply cannot do without these basic assumptions. A more thorough appreciation of them will have to be reserved for a later stage.

If I stress the idea of the two psychical agencies and how they relate to consciousness, a wholly congruent analogy for the remarkable tenderness that I feel in the dream towards my friend R., who is so disparaged in the relevant dream-interpretation, can be seen in the political life of mankind. I imagine myself in a situation in which a ruler who is jealous of his power and a lively public opinion are locked in combat. Furious about an official whom they do not like, the people are calling for his dismissal; to show that he need take no account of what the people want, the autocrat will bestow some high honour upon the official at the very moment when there would not normally be any occasion for him to do so. In the same way, my second agency, which controls access to consciousness, 'decorates' my friend R. with an outpouring of excessive tenderness because the wishful endeavours of the first system, prompted by a particular interest to which they are currently in thrall, would like to brand him a dimwit.[13]

A suspicion may strike us at this point: dream-interpretation could perhaps supply information about the structure of our mental apparatus that we had (hitherto vainly) expected philosophy to provide. However, we shall not be following this trail; instead, once we have explained dream-distortion, we shall return to the question we asked at the outset – namely, how can dreams with a painfully embarrassing content be resolved into wish-fulfilments? We now see that this can in fact happen if dream-distortion has taken place and the painful content serves simply to disguise something wished for. In the light of our assumptions regarding the two psychical agencies, we can now say that painful dreams do indeed contain something that, while painful for the second agency, at the same time fulfil a wish so far as the first agency is concerned. They are wish-dreams in so far as all dreams proceed from the first agency, with the second agency playing only a defensive, non-creative role.[14] If we confine ourselves to appreciating what the second agency contributes to dream, we shall never understand the phenomenon. All the riddles that the literature has raised in connection with dream will still exist.

That dream really does have a secret meaning (as wish-fulfilment) needs to be shown by analysis in each and every case. So I shall pick out a number of dreams having a painfully embarrassing content and try to analyse them. Some of them were dreamed by hysterics and need a lengthy introduction and in places a deeper understanding of the psychical processes at work in hysteria. However, I see no way around this presentational difficulty.

If I accept a psychoneurotic for analytical treatment, the patient's dreams, as I have said, regularly form the subject of our discussions. I have to give the patient all the psychological explanations that have helped me to reach an understanding of his or her symptoms, and in the process I suffer relentless criticism of a severity that, in my view, fellow professionals could scarcely exceed. It very regularly happens that my patients protest against the theory that all dreams are wish-fulfilment. Here are some examples from this body of dream-material that were held up to me as proving the opposite.

'You always say that a dream is a wish fulfilled,' one bright [female] patient begins. 'Now I want to recount to you a dream whose content points in completely the opposite direction, namely that a wish of mine is *not* fulfilled. How do you reconcile that with your theory?' The dream goes like this:

'I want to give a supper party but have nothing in the larder except some smoked salmon. I think about going shopping but remember that it's Sunday afternoon, when all the shops are shut. I then want to telephone some suppliers, but the telephone is not working. So I have to abandon my wish to give a dinner party.'

I of course reply that only analysis can decide what the dream means, although I concede that it seems at first glance to be rational and coherent and looks like the opposite of an act of wish-fulfilment. 'But from what material did this dream proceed? As you know, the stimulus to a dream always lies in the experiences of the foregoing day.'

Analysis: The patient's husband, a worthy and virtuous wholesale butcher, had told her the day before that he was becoming too fat, so wanted to start a slimming-course. He would rise early, do exercises, observe a strict diet, and above all accept no more dinner invitations. With a laugh, she goes on to say of her husband that, at the pub, he had met a painter who very much wanted to paint his portrait because he had never, he said, come across such an expressive head before. Her husband, however, had replied in that dry manner of his that he was most grateful and was quite sure that the painter would prefer part of a lovely girl's bottom to his entire face.[15] She is currently very much in love with her husband, she says, and teases him all the time. She has also asked him not to give her caviar. I ask: 'What is that supposed to mean?'

The fact is, she has long wished to be in a position to enjoy a caviar roll every morning, but she begrudges the expense. She would of course have the caviar provided immediately by her hus-

band, were she to ask him for it. However, she has asked him not
to buy her caviar in order that she can go on teasing him about it.

(This justification strikes me as flimsy. Such unsatisfactory pieces
of information usually conceal unadmitted motives. One thinks of
Bernheim's hypnotized patients, who execute a post-hypnotic task
and, when asked about their motives, rather than answer, 'I don't
know why I did that', have to make up some (clearly inadequate)
justification. No doubt something like that is happening with my
patient and her caviar. I note that she is compelled to create an
unfulfilled wish for herself in life. Her dream also shows her this
wish-denial coming true. But why does she need an unfulfilled
wish?)

The things that have occurred to her so far in connection with
interpreting the dream have not sufficed. I insist on others. After a
brief pause (such as would indeed correspond to a certain resistance
being overcome), she goes on to report that the day before she had
called on a girlfriend of whom she is in fact jealous because her
husband always speaks so highly of her. Fortunately, the girlfriend
is extremely thin and scrawny and her husband is an admirer of the
fuller figure. And what did this skinny person talk about? Her desire
to put on weight, of course. She also asked my patient, 'When are
you going to invite us again? One always eats so well at your place.'

Now the meaning of the dream is clear. I am able to tell the
patient, 'It's just as if you had thought when thus challenged: "Oh
yes, very likely – I invite you around in order that you can eat your
fill at my place, grow fat and appeal to my husband even more! I'd
rather give no more dinner parties." Dream then tells you that you
cannot give a dinner party; in other words, it fulfils your wish to do
nothing towards enhancing your friend's figure. That a person does
grow fat from the things on offer at parties is demonstrated by your
husband's resolution to stop accepting dinner invitations in the
interests of his slimming-course.'

The only thing missing now is some sort of link to corroborate
the solution. Also, the 'smoked salmon' of the dream-content has
yet to be traced. 'How do you get to the salmon mentioned in the
dream?' 'Smoked salmon is my friend's favourite food,' she replies.

I happen to know the lady too and can confirm that she has just as soft a spot for salmon as my patient has for caviar.

The same dream admits of a further, subtler interpretation that a secondary circumstance makes necessary. The two interpretations, far from contradicting each other, in fact overlap and provide a splendid example of the customary ambiguous quality of dreams, as of all other psychopathological formations. We have heard that, at the same time as she was dreaming of a wish being denied, the patient was endeavouring to make a frustrated wish come true (the caviar roll). Her friend had also expressed a wish: she would like to be a bit fatter. It would not surprise us if our patient had dreamed that her friend's wish remained unfulfilled. The fact is, it is her own wish that her friend's wish (to put on weight) should remain unfulfilled. Instead, though, she dreams that she is the one to whom a wish is denied. The dream takes on another meaning if, in it, she means not herself but her friend, if she substitutes herself for her friend, or if, as we might say, she has *identified* with her.

I believe she really had done so, and as a sign of that identification she had turned the frustrated wish into a reality. But what does such hysterical identification mean? Explaining this will involve going into things in greater detail. Identification is an extremely important factor so far as the mechanism of hysterical symptoms is concerned; it is how patients contrive to express in their symptoms the experiences of a large number of people, not just their own – to suffer on behalf of a whole crowd of people, as it were, and enact each one of the parts in a play, drawing only on their own personal resources. It will be objected that this is the well-known phenomenon of hysterical imitation, the ability of hysterics to imitate all the symptoms that impress them in others, almost like a kind of empathy heightened to the point of reproduction. However, that only indicates the path along which the psychical process involved in hysterical imitation unfolds; there is a difference between the path and the mental act that takes that path. The latter is slightly more complicated than people normally like to imagine hysterical imitation; it corresponds to an unconscious conclusion-process, as an example will make clear.

A hospital doctor who has a patient with a particular type of twitch, in the same ward as other patients, is not surprised to discover one morning that this particular hysterical fit has found imitators. He simply says to himself, 'The others have seen it and copied it; it's a case of psychical infection.' Yes, but psychical infection occurs in more or less the following fashion. Patients usually know more about one another than the doctor knows about each one of them, and they feel concern for one another when the doctor's round is finished. One woman has her fit today; it very soon becomes known to the others that a letter from home, a stirring of the pangs of love, or some such thing is the cause of it. Their sympathy is aroused, and without doing so consciously they reach the following conclusion: if it is possible to have such fits from such causes, I too can have such fits, because I have as much occasion. Were this conclusion capable of becoming conscious, it might result in the *fear* of having the same fit; however, it is reached on different psychical terrain and therefore culminates in the feared symptom becoming reality. In other words, identification is not mere imitation but *appropriation* on the basis of the same aetiological requirement; it gives expression to a 'just as' and relates to a common factor that has remained unconscious.

Identification is most frequently used in hysteria to express a sexual common factor. The hysteric identifies in terms of her symptoms most often (though not exclusively) with persons with whom she has had sexual relations in the past or who are in sexual relationships with the same persons as herself. Language takes similar account of such a view. Two lovers are 'one'. In the hysterical imagination, as in dream, all that is necessary for identification is that the subject should think of sexual relations; such relations need not be real. My patient, then, is simply following the rules of hysterical thought-processes in expressing her jealous feelings towards her friend (feelings that, incidentially, she herself acknowledges to be unjustified) in that in dream she puts herself in the friend's place and, by creating a symptom (the frustrated wish), identifies with her. Linguistically, one might explain the process as follows: she puts herself in her friend's place in the dream because her friend takes her place in her husband's eyes, because she would like to enjoy her friend's standing in her husband's estimation.[16]

In a simpler fashion, yet still along the lines that non-fulfilment of one wish means fulfilment of another, a conflict with my dream-theory was resolved in another patient, the most amusing of all my [female] dreamers. I had been explaining to her one day how dream is wish-fulfilment; next day she brought me a dream in which she is travelling in the company of her mother-in-law to the place in the country that they have taken together. I was aware, in fact, that she had put up fierce resistance to the idea of spending the summer in the vicinity of her mother-in-law; I was also aware that in the last few days she had happily found a way out of the situation she so dreaded by renting a house in the country nowhere near her mother-in-law's place. Now dream had unpicked this much-desired solution; was this not in diametrical opposition to my theory of wish-fulfilment through dream? Of course, one needed only to draw the obvious conclusion from this dream and there was the interpretation. According to the dream, I was wrong: *so it was her wish that I should be wrong, and dream fulfilled it for her*. The wish that I should be wrong, which found fulfilment in the matter of the place in the country, actually referred to a different, more serious topic. Around the same time, I had concluded from the material furnished by her analysis that at a certain period in her life something must have occurred that was significant so far as her illness was concerned. She had questioned this, having no memory of such an event. We soon found out that I was right. In other words, her wish that I might be wrong, transformed into the dream that she is travelling to the country with her mother-in-law, corresponded to the legitimate wish that the things she had only just begun to suspect might never in fact have happened.

Without analysis, solely through the medium of conjecture, I took the liberty of interpreting a small incident in connection with a friend, someone who had been with me through the eight years of our secondary education. He once heard, in a small group, a lecture of mine about the novel idea that dream is wish-fulfilment, after which he went home and dreamed *that he had lost all his cases* (he was a barrister); he complained to me about this. I resorted to the excuse: 'No one can win all his cases.' But what I thought to myself was: 'If for eight years I sat at the top of the class while he fluctuated somewhere around the middle, will he never, throughout those boyhood years, have conceived the wish that I should one day fall flat on my face?'

A different dream of a rather darker character was also recounted to me by a patient as an objection to the wish-dream theory. The patient (she was a young woman) began: 'You remember that my sister now has only one boy, Karl; she lost the elder one, Otto, while I was still living with her. Otto was my favourite; I actually brought him up. I like his little brother too, but of course not nearly as much as the one who died. Well, last night, I dream *that I can see Karl laid out dead in front of me. He is lying in his little coffin, hands folded, surrounded by candles – in short, just the way little Otto had once, the boy whose death had so affected me.* All right, then – what's this supposed to mean? You know me, after all; am I so awful a person that I could wish upon my sister the loss of the only child still remaining to her? Or does the dream mean that I would rather Karl had died instead of Otto, whom I loved so much more?'

I reassured her that the latter meaning was quite out of the question. After a brief reflection, I was able to tell her the correct interpretation of the dream, which I then had her confirm. This I was able to do because I knew the whole of the dreamer's previous history.

Orphaned at an early age, the girl had been brought up in the house of her very much older sister, where among the friends and acquaintances who visited the house she met the man who made a lasting impression on her heart. It looked for a while as if these scarcely voiced relations were to culminate in marriage, but that happy outcome was frustrated by the sister, whose motives have never been satisfactorily explained. Following the rupture, the man whom our patient loved avoided the house; she too, some time after the death of little Otto, on whom she had meanwhile expended her tenderness, left to live her own life. She failed completely, however, to free herself from the dependency into which her attachment to her sister's friend had plunged her. Pride demanded that she keep out of his way; however, she found it impossible to transfer her love to any of the other suitors who presented themselves subsequently. If the man she loved (a literary figure in the academic world) announced a lecture somewhere, she was invariably to be found in the audience; she also seized every other opportunity to see him (from a distance) elsewhere. I remembered her telling me the day before that the professor would be attending a particular concert to which she meant to go also in order once again to enjoy a glimpse of him. That was on the day preceding the dream; the day she recounted the dream to me was the day when the concert was to take place. It was then easy for me to construe the correct interpretation, and I asked her whether any event sprang to mind that had occurred after little Otto's death. She replied immediately, 'It certainly does. That was when the professor, having stayed away for a long time, came back and I saw him once again over little Otto's coffin.' It was just as I had expected. So I interpreted the dream as follows: 'If the other boy were now to die, the same thing would happen again. You would spend the day at your sister's, the professor would undoubtedly call in to offer his condolences, and you would see him again in the same circumstances as before. All the dream signifies is this wish of yours to see him again, against which you are inwardly struggling. I know you have a ticket for today's concert in your bag. Your dream is an impatience-dream; it anticipated your seeing him again, as you will today, by several hours.'

To cover up her wish, she had obviously chosen a situation in which such wishes are customarily suppressed, a situation in which everyone is so preoccupied with mourning, no one thinks of love. And yet it is entirely possible that in the real situation, too, which the dream faithfully reproduced, she had been unable, at the coffin of the elder son (whom she had loved more intensely), to suppress her feelings of tenderness towards the long-missed visitor.

A different explanation was invoked by a similar dream recounted by another patient, who in her younger years had been known for her quick wit and merry moods and who still, at least so far as her associations of ideas during treatment were concerned, evinced those qualities. In the context of a more extended dream, this woman saw her fifteen-year-old only daughter lying dead in a box [*Schachtel*]. She would quite have liked to use this dream-manifestation as an objection to the wish-fulfilment theory; but she herself had an inkling that the detail of the box must point the way towards a different perception of the dream.[17] During analysis, she recalled that the previous evening people had been talking about the English word 'box' and how it corresponded to many different German words: *Schachtel* [an ordinary, possibly cardboard box], *Loge* [a box at the theatre], *Kasten* [a tea-chest, say], *Ohrfeige* [a box on the ears] and so on. From other components of the same dream, it became possible to add that, having hit upon how the English word 'box' is related to the German word *Büchse*, she was subsequently haunted by the memory that *Büchse* is also used as a vulgar appellation for the female genitalia. Consequently, taking a lenient view of her knowledge of topographical anatomy, one might assume that the child lying in the *Schachtel* represented a foetus in the womb. When all this had been explained to her, she no longer denied that the dream-image really did correspond to a wish of hers. Like so many young women, she was far from happy to find herself pregnant, and she admitted to herself having wished more than once that the child should die in her womb; indeed, in a fit of rage following a fierce row with her husband, she had pummelled her abdomen with her fists, hoping to land a blow on the child inside. So the dead child actually was a wish-fulfilment, albeit of a wish that had been set aside fifteen years earlier, and it is not surprising that, arriving so belatedly, the wish-fulfilment was no longer recognized. Too much has changed in the mean time.

The group to which both the last two dreams belong (dreams that have as their content the deaths of loved family members) will be re-examined in the next chapter, under 'Typical dreams'.[18] There I shall be able to show with fresh examples how, their unwished-for content notwithstanding, all these dreams should be interpreted as wish-fulfilments. It is not to a patient but to a highly intelligent legal scholar of my acquaintance that I am indebted for the following dream, which again was recounted to me with the object of holding me back from precipitately generalizing the wish-dream theory.

'*In my dream*,' reports my source, '*I arrive in front of my house with a lady on my arm. A closed carriage is parked there. A gentleman comes up to me, identifies himself as a police officer and asks me to follow him. I plead simply for time enough to put my affairs in order.* Is it your belief that I perhaps wish to be arrested?'

'Certainly not,' I have to concede. 'Do you happen to know on what charge you were being arrested?'

'Yes, I believe it was infanticide.'

'Infanticide? Surely you know that infanticide is a crime that only a mother can commit against her new-born child?'

'That is correct.'[19]

'And in what circumstances did you dream? What happened the evening before?'

'I'd rather not say. It's a matter of some delicacy.'

'But I need to know, otherwise we must give up the idea of interpreting the dream.'

'All right, listen: I did not spend the night at home but with a lady who means a great deal to me. When we woke up in the morning, once again something happened between us. Afterwards I fell asleep again and dreamed what you know.'

'She's a married woman?'

'Yes.'

'And you don't want to have a child with her?'

'No, no. That might give us away.'

'So you don't have normal intercourse?'

'I take the precaution of withdrawing before ejaculation.'

'Can I assume you had performed this trick several times during the course of the night, and after the repetition in the morning you were slightly unsure whether you had been successful?'

'It's quite possible.'

'In that case your dream is an act of wish-fulfilment. Through it you receive reassurance that you have not created a child – or what comes to almost the same thing: your having killed a child. The intermediate links I can easily demonstrate to you. You remember how, several days ago, we were talking about forced marriage and about the illogicality of its being permitted to have intercourse in such a way that conception does not take place whereas every act in which egg and sperm do happen to meet and a foetus is formed is punished as a crime. We went on to recall the medieval dispute about the precise moment at which the soul enters the foetus, because only then does the term "murder" become admissible. You are surely also aware of that dreadful poem of Lenau's that equates infanticide with contraception.'

'That's interesting: Lenau popped into my mind only this morning.'

'Another echo of your dream. And now I want to show you a small additional piece of wish-fulfilment in your dream. You arrive in front of your house with the lady on your arm. In other words, you are *taking her home*, whereas in reality you spend the night at her place. There may be more than one reason for the wish-fulfilment that forms the nucleus of the dream taking so unpleasant a form. You could have discovered from my essay on the aetiology of the anxiety neurosis that I name *coitus interruptus* as one of the factors giving rise to neurotic anxiety. It would chime with this if, after practising intercourse of this kind several times, you were left with a sense of unease that then became a factor in the composition of your dream. This feeling of disgruntlement you also make use of to disguise your wish-fulfilment. By the way, the mention of infanticide is also unaccounted for. What put that specifically female crime into your head?'

'I'll make a confession to you. Some years ago I was in fact involved in such an affair. I was to blame for the fact that a girl tried by having an abortion to protect herself from the consequences of a relationship with me. I had nothing whatsoever to do with the execution of the deed, but for a long time I was understandably anxious lest the thing be discovered.'

'I do understand. The memory provided you with a second reason why supposing you had performed your trick badly must have been painful for you.'

A young doctor who heard this dream narrated in my lecture

must have felt that it applied to him because he lost no time in dreaming it himself, adapting its train of thought to a different topic. The previous day he had submitted his declaration of income, which he had drawn up in all honesty, having only a small income to declare. What he dreamed was that an acquaintance came to him from the meeting of the tax committee and told him that every other tax declaration had been accepted without query but that his had aroused general suspicion and would earn him a heavy fine. The dream is a carelessly disguised piece of wish-fulfilment: he wished to be taken for a doctor with a large income. Incidentally, it reminds one of the well-known story of the girl who is advised not to accept her suitor because he has a violent temper and, once married to her, will surely beat her. The girl's answer is, 'Let him!' So strong is her desire to be wed that she accepts the unpleasantness that people tell her will be associated with this particular marriage, even wishing it.

If I group the very frequent dreams of this kind, which appear directly to contradict my theory in that they have as their content the failure of a wish or the occurrence of something clearly not wished for – if I group these together as *'counter-wish dreams'*, I see that they generally stem from two principles, one of which has not yet been mentioned, although it plays a major part in people's lives as in their dreams. One of the driving forces behind such dreams is the wish that I should be wrong. These dreams occur regularly during my treatments if the patient is in resistance against me, and I can expect with a high degree of certainty to provoke such a dream after the first time I introduce the patient to the theory that dream is wish-fulfilment.[20] Indeed, I can expect many a reader to react in the same way: to be quite prepared to sacrifice a wish in dream simply in order to have the wish that I might be wrong fulfilled. The last treatment dream of this kind that I should like to report again shows the same thing. A girl who fiercely resisted continuance of my treatment, in defiance both of her family and of the authorities upon whose advice they had called, told me the following dream: *At home they forbid her to go on coming to me. She then appeals to me, referring to a promise I had once given her to treat her for nothing if it should come to that, and I say to her, 'In money matters I can make no allowances.'*

This time, it really is not easy to prove wish-fulfilment. However, in all such cases, as well as the one riddle there is another, solving which will also help to solve the first. Where do the words come from that she puts into my mouth? Naturally, I have never told her anything of the kind, but one of her brothers (the very one who has most influence over her) was good enough to make this remark about me. In other words, the result that the dream wishes to achieve is that the brother should be proved right, and it is not just in dream that she seeks justice for this brother; it is the substance of her life and the reason why she is ill.

A dream that at first glance poses particular problems for the wish-fulfilment theory was dreamed and interpreted by a doctor (August Stärcke [1911–12]): *'I have and can see on the index finger of my left hand a syphilitic primary affect on the last phalanx.'*

One might let oneself be dissuaded from analysing this dream by assuming that, apart from its undesirable content, it appears clear and coherent. Only by bothering to embark on an analysis does one discover that 'primary affect' is just like *prima affectio* ('first love') and that, as Stärcke himself puts it, the repulsive sore proves to 'stand for wish-fulfilments filled with great emotion'.[21]

The other motive of counter-wish dreams is so obvious that there is a great danger of our overlooking it, as I did myself for quite a long time. The sexual make-up of so many people contains a masochistic element that as a result of total reversal stems from the aggressive, sadistic side. Such people are termed 'ideational' masochists if they seek pleasure not from having physical pain inflicted on them but from humiliation and mental torment. It is immediately apparent that such people may entertain counter-wish dreams and aversion dreams that so far as they are concerned are in fact wish-fulfilments, satisfying their masochistic tendencies. Here is one such dream:

A young man who in earlier years had given his elder brother, towards whom he experienced a homosexual attraction, a very bad time but had since undergone a radical character transformation, now dreams a dream comprising three parts: *I. How his elder brother 'pesters' him.*[22] *II. How two adults flirt together with homo-sexual intent. III. His brother has sold the business that he* [the dreamer] *had been looking forward to managing in future.* He wakes from this dream with the most painful feelings; even so, it is a masochistic wish-dream that might be translated thus: it would serve me right if my brother had inflicted that sale on me as punishment for all the torments he had suffered at my hands.

I hope that the foregoing examples will suffice to make it seem plausible (until further objection) that even dreams having a painful content should be resolved as wish-fulfilments.[23] And no one will see it as accidental that, each time such dreams are interpreted, one comes up against subjects that people are reluctant to speak of or do not like thinking about. No doubt the painful feeling that such dreams arouse is simply the same as the reluctance that seeks to keep us (usually with success) from dealing with or even contemplating such subjects and that has to be overcome by each one of us if we find ourselves obliged to tackle it none the less. However, this feeling of aversion that recurs in dream does not mean that no wish exists; everyone has wishes that he would rather not share with others – and wishes that he refuses to admit to himself. On the other hand, we feel justified in connecting the aversion character of all these dreams with the fact of dream-distortion and in conclud-ing that the reason why such dreams are so distorted and the wish-fulfilment in them disguised beyond recognition is precisely that there exists a reluctance towards or repressive intention directed against the topic of the dream or the wish that is drawn therefrom. Dream-distortion, then, turns out to be a real act of censorship. How-ever, everything that analysing aversion-dreams has brought to light is in fact allowed for if we revise our definition (meant to convey the essence of dream) as follows: *Dream is the (disguised) fulfilment of a (suppressed* [unterdrückten] *or repressed) wish.*[24]

Anxiety-dreams are in fact superfluous as a separate sub-species of the dreams having a painful content that the ignorant are least willing to accept as wish-dreams. Yet I can dismiss anxiety-dreams very briefly here. It is not a case of these showing us a fresh aspect of the dream-problem; this is about our understanding neurotic anxiety in general. The anxiety that we feel in dream only seems to be explained by the content of the dream. Subjecting that content to interpretation, we find dream-anxiety to be no better justified by dream-content than, say, the anxiety of a phobia by the idea on which that phobia depends. While it is true that, for example, one can fall from a window so has reason to exercise a certain caution when standing by a window, there is no understanding why, in connection with the corresponding phobia, the anxiety is so great and haunts the patient so far beyond what causes it. The same explanation then turns out to be valid both for phobia and for the anxiety-dream. In both cases, anxiety is simply *soldered on to* the accompanying idea; it stems from a different source.

Because of this close connection between dream-anxiety and neurotic anxiety, in discussing the former in this context I have to refer to the latter. In a short essay on 'Anxiety neurosis',[25] I once maintained that neurotic anxiety stems from the sexual life and corresponds to a libido that has been diverted from its purpose and remained unused. That formulation has always turned out to be more than sound since. From it can now be derived the principle that anxiety-dreams are dreams with a sexual content, the attendant libido of which has undergone a transformation into anxiety. Later there will be an opportunity to back up this assertion by analysing a number of dreams experienced by neurotics. I shall also, in connection with further attempts to move closer to a theory of dream, be returning to the condition of anxiety-dreams and their compatibility with the wish-fulfilment theory.

Notes

1. See Radestock [1878], pp. 137–8, Volkelt [1875], pp. 110–11, Purkinje [1846], p. 456, Tissié [1898], p. 70, Simon [1888], p. 42, on the imprisoned Baron Trenck's hunger dreams, and the passage in Griesinger [1871], p. 111.

As early as the third century the Neoplatonist Plotinus [CE 205–70] wrote: 'If longing stirs, imagination comes along and presents us with (as it were) the object longed for' (Du Prel, p. 276).

2. [Eduard von Hartmann, *Philosophie des Unbewussten*, Part II, stereo-typed edition, p. 344.]

3. See, among others, Scholz [1887], p. 33, and Volkelt [1875], p. 80.

4. [*Angstträume*; 'anxiety-dreams' is the usual English translation, but the reader should bear in mind that *Angst* covers naked dread as well as niggling worry. Interestingly, English has adopted the German word; 'angst' is defined in the *COD* not only as 'anxiety' but also as 'a feeling of guilt or remorse'. It is as if English speakers were aware of a gap in their own language; when they say 'angst' they perhaps *feel* they are saying more than 'anxiety'.]

5. See Debacker [1881] on *pavor nocturnus*.

6. It is quite incredible how stubbornly readers and critics close their minds to this consideration and continue to leave the fundamental difference between manifest and latent dream-content entirely out of account. How-ever, none of the accounts set down in the literature comes so close to this idea of mine as a passage in J. Sully's 1893 essay 'Dreams as a revelation' (the merit of which ought not to be diminished by the fact that I have not mentioned it before): 'It would seem then, after all, that dreams are not the utter nonsense they have been said to be by such authorities as Chaucer, Shakespeare and Milton. The chaotic aggregations of our night-fancy have a significance and communicate new knowledge. *Like some letter in cipher, the dream-inscription when scrutinized closely loses its first look of balder-dash and takes on the aspect of a serious, intelligible message. Or, to vary the figure slightly, we may say that, like some palimpsest, the dream discloses beneath its worthless surface-characters traces of an old and precious communication*' (op. cit. p. 364).

7. ['Adjunct professor', 'associate professor' and 'titular professor' have all been suggested, but there is no precise equivalent for this largely honorific title at either a British or an American university (I am grateful to John Forrester for this information).

8. It is remarkable how here my memory (in the waking state) economizes for the purposes of the analysis. I knew five of my uncles, and there was one of them I loved and looked up to. Yet in the moment of overcoming my reluctance, I say to myself, 'I had only one uncle' – the one meant in the dream.

9. ['Feeble head', actually, but the word is quite insulting.]

10. [The words Freud uses for 'distortion' and 'disguise' are even more closely related than the English words I use to render them; they are, respectively, '*Entstellung*' and '*Verstellung*' – as one might say, 'locating in the wrong place' and 'wrongly locating'.]

11.   [*Das Beste, was du wissen kannst,*
        Darfst du den Buben doch nicht sagen.

The lines, spoken by Mephistopheles, are from Goethe's *Faust* (Part I, scene 4). Freud quoted them often (see below, p. 467).]

12. Writing in 1915 (*Internationale Zeitschrift für ärztliche Psychoanalyse* ['International journal for medical psychoanalysis'], III), Dr H. von Hug-Hellmuth recounts a dream that is perhaps better suited than any other to justifying my nomenclature. In this example, dream-distortion operates with the same instruments as postal censorship to get rid of passages it finds offensive. Postal censorship makes such passages illegible by crossing them out; dream-distortion replaces them with an incomprehensible murmur.

To understand the dream, it is necessary to know that the dreamer is a most respectable, highly educated lady of fifty, widow of a high-ranking officer who had died some twelve years previously and mother of grown-up sons, one of whom is on active service at the time of the dream.

And now the dream of the '*sexual favours*' [*Liebesdienste* – literally, 'love services']:

> She goes to Garrison Hospital No. 1 and tells the sentry at the gate that she needs to speak to the Chief Medical Officer . . . (she gives a name she does not know) because she wishes to serve in the hospital. She stresses the word 'serve' in such a way that the subaltern is immediately aware that she is talking about sexual favours. Since she is an elderly woman, after a moment's hesitation he lets her pass. However, instead of meeting the CMO she finds herself in a large, dimly lit room in which a great many officers and army doctors are standing around or sitting at a long table. She addresses her request to a medical-corps captain, who understands her meaning after only a few words. The wording she employs in the dream is: 'I and many other Viennese women and girls are prepared to provide the soldiers, no matter whether other ranks or officers, with . . .' There follows, in the dream, a murmur. However, she knows that her words have been correctly understood by all present from the expressions (embarrassed in some cases, in others gloating) on the officers' faces. The lady goes on, 'I know our decision will sound disconcerting, but we mean it in all seriousness. The soldier on active service is also never asked whether or not he wishes to die.' A minute's painful silence ensues. The captain passes an arm around her waist and says, 'My good woman, let's assume for a moment that it actually comes to . . .' (more murmuring). She eludes his embrace, thinking, 'They really are all the

same.' She retorts, 'God, I'm an old woman and will possibly never be in that situation. Anyway, one condition would have to be observed: respect for age; an elderly woman and a boy in the first flush of youth must never ... (murmuring again). That would be dreadful.' The captain replies, 'I understand perfectly.' A number of officers, including one who had once, in her younger days, asked for her hand in marriage, burst out laughing, and the lady asks to be taken to the CMO, whom she knows, in order for everything to be clarified. To her deep dismay, however, she realizes that she does not know his name. The captain nevertheless most courteously and respectfully orders her to climb to the second storey by way of a very narrow iron spiral staircase that leads directly from the room they are in to the upper floors. As she climbs, she hears an officer say, 'That's a huge decision, never mind whether you're young or old; hats off to her!'

Feeling that she is simply doing her duty, she climbs the endless staircase.

The dream recurred twice more in the space of a few weeks with (as the lady commented) quite unimportant and utterly meaningless changes.

13. Neither in my own case nor in that of others are such hypocritical dreams a rare occurrence. When I am busy working on a certain scientific problem, I am visited on several nights in swift succession by a mildly confusing dream that has as its content a reconciliation with a friend long since thrust aside. On the fourth or fifth occasion, I do eventually succeed in grasping the meaning of these dreams. It lies in a recommendation that I finally abandon the last remaining shreds of consideration for the person concerned, freeing myself entirely from that person, and in this hypocritical fashion it appears disguised as the contrary suggestion. Someone once told me of a 'hypocritical Oedipus dream' in which the hostile stirrings and murderous desires of the dream-thoughts are replaced by a manifest tenderness ('Typical instance of an undiagnosed Oedipus dream'). Another kind of hypocritical dreaming will be mentioned later (see Chapter 6, 'Dream-Work').

14. Later we shall also come across the opposite case – where dream voices a wish on the part of this second agency.

15. One 'sits' for one's portrait painter. As Goethe writes:

> *Und wenn er keinen Hintern hat*
> *Wie kann der Edle sitzen?*

[And if he has no bottom / How can the noble sit?]

16. I myself regret interpolating such material from the psychopathology of hysteria, which being presented in this fragmentary fashion and taken completely out of context can scarcely shed much light. If it does manage to point the reader in the direction of the very close relations between dream and psychoneuroses, it will have served the purpose for which I intended it.

17. As in the dream of the smoked salmon and the frustrated dinner-party [see pp. 158ff.].

18. [See Chapter 5, section D.]

19. It frequently happens that a dream is recounted incomplete and that it is only during analysis that the omitted portions are recalled. These portions inserted at a later stage regularly provide the key to interpreting the dream. See below for a discussion of forgetting dreams [Chapter 7, section A].

20. Similar counter-wish dreams have been recounted to me by my students many times in recent years as their reaction to their first encounter with the 'wish-theory of dream'.

21. *Zentralblatt für Psycho-Analyse*, II, 1911–12.

22. [The word Freud uses, also placing it between inverted commas, is the peculiarly Austrian *'sekkiert'*.]

23. I would point out that I have not finished with this topic and will be returning to it later.

24. A major living writer who (I am told) claims to know nothing of psychoanalysis and interpreting dreams nevertheless arrives independently at an almost identical form of words to define the essence of dream: 'Unauthorized appearance of suppressed longings behind a false face and under a false name' (C[arl] Spitteler, *Meine frühesten Erlebnisse* ['My earliest experiences'], one of the *Süddeutsche Monatshefte*, October 1913).

Let me anticipate by quoting Otto Rank's extension and modification of the foregoing basic formula: 'Dream regularly represents, on the basis and with the help of repressed infantile-sexual material, current wishes, usually likewise of an erotic nature, in concealed, symbolically disguised form as having found fulfilment' ('Ein Traum, der sich selbst deutet' ['A dream that interprets itself', 1910, see Other Literature]).

Nowhere have I claimed Rank's formula as my own. The shorter version given in my text strikes me as adequate. But the fact that [in earlier editions of this book] I mentioned Rank's modification at all was enough to earn psychoanalysis the oft-repeated charge that it says *all dreams have a sexual content*. If we understand the charge as it is meant, all it proves is how little conscientiousness critics employ as they go about their business and how readily opponents will overlook the clearest statements when those statements do not fit in with their aggressive tendencies. The fact is, a few pages earlier I talk about the many and varied wish-fulfilments of children's dreams (a country excursion, a lake trip, catching up on a missed meal and so on), while elsewhere I deal with hunger dreams, dreams prompted by the thirst stimulus, by the excretory stimulus, and pure comfort-dreams. Even Rank qualifies his assertion. He says 'usually likewise of an erotic nature', and so far as most adult dreams are concerned that is very much corroborated.

The picture changes if the word 'sexual' is used in the sense usually given to it in psychoanalysis, namely that of 'eros'. However, the interesting problem of whether all dreams are not in fact created by 'libidinal' (as opposed to 'destructive') driving forces is scarcely what opponents will have had in mind.

25. 'Die Angstneurose', in *Neurologisches Zentralblatt*, 1895 (*Gesammelte Schriften*, vol. I).

5

Dream-Material and Sources of Dream

When we saw from the analysis of the dream of Irma's injection [see pp. 120ff.] that dream is wish-fulfilment, initially our interest was caught by whether we had here discovered a general character-istic of dream, and we provisionally silenced whatever other kinds of scientific curiosity may have been stimulated in us during that interpretation. Now, however, having reached our goal along one path, we can go back and select a fresh starting-point for our rambles through the problems of dream. So let us, although we have by no means exhausted the subject of wish-fulfilment, for a moment turn our attention elsewhere.

Having been able, by applying our method of interpreting dreams, to uncover a *latent* dream-content that is of far greater importance than the *manifest* dream-content, we are inevitably driven to take up the individual problems of dream once again in order to try to find a satisfactory solution to puzzles and contradic-tions that, while all we knew of was the manifest content of dreams, appeared impregnable.

What the literature has to say about the connection between dream and waking life and about where dream-material comes from was dealt with thoroughly in our opening chapter. Let us also recall those three distinguishing features of dream-memory that have been so frequently remarked upon but never explained:

1)   that dream has a clear preference for the impressions of the last few days (Robert [1886], Strümpell [1877], Hildebrandt [1875], and also Weed and Hallam [1896]);

2) that dream makes its selection according to different principles than those used by our waking memory in that it remembers not what is essential and significant but what is peripheral and disregarded;

3) that dream has access to our earliest childhood impressions and even fetches out details from that period in our lives that once again seem trivial to us and that in the waking state we deemed long forgotten.[1]

These peculiarities in the choice of dream-material are of course observed by the authors of the literature in terms of manifest dream-content.

A *The live and the neutral in dream*[2]

If I now consult my own experience with regard to the origin of the elements appearing in dream-content, I must first advance the claim that in every dream it is possible to trace a link to the experiences of the *day that has just passed*. No matter what dream I take, be it one of my own or someone else's, I invariably find this fact confirmed. Knowing this, I may well begin a dream-interpretation by first enquiring about the events of the day that prompted the dream; in many cases, this is in fact the shortest route. In the two dreams I analyse in previous chapters (that of Irma's injection [pp. 119ff.], that of my uncle with the yellow beard [pp. 151ff.]), the connection with the day is so striking as to need no further elucidation. However, to show how regularly that connection can be shown, I propose to examine an extract from my own dream-diary from that angle. I recount the dreams only to the extent that this is necessary for uncovering the source I am looking for.

1) *I call at a house where I gain admission only with difficulty, etc. meanwhile keeping a woman waiting.*
   Source: Conversation with a relation that evening about the fact that an acquisition that she had asked for must *wait* until etc.
2) *I have written a* monograph *about a certain* (not clear) *type of plant.*
   Source: Seen that morning, in the window of a bookshop, a *monograph* about the genus Cyclamen.

3) *I see two women in the street,* mother and daughter, *the latter of whom was a patient of mine.*
   Source: That evening a patient whom I was treating had told me what difficulties her *mother* was putting in the way of the treatment continuing.

4) *In the S. and R. bookshop I take out a subscription to a periodical costing twenty florins [Gulden] a year.*
   Source: My wife had reminded me that day that I still owed her twenty florins' housekeeping money.

5) *I receive a communication from the Social-Democratic Committee in which I am treated as a member.*
   Source: *Communications* received simultaneously from the Liberal Election Committee and the Committee of the Humanitarian Society, to which I do actually belong.

6) *A man on a precipitous rock in the middle of the sea, in the style of Böcklin.*
   Source: Dreyfus on *Devil's Island*, simultaneously news of my relations in *England*, etc.

It might be asked whether the dream-link always relates to events of the past day or whether it can extend to impressions received during a longer period in the recent past. Probably the object cannot lay claim to any importance of principle, but I should still be inclined to opt for the exclusive prerogative of the day before the dream (the dream-day). Wherever I felt that an impression from two or three days earlier had been the source of the dream, I was able on closer examination to satisfy myself that that impression had been recalled on the day preceding the dream – in other words that a verifiable reproduction on the previous day had interposed itself between the day of the event and the time when the dream occurred; I was also able to verify the still-vivid occasion from which the memory of the earlier impression might have stemmed. On the other hand, I was unable to convince myself that a regular interval of biological significance (the first of this kind is put by Hermann Swoboda [1904] at eighteen hours)[3] had interposed itself between the triggering daytime impression and its recurrence in dream.

Havelock Ellis, too, who has devoted some attention to this question, admits that 'despite looking out for it' he failed to find any such periodicity of reproduction in his dreams. He recounts a dream in which he was in Spain and wished to travel to a town called *Daraus, Varaus* or *Zaraus*. On waking, he could remember no such place-name and disregarded the dream. Some months later he did indeed find the name *Zaraus* [Zardúz] as that of a station between San Sebastian and Bilbao that his train had passed through 250 days before the dream (p. 227).

I believe, then, that for every dream there is a dream-trigger arising out of the experiences over which 'one has not yet slept a night'.

In other words, the experiences of the immediate past (with the exception of the day preceding the dream-night) stand in no different a relationship to dream-content than other impressions from never mind how long ago. Dream can choose its material from any time of life, provided only that there is a mental thread connecting the experiences of the dream-day ('still-vivid' impressions) with those earlier experiences.

But why this preference for impressions that are still 'live'? We shall reach certain conjectures on this point if we subject one of the above-mentioned dreams to more detailed analysis. I have chosen the

DREAM OF THE BOTANICAL MONOGRAPH

I have written a monograph on a certain plant. I have the book before me, and I am just turning over one of the tipped-in colour plates. Each copy has a dried specimen of the plant bound in with it, as if from a herbarium.

ANALYSIS:

That morning I had seen in the window of a bookshop a book entitled *The Genus Cyclamen* – clearly a *monograph* about the plant.

Cyclamen is my wife's *favourite flower*. I reproach myself for so seldom *buying her flowers*, as she would wish. On the subject of *buying flowers*, I recall a story I recently told among friends, using it in support of my claim that forgetting is very often the execution of an intention of the unconscious and certainly permits a conclusion to be drawn regarding the secret state of mind of the person doing the forgetting. A young woman who has become accustomed to receiving a bunch of flowers from her husband for her birthday misses this token of affection on one such occasion and bursts into tears over the omission. Her husband arrives and is unable to account for her tears until she tells him, 'It's my birthday today.' Whereupon he slaps his forehead, exclaims, 'I'm so sorry, I'd quite forgotten!' and is about to go out and get her some flowers. She, however, is inconsolable, seeing her husband's forgetfulness as proof that she no longer occupies the place in his thoughts that she once enjoyed. This Mrs L. bumped into my wife a couple of days ago, told her how well she was feeling, and asked after me. Some years ago she was a patient of mine.

Another link: I did indeed once write something like a *monograph* about a plant, namely an essay about the *coca plant*, which drew the attention of K. Koller to the anaesthetizing property of cocaine. I had myself touched on this use of the alkaloid in my publication but lacked the thoroughness to go further into the matter. In this connection, it occurs to me that on the morning of the day following the dream (I did not find time to interpret it until that evening) I thought about cocaine in a kind of waking fantasy. If I ever got glaucoma, I fantasized, I should travel to Berlin, ask my friend to recommend an eye surgeon, and have that surgeon operate on me *incognito*. The surgeon, unaware of the identity of his patient, would once again boast of how easy this operation had become to perform since the introduction of cocaine; I should never once let my face betray the fact that I had had a part in that discovery myself. The fantasy prompted other thoughts such as how awkward it is for a doctor to ask colleagues to provide medical services for himself. The Berlin eye surgeon would not know who I was, so I should be able to pay him like any other patient. It was only after this day-dream had come to me that I became aware that a memory of a specific experience lay behind it. The fact was, shortly after Koller's discovery my father contracted glaucoma; he was operated on by my friend Dr Königstein, with Dr Koller providing the cocaine anaesthesis, in connection with which he pointed out that this case brought together all three of the people who had had a hand in the introduction of cocaine.

This in turn prompts another thought: when had I last been reminded of this cocaine story? It had been a few days earlier, when I had received a copy of the commemorative publication with which grateful students had celebrated the jubilee of their teacher and head of laboratory. Among the laboratory's claims to fame I found listed the fact that it was there that the discovery of the anaesthetizing property of cocaine by K. Koller had occurred. At this point I suddenly become aware that my dream has a connection with an experience of the evening before. I had just accompanied Dr Königstein home, having become involved with him in a discussion concerning a subject that excites me keenly every time it comes up. As I stood talking to him in the hallway of his apartment building, we were joined by Professor *Gärtner* and his young wife. I could not help but congratulate them both on how *blooming* they looked. Now, Professor Gärtner is one of the authors of the *Festschrift* I just mentioned [the 'commemorative publication'] and may well have put me in mind of it. And Mrs L., whose birthday disappointment I mentioned earlier, had come up in my conversation with Dr Königstein, albeit in a different context.

Let me try to interpret the other determining characteristics of the dream-content as well. A *dried specimen* of the plant accompanies the monograph as if it were a *herbarium*. The herbarium takes me back to my schooldays. Our headmaster once called the senior pupils together to give them the school herbarium to examine and clean. Little *worms* had been found – bookworms. He appears to have shown no confidence in my assistance since he gave only a few sheets to me. I still remember that they contained Crucifers. I was never on particularly good terms with botany. In my botanical preliminary examination I was again given a Crucifer to identify –

and failed to recognize it. I should have been in trouble, had not my knowledge of theory come to my rescue. Crucifers bring me to Compositae. Actually, the artichoke is also a member of the Compositae, in fact the one I might call my *favourite flower*. Being a nicer person than myself, my wife regularly brings this favourite flower home from market for me.

I can see the monograph I have written *lying before me*. This too has a bearing. My clairvoyant friend wrote to me yesterday from Berlin, 'Your *dream-book is preoccupying me a great deal. I see it lying before me, finished, and I am leafing through it.*' How I envy him his gift! If only I could already see it lying before me, finished!

The tipped-in colour plate: When I was a medical student I suffered from the impulse of only wanting to learn from *monographs*. At the time, despite my limited means, I subscribed to several medical archives whose *colour plates* were my delight. I was proud of this leaning towards thoroughness. When I then began publishing myself, I also had to draw the plates for my treatises, and I know that one of them came out so wretchedly that a well-meaning colleague teased me about it. In this connection (I cannot think how) a very early memory of my younger days also comes back to me. Once, as a joke, my father gave me and my eldest sister a book with *colour plates* (description of a journey in Persia) to destroy. Educationally, it would have been hard to justify. I was five at the time, my sister less than three, and the image of us two children rapturously pulling that book to pieces (like *plucking an artichoke* leaf by leaf, I have to say) is virtually the only concrete memory left to me from that period in my life. When I became a student, there developed in me a marked predilection for collecting and owning books (like the inclination to study from monographs, a *fancy*, as already comes out in the dream-thoughts regarding cyclamen and artichoke). I became a *bookworm* (see the *herbarium*). I have always, since I have been reflecting about myself, traced this first passion in my life back to that childhood impression, or rather I recognized that that childhood scene was a 'covering memory' for my later bibliophilia.[4] Of course, I also learned at an early age that passions [*Leidenschaften*] can easily lead to suffering [*Leiden*].

When I was seventeen years old I had a substantial account at a bookshop and no money with which to settle it, and my father had little sympathy with the excuse that my inclinations had plumped for nothing worse. However, mentioning this later experience of my younger years brings me straight back to the conversation with my friend Dr Königstein. Because that conversation, too, which had taken place on the evening of the dream-day, was about the same reproach as was levelled at me back then, namely that I indulged my *fancies* to excess.

For reasons that have no place here I intend to pursue the interpretation of this dream no further but simply to indicate the route leading to it. During the work of interpretation I am reminded of the conversation with Dr Königstein – not once but from several standpoints simultaneously. When I consider the things that were touched on in that conversation, the meaning of the dream becomes clear to me. All the chains of thought begun here – about my wife's and my own fancies, about cocaine, about the difficulties surrounding medical treatment among colleagues, about my predilection for monographic studies and my neglect of certain subjects such as botany – all this finds its continuation here and feeds one of the streams of the many-branched discussion. Once again, dream takes on the character of a justification, a plea for my rights – like the dream I analysed first, the one about Irma's injection. Indeed, it continues the theme broached there, discussing it in terms of the fresh material that has accumulated in the interval between the two dreams. Even dream's apparently indifferent form of expression acquires a new emphasis. This time it means: Yes, I am the man who wrote this valuable and successful treatise (about cocaine), rather as I had asserted at the time by way of self-justification: Look, I am a competent, hard-working student; in both cases, then: I am justified in doing this. However, I can decline to continue the task of interpretation at this point since what prompted me to disclose the dream was purely my intention to study, through the medium of an example, the relationship between dream-content and the triggering experience of the previous day. As long as the only thing I know about this dream is its manifest content, only one link between the dream and a daytime impression will be obvious to me; once I have done the analysis, a second dream-source emerges from a different experience of the same day. The first impression to which the dream relates is a trivial, incidental one. I see, displayed in a shop window, a book whose title briefly excites me but whose contents would doubtless be of little interest. The second experience was of high psychical value; I had had probably an hour's spirited conversation with my ophthalmologist friend, making suggestions to him that inevitably affected us both closely and that aroused memories within myself in connection with which I became aware of the most varied arousals of my inner being. Furthermore, that conversation had been broken off incomplete because acquaintances joined us. So how do the day's two experiences relate to each other and to the following night's dream?

In the dream-content, I find only an allusion to the trivial impression and can therefore confirm that dream has a preference for including life's trivialities in its content. In dream-interpretation, on the other hand, everything leads to the important, rightly arousing experience. If I judge the meaning of a dream, its only correct meaning, by the latent content that analysis has brought to light, I unexpectedly make a new and important discovery. I now witness the collapse of the riddle that dream is interested only in the worthless scraps of daily life; I must also counter the claim that the life of the waking mind does not continue in dream and that dream therefore squanders psychical activity on silly material. The opposite is true: what preoccupied us during the day also dominates our dream-thoughts, and we take the trouble to dream only in connection with such materials as would have given us food for thought during the day.

The most obvious explanation of the fact that I still dream about the trivial daytime impression, whereas it was the rightly stimulating impression that caused me to dream, is presumably that here we have another phenomenon of dream-distortion such as we previously traced back to a psychical power operating in terms of censorship. My remembering the monograph about the genus Cyclamen is used as if it was an *allusion* to the conversation with my friend in much the same way as, in the dream of the frustrated supper-party, mention of the dreamer's female acquaintance was represented by the 'smoked-salmon' allusion. The only question is: through what intermediaries can the monograph impression be brought into an allusive relationship to the conversation with the ophthalmologist (because such a relationship is not at first apparent)? In the example of the foiled supper, the relationship is given in advance: 'smoked salmon' as the friend's favourite food falls quite naturally within the range of ideas that the friend's person is likely to evoke in the dreamer. In this new example, we are dealing with two discrete impressions that at first have nothing in common except that they occurred on the same day. The monograph I notice in the morning; the conversation I have in the evening. The answer suggested by analysis is this: such links between the two impressions, which were initially not present, were developed subsequently between the ideational content of the former and the ideational content of the latter. I highlighted the intermediaries involved when I wrote the analysis down. In the absence of outside influences, the only notion capable of linking up with the idea of the Cyclamen monograph was the fact of this being my wife's favourite flower – and possibly also the reminder of Mrs L.'s missed bunch of flowers. I do not believe these secondary thoughts would have sufficed to provoke a dream.

> There needs no ghost, my lord, come from the grave
> To tell us this

it says in *Hamlet*. But lo and behold, in the course of analysing the dream I am reminded that the man who interrupted our conversation is called *Gärtner* [or 'Gardener'] and that I found his wife *blooming*; in fact, it occurs to me now, belatedly, that a patient of mine who goes by the lovely name of *Flora* was for a while the focus of our conversation. What must have happened is that it was through these intermediaries from the realm of botanical ideas that the link between the two daytime experiences, the trivial one and the arousing one, came about. Then other connections appeared (the one with cocaine, which is able quite justifiably to mediate between the person of Dr Königstein and a botanical monograph written by myself) that reinforce this merging of the two ideational realms into one in such a way that a fragment of the first experience could now be used to allude to the second.

I am prepared for this explanation to be challenged as arbitrary or artificial. What would have happened if Dr *Gärtner* and his wife of the *blooming* appearance had not come along or if the patient we were discussing had been called not *Flora* but *Anna*? Yet the answer is simple. If these thought-connections had not arisen, in all likelihood others would have been chosen. It is easy to manufacture such links – as indeed the joke questions and riddles with which we enliven the day adequately prove. The dominion of jest knows no bounds. To take the argument a step further, had it proved impossible to manufacture satisfactorily ample connections linking the two experiences of the day, the dream would have turned out differently; a different trivial impression of the day, vast numbers of which present themselves to us and are forgotten, would for the purposes of dream have taken the place of the 'monograph', would have found a connection with the substance of the conversation, and would have represented this in the dream-content. Since this was the fate of no other impression but that of the monograph, presumably the monograph was best suited to form the connection. One need never, like Lessing's Hänschen Schlau, be amazed that 'it's only the wealthy in this world who have most money'.

The psychological process whereby, as we have described it, the trivial experience comes to stand for the psychically more valuable one will inevitably strike us as questionable and disconcerting. In a later passage we shall find ourselves confronted with the task of bringing the peculiarities of this apparently incorrect operation closer to our understanding. Here we are concerned only with the outcome of a process that innumerable, regularly recurring experiences in connection with dream-analysis have compelled us to accept. However, the process is as if a *shift* (of psychical emphasis, let us say) occurred by way of this intermediary until ideas that initially carried a low-intensity charge, by borrowing from those initially carrying a high-intensity charge, acquire sufficient power to enable them to force their way into consciousness. Shifts of this kind come as no surprise to us where it is a question of inserting quantities of affect or motor actions generally. That the spinster still living on her own transfers her affection to animals, that the bachelor becomes a passionate collector, that the soldier defends a strip of coloured material (the flag) to his last drop of blood, that in a love relationship a handshake prolonged by a matter of seconds generates bliss or, as in *Othello*, a mislaid handkerchief provokes an angry outburst – these are all examples of psychical shifts that seem to us incontestable. But that by the same avenue and following the same principles a decision should be made about what reaches consciousness in us and what is kept back from it – in other words, what we think – that strikes us as morbid, and we call it a mistake of logic when it occurs in the waking state. Let me reveal here, as the outcome of observations we shall be making later, that the psychical process we have noted as dream-displacement in fact turns out not to be something morbidly disturbed, although it does differ from the normal; it turns out to be a process of a more *primary* nature.

That is to say, we interpret the fact that dream-content takes into itself leftovers of trivial experiences as an expression of *dream-distortion* (as a result of a shift or displacement) and remind the reader that we have recognized dream-distortion as a consequence of the transit censorship existing between two psychical authorities. In this connection, we expect dream-analysis regularly to reveal to us the true, psychically significant dream-source from daily life, remembering which shifted the emphasis on to the trivial memory. This view places us in total opposition to Robert's theory [1886], which for us has become unusable. The fact that Robert was trying to explain is not actually a fact at all; assuming that it is rests on a misunderstanding, on neglecting to substitute the true meaning of a dream for the ostensible dream-content. A further objection can be levelled against the Robert theory: if the function of dream really was to rid our memory, by performing particular psychical work, of the [in the physiological sense] 'waste products' of the day's recollections, our sleep would inevitably be more tormented and taken up with more strenuous work than we can claim in relation to our waking intellectual life. Because the number of neutral impressions of the day from which we should need to shield our memory is clearly immeasurable; the night would not be long enough to deal with them all. It is very much more likely that forgetting the trivial impressions takes place without the active intervention of our mental powers.

Nevertheless, we sense a warning against dismissing Robert's ideas out of hand. We have left unexplained the fact that one of the day's (and I am talking about the last day) neutral impressions makes a regular contribution to dream-content. The links between that impression and the true dream-source in the unconscious do not always exist in advance; as we have seen, they are manufactured only subsequently, during the process of dream-work, as it were in the service of the proposed shift. So there must be some compulsion present to initiate connections particularly in the direction of the still-vivid (albeit neutral) impression, which must exhibit a special propensity for the purpose as a result of some property or other. Otherwise, surely it would be just as easy to have the dream-thoughts shift their emphasis to some unimportant component of their own circle of ideas?

The following experiences are capable of guiding us towards an explanation here. If a day has brought us two or more experiences worthy of stimulating dreams, dream combines the mention of both in a single whole; it obeys a *compulsion to form an entity from them.* Here is an example: One summer afternoon I climbed into a railway carriage in which I met two people known to me but strangers to each other. One was an influential colleague, the other a member of a distinguished family in which I had some involvement as a physician. I introduced the two gentlemen to each other; however, communication between them took the long way round via myself, with the result that I found myself talking now with one, now with the other, but dealing with the same topic of conversation. I asked the colleague to lend his recommendation to a mutual acquaintance who had just begun to practise as a doctor. The colleague replied that he was confident the young man was a good doctor but afraid that his unprepossessing manner would make it difficult for him to gain access to upper-class households. To which I replied that it was precisely for that reason his recommendation was required. Shortly afterwards I enquired of my other travelling companion how his aunt (the mother of one of my patients) was bearing up, knowing her to be very ill at the time and confined to her bed. In the night following that journey I dreamed that the young friend for whom I had requested protection was on his feet in an elegant drawing-room, before a select audience that my dream crammed with all the respectable, wealthy people I knew, delivering an obituary oration, which he accompanied with all manner of sophisticated gestures, for the elderly (in my dream she was already dead) aunt of my second travelling companion. (I admit quite frankly that I had not been on good terms with the lady in question.) My dream, in other words, had again found links between the two impressions of the day and used them to compose a single situation.

On the basis of many similar experiences I must advance the proposition that dream-work is under a kind of compulsion to combine, in dream, all available sources of dream-stimulus into a single entity.[5]

I should now like to draw into the discussion the question of whether the dream-triggering source to which analysis leads must always be a still-vivid (and significant) occurrence or whether an inner experience (the memory of a psychically valuable event, say, or a train of thought) may act as dream-trigger. The answer provided by many analyses in the most categorical fashion indicates the latter. The dream-trigger may be an inner process that daytime thought-work has somehow revivified. This is the moment, I think, to bring together schematically the various requirements that mark out dream-sources.

The dream-source may be:

a)   A still-vivid, psychically significant experience that is directly represented in dream.[6]

b)   Several still-vivid significant experiences that dream combines into an entity.[7]

c) One or more still-vivid significant experiences that are represented in the dream-content by the mention of an experience occurring at the same time, but a neutral [*indifferent*] one.[8]

d) A significant inner experience (memory, train of thought) that is *regularly* represented in dream by the mention of a still-vivid but neutral impression.[9]

As we see, so far as dream-interpretation is concerned, in every case the requirement is met that a component of the dream-content echoes a still-vivid impression of the previous day. This constituent element, which is destined to be represented in dream, may either belong to the ideational sphere of the dream-trigger proper (and either, be it noted, as an essential or as an unimportant component of the same) or have its roots in the sphere of a neutral impression that through a richer or poorer association has become associated with the sphere of the dream-trigger. The apparent plurality of requirements here results from the *alternative* that *a shift or displacement has or has not taken place*, and we note at this point that such an alternative makes it as easy for us to explain the contrasts of dream as the series of states from partial to complete wakefulness of the brain cells makes it for the medical theory of dream (see above, pp. 90ff.).

Another thing one notices in connection with this list of requirements is that the psychically valuable but not still-vivid element (the train of thought, the memory) may for the purposes of dream-formation be replaced by a still-vivid but psychically neutral element, provided only that the two requirements are adhered to that 1) the dream-content can be linked to still-vivid experience and 2) the dream-trigger remains a psychically valuable process. In only a single instance (namely *a*) are both requirements supplied by the same impression. If one further bears in mind that the same neutral impressions as are used for the dream, so long as they are still-vivid, forfeit that suitability as soon as they become a day (at most several days) older, one is obliged to accept that the freshness of an impression itself lends it a certain psychical value for dream-formation that is in some way equal to the valency[10] of affect-accentuated memories or trains of thought. Only later, in the context of certain psychological considerations, shall we be able to guess in what this value of *still-vivid* impressions with regard to dream-formation may have its roots.[11]

Incidentally, our attention is directed in this context to the fact that, at night and unnoticed by our conscious mind, the stuff of memory and imagination may undergo important changes. The demand that we 'sleep on' a matter before making a final decision about it is clearly quite justified. However, we note that at this point we have crossed over from the psychology of dreaming to that of sleep – a step that we shall have further occasion to take from time to time.[12]

But there is an objection that threatens to overturn the last few conclusions. If neutral impressions can make their way into dream-content only if they are still vivid, how is it that we also find in dream-content elements from earlier life periods that, at the time when they were still vivid, did not (according to Strümpell [1877]) possess any psychical value, i.e. should have been long forgotten – elements, in other words, that are neither fresh in the mind nor psychically significant?

The objection can be dealt with completely if one takes as one's basis the findings of psychoanalysis in connection with neurotics. The solution, in fact, is that the shift replacing psychically important material with material that is neutral (for dreaming as for thinking) here occurred back in those early periods of life and has since become fixed in memory. The originally neutral elements are no longer neutral once they have, through displacement, taken on the valency of psychically significant material. What really is still neutral can no longer be reproduced in dream.

It will rightly be concluded from the foregoing remarks that I am advancing the claim that there are no neutral dream-triggers, therefore no innocuous dreams either. This is in all strictness and exclusiveness my view, leaving aside the dreams of children and possibly the brief dream-reactions to nocturnal sensations. Otherwise, what a person dreams is either manifestly recognizable as psychically significant or it is distorted, in which case it can only be assessed after a full dream-interpretation, whereupon it will again become recognizable as significant. Dream never bothers with minor matters; we do not let details disturb our sleep.[13] The dreams that seem innocuous turn out to be evil when one takes the trouble to interpret them; if the reader will forgive the expression, there is 'more to them than meets the eye'. Since this is another point in connection with which I can expect contradiction, and since I welcome the opportunity to show dream-distortion at work, I should like to take a series of *'innocuous dreams'* from my collection and subject them to analysis.

I

A shrewd, sensitive young lady, though one who in life, too, is among those of whom it is said that 'still waters run deep', narrates as follows: *I dreamed that I arrive at market too late and get nothing from the butcher or from the vegetable woman.* An innocuous dream, certainly, but a dream never looks like that; I ask her to give me details. She then reports as follows: *She goes to market with her cook, who carries the basket. The butcher tells her, after she has asked for something, 'That's no longer to be had', and he wants to give her something else, saying, 'That is good too.' She declines and goes to the vegetable woman, who tries to sell her a peculiar vegetable done up in bundles but black in colour. She says, 'That's new to me, I shan't have any.'*

The dream's daytime link is simple enough. She really had arrived late at the market and come away empty-handed. *The meat stall was closed already*, is what springs to mind as a description of the occurrence. But wait – is that not a very vulgar expression (or rather its opposite) that refers to a certain negligence in a man's dress?[14] The dreamer did not use these words, by the way; she may have avoided them. Let us investigate the meaning of the details contained in the dream.

Where something in a dream has the character of a speech, i.e. is spoken or heard rather than simply thought (a distinction that can usually be drawn with certainty), it originates from things said in waking life – but treated as raw material, of course, fragmented, slightly altered, and above all wrenched completely out of context.[15] In interpreting a dream, one approach is to start out from such speeches. So when the butcher says, *'That's no longer to be had'*, where does his speech come from? From myself; a few days before this I had told her 'that the earliest childhood experiences are *no longer to be had* as such but are replaced by "transferences" and dreams during analysis'. I am the butcher, then, and she is rejecting such transferences of old ways of thinking and feeling on to the present. And her own speech in the dream (*'That's new to me, I shan't have any'*), what is that based on? For the purposes of analysis, this needs to be split into two. *'That's new to me'* was something she had said to her cook the day before during a row with her, but at the time she had added, *'Behave yourself!'* Here is a tangible instance of displacement. Of the two things she had flung at her cook, it was the insignificant one she taken into her dream; however, the one she had suppressed (*'Behave yourself'*) is the only one that fits with the rest of the dream-content. That is something one might call out after someone who is making rude suggestions and has forgotten to 'close the meat stall'. That we really are on the trail of the meaning is revealed subsequently by the harmony with the allusions made in the business with the vegetable woman. A vegetable that is sold in bundles (elongated in shape, as she adds subsequently) and also black – what else can that be but a dream-conflation of asparagus and black radish? Asparagus is not something I need interpret to initiates of either sex, but the other vegetable, too, seems to me to point to the same sexual theme as we guessed at the outset,[16] when for the dream-narration we wanted to substitute: the meat stall was closed. It is not a matter of recognizing the meaning of this dream completely; we know already that it is rich in meaning and not by any means innocuous.[17]

II

Another innocuous dream by the same patient, in a sense a counterpart to the previous one: *Her husband asks, 'Shouldn't we have the piano tuned?' She: 'It's not worth it, the hammers need re-covering anyway.'* Again, repetition of a real event of the previous day. Her husband did ask such a question, and she replied to much that effect. But what is the significance of her dreaming it? She says of the piano that it is in fact a *dreadful old box* with a *terrible sound*, a thing that her husband had possessed before their marriage,[18] and so on. But the key to the solution emerges only with the speech: *'It's not worth it.'* This comes from a visit made to a friend the day before, when she was asked to take off her jacket and declined with the words: *'It's not worth it. I have to leave soon.'* In narrating this I am forcibly reminded that yesterday, while I was working on her analysis, she suddenly put a hand to her jacket, on which a button had come undone. It is as if she wanted to say, *'Please don't look, it's not worth it.'* The *Kasten* ['old box'] expands to become a *Brustkasten* ['thorax' or 'chest'], and the interpretation of the dream leads straight back to the time of her physical development, when she began to be unhappy about the shape her body was assuming. And it presumably leads back to earlier times if we consider the *'dreadful'* and the *'terrible sound'* and recall how often the small hemispheres of the female body (as opposite and as substitute) deputize for the large ones – in allusion and in dream.

III

I interrupt this sequence to insert a brief innocuous dream had by a young man. He dreamed *that he is putting on his winter coat again, which is terrible*. What prompts this dream, according to him, is the sudden return of cold weather. A more discerning judgement, however, will note that the two short fragments of the dream do not fit together very well, because what could be so 'terrible' about wearing the heavy or thick coat in cold weather? To the detriment of the 'innocuous' nature of the dream, the first thing he thinks of in his analysis reminds him that a woman told him in confidence yesterday that her last child owes its existence to a burst condom. He now reconstructs what he thought on hearing this: A thin condom is dangerous, a thick one no good. A condom is rightly referred to [in German] as an *Überzieher*, since one 'pulls' it 'over', and an *Überzieher* is another name for a light overcoat. An occurrence such as the one reported by the lady would certainly be 'terrible' for an unmarried man.

Let us return to our dreamer of innocuous dreams.

IV

She is sticking a candle into the candelabrum; the candle is broken, though, so will not stand properly. The girls at school call her clumsy; the teacher, however, says it is not her fault.

Here again there is a real occasion; yesterday she really did insert a candle in the candelabrum; however, this one was not broken. The symbolism used here is transparent. The candle is an object that can stimulate the female genitalia; if it is broken and will not stand properly, it means that the man is impotent (*'it is not her fault'*). But is the carefully brought-up young woman, to whom everything unseemly is a closed book, familiar with this use of the candle? It so happens that she is still able to indicate the experience as a result of which she came to that knowledge. Out rowing on the Rhine, she and her husband were passed by a boat full of students, who with huge contentment were singing or rather shouting a song about the Queen of Sweden, some closed shutters and a so-called 'Apollo' candle . . .

She failed to hear or could not understand the last word. Her husband had to supply the requested explanation. The lines of the song were then replaced in the dream-content by an innocuous memory of a task that she once performed *clumsily* at boarding-school – by dint of the shared element of *closed shutters*. The connection of the masturbation theme with impotence is clear enough. 'Apollo' in the latent dream-content links this dream with an earlier one featuring the virginal Pallas. Innocuous? Not by a long chalk.

V

Lest anyone form too easy an idea of the conclusions drawn from dreams as regards the true-life circumstances of the dreamer, let me add one more dream that is also apparently innocuous and stems from the same person. *I dreamed something*, she reports, *that I had actually done that day, namely filled a small suitcase so full of books that I had trouble closing it, and I dreamed it the way it really happened*. Here the narrator herself places the main emphasis on the correspondence between dream and reality. All such verdicts about dream and comments on dream, although they have created a place for themselves in waking thought, actually belong (as a general rule) in latent dream-content, as subsequent examples will make clear to us. So we are being told that what the dream narrates did actually occur on the previous day. Now, it would take too long to explain by what route we arrive at the idea of drawing upon the English language as an aid to interpretation. Suffice it to say that we are once again talking about a small *box* (see the dream of the small child in the carton above, p. 165) filled so full that nothing more will go in it. At least nothing bad this time.

In all these 'innocuous' dreams, the sexual factor as motive for censorship is strikingly in evidence. Yet this is a topic of fundamental importance that we must put to one side.

Notes

1. Clearly the view taken by Roberts [1886] that the purpose of dream is to disburden memory of the day's worthless impressions is no longer tenable if there appear in dream with any frequency unimportant memory images

from our childhood. One would have to conclude that dream is in the habit of performing its allotted task most inadequately.

2. [There's a bit of translator's sleight of hand here, so let me explain. Freud's title for this section is '*Das Rezente und das Indifferente im Traum*'. I am concerned to highlight the fact that 'recent' and 'indifferent' (the English words normally used to translate these terms) are what language teachers like to call 'false friends'; they do not entirely coincide with their apparent equivalents.

Of the German words employed, '*rezent*' is in fact quite uncommon; in biology and geology, it is a technical term denoting a period of time (and everything belonging to it) extending from a moment in the near past *up to and including the present*. Various dictionaries translate it as 'living', 'fresh'. ('*Rezent*' also has a secondary connotation that is more likely to evoke a pungent cheese than a temporal relationship.) '*Indifferent*', in addition to its ordinary meaning, is also (in English, too) a technical term in the natural sciences denoting 'neutral' or 'inert'. It seems to me impossible that an educated man, writing in Vienna in 1899, will have been unaware of these connotations. When he used these words, their connotations will have been present to his mind. To highlight this fact, I have chosen in this important sub-title to transfer the terms to the domain of electricity (as I do in connection with Freud's use of '*Besetzung*'), though elsewhere in the text I render '*rezent*' as 'still vivid'. The point is, Freud is saying that some things in the past retain an ability to influence mental activity in the present (by forming associations, for instance) while others do not.

If I may cite two pieces of evidence in support of this contention, in one of Freud's own notes (p. 420, note 73,) Rank is quoted as placing the word '*rezent*' in inverted commas, which perhaps suggests that Freud's use of it had an extra dimension, and in Freud's text (Chapter 7) he writes '. . . *auf sinnliche Qualitäten rezenter und kürzlich erfolgte Eindrücke* . . .', which I translate as '. . . to sensory qualities of still-vivid impressions recently received' (p. 564) but which past translators all fudge.

In this translation, therefore, the reader will find '*rezent*' rendered as 'still-vivid' and '*indifferent*' as 'indifferent' – the 'friend' being in this case slightly less false in that it does in fact bear the 'neutral/inert' connotation (in a psychoanalytical context, 'incapable of forming associations') that must surely have been present to Freud's mind when he wrote it.]

3. Hermann Swoboda (see Chapter 1, section H, note 2) tells how the biological intervals of 23 and 28 days discovered by Wilhelm Fliess can to a great extent be transferred to what happens in the mind; in particular,

he claims that these times are crucial as regards the appearance of dream-elements in dreams. The interpretation of dreams would not be materially affected if such were to be proven, but as regards the origin of dream-material there would be an additional source. It so happens that I have recently carried out certain investigations into dreams of my own in order to test the applicability of the 'period theory' to dream-material, choosing to this end particularly striking elements of dream-content whose appearance in life could be determined with chronological certitude.

I DREAM OF 1/2 OCTOBER 1910

(Fragment) ... *Somewhere in Italy. Three little girls are showing me some small treasures, as in an antique shop, sitting in my lap as they do so. Of one of the pieces I say, 'That one you have from me'. As I say it, I have a clear view of a profile mask with the clear-cut features of Savonarola.*

When did I last see a portrait of Savonarola? According to my travel-journal, I was in Florence on 4 and 5 September; there I had the idea of showing my travelling companion the medallion with the fanatical monk's features on it set in the pavement of the Piazza Signoria, marking the spot where he was burned to death, and I believe that on the morning of the 5th I did in fact draw it to his attention. Now, between that impression and its recurrence in dream a total of 27 + 1 days elapsed – what Fliess would call a 'feminine period'. However, unfortunately for the evidential value of this example I have to point out that *on the dream-day itself* I had a visit (the first since my return) from the capable but rather lugubrious-looking colleague for whom some years before this I had coined the nickname 'Rabbi Savonarola'. He introduced me to a patient who had been in an accident on the Pontebba railway, on which I had myself travelled eight days earlier. In so doing, he led me to think of my last Italian trip. The appearance in the dream-content of the striking 'Savonarola' element is explained by this visit from my colleague on the dream-day, depriving the twenty-eight-day interval of its significance in terms of the derivation thereof.

II DREAM OF 10/11 OCTOBER

I am back doing chemistry in the university laboratory. Counsellor L. invites me to another place and goes ahead of me out into the corridor, bearing a lamp or some other instrument as if sharp-wittedly ['scharf-sinning'] *(?) (sharp-sightedly?* ['scharfsichtig?']*) before him in his raised hand; his whole posture is curious, the way his head is stretched forward. We then cross an open space and come* ... (rest forgotten).

The most striking part of this dream-content is the way in which Counsellor L. carries the lamp (or magnifying-glass) before him, his eye peering fixedly into the distance. I have not seen L. for many years now, but I am already aware that he is simply a substitute for another, greater figure, namely [the statue of] Archimedes near the Arethusa spring in *Syracuse*, who is standing exactly like the man in the dream as he holds up the burning-glass to peer at the besieging Roman army. When did I first (and most recently) see that monument? According to my notes it was on 17 September, in the evening, and from that day to the dream it was true: 13 + 10 = 23 days had elapsed – a 'masculine period', according to Fliess.

Here too, unfortunately, pursuing the interpretation of the dream makes this connection seem somewhat less imperative. What prompted the dream was the news, received on the dream-day, that the hospital in whose lecture-theatre I was currently making guest appearances was soon to be moved elsewhere. I assumed that the new locality would be very inconveniently situated, and I told myself that it would be as if I had no lecture-theatre available to me at all. From there my thoughts must have gone back to the beginnings of my lecturing career, when I really did not have a lecture-theatre and my efforts to obtain one had met with little sympathy from the wealthy counsellors and professors. At the time I had gone to L., who then held the high office of dean and whom I considered a patron, to complain of my plight to him. He promised to help me but was not heard from again. In the dream he is Archimedes, who gives me ποῦ στῶ 'somewhere to brace my feet' and himself leads me to the other locality. That dream-thoughts are strangers neither to vindictiveness nor to bigheadedness will be easily guessed by anyone who knows anything about interpreting dreams. I have to say, though, that but for this dream-content Archimedes would scarcely have made it into that night's dream; I am not at all sure whether the powerful and still-vivid impression of the statue in Syracuse would not equally well have asserted itself at a different time-interval.

III DREAM OF 2/3 OCTOBER 1910

(Fragment) ... *Something about Professor Oser, having drawn up the menu for me himself, which has a very soothing effect* (other parts forgotten).

The dream is a reaction to a stomach-upset, experienced that day, that had led me to consider whether I should not ask a colleague to prescribe me a diet. My assigning the task (in dream) to Oser, who had died that summer, had to do with the death (which had taken place very recently, on 1 October) of another university teacher whom I held in very high regard. But when had Oser died, and when had I learned of his death? According to the newspaper, [he died] on 22 August; since I was in Holland at the time and having the *Wiener Zeitung* [Vienna's main daily newspaper] regularly forwarded to me, I must have read the announcement of his death on 24 or 25 August. However, this interval no longer corresponds to one of the periods, comprising as it does 7 + 30 + 2 = 39 days or possibly 40 days. I have no recollection of hearing about or thinking about Oser in the mean time.

The fact is, intervals like that, which are of no use to the period theory without more work being done on them, arise out of my dreams with incomparably greater frequency than regular ones. I find the only constancy (as I say in the text) in the link to an impression received on the dream-day itself.

4. See my essay 'Über Deckerinnerungen' in *Monatsschrift für Psychiatrie und Neurologie*, 1899 ['Screen memories', *Standard Edition*, vol. III, p. 301; there is a new translation by David McLintock in the New Penguin Freud, *The Uncanny*, London 2003].

[The usual translation of Freud's *Deckerinnerungen* is indeed 'screen memories'. I choose to call them 'covering memories' because, to the modern mind, a 'screen' is more likely to evoke a surface on which things are projected than a piece of furniture designed to hide things (presumably the source of Freud's metaphor for the vivid childhood memories that overlay other, more important, subconscious ones); see Jean Laplanche and Jean-Bertrand Pontalis, *The Language of Psychoanalysis* (1973) (tr. Donald Nicholson-Smith), London, reprinted 1988, pp. 410–11.]

5. The tendency of dream-work simultaneously to meld interesting available facts into a single plot has already been remarked on by a number of authors, e.g. by Delage [1891], p. 41, and Delboeuf [1885], who refers to it as *rapprochement forcé* (p. 237).

6. Dream of Irma's injection; dream of the friend who is my uncle.

7. Dream of the young doctor's obituary oration.

8. Dream of the botanical monograph.

9. Most of my patients' dreams during analysis are of this kind.

10. [*Wertigkeit*; here Freud borrows a technical term from chemistry (now also used in linguistics) denoting the number and type of bonds that a substance may form with others.]

11. See below, Chapter 7, on 'transference', pp. 569ff.

12. An important contribution on the role of the still-vivid in dream-formation is made by O. Pötzl in an article that offers a huge number of links ('Experimentell erregte Traumbilder in ihren Beziehungen zum

indirekten Sehen' ['Experimentally stimulated dream-images in their connections with indirect sight'] in *Zeitschrift für die ges. Neurologie und
Psychiatrie*, XXXVII, 1917). Pötzl asked various experimental subjects to
capture in drawings what they had consciously retained from an image
displayed tachystoscopically [or 'flashed up']. He then turned his attention
to what the subject dreamed the following night and again had the subject
represent suitable portions of that dream in a drawing. The result was
unmistakable: the details of the displayed image that the experimental
subject had not taken in supplied material for dream-formation, whereas
the details that had been consciously perceived and subsequently recorded
in the drawing made after the image had been displayed did not reappear
in the manifest dream-content. The material taken up by dream-work was
processed by it in the familiar 'arbitrary' (better: self-possessed, magisterial)
fashion in the service of the dream-forming tendencies. The ideas stimulated by Pötzl's study go well beyond the intentions of the kind of dream-
interpretation attempted in this book. Let me just briefly point out how far
removed this new way of studying dream-formation experimentally is from
the earlier, clumsy technique that consisted of introducing into the dream-
content stimuli that themselves disturbed sleep.

13. H[avelock] Ellis, the kindly critic of *Interpreting Dreams*, writes [in
The World of Dreams, London 1911] (p. 166): 'This is the point at which
many of us are no longer able to follow Freud.' The only trouble is, H.
Ellis has undertaken no analyses of dreams and refuses to believe how
unwarranted it is to judge from manifest dream-content.

14. [Yes, Austrians do indeed sometimes say, when they notice a man's
fly-buttons are undone, that 'the meat stall is open'.]

15. On the subject of speeches in dream, see also Chapter 6, 'Dream-Work'.
Only one writer appears to have recognized the origin of dream-speeches;
this is Delboeuf [1885] (p. 226), who compares them to '*clichés*'.

16. [I have omitted a parenthesis here (– *als Zuruf: Schwarzer, rett' dich* –)
that is wholly obscure to me. It would clearly require a great deal of
explanation, but it seems to me to add nothing to the sense.]

17. For those with a thirst for knowledge, let me add that, concealed
behind the dream there is a fantasy of improper, sexually provocative
behaviour on my part and defence on the part of the lady. Anyone who
finds this interpretation incredible I would remind of the many cases where
doctors have experienced such complaints from hysterical women for whom
the same fantasy, rather than appearing in distorted form and as a dream,
becomes plainly conscious and delusive. This dream marked the beginning
of the patient's psychoanalytical treatment. Only later did I come to under-

stand that with it she was repeating the initial trauma from which the neurosis proceeded, and I have since found the same behaviour in other persons who, having been exposed to sexual assaults in childhood, wanted now, as it were, to go through them again in dream.

18. A replacement by the opposite, as will become clear to us after interpretation.

B *The infantile as dream-source*

Along with all the authors of the literature (with the exception of Robert [1886]), we place third in the list of the distinguishing features of dream-content the fact that dreams may reproduce impressions from the earliest years of life to which in the waking state memory apparently has no access. How rarely or how frequently this occurs is understandably difficult to judge since, after waking, the relevant ingredients of dream are not identified in terms of their origin. The proof that childhood impressions are involved here must therefore be furnished objectively, and for this conditions are rarely favourable. Particular evidential value attaches to a story that A. Maury tells of a man who decided one day, after a twenty-year absence, to revisit the town of his birth. On the night before the trip he dreamed that he was in a place he did not know at all and that there, in the street, he met a man he likewise did not know but with whom he had a conversation. Once back in his native town, he was able to confirm that the strange place really did exist (it was a village in the immediate environs), and the strange man turned out to be a friend of his late father who lived there – compelling proof, surely, that he had seen both man and village in his childhood. Incidentally, this should be interpreted as an impatience-dream like those of the girl with the concert ticket in her handbag (see above, p. 164), the child whose father had promised her a visit to the Hameau [see above, p. 142], and so on. The motives prompting the dreamer to produce precisely this impression from his or her childhood can of course only be uncovered by analysis.

A member of my lecture audience who boasted that only very

seldom were his dreams subject to dream-distortion once told me that, some time before, he had seen in a dream that *his former tutor was in bed with the maid* (who had lived in the house until he was eleven). Even the location of the scene had come to him in the dream. His interest thoroughly roused, he recounted the dream to his elder brother, who confirmed with a laugh that it was true. He remembered vividly, having been six at the time. The lovers used to make him, the older boy, drunk on beer when circumstances favoured a nocturnal tryst. The smaller child, then three years old (our dreamer), who slept in the maid's room, was not regarded as a disturbance.

In a further case it is possible, without benefit of interpretation, to say with certainty that a dream contains elements from childhood, and that when the dream is a so-called *perennial* one, first dreamed in childhood, it recurs from time to time subsequently during the sleep of the adult. To the well-known examples of this type I can add one or two from my own experience, although I have never had personal knowledge of such a perennial dream. A doctor in his thirties once told me that there often appeared in his dream-life, and had done ever since his earliest childhood, a yellow lion, which he was able to describe in minute detail. Long familiar to him from dreams, this lion one day confronted him *in natura* as a long-disappeared porcelain *objet*, and the young man's mother had then told him that the porcelain lion had been the best-loved toy of his earliest childhood years, though he himself had no memory of this.

If we now turn from manifest dream-content to dream-thoughts, which only analysis uncovers, it is possible, astonishingly, to identify the influence of childhood experiences even in dreams whose content would have aroused no such suspicion. I am grateful to my esteemed 'yellow lion' colleague for a particularly charming and instructive instance of such a dream. After reading Nansen's account of his polar expedition, he dreamed that in the middle of a snowy wilderness he gave the bold explorer electric-shock treatment for a sciatica that the latter had been complaining of. While analysing this dream, he was suddenly struck by a story from his childhood, without which the dream in fact remains incomprehensible. As a three- or four-year-old child, he one day listened avidly as the grown-ups discussed voyages [*Reisen*] of discovery, and afterwards he asked his father whether that was a serious condition. Clearly, he had confused *Reisen* with *Reissen* [ache], and sibling teasing ensured that the embarrassing experience was never forgotten.

A very similar case is my coming across, while analysing the dream about the monograph on the genus Cyclamen, a still-intact childhood memory of my father giving his five-year-old son a book with colour plates to destroy [see above, p. 184]. Some may perhaps doubt whether that memory really did contribute towards shaping the relevant dream-content and wonder instead whether the work of analysis did not manufacture a connection subsequently. However, the abundance and intricacy of the associative links vouch for the former view. (Cyclamen – favourite flower – favourite food – artichoke; to pluck like an artichoke, leaf by leaf [an expression one hears daily in connection with the division of the Chinese Empire];[1] herbarium – bookworm, of which the favourite food is books.) Moreover, I can assure readers that the ultimate meaning of the dream, which I have not set out here, is very closely related to the content of the childhood scene.

In connection with another series of dreams, analysis teaches us that the very wish that aroused a particular dream, fulfilment of which that dream seeks to represent, itself stems from childhood, with the result that, much to our surprise, *we find in dream the child and its impulses living on.*

At this point I shall continue with the interpretation of a dream that has already taught us something new. I mean the dream: my friend R. is my uncle [see above, pp. 151ff.]. We took this interpretation to the point where the wish-motive to be made *professor extraordinarius* became tangible, and we explained the affection felt in the dream for my friend R. as an oppositional, defiance creation against the abuse directed at the two colleagues that was contained in the dream-thoughts. The dream was my own; I may therefore continue analysis of it by saying that my feelings were still not satisfied by the solution reached. I was aware that my verdict on the colleagues abused in the dream-thoughts would have been quite different in the waking state; the strength of the desire not to share their fate in the matter of appointment struck me as inadequate to explain in full the contrast between my waking and dream assessments. If my need to be addressed with a different title was apparently so great, it suggests a morbid ambition that I fail to recognize in myself – to which, in fact, I believe I am a complete stranger. I am not aware how others who think they know me would judge me on this point; perhaps I really did possess ambition; but if I did, a long time back, it became focused on other things than the title and status of a *professor extraordinarius*.

So where did it come from, the ambition that inspired my dream? Here something occurs to me that I heard repeated so often during my childhood: when I was born an old peasant woman is said to have prophesied to my mother, who was delighted at the birth of her first child, that she had given the world a great man. Such prophecies must occur very frequently; there are so many expectant mothers and so many aged peasants or other old women who, having lost all their power on earth, have turned to the future. Nor will it have been to the prophetess's disadvantage. Was that the source of my yearning for greatness? But here I recall a different impression from my later childhood years that would provide an even more apt explanation. It was an evening in one of the Prater restaurants where my parents were in the habit of taking their eleven- or twelve-year-old son: we noticed a man going from table to table who, for a small tip, improvised verses on a set subject. I was despatched to ask the poet to come to our table, and he showed himself grateful to the messenger. Before enquiring what his task was to be, he let fall a number of lines concerning myself and in his inspired state pronounced it likely that I should, again, one day be a [government] 'minister'. I still remember the impression of this second prophecy very well. This was at the time of the *Bürgerminis-terium* [the 'bourgeois cabinet'], and my father had recently brought home pictures of bourgeois Drs Herbst, Giskra, Unger, Berger, etc., in whose honour we had made a kind of illuminated shrine. Some of them were even Jews, so that every hard-working Jewish boy carried a ministerial portfolio in his school-bag. In fact, it must have had to do with the impressions of that period that, until shortly before matriculating at university, I intended to study law, switching only at the last moment. A ministerial career, you see, is closed to a medical doctor. And now my dream! For the first time I notice that it transplants me from the dreary present back to the optimistic years of the *Bürgerministerium* and does its best to fulfil what was my wish at the time. In treating my two learned and estimable colleagues so badly because they are Jews – one as if he were a dimwit, the other as if he were a criminal – in doing this I am behaving as if I were the minister, I have put myself in the minister's place. What radical revenge on His Excellency! He refuses to make me a *professor extraordinarius*, so in return I supplant him in the dream!

In another case I was able to observe that the wish that arouses dream, albeit a current one, nevertheless draws powerful reinforcement from deep-seated childhood memories. I am talking about a series of dreams based on a yearning to visit Rome. This is a yearning that I shall no doubt have to go on fulfilling through dreams for some time to come, because at the time of year available to me for a major trip a visit to Rome is to be avoided on health grounds.[2] Consequently, I dream on one occasion that I am looking out of a carriage window at the [River] Tiber and the Ponte Sant' Angelo; the train then starts to move, and I realize I have never set foot in the city. The view I saw in the dream was taken from a well-known engraving that I had fleetingly seen on a patient's drawing-room wall the day before. Another time, someone takes me up a hill and shows me Rome, half-veiled in mist and so distant that I am astonished at how clear the view is. The content of this dream is richer than I wish to set out here. In it, the theme of 'seeing the Promised Land from afar' is clearly recognizable. The city that I first saw shrouded in mist like that is – *Lübeck*; the hill is modelled on – the *Gleichenberg*. In a third dream I am in Rome at last (as the dream tells me). However, to my disappointment the scenery is not at all urban; I can see *a small river of dark water with, on the one side, black cliffs and on the other meadows with large white flowers. I spot a Mr Zucker* (a superficial acquaintance) *and decide to ask him the way into the city.* Evidently, I am trying in vain to see, in dream, a city that in the waking state I have not seen. When I break the landscape of the dream down into its components, the white flowers point me in the direction of a city I do know, namely *Ravenna*, which at least for a time had taken precedence over Rome as Italy's capital. In the swamps around Ravenna we had found the most beautiful water-lilies growing in the black water; the dream has them growing in meadows like the daffodils in our *Aussee*, because at the time it was so laborious, hauling them out of the water. The dark cliff so close to the water vividly recalls the *Tepl Valley* near *Karlsbad*. 'Karlsbad' now puts me in a position where I can account for the curious fact of my having asked the way of Mr Zucker. At this point in the material from which the dream is woven, two of those amusing Jewish anecdotes become recognizable that contain so much profound, often bitter wisdom and that we dearly love to quote in conversation and correspondence. One is the 'constitution' story, which tells how a poor Jew, having gained access by guile to the Karlsbad Express, is then caught, thrown off whenever the tickets are checked on the train, and treated more harshly each time; eventually a friend, coming across him at one stage of his sufferings, asks him where he is going, whereupon he replies 'To *Karlsbad* – if my constitution holds out.' Lying close by in memory is another story, the one about the Jew who, knowing no French, is urged when in Paris to ask the way to the rue [de] Richelieu. *Paris* was another city that for years I had longed to visit, and I took the sheer bliss with which I walked the streets of Paris for the first time as a guarantee that I should also fulfil other wishes. Asking the way is a further direct allusion to Rome, because everyone knows that 'all roads lead to Rome'.[3] Incidentally, the name 'Zucker' [literally, sugar] also points to *Karlsbad*, which is where we send all patients suffering from the *constitutional* condition known as diabetes.[4] What prompted this dream was a suggestion by my Berlin friend that we meet in Prague at Easter. The things I had to discuss with him would have given rise to another connection with 'Zucker' and 'diabetes'.

A fourth dream, shortly after the one I have just mentioned, brings me back to Rome. I can see a street corner before me and am surprised that so many German posters are displayed there. The previous day I had written to my friend with prophetic foresight that, for German people strolling about, Prague was probably not a comfortable place to be. So the dream simultaneously expressed the desire to meet him in Rome rather than in a city in Bohemia and the interest, doubtless stemming from student days, that the German language should be tolerated more in Prague. I must of course have understood the Czech language in my earliest childhood years, because I was born in a small town in Moravia with a Slavonic population.[5] A Czech children's poem that I heard when I was seventeen impressed itself on my memory with such ease that I can still recite it today, although I have no idea what it means. So these dreams, too, exhibit a wide variety of connections with impressions received in my earliest years.

On my last Italian trip, which among other places took me past Lake Trasimeno, I did eventually, having seen the River Tiber and turned back in a state of deep emotion 80 kilometres short of Rome, find the extra strength that my longing for the eternal city draws from youthful impressions. I was just considering a plan (for another year) to bypass Rome to visit Naples when something occurred to me that I must have read in one of our classical writers:[6] It is questionable who paced his room with a livelier step after forming the project to go to Rome – Deputy Principal *Winckelmann* or Commander-in-Chief *Hannibal*.[7] I had in fact been travelling in the footsteps of Hannibal. Like me, he had never been granted the privilege of seeing Rome, and he too had proceeded to *Campania* when everyone had expected him in the imperial capital. But Hannibal, with whom I now had this in common, had been the hero of my schooldays. Like so many at that age, I had bestowed my sympathies during the Punic Wars not on the Romans but on the Carthaginians. When in my later schoolboy years some understanding began to dawn on me of the consequences of being descended from a foreign race, and anti-Semitic stirrings among my friends urged me to take a stand, the figure of the Semitic general rose even further in my estimation. In the eyes of the youth that I was, *Hannibal* and *Rome* symbolized the contrast between the toughness of Jewry and the organization of the Catholic Church. The significance that the anti-Semitic movement has since acquired for our emotional life helped the thoughts and feelings of that earlier time to become fixed. For the life of dream, therefore, the desire to visit Rome came to cloak and symbolize a number of other much longed-for desires towards the realization of which one would like to work with the endurance and single-mindedness of the Carthaginian and the fulfilment of which seems sometimes as little favoured by fate as Hannibal's lifelong wish to enter Rome.

And it is at this point that I stumble across the childhood experience that to this day continues, in all these feelings and dreams, to wield its power. I was perhaps ten or twelve years old when my father started taking me with him on his walks and sharing with me, in our conversations, his thoughts on the things of this world. Once, for example, to show me how much more favourable were the times I had been born into than those he had, he told me this story: 'One Saturday when I was young I was walking along the street in the town where you were born, dressed in my best clothes and wearing a new fur cap. A Christian comes past, swipes my cap off, sending it into the mud, and says, "Down off the pavement, Jewboy!"' 'And what did you do?' I asked. 'Stepped into the roadway and recovered my cap,' was his calm reply. That struck me as unheroic on the part of the big strong man holding little me by the hand. I compared this situation, which I found unsatisfactory, with another that suited my feelings better, namely the scene in which Hannibal's father, Hamilcar Barca, has his boy swear before the house altar that he will wreak vengeance on the Romans.[8] Hannibal has had a place in my fantasies ever since.

I believe I can trace this enthusiasm for the Carthaginian general some way further back into my childhood, meaning that here again it may be that we are simply dealing with the transference of an already formed affect relationship on to a fresh vehicle. One of the first books that came this young reader's way was Thiers' *Consulate and Empire*;[9] I remember sticking little labels bearing the names of the imperial marshals on the flat backs of my wooden soldiers, and that already then Masséna[10] (as a Jew: Menasseh) was my avowed favourite.[11] (This preference can no doubt also be explained by the accident of the same date of birth, one hundred years later.) Napoleon himself follows Hannibal in having also crossed the Alps. And possibly the development of this warrior ideal might be traced even further back into childhood, all the way to wishes that the now benevolent, now bellicose relations during the first three years with a boy who was a year older inevitably evoked in the weaker of the two playmates.

The deeper one allows oneself to become involved in analysing dreams, the more often one is put on the track of childhood experiences that play a part, as dream-sources, in the latent dream-content.

We learned earlier [see above, pp. 31ff.] that very seldom does dream reproduce recollections in such a way that, unabridged and unamended, they form the only manifest dream-content. Nevertheless, a few examples of this happening are attested to, and to these I can add a few new ones that again relate to infantile scenes. One of my patients was once presented, in dream, with a scarcely distorted reproduction of a sexual incident that he immediately recognized as a faithful memory. While the memory of it had never completely disappeared in the waking state, it had become very obscure, and reviving it was a consequence of the analytical work that had gone before. At the age of twelve the dreamer had gone to see a bedridden friend who, probably by accident, as a result of his changing his position in bed, had exposed himself. Seized by a sort of compulsion on seeing the other's genitalia, my patient had exposed himself in turn and grasped his friend's penis. His friend, however, gave him a look of indignation and surprise, whereupon he became embarrassed and let go. This scene was repeated by a dream twenty-three years later, including every detail of the sensations that had accompanied it, though the dream changed it in such a way that the dreamer, instead of playing the active role, played the passive one, while the person of the school-friend was replaced by a friend belonging to the present.

As a rule, of course, the infantile scene is represented in the manifest dream-content only by an allusion and needs to be unpacked from the dream by the process of interpretation. Reporting such examples can have little evidential value. The fact is, there is usually no other guarantee for these childhood experiences; if they date from an early age, memory can no longer vouch for them. The right to conclude from dreams that such childhood experiences even existed flows, so far as the work of psychoanalysis is concerned, from a whole series of factors that, interacting with one another, seem reliable enough. Wrenched out of context for the purpose of interpreting a dream, such trackings-back to childhood experiences may make little impression, particularly since I am not even reporting all the material on which the interpretation is based. Nevertheless, I refuse to accept this as a reason for not reporting such things.

I

In the case of one of my patients, all her dreams have a *'hurried/ harried'* quality: she is rushing to be in time, not to miss the train – that sort of thing. In one dream *she is supposed to be visiting her friend; her mother has said she should take some form of transport, not walk; she does walk, however, and keeps tripping over*. The material cropping up in connection with her analysis makes it possible to recognize a memory of childhood joshing (we all know what Viennese people mean by a *Hetz* [a joke, a bit of fun]) and for one dream in particular gives a derivation from that joke so popular with children, namely making someone say the sentence '*Die Kuh rannte, bis sie fiel*' [literally: 'the cow ran until it fell'] as quickly as if it were a single word, which is another form of tease.[12] All this harmless mischief among small girls is remembered because it takes the place of other, less innocent japes.

II

From another patient, the following dream: *She is in a large room in which there are all kinds of machines – rather as she imagines an orthopaedic establishment to be. She hears that I have no time and that she must undergo her treatment along with five other people. She shows reluctance, however, and refuses to get into the bed – or whatever it is – that has been allotted to her. She stands in a corner and waits for me to say it is not true. Meanwhile the others laugh at her, saying she is simply fooling around.* Also, and at the same time, *as if she was making a lot of little squares*.

The first part of this dream-content links up with the treatment and constitutes a transference to myself. The second contains the allusion to the childhood scene; mention of the bed welds the two fragments together. The orthopaedic establishment goes back to something I said about the treatment being comparable in length and nature to a course of *orthopaedic* treatment. I had had to tell her at the beginning of the treatment that *I did not have much time for her at present* but that later on I should be giving her a full hour a day. This stirred the old hypersensitivity in her that is one of the chief characteristics of children destined for hysteria. They have an insatiable thirst for love. My patient was the youngest of six siblings (hence: *along with five other people*) and as such was her father's darling, yet she seems to have found that her beloved father still gave her too little time and attention. Her waiting for me to say it is not true has the following derivation: A young tailor's apprentice had brought her a dress, and she had given him the money for it. She then asked her husband whether she would have to pay the money again if he lost it. As a tease, her husband said yes, she would (the *laughter* directed at her in the dream-content), and she kept on asking, over and over again, *waiting for him to say eventually that it is not true*. The thought can in fact be construed, so far as the latent dream-content is concerned: presumably she would have to pay me twice the amount if I gave her twice the time – a thought that is stingy or *dirty*. (A very frequent dream-substitute for the

uncleanness of childhood is money-grubbing, the word 'dirty' forming the bridge here.) If all the stuff about waiting for me to say,
etc., is meant to be referred to obliquely in the dream by the word
'dirty', the *standing in the corner* and *not getting into bed* fit in as
components of a childhood scene in which she has evidently soiled
the bed and *been made to stand in the corner* as a punishment, with
the threat of Daddy no longer loving her, the siblings laughing at
her, and so on. The *little squares* point to her young niece who is
demonstrating some arithmetic to her, showing her how in nine
squares (I think it is) you can enter numbers in such a way that they
add up to fifteen in each direction.

III

A man's dream: *He sees two boys scrapping – cooper's boys, he
deduces from the tools lying around; one of the boys has thrown the
other to the ground; the one on the ground has earrings with
blue stones. He hurries over to the miscreant with his stick raised,
intending to teach him a lesson. The boy flees to a woman standing
by a fence as if she was his mother. She is a day-labourer's wife,
and she has her back to the dreamer. Eventually she turns around
and gives him such a hideous look that he runs off in fright. In her
eyes he can see the red lining of the lower lid protruding.*

The dream has made plentiful use of trivial events of the previous
day. He did indeed see two boys the day before, one of whom threw
the other to the ground. As he hurried over to intervene, they took
flight. Cooper's boys: this is explained only by a subsequent dream,
during analysis of which he uses the saying: *that knocks the bottom
out of the barrel* ['that's the last straw', in the sense that nothing
more/worse is possible]. Earrings with blue stones he has mostly
seen *prostitutes* wearing. There is a well-known nonsense verse
about *two boys* that goes: 'the other boy's name was Mary' (i.e. 'he'
was a girl). The *woman standing*: After the scene with the two boys
he went for a walk by the Danube and took advantage of the
seclusion there to urinate *against a fence*. As he walked on, a

respectably dressed elderly woman gave him a very friendly smile and wanted to give him her visiting-card.

Since the woman in the dream stands like he does while urinating, what we are dealing with is a urinating member of the female sex, and part of this is the hideous 'sight',[13] the protruding red flesh, which must relate to the genitalia, gaping wide in the crouching position, as seen in childhood and subsequently reappearing in memory as 'proud flesh' [in the medical sense] or a 'wound'. The dream combines two occasions when the small boy was able to see little girls' genitalia – when they were *thrown to the ground* and when they were *urinating* – and as emerges from the rest of the context he retains the memory of a punishment or threat from his father on account of the sexual curiosity that the small boy had manifested on such occasions.

IV

A whole host of childhood memories, hurriedly cleaned up to form a fantasy, lie behind the following dream, had by an elderly lady.

She rushes out to do some shopping. In the Graben [a well-known square in Vienna], *she sinks to her knees, as if collapsing. Large numbers of people gather around her, particularly the cabbies; however, no one helps her up. She makes many vain attempts; in the end she must have succeeded, because she is being put into a cab, which is to take her home; through the window a large, heavily laden basket (like a shopping-basket) is thrown in after her.*

It is the same thing that is always harried in her dreams as harried her as a child. The first situation in the dream clearly derives from the sight of a horse that has fallen; the 'collapsing' also points to the idea of racing. In her younger years she had *ridden*; even further back she had probably also been a *horse*. Part of the falling down is her earliest childhood memory of the doorman's seven-year-old son who, overcome by epileptic convulsions in the street, had been brought home in a carriage. She had only heard about that, of course, but the idea of epileptic convulsions, of the 'boy who *fell down'*, had gained great power over her imagination and had sub-sequently influenced the form of her own fits of hysteria. When a female person dreams of falling, this doubtless regularly carries a sexual connotation in that she becomes a *'fallen woman'*; for our dream, this interpretation becomes virtually certain since the place where she falls down is the *Graben*, the square in Vienna that has the reputation of being a parade-ground for prostitutes. The *shopping-basket* offers more than one interpretation. As a *Korb* ['basket'] it recalls the many *rebuffs* [a metaphorical meaning of *Korb*] that she initially administered to her suitors and subsequently, as she believes, received herself. Part of that is also the fact that *no one is willing to help her up*, which she takes personally as rejection. The *shopping-basket* also calls to mind fantasies that her analysis has already exposed, fantasies of having married well below her station and now going to market herself. Eventually, however, it became possible to interpret the shopping-basket as indicating a *servant* of some kind. Here, other memories of childhood come into play: a *cook* who was dismissed because she stole; she too *sank to her knees* and pleaded. The dreamer was twelve years old at the time. Then there was a chambermaid, dismissed because she had become involved with the *coachman* of the house (who later married her, actually). So this memory gives us a source for the *coachmen* in the dream (who in contrast to reality do not touch fallen women). But that still leaves the throwing of the basket after her *through the window* ['*Fenster*'] to be explained. This reminds her of luggage being despatched by rail, of the rustic custom of *Fensterln* [when the suitor climbs through his sweetheart's bedroom window], of brief impressions of stays in the country, the way a man tossed *blue plums* through the window of a lady's room, the way her little sister took fright because a passing yokel saw into her room through the window. And now, underneath all this, a dim memory surfaces from her tenth year – a maid who, in the country, dallying with a servant of the house, performed love scenes of which the child might in fact have caught a glimpse, and who, together with her lover, was *'sent packing'*, was *'thrown out'* (in the dream it was the other way around: *'thrown in'*). It was a story, incidentally, that we had approached from several other directions. A servant's luggage or 'stuff' is referred to in Vienna disparagingly as his or her 'seven *plums*', as in: 'Pack your seven plums and get out.'

My collection, of course, has an overabundance of such dreams of patients, analysis of which leads back to dimly remembered or wholly forgotten impressions of childhood, often of the first three years of life. However, it would be unfortunate if, from them, we were to draw conclusions assumed to apply to dream in general; for the most part, after all, these are neurotic and in particular hysterical people, and the role assigned to childhood scenes in their dreams might be governed by the nature of their neurosis rather than by the essence of dream. However, when interpreting my own dreams, which is not something I undertake because of clear symptoms of illness, I find equally often that in the latent dream-content I stumble unexpectedly across an infantile scene, and that a whole series of my dreams suddenly come together into avenues proceeding from a childhood experience. I have already cited instances of this, and there will be various occasions for me to cite others. Possibly the best way of concluding this whole section is by recounting some of my own dreams in which still-vivid promptings and long-forgotten childhood experiences appear together as dream-sources.

I) After returning from a trip tired and hungry, I go to bed; in sleep, life's major requirements assert themselves and I dream: *I enter a kitchen to ask for some pudding.*[14] *Three women are standing there, one of whom is the landlady, and she is turning something over in her hand as if making dumplings. She replies that I must wait until she has finished* (unclear as speech). *I grow impatient and go off in a huff. I pull on an overcoat; however, the first one I try is too long for me. I take it off again, somewhat surprised that it sports fur trimmings. A second one that I put on has a long strip of Turkish patterning let into it. A stranger with a long face and a short goatee comes up and stops me putting the coat on by saying that it is his. I proceed to show him that it has Turkish embroidery all over it. He asks, 'What business is the Turkish (patterning, strip . . .) of yours?' Afterwards, though, we are perfectly friendly with each other.*

In analysing this dream I am most unexpectedly reminded of the first novel (I was perhaps thirteen at the time) that I read, i.e. I started with the end of the first volume. The title of the novel and its author I never knew, but I still vividly remember the end. The hero succumbs to madness, repeatedly calling out the three women's names that have meant the greatest happiness and misfortune in his life. One of those names is *Pélagie*. I do not yet know what I shall do with this notion in the analysis. Then, in addition to the three women, the Three Fates appear, those figures who weave the destiny of mankind, and I know that one of the three women, the landlady in the dream, is my mother, giver of life, including (as in my case) the first feed to the living. The female breast is where love and hunger meet. A young man (so the story goes) who became a great admirer of female beauty once said, when the conversation turned to the beautiful nurse who had fed him as a 'suckling',[15] that he regretted not having made better use of the opportunity at the time. I like to use the anecdote to explain the *subsequentiality* factor in the mechanism of psychoneuroses.[16] So, one of the Fates is rubbing her hands together as if making *dumplings*. A strange thing for one of the Fates to be doing, and something that urgently needs explaining! The explanation in fact comes from another, earlier childhood memory. When I was six years old and receiving my first instruction from my mother, I was asked to believe that we are made of dust ['earth' in German] and must therefore go back to being dust.[17] However, I felt uncomfortable about this and questioned the teaching. Whereupon my mother rubbed her hands together (very much as if she was making dumplings, only there was no dough between them this time) and pointed to the dusky *epidermis* flakes that had rubbed off as a specimen of the dust of which we are made. I was immensely struck by this *ad oculos* demonstration and gave myself up to a feeling that I later heard expressed verbally as: 'You owe nature a death.'[18] So these really are Fates that I go to in the kitchen, as I did so often in childhood when I felt hungry and my mother at the stove told me to wait until lunch was ready. And now for the dumplings [the German word is *Knödel*]! At least one of my university teachers – the very one, indeed, who taught me what I know of *histology* (*epidermis*) – will remember the name *Knödl* as being that of someone he had to prosecute for having committed an act of *plagiarism* [*Plagiat*] against him. Committing plagiarism, appropriating something one is able to obtain, even if it belongs to someone else, obviously leads to the second part of the dream, in which I am treated like the *overcoat thief* who haunted the lecture-rooms for a while. I put down the word *Plagiat* unintentionally, because it was there to be used, and now I become aware that it can serve as a word-bridge between different pieces of the manifest dream-content. The chain of association *Pélagie* – *Plagiat* – *Plagiostomen*[19] (sharks) – *swim bladder* connects the old novel with the Knödl affair and with the overcoats [*Überzieher*; literally: 'draw-overs'], which clearly denote an item of sexual technology (see also Maury's *kilo–lotto* dream on p. 70). A highly contrived and nonsensical chain it might be, but not one I could have put together in the waking state if it had not already been assembled by dream-work. Indeed, as if nothing was sacred to the urge to force connections, the dear name of *Brücke* ['bridge'] (see 'word-bridge' above) now serves to remind me of the eponymous establishment in which I spent my happiest hours as a student,[20] otherwise entirely need-free ('Thus will you at wisdom's *bosom* daily long for more'),[21] in the most complete contrast to the cravings that plague me as I dream. And finally the memory of another dear teacher surfaces, whose name again suggests something edible (*Fleischl* [*Fleisch* = 'meat'], like *Knödl*) and calls up an unhappy scene in which *epidermis flakes* are involved (mother – landlady) and mental disturbance (the novel) and a preparation from the Latin *kitchen* [*coquo* = 'to cook'] that stills *hunger*, namely cocaine.

I might, following this route, pursue the intertwined trains of thought further and explain in full the part of the dream that is missing from the analysis, but I must refrain from doing so because the personal sacrifices that would entail are too great. I shall pick up just one of the threads capable of leading straight to one of the dream-thoughts underlying the confusion. The stranger with the long face and the goatee who tries to prevent me from donning the overcoat looks just like a shopkeeper in Spalato from whom my wife bought a great deal of *Turkish* material. He was called *Popović*, a suspicious-sounding name that also prompted the humorist Stettenheim to make a suggestive remark. ('He announced his name and shook hands with me as the blush rose.')[22] The same abuse of names, incidentally, as above with *Pélagie, Knödl, Brücke* and *Fleischl*. That such name-games are a bad habit with children no one will deny; but if I indulge in them myself, it is an act of revenge, my own name having fallen victim to similarly feeble witticisms on many, many occasions.[23] Goethe once noted how sensitive we are about our names, in which we feel as comfortable as in our *skin*, when Herder wrote the following lines on the older man's name:

Der du von Göttern[24] *abstammst, von Gothen oder vom Kote –*
So seid ihr Götterbilder *auch zu Staub.*

[You who are descended from gods, from Goths, or from dung –
May your idols also become dust.]

I note that this digression about improper use of names was simply in order to pave the way for this complaint. But let us change the subject. The purchase in Spalato reminds me of another shopping expedition, in Cattaro, when I was altogether too restrained and missed the opportunity for some fine acquisitions. (The missed opportunity with the wet-nurse; see above.) Among the dream-thoughts that hunger inspires in the dreamer is this: *One should let nothing go by, one should take what one can, even if a little wrong-doing is involved; one should miss no opportunity, life is so short, death inevitable*. Because this is also meant sexually, and because desire refuses to stop at wrongdoing, this *carpe diem* must go in fear of censorship and therefore hide behind dream. Then, too, all counter-thoughts find expression, remembering the time when *intellectual nourishment* alone was sufficient for the dreamer, all preventive corrections, even those threats with nasty sexual punishments.

°

II) A second dream calls for a longer *introduction*:

I have driven to [Vienna's] West Station to begin my holiday trip to Aussee, but I access the platform for the [Bad] Ischl train, which leaves earlier. Standing there is Count Thun, who is once again off to Ischl to see the Emperor.[25] Despite the rain he had arrived in an open carriage, descended right by the barrier for local trains, and when the ticket-collector, who did not know him, tried to take his ticket, waved the man away with a curt gesture and no explanation. When the Ischl train has pulled out, with him on board, I am supposed to leave the platform and return to the waiting-room, but with much difficulty I obtain permission to stay. I while away the time by watching out for anyone who arrives and tries by offering a bribe to have himself allocated a compartment; I intend then to kick up a stink, demanding the same right. Meanwhile, I sing something to myself that I subsequently recognize as an aria from *The Marriage of Figaro*:

> *Will der Herr Graf ein Tänzelein wagen, Tänzelein wagen,*
> *Soll er's nur sagen,*
> *Ich spiel' ihm eins auf.*

> [If my Lord Count would like a little dance, like a little dance, he need only say, a dance I shall play.]

(Someone else might not have recognized the song.)

The whole evening I have been in a boisterous, aggressive mood, teasing waiters and cabbies – without causing offence, I hope. Now all sorts of bold, revolutionary thoughts are running through my head, such as might fit Figaro's quips and my memory of the Beaumarchais play, which I saw performed at the *Comédie française*. The one about the grand gentlemen who have taken the trouble to be born; the *droit de seigneur* that Count Almaviva means to assert over Susanna; the jokes that our mischievous opposition journalists make about Count Thun's name, calling him Count *Nichtstun*.[26] I do not envy him, truly; he now faces the problem of gaining the Emperor's ear, and the real Count *Inaction* is me: I'm off on holiday. All sorts of jolly holiday plans follow. A gentleman now arrives who is known to me as the government representative overseeing medical exams and who by his accomplishments in that role has earned himself the flattering nickname 'the government concubine'. Citing his official capacity, he demands a first-class half-compartment, and I hear the official saying to a colleague, 'Where shall we put the gentleman with the half-first?' A clear case of preferential treatment; I pay my first class in full. I am then also given a compartment to myself, but not in a walk-through carriage, which means that I have no access to a toilet during the night. My complaint to the official is unsuccessful; I take my revenge by suggesting to him that in this compartment at least a hole should be made in the floor for any calls of nature that the traveller might experience. I do actually wake, at 2:45 a.m., needing to pee, from the following dream:

A crowd of people, a student gathering. A count (Thun or Taafe)[27] *is speaking. Called upon to say something about the Germans, he states mockingly that their favourite flower is the coltsfoot and then sticks something that looks like a shredded leaf but is actually a crumpled leaf-skeleton in his buttonhole. I fly into a rage, I react furiously*[28] *but do in fact feel surprised at this attitude of mine.* Then less clearly: *As if this was the assembly-hall* ['Aula'], *all the entrances were blocked, and there was a need to escape. I fight my way through a series of beautifully appointed rooms, obviously government rooms, with furniture in a colour between brown and purple, and at last I come into a corridor where a housekeeper, a fat elderly woman, is sitting. I avoid talking to her; but she evidently thinks I am entitled to pass here since she asks whether she should accompany me with the lamp. I indicate to her or tell her to stay on the stairs, and in doing so I feel cunning in (when all is said and done) slipping through this checkpoint. Then I am at the bottom, where I find a narrow, steeply climbing path, which I take.*

Another unclear bit . . . *As if this, now, is the second task – getting out of the town, as previously out of the house. I am riding in a one-horse carriage and tell the driver to go to a station. 'I can't make the actual rail trip with you,' I say, he having first raised some*

objection as if I had overtired him. At the same time it is as if I had
already come some way with him, covering a stretch for which one
would normally have taken the train. The stations are busy; I am
wondering whether to go to Krems or Znaim, but then I think, 'The
[Emperor's] court will be there', and I decide in favour of Graz or
some such place. Now I am sitting in the carriage, which resembles
a tram, and in my buttonhole I am wearing a curiously woven
elongated thing with purple-brown violets on it, made from some
stiff fabric, that people find very striking. The scene breaks off at
this point.

I am once again outside the station, this time accompanied by an
elderly gentleman. I devise a plan to remain incognito but then see
the plan already implemented. Thinking and experiencing are one
and the same. He pretends to be blind, at least in one eye, and I
hold up a male urine glass in front of him (which we had to buy or
had bought in town). So I am a nurse and have to give him the glass
because he is blind. If the conductor sees us like this he will have to
let us get away with it, ignore us as being inconspicuous. In the
process the stance of the gentleman concerned and the position of
his urinating member are seen vividly. At this point I wake up,
needing to pass water.

The whole dream rather gives the impression of being a fantasy
that transports the dreamer back to 1848, the year of the Revolution,
the memory of which was of course revived by the 1898 jubilee –
as it was, moreover, by a small excursion to the *Wachau* district on
which I first made the acquaintance of Emmersdorf,[29] the refuge
of the student leader Fischhof, to whom certain features of the
manifest dream-content may point. Association of ideas now takes
me to England, to the house of my brother, whose wife was in the
habit of saying reproachfully to him, as a joke, *'Fifty years ago'*,
after the title of a poem by Lord Tennyson, whereupon the children
used to correct, *'Fifteen years ago.'* However, this fantasy, which
follows on from the ideas evoked by the sight of Count Thun, is
like the façades of Italian churches, which have no organic connection with the building behind; unlike those façades, incidentally, it
is full of holes, confused, and in many places portions of the interior

poke through. The first situation is cobbled together from several scenes, into which I can break it down. The arrogant attitude of the count in the dream is copied from a school scene when I was *fifteen*. We had fomented a plot against an unpopular and ignorant teacher, and at the heart of the plot was a friend of mine who since then appears to have modelled himself on *Henry VIII of England*. It fell to me to deliver the principal blow, and a discussion about the significance of the Danube so far as Austria was concerned (the *Wachau!*) was the occasion when open rebellion broke out. One of the conspirators was the only aristocratic member of the class, whom we dubbed '*Giraffe*' on account of his striking height and who, when taken to task by the school tyrant, the *German-language* teacher, stood there like the count in the dream. Explaining the *favourite flower* and *my putting in my buttonhole* something that must also be a flower (a reminder of the orchids I had given a girlfriend on the same day as well as of a rose of Jericho) strikingly recalls the scene from Shakespeare's history plays that marks the opening of the Wars of the Roses, the civil war between supporters of the *white* and *red* roses; the mention of *Henry VIII* paved the way for this reminiscence. After that, it is not far from roses to red and white carnations. (In between, two couplets squeeze their way into the analysis: one *German*, the other *Spanish. Rosen, Tulpen, Nelken,/ alle Blumen welken* ['roses, tulips, carnations, all flowers wilt']. *Isabelita, no llores,/ que se marchitan las flores* ['Isabelita, cry not because flowers fade']. The *Spanish* comes from *Figaro*). For us in Vienna, white carnations have become the badge of the *anti-Semites*, red that of the *Social Democrats*. In the background, a memory of an anti-Semitic challenge during a railway journey in beautiful Saxony (*Anglo-Saxons*). The third scene, which yielded components for forming the first dream-situation, takes place in my earliest student days. In a *German* students' association there was a debate about the relationship of philosophy to the natural sciences. I, a green youngster full of materialistic theory, thrust myself forward to argue for a thoroughly one-sided viewpoint. Whereupon a superior older student, who has since shown proof of his ability to lead people and organize crowds (and who happens, too, to bear a name from the animal kingdom), gave us a good ticking off: he had likewise looked after pigs in his youth and had then returned to his father's house in remorse. *I flew into a rage* (as in the dream), became *extremely coarse* ['*saugrob*'; literally: 'sow-coarse'], and replied that, since knowing he had tended *pigs*, I was *no longer surprised* at the tone of his speeches. (In the dream I feel *surprised* at my German national feeling.) Huge uproar; called upon from many quarters to withdraw my words, I nevertheless stood my ground. The man I had insulted was too sensible to take up the idea of a *challenge* directed at himself; he let the matter rest.

The remaining elements of the dream-scene come from deeper levels. What is the meaning of the count proclaiming 'coltsfoot' [*'Huflattich'*; literally: 'hoof-lettuce']? Here I must consult my chain of association. *Huflattich – lattice*[30] *– salad – salad hound* (dog that begrudges others what it refuses to eat itself). Here we see through to a fund of insults: *Gir-affe* ['*Affe*' = 'monkey'], *Schwein* ['pig'], *Sau* ['sow'], *Hund* ['dog']. I was also able, via a detour using a name, to reach *Esel* ['ass'] and come back to mocking an academic teacher. I further equate *Huflattich* (here I am not sure whether I am right) with the French '*pisse-en-lit*'. I know this from Zola's *Germinal*, in which the children are asked to bring back some of this salad. 'Dog' (in French: '*chien*') carries an echo of the bodily function sometimes referred to as 'number twos' ('*chier*' = to shit; as '*pisser*' refers to 'number ones'). Now we shall soon have the dirty bits in all three states together; because in the same *Germinal*, with its many references to the coming Revolution, there is a very curious competition having to do with the production of gaseous excretions known as *flatus*.[31] And here I am made aware that the trail to this *flatus* was laid long ago, from *flowers* via the *Spanish* couplet to *Isabelita*, then to *Isabella* and *Ferdinand* by way of *Henry VIII* and English history to the Battle of the Armada against *England*, after the victorious conclusion of which the English cast a medal bearing the inscription '*Flavit* et dissipati sunt' ['(He) blew and they are scattered'], a fierce wind having dispersed the Spanish fleet.[32] I was thinking of using the line half in jest as the title of the 'Therapy' chapter, should I ever get around to writing a thorough account of my view of and treatment of hysteria.

As regards the second scene of the dream, the reason why I cannot give so detailed a breakdown is censorship. The fact is, I put myself in the place of a major figure of that revolutionary period, who is also supposed to have had an adventure with an *eagle*, to have suffered from *incontinentia alvi*, and so on, and I believe *I should have no right to evade* censorship here, despite the fact that a *Hofrat* [formerly an Aulic councillor] (*Aula, consilarius aulicus*) told me most of these stories. The suite of rooms [*Zimmer*] in the dream was prompted by His Excellency's saloon carriage, of which I caught a brief glimpse; however, as so often in dreams it means *females* ['*Frauenzimmer*'] (Treasury *Frauenzimmer*).[33] With the person of the housekeeper I am offering a quick-witted elderly lady inadequate thanks for the hospitality and the many excellent stories recounted to me in her house. The business with the lamp goes back to Grillparzer, who noted a charming experience of similar content and then used it in his version of the Hero and Leander story (*Des Meeres und der Liebe Wellen* [literally: 'The Waves of Sea and Love']34 – the Armada and the *storm*).[35]

I must also hold back any detailed analysis of the two remaining dream-fragments, simply picking out those elements that led to the two childhood scenes for the sake of which I took up this dream in the first place. One would be right in surmising that it is sexual material that compels me to make this suppression; however, no one need be satisfied with that explanation. After all, a person does not keep secret from himself much that he must treat as secret in front of others, and here it is a question not of the reasons that require me to hide the solution but of the motives of internal censorship that conceal the real content of the dream from myself. That is why I have to say that analysis reveals these three dream-fragments as impertinent boasts flowing from a ludicrous and (so far as my waking life is concerned) long-suppressed delusion of grandeur, individual 'runners' of which have ventured as far as the manifest dream-content (*I feel cunning*), although it makes the superior mood of the evening before the dream strikingly under-standable. Boasting in all areas, in fact; for instance, the mention of Graz alludes to the question 'What price Graz?' in which a person will indulge when feeling particularly well-off financially. If anyone cares to think of Maître Rabelais' unsurpassed account of the life and deeds of Gargantua and his son Pantagruel, he will also be able to categorize the suggested content of the first dream-fragment as an instance of boasting. However, the following material belongs to the two promised childhood scenes: For this trip I had bought a *new* suitcase, the colour of which (a *brownish purple*) crops up several times in the dream (*purple-brown violets of some stiff fabric* next to a thing called a '*girl-catcher*' [literally, but see note 38] – the furniture in the government offices). Everyone knows that children believe *something new attracts people's attention*. Well, the following scene from my childhood is one I have been told about; any memory of it has been replaced by a memory of the telling. Apparently, when I was two years old I still *wet the bed* occasionally, and on one such occasion, on being told off about it, I *consoled* my father by promising that I would go to N. (the nearest town of any size) and buy him a new bed, a beautiful *red* one. (Which is why the dream contains the parenthesis about the glass: *which we had bought or would have to buy in town;* one *must* keep one's promises.) [Notice, by the way, the juxtaposition of the male glass and the female 'box'.][36] This promise encapsulates the child's entire delusion of grandeur. The significance of the child's urinary problems for the dream is something that already struck us when interpreting an earlier dream (see the dream told on pp. 216f.). We are also familiar, from psychoanalyses of neurotics, with the close connection between bed-wetting and the character-trait ambition.

But then, on one occasion, there was a different domestic upset; it happened when I was seven or eight years old, and this one I remember very well. One evening before going to bed I disregarded the ban, imposed for the sake of discretion, on relieving oneself in the parents' bedroom, in their presence. In the lecture that my father gave me he let fall the remark, 'The boy will come to nothing.'

It must have constituted a fearful blow to my ambition, because allusions to this scene recur constantly in my dreams and are regularly associated with recitals of my achievements and successes, as if I was trying to say, 'You see – I have in fact come to something.' This childhood scene provides the material for the final image of the dream, in which of course for the purposes of revenge the roles are reversed. The elderly gentleman (obviously my father, since the blindness in one eye signifies his unilateral glaucoma)[37] now urinates in my presence, as I formerly had in his. With the glaucoma I am reminding him of the cocaine from which he benefited at the time of the operation, as if with this I had kept my promise. I also laugh at him; because he is blind I have to hold the glass for him, and I revel in allusions to my knowledge of the theory of hysteria, of which I am proud.[38]

If the two urination scenes from childhood are certainly, in my case, closely bound up with the subject of megalomania, their awakening on the journey to Aussee was further favoured by the accidental circumstance that my compartment had no lavatory and I must be prepared to be caught short during the journey, as indeed I was in the morning. I woke up with the sensations of physical need. One might, it seems to me, be inclined to cast those sensations in the role of the actual dream-trigger, but I prefer a different view, namely that it was dream-thoughts that brought on the need to pee. It is most unusual for me to have my sleep disturbed by needs of any kind, least of all at the time of this particular waking, which was a quarter to three in the morning. I counter a further objection by remarking that, on other journeys in more comfortable surroundings, I almost never felt the need to pass water after waking prematurely. Anyway, no harm will be done if I leave this point undecided.

Since becoming aware, through further experiences in dream-analysis, that even from dreams whose interpretation at first appears complete, because dream-sources and wish-trigger can easily be proved – that even from such dreams important trains of thought proceed that reach back into the earliest days of childhood, I have had to ask myself: 'Does this feature too perhaps constitute an essential requirement of dream?' If I may be permitted to generalize from these thoughts, every dream would have in its manifest content some connection with recent experience but in its latent content some connection with a person's earliest experience, regarding which I am truly, from my analysis of hysteria, able to show that in the best sense it has remained recent [i.e. has retained its freshness]³⁹ right up until the present. However, this supposition still seems very difficult to prove; I shall need to return to the probable role of very early childhood experiences as regards dream-formation in a different context (Chapter 7).

Of the three peculiarities of dream-memory that we looked at initially, one (the preference, in dream-content, for what is trivial) has been satisfactorily solved by tracing it back to *dream-distortion*. The other two (the elevation of the still-vivid and of the infantile) we have been able to corroborate but not derive from the motives of dreaming. These two characteristics, which it would be superfluous for us to explain or evaluate, we intend to keep in mind; they will have to find their place elsewhere, either in the psychology of the sleeping state or in connection with the considerations of the structure of the mental apparatus that we shall embark upon later, having first observed that interpreting dreams affords us a glimpse inside that apparatus, as if through a peephole.

But there is one other finding of the last few dream-analyses that I wish to highlight immediately. Dream often appears to have *several meanings*. Not only (as our examples show) may several wish-fulfilments be combined; it is also possible for one meaning or one wish-fulfilment to hide others, down and down until one encounters the fulfilment of a wish from earliest childhood, and here too the consideration, once again, whether the 'often' in the foregoing sentence ought not more properly to read 'as a rule'.⁴⁰

Notes

1. [These square brackets are Freud's. At the time when he was writing this book, the disintegration of the Chinese Empire was indeed much in the news.]

2. I discovered quite a while back that all it takes to fulfil such wishes (wishes long deemed unattainable) is a little courage, and I am now an assiduous *Rome* pilgrim.

3. [This sentence works better in German (and hence for Freud's purposes) because the same German word (*Weg/e*) serves for 'way' and 'roads'.]

4. [Commonly known, in German, as '*die Zuckerkrankheit*' (literally: 'sugar sickness').]

5. [Freud was born into a German-speaking Jewish family in Freiburg, Moravia (now Pribor in the Czech Republic), in 1856; the family moved to Vienna in 1860.]

6. The writer in whose work I came across this passage must have been Jean Paul [1763–1825].

7. [The latter is a familiar figure, the former perhaps less so. Long-time schoolmaster and later historian of classical art, Johann Joachim Winckelmann (1717–68) paid his first visit to Rome in 1755, having converted to Roman Catholicism in the previous year, allegedly to facilitate the trip.]

8. In the first edition the name Hasdrubal occurred here, a disconcerting error that I explain in my *Psychopathologie des Alltagslebens* (eleventh edition, 1929 [see the new translation by Anthea Bell in *The Psychopathology of Everyday Life*, London 2002, p. 210]).

9. [Adolphe Thiers (1797–1877), *Histoire du consulat et de l'empire*, 1845–62.]

10. [André Masséna (1758–1817) was one of Napoleon's original eighteen '*Maréchaux de l'empire*'.]

11. Incidentally, doubt has been cast on the Marshal's Jewish descent.

12. [All of which demands either some very agile translation (which I decline to perform) or some rather prosaic explanation. The German verb '*hetzen*' corresponds to the English 'to hurry' and also 'to cause to hurry' ('harry'), hence my admittedly inelegant device coupling these intransitive and transitive connotations in order to highlight the fact that the German original combines both. In Austria, the associated noun ('*Hetz*') denotes a 'joke' or 'bit of fun' ('joshing') – like saying a sentence (possibly, borrowing from Freud's example, 'the cow chose buttercups') so quickly that it becomes amusing nonsense ('the couch owes buttercups').]

13. [*Anblick*; the German words for a 'sight' and a 'look' (*Blick*) are very close.]

14. [*Mehlspeise* = a cereal-based dessert course, which may range from pancakes to rice pudding; something sweet, anyway.]

15. [As German (in which a baby is a *Säugling*) still says, of course.]

16. [The word I have chosen to render as 'subsequentiality' is pretty awful in German too (*Nachträglichkeit*). But at least it conveys the notion (very important to Freud) that, while infant sexuality lays down much of our being, we do a certain amount of self-creation 'after the event', as it were – by 'revising' some of the things we learn about ourselves. Previous translators have talked in terms of 'deferred action' – which rather misses the point, I feel. For more on this, see Jean Laplanche and Jean-Bertrand Pontalis, *The Language of Psychoanalysis* (1973) (tr. Donald Nicholson-Smith), London 1988, pp. 111ff.]

17. [Gen. 3:19 (RSV): 'You are dust, and to dust you shall return.']

18. Both affects belonging to these childhood scenes, namely astonishment and surrender to the inevitable, had come up in a slightly earlier dream that was what first brought this childhood experience back to me.

19. I do not add the *plagiostomes* arbitrarily; they remind me of an irritating occasion when I disgraced myself in front of the same teacher.

20. [Freud is referring to the Physiological Institute in Vienna, headed by Ernst Brücke, where he worked as an assistant in 1882.]

21. ['So wird's Euch an der Weisheit Brüsten mit jedem Tage mehr gelüsten'. Goethe, *Faust* I:4]

22. [Popović is in fact a very common name. Freud may have been alluding to Cvijetko Popović, one of the members of the plot to assassinate Archduke Ferdinand in 1914. Julius Stettenheim (1831–1916) was a prominent German satirist.]

23. [In German, *'Freud'* is the root of 'pleasure, joy'.]

24. [The writer's name is of course pronounced 'gerter'; the *'Göttern'* and *'Göttenbilder'* in Herder's ditty begin with a similar sound. Herder's lines were not meant seriously, though Goethe took enormous offence at them (whence his comment). Incidentally, the original wording was 'Der von Göttern Du abstammst . . .']

25. [Count Thun was the Austrian prime minister at the time. Emperor Franz Josef had left Vienna temporarily, together with his court, and taken up residence in the spa town of Bad Ischl, near Salzburg.]

26. [The point being that the count's name sounds like *'tun'* ('to do' or simply 'action') and lends itself readily to being turned around.]

27. [Count Eduard von Taafe was a former Austrian prime minister.]

28. This repetition slipped into the text of the dream, apparently through absent-mindedness, and I have left it because the analysis shows that it is not without significance.

29. An error, but this time not a 'slip'! [*Fehlleistung*; on some of the problems associated with translating the word Freud himself used for what we have come to call a 'Freudian slip', see Anthea Bell's Translator's

Preface in Sigmund Freud, *The Psychopathology of Everyday Life*, London 2002. The Wachau, incidentally, is a wine-growing district lying along the Danube to the west of Vienna.] I learned later that the Wachau Emmersdorf is not the same as the homonymous village in which the revolutionary Fischhof found asylum. [At the age of thirty-two, Adolf Fischhof became one of the leaders of the 1848 revolutionary uprising in Vienna. Subsequently amnestied, he lived a quiet life in one of several villages in Austria called Emmersdorf.]

30. [*Sic*. Did Freud perhaps mean to write the English word 'lettuce' here?]

31. Not in *Germinal*; in *La Terre*. A mistake of which I became aware only after the analysis. Incidentally, let me point out the identical letters in '*Huflat*tich' and '*Flatus*'.

32. The uninvited biographer whom I have found, Dr Fritz *Wittels*, tells me that in citing this motto I have left out the name *Jehovah*. On the English medal the divine name is written in Hebrew letters; it appears on the cloud background, but in such a way that it can be seen as part of the image as much as belonging to the inscription. [The first word of the Latin inscription is variously given as '*Flavit* . . .' and '*Afflavit* . . .' – the version Freud cites in his second reference (see below, p. 485).]

33. [The German word *Frauenzimmer*, which in sixteenth-century courtly language denoted 'all the women in the room', declined during the nineteenth century to become a derogatory term for 'females in general'. The *ärarische Frauenzimmer* to whom Freud alludes in brackets are a mystery to me. The Greek word αὐλή originally denoted a cattle fence surrounding a house; in the sixteenth century, by which time the German version (*Aula*) had acquired a more exalted meaning, the Aulic Council became the supreme executive and judicial organ of the Holy Roman Empire; nowadays, throughout the German-speaking world, *Aula* most commonly denotes the assembly-hall of a school or college.]

34. [*Des Meeres und der Liebe Wellen* (1831) is often judged the greatest tragedy written by the Viennese playwright Franz Grillparzer (1791–1872). An English translation, which appeared in 1938, was actually entitled *Hero and Leander*.]

35. Regarding this part of the dream, Herbert Silberer tried in a very full piece of work (*Phantasie und Mythos*, 1910) to show that dream-work is able to reproduce not only the latent dream-thoughts but also the psychical processes that accompany dream-formation ('The functional phenomenon'). However, I think he overlooks the fact that, for me, the 'psychical processes that accompany dream-formation' constitute *material* for thought

like everything else. In this very arrogant dream I am clearly proud of having discovered those processes.

36. [These square brackets are Freud's own, and he gives the word 'box' in English.]

37. Another interpretation: He is one-eyed like Odin, the father of the gods. Odin's *consolation*. The *consolation* from the childhood scene, that I will buy him a new bed.

38. Some additional interpretation material: Holding out the glass recalls the story of the peasant [*Bauer*] at the optician's, who tries glass after glass but cannot read. (*Bauernfänger* ['con-man'] – *Mädchenfänger* ['sweet-talker'] in the previous dream-fragment.) The treatment of the now feeble-minded father among the peasants in Zola's *La Terre*. The sad satisfaction that my father, in the last days of his life, soiled the bed like a child; that is why in the dream I am his *nurse*. 'Thinking and experiencing are here as one' recalls a strongly revolutionary book by Oskar Panizza in which God the Father is dealt with quite shamelessly as a paralytic old man; there the words are 'With him, intention and deed are one', and he has to be prevented by his archangel, a sort of Ganymede, from grumbling and cursing because those curses would immediately come true. The making of *plans* is a reproach aimed at my father stemming from a later period of criticism, as indeed the whole rebellious dream-content with its offensive attitude towards royalty and its mockery of officialdom goes back to a revolt against my father. The ruler is called the father of his country, and a person's father is the oldest, first and (for the child) only authority, from whose perfect power the other social authorities have proceeded over the course of human cultural history (in so far as 'matriarchy' does not need to qualify this proposition). The dream version 'Thinking and experiencing are one and the same' points to the elucidation of the symptoms of hysteria, to which the *male glass* also relates. To a person from Vienna I should not need to explain the *Gschnas* principle; *Gschnas* consists in fabricating objects of rare and beautiful aspect from trivial and preferably comical and worthless materials, e.g. weapons from pots and pans, small straw brooms and pretzel sticks, as our artists like to as they make merry of an evening. The fact is, I had noticed that hysterics do the same; on top of the things that really happened to them, they unconsciously make up hideous or wild fantasy occurrences, which they put together using the most innocent, most commonplace material drawn from their daily lives. It is from these fantasies that the symptoms hang, not from memories of real events, be they serious or similarly innocent. This explanation had helped me over many difficulties and gave me great joy. I was able to suggest it with the

dream-element of the *'male glass'* because I had been told that at the last *Gschnas* session one of Lucrezia Borgia's poison cups had been displayed, the core component of which was a *male urine glass* as used in hospitals.

39. [May I repeat (see p. 199, note 2): I introduce this parenthesis to stress that, as Freud used it, the word *rezent* is both quantitative (in this case belonging to the immediate past, namely the day preceding the dream) and qualitative (in the sense of 'fresh', 'still vivid'). I have become convinced that *rezent*, for Freud, covers a broader area of meaning than the English word 'recent', which is why I usually render it as 'still vivid'.]

40. The multi-layeredness of the meanings of dream is one of the trickiest but at the same time one of the richest (in terms of content) problems of dream-interpretation. Anyone forgetting this possibility will easily go astray and be misled into positing untenable assertions regarding the nature of dream. However, far too few studies have addressed themselves to this topic as yet. Up to now, only the somewhat regular layering of symbols in the urinary-stimulus dream has been thoroughly investigated, by O[tto] Rank.

C *Somatic dream-sources*

If, seeking to interest an educated layman in the problems of dream, one asks where he thinks the sources of dream spring from, one will usually find that the person asked believes himself to be in assured possession of this part of the solution. He will immediately think of how a disturbed or impeded digestion ('dreams come from the stomach'), the way the body happens to be lying, and minor experiences during sleep will influence dream-formation, and he seems to have no idea that, after all these factors have been taken into account, there is still something left that needs explaining.

The role that the scientific literature assigns to somatic stimuli as regards dream-formation is something we dealt with thoroughly in Chapter 1, section C; here we need only remind ourselves of the findings of that investigation. We heard that three different somatic stimuli have been identified as dream-sources (objective sensory stimuli proceeding from external objects, purely subjectively grounded internal states of arousal on the part of the sense organs, and corporeal stimuli coming from inside the body), and we noted that authors tend, when considering those somatic stimuli, to thrust into the background or even eliminate altogether any psychical sources of dream (see pp. 50f.). In examining the claims put forward in favour of somatic stimuli, we found that the importance of objective sense-organ arousals (sometimes chance stimuli during sleep, sometimes ones that do not keep their distance even from the sleeping life of the mind) has been established by many observations; we found also that it has been corroborated experimentally (see pp. 36f.) that the role of subjective arousals of the senses appears to be demon-

237

strated by the recurrence of hypnagogic sense-images in dreams (see pp. 42ff.), and that the almost universal assumption that our dream-images and dream-ideas derive from internal corporeal stimuli, while it cannot be proven across its entire breadth, is able to draw support from the general recognition that a state of arousal in the digestive, urinary and sexual organs can influence the content of our dreams.

So *'nerve stimuli'* and *'corporeal stimuli'* are said to be the somatic sources of dream; several writers say they are the only sources of dream that exist.

However, we have already entertained a series of doubts that appear to attack not so much the correctness as the adequacy of the somatic-stimulus theory.

Confident as all the champions of this theory must have felt in relation to the actual foundations of it (particularly as regards the accidental and external nerve stimuli that are not at all hard to find in dream-content), none of them was a stranger to the recognition that the rich ideational content of dreams scarcely admits of a derivation from external nerve stimuli alone. Mary Whiton Calkins [1893] examined her own and another person's dreams from this standpoint over a period of six weeks, and found only 13.2 per cent (and 6.7 per cent) in which the external sense-perception element could be proved; only two cases in the collection could be traced back to organic sensations. Here statistics confirm what even a fleeting survey of our own experience would have led us to surmise.

People were often content to single out the 'nerve-stimulus dream' from other forms of dream as a well-researched sub-species of dream. Spitta [1882] divides dreams into *nerve-stimulus* and *associative* dreams. But clearly the solution remained unsatisfactory as long as the link between the somatic sources of a dream and that dream's ideational content could not be demonstrated.

So in addition to the first objection (the inadequate frequency of external stimuli as dream-sources) there is a second, namely the inadequate explanation of dream achievable by introducing this type of dream-source. The champions of the theory owe us two explanations: first, why is the external stimulus not seen in the dream in its true nature but instead regularly goes unrecognized (see the alarm-clock dreams on pp. 39f.); and secondly, why can the result of the reaction of the perceiving mind to this unrecognized stimulus turn out so indeterminably varied? In answer to these questions we heard from Strümpell [1877] that, as a result of its turning-away from the external world during sleep, the mind is not able to give the correct interpretation of the objective sensory stimulus, but is compelled, on the basis of what is in many ways an indeterminate prompting, to form illusions, or as he puts it:

> As soon as an external or internal nerve stimulus experienced during sleep gives rise in the mind to a sensation or complex of sensations, or to a feeling, or to any kind of psychical process that the mind perceives, the process calls up sensation images from the sphere of experience left to the mind from the waking state, i.e. earlier perceptions, either unadorned or with attendant psychical values. It gathers around itself, as it were, a larger or smaller number of such images, through which the impression stemming from the nerve stimulus receives its psychical value. We usually say here too, as popular usage does in relation to waking behaviour, that in sleep the mind *interprets* the nerve-stimulus impressions. The result of that interpretation is the so-called *nerve-stimulus dream* – that is to say, a dream whose components are conditioned by the fact that a nerve stimulus exerts its psychical effect on the life of the mind in accordance with the laws of reproduction.[1]

Identical with this theory in all essentials is what Wundt [1880] says about how the ideas of dream likewise, for the most part, proceed from sensory stimuli, including those of the general senses, and therefore represent mainly fantastic illusions, probably only a small number of which are pure memory ideas intensified to the point where they become illusions. As regards the relationship of dream-content to dream-stimuli that arises out of this theory, Strümpell finds an apt simile when he writes (on p. 84 of his book) that it is as if 'the ten fingers of someone who knows nothing of music were to ripple over the keys of the instrument'. Looked at in this way, dream would appear not as a mental phenomenon sprung from psychical motives but as the upshot of a physiological stimulus finding expression in psychical symptomatology, since the apparatus affected by the stimulus is capable of no other expression. A similar assumption underlies the explanation of obsessions, for example, that Meynert tried to provide with the famous simile of the clock face on which some numbers stand out in stronger relief.

Popular though the theory of somatic dream-stimuli has become and attractive though it may seem, we shall have no difficulty in demonstrating its weak point. Every somatic dream-stimulus that in sleep challenges the mental apparatus to interpret it by forming illusions may in fact prompt countless such attempts at interpretation – may in other words achieve representation in the dream-content in tremendously varied ideas.[2] However, the theory put forward by Strümpell and Wundt is incapable of supplying any motive whatsoever governing the relationship between the external stimulus and the dream-idea chosen to interpret it – that is to say, of explaining the 'special selection' that the stimuli 'quite often make in taking productive effect'.[3] Other objections concern the basic assumption of illusion theory as a whole, which is that the mind is not capable, in sleep, of recognizing the true nature of objective sensory stimuli. The old physiologist Burdach [1830] proves to us that even in sleep the mind is quite capable of correctly interpreting the sense impressions that reach it and of reacting in accordance with the correct interpretation. He does so by setting out how certain sense impressions that seem important to the individual can be exempted from neglect during sleep (wet-nurse and child) and by showing that a person is far more likely to be woken by his own name than by any old auditory impression, which presupposes that even in sleep the mind distinguishes between sensations (see above pp. 64f.). Burdach deduced from these observations that what one can assume in the sleeping state is not an inability to interpret sense impressions but a *lack of interest in them*. The same arguments as Burdach employs in 1830 recur unchanged in Lipps in 1883 to combat the somatic-stimulus theory. The mind, in those arguments, is like the sleeper in the story, who when asked 'Are you asleep?' replies 'No,' but when asked the second question,

'Then lend me a quid,' takes refuge behind the excuse, 'I'm asleep.'

The inadequacy of the theory of somatic dream-stimuli can be demonstrated in other ways as well. Observation shows that external stimuli do not make me dream, despite the fact that such stimuli appear in the dream-content, as soon as (and in the event that) I dream. Against a skin or pressure stimulus, for example, I have various reactions at my disposal. I may ignore it and then, on waking, find that a leg was uncovered, for example, or an arm squashed; pathology shows me countless instances of a wide variety of powerfully arousing sensory and motor stimuli having no effect during sleep. I may feel the sensation during sleep – through my sleep, as it were, which is what usually happens with painful stimuli, though without using the pain in a dream. And thirdly I may wake up at the stimulus in order to get rid of it.[4] A fourth possible reaction (but it is only a possibility) is for the nerve stimulus to make me dream; however, the other possibilities will occur at least as often in connection with dream-formation. This could not be *unless the motive of dreaming lay outside somatic stimulus sources.*

In due appreciation of the gaps (as we have exposed them above) in the explanation of dream by somatic stimuli, other writers (Scherner [1861], followed by the philosopher Volkelt [1875]) have sought to define more closely the mental activities that cause such colourful dream-images to spring from somatic stimuli – in other words, to shift the essence of dream back into the mental sphere, making it a psychical activity. Not only did Scherner give us a poetically sensitive and most vivid account of the psychical characteristics that unfold in dream-formation; he also believed he had guessed the principle by which the mind deals with the stimuli presented to it. In Scherner's view, dream-work, giving free play to an imagination freed of its everyday bonds, seeks to portray the essence of the organ from which the stimulus proceeds and the nature of that stimulus *by symbolic means*. The result is a kind of dream-book that can be used as an instruction manual for interpreting dreams, making it possible to trace dream-images back to physical sensations, conditions of organs and states of arousal. 'Thus the image of the cat expresses a mood of intense irritation, the image of light-coloured, smooth pastry expresses physical nakedness. The human body as a whole is represented by dream-imagination as a house, individual organs as parts of that house. In "dental-stimulus dreams", the mouth corresponds to a high-arched hallway and the dropping-away from the fauces to the gullet a staircase; in the "headache dream", what is chosen to denote the upper part of the head is the ceiling of a room covered with hideous, toad-like spiders.' (K. A. Scherner, *Das Leben des Traumes* ['The life of dream'], Berlin 1861, pp. 33f.). 'A number of such symbols are used by dream for the same organ; the breathing lungs find their symbol in the flame-filled oven with its roaring, the heart in hollow boxes and baskets, the bladder in round, pouch-shaped or simply hollowed-out objects' (ibid., p. 34). 'A particularly important feature is that sometimes at the end of the dream the organ doing the arousing or the function of that organ is represented undisguised – usually on the dreamer's own body. The "dental-stimulus dream", for instance, usually ends with the dreamer pulling a tooth from his mouth' (ibid., p. 35). This theory of dream-interpretation cannot be said to have found much favour in the literature. Above all it seemed extravagant; people even hesitated to identify the element of justification to which in my view it can lay claim. It leads, as we see, to a revival of interpreting dreams by means of *symbolism*, as used by the ancients, the only difference being that the area from which interpretation is to be drawn is limited to the scope of human physicality. The lack of a scientifically comprehensible technique of interpretation inevitably reduces the applicability of Scherner's theory very considerably. Arbitrariness in dream-interpretation seems by no means ruled out, particularly since here too a stimulus may find expression in dream-content in a multiplicity of representations; Scherner's supporter Volkelt, for instance, was already unable to confirm the representation of the body as a house. It is also bound to cause offence that here again the mind has dreamwork thrust upon it as a useless and pointless activity, since according to the theory under discussion the mind is content to fantasize about the stimulus preoccupying it with no prospect of the stimulus being responded to in some way.

But there is one objection that would seriously affect Scherner's theory of the symbolization of corporeal stimuli by dream. Such corporeal stimuli are present all the time, and the general consensus is that the mind is more accessible to them during sleep than in the waking state. So one fails to understand why the mind does not dream continuously throughout the night, every night, about every single organ. If one seeks to escape this objection by advancing the condition that special stimuli would have to proceed from eyes, ears, teeth, digestive organs and so on for dream-activity to be aroused, one is faced with the difficulty of proving these stimulus enhancements to be objective, which is possible only in a small number of cases. If the dream of flying constitutes a symbolization of the rising and falling of the lungs during breathing, either this dream (as Strümpell remarked) would have to be dreamed far more frequently or there would have to be evidence of increased respiratory activity during it. There is a third possibility (the most likely of all), namely that there are, at times, special motives at work to direct attention at visceral sensations that are present constantly and to the same degree, but this already takes us beyond Scherner's theory.

The value of the discussions in the works of Scherner and Volkelt lies in the fact that they draw attention to a series of characteristics of dream-content that need explaining and seem to conceal new findings. It is quite true that dreams do contain symbolizations of bodily organs and functions, that water in dreams often indicates an urge to pass it, that the male member may be represented by an upright stick or column – that sort of thing. In dreams that portray a very animated field of vision in glowing colours, in contrast to the dreariness of other dreams, one can scarcely reject the interpretation 'facial-stimulus dream', any more than one can dispute the contribution to illusion-forming in dreams made by noise and the babble of voices. A dream such as Scherner's, where two rows of beautiful, fair-haired boys confront each other on a bridge, attack, then resume their former positions, until in the end the dreamer sits down on a bridge and pulls a long tooth from his jaw (or a similar one recounted by Volkelt concerning two rows of drawers and again ending with the extraction of a tooth) – such dream-images, described by both writers in great numbers, will not permit us to dismiss Scherner's theory as idle invention without searching for its core of truth. The task is then to find a different sort of explanation for the putative symbolization of the alleged dental stimulus.

All the time we have been discussing the theory of somatic dream-sources I have refrained from putting forward the argument derived from our own dream-analyses. If, using a method that other writers had not applied to their dream-material, we have successfully shown that dream has a value of its own as psychical action, that a wish is the motive behind its formation and that the experiences of the previous day provide the immediate material for its content, then every other dream-theory that neglects so important a method of investigation, allowing dream to appear as a useless and puzzling psychical reaction to somatic stimuli, stands condemned without specific criticism. That would inevitably mean (which is most unlikely) that there were two quite different types of dream, one of which has visited only us, the other only the earlier judges of dream. All we need do is take the facts on which the conventional theory of somatic dream-stimuli is based and accommodate them within our theory of dream.

We have already taken the first step in this direction. This was when we posited that dream-work is compelled to process all simultaneously present dream-stimuli until they form an entity (see pp. 190f.). We saw that when two or more experiences capable of making an impression are left over from the previous day, the wishes proceeding from them are combined in a dream; we also saw that the psychically valuable impression and the indifferent [trivial, inert] experiences of the previous day come together to furnish the dream-material, provided that reciprocally communicating ideas can be established between them. Dream thus appears as a reaction to everything that is simultaneously present in the sleeping psyche as being of relevance to the current situation. In other words, where we have analysed dream-material hitherto, we have found it to be a collection of psychical residues and memory traces to which (because of the privileged treatment accorded to material that is still vivid and to infantile material) we had to attribute a quality of relevance that at the time was psychologically indeterminable. Now, it is not particularly hard for us to predict what will happen when new material, in terms of sensations felt during sleep, is added to these memories of current relevance. Such stimuli in turn acquire importance for dream in that they too are of current relevance; they become combined with the other matters of psychical relevance to provide the material for dream-formation. Stimuli experienced during sleep are (to put it another way) processed into a wish-fulfilment, the other components of which are the day's psychical residues, as we have seen. That combination does not *necessarily* take place; we know already that more than one type of behaviour is possible in the face of corporeal stimuli experienced during sleep. Where it does take place, ideational material for dream-content has successfully been found that is capable of representing both dream-sources, the somatic and the psychical.

The nature of dream remains unchanged when somatic material is added to psychical dream-sources; it is still wish-fulfilment, no matter how the expression of that wish-fulfilment is determined by the material of current relevance.

I should very much like to make room here for a series of characteristics capable of shaping the importance of external stimuli (so far as dream is concerned) in a variety of ways. I can imagine that a combination of personal physiological factors and accidental factors arising out of the circumstances of a particular time determines how a person will behave in individual instances of intensive objective stimulation during sleep; that person's habitual, accidental depth of sleep, in conjunction with the intensity of the stimulus, will on one occasion enable him to suppress the stimulus in such a way that it does not disturb his sleep, and on another occasion force him to wake up or support the attempt to overcome the stimulus by weaving it into a dream. In line with the very wide range of possible situations, external objective stimuli may find expression in dream with greater or lesser frequency in one individual than in another. In myself (an excellent sleeper who obstinately insists on ensuring that nothing disturbs my sleep), it is very rare for external causes of arousal to become mixed up in dreams, whereas it is clear that psychical motives will very readily make me dream. In fact, I have recorded only a single dream in which an objective, painful source of arousal is recognizable, and in this dream in particular it will be highly instructive to examine how that external stimulus affected the dream.

I am riding a grey horse, timidly and clumsily at first as if not seated properly. I then meet P., a colleague of mine, who is dressed in his loden suit and sitting upright in the saddle and who delivers some sort of rebuke to me (probably because I am sitting badly). I now feel better and better all the time on this highly intelligent horse; I am sitting comfortably and increasingly feel very much at home up here. My saddle is a sort of cushion that completely fills the space between the horse's neck and its croup. In this way I ride neatly between two freight carts. After riding some way down the street, I turn around and am about to dismount, initially in front of a small, open chapel lying flush with the façades. Then I do actually dismount in front of one near it; the hotel is in the same street; I could let the horse find its way on its own but I choose to lead it there. It is as if I would feel ashamed of myself, arriving there on horseback. Standing outside the hotel is a page boy, who shows me a note that I had found and teases me about it. On the note, underlined twice, are the words, 'Do not eat anything', then a second instruction (unclear) like 'Do no work'; at the same time a vague notion that I am in a foreign city, where I am doing no work.

It is not immediately apparent that this dream came about under the influence (or, rather, under the compulsion) of a pain stimulus. The fact is, the previous day I had suffered from boils that made every movement a torment to me, and most recently one boil at the base of the scrotum had grown as large as an apple, causing me the most intolerable discomfort at each step; on top of which a feverish fatigue, loss of appetite and a hard day's work (which I had adhered to none the less) combined with the pain to upset my mood. I was not properly able to carry out my medical duties, but because of the nature and location of the malady I was put in mind of another activity of which I would undoubtedly have been uniquely incapable, and that is *riding*. Riding is the very activity that dream has me perform; it is the most forceful negation of my suffering that imagination could have come up with. I cannot ride at all and do not normally dream about it; in fact, I have only ever sat on a horse once, when I had no saddle and took no pleasure in the occasion. However, in this dream I am riding as if I had no boil on my perineum – *or rather: precisely because I do not want to have one*. My saddle, to judge from the description, is the poultice that enabled me to get to sleep. I probably (thus protected) felt no discomfort during the first few hours of sleep. Then the painful sensations made themselves felt and tried to wake me up, whereupon the dream came along and said soothingly, 'No, sleep on, you're not going to wake up! In fact, you don't have a boil at all, because you're on horseback, and with a boil just there no one could ride a horse!' Moreover, the dream succeeded: the pain was deadened, and I stayed asleep.

But my dream was not content with 'de-suggesting' the boil by stubbornly insisting on an idea that was incompatible with the pain – in doing which it had behaved like the hallucinatory insanity of the mother who has lost her child[5] or of the businessman whose losses have stripped him of his fortune. It went further: the details of the sensation it is denying and of the image it is using to repress that sensation also supply it with material with which to link whatever other things are freshly present in my mind to the dreamed situation and to body those things forth. I am riding a *grey* horse, which is precisely the colour of the *pepper-and-salt-coloured* outfit I had been wearing when I last met my friend P. in the country. *Spicy* food had been suggested to me as the cause of my furunculosis – a preferable aetiology to *sugar*, incidentally, which may suggest itself in connection with boils. My friend P. has been fond of lording it over me (*sitting upright in the saddle* or 'sitting on his high horse') ever since he took over one of my female patients in connection with whom I had demonstrated *great skill* (in the dream I am sitting on the horse at an angle, like a *trick rider*) but who had actually, like the horse in the story about the Sunday rider, taken me where she wanted to go. The horse thus comes to symbolize a female patient (in the dream it is *highly intelligent*). '*I [. . .] increasingly feel very much at home up here*' alludes to the position I occupied in the house before P. took my place.[6] '*I thought you were sitting firmly in the saddle up there*' [i.e. 'I thought nothing could dislodge you'], one of my few well-wishers among the great doctors of this city told me recently in relation to that same hospital. It also demonstrated *great skill* to practise psychotherapy for eight to ten hours a day in such pain, but I know that unless I enjoy complete physical well-being I cannot keep up my particularly difficult work for long, and the dream is full of dark suggestions as to the situation that must then arise (the *note*, such as neurasthenics have and show the doctor): *No working and no eating.* Further interpretation shows me that dream-work has managed to find the way from the wish-situation of riding to very early childhood disputation scenes that must have taken place between myself and a nephew (a year older than me, incidentally), who now lives in England. It has also picked up bits from my travels in Italy; the street in the dream is made up of impressions of Verona and Siena. Even more intensive interpretation leads to sexual dream-thoughts, and I remember what dream-allusions to that lovely country apparently meant for a female patient who had never been to Italy (*gen Italien – Genitalien*)[7] – not unconnected, at the same time, with the establishment in which I was a doctor before my friend P., as well as with the site of my boil.

In another dream I managed in a similar fashion to ward off a sleep-disturbance, which *this time* threatened to come from a sensory stimulus. However, only an accident enabled me to uncover the link between the dream and the chance dream-stimulus and consequently understand the dream. I woke up one morning (this was in high summer, in a Tyrolean mountain resort), aware that I had dreamed: *The Pope has died.* I was unable to interpret this brief, non-visual dream. All I remembered was one 'leg' of the dream, so to speak: shortly before this I had read in the paper a report of His Holiness suffering a mild indisposition. But during the morning my wife asked, 'Did you hear all that dreadful bell-ringing earlier?' I was not aware of having heard it, but now I understood my dream. It had been the reaction of my requirement for sleep to the noise with which the pious Tyroleans had attempted to rouse me. I avenged myself on them with the deduction that forms the content of the dream, and as a result slept on in total indifference to the bell-ringing.

Several of the dreams mentioned in previous chapters might serve as examples of the processing of what I call 'nerve stimuli'. The dream about drinking in deep draughts [p. 137] is one such; in it the somatic stimulus is apparently the sole dream-source and the wish proceeding from the sensation (thirst) the only dream-motive. The situation is much the same in other simple dreams, where the somatic stimulus is able to formulate a wish on its own. The dream by a patient who slid the cooling appliance off her cheek at night [p. 139] demonstrates an unusual way of reacting to pain stimuli with wish-fulfilment; the patient appears to have succeeded in making herself temporarily pain-free, shifting her pain on to some-one else.

My dream about the Three Fates [p. 220] is clearly a hunger-dream, but it contrives to shift the need for food back to the child's yearning for its mother's breast, and to use this innocent desire as cover for a more serious one, which is not permitted to express itself in such plain terms. The dream about Count Thun [p. 223] showed us how an accidentally given bodily need can be brought into association with the most powerful but also most powerfully repressed stirrings of the life of the mind. And if, as in the case reported by Garnier, the First Consul incorporated the sound of the exploding time bomb in a battle-dream before it woke him up [p. 38], we find revealed here with especial clarity the endeavour in whose service mental activity takes note of sensations felt during sleep in the first place. A young lawyer who, full of his first big bankruptcy, falls asleep one afternoon, behaves just like the great Napoleon. He dreams about one G. Reich of *Hussiatyn*, whom he knows from a bankruptcy case, but *Hussiatyn* goes on and on – demanding his urgent attention; he has to wake up and hears his wife (who has a bad case of bronchial catarrh) loudly coughing [German: 'husten'].

Let us take this dream by Napoleon I (who incidentally was an excellent sleeper) in conjunction with that other one by the oversleeping student [p. 138], who when his landlady woke him, saying he must leave for the hospital, dreamed that he was lying in a hospital bed and slept on, with the motivation: 'If I'm already at the hospital, I don't need to get up and go there, do I?' The latter is an obvious comfort-dream; the dreamer is quite open with himself about the motive of the dream but in the process uncovers one of the secrets of all dreaming. In a sense, all dreams are *comfort-dreams*, serving the intention of maintaining the state of sleep rather than waking up. *Dream is the guardian of sleep, not its spoiler.* Confronted by psychically waking factors, we shall be justifying this view elsewhere; its applicability to the role of objective external stimuli we can already show here. The mind either takes no notice whatsoever of what causes sensations during sleep, where it is able to in the face of the intensity and what it clearly understands to be the significance of those stimuli, or it uses dream to deny them, or thirdly, if forced to acknowledge such stimuli, it seeks to interpret them in a way that represents the particular current sensation as one component of a desired situation favouring sleep. The current sensation is woven into a dream *in order to rob it of reality*. Napoleon may sleep on; after all, it is only a dream-reminiscence of the thunder of the guns of Arcole trying to disturb him.[8]

The wish to sleep that the conscious 'I' has arrived at (and which, together with dream-censorship and the 'secondary processing' that we shall be looking at later and that represents the contribution made by the 'I' towards dreaming) must therefore be allowed for each time as a motive in dream-formation, and every successful dream is a fulfilment of the same. How this universal, ever-present, unvarying wish to sleep relates to the other wishes of which sometimes this one, sometimes that one is fulfilled by the dream-content will form the object of a separate discussion. But in the wish to sleep we have discovered the factor that is capable of plugging the gap in the Strümpell–Wundt theory and throwing light on the distorted and capricious manner in which the external stimulus is interpreted. The correct interpretation, of which the sleeping mind is quite capable, would claim an active interest, demanding that an end be made to sleep; that is why, of the interpretations that are at all possible, only those are admitted that are compatible with the absolutist censorship of the wish to sleep. For instance: 'It was the nightingale, and not the lark.'[9] Because, if it is the lark, the night of love has come to an end. Among the interpretations of the stimulus deemed admissible, that one will be chosen that best ties in with the wish-stirrings lurking in the mind. In that way, everything is unambiguously laid down and nothing left to chance. The misinterpretation is not an illusion; if you like, it is an excuse. But again, what we have here, as with substitution by distortion for the purposes of dream-censorship, is an act of diffraction of the normal psychical process.

If the external nerve stimulus and the internal corporeal stimulus are sufficiently intense to compel psychical attention, they constitute (if in fact they result in dreaming and not in waking) a fixed point for dream-formation, a nucleus in the dream-material to which a corresponding wish-fulfilment is sought in a similar way to (see above) the ideas linking two psychical dream-stimuli. To that extent it is correct to say of a certain number of dreams that in them the somatic element controls the dream-content. In this extreme case, merely for the purpose of dream-formation a wish is aroused that is specifically not relevant to the current situation. Dream, however, cannot help but represent a wish in a particular situation as fulfilled; it is faced with the task, as it were, of finding which wish can be represented as fulfilled by the sensation that has come to the fore. If the material that has now acquired current relevance is of a painful or embarrassing nature, for that very reason it is not unusable for the purpose of dream-formation. Mental life also has access to wishes whose fulfilment evokes aversion, which may appear to be a contradiction but becomes explicable by reference to the presence of two psychical authorities and the censorship existing between them.

We have heard how the life of the mind contains *repressed* wishes that belong to the first system but whose fulfilment the second system endeavours to frustrate. This is not meant historically (in the sense that such wishes once existed and have since been destroyed); the theory of repression, which is necessary in dealing with psychoneurosis, states on the contrary that such repressed wishes continue to exist, though with a simultaneous inhibition weighing heavy upon them. Language [the relevant German word is *Unterdrücken*] gets it right when it speaks of 'pressing down' such impulses. The psychical arrangement whereby such repressed wishes break through to realization remains in place and still works. However, should such a repressed wish reach fulfilment after all, the conquered inhibition that came from the second system (capable of consciousness) finds expression as aversion. To close this [parenthetical] discussion, if sensations of an unpleasant nature are present in sleep from somatic sources, the situation is exploited by dream-work to represent the fulfilment of a normally repressed wish – while retaining any censorship to a greater or lesser degree.

This state of affairs makes possible a series of anxiety-dreams, while a different series of these dreams that appear to negate the wish-theory reveals a different mechanism. Anxiety in dreams may in fact be of a psychoneurotic nature, it may stem from psychosexual states of arousal, with the anxiety corresponding to suppressed libido. In which case such anxiety, like the anxiety-dream as a whole, has the significance of a neurotic symptom, and we find ourselves at the outer limit, where the wish-fulfilling tendency of dream fails. In other anxiety-dreams, however, the feeling of anxiety is somatically present (in people with lung or heart disease, for instance, when they happen to find themselves short of breath), in which case it is exploited in order to help such vigorously suppressed wishes find fulfilment in dream, dreaming which would for psychical reasons have resulted in the same release from anxiety. It is not hard to combine the two apparently separate cases. Of two psychical formations (an emotional inclination and an ideational content) that belong intimately together, one that exists currently also, in dream, brings out the other; now the somatically occasioned anxiety brings out the suppressed ideational content, now the ideational content, freed from repression and accompanied by sexual arousal, brings out the release from anxiety. Of the one case we can say that a somatically occasioned affect is interpreted psychically; in the other case everything is psychically occasioned, but the formerly suppressed content easily lets itself be replaced by a somatic interpretation suiting the anxiety. The difficulties that arise here so far as understanding is concerned have little to do with dream; they stem from the fact that, with these discussions, we are touching on the problems of how anxiety unfolds and of repression.

One of the controlling dream-stimuli from the internal corporeal sphere is undoubtedly overall bodily mood. Not that it would be capable of furnishing dream-content, but it forces dream-thoughts to make a selection from the material intended to serve the purposes of portrayal in the relevant dream-content by putting forward part of that material as suiting its nature and holding back the rest. Moreover, this general mood left over from the day is presumably bound up with the psychical residues that are important for dream-purposes. Yet that mood may itself, in dream, be retained or overcome, with the result that a mood of bored listlessness will change into its opposite.

If somatic stimuli felt during sleep (sleep-sensations, in other words) are not unusually intense, my supposition is that they play a similar role in dream-formation as still-vivid but insignificant impressions left over from the day. What I mean is, they will be drawn into the process of dream-formation if they lend themselves to combination with the ideational content of the psychical dream-sources – otherwise not. They are treated as inexpensive, always-available material that is drawn on whenever required rather than as some costly fabric that partly dictates the use to which it will be put. The case is not unlike when a patron brings the artist a rare stone (an onyx, say) for him to fashion into a work of art. The size of the stone, its colour and its markings help to decide what portrait head or what scene shall be represented with it, whereas in the case of a regular, plentiful material (marble, say, or sandstone) the artist simply pursues the idea that takes shape in his head. This strikes me as the only way to understand the fact that the dream-content provided by bodily stimuli that fail to attain unusual heights does not in fact recur in every dream and is not dreamed of every night.[10]

Possibly an example that takes us back to dream-interpretation will best explain my view. One day I was struggling to understand what the feeling of being inhibited, of being unable to move, of not managing to do something (that sort of feeling, which so often features in dreams and is so closely related to anxiety) – what in fact it might mean. The next night I had the following dream: *Very inadequately dressed, I am making my way from a ground-floor flat up the stairs to a higher floor. I take four steps at a time, pleased that I am able to climb stairs so nimbly. Suddenly I see a maid descending the stairs towards me – and I know we shall meet. I feel ashamed and try to hurry, and at this point the feeling of inhibition comes over me, I am glued to the spot and cannot move.*

Analysis: The situation in the dream is taken from everyday reality. I have two flats in a house in Vienna, connected only by the main staircase. On the raised ground floor is a flat accommodating my medical practice and my study; on the floor above are my living quarters. When in the late evening I have finished working down below, I climb the stairs to bed. The evening before the dream I had indeed made the short journey in some disarray – that is to say, I had removed my collar, tie and cuffs; in the dream this had become a more advanced but as usual indeterminate state of undress. Taking several steps at a stride is my usual way of climbing stairs (in the dream, incidentally, this is already an acknowledged piece of wish-fulfilment, the ease with which I perform this activity reassuring me as to the state of my heart). Furthermore, it forms an effective contrast to the inhibition experienced in the second half of the dream. It shows me (which did not need proving) that dream has no difficulty in imagining motor actions performed to perfection; think of flying in dreams!

However, the staircase I am negotiating is not the one in my house. I do not recognize it at first; only the person descending towards me enlightens me as to the place meant. That person is the maid of the old lady whom I visit twice daily to administer injections; the staircase is also very similar to the one I have to climb there twice every day.

Now, how do that staircase and that woman find their way into my dream? The sense of shame at being incompletely dressed is undoubtedly sexual in nature; the maid about whom I dream is older than myself, surly and not in the least attractive. As I ask myself these questions, what occurs to me is precisely this: when I make my morning visit to this house I usually feel the need, when climbing the stairs, to clear my throat; the product of the expectoration ends up on one of the treads. The fact is, on those two floors there is no spittoon, and I take the view that keeping the staircase clean should not be effected at my expense but should be done by providing a spittoon. The janitor, who is also an elderly lady of surly appearance but, as I am prepared to concede, cleanly instincts, takes a different view of the matter. She lies in wait to see whether I will once again take the aforementioned liberty, and if she finds that I do I hear her mutter audibly. She also, for days thereafter, denies me the usual respectful greeting when we meet. It so happened that, the day prior to the dream, the janitor's side had also been taken by the maid. In my customary haste, I had completed my sick visit when the maid accosted me in the hallway and remarked, 'Sir might at least have wiped his feet before entering the bedroom today. The red carpet is all dirty again from your boots!' That is the only claim that staircase and maid can assert as regards featuring in my dream.

Between my flying-up-the-stairs and the spitting-on-the-stairs there is a close connection. Pharyngitis and heart problems are both deemed to represent penalties for the sin of smoking, because of which I do not enjoy a reputation for enormous niceness even with my own janitor – that is to say, either in the one house or in the other, my dream blending them into one.

I must postpone further interpretation until I can report where the typical dream of not being fully dressed comes from. I simply note, as a preliminary finding from the dream I have told you about, that the dream-sensation of inhibited movement is evoked wherever a certain context requires it. A particular state of my motility in sleep cannot be the cause of such dream-content, since a moment earlier I saw myself (as if to confirm this realization) running nimbly up the stairs.

Notes

1. [L. Strümpell, *Die Natur und Entstehung der Träume* ('Nature and origin of dreams'), Leipzig 1877, p. 108.]

2. I should like to advise everyone to read the two volumes of Mourly Vold's thorough and precise record of experimentally generated dreams in order to be convinced of how little explanation of the content of the individual dream is contained in the relevant experimental conditions described and of how relatively useless such experiments are as regards understanding dream-problems.

3. [T. Lipps, *Grundtatsachen des Seelenlebens* ('Fundamentals of the life of the mind'), Bonn 1883, p. 170.]

4. See also K. Landauer, 'Handlungen des Schlafenden' ['Actions of the sleeper'], in *Zeitschrift f. d. ges. Neurologie und Psychiatrie*, XXXIX, 1918. For every observer there are visible, meaningful actions performed by the sleeper. The sleeper is not completely stupefied; on the contrary, he is capable of acting logically and with determination.

5. See also the passage in Griesinger [1871] and the comment in my second essay on the psychoneuroses of defence ['Further remarks on the psychoneuroses of defence', in *Standard Edition*, vol. III, p. 159].

6. [Freud does indeed simply say '*das Haus*'. He is referring to the psychiatric clinic, where he worked under Theodor Meynert in 1883.]

7. [This works better in German, of course, where since all 'g's are hard the sound of the two elements is identical. '*Gen*' is an old-fashioned, literary German word for 'towards'.]

8. The content of this dream is given in different ways in the two sources from which I learned it.

9. [*Romeo and Juliet*, Act III, scene v.]

10. Rank has shown in a series of essays that certain dreams evoked by organ stimuli that wake the dreamer up (dreams provoked by the urge to urinate, emission dreams) are particularly apt to illustrate the struggle between the requirement for sleep and the demands of organic need, demonstrating how the latter influences dream-content.

D *Typical dreams*

We are not, as a rule, able to interpret another person's dream if that person refuses to provide us with the unconscious thoughts underlying the relevant dream-content, and this seriously reduces the practicability of our method of dream-interpretation.[1] However, in diametrical contrast to the individual's normal freedom to furnish his dream-world in particular, private ways, thus rendering it inaccessible to other people's understanding, there exist a certain number of dreams that almost everyone has dreamed in the same fashion and in connection with which we customarily assume that they also have the same meaning in every case. Moreover, particular interest attaches to such typical dreams because they presumably stem from the same sources for all people, which seems to make them especially apt to provide us with information about where dreams come from.

So it is with very particular expectations that we shall set about trying our method of dream-interpretation on these typical dreams, and we shall be very loath to concede defeat if our technique fails to prove its worth on precisely this material. When it comes to interpreting typical dreams, the dreamer's own ideas, which have been our usual guide to understanding dream, are in fact no use or become blurred and inadequate, with the result that we cannot solve our task with their help.

Why this is, and how we correct this defect in our technique, will become apparent at a later stage of our study. The reader will then also understand why at this point I can deal only with a few specimens from the group of typical dreams, and why I postpone discussion of the others to that later stage.

i The embarrassment-dream of being naked

The dream in which one is naked or poorly clad in the presence of strangers also comes with the additional feature that one felt no shame at the fact – nothing of that kind. However, our interest in dreams of being naked concerns only those where the dreamer experiences shame and embarrassment, wishes to flee or hide, and in the process suffers the curious inhibition of being unable to move and feels incapable of altering what is a painfully awkward situation. Only in this combination is the dream typical; in other respects, the core content may involve all kinds of other associations or contain individual ingredients. Essentially, it is about the embarrassing experience of the nature of shame, about wishing to hide one's nakedness, usually by means of locomotion, and not being able to. I believe the vast majority of my readers will, in dream, have found themselves in this situation at one time or another.

Usually the way in which a person loses his [or her] clothes is unclear. Sometimes one will hear, 'I was wearing a shirt [or blouse]', but rarely is the picture definite; in most cases the state of undress is so unspecific that it is narrated as an alternative: 'I was in my blouse or chemise.' As a rule, the sartorial defect is not so serious as to appear to justify the accompanying feeling of shame. For someone who has worn the Emperor's uniform, nakedness is frequently replaced by an infringement of dress regulations. 'I am in the street without a sword and see officers coming towards me, or without a collar, or I am wearing check civilian trousers' – that sort of thing.

The people in whose presence one feels ashamed are almost invariably strangers with faces left indistinct. It never happens in the typical dream that one is reprimanded or even simply noticed because of one's dress, even when it occasions such embarrassment. On the contrary, people appear indifferent or, as I was able to perceive in a particularly clear dream, solemnly stiff-featured. This is interesting.

The dreamer's embarrassed sense of shame and people's indifference together produce a contradiction such as often occurs in dream. After all, the only thing that would accord with the way the dreamer feels would be if strangers stare at him in amazement and laugh at or get angry with him. What I think is that the one offensive feature has been removed by wish-fulfilment, while the other, preserved by some power, has remained intact, and as a result the two pieces fit ill together. We have here interesting proof that, because its form is partly distorted by wish-fulfilment, the nakedness dream has not been properly understood. The fact is, it has become the basis of a folk tale, familiar to all of us in Andersen's version ('The Emperor's New Clothes') and recently put to poetic use in Fulda's *The Talisman*.[2] The Andersen story tells of two swindlers who weave a costly garment for the Emperor that, they say, only the good and true will be able to see. The Emperor goes out one day, wearing this invisible garment, and all the people, intimidated by the touchstone-like power of the fabric, pretend to be unaware of the Emperor's nakedness.

This, however, is the situation of our dream. It hardly takes great boldness to assume that an incomprehensible dream-content has provided the stimulus to inventing some sort of dressing-up, some sort of investiture in which the situation being remembered becomes meaningful. In the process, though, the situation has been stripped of its original significance and made to serve other ends. However, we shall hear that this kind of misunderstanding of dream-content by the conscious ratiocination of a second psychical system occurs often and should be recognized as a factor in the definitive structuring of dream; also that similar misunderstandings (likewise within the same psychical personality) play a major role in the formation of compulsive ideas and phobias. As regards our dream, too, it is possible to suggest where the material for the reinterpretation is taken from. The swindler is the dream, the Emperor is the dreamer, and the moralizing tendency betrays a dim sense that the latent dream-content concerns forbidden wishes sacrificed to repression. The fact is, the context in which such dreams appear during my analyses of neurotics puts it beyond doubt that this dream is based on a memory of earliest childhood. Only in our childhood was there time for us to appear less than fully clothed in the presence of members of our family as well as unrelated nurses, maids and visitors, and then we were not ashamed of our nakedness.[3] In many children, even when they are older, it is possible to observe how nakedness has an almost intoxicating effect on them, rather than making them feel ashamed. They laugh, they jump around, they punch one another, and their mother or whoever is there chides them for it, saying, 'Stop it, that's disgusting, you shouldn't do that.' Children often show a tendency to exhibitionism; one can scarcely walk through a village in this part of the world without meeting a two- or three-year-old youngster who will lift his or her little shirt in front of the stroller, possibly in the stroller's honour. One of my patients has retained in conscious memory a scene from when he was eight, showing how, after undressing for bed, he wants to go dancing in to his little sister in the next room wearing only his nightshirt and how the servant forbids him. In the juvenile histories of neurotics, self-exposure to children of the opposite sex features heavily; in paranoia, the delusion that one is being watched while dressing and undressing stems from such experiences; those who remain perverted include a category (*exhibitionists*) in which the infantile impulse is elevated to the status of symbol.

This childhood devoid of shame, when we look back on it later, seems like a paradise, and paradise itself is nothing but a mass fantasy of the childhood of the individual. That is why in paradise, too, people are naked and not ashamed – until a time comes when shame and fear arise, expulsion follows, and sexual life and cultural activities commence. Only dream is capable of returning us to that paradise every night; we have already voiced the supposition that the impressions of earliest childhood (the 'prehistoric'[4] period up until around the third birthday), possibly regardless of their content, inherently demand reproduction, that their repetition is an act of wish-fulfilment. In other words, dreams of being naked are *exhibitionist dreams*.[5]

The exhibitionist dream revolves around the figure of the dreamer, which is not that of a child but as the dreamer appears at present, and around his [or her] inadequate attire, which as a result of the overlaying of so many subsequent dishabille memories or for censorship's sake comes out only vaguely; a third element are the persons in whose presence the dreamer feels ashamed. I do not know of a single instance of the actual observers of that infantile exposure reappearing in dream. Hardly ever, in fact, is dream mere memory. Remarkably, the persons who had our sexual interest during childhood are omitted from all reproductions in dream, in hysteria and in obsessional neurosis; only paranoia reinserts the observers and concludes with fanatical conviction that, though remaining invisible, they are present. What dream inserts in their stead (namely, 'a lot of strangers' who take no notice of the proffered exhibition) is precisely the *wish-opposite* to the familiar, trusted individual for whom the exhibition was intended. Incidentally, 'a lot of strangers' also make frequent dream appearances in a great many other contexts; they invariably mean 'secret' as wish-opposite.[6] Notice how even the restitution of the original circumstances that occurs in paranoia takes account of this contrast. One is no longer alone, one is undoubtedly being watched, but the observers are 'a lot of strangers, left curiously indistinct'.

Another thing that comes out in the exhibitionist dream is repression. The embarrassment felt in the dream is the reaction of the second psychical system to the fact that the content of the exhibition scene rejected by it has nevertheless found expression. To spare it, the scene should not have been revived.

We shall deal again later on with the question of being unable to move. In dream it serves primarily to represent *conflict of wills*, the *no*. The unconscious intention is that the exhibition shall continue; censorship demands that it be broken off.

The links between our typical dreams and folk tales and other writings are of course neither isolated nor accidental. Every now and then the transformation process (whose instrument the writer usually represents) is seen analytically by some sharp-eyed poet and traced in the opposite direction – in other words, the tale goes back to the dream. A friend drew my attention to the following passage in Gottfried Keller's *Der Grüne Heinrich* ['Green Henry']:

> I would not wish, my dear Lee, that you should ever learn from experience, so to speak, the very piquant truth of the situation Odysseus finds himself in when, naked and covered with mud, he appears before Nausicaa and her playmates. Do you want to know how that happens? Let us hold fast to our example. Should you ever, cut off from your homeland and from all that is dear to you, wander far afield among strangers, seeing many things, experiencing many things, should you have cares and woes, even know poverty and feel abandoned, then one night, without fail, you will dream that you are drawing near to your homeland; you spy it gleaming and sparkling in the loveliest colours, you see dear, fond, beloved beings coming towards you; and all of a sudden you discover that you are wandering about in rags or naked and covered in dust. A nameless shame and fear overcome you, you try to cover yourself up or hide, and you wake up bathed in sweat. Such, so long as he has walked the earth, has been the dream of sorrowful, storm-tossed man, and in such terms did Homer distil the situation from the inmost, ageless essence of mankind.

The inmost, ageless essence of mankind, which is what poets and storytellers usually rely on arousing among their audience, consists of those stirrings of the life of the mind that have their roots in a childhood subsequently become 'prehistoric'. Behind the irreproachable wishes of the homeless wanderer, which are accessible to consciousness, other dreams break through, dreams of childhood that have been suppressed as inadmissible, and this is why the dream objectified in the Nausicaa legend regularly tips over into an anxiety-dream.

My own dream (see above, page 254) of hurrying up some stairs, which soon afterwards turns into a rooted-to-the-spot dream, is also an exhibitionist dream, presenting as it does the essential components of one. So it should be traceable back to childhood experiences, and being aware of that should tell us how far the maid's treatment of me (her reproach that I have made the carpet dirty) helps her towards the position she occupies in the dream. Now I can really provide the explanations we are after. In performing a psychoanalysis, one learns to reinterpret closeness in time as connectedness in meaning; two thoughts that seem unconnected but follow immediately upon each other form an entity that needs to be guessed at – just as an *a* and a *t*, placed together on the page, should be pronounced as a single syllable: *at*. Dreams are interrelated in a similar fashion. The aforementioned dream about the staircase is plucked from a series of dreams, the other components of which are known to me in terms of their interpretation. Being embedded in a series, the dream must belong in the same context. Now, those other, enclosing dreams are based on my memories of a nanny who looked after me from some time prior to weaning until I was two and a half years old and of whom I have a dim conscious recollection. To judge from information recently gleaned from my mother, she was old and ugly but very clever and capable; to judge from the conclusions I may be permitted to draw from my dreams, she did not always accord me the most loving treatment, in fact she had harsh words for me when I did not show adequate understanding of her training in cleanliness. So by endeavouring to continue that instruction, the maid acquired the right to be treated by me, in dream, as an embodiment of the 'prehistoric' old woman. Presumably the child, despite that instructress's poor treatment of him, gave her his love.[7]

ii *Dreams of the deaths of loved ones*

Another series of dreams that may be termed typical are those in which a loved relative (parent, sibling, offspring – someone like that) has died. From the outset, such dreams must be divided into two categories: one in which the mourning dreamed of leaves the dreamer unaffected, with the result that, on waking, one is surprised at one's lack of feeling, the other in which one feels deep sorrow at the death, even giving expression to one's grief by shedding fervent tears while asleep.

We can disregard the first group of dreams; they have no claim to being deemed typical. Analysing them, one finds that they mean something other than what they contain, that their purpose is to conceal a different wish. An example is the dream of the aunt who sees her sister's only son laid out in his coffin before her (see p. 163). This does not mean that she wishes the young nephew dead but simply conceals, as we discovered, the wish that she should once again, after missing him for a long time, see a certain loved person – the same one as, after a similarly long interval, she had re-encountered once before over the corpse of another nephew. This wish, which constitutes the true content of the dream, offers no reason for mourning, which is why in the dream, too, no grief is felt. Note that in this instance the feeling experienced in the dream belongs not to the manifest dream-content but to the latent, and that the emotional substance of the dream has remained free from the distortion affecting the ideational substance.

Quite different are the dreams in which the death of a loved relative is portrayed and painful emotion is experienced. Such dreams signify what their content suggests, namely the wish that the person concerned should die, and since I can expect at this point that the feelings of every reader and of every person who has dreamed something similar will rebel against my explanation, I must strive to prove the point on the broadest possible basis.

We commented earlier on a dream from which we were able to learn that the wishes that represent themselves as fulfilled in dreams are not always of current relevance. They may also be bygone, worn-out, overlaid, repressed wishes to which, merely because they have cropped up again in dream, we have to grant a kind of continuance, a kind of continued existence. They are not dead as we understand people to be dead; they are like the Shades of the *Odyssey*, which awake to a certain life as soon as they have drunk blood. The dream of the dead child in the box (see p. 165) deals with a wish that was relevant fifteen years earlier and had been frankly admitted ever since. It is perhaps not unimportant as regards the theory of dream if I add: even that wish was based on a memory of earliest childhood. The dreamer had heard as a small child (the precise time cannot be ascertained) that her mother, during the pregnancy that was to result in herself, fell into a mood of deep disgruntlement and earnestly wished that the child in her womb should die. Grown up now and herself with child, she was simply following her mother's example.

When someone dreams, with expressions of pain, that his father or mother or brother or sister is dead, I never use that dream as proof that he wishes them dead *now*. The theory of dream is not so exigent; it is content to conclude that the dreamer did wish them dead at some time in childhood. However, I fear that this qualification will do little to soothe the complainants, who will doubtless as vigorously deny ever having thought this way in the past as they feel confident of harbouring no such wishes in the present. So I am going to have to reconstitute a portion of the extinct life of the child's mind from testimony still available today.[8]

Let us start by looking at children's relationship to their siblings. I do not know why we assume this should be one of affection; after all, examples of sibling hostility among adults form a prominent part of the experience of each one of us, and we can often see that such divisions stem from childhood or have always existed. Equally, though, a great many adults who today are very fond of their siblings and give them much support used once, in childhood, to live in almost unbroken hostility with them. The elder child maltreated the younger, told lies about it, stole its toys; the younger child, consumed with helpless rage against the elder, envied and feared it, or the first stirrings of its own desire for freedom and sense of justice were turned against the oppressor. The parents say, 'The children don't get on', and they cannot understand why. It is not hard to see that even the character of the good child differs from that which we should wish to find in an adult. The child is wholly egoistic, experiencing its needs intensely and striving ruthlessly to satisfy them, particularly against its rivals – other children, but in the first instance its own siblings. However, we do not call the child 'bad' because of that; we call it 'naughty'. It is not responsible for its misdeeds, either before our judgement or before the law. And rightly so; because even within phases of existence that we include within childhood we can expect the little egoist to show stirrings of altruism and morality that, as Meynert puts it, will overlay the primary 'I' with a secondary 'I', thus inhibiting it.[9] No doubt morality does not arise simultaneously all along the line; also, the duration of the amoral childhood period differs from individual to individual. Where such morality fails to develop, we often speak of 'degeneration'; this is clearly a case of arrested development. Where the primary character is already overlaid by the later development, it may be at least partially re-exposed by the person's succumbing to hysteria. The similarity between the so-called 'hysterical character' and that of a naughty child is in fact very striking. Compulsive neurosis, on the other hand, corresponds to an extra morality [*Übermoralität*], imposed on the re-aroused primary character as a strengthening burden.

In other words, many people who today love their siblings and would feel deprived by their demise unconsciously carry with them, from an earlier period, ill-will against the latter in the form of wishes that may emerge in dreams. But it is of very particular interest to observe small children of up to three years of age or slightly over in their behaviour towards younger siblings. Hitherto the child was unique; now he is told that the stork has brought a new child. Eyeing the newcomer, the child avers determinedly, 'The stork should take it away again.'[10]

I quite seriously take the view that the child is able to work out what disadvantages it can expect from the new arrival. A lady of my acquaintance, who now gets on very well with the sister who is four years younger than herself, told me that she greeted the news of her sister's birth with the reservation, 'But she can't have my red bonnet, I'm not giving her that.' Should the child fail to reach this recognition until later, the hostility will arise when it does so. I know of a case where a girl not yet three tried to strangle in the cradle the infant whose further presence, she felt, boded no good so far as she was concerned. Jealousy is something that children of that age are capable of in all its clarity and power. Or the little sibling really does soon disappear, the child has managed to refocus all the love and affection in the household on itself, and the stork promptly sends another present; is it not then perfectly in order that our little darling should conceive and nourish the wish that the new rival might suffer the same fate as the one before, leaving the child free to enjoy the same fine conditions as it had enjoyed previously and in the interim?[11] In normal circumstances, of course, such behaviour by the child towards the new-born baby is a simple function of age difference. Where the gap is sufficient, the elder girl's maternal instincts towards the helpless newborn will already be coming into play.

Feelings of hostility towards siblings must be far more common in young children than the dull observation of adults takes them to be.[12]

In the case of my own children, who followed one another in quick succession, I neglected the opportunity to make such observations; I am making up for it now in the case of my young nephew, whose monopoly was disturbed after fifteen months by the appearance on the scene of a competitor. I hear, in fact, that the young man behaves in a most courtly fashion to his little sister, kissing her hand and caressing her; I am convinced, however, that even before turning two he was using his ability to speak to voice criticism of someone who seems to him wholly superfluous. Each time the talk turns to her, he butts in and cries indignantly, 'Too (s)mall, too (s)mall!' In the last few months, the child having developed superbly and outgrown such disparagement, he has learned to give a different reason for his admonition that the girl does not deserve so much attention. Whenever the occasion presents itself, he reminds people that 'She's got no teeth.'[13] And none of us will ever forget how, at the age of six, the eldest girl of another of my sisters spent half an hour having all her aunts confirm, 'Lucy can't understand that yet, can she?' Lucy was her two-and-a-half-year-younger rival.

The dream of the death of a sibling (as corresponding to this increased hostility) is one that, for instance, comes up without fail in analyses of my female patients. I have found only a single exception, in fact – and that lent itself readily to reinterpretation as confirming the rule. Once when, during a session, I was explaining this matter to a lady (in view of her symptom, it seemed to me an apt item for discussion), she astonished me by replying that she had never had such dreams. However, she did recall another dream that she said was of no relevance, a dream that she had first had at the age of four, when she was the youngest, and had had repeatedly since. '*A crowd of children, all her brothers and sisters and cousins, were romping about in a field. Suddenly they grew wings, took flight and were gone.*' She had no idea what the dream meant; we shall have no difficulty in recognizing it as a dream of the death of all a person's siblings in its original form, almost untouched by censorship. I venture to put forward the following analysis. On the occasion of the death of one of the crowd of children (the children of two brothers were in this case brought up together, virtually as siblings), our not yet four-year-old dreamer will have asked a wise grown-up, 'What happens to children after they die?' The answer will have been, 'They sprout wings and become angels.' In the dream that followed this explanation, the siblings do all have wings like angels, and (which is the main thing) they fly away. Our little angel-maker is left on her own, imagine, the only one of such a crowd! The fact that the children are romping about in a field, from which they fly off, almost certainly points to butterflies – as if the same thought-association guided the child as prompted the ancients to depict Psyche with butterfly's wings.

Someone may object at this point that, while the hostile impulses of children towards their siblings can possibly be conceded, how does it happen that this childish ill-will reaches such a pitch of wickedness as to wish the rival or stronger playmate dead, as if every misdemeanour can be atoned for only by the death penalty? Anyone who does so object is forgetting that the child's idea of 'being dead' has little in common with our own. It uses the same word, that's about all. The child knows nothing of the horrors of decay, of shuddering in an icy tomb, of the dread of everlasting night that the adult imagination, as all myths of the beyond bear witness, tolerates so ill. Fear of death is foreign to the child, which is why children toy with the ghastly word, saying menacingly to other children, 'If you do that once more you'll die the way Franz died', which sends shivers down the poor mother's spine, possibly because she cannot put out of her mind the fact that most people born on this earth do not survive their childhood years. Even at eight, a child returning from a visit to the Natural History Museum can tell its mother, 'Mummy, I love you so much; when you die I'm going to have you stuffed and stand you in the room here; that way I'll always be able to see you!' So little does the child's idea of being dead resemble our own.[14]

To the child (who has in any case been spared from witnessing the scenes of suffering that precede death), having died means the same as having 'gone away', no longer bothering the survivors. The child does not distinguish how such absence comes about – whether by departure, abandonment, estrangement or death.[15] If in the prehistoric years of a child's life its nurse has been dismissed and shortly afterwards its mother dies, so far as its memory is concerned (as analysis will reveal) the two events merge to form a single sequence. The child does not miss the absent one very intensively, as many a mother has found to her regret when, returning home after several weeks away in the summer, she is told in answer to her enquiries, 'The children didn't ask after mummy once.' But when she really has journeyed to that 'undiscover'd country, from whose bourn no traveller returns', the children seem at first to have forgotten her; only *some time later* do they start to recall the dead person.

So when the child has a motive for wishing another child absent, there is nothing to stop it from clothing such a desire in the form of wishing that child dead, and the psychical reaction to the death-invoking dream shows that, all differences of substance notwithstanding, such a wish is in some way the same for the child as a similar wish expressed by an adult.

But if the child's wish invoking the death of siblings is explained in terms of the child's egoism, which causes it to see the siblings as rivals, how is one to explain the wish invoking the deaths of parents, who so far as the child is concerned are the fount of love and fulfilment of its needs and whose preservation is desirable from just such egoistical motives?

As regards solving this problem, experience teaches us that

dreams of the deaths of parents predominantly concern that particular parent who shares the sex of the dreamer – in other words, that the male usually dreams of the death of his father and the female of the death of her mother. I cannot put this forward as a rule, but the predominance in the sense indicated is so marked as to demand explanation in terms of some factor of universal significance.[16] Roughly speaking, it is as if a sexual preference were to assert itself prematurely, as if the boy saw his father and the girl her mother as a rival in love, removing whom can only redound to the child's advantage.

Before anyone rejects this notion as monstrous, let him take a good look, here too, at the real relations between parents and children. We need to separate what the cultural requirement of respect demands of this relationship and what daily observation reveals to be actually the case. The relationship between parents and children harbours more than one occasion for hostility; conditions in which wishes may be engendered that do not stand up to censorship exist in plenty. Let us dwell for a moment on the father/son relationship. I believe that the sacred nature we ascribe to the prescriptions of the Decalogue dulls our faculty for perceiving reality. We scarcely dare notice, perhaps, that the majority of mankind feels that the fourth Commandment does not apply to it.[17] At the lowest as at the highest levels of human society, respect for parents tends to be overshadowed by other interests. The sombre messages that myth and legend bring us from the primeval years of human society give a nasty impression of the power of the father and the ruthlessness with which it has been wielded. Cronus eats his children, rather as the boar eats the sow's litter, and Zeus castrates his father[18] and rules in his stead. The more absolutely the father lorded it over the ancient family, the more the son (as designated successor) must have moved into the position of enemy and the greater his impatience must have become to attain dominion himself as a result of the father's death. Even nowadays, in our bourgeois families, the father, by refusing to grant his son self-determination and the requisite means thereto, tends to foster the natural seed of enmity that lies in their relationship and to help it grow. Doctors, in going about their business, are often able to observe how grief over the loss of his father cannot suppress the son's delight at finally obtaining his freedom. The residue of what in our present-day society is a sadly old-fashioned *potestas patris familias* tends to be clung to desperately by every father, and every writer can be confident of his effect if, like Ibsen, he sets the age-old struggle between father and son at the forefront of his plots. Occasions for conflict between mother and daughter occur when the daughter grows up and finds her mother standing guard while she longs for sexual freedom, whereas the mother, alerted by her daughter's blooming, realizes that the time has come for her to forgo sexual desires.

Such matters are plain for all to see. But they get us no further as regards explaining dreams of parental death in people whose piety towards their parents has long possessed a sacrosanct quality.[19] Also, what we were saying earlier has prepared us to derive such wishes invoking the deaths of parents from the years of earliest childhood.

It can be confirmed with a certainty excluding all doubt that this supposition holds for psychoneurotics so far as analyses conducted with them are concerned. One learns in this connection that the child's sexual desires (so far as they merit the name in their embryonic state) awaken very early on, and that the girl's first inclination is towards her father, the boy's first infantile yearnings are for his mother. His father is thus, for the boy, an unwelcome rival, as is her mother for the girl; and how little it takes, so far as the child is concerned, for this feeling to lead to a wish for the relevant parent's death is something we have already set out in regard to siblings. Sexual choice is usually made early, falling on one of the child's parents; a natural trait ensures that the husband pampers his little daughters and the wife sticks up for her sons, while both of them, where the magic of sex does not cloud their judgement, work sternly towards bringing up their children. The child, well aware of the preference, tends to rebel against the parent who opposes it. To find love among adults is not only, so far as the child is concerned, to satisfy a particular requirement; finding such love also means that the child's wishes will be complied with in every other matter.

So it is obeying its own sexual drive and at the same time reinforcing the stimulus coming from the respective parent when its choice between the parents falls in the same way as their own.

We are in the habit of overlooking most of the signs of these infantile leanings on the part of children, some of which are even detectable after the earliest childhood years. An eight-year-old girl of my acquaintance, when her mother is called away from the table, takes the opportunity to proclaim her own succession. 'Now I'm going to be Mummy. Karl, would you like more vegetables? Help yourself, do', and so on. A particularly gifted and lively girl of four, in whom this piece of child psychology is particularly transparent, will say straight out, 'Mummy can go off now, then Daddy will have to marry me and I'll be his wife.' In childhood, such a wish is by no means incompatible with the child being very fond of its mother. If a small boy is allowed to sleep in his mother's bed when his father goes away and, as soon as his father returns, has to go back to the nursery and sleep with someone of whom he is very much less fond, there may easily take shape within him the wish that his father might always be away and he, in consequence, might retain his place beside dear, lovely Mummy. And one way of achieving that wish is obviously for his father to be dead, because if experience has taught the boy anything it is that 'dead' people (Grandpa, for example) are always absent; they never come back.

If such observations of small children effortlessly accommodate the interpretation suggested, they fail to provide the unreserved conviction that psychoanalyses of adult neurotics force upon the doctor. Here, the relevant dreams are narrated with introductions that render their interpretation as wish-dreams unavoidable. One day, I find a lady distressed and tearful. She says, 'I don't want to see my relatives any more, they must find me frightening.' Then, almost without transition, she tells me that she recalls a dream of which she does not, of course, know the meaning. She had the dream when she was four, and it runs as follows: *A lynx* [Luchs] *or a fox* [Fuchs] *is walking on the roof, then something falls down or she falls down, then her mother is being carried out of the house, dead*, at which point she begins to weep with grief. Scarcely have I informed her that this dream must represent her childhood wish to see her mother dead and that it must be this dream that is making her think her relatives find her frightening than she comes out with some material explaining the dream. 'Lynx-eye' is an insult that was once, when she was a very small child, hurled at her by a street urchin; when the child was three, her mother had had a roof-tile fall on her head, causing it to bleed profusely.

I once had the opportunity of making a thorough study of a girl who went through various psychical states. In the raving confusion that marked the beginning of her illness, the patient showed a quite exceptional aversion to her mother, hitting out at and cursing the woman as soon as she approached the bed, while at the same time remaining affectionate and submissive in her behaviour towards a much older sister. There followed a lucid but somewhat apathetic state with very disturbed sleep; the treatment began during this phase with me analysing her dreams. A vast number of these dealt in a more or less disguised fashion with the mother's death; in one she was at the funeral of an elderly woman; in another she saw herself and her sister sitting at a table dressed in mourning; the meaning of the dreams was beyond doubt. As the patient continued to show improvement, hysterical phobias appeared; the most agonizing of these was that something had happened to her mother. Wherever she was, she then had to hurry home to satisfy herself that her mother was still alive. Taken in conjunction with my other experiences, the case was most instructive; it showed (translated into several languages, as it were) various ways in which the psychical system reacted to the same ideational stimulus. In the confusion, which I understand as the *overcoming* of the second psychical agency by the normally suppressed first, the patient's unconscious hostility towards her mother received motor expression; then, when the first period of calm occurred and, with the tumult suppressed, the rule of censorship was restored, only the field of dreaming was left open to that hostility as a place where the wish for the mother's death might be realized; as normality further asserted itself it produced, as a hysterical counter-reaction and defence manifestation, an excessive level of concern for the mother's well-being. In this context it is no longer inexplicable that hysterical young women should so often show excessive tenderness towards their mothers.

On another occasion I was able to gain deep insights into the unconscious mental life of a young man whose existence compulsive neurosis had rendered virtually unviable; he could not leave the house for fear (excruciating fear) that he would kill every passer-by. He spent his time tending the evidence for his alibi, in case he should be charged with committing one of the murders that occurred in the city. Needless to say, he was as moral a person as he was well educated. His analysis (which incidentally led to a cure) showed the reason for this embarrassing obsession to be murderous impulses towards his somewhat over-strict father. Those impulses had to his astonishment found conscious expression when he was seven years old but of course stem from much further back in his childhood. Following the painful illness and death of his father, my patient was assailed at the age of thirty by a compulsive reproach that transferred itself to strangers in the form of the said phobia. Anyone capable of wanting to push his own father off a mountaintop into empty space can be expected not to spare the lives of persons unrelated to him, either; so he was quite right to lock himself in his room.

In my experience (and it has been extensive), parents share the leading role in the infant mental lives of all subsequent psychoneurotics, and being in love with one parent and hating the other constitute an integral part of the stock of psychical stirrings that is formed at that time and is of such importance for the symptomatology of the neurosis to come. However, I do not believe that psychoneurotics differ sharply in this respect from other human children who remain normal; they are not, in my view, capable of creating something wholly new and peculiar to themselves. It is far more probable, as occasional observations of normal children corroborate, that even with these adoring and inimical wishes directed at their parents they simply make recognizable to us, by enlargement, what occurs with a lesser degree of clarity and intensity in the minds of most children. Antiquity has handed down to us, in support of this finding, a myth whose far-reaching, universal effectiveness is explicable only in terms of a similar universal validity for the foregoing premise from the field of child psychology.

I refer to the saga of King Oedipus and the drama of the same name by Sophocles. Oedipus, son of Laius, King of Thebes, and Jocasta, is exposed as an infant because an oracle had told the father that his as yet unborn son would be his murderer. He is rescued and grows up as the son of the king at a foreign court until, unsure of his origins, he consults the oracle himself and is advised to avoid going home since he is destined to become the murderer of his father and husband to his mother. On the way from what he thinks of as home, he encounters King Laius and kills him in a fight that erupts swiftly. He then approaches Thebes, where he solves the riddle posed by the Sphinx barring the way; the grateful Thebans express their thanks by making him king and giving him Jocasta's hand in marriage. He rules for many years in peace and honour and, together with the woman he does not know to be his mother, has two sons and two daughters – until a plague breaks out, occasioning a fresh consultation of the oracle, this time by the Thebans. This is where Sophocles' tragedy begins. Messengers bring the information that the plague will cease when the murderer of Laius is driven from the land. But where is he now?

> [. . .] Where shall we hope to uncover
> The faded traces of that far-distant crime?[20]

The plot of the play consists quite simply of the gradually intensifying and elaborately delayed exposure (not unlike the task of a psychoanalysis) of the fact that Oedipus is himself the murderer of Laius as well as the son of the murdered man and of Jocasta. Shattered by his unwittingly performed atrocity, Oedipus blinds himself and abandons his homeland. The words of the oracle are fulfilled.

King Oedipus is what is called a 'tragedy of fate'; its tragic effect is said to rest on the contrast between the all-powerful will of the gods and the vain efforts of mankind, threatened with disaster, to thwart it; surrender to the divine will and an understanding of their own powerlessness are the lessons the deeply moved audience is meant to take away from the tragedy. With logical consistency, modern playwrights have tried to achieve a similarly tragic effect by setting up the same contrast with a story of their own invention. However, audiences look on unmoved as, despite all the flailings of innocent men, some curse or prophecy finds fulfilment at their expense; subsequent 'tragedies of fate' have remained without effect.

If *King Oedipus* is no less unsettling for modern man than it was for contemporary Greeks, the answer can presumably only be that the effect of Greek tragedy does not rest on the contrast between fate and human will but must be sought in the special nature of the material used to demonstrate that contrast. There must be a voice deep inside us that is prepared to acknowledge the compelling power of fate in the case of Oedipus whereas we are able to reject as arbitrary the dispositions made in *The Ancestress* or in other tragedies of fate.[21] And such an element is indeed contained in the story of King Oedipus. The only reason why his fate grips us is because it might also have been our own, because prior to our birth the oracle uttered the same curse over us as over him. It was given to us all, possibly, to direct our first sexual stirring at our mother, our first hatred and violent wish at our father; our dreams persuade us of that. King Oedipus, who struck his father Laius dead and married his mother Jocasta, is simply the wish-fulfilment of our childhood years. But we have been more fortunate than he: we have since managed (those of us who have not become psychoneurotics) to detach our sexual stirrings from our mothers and forget our jealousy of our fathers. Confronted by the person in whom that primeval childhood wish found fulfilment, we shy away with the sum total of the repression that those wishes have since suffered in our inner lives. As the playwright, in the course of his investigation, brings to light Oedipus' guilt, he forces us to acknowledge our own inner life – in which such impulses, albeit suppressed, are still present. The comparison with which the chorus leaves us,

[. . .] behold: this was Oedipus,
Greatest of men; he held the key to the deepest mysteries;
Was envied by all his fellow men for his great prosperity;
Behold, what a full tide of misfortune swept over his head![22]

is a warning to ourselves and to our pride in how wise we have become since infancy and how sure in our reckoning. Like Oedipus, we live in ignorance of the wishes so offensive to morality with which nature has burdened us and following the unveiling of which we should no doubt all rather look away from the scenes of our childhood.[23]

We know that the Oedipus legend sprang from age-old dream-material revolving around the painful disturbance of the child's relationship to its parents as a result of the first stirrings of sexuality because there is an unmistakable allusion to that effect in the text of the Sophoclean tragedy itself. In this passage, Jocasta is consoling Oedipus (who has still not discovered the truth but who has begun to worry after remembering what the oracle said) by speaking of a dream that many men have but that does not, she thinks, mean anything:

Nor need this mother-marrying frighten you;
Many a man has dreamt as much. Such things
Must be forgotten, if life is to be endured.[24]

The dream of having sexual intercourse with one's mother is also, then as now, a dream that many men share – and recount in outraged amazement. For obvious reasons, it is the key to the tragedy and complements the dream of the father's death. The Oedipus story is the imagination's reaction to these two typical dreams, and as the dreams are experienced by the adult with feelings of disapproval, the legend must include in its content horror and self-punishment. Its further structuring is again based on an erroneous secondary processing of the material in an endeavour to harness it for a theologizing purpose. (See also the dream-material concerning self-exposure on pp. 258ff.) The attempt to combine divine omnipotence with human responsibility will of course fail in connection with this material as with any other.

Rooted in the same soil as *King Oedipus* is another great tragic literary creation, Shakespeare's *Hamlet*. However, the altered way in which the latter play deals with the same material highlights the whole difference between the mental lives of the two widely separated cultural periods; it reveals the huge advance made by repression in the emotional life of mankind. In *King Oedipus* the underlying wish-fantasy of the child is exposed and finds realization as in dream; in *Hamlet* it remains repressed, and we learn of its existence (much as we uncover the facts in a case of neurosis) only through the inhibitory effects that flow therefrom. In a curious way it has turned out to be consistent with the overwhelming effect of the more modern drama that one may remain completely in the dark as regards the hero's character. The play rests on Hamlet's reluctance to carry out the task of revenge assigned to him; what the reasons for or motives behind that reluctance are the text does not say; the most diverse attempts at interpretation have been unable to spell them out. According to what is still the prevalent version, as substantiated by Goethe, Hamlet represents the type of person in whom spontaneity of action is paralysed by the rampant overgrowth of ratiocination ('sicklied o'er with the pale cast of thought').[25] According to others, the poet has tried to describe a morbid, vacillating, almost neurasthenic character. But the storyline tells us that Hamlet is not by any means meant to appear as someone quite incapable of taking action. We see him twice proceeding to action: once in a swift fit of passion, when he stabs to death the person listening behind the wall-hanging, another time deliberately (almost cunningly, indeed) when with all the nonchalance of a Renaissance prince he sends two courtiers into the ambush intended for himself. So what holds him back from performing the task his father's ghost has set him? Again, the suggestion is that it is in the special nature of that task that Hamlet can do anything but take vengeance on the man who has removed his father and taken the father's place beside his mother, on the man who has shown him the realization of his repressed childhood wishes. The repulsion that is supposed to drive him to revenge is replaced in him by self-reproaches, scruples of conscience that put it to him that, literally speaking, he is himself no better than the sinner he is asked to punish. Here I have translated into consciousness what in the hero's mind has to remain unconscious; if anyone feels inclined to call Hamlet a hysteric, I can only acknowledge this as following from my interpretation. Very probably in line with this is the sexual aversion that Hamlet subsequently voices in conversation with Ophelia, the same sexual aversion as was to take increasing possession of the poet's mind over the next few years until its culminating expressions in *Timon of Athens*. It can of course only have been the poet's own mental life that we encounter in Hamlet; I gather from the 1896 biography of Shakespeare by Georg Brandes that the drama was written immediately after the death of Shakespeare's father (1601) – that is to say, in the first flush of mourning for him and at a time, we may assume, of revived childhood feelings towards him. We also know that Shakespeare's son, who died young, bore the name Hamnet (identical to Hamlet). As *Hamlet* deals with the son's relationship with his parents, the slightly later *Macbeth* is based on the subject of childlessness. Like every neurotic symptom, in fact (like dream itself, which is capable of repeated interpretation, at a deeper and deeper level[26] – even requires it if the dream in question is to be fully understood), every genuine poetic creation will also have proceeded from more than one motive and more than one stimulus in the poet's mind and admit of more than one interpretation. Here I have sought only to interpret the deepest stratum of stimuli in the sleeping writer's mind.[27]

I cannot leave these typical dreams of the deaths of dear relatives without devoting a few words to explaining their wider importance for the theory of dream. Such dreams embody for us the most unusual case of the dream-thought formed by the repressed wish eluding all censorship and making the transition to dream unchanged. Special circumstances must be present to make such a thing possible. I find that dreams of this kind are favoured by the following two factors:

First, there is no wish that we supposed further removed from our mind: 'never in our wildest dreams' (so we believed) could such wishes occur to us; dream-censorship is therefore unprepared for such monstrosities, much as the laws of Solon[28] failed to provide any penalty for patricide. But secondly it is precisely here that the repressed and unsuspected wish encounters with particular frequency a day's residue that takes the form of some *concern* about the life of the loved person. Such a concern cannot register in dream otherwise than by using the corresponding wish; the wish, however, is able to mask itself with the concern that the day has revived. To think that all this happens in a much simpler fashion – that all a person does at night, in dream, is continue the tale he has been weaving by day – is to leave dreams of the deaths of loved ones quite out of account in terms of explaining dreams and to cling unnecessarily to a riddle that can very easily be made less puzzling.

It is also instructive to explore the relationship between these dreams and anxiety-dreams. In dreams of the deaths of loved ones, the repressed wish has found a way of escaping censorship (as well as the resultant distortion). The inevitable side effect is then that painful sensations are experienced in dream. Similarly, the anxiety-dream comes about only if censorship is partially or wholly over-come, and on the other hand it facilitates the overcoming of censorship if anxiety is already present as an actual sensation stemming from physical sources. This makes it clear to what end censorship performs its duties, why it practises dream-distortion: censorship seeks *to prevent the growth of anxiety or other forms of painful affect*.

I spoke above of the egoism of the infant mind; I now return to that theme with the intention of suggesting a connection here: dreams, too, retain that character. They are without exception totally egoistic; they all feature the beloved 'I', even if it is in disguise. The wishes that are fulfilled in dreams are, as a rule, wishes of that 'I'; it is simply a sham and a deception if a dream ever happens to evoke interest in someone else. I want to analyse a few examples that contradict this assertion.

I

A not yet four-year-old boy recounts: *He saw a large, full bowl of food on top of which lay a large piece of roast meat, and all of a sudden the piece of meat was swallowed whole – not cut into slices. The person who had eaten it he did not see.*[29]

Who can he be, the stranger about whose lavish meal of meat our youngster dreamed? Only the experiences of the dream-day can explain this. The boy has for some days, on doctor's orders, been on a milk diet; on the evening of the dream-day, however, he was naughty, and for punishment he was sent to bed with no supper. He had endured such a fasting cure once before and been very brave about it. He knew he would receive nothing but did not venture a single word that might suggest he was hungry. Training is starting to work with him; it finds early expression in this dream, which already shows a degree of dream-distortion. There is no doubt that he is himself the person whose wishes are directed at so sumptuous a meal – even a roast-meat meal. However, knowing that this is forbidden him, he does not dare do what hungry children do in dream (see my little Anna's strawberry dream on page 143), which is to sit down at table themselves. The person remains anonymous.

II

I dream on one occasion that I see in the window of a bookshop a new issue of the 'collections for connoisseurs' series that I usually buy (monographs about artists, about history, about famous cultural sites, etc.). *The new collection is called 'Famous speakers' (or speeches), and issue 1 bears the name of Dr Lecher.*[30]

In analysis I come to see the unlikelihood of the fame of Dr Lecher, a so-called 'Obstructionist' in the Austrian Parliament, pre-occupying my dreams. The fact of the matter is that several days previously I had taken on some new patients for psychical treatment and was now obliged to speak for ten to eleven hours a day. This makes me something of an interminable speaker myself.

III

On another occasion I dream that a teacher of my acquaintance at our university says: *My son, the myopic.* There then follows a dialogue of short speeches and replies. But then there is a third dream-fragment in which I and my sons appear, and as regards the latent dream-content father and son, Professor M., are simply fronts for myself and my eldest. I shall deal with this dream again later because of another peculiar characteristic.

IV

An example of really base egoistical feelings hiding behind tender concern may be found in the following dream.

My friend Otto looks bad; his complexion is brown and his eyes bulge.

Otto is my family doctor, and I am hopelessly in his debt because for years he has kept an eye on my children, treated them successfully when they were ill, and furthermore given them gifts on every conceivable occasion. On the dream-day he had called on us, and my wife had noticed that he looked tired and run-down. That night the dream came to me and lent him some of the indications of Basedow's disease [= hyperthyroidism, also known as Graves' disease]. Anyone who repudiates my rules of dream-interpretation will understand this dream to mean that I am concerned about my friend's health and that this worry has found expression in dream. This would be in contradiction not only of the assertion that dream is an act of wish-fulfilment but also of the other claim that it is accessible to none but egoistical stimuli. But in that case, let that person explain why I am afraid Otto has Basedow's disease – a diagnosis for which his appearance does not offer the slightest occasion. My analysis, on the other hand, supplies the following material from something that had occurred six years previously. We were driving (a small party of us that included Professor R.) in deep darkness through the Forest of N., several hours away from the place where we were staying that summer. The coachman, who was not entirely sober, pitched us and the carriage down a slope, and we were lucky to come away unhurt. However, we did have to spend the night at the next inn, where the news of our accident earned us much sympathy. A gentleman who bore the unmistakable signs of *morbus Basedowii* – only browning of the complexion, incidentally, and bulging eyes, just like in the dream; no goitre – placed himself at our entire disposal and asked what he might do for us. Professor R. replied in his distinctive manner, 'Just one thing: could you lend me a nightshirt?' To which the aristocrat responded, 'That I can't do, I'm afraid', and withdrew.

To take the analysis further, it occurs to me that Basedow is not only the name of a doctor; it is also that of a famous pedagogue. (Now, in the waking state, I am not entirely sure of this piece of knowledge.)[31] My friend Otto, however, is the person whom I asked, in the event of anything happening to me, to oversee the physical upbringing of my children, notably during puberty (hence the nightshirt). In seeing my friend Otto in my dream with the morbid symptoms of our noble helper, I am clearly trying to say, 'If anything does happen to me, there will be as little for my children to have from him as Baron L. was able to provide on that occasion, for all his kind offers.' The egoistical cast of this dream is presumably now well and truly exposed.[32]

Where is the wish-fulfilment here, then? Not in vengeance on my friend Otto, who is quite simply fated to be treated badly in my dreams, but in the following circumstance. By representing Otto, in the dream, as Baron L., I was at the same time identifying myself with another person, namely Professor R., because I am asking something of Otto as, on that occasion, R. asked something of Baron L. And that is the point. Professor R., with whom I do not normally make so bold as to compare myself, made a career for himself independently, like me, outside the school, and only late in life achieved the title he had long deserved. So I want that professorship again! Even the 'late in life' is a piece of wish-fulfilment, because it implies I live long enough to see my boys through puberty myself.

As for other typical dreams – of flying with a sense of contentment or falling with feelings of anxiety – I know nothing of these from my own experience and owe everything I have to say about them to psychoanalysis. From the information gleaned from psychoanalyses, it must be concluded that these dreams, too, reiterate impressions from childhood, relating specifically to those active games that hold such an extraordinary attraction for children. What uncle has not made a child fly by running through the room with him, arms outstretched, or played falling with him by rocking him on his knees and suddenly sticking one leg out straight or holding him high and suddenly pretending to withdraw all support. Children shriek with delight on such occasions and tirelessly ask for more, especially if there is an element of fright and giddiness involved; then, years later, they re-create the experience in dream except that, in dream, they leave out the hands that held them, with the result that they now swoop and plummet freely. All small children love such games as well as playing on swings and seesaws; everyone knows that. And when, later on, they see gymnastic tricks performed at the circus, memories are refreshed once more.[33] In many boys, hysterical fits consist only of reproductions of such tricks, which they execute with great skill. And it is not unusual for these inherently innocent games to reawaken sexual feelings as well.[34] To use a word that we [German-speakers] draw on frequently to cover all these activities, it is the *Hetzen* [= 'hurrying/harrying', 'rough-and-tumble'] of childhood that dreams of flying, falling, losing one's balance, etc. pick up on and repeat, this time with the feelings of pleasure turned to fear. But as every mother knows, in reality children's *Hetzen*, too, quite often ends in strife and tears.

So I have good reason to dismiss the explanation that it is the state of our cutaneous sensations during sleep, the sensations created by the movement of our lungs, and so on – that it is these things that evoke dreams of flying and falling. I can see that such feelings are themselves reproduced from the memories to which dreams relate – in other words, that they constitute dream-content rather than dream-sources.

However, I am in no way blinding myself to the fact that I cannot supply a complete explanation for this series of typical dreams. Particularly here, my material leaves me in the lurch. I must hold fast to the general view that all the cutaneous and movement sensations of these typical dreams are evoked as soon as some psychical motive requires them and are capable of being ignored if no such requirement is encountered. Also, the connection with infantile experiences seems to me to proceed without doubt from hints I have received while analysing psychoneurotics. But what other meanings may in the course of life have become attached to the memory of those sensations (possibly different ones in each individual case, despite the typical appearance of such dreams) – that I cannot say; I should like, in fact, to be able one day to plug this gap by carefully analysing good examples. If anyone is surprised that, despite the frequency of precisely these dreams of flying, falling, having teeth pulled and so on, I complain of being short of material, I owe it to that person to explain that, since devoting my attention to the subject of interpreting dreams, I have not had the experience of dreaming such dreams myself. The dreams of neurotics, which are what is normally available to me, are not all (and often not right to the end of their hidden purpose) open to interpretation; a certain psychical force, which was involved in constructing the neurosis and is restored to effectiveness once the neurosis has been resolved, resists exhaustive interpretation – that is to say, interpretation going all the way to the final riddle.

iii The examination dream

Everyone who, after attending a *Gymnasium*, concludes his schooling with the *Matura* examination complains about the persistence with which he is plagued by the anxiety-dream that he has failed, has to do the final year again, and so on.[35] For the holder of an academic degree, this typical dream is replaced by another that rebukes him for not having passed the viva and against which he protests in vain, in his sleep, that he has been working as a doctor for years or that he is an outside lecturer or heads a group practice. It is the indelible memories of the punishments we suffered in childhood for misdeeds committed that are thus reawakened, deep inside us, at the two nodal points of our studies, the *dies irae, dies illa* of these rigorous exams. The neurotic's 'examination fear'[36] also draws its reinforcement from such childhood anxiety. After we cease to be schoolchildren, it is no longer, as initially, parents and governesses or at a later stage teachers who see to it that we are punished; life's relentless chain of cause and effect has taken over our further education, and now we dream about the *Matura* or that viva (and which of us did not quail then, even if he knew he was right?) every time we expect an outcome to punish us because we have not got something right or not done something properly, every time we feel the pressure of some responsibility.

I owe further elucidation of the examination dream to a comment made by a learned colleague during a scientific discussion once. He said on that occasion that, so far as he is aware, the *Matura*-dream occurs only in persons who passed the examination, never in those who failed it. In other words, the anxious examination dream that, as is confirmed repeatedly, comes when one faces a responsible task next day or is expecting the possibility of disgrace has (it would appear) sought out an occasion in the past when one's great anxiety turned out to have been unjustified and was refuted by the result. This would be a very striking example of the dream-content being misunderstood by the waking mind. The kind of indignant objection framed against the dream ('But I'm already a doctor, I tell you!') would in reality be the consolation offered by the dream, so would run, 'Don't worry about tomorrow; think how anxious you were before your *Matura* exam, and nothing happened to you. Today you're already a doctor' (or whatever it might be). However, the fear that we ascribe to the dream stems (according to my colleague) from the day's residues.

The tests of this explanation that I have been able to make on myself and others have all, though there have not been enough of them, said much the same thing. I, for instance, failed my viva in forensic medicine; not once has this fact troubled me in dream, whereas I have quite often been examined in botany, zoology or chemistry, in which subjects I went into the exam with well-justified anxiety but avoided punishment through the favour of fate or of the examiner. In the dream about the *Gymnasium* exam I am regularly examined in history, which I passed with flying colours at the time, though only because my dear teacher (the one-eyed helper of another dream, recounted on p. 28) had not omitted to notice that on the exam paper I handed back to him the middle question of three had been scored through with a fingernail to encourage him not to insist on that one. One of my patients, who had withdrawn from the *Matura* exam and then taken it later but had subsequently failed the officer's examination and not become an officer, told me that he quite often dreamed of the former examination but never of the latter.

Examination dreams pose the same problem, so far as interpretation is concerned, as I mentioned previously as characterizing most typical dreams. The associative material that the dreamer places at our disposal only rarely suffices for purposes of interpretation. We have to assemble a larger collection of examples if we are to reach a better understanding of such dreams. I recently became convinced that the objection, 'You're a doctor already' (or whatever) does not merely conceal consolation; it also hints at a reproach. It might have run, 'You're already so old, you've come so far in life, and you're still involved in such stupidities, such childish nonsense.' This blend of self-criticism and consolation would correspond to the latent content of the examination dream. It is then no longer particularly striking if in the examples analysed most recently the accusations of 'stupidities' and 'childish nonsense' relate to the repetition of sexual acts complained of.

W[ilhelm] Stekel, who advanced the first interpretation of the *Matura* dream, takes the view that it regularly relates to sexual experimentation and sexual maturity. My experience has often been able to corroborate this.

Notes

1. The proposition that our method of dream-interpretation becomes inapplicable if we do not have the dreamer's associative material available needs to be qualified by adding that there is one case in which our interpretative work is independent of such associations, and that is when the dreamer has employed *symbolic* elements in the dream-content. We then, strictly speaking, use a second, *auxiliary* method of dream-interpretation (see below).

2. [The stories of Hans Christian Andersen (1805–75), including 'The Emperor's new clothes', became famous around the middle of the nineteenth century; *Der Talisman*, a play written in 1894 by Ludwig Fulda (1862–1939), was notoriously banned by a real emperor (Wilhelm II) in 1903.]

3. A child figure also appears in the story, though, because all of a sudden a youngster pipes up, 'But he hasn't got anything on!'

4. [The inverted commas are my own, designed to highlight the fact that, in the context of psychoanalysis, Freud gave this ordinary word the special meaning defined in this parenthesis.]

5. Ferenczi tells of a number of interesting nakedness dreams had by women that could easily be traced back to the infantile desire to expose oneself but differ in many respects from the 'typical' nakedness dream discussed above.

6. The same meaning, for understandable reasons, attaches in dream to the presence of the 'whole family'.

7. A supplementary interpretation [*Überdeutung*] of this dream: spitting [*spuken*] on the stairs leads by a loose translation (haunting [*Spuken*] being an activity of ghosts [*Geister*; *Geist* also means 'spirit' or 'intellect']) to [the French expression] *esprit de l'escalier*, which suggests a lack of quick-wittedness. This is something I really can reproach myself with. But I wonder if the nanny lacked '*quick-wittedness*'?

8. See also, in this connection, the article referred to in Chapter 3, note 9, and my 'On the sexual theories of children' ['Über infantile Sexualtheorien'] (1908), in *Sammlung kleiner Schriften zur Neurosenlehre*, second series [*Standard Edition*, vol. IX, p. 207].

9. [The reader will have noticed by now that I have decided, all things considered, to translate Freud's *das Ich*, *das Es* and *das Über-Ich* not into Latin, as is usually done, but into the English terms 'the "I"', 'the "It"', and 'the "Above-I" '. Incidentally, the terms 'egoist' and 'altruism', also used in this passage, pre-date Freud by some hundred years and fifty years respectively.]

10. Three-and-a-half-year-old Hans, whose phobia forms the object of the analysis referred to earlier [see Chapter 3, note 9], calls out in a fever shortly after the birth of a sister, 'But I don't want a little sister.' In his neurosis, eighteen months later, he frankly admits to wishing that his mother would drop the baby in the bathtub so that it died. Yet Hans is a good-natured, affectionate child who has quickly become fond of this sister, too, being particularly keen to protect her.

11. Such deaths experienced during childhood may soon pass into oblivion within the family, but psychoanalytical research shows that, so far as the later neurosis is concerned, they were highly significant.

12. Observations relating to the originally hostile behaviour of children towards siblings and one parent have since been conducted in great numbers and recorded in the psychoanalytical literature. [Swiss poet and novelist Carl] Spitteler gives a particularly genuine and naive description of this typical childhood attitude from his own earliest years:

> Actually there was a second person present – Adolf. A little fellow who people said was my brother, though I could never understand what use he was; even less could I understand why they were making the same sort of creature out of him as they were out of me. I was all I wanted, what did I need a brother for? And not only was he no use, he sometimes even got in the way. When I pestered Grandma, he wanted to pester her too: when I was taken out in the pram, he sat opposite and took up half my space, with the result that our feet had to touch.

13. Three-and-a-half-year-old Hans (see Chapter 3, note 9) clothes his withering criticism of his sister in the same words. He assumes that it is this lack of teeth that prevents her from talking.

14. I was astonished to hear a gifted ten-year-old, whose father had died suddenly, say, 'I can understand my father having died; what I can't explain is why he doesn't come home to supper.'

Further material on this topic can be found in Dr von Hug-Hellmuth's 'Kinderseele' ['The child mind'] column in *Imago, Zeitschrift für Anwendung des Psychoanalyse auf die Geisteswissenschaften*, vols I–V, 1912–18.

15. Observation by a psychoanalytically trained father even catches the moment at which his intellectually precocious four-year-old daughter recognizes the difference between 'being away' and 'being dead'. The child

was causing problems at mealtimes and felt she was being watched in a malevolent way by one of the waitresses in the guesthouse. So she tells her father, 'I want Josephine to be dead.' 'Why dead?' her father asks soothingly. 'Isn't it enough if she just goes away?' 'No,' the child replies, 'then she'll come back.' For the boundless self-love (narcissism) of the child, any disturbance is a *crimen laesae majestatis*, and like a draconian body of laws the child's emotional reaction to any such offence allows of only one punishment – there are no half-measures.

16. The facts are often obscured by the appearance of a tendency to punish, which by way of a moral reaction threatens to remove the parent who is loved.

17. ['Honour your father and your mother . . .' (Ex. 20:12; Deut. 5:16).]

18. In some mythological accounts, at least; according to others, the only castration is performed by Cronus on his father, Uranus.

Regarding the mythological significance of this subject, see also Otto Rank, *Der Mythus von der Geburt des Helden* ['The myth of the birth of the hero'], issue 5 of *Schriften zur angewandten Seelenkunde*, 1909, and *Das Inzestmotiv in Dichtung und Sage* ['The incest theme in poetry and legend'], 1912, chapter IX, p. 2.

19. [We talk of 'filial piety'. *'Pietät'* is in fact the German word I render by 'respect'.]

20. [This and the following quotations from *King Oedipus* are taken from Sophocles, *The Theban Plays*, translated by E. F. Watling, London 1947, p. 28.]

21. [*Die Ahnfrau* ('The ancestress') is a five-act verse tragedy by Austrian playwright Franz Grillparzer that was first performed and published in 1817. Like the Sophocles play (though not in the same way), *Die Ahnfrau* deals with themes of patricide and incest.]

22. [Op. cit. (see note 20 above), p. 68.]

23. None of the findings of psychoanalytic research has given rise to such bitter contradiction, such determined resistance and such (it has to be said) exquisite critical contortions as this indication of childhood leanings towards incest that have remained preserved in the unconscious. Recently, there has even been an attempt to give incest, in defiance of all experience, a purely 'symbolic' status. An ingenious reinterpretation of the Oedipus myth, based on a passage in one of Schopenhauer's letters, has been supplied by Ferenczi in *Imago*, I, 1912. [Sandor Ferenczi (1873–1933) was for most of his life a cherished if somewhat unorthodox member of Freud's inner circle.]

The 'Oedipus complex', first touched on in *Interpreting Dreams*, has as a result of further studies attained unexpectedly huge importance for understanding the history of mankind and the development of religion and morality (see my *Totem und Tabu* [1913; *Selected Edition*, vol. XIII, p. 1; a new translation by Shaun Whiteside appears in *On Murder, Mourning and Melancholia*, London 2005 in the New Penguin Freud series]).

24. [Op. cit. (see note 20 above), p. 52. The italics are Freud's.]

25. [Shakespeare, *Hamlet*, Act III, scene 1.]

26. [*Überdeutung*. Wrongly, in my view, this has acquired the status of a technical term of Freudianism; certainly such translations as 'over-interpretation' and 'super-interpretation' are misleading. Freud does indeed use the word *Überdeutung* several times. As so often in German, the *über-* prefix confers a purely topographical relation, and what Freud meant was that dream-interpretation is never complete; one can always add (or uncover) another layer.]

27. These suggestions towards an analytical understanding of *Hamlet* have been added to by E[rnest] Jones and defended by him against other views set out in the literature ('The Oedipus Complex as an explanation of Hamlet's mystery: A study in motive', in *American Journal of Psychology*, January 1910, pp. 72–113). I say above that the author of the works of Shakespeare was the man from Stratford; I have since lost faith in this assumption.

Other attempts to analyse *Macbeth* will be found in my essay 'Einiger Charaktertypen aus der psychoanalytischen Arbeit' ['Some Character-Types Met with in Psycho-Analytical Work', *Standard Edition*, vol. XIV, p. 311] and in L. Jekels, 'Shakespeare's *Macbeth*', in *Imago*, V, 1918.

28. [Solon, *c.* 630–*c.* 560 BCE, a reforming Athenian legislator.]

29. Everything large, overabundant, immoderate and exaggerated in dreams may also possess a childish character. Children know no more eager wish than to grow up, to receive as much of everything as the grown-ups; they are hard to satisfy, never know when they have had enough, demand incessant repetition of whatever has pleased or appealed to them. *Moderation*, contentment, resignation – these are things children learn only through the civilizing effect of training. Neurotics, too, tend famously towards excess, towards lack of moderation.

30. [Dr Lecher, an opposition representative in the Austro-Hungarian Parliament, once famously spoke for twelve hours. The incident is amusingly described by Mark Twain, who was in Vienna shortly before Freud wrote this book. See Mark Twain, 'Stirring Times in Austria', in *Harper's New Monthly Magazine*, March 1898, pp. 530–40 (available on the internet).]

31. [Which was in fact correct: German educational reformer Johann Bernhard Basedow (1723–90) was a slightly younger contemporary of Rousseau.]

32. When Ernest Jones, giving a scientific lecture to an American society, spoke of the egoism of dreams, a learned lady disputed this unscientific generalization by objecting that surely the author could judge only the dreams of Austrians and was not entitled to say anything about the dreams of Americans. So far as she was concerned, she was convinced all her dreams were strictly altruistic.

Incidentally, to excuse that race-proud lady, let it be said that the proposition that dreams are thoroughly egoistical should not be misunderstood. Since absolutely everything that occurs in preconscious thought can make the transition to dream (content as well as latent dream-thoughts), that possibility is also open to altruistic stimuli. Similarly, a tender or loving feeling for another person, if it is present in the unconscious, may appear in dream. So what is correct about the said proposition is limited to the fact that, among the unconscious stimuli of dream, one very often finds egoistical tendencies that appear to have been overcome in the waking state.

33. Analytical study has enabled us to guess that in children's predilection for gymnastic displays and their repetition in hysterical fits there is another factor present, apart from organ-pleasure, and that is the (often unconscious) memory of (human or animal) observed sexual intercourse.

34. A young colleague, who is entirely free of nervous tension, informs me, 'I know from experience that I used, when swinging – in fact, at the precise moment when the downwards movement has its greatest momentum – to get a curious feeling in my genitals that, although it was not actually pleasant, I have to describe as a feeling of desire.' Patients have often told me that the first erections coupled with sexual desire that they remember from their boyhood came to them when climbing. Psychoanalysis teaches us with absolute certainty that a person's earliest sexual stirrings are rooted in the fighting and wrestling games of childhood.

35. [There seems little point in translating these terms, so different are the educational systems of the German-speaking world from those of the English-speaking world. A *Gymnasium* provides the most academic type of secondary education, usually leading to university; the *Matura* examination that concludes that education (and provides access to university) can be retaken if necessary after the student has repeated the final year.]

36. [Also *Angst*, but 'anxiety' does not seem quite raw enough here, and the German word certainly stretches to 'fear'.]

6

Dream-Work

All other previous attempts to settle the problems of dream have been directly linked to the memory of a given manifest dream-content and sought to wrest the dream-interpretation from that or, if they abstained from making an interpretation, endeavoured to justify their verdict on a dream with reference to the relevant dream-content. We are the only ones to have confronted a different set of facts; in our view, a new body of psychical material forces its way between a specific dream-content and the outcome of our examination, namely what our methods have brought to light as the *latent* dream-content or dream-thoughts. It is from these rather than from the manifest dream-content that we derive the solution of the phenomenon of dream. We therefore also face a fresh task – one that did not exist before. This is the task of studying the links between manifest dream-content and latent dream-thoughts and tracing the processes by which the latter have become the former.

Dream-thoughts and dream-content lie before us like two representations of the same content in two different languages – or, rather, a particular dream-content appears to us as a version of the relevant dream-thoughts rendered into a different mode of expression, the characters and syntax of which we are meant to learn by comparing the original with the translation. Dream-thoughts are comprehensible to us anyway, as soon as we have found out what they are. Dream-content is embedded, as it were, in a hieroglyphic script whose characters need to be translated one by one into the language of the dream-thoughts. One would clearly be led astray if one tried to read those characters in accordance with their pictorial value rather than with their significance. Imagine I have a picture-puzzle (a rebus) in front of me: a house with a boat on the roof, then a single letter, then a running figure with an apostrophe for a head, and so on. I could drop into a critical stance and say that such a combination and its components are nonsense. A boat does not belong on the roof of a house, and a person without a head cannot run; also, the person is bigger than the house, and if the whole thing is intended to represent a landscape, the individual letters do not fit in since they do not occur in nature. Obviously, the correct assessment of the rebus emerges only if I raise no such objections to the overall thing and the details thereof but try to replace each image by a syllable or a word that may, by some link or other, be represented by the image. The words assembled in this way are no longer meaningless; in fact, they can produce the most beautiful and most meaningful poetic aphorism. Well, a dream is a picture-puzzle like that, and our precursors in the field of dream-interpretation made the mistake of judging the rebus as a pictorial composition. As such, it struck them as nonsensical and valueless.

A *Compression*[1]

The first thing that comparing dream-content and dream-thoughts makes clear to the investigator is that a splendid job of *compression* has been done here. The actual dream is paltry, laconic, terse, compared to the broad compass and richly varied nature of the dream-thoughts. A dream, written down, fills half a page; analysis of it, which includes the dream-thoughts, requires six, eight, twelve times as much space. The ratio is different for different dreams; it never, so far as I have been able to ascertain, comes out the other way around. As a rule one underestimates the amount of compression going on in that one takes the dream-thoughts brought to light to constitute the sum total of the material, whereas further interpretation may expose fresh thoughts concealed behind the dream. We have already had occasion to point out that one can never in fact be sure of having interpreted a dream completely; even when the solution appears satisfying and entire, there always remains the possibility that yet another meaning will announce itself through the same dream. So the *compression ratio*, strictly speaking, is indeterminable. One might, faced with the claim that the disproportion between dream-content and dream-thoughts invites the conclusion that substantial compression of the psychical material takes place during dream-formation, raise an objection that seems on first impression to be most pertinent. We so often, do we not, have the feeling that we dreamed very extensively the whole night through but have forgotten the greater part. The dream that we remember on waking would then be a mere fragment of the whole dream-work, which would probably have equalled the dream-

295

thoughts in extent had we but been able to recall it in full. Part of this is undoubtedly correct: there is no mistaking the impression that a dream is most faithfully reproduced when one tries to remember it soon after waking and that one's memory of it becomes increasingly patchy towards evening. On the other hand, the sense that one dreamed a great deal more than one can reproduce is known in very many instances to rest on an illusion, the origin of which we shall have to go into later. Moreover, the assumption of compression forming part of dream-work is not affected by the possibility of forgetting dream, since it is proven by the large amounts of ideational material belonging to the individual fragments of the dream that have survived. If a sizeable fragment of dream has indeed been lost to memory, among the things barred to us as a result is access to a fresh series of dream-thoughts. There is nothing to support the expectation that the extinct dream-fragments would also have related purely to the thoughts already known to us from our analysis of the dream-fragments that survived.[2]

Given the vast number of ideational associations that analysis contributes to each individual element of the dream-content, many readers will find themselves doubting as a matter of principle whether all the things that occur to a person subsequently during analysis can be attributed to the dream-thoughts – in other words, is one entitled to assume that all these thoughts were in fact active during sleep and involved in dream-formation? Is it not far more likely that fresh thought-associations arise during the process of analysis that played no part in dream-formation? I can entertain this doubt only to a limited extent. It is of course true that individual thought-associations arise only during analysis; however, on each occasion one is able to satisfy oneself that such fresh associations arise only between thoughts that are already connected in a different fashion in the dream-thoughts; the fresh associations are supplementary conclusions, as it were, short-cuts made possible by the existence of other, deeper-seated connecting channels. So far as the vast majority of thought-masses uncovered during analysis is concerned, one is forced to concede that they were already actively involved in dream-formation, because, having worked through a chain of such thoughts that appeared to have no connection with dream-formation, one suddenly comes across a thought that is represented in the dream-content, is essential as regards interpreting the relevant dream, yet could not have been accessed in any other way than via that chain of ideas. See in this respect my dream of the botanical monograph [p. 181], which appears to be the outcome of an astonishing feat of compression, even though I have not given the analysis of it in full.

But how, then, is one to picture the psychical state during the sleep that precedes dreaming? Do all the dream-thoughts exist alongside one another, or are they run through in sequence, or are several trains of thought generated simultaneously from various centres, coming together later? I think there is as yet no need to create a concrete image of the psychical state associated with dream-formation. Let us just remember that we are dealing with unconscious thought here and that the process may well differ from the one we are aware of in ourselves in connection with deliberate reflection accompanied by consciousness.

However, the fact that dream-formation is based on compression is beyond dispute. The question is, by what means does that compression come about?

Considering that very few of the dream-thoughts discovered are represented in dream by one of their ideational elements, the conclusion should be that compression occurs by way of *omission*, in that a dream is not a faithful translation or point-by-point projection of dream-thoughts but an extremely sketchy and incomplete reproduction of the same. This view, as we shall soon find out, is a most inadequate one. However, let us take it as our initial basis and ask ourselves further: if only a few elements make it from dream-thoughts to dream-content, what conditions govern the selection process?

To gain an explanation of this, let us turn our attention to those elements of dream-content that evidently met the conditions we are looking for. A dream in the formation of which compression played a particularly large part will furnish the most suitable material for such an investigation. I choose the one I recounted on p. 181:

I Dream of the botanical monograph

Dream-content: *I have written a monograph about a type of plant (left unspecified). I have the book in front of me and I am just turning over a tipped-in colour plate. Bound in with the copy is a dried specimen of the plant.*

The most conspicuous element of this dream is the *botanical monograph*. This stems from the impressions of the dream-day; I had actually seen, in a bookshop window, a *monograph on the genus 'Cyclamen'*. There is no mention of this in the dream-content, in which only the monograph and its connection with botany remain. The 'botanical monograph' immediately proves to be related to the *essay on cocaine* that I once wrote; from cocaine, the train of thought proceeds on the one hand to the 'commemorative publication' [the *Festschrift* referred to on p. 183] and to certain events in a university laboratory, on the other hand to my friend, eye specialist Dr Königstein, who played a part in the exploitation of cocaine. The person of Dr K. provides a further link to the memory of the interrupted conversation I had had with him the previous evening and to the diverse thoughts it had prompted with regard to payment for medical services rendered among colleagues. That conversation, in fact, is the real currently relevant dream-trigger; the monograph about cyclamen also possesses current relevance but of a more indifferent kind; the 'botanical monograph' of the dream, I see, turns out to be a *median common factor* between the two experiences of the day, taken over unchanged from the indifferent impression, coupled with the psychically significant experience by a wealth of associative links.

However, not only the composite idea 'botanical monograph' but also its separate elements 'botanical' and 'monograph' penetrate more and more deeply, as a result of multiple associations, into the jumble of the dream-thoughts. Belonging to 'botanical' are memories of the person of Professor *Gärtner* [the name means 'gardener', remember], of his wife, who looked *blooming*, of my patient, named *Flora*, and of the lady who had told me the story of the *flowers* that had been forgotten. [The name] *Gärtner* leads in turn to the laboratory and the conversation with Königstein; mention of the two patients belongs to the same conversation. From the woman with the flowers, a train of thought forks off to my wife's *favourite flower*, the other exit of which lies in the title of the monograph glimpsed briefly during the day. 'Botanical' further recalls an episode at secondary school and an examination during my university years, and another topic touched on in that conversation (my hobbies) links up, through the medium of what is jokingly referred to as my *'favourite flower'*, the artichoke, with the train of thought proceeding from the flowers that had been forgotten; behind 'artichoke' is my memory of Italy on the one hand and, on the other, of a scene from my childhood with which I began what has since become an intimate relationship with books. So 'botanical' is a real nodal point at which numerous trains of thought pertaining to the dream come together – trains of thought that, as I can confirm, were with full justification connected up with one another in that conversation. We find ourselves here in the middle of an associative fabric in which, as in the weaver's masterpiece [in Goethe's *Faust*]:

> One treadle-thrust a thousand threads bestirs,
> The shuttles shoot over, shoot under,
> The threads flow unseen,
> A thousand links are forged at a stroke.[3]

'Monograph' in the dream again touches on two themes: the imbalance of my studies and the expensive nature of my hobbies.

From this initial investigation, one gets the impression that the reason why the elements 'botanical' and 'monograph' have found a place in the dream-content is because they are able to show the amplest points of contact with most dream-thoughts – in other words, they represent nodal points at which a very large number of dream-thoughts meet; it is because as regards dream-interpretation they are *open to many interpretations*. The circumstance behind this explanation can also be expressed differently. One would then say: Each element of the dream-content turns out to be *multiply determined*[4] – represented in the dream-thoughts several times.

We learn more if we examine the other components of the dream as to whether they appear in the dream-thoughts. The *colour plate* that I turn to leads on (see also the analysis on pp. 181ff.) to a fresh theme, namely colleagues' criticism of my essays, and to one that is already represented in the dream, namely my hobbies, as well as to the childhood memory in which I am pulling apart a book with colour plates; the dried plant specimen touches on the schoolboy memory of the herbarium and gives that memory special prominence. So I see what sort of relationship exists between dream-content and dream-thoughts: not only are the elements of the dream determined *several times* by dream-thoughts; individual dream-thoughts are also represented in the dream by several elements. From one element of the dream, the avenue of association leads to several dream-thoughts, from one dream-thought to several dream-elements. In other words, dream-formation does not proceed in such a way that an individual dream-thought or a group of dream-thoughts furnishes an abbreviation for the dream-content, then the next dream-thought furnishes another abbreviation to represent it, rather as [political] representatives are elected from among a people; rather, the whole body of the dream-thoughts undergoes a certain process whereby the most supported and best supported elements stand out prominently for inclusion in the dream-content, with the analogy here being voting for a party list rather than an individual. No matter what dream I subject to this kind of dissection, I always find the same principles corroborated, namely that the dream-elements are formed from the entire body of dream-thoughts and that each of them appears to be determined a number of times in relation to the dream-thoughts.

It will certainly not be superfluous to demonstrate this relationship between dream-content and dream-thoughts in terms of a further example that is distinguished by a particularly elaborate intertwining of such reciprocal links. The dream comes from a male patient whom I am treating for anxiety in enclosed spaces. It will soon become apparent why I feel prompted to give this exceptionally ingenious piece of dreaming the following title:

II 'A lovely dream'

He is driving with a large party of people along X Street, where there is a modest inn (there is not, in fact). A play is being performed on the premises; at one moment he is the audience, at another an actor. At the end there is a question of people having to change to go out again. Part of the staff is shown to the stalls areas, another part to the first floor. Then there is an argument. The ones up above are irritated that those downstairs are not yet ready, thus preventing them from descending. His brother is upstairs, he down below, and he is irritated with his brother because there is such a crush. (This part is unclear.) *Actually, the decision had been made on arrival and people had been divided into who was to be upstairs and who down. Then he is walking alone up the hill that X Street forms towards the city, and his gait is so slow, so laboured, that he makes no progress whatever. An elderly gentleman joins him, complaining about the King of Italy. At the end of the rise, the going gets much easier.*

The problems with climbing were so great that, after waking, he wondered for a while whether this was dream or reality.

In terms of the manifest content, the dream is scarcely praiseworthy. Breaking the rules, I want to begin the interpretation with that part of the dream that the dreamer would describe as the clearest.

The difficulty that he dreamed and probably, in the dream, actually felt, the laboured climbing accompanied by dyspnoea, is one of the symptoms that the patient really did present some years ago, when in conjunction with other manifestations it was related to a (probably hysterically feigned) case of tuberculosis. This sensation of inhibited movement, which is characteristic of dream, is one we know of already from exhibitionist dreams, and once again we find that, as an ever-available piece of material, it is used here for the purposes of some other representation. The fragment of the dream-content that describes how climbing was difficult initially and became easier at the end of the rise reminded me, as the dream was being recounted, of that well-known, masterly introduction to *Sapho* by Alphonse Daudet, where a young man is carrying his beloved up some stairs; at first she is as light as a feather, but the higher he climbs the heavier the burden in his arms becomes. The scene exemplifies the course of the relationship, by portraying which *Daudet* seeks to warn young men against squandering a serious inclination on girls of humble origin and dubious background.[5] Though I was aware that my patient had recently entertained and terminated a love affair with a lady of the theatre, I certainly did not expect to find my interpretative intuition corroborated. Also, in *Sapho* it was the *other way around* than in the dream; in the latter, the climbing was initially hard and became easier; in the novel, symbolism required that what had at first been easy should in the end turn out to represent a heavy burden. To my astonishment, the patient commented that the interpretation was very much in line with the substance of the play he had seen at the theatre the previous evening. The play was called *Rund um Wien* ['Around Vienna'] and told the life-story of a girl who, from being respectable, passed over to the *demi-monde*, had affairs with members of high society, hence 'went up in the world', but in the end went increasingly 'into decline'. The play had also reminded him of one he had seen years before. That had borne the title *Von Stufe zu Stufe* ['Step by step'], and the poster had featured a *flight of stairs*.

Now the wider interpretation. X Street had been the address of the actress with whom he had had the most recent affair – one having many associations. The street does not contain an inn. However, when for the lady's sake he had spent part of one summer in Vienna he had *stayed*[6] at a small hotel nearby. On leaving the hotel, he had told the coachman, 'I'm glad that at least I didn't catch any lice!' (Another of his phobias, incidentally.) The coachman's response had been, 'How could anyone stay there? That's no hotel, it's more like a *country pub*.'[7]

This immediately, for him, ties in with a remembered quotation:

> A country landlord, wondrous mild,
> Was recently my host.

But the landlord in Uhland's poem is in fact an *apple tree*. At this point a second quotation continues the train of thought:

> FAUST (*dancing with the girl*)
> Once I dreamed a lovely dream;
> I saw an *apple tree*,
> Two lovely apples gleamed thereon,
> Tempting; up I climbed.
>
> THE BEAUTY
> Apples have been objects of desire
> For you since Paradise.
> How glad I am, how very glad
> That my grove too grows apples.

There cannot be the slightest doubt what is meant by the apple tree and the apples. A lovely bosom topped the list of the charms by which the actress had ensnared my dreamer.

In the context of the analysis we had every reason to assume that the dream went back to an impression from childhood. If this was so, it must relate to the man's wet-nurse, he being now almost thirty. For the child, the wet-nurse's bosom really is a refreshment stop [as *Einkehrwirtshaus* can be rendered]. Both the wet-nurse and Daudet's Sappho thus allude to the lover he had recently left.

In the dream-content the patient's (elder) brother also appears – as being *upstairs*, while he himself is *below*. This is another *reversal* of an actual state of affairs, since the brother, as I know, has lost his position in society, whereas my patient has retained his. When reproducing the dream-content, the dreamer avoided saying that his brother had been upstairs, he himself *parterre*. That would have been to state the case too clearly, because we tend to say of a person who has lost fortune and position that he is *parterre* – as one might say, he has '*come down in the world*'. Now, it must be significant that at this point in the dream something is portrayed as *reversed*. The reversal must also stand for a different relationship between dream-thoughts and dream-content. There is a hint as to how that reversal is to be undertaken. Obviously at the end of the dream, where the business with the climbing is again *the other way around* than in *Sapho*. Then it is easy to see what kind of reversal is intended. In *Sapho*, the man carries the woman with whom he is having sexual relations; in the dream-content, therefore, it is *conversely*[8] a woman carrying a man, and since this is something that can only occur in childhood, it is a further reference to the wet-nurse, who is having difficulty in carrying the suckling child. So the end of the dream hits upon the idea of portraying Sappho and the wet-nurse in the same suggestive role.

Just as the name 'Sappho' was not chosen by the writer without reference to a lesbian habit, so too the fragments of the dream in which persons are busy *upstairs* and *downstairs* suggest fantasies of a sexual nature preoccupying the dreamer that, as suppressed desires, are not unconnected with his neurosis. That they are fantasies and not memories of actual events that are portrayed in the dream in this way is not something that interpreting the dream itself indicates; interpreting the dream gives us only a thought-content, leaving us to ascertain the reality-value of that thought-content. Here (and not only here; also in the generation of more important psychical creations than dreams), real and fantasized events appear initially as having the same value. A 'large party' means, as we already know, a secret. The brother is simply the representative (registered in the childhood scene by 'back-fantasizing') of all subsequent rivals for women. The episode of the gentleman complaining about the King of Italy again relates (through the medium of a still-vivid and inherently unimportant experience) to the intrusion of people of low standing into high society. It is as if the warning that Daudet wishes to give the youth were to be coupled with a similar warning aimed at the suckling infant.[9]

In order to have a third example to hand for the study of compression in dream-formation, let me recount my partial analysis of another dream, which I owe to an elderly lady undergoing psycho-analytical treatment. In line with the severe anxiety states that the patient was suffering, her dreams contained an overabundance of sexual thought-material, becoming aware of which initially surprised her as much as it shocked her. Since I am not able to complete my analysis of the dream, the dream-material appears to fall into several groups without apparent coherence.

III 'The beetle dream'

Dream-content: *She remembers that she has two cockchafers [Mai-käfer, also called 'maybugs' or 'May-beetles'] in a box that she must set free, since otherwise they will suffocate. She opens the box, the beetles are very sluggish; one flies out of the open window, but the other is crushed by the casement as she closes the window at some-body or other's request (expressions of revulsion).*

Analysis: Her husband is away, their fourteen-year-old daughter sleeps in the bed at her side. In the evening the girl points out to her that a moth has fallen into her water-glass; however, she neglects to take it out and in the morning feels sorry for the poor creature. Her bedtime reading had contained the story of how some boys had thrown a cat into boiling water and had described the animal's convulsive movements. These are the two inherently unimportant dream-prompts. The subject of *cruelty to animals* continues to preoccupy her. Years before, when they were spending the summer in a certain area, her daughter had behaved very cruelly to small creatures. She started a butterfly collection and asked her for *arsenic* to kill the butterflies. On one occasion a moth with a pin through its body went on flying around the room for a long time; another time, several caterpillars that she had kept for pupating starved to death. The same child was in the habit, whilst yet at a tender age, of pulling the wings off *beetles* and butterflies; today, all such cruelties would appal her; she has become so kind-hearted. This contradiction preoccupies her, reminding her of another contradiction, that between *appearance* and character as portrayed in Eliot's *Adam Bede*. A beautiful but vain and thoroughly stupid girl alongside an ugly but noble one. The *aristocrat* who seduces the little goose; the workman who feels himself high-born and behaves accordingly. These things cannot be told from the appearance of the people concerned. Who would see, looking at *her*, that she is plagued by sensual desires?

In the same year as the girl started her butterfly collection, the area suffered a terrible plague of *May-beetles*. The children went mad, swiping at the beetles and *squashing* them cruelly. She saw one person, at the time, tearing the wings off the May-beetles and then eating the bodies. She herself had been born in *May* and had a *May* wedding. Three days after her marriage she wrote a letter to her parents back home, telling them how happy she was. But she wasn't at all.

On the evening before the dream she had been going through old letters and reading various earnest and comical letters aloud to the family, including a quite ridiculous letter from a piano teacher who had paid court to her as a girl and one from an *aristocratic* suitor.[10]

She blames herself for the fact that one of her daughters has got her hands on a bad book by Maupassant.[11] The arsenic that her little girl asks for makes her think of the arsenic pills that give the Duc de Mora back the power of youth in *Le Nabab*.[12]

On 'setting them free', she recalls the passage from *The Magic Flute*:

> *Zur Liebe kann ich dich nicht zwingen,*
> *Doch geb ich dir* die Freiheit *nicht.*

[I cannot make you love me, yet neither shall I *set you free*.]

On 'May-beetles', there is Käthchen's line:[13]

> *Verliebt ja wie ein* Käfer *bist du mir.*

[You're in love with me as a *beetle* might be.]

And between them Tannhäuser's line:

> *Weil du von* böser Lust *beseelt* –

> [For you, being filled with *evil lusts* –]

She lives in anxiety and concern for her absent husband. The fear that something will *happen* to him on the trip comes out in numerous daytime fantasies. Shortly before, in her unconscious thoughts during analysis, she had found a complaint about his 'extreme old age'. The wish veiled by this dream can perhaps best be guessed if I say that several days prior to the dream she had suddenly, in the middle of what she was doing, been startled by the order, directed at her husband, *'Go hang yourself!'* It transpired that, only hours previously, she had read somewhere that, when a man is hanged, a powerful erection results. It was a desire for such an erection that emerged in this startling disguise from her repressed thoughts. 'Go hang yourself!' is tantamount to saying 'Whatever it costs, get a hard-on.' Dr Jenkins's arsenic pills in *Le Nabab* belong in this context; but the patient was also aware that the most powerful aphrodisiac, *cantharides*, is made from *squashed beetles* (so-called 'Spanish fly'). This is the direction the chief component of the dream-content is going in.

Opening and closing the *window* is always a bone of contention with her husband. She likes to sleep with it open, he likes it closed. *Sluggishness* is the main symptom she had to complain of at the time.

In all three of the dreams recounted here I have used *italic* type to stress where a particular dream-element recurs in the dream-thoughts, my purpose being to highlight the multiple relatedness of the former. However, since for none of these dreams is the analysis taken to its conclusion, it is probably worth examining a dream whose analysis has already been communicated in greater detail in order to show this multiple determination of dream-content. My choice falls on the dream of Irma's injection [see pp. 119ff.]. We shall have no trouble in recognizing from this example that the work of compression in dream-formation employs more than one means.

The chief character in the dream-content is the patient, Irma, who is seen the way she actually looks in life, so initially represents herself. However, the position in which I examine her by the window is taken from a memory of another person, namely from the lady for whom I should like to exchange my patient, as the dream-thoughts reveal. By presenting a diphtheritic coating, which calls to mind my concern about my eldest daughter, Irma contrives to portray this child of mine, concealed behind whom (and associated with whom by having the same name) is the person of a patient lost through intoxication. As the dream goes on, the significance of Irma's personality undergoes a change (without her image changing, as seen in the dream); she becomes one of the children we examine at the public surgery of the children's hospital, in connection with which my friends show their very different intellectual gifts. The transition was clearly effected by the idea of my young daughter. Through her reluctance when asked to open her mouth, the same Irma becomes an allusion to another lady I once examined; she also, in the same context, becomes an allusion to my own wife. Moreover, in the morbid changes that I discover in her throat I have assembled allusions to a whole range of further persons.

All these persons encountered as I pursue 'Irma' do not appear in the dream 'in person', as it were; they hide behind the dream-person 'Irma', who is thus built up into a collective image, though one with contradictory features. Irma comes to stand for these other persons sacrificed by the process of compression in that I have happen to her all the things that, one by one, remind me of those persons.

There is another way in which I can constitute a *collective person* for myself for the purposes of dream-compression: I can combine actual features of two or more persons into a dream-image. That is how the Dr M. of my dream came about; he bears the name of Dr M., he speaks and acts like Dr M., but his physical characteristics and his illness are those of another person, namely my elder brother. Only one feature (the pale appearance) is doubly determined in that in reality it is common to both men. A similarly mixed figure is Dr R. in my uncle dream [see pp. 151ff.]. Here, though, the dream-image was produced in yet another way. I did not combine features peculiar to one with the features of the other, thereby reducing the memory-image of each one by certain features; instead I adopted the process that Galton used to generate his family portraits;[14] that is to say, I projected both pictures one on top of the other in such a way that the shared features emerge more strongly and those that do not harmonize cancel one another out, becoming fuzzy in the final picture. In the uncle dream, for instance, a prominent feature to emerge from the physiognomy belonging to two persons and therefore blurred is the fair-coloured beard – which moreover constitutes an allusion to my father and to myself, conveyed by the reference to going grey.

The production of collective persons and mixed persons is one of the chief ways in which dream-compression operates. We shall have occasion, shortly, to deal with it in a different context.

The 'dysentery' association in the injection dream is likewise multiply determined – on the one hand because it sounds not unlike 'diphtheria', on the other hand because of the link with the patient I had sent to the Middle East, where his hysteria went unrecognized.

Another interesting case of compression is the mention of *'propylene'* in the dream. The word contained in the dream-thoughts was not *'propylene'* but *'amylene'*. One might suppose that here simple displacement had affected the dream-formation process. And so it has, only this displacement serves the purposes of compression, as the following postscript to the dream-analysis shows. If my attention lingers for a moment on the word *'propylene'*, I am struck by the similarity of the sound to the word *'Propylaea'*. However, *Propylaea* are to be found not only in Athens but also in Munich.[15] In that city, a year before the dream, I visited a friend of mine who was then very ill – and who is unmistakably referred to by the *trimethylamine* that follows shortly after *propylene*.

Disregarding the striking circumstance that, here and elsewhere in connection with dream-analysis, associations of very different valency are used as if of equal value in the formation of trains of thought, I surrender to the temptation to picture the process involved in the replacement of *amylene* in the dream-thoughts by *propylene* in the dream-content as it were in three dimensions.

On the one hand, we have here the group of ideas associated with my friend Otto, who does not understand me, says I am wrong, and pours me a drink smelling of amylene; on the other hand, bound together by contrast, the one belonging to my Berlin friend, who does understand me, would say I am right, and to whom I owe so many valuable communications, including some about the chemistry of sexual processes.

What is particularly going to excite my attention from the Otto group is determined by the still-vivid occasions stimulating the dream; *amylene* is one of these elements, marked out and predestined for the dream-content. The rich 'Wilhelm' group of ideas is activated precisely by the contrast with Otto, and those elements in it are highlighted that recall the ones already stimulated in Otto. The fact is, in this entire dream I am appealing from a person who excites my displeasure to another person whom I am able, at will, to set against the first, constantly, repeatedly invoking my friend against my adversary. For example, the amylene in the Otto group also awakens memories from the chemical sphere in the other group; trimethylamine, with backing from several directions, reaches the dream-content. 'Amylene' might also reach the dream-content unchanged, but it succumbs to the influence of the 'Wilhelm' group in that, from the whole range of recollection covered by that name, one element is sought out that can provide a dual determination for amylene. In the vicinity of amylene, so far as association is concerned, lies 'propylene'; from the 'Wilhelm' group it is met by Munich with its *'Propyläen'*. In propylene-Propylaea[16] the two groups of ideas come together. As if through a compromise this median element makes it into the dream-content. A collective average has here been created that permits multiple determination. This makes it quite clear to us that multiple determination must facilitate the breakthrough to dream-content. For the purpose of forming this average a shift of attention has occurred, without benefit of thought, from what is really meant to something close to it by association.

Studying the injection dream allows us to gain a certain general understanding of the compression processes involved in dream-formation. We have been able to identify the following particulars as characterizing the part of dream-work we have called 'compression': selection of elements occurring in the dream-thoughts on multiple occasions, formation of new entities (collective persons, composite structures) and production of median, shared elements. What purpose compression serves and how it is called up are questions we shall not be asking until we are ready to look at all the psychical processes involved in dream-formation together. Let us, at this point, simply register the phenomenon of dream-compression as an interesting relationship between dream-thoughts and dream-content.

The compression-work performed by dream is at its most tangible when it has chosen words and names as its object. Words, in dream, are in fact often treated as things and are put together in the same ways as thing-concepts. Comical and curious creations spring from such dreams.

1) When a colleague once sent me an essay he had written in which a recent physiological discovery was, to my mind, overestimated and above all dealt with in gushing terms, I dreamed the next night of a sentence that clearly had to do with such treatment: *'This is true Norekdal style.'* Breaking down the neologism caused me some difficulty at first; there was no doubt that it parodied the superlatives 'huge, colossal'; but where it came from was not easy to say. Eventually the monstrous creation fell apart into the two names *'Nora'* and *'Ekdal'* from two well-known Ibsen plays. The same author (the one whose latest *opus* I was criticizing in this dream) had previously penned a newspaper article about Ibsen, which I had read.

2) A patient of mine tells me of a brief dream that culminates in a nonsensical word-combination. She and her husband are at some rural festivity when she says: *'This will end in a general "Maistollmütz".'* I should add that in the dream she had felt vaguely that this was some kind of flour preparation made from maize, a sort of polenta. Analysis broke the word down into *Mais* ['maize'] – *toll* ['mad'] – *mannstoll* ['nymphomaniac'] – *Olmütz* [a place-name] –

all of which are recognizably fragments of a mealtime conversation with members of her family. The word *Mais* [pronounced 'mice'] conceals not only an allusion to the recently opened jubilee exhibition but also: *Meissen* (a *Meissen* porcelain figure representing a bird), *Miss* (the Englishwoman among her relatives who had travelled to Olmütz), *mies* (jocular Jewish slang for 'nasty, disgusting'), and a long train of thoughts and associations proceeded from each syllable of the verbal accretion.

3) A young man whose doorbell an acquaintance rings late one evening in order to leave a visiting-card dreams in the night thereafter: *A tradesman attends late one evening to repair the room-telegraph* [Zimmertelegraph]. *After he has left, it goes on ringing, not continuously but only in individual bursts. The servant calls the man back, and the man says, 'Isn't it strange how even normally* tutelrein *people do not know how to deal with such matters?'*

The indifferent dream-prompt, as we see, covers only one element of the dream. It has only acquired importance at all in that it followed an earlier experience of the dreamer, also trivial in itself but that his imagination had invested with representative significance. As a boy living with his father he had once, dazed with sleep, upset a glass of water on to the floor in such a way that the telegraph cable became soaked right through and the *continuous ringing* disturbed his father's sleep. Since the continuous ringing corresponds to the cable getting wet, *'individual bursts'* are used to portray the *dripping*. The word *'tutelrein'*, however, breaks down three ways, thus aiming at three of the matters represented in the dream-thoughts: *'Tutel'* = *Kuratel* means guardianship; *Tutel* (possibly *'Tuttel'*) is a vulgar term for the female breast, and the element *'rein'* [one meaning of which is 'clean'] borrows the first part of *Zimmertelegraph* to form the word *Zimmerrein*, which has a lot to do with making the floor wet and also sounds like a name represented in the dreamer's family.[17]

4) In an extended, desolate dream of mine that seems to revolve around a boat trip, it so happens that the next port of call is named *'Hearsing'* but the one after that *'Fliess'*. The latter is the name of

my friend in B., who has often formed the goal of my trip. But *'Hearsing'* is a combination of the place-names on our Viennese local line, so many of which end in 'ing': *Hietzing, Liesing, Mödling* (once known as Medelitz, *meae deliciae* – that is to say, *'meine Freud'* ['my delight']), and the English word *'hearsay'*, which suggests slander and constitutes the link to that day's indifferent dream-trigger, a poem in the popular magazine *Fliegende Blätter* by a slanderous dwarf called *Sagter Hatergesagt* ['Says-he Hesaid']. Linking the final syllable *'ing'* to the name *'Fliess'* gives *'Vlissingen'*, which actually is where my brother steps off the ferry when he visits us from England. But the English name for *Vlissingen* is *Flushing*, which in the English language is like 'blushing' and reminds me of the patient who suffered a 'fear of blushing'; it also puts me in mind of a recent publication by Bechterev about this neurosis, which caused me some irritation.

5) On another occasion I have a dream that consists of two separate fragments. The first is the vividly remembered word *'Autodidasker'*, the second faithfully matches a brief, harmless fantasy produced some days earlier to the effect that when I see Professor N. soon I must tell him, 'That patient about whose condition I consulted you last really does only have a neurosis, just as you supposed.' So the neologism *'Autodidasker'* must not only meet the demand that it contains or represents compressed meaning; that meaning must also be closely connected with my intention, voiced repeatedly in the waking state, to give Professor N. such satisfaction.

The word *'Autodidasker'* breaks down easily into *'author'*, *'autodidact'* and *'Lasker'*, with the attached name *Lassalle*. The first of these leads to the (this time significant) cause of the dream. I had given my wife several books by a well-known author who is a friend of my brother and who, as I have discovered, comes from the same town as I do (J. J. David). One evening she spoke to me of the deep impression made on her by the touching story of a talent wasted in dissipation told in one of David's novellas, and our conversation then turned to the signs of giftedness that we saw in our own children. Under the influence of what she had just read, she expressed a concern relating to the children, and I consoled her by remarking that just such dangers can be averted by education. In the night, my train of thought continued, took up my wife's concerns and wove all sorts of other things in with them. Something the writer had said to my brother about marrying ushered my thoughts down a by-road that successfully led to their being portrayed in dream. The by-road took me to Breslau, where a great friend of ours had married and settled. As for the worry about being ruined by women that formed the core of my dream-thoughts, in Breslau I found the examples of Lasker and Lassalle, which allowed me to portray the two types of this disastrous influence simultaneously.[18] 'Cherchez la femme', the phrase in which such thoughts can be summarized, brings me in a different sense to my still-unmarried brother, whose name is *Alexander*. At this point I become aware that *Alex*, as we call him for short, sounds almost like *Lasker* jumbled up and that this factor must have helped to tell my thoughts about the detour via Breslau.

However, the playing around with names and syllables in which I am indulging here has yet another sense. It represents the wish for a happy family life for my brother, and this is how: In *L'oeuvre*, the novel about an artist which must have suggested the substance of my dream, we know that from time to time the author [Émile Zola] describes himself and his familial contentment, appearing under the name of '*Sandoz*'. Probably he went about transforming the name in the following way. '*Zola*', read backwards (as children love to do), is '*Aloz*'. Probably this was too obvious for him; so the syllable '*Al*', which also introduces the name '*Alexander*', was supplanted by the third syllable of the same name, giving '*Sandoz*'. My '*Autodidasker*' came about in a similar fashion.

As for my fantasy of telling Professor N. that the patient we had both seen was suffering from a simple neurosis – that got into the dream in the following manner. Shortly before the end of my working year a man came to see me, in connection with whom my diagnosis let me down. A severe organic complaint, possibly a case of myelomalacia [a condition of the bone marrow], was indicated but could not be proven. Diagnosing a neurosis would have been tempting and would have removed all the problems but for the fact that the sexual case history, without which I refuse to recognize any neurosis, was so vigorously disputed by the patient. In my embarrassment, I turned for help to the doctor for whom I have the greatest admiration personally (as do others) and to whose authority I am most likely to cede. He listened to my doubts, pronounced them justified, and then said, 'Keep an eye on the man – it'll be a neurosis.' Knowing he does not share my views on the aetiology of neurosis, I refrained from contradicting him, though without hiding my incredulity. Several days later I told the patient I could do nothing for him and advised him to consult another doctor. Whereupon to my enormous astonishment he began to beg for my forgiveness, saying that he had lied to me; he had been so ashamed, he told me, and proceeded to reveal the very fragment of sexual aetiology that I had expected and that I required for my assumption of neurosis. I was relieved, but at the same time I felt ashamed; I was forced to admit to myself that my senior colleague, unflustered by considerations of medical history, had seen more clearly than I. I resolved to tell him so when I saw him again, to tell him that he had been right and I had been wrong.

Which is precisely what I do in my dream. But what kind of wish-fulfilment can be involved in my admitting that I am wrong? Precisely that is my wish; I want to be wrong about my fears, or rather I want my wife, whose fears I have made my own in the dream-thoughts, to be wrong. The subject to which being right or being wrong relates in the dream is not far removed from what for the dream-thoughts is really interesting. The same alternative of either organic or functional impairment by woman – by sexual life, in fact: tabetic paralysis or neurosis, to the second of which the manner of Lassalle's demise is more loosely attached.

Professor N. plays a part in this firmly structured (and, if interpreted with care, thoroughly transparent) dream not only because of the foregoing analogy and because of my wish to be proved wrong – nor simply because of his concomitant links to Breslau and the family of our friend who married a man from that city; his featuring in it is partly due to the following minor event that occurred after our consultation. Having discharged his medical functions with that supposition, he turned his attention to personal matters. 'How many children do you have now?' 'Six.' A gesture of respect coupled with misgiving. 'Girls, boys?' 'Three of each – my pride and my fortune.' 'Well, have a care. With girls there's no problem, but the boys, later on, will cause problems so far as their upbringing is concerned.' I objected that they have remained most biddable up to now; clearly this second diagnosis with regard to my boys pleases me no better than the one made earlier (to the effect that my patient only had a neurosis). So these two impressions are bound together by their contiguity, by their being experienced as one, so to speak. And if I take the story of the neurosis into the dream, I substitute it for what N. said about upbringing, which shows more connection with the dream-thoughts, coming as it does so close to the concerns expressed later by my wife. In this way, even my fear that N. might be right with his remarks about educational problems with boys finds its way into the dream-content by hiding behind the portrayal of my wish to be wrong in having such apprehensions. The same fantasy serves unchanged to portray the two divergent terms of the alternative.

6) Marcinowski [1911–12]: 'Early this morning, between dream and waking, I experienced a lovely piece of word-compression. In the course of a wealth of dream-fragments that I could barely recall, I stumbled (as it were) over a word that I see before me half as if written down, half as if printed. The [invented] word is *"erzefilisch"*, and it belongs to a sentence that, in total isolation, outside any sort of context, slipped over into my conscious memory: *"That has an* erzefilisch *effect on sexual feeling."* I knew immediately that the word should really have been *erzieherisch* ["educative"], but I also wavered once or twice, wondering whether it should not more correctly be *erzifilisch*. Here the word "syphilis" occurred to me, and I racked my brains, embarking on an analysis while still half asleep, as to how that could have come into my dream, since neither personally nor professionally have I ever had anything to do with that disease. Then *erzehlerisch* occurred to me, accounting for the

e and at the same time explaining my having been asked by our *Erzieherin* ["teacher"] the previous afternoon to talk about the problem of prostitution, in which connection I had, in order to bring an "educative" effect to bear on her not quite normally developed emotional life, given her Hesse's book *On Prostitution*, after telling her all manner of things about the problem. And now, all of a sudden, it was clear to me that the word "syphilis" was not to be taken literally but stood for poison – in connection with the sexual life, of course. So the sentence, translated, runs quite logically, "With my *Erzählung* ['story'] I tried to have an *erzieherisch* ['educative'] effect on the emotional life of my *Erzieherin* ['teacher'], but I rather fear that at the same time it may have had a *poisonous* effect." *Erzefilisch* = *erzäh* – (*erzieh* –) (*erzefilisch*).'

The word-deformations of dream are very like those that we came across in connection with paranoia – but also, invariably, in connection with hysteria and obsessions. The linguistic skills of children, who at times do indeed treat words as objects, as well as inventing new languages and artificial verbal constructions, are in this case the joint source for dream and for psychoneuroses.

Analysing nonsensical word-formations in dreams is a particularly good way of demonstrating the compression performed by dream-work. No one should conclude from the small selection of examples used here that such material is observed only rarely or indeed constitutes the exception; on the contrary, it occurs with great frequency. However, the consequence of dream-interpretation being dependent on psychoanalytic treatment is that a very small number of examples are noted and recounted and that most of the analyses that are passed on are comprehensible only to experts in the pathology of the neuroses. This is the case with a dream reported by Dr v. Karpinska (*Internationale Zeitschrift für Psychoanalyse*, II, 1914), which includes the senseless word-formation '*Svingnum elvi*'. Also worth mentioning is the case where a word appears in dream that is not meaningless in itself but that, alienated from its true meaning, collects together a variety of other meanings, in relation to which it assumes the character of a 'senseless' word. This is the case in the 'category' dream had by a ten-year-old boy and reported by V. Tausk ('Zur Psychologie der Kindersexualität' ['On the psychology of child sexuality'], in *Internationale Zeitschrift für Psychoanalyse*, I, 1913). 'Category' here refers to the female genitalia, and 'to categorize' implies 'to urinate'.

Where, in a dream, speeches occur that are explicitly different from thoughts, the invariable rule is that dream-speech derives from remembered speech in the relevant dream-material. The wording of the speech is either retained intact or gently shifted in terms of expression; often dream-speech is pieced together from various speech memories, with the wording in this connection remaining the same while the sense is if possible altered to produce multiple or simply different meanings. Dream-speech not infrequently serves merely to allude to an event in connection with which the remembered speech occurred.[19]

Notes

1. [Freud's *'Verdichtung'* is usually rendered as 'condensation' in English; I have chosen 'compression' because, although the process clearly includes condensation (the reduction of a single element), it also embraces the bringing together, in abbreviated form, of a multiplicity of elements (something that 'condensation' cannot properly imply). Really, Freud's *'Verdichtung'* is a process of 'making denser', of 'concentration'.]

2. References to compression in dream may be found in the works of many writers. Du Prel says at one point (p. 85) that it is absolutely certain that a process of compression of the ideational sequence has taken place.

3. [Goethe, *Faust*, Pt 1, scene 4.]

4. [*Überdeterminiert*; not 'over-determined' but 'springing from a number of factors'.]

5. In tribute to the writer's account, the reader is referred to the meaning of climbing dreams given in the section on symbolism. [Chapter 6, section E, especially sub-section 7. The novel *Sapho* (the French spelling of 'Sappho') by Alphonse Daudet was published in Paris in 1884. It concerns a young man from the provinces who comes to the capital and there forms a liaison with a model, to whom he becomes completely subjected.]

6. [*Abgestiegen*; literally, 'stepped down'.]

7. [*Einkehrwirtshaus* (incidentally, the word in the first sentence of the

dream that I translate as 'inn' suggests a place where one 'calls in' (*Ein-kehren*) for refreshment during a country walk rather than an establishment where one would seek accommodation. Hence, no doubt, the coachman's evident disparagement.]

8. [My 'conversely', 'the other way around' and 'reversed' are all, in German, *umgekehrt*.]

9. The fantastical nature of the situation in relation to the dreamer's wet-nurse is proven by the fact, objectively ascertained, that in this instance the wet-nurse was his mother. Incidentally, may I remind the reader of the regret mentioned on p. 220 as having been experienced by the young man of the anecdote at not having taken better advantage of the situation with his own wet-nurse, a regret which is no doubt the source of this dream.

10. This was the actual dream-trigger.

11. Let me add that, in her view, such reading was *poison* for a young girl. She herself, she told me, had in her youth garnered much from banned books.

12. [*Le Nabab* is another novel by Alphonse Daudet, published in 1877.]

13. A further train of thought leads to the same author's *Penthesilea: cruelty* towards one's beloved. [The author of *Das Käthchen von Heilbronn* and *Penthesilea*, two blank-verse plays, is the great German writer Heinrich von Kleist (1777–1811), as Freud was evidently confident all his readers would know. One thing that English readers might need to know is that *Käfer* ('beetle') is also used in much the same sense as our 'bird' or 'chick' as a somewhat lightweight term for a young woman.]

14. [Sir Francis Galton (1822–1911), explorer and anthropologist, made pioneering studies of eugenics using superimposed photographs.]

15. [Examples of these monumental gateways of Greek architecture are the Athens Propylaea (built on the Acropolis in the fifth century BCE) and the Munich Propyläen (built 1862).]

16. [Much closer in German, of course: *Propylen-Propyläen*.]

17. This kind of dismantling and reassembling of syllables ('syllable chemistry', one might almost call it) is something we use in the waking state to make all kinds of jokes. 'What's the cheapest way to get silver? Find an avenue of *Silberpappeln* ["white poplars"] and ask for quiet, whereupon the *Pappeln* ["chattering"] will break off, leaving the silver.' The first reader and critic of this book objected (and subsequent ones will doubtless agree) that 'the dreamer often appears too witty'. This is true – provided that it relates only to the dreamer; it constitutes a reproach only when it is supposed to extend to the interpreter. In waking reality I can lay little claim to the epithet 'witty'; if my dreams appear witty, it has nothing to do with

me personally but with the curious psychological conditions in which dream is processed, and it is closely bound up with the theory of the witty and comical. Dream becomes witty because the straightforward, obvious way to express its thoughts is barred to it; it becomes so of necessity. Readers can see for themselves that dreams recounted by my patients impress as witty (jesting) in the same degree as (sometimes in greater degree than) my own. Still, the charge did prompt me to compare the techniques of joke-making and dream-work, as I did in my 1905 study *Der Witz und seine Beziehung zum Unbewussten* [*Jokes and their Relation to the Unconscious, Standard Edition*, vol. VIII; a new translation by Joyce Crick appears in the New Penguin Freud: Sigmund Freud, *The Joke and Its Relation to the Unconscious*, London 2002].

18. Lasker died of progressive paralysis – that is to say, of the consequences of an infection (lues [syphilis]) caught from women; Lassalle, notoriously, died in a duel over a woman. [Both writers had been born in Breslau, now Wrocław in Poland.]

19. In connection with a young man suffering from obsessions, though with unimpaired, highly developed intellectual functions, I recently came across the sole exception to this rule. The speeches that occurred in his dreams did not derive from overheard or self-delivered utterances but corresponded to the undistorted wordings of his obsessive thoughts, of which he became conscious in the waking state only in an altered form.

B *Displacement*

Another, probably no less important connection inevitably struck us while we were putting together examples of dream-compression. It came to our attention that those elements that in dream-content stand out as essential components do not play at all the same role in the relevant dream-thoughts. Conversely, the same proposition may be said to apply the other way around: what is clearly the essential substance of those dream-thoughts need not be represented in dream at all. A dream, one might say, is *centred differently*; its content is arranged around and revolves around other elements than the dream-thoughts. For instance, in the dream of the botanical monograph [see pp. 181ff.], what clearly constitutes the focal point of the dream-content is the element 'botanical'; the dream-thoughts have to do with complications and conflicts arising out of binding commitments between colleagues and subsequently with the accusation that I sacrifice far too much to my hobbies, and the element 'botanical' has no place at all in this core of dream-thoughts, unless it is loosely connected by way of contrast, botany having never been one of my favourite subjects. In my patient's Sappho dream [see pp. 301ff.] the focus is on *climbing* and *descending*, on being *above* and *below*; the dream, however, is about the dangers of sexual relationships with persons of *lower* rank. So only one element of the dream-thoughts (but this one to an uncalled-for degree) appears to have entered the dream-content. Similarly, in the cockchafer dream [see pp. 305ff.], which is about the links between sexuality and cruelty, the cruelty factor does in fact reappear in the dream-content but in a different kind of connection and with no mention of sexuality

– in other words, it is torn out of context and in the process transformed into something alien. Again, in the uncle dream [pp. 151ff.], the blond beard at its centre appears to have no meaningful connection with the megalomaniac desires that we recognized as forming the core of the dream-thoughts. Such dreams rightly give one an impression of '*displacement*'. In complete contrast to these examples, the dream of Irma's injection [pp. 119ff.] shows that during the process of dream-formation the individual elements are well able to lay claim to the place that they occupy in the relevant dream-thoughts. Becoming aware of this new and (in terms of its meaning) thoroughly inconstant relationship between dream-thoughts and dream-content is likely, at first, to excite our surprise. If in connection with a psychical process of normal life we find that an idea has been plucked out of several others and has achieved especial vividness so far as consciousness is concerned, we usually regard that outcome as proving that the victorious idea possesses particularly great psychical valency (a certain degree of interest). We now discover that that valency of the individual elements in the dream-thoughts is not preserved or is left out of account as regards the process of dream-formation. After all, there is no doubt about what are the highest-value elements in the dream-thoughts; our judgement tells us immediately. But the fact is, in dream-formation these key elements, highlighted with especial interest, may be treated as if of lesser value and supplanted in the dream by other elements that in the dream-thoughts certainly were of lesser value. One's initial impression is as if the psychical intensity[1] of the individual ideas were left quite out of account so far as dream-selection is concerned, only the more or less multiple determination of those same ideas ever coming into consideration. It is not what is important in the dream-thoughts that enters the dream, one might think, but what is contained in them several times over; however, our understanding of dream-formation is not greatly advanced by this assumption, because from the outset it will be impossible to believe that the two factors of multiple determination and inherent valency can affect dream-selection otherwise than in the same sense. The ideas that are most important in the dream-thoughts will no doubt also be the ones that recur in them most often, since it is from them that the individual dream-thoughts radiate like spokes. Yet dream may reject these intensively highlighted and multiply supported elements and take other elements possessing only the latter quality into its content.

To resolve this difficulty we shall use another impression obtained while investigating multiple determination of dream-content. Possibly some readers will already have judged that investigation for themselves and concluded that multiple determination of dream-content is no big discovery since it is self-evident. The fact is, one proceeds during analysis from the dream-elements and records all the ideas associated with them; not surprisingly, then, in the thought-material thus obtained those very elements are found with particular frequency. I might invalidate that objection, but I am about to say something that sounds similar myself: among the thoughts that analysis brings to light are many that are further from the core of the dream and that behave like artificial interpolations for a specific purpose. The purpose is not hard to find; it is precisely they that establish a connection, often a forced and contrived connection, between dream-content and dream-thoughts, and if these elements were to be obliterated from the analysis the components of the dream-content would often lose not only their multiple determination but any adequate determination by the dream-thoughts at all. This leads us to conclude that multiple determination, crucial as regards dream-selection, is not in fact always a primary factor in dream-formation but is often a secondary product of a psychical power of which we are as yet unaware. But it must, for all that, be important as regards individual elements entering into a dream, because our observations show that it is manufactured at a certain cost where it does not spring unaided from the dream-material.

The suggestion is that a psychical power finds expression in dream-work that on the one hand strips the psychically high-value elements of their intensity and on the other hand, *using the channel of multiple determination*, takes elements of lower value and creates new valencies that then find their way into the dream-content. If that is what happens, in dream-formation a *transferral and displacement of the psychical intensities* of the individual elements has taken place, as a result of which a textual difference between dream-content and dream-thoughts appears. The process we are supposing here is the very essence of dream-work: it merits the name *dream-displacement*. *Dream-displacement* and *dream-compression* are the two foremen to whose labours we can chiefly ascribe the creation of dream.

I believe that it is no harder for us to discern the psychical power that finds expression in the facts of dream-displacement. The outcome of such displacement is that the dream-content no longer looks the same as the core of the dream-thoughts, that the dream in question simply reflects a distortion of the dream-wish in the unconscious. But dream-distortion is something with which we are already familiar; we traced it back to the censorship that one psychical authority in the life of the mind practises against another. Dream-displacement is one of the chief means by which such distortion is achieved. *Is fecit, cui profuit* ['He did the deed who gained by it']. We can assume that dream-displacement comes about through the influence of that censorship, namely endopsychical defence.[2]

We are inclined to reserve for subsequent examinations the manner in which the factors of displacement, compression and multiple determination interact with one another in dream-formation, which becomes the dominant and which the secondary factor. For the time being we can state, as a second condition that elements reaching dream must satisfy, *that they should be removed from the censorship of resistance*. But from now on we intend to take dream-displacement into account as an indubitable fact in connection with dream-interpretation.

Notes

1. Psychical intensity, valency and interest-emphasis of an idea should of course be kept separate from sensory intensity, the intensity of the thing imagined.

2. Since I might describe this tracing of dream-distortion back to censorship as the core of my view of dream, let me quote here the final fragment of the story 'Träumen wie Wachen' ['Dreaming like being awake'] from *Phantasien eines Realisten* ['Fantasies of a realist'] by Lynkeus (Vienna, second edition, 1900), in which I rediscover this principal feature of my theory:

'Of a man who has the remarkable quality of never dreaming nonsense . . .

' "Your marvellous quality of dreaming like lying awake rests on your virtues, on your goodness, your fairness, your love of truth; it is the moral transparency of your nature that makes everything about you comprehensible to me."

' "But giving the matter due consideration," the other replied, "I tend to think all men are like me and no one ever dreams nonsense! A dream one remembers so clearly as to be able to recount it (not a delirious dream, then) *always* makes sense, nor can it ever be otherwise! Because things that are mutually contradictory could never come together to form a whole. The fact that time and space are often confused detracts not at all from the true substance of a dream, for both were undoubtedly of no consequence as regards its essential content. We often do the same thing when awake; think of folk tales, of all those bold and meaningful fantasy images of which only an ignorant person would say, 'That's nonsense! It couldn't happen!' "

' "If only people could interpret dreams correctly every time, the way you've just interpreted mine!" said his friend.

' "It's no easy task, I'll grant you that, but it should always be possible, given a certain amount of attentiveness on the part of the dreamer. Why does it usually fail? There seems to be, with you, something hidden about dreams, a peculiar, superior unchastity, a certain secretiveness in your nature that is hard to fathom; and that is why your dreams so frequently appear meaningless, even nonsensical. Deep down, however, this is quite untrue; indeed, it cannot possibly be true, for a person is always the same, be he awake or dreaming." '

C *Dream's modes of representation*

In addition to the two factors of dream-*compression* and dream-*displacement* that we have found to influence the transformation of latent thought-material into manifest dream-content, as we continue this investigation we shall come across two further conditions that undoubtedly affect the choice of material that finds its way into dream. But first, even at the risk of appearing to pause on our way, I should like to cast an initial glance at the processes involved in practising dream-interpretation. I do not close my eyes to the fact that I am most likely to succeed in clarifying those processes and defending their soundness against objections if I take an actual dream as a specimen, proceed to interpret it (as I illustrated in Chapter 2 in connection with the dream of Irma's injection [see pp. 119ff.]), but then gather together the dream-thoughts that I have uncovered and go on to reconstruct from them the formation of the dream – in other words, if I supplement my analyses of dreams with syntheses of the same. I have done this with several examples, and I have learned from it; however, I cannot undertake it here because a wide variety of considerations (of which every right-minded person will approve) relating to the psychical material involved in such a demonstration hold me back. In connection with dream-analysis, such considerations were less inhibiting because analysis might be less than total, retaining its value even where it led only a little way into the fabric of a particular dream. With regard to synthesis, I knew only that, to be convincing, it must be complete. I could provide a full synthesis only of dreams of persons unknown to the reading public. But since it is only patients, neurotics, who offer me the relevant means, this part of my account of dream must be postponed until such time as I am able (elsewhere) to take the psychological elucidation of neurosis to the point where the link to our present topic can be shown.[1]

I know from my attempts to produce dreams synthetically from dream-thoughts that the material that emerges during interpretation varies in value. One part consists of the essential dream-thoughts, which in other words entirely replace the particular dream and would suffice in themselves as a substitute for it if dream were not subject to censorship. The other part is usually deemed unimportant. Nor does any value attach to the claim that all these thoughts played a part in dream-formation; the fact is, they may include ideas that link up with experiences subsequent to the dream, in the period between the dream and its interpretation. This part embraces all the connecting avenues that led from the manifest dream-content to the latent dream-thoughts but also the mediating and approximative associations through which, during the work of interpretation, one had reached a knowledge of those connecting avenues.

At this point, we are interested solely in the essential dream-thoughts. These usually reveal themselves as a complex of thoughts and memories with the most intricate structure and possessing all the qualities of the thought-processes familiar to us from the waking state. Not infrequently they are trains of thought proceeding from more than one centre but not lacking in points of contact; almost invariably one train of thought will be accompanied by its own contradiction, to which it is bound by contrast-association.

It goes without saying that the individual pieces of this complicated structure stand in the most widely varied logical relationships to one another. They form foreground and background, digressions and explanations, conditions, lines of argument and objections. If the whole mass of these dream-thoughts then undergoes the squeezing effect of dream-work in which the pieces are twisted around, broken up and thrust against one another, rather like drifting ice-floes, the question arises: what happens to the logical ties that had formed the structure hitherto? How are they represented in dream – the 'when, wherefore, just as, albeit, either/or', and all the other connecting words without which we cannot make sense of what we are told?

Our initial answer must be that, so far as these logical relationships among dream-thoughts are concerned, dream has no means of representation at its disposal. It usually leaves such connecting words out of account, taking over only the objective substance of the dream-thoughts for processing. It is up to dream-interpretation to restore the context that dream-work has destroyed.

Evidently, responsibility for the fact that dream lacks this ability to express itself lies with the psychical material from which it is fashioned. A similar restriction afflicts the pictorial arts, of course, namely painting and sculpture (in comparison with poetry, which is able to use language), and here too the reason for the inability lies in the material that these two arts take and fashion in an attempt to give expression to something. Before painting became aware of the laws of expression that govern it, it kept trying to compensate for this disadvantage. In old paintings, little labels were left dangling from the mouths of the persons portrayed, using speech, in the form of writing, to represent in the painting what the artist despaired of conveying.

An objection might arise here that, so far as dream is concerned, challenges this refusal to portray logical relationships. After all, there are dreams in which the most complicated intellectual operations unfold, are justified and contradicted, joked about and compared, as in waking thought. But here again appearances are deceptive; proceeding to analyse such dreams, one learns that this is all *dream-material*, not *portrayal of intellectual work in dream*. The *content* of dream-thoughts is reflected by the ostensible thinking of the relevant dream, not *the relationships of those dream-thoughts among one another*, in ascertaining which such thinking consists. I shall be citing examples of this. But it is easiest to note that all spoken language that features in dreaming and is expressly described as such consists of intact or only slightly modified reproductions of remarks that likewise appear in recollections of the dream-material. Such remarks are often only allusions to events contained in the dream-thoughts; the meaning of the relevant dream is something quite different.

Nevertheless, I would not deny that critical thought-work that does not simply echo material from the dream-thoughts also plays a part in dream-formation. I shall need to shed light on this factor at the end of this discussion. It will then be seen that such thought-work is evoked not by the dream-thoughts but by what is in a sense already the finished dream.

So for the time being it remains the case that the logical relationships among dream-thoughts find no special representation in dream. For instance, where there is contradiction in a particular dream it is either contradiction of the dream itself or contradiction arising from the substance of one of the dream-thoughts; in dream, any contradiction corresponds to a contradiction *among* the dream-thoughts only in the most indirect manner.

However, just as painting did eventually manage to convey the outward intentions of the persons portrayed (affection, threat, admonition, and so on) otherwise than through the banner streaming in the wind, so too did dream find a way of taking some of the logical relationships among dream-thoughts into account by appropriately modifying the particular dream-representation involved. Some dreams may be found to go further than others in this; while one dream places itself quite outside the logical structure of its material, another will seek to suggest that structure as fully as possible. Dream, in doing this, withdraws to a greater or lesser distance from the text placed before it for processing. Incidentally, it also behaves in a similar way towards the time-structure of the dream-thoughts, where such a structure has been fashioned in the unconscious (as, for example, in the dream of Irma's injection [see pp. 119ff.]).

But by means of what techniques is dream-work able to suggest such relations (which are difficult to portray) in dream-material? I shall try to enumerate them one by one.

Initially, a dream will on the whole do justice to the undeniable presence of a coherence among all the pieces of the relevant dream-thoughts by bringing that material together into a summary as a particular situation or chain of events. It will reflect *logical coherence* as *simultaneity*; here dream is doing a similar thing to the painter who assembles all the philosophers or poets for a painting of the School of Athens or Parnassus – people who were never together in the same room or on the same mountain-top but who for the purposes of intellectual contemplation form a community.

This mode of representation is one that dream continues in detail. Whenever it shows two elements close together it guarantees a special inner connection between their equivalents in the dream-thoughts. It is like in our system of writing: *ab* means that the two letters are to be pronounced as a single syllable; *a* followed by *b* after an empty space indicates that *a* is the last letter of one word and *b* the first letter of another. Accordingly, dream-combinations are formed not from arbitrary, wholly disparate components of the relevant dream-material; they are formed from components that in the dream-thoughts, too, belong intimately together.

As regards representing *causal relationships*, dream has two procedures, which are in essence one and the same. The more frequent mode of representation (when the dream-thoughts say something like, 'Because this was the way it was, such and such had to happen') consists in taking the subordinate clause as the preliminary dream and then adding the main clause as the principal dream. If I am right in my interpretation, the temporal order may also be reversed. The main clause always corresponds to the more expansive portion of the particular dream.

A fine example of such representation of causality was once supplied by a patient of mine whose dream I shall be giving in full later [see below, pp. 361ff.]. It consisted of a brief prelude and a very rambling dream-fragment that was highly centred and might have been entitled 'Through the Flowers'. The preliminary dream went like this: *She goes into the kitchen where the two maids are and scolds them for not being ready 'with that little snack'. In the kitchen she sees a very large number of heavy pots and pans turned upside-down to drain; they are all over the place, piled in heaps. The two maids go to fetch water, for which they have to step into a river, which comes up as far as the house or the yard.*

The main dream follows, and it begins like this: *She is descending from higher up over a strangely formed landscape, and she is glad that, as she does so, her dress does not get caught up anywhere*, etc. The preliminary dream in fact relates to the woman's parental home. The words spoken in the kitchen are presumably ones she had often heard her mother say. The piles of unfinished washing-up derive from the simple way in which washing-up was done in that house. The other portion of the dream contains an allusion to her father, who spent a lot of time with the servant-girls and who later, when there was a flood (the house stood near the river bank), caught a fatal disease. So the thinking concealed behind the preliminary dream is this: Because I come from this house, from such petty, unedifying circumstances. The principal dream takes up the same thoughts and delivers them in a way that is transformed by wish-fulfilment: I spring from superior origins. Which actually means: Because I spring from such humble origins, my life has taken this and this course.

So far as I can see, division of a dream into two unequal parts does not always imply a causal relationship between the thoughts of the two parts. Often it seems as if the same material has been represented in the two parts from different points of view; this is certainly true of a single night's dream-sequence, culminating in an emission, where the somatic need compels clearer and clearer expression. Or the two dreams proceed from separate centres in the dream-material and overlap in terms of content, with the result that something is central in one dream that in the other appears as a suggestion, and the other way around. However, in a certain number of dreams this split into a shorter preliminary dream and a longer subsequent dream does in fact imply a causal relationship between the two parts. The other technique for representing the causal relationship is used in the case of less extensive material and consists of an image in the dream (be it a person or a thing) turning into something else. Only where we see this transformation happening in a dream is a causal relationship being seriously asserted; not where we simply become aware that in place of one thing we now have the other. I said that the two ways of representing a causal relationship ultimately amounted to the same; in both cases the *occasioning* is represented by a *sequence* – sometimes through succession of dreams, at other times through the immediate transformation of one image into another. In most instances, of course, the causal relationship is not represented at all but falls into what in the dream-process, too, is the unavoidable sequence of elements.

The 'either–or' alternative is one that dream cannot express at all; it tends to absorb the two halves of the alternative into a single context, as if they enjoyed equal validity. A classic instance of this is to be found in the dream of Irma's injection [see pp. 119ff.]. One of the latent thoughts here is clearly, 'I am innocent of the fact that Irma's pain continues; the blame lies *either* with her resistance to accepting the solution *or* in the fact that she is living in unhappy sexual circumstances that I am powerless to change, *or* her pain is not hysterical at all but organic in nature. However, dream runs through these almost mutually exclusive possibilities and takes no exception to adding a fourth such solution from the dream-wish. The 'either–or' is something that I have then inserted in the context of the dream-thoughts after the dream-interpretation.

But where the narrator, reproducing a dream, wishes to use an 'either–or' ('It was either a garden or a room' – that sort of thing), what happens in the dream-thoughts is not so much an alternative as an 'and', a simple following on. We generally use 'either–or' to describe a still resolvable character of vagueness about a dream-element. The rule for interpreting such a case is: the individual terms of the apparent alternative must be equated with each other and connected by 'and'. For instance, having waited in vain for a long time for the address of a friend of mine who is staying in Italy, I dream that I receive a telegram telling me the address. I see it printed in blue on the paper-tape of the telegram; the first word is fuzzy,

perhaps *via*

or *Villa*   the second clear: *Sezerno*

or even (*Casa*)

The second word, which sounds like an Italian name [*Secerno*] and reminds me of our etymological discussions, also expresses my irritation at his having kept his address *secret* from me for so long; but each term of the threefold proposal for the first word is recognizable, when analysed, as an independent starting point, enjoying entirely equal rights, for the train of thought.

In the night before my father's funeral I dream of a printed label, a plaque or notice (not unlike the sign in station waiting-rooms telling people that smoking is forbidden) on which the message is either

> *You are requested to close your eyes*

or

> *You are requested to close an eye*

which I am in the habit of representing in the following form:

$$\text{\textit{You are requested to close}} \quad \substack{\textit{your} \\ \\ \textit{an}} \quad \textit{eye(s)}$$

Each version has its own meaning and leads in dream-interpretation along particular paths. I had kept the ceremonial as simple as possible, knowing what the deceased had thought about such occasions. But other members of the family did not agree with such puritanical simplicity; they thought we should inevitably lose face in front of the mourners. That is why one version of the dream-wording asks people to 'close an eye' – in other words, to exercise forbearance. The significance of the vagueness that we describe with an 'either–or' is particularly easy to grasp here. The relevant dream-work has failed to produce a uniform but at the same time ambiguous wording for the dream-thoughts. As a result, the two main trains of thought split apart as early as the dream-content.

In certain cases, bisection of a dream into two pieces of equal size expresses the alternative that is so hard to represent.

Particularly striking is the way dream behaves towards the *conflict* and *contradiction* category. It is quite simply ignored; so far as dream is concerned, 'no' appears not to exist. Dream has a particular predilection for drawing opposites together to form a single entity or representing them as such. Indeed, it even takes the liberty of representing any element by its optative opposite, with the result that one cannot, at first, know of any element capable of having an opposite whether in the relevant dream-thoughts it bears a positive or negative connotation.[2] In one of the dreams last mentioned [pp. 331, 362], the prelude to which we have already interpreted ('because I spring from such origins'), the dreamer is walking down through a field, holding a flowering twig in her hands. Since it occurs to her, in connection with this image, that the angel is always carrying a lily stem in pictures of the Annunciation (she shares the same name as the Virgin; she is also a 'Maria'), and that the white-clad maidens accompanying the Corpus Christi procession walk along streets decorated with greenery, it is quite obvious that the flowering twig in the dream alludes to sexual innocence. However, the twig bears a great many red flowers, each resembling a camellia. When the maidens reach the end, the dream further relates, the flowers are already somewhat wilted; there then follow unmistakable allusions to the monthly period. Thus the same twig as is borne like a lily as if by an innocent maiden is simultaneously an allusion to '*la dame aux camélias*', who, as we know, always wore a white camellia, except when she had her period, when it was red.[3] The same flowering twig ('the maiden's flowers', in Goethe's songs about the miller's daughter) represents sexual innocence and also its opposite. And the same dream which expresses the joy of having successfully gone through life unstained also, at certain points (the wilting of the flowers, for instance), allows the contrary train of thought to show through, namely that the dreamer has been guilty of committing various sins against sexual purity (in childhood, that is). When it comes to interpreting the dream, we can clearly distinguish the two thought-processes (with the comforting one seeming more superficial and the accusatory one apparently lying deeper) and see that they are diametrically opposed to each other; we see too that their equal but opposite elements have found representation through the same dream-elements.

Only one of the logical relationships benefits to the greatest extent from the mechanism of dream-formation. This is the relationship of similarity, of correspondence, of contact, the *'as if'* that dream is able to represent like nothing else with a wide variety of means.[4] The correspondences or instances of 'as if' present in the dream-material are of course the first points of support of dream-formation, and a substantial portion of dream-work consists in creating fresh correspondences of this kind in case, because of resistance censorship, the existing ones fail to reach the relevant dream. The compression effort of dream-work assists the representation of the similarity relationship.

Similarity, correspondence, common ground – these dreams usually represents by drawing [the two terms concerned] together into one, forming a *single entity* that is either already present in the relevant dream-material or is constructed from scratch. The former instance we can call *identification*, the latter *blending*. Identification is used when people are involved, blending where things constitute the material to be joined together, although blending may also occur with people. Places are often treated like people.

Identification consists in only one of the persons sharing a common characteristic that reaches the dream-content for the purpose of representation, whereas the other person or persons seem(s) to be suppressed so far as the relevant dream is concerned. However, in the dream that one covering person ['umbrella' person, almost] enters into all the relationships and all the situations that stem from him or from the other persons covered. In blending, when extended to persons, the relevant dream-image already contains traits that are peculiar to those individuals rather than common to them – with the result that combining those traits definitely gives rise to a fresh entity, a mixed or composite person. Blending itself may be effected in various ways. Either the dream-person has the name of one of the related persons (in which case we know in a way that is entirely analogous to knowing in the waking state that this or that person is meant) while the visual traits are those of the other person; or the dream-image is itself made up of visual traits that are in reality drawn from one or the other. Rather than by visual traits the presence of the second person may also be represented by gestures associated with that person, the words the dreamer has that person speak, or the situation in which he is placed. In connection with the latter type of characterization, the sharp distinction between identification and blending begins to dissipate. However, it can also happen that the forming of such a composite person fails. Then the scene of the relevant dream is attributed to one person, while the other (usually the more important one) steps aside as someone present but otherwise uninvolved. The dreamer narrates, say, 'My mother was there too' (Stekel). Such an element in the dream-content should then be compared to a determinative in hieroglyphic script, which is not pronounced but is there to clarify another sign.

The common ground that justifies or rather occasions the union of the two persons may or may not be represented in dream. As a rule, identification or blending of persons serves in fact to render such representation unnecessary. Instead of repeating, 'A is hostile to me, but so is B', in the relevant dream I constitute a blend of A and B, or I imagine A behaving in a different way than we associate with B. The dream-person thus obtained engages me in the dream in some new association, and from the circumstance that that person implies both A and B I derive the justification for inserting in the relevant place in the dream-interpretation what the two persons have in common, namely a hostile relationship to myself. In this way I often achieve a quite extraordinary degree of compression so far as the dream-content is concerned; I am able to dispense with direct representation of highly complicated relationships having to do with one person if for that person I have found another who has the same right to some of those relationships. It is easy to understand how far such representation through identification can also serve to bypass resistance censorship, which places dream-work under such harsh conditions. The impulse for censorship may lie in precisely those ideas that in the material are associated with one person; I now find a second person who likewise has links to the offending material, though only to some of it. Contact at that point not free of censorship now gives me the right to form a composite person characterized in both directions by indifferent features. This composite or identifying person is now, being free of censorship, fit for admission to the dream-content, and I have met the demands of dream-censorship by applying dream-compression.

Where in dream something common to both persons is represented, this is usually a hint in the direction of looking for another disguised common feature that censorship makes it impossible to represent. What has happened here (as it were, for the sake of representability) is a displacement with regard to the common feature. As a consequence of my being shown the composite person, in dream, with an indifferent common feature, I am supposed to deduce, in the dream-thoughts, another common feature, this one not at all indifferent.

Accordingly, identification or the formation of a composite person serves various purposes in dream: first, to represent something that both persons have in common; secondly, to represent a *displaced* common feature; but thirdly, to give expression to a common feature that is merely *desired*. Since desiring a common feature between two persons often coincides with an *interchange* of the same, this relationship too is expressed in dream through identification. In the dream of Irma's injection [see pp. 119ff.] I wish to exchange this patient for another one – that is to say, I wish the other woman could be my patient as this one is; the dream takes this wish into account by showing a person who is called Irma but is being examined in a position that I had occasion to see only in connection with the other. In the uncle dream [see pp. 151ff.] such an exchange becomes the hub of the dream; I identify with the minister in that I treat and pass judgement on my colleagues no better than he did.

It has been my experience (and I have found no exception to this) that every dream deals with the person of the dreamer. Dreams are wholly egoistical.[5] Where in the content of a particular dream it is not my 'I' that appears but simply a stranger, I can confidently assume that my 'I' is hidden behind that person as a result of identification. I may add my own 'I'. Other times when my 'I' does appear in a dream, the situation in which it finds itself tells me that another person is hidden behind the 'I' through identification. The dream is then meant to remind me to take something that in the dream-interpretation is attached to that person (the disguised common feature) and transfer it to myself. There are also dreams in which my 'I' appears alongside other persons who, once the identification has been resolved, in turn reveal themselves as my 'I'. It seems that, by means of such identifications, I combine certain ideas with my 'I' that censorship objects to my accepting. So I am able to represent my 'I' in a dream several times – now directly, now through identification with others. With several such identifications, an immensely rich thought-material can be compressed.[6] That my own 'I' should appear in a dream several times or in several guises is basically no more surprising than that it should be contained several times and in various places or in different connections in a conscious thought. Take, for example, the words 'When *I* think what a healthy child *I* was . . .'

Even more transparent than in the case of persons is the resolving of identifications in the case of places described with proper names because here there is no disturbance by the 'I' (so overpowering in dream). In one of my Rome dreams (see p. 211) the name of the place I am in is Rome; but I am surprised to find so many German posters on one street corner. The latter is a piece of wish-fulfilment, in connection with which the name Prague immediately springs to mind; the wish itself may derive from a period (now behind me) of German nationalism in my youth. At the time of my dream I was considering a meeting with my friend in Prague; so the identification of Rome and Prague is explained by a wished-for common feature: I should prefer to meet my friend in Rome than in Prague, exchanging Prague and Rome for our meeting.

The possibility of creating composite formations heads the list of features to which dream so often lends a fantastic character in that through it elements are introduced into the content of a dream that could never be an object of perception. The psychical process involved in the forming of composites in dream is evidently the same as when in the waking state we picture to ourselves or reproduce a centaur or a dragon. The difference is only that in the case of the fantastical creation in the waking state the impression that the new creature is intended to make is itself what matters, whereas the dreamed composite formation is determined by a factor that lies outside its creation, namely the common feature in the relevant dream-thoughts. The composite formation of dream can be executed in a wide variety of ways. In the least sophisticated execution, only the qualities of one thing are represented, and that representation is accompanied by the knowledge that it is also valid for a different object. A more careful technique combines features from one object with features from the other to form a fresh image, making clever use in the process of such similarities between the two objects as may exist in reality. The new formation may look wholly absurd or even fantastically successful, depending on what material and wit make possible when it is being put together. If the objects that are to be compressed into a single entity are in fact too disparate, dream-work is often content to create a composite formation with a clearer nucleus around which less clear determinants are added on. Unification into a single image has here not worked, as it were; the two representations overlap and generate something like a contest of visual images. Were one to try to present the formation of a concept from individual perceptual images, one might arrive at similar representations in a drawing.

Dreams of course teem with such blendings, such composite images; I have already cited a few examples in the dreams I have analysed hitherto; I shall now add some more. In the dream on pp. 330 and 361ff., which describes the patient's life-story 'through the flowers' or in a 'flowery' way, the dream-'I' is holding a flowering twig that, as we learned, simultaneously indicates innocence and sexual sinfulness. Because of the way the flowers grow on it, the twig also recalls *cherry* blossom; the flowers themselves, taken individually, are camellias, with the whole thing giving the further impression of an *exotic* plant. What is common to the elements of this composite structure emerges from the relevant dream-thoughts. The flowering twig is made up of allusions to gifts by means of which she had been persuaded or was to be persuaded to exhibit complaisance. Thus the cherry in childhood, in later years a sprig of camellia; the exotic quality alludes to a much-travelled

339

naturalist who sought to gain her favour with a flower-drawing. Another patient creates for herself in dream a cross between a *bathing-cabin* at a seaside spa, an *outside lavatory* in the country, and an *attic-compartment*, as in one of our urban blocks of flats. The first two elements share a connection with human nakedness and exposure; their being associated with the third element suggests that (back in her childhood) the attic-compartment was also a scene of self-exposure. One dreamer creates for himself a blend of two localities in which 'treatment' is administered: my consulting-room and the public place of entertainment where he first met his wife. A girl dreams, after her elder brother has promised to regale her with caviar, that the same brother's legs are *covered with black beads of caviar*. The elements 'infection' in the moral sense and her recollection of a childhood *rash* that had made her legs look as if they were covered with red rather than black spots have here combined with the beads of caviar to form a new concept of *'something she caught from her brother'*. In this dream, parts of the human body are treated as objects – as they are in other dreams, too. In a dream recounted by Ferenczi there was a composite creation made up of the person of a *doctor* and a *horse*, the whole wearing a *nightshirt*. What these three components had in common was revealed by analysis, once the nightshirt had been shown to be an allusion to the dreamer's father in a childhood scene. All three turned out to be objects of sexual curiosity. As a child, she had often been taken by her nanny to the army's stud farm, where she had ample opportunity to sate her (then still uninhibited) curiosity.

I said before that dream has no technique for expressing the contradiction relation, opposition, the 'no'. I am about to contradict that statement for the first time. Some of the cases that may be summarized as 'opposition' do find representation through simple identification, as we have seen – namely when such an 'over against each other' can be associated with an exchange, an 'in place of'. We have made repeated mention of examples of this. Another set of oppositions in dream-thoughts, those that can perhaps be categorized as *'the other way around, on the contrary'*, achieve representation in dream in the following remarkable (one might almost say, witty) fashion. The 'the other way around' does not itself find its way into the dream-content; instead, it indicates its presence in the dream-material by the fact that a portion of the already formed dream-content that suggests itself for other reasons is turned *the other way around* – after the event, so to speak. The process is easier to illustrate than to describe. In the beautiful 'up and down' dream (see pp. 301ff.) the dream-representation of climbing is the other way around from the model in the dream-thoughts, namely the introductory scene of Daudet's *Sapho*; in the dream the going is difficult at first, then easy, whereas in the scene the climbing is easy at first and subsequently becomes more and more difficult. The 'above' and 'below' in relation to the brothers is also, in the dream, represented in reverse. This points to a relationship of reversal or opposition that exists between two parts of the material in the dream-thoughts and that we found in the fact that in the dreamer's childhood fantasy he is being carried by his nurse, whereas in the novel it is the other way around: the hero carries his beloved. My dream of Goethe's attack on Mr M. (see pp. 454ff.) also contains such a reversal, which must first be corrected before the dream can be interpreted. In the dream, Goethe attacked a young man, Mr M.; in reality, as contained in the relevant dream-thoughts, an important man, a friend of mine, was attacked by an unknown young author. In the dream, I count from the year of Goethe's death; in reality, the counting started from the year of the paralytic's birth.[7] The crucial thought so far as the dream-material is concerned arises out of the denial that Goethe should be treated as if he were a madman. On the contrary, says the dream, if you do not understand the book you are the mentally deficient one, not the author. In all these dreams of reversal there seems to me to be a further link to the contemptuous expression 'to turn one's back on someone'[8] (note the reversal in relation to the brother in the *Sapho* dream [see pp. 301ff.]). Also remarkable is how often reversal is used in dreams prompted by repressed homosexual urges.

Reversal, transformation of a thing into its opposite, is in fact one of dream-work's favourite techniques of representation, capable of being used in a wide variety of ways. In the first place, it serves to reinforce wish-fulfilment against a specific element in the dream-thoughts. 'If only it had been the other way around!' is often the best expression for the reaction of the 'I' to an embarrassing memory. But reversal is particularly valuable in the service of censorship in that it brings about a measure of distortion of what is to be represented that for a time virtually paralyses understanding of the dream concerned. For that reason, whenever a dream stubbornly refuses to yield its meaning one can try reversing specific portions of its manifest content, whereupon everything, quite often, will become clear immediately.

As well as reversal of content, reversal of time should not be overlooked. A very common technique of dream-distortion consists in representing the outcome of an event or the conclusion of a train of thought at the beginning of a dream and adding the assumptions behind the conclusion or the causes of the event on at the end. Anyone who has not thought of this technical resource of dream-distortion will be at a loss when faced with the task of interpreting a dream.[9]

Indeed, in many cases one does not get the meaning of a dream until one has turned the dream-content around several times, tracing different relationships. For instance, in the dream of one young compulsive neurotic a recollection of a childhood death-wish against his father is concealed behind the following wording: *His father scolds him for coming home so late*. Only the context of psychoanalytical treatment and the ideas occurring to the dreamer reveal that this must originally have been: *He is cross with his father*, the reason being that so far as he was concerned his father always came home *too early* (i.e. too soon). He would have preferred his father never to come home, which is the same thing as wishing one's father dead (see p. 269ff.). The fact is, as a small boy, during a lengthy absence on his father's part, the dreamer had been accused of committing an act of sexual aggression against another person and incurred the threat: 'Just you wait till your father gets back!'

If we wish to pursue the links between dream-content and dream-thoughts, the best way of doing so will be to take an actual dream as our starting point and [in that context] ask what specific formal characteristics of that dream's portrayal mean in relation to the dream-thoughts. The chief formal characteristics that inevitably strike us in connection with dreams include differences in the sensory intensity of individual dream-creations and in the clarity of individual parts of dreams or entire dreams, as compared with one another. Differences in the intensity of individual dream-creations cover a whole scale from a sharpness of definition that one is inclined (albeit without guarantee) to place above that of reality to an irritating blur deemed characteristic of dream because in fact it is not quite like any of the degrees of fuzziness that we sometimes perceive in relation to real objects. Furthermore, we usually describe the impression we receive from an unclear dream-object as 'fleeting', whereas we say of clearer dream-images that they have stood the test of perception even for quite some time. The question now is: what conditions in the dream-material give rise to these differences in the vividness of individual parts of the dream-content?

The first thing one must do here is counter certain expectations that almost inevitably present themselves. Since actual sensations during sleep can themselves form part of the material of a dream, it will no doubt be assumed that these or the dream-elements derived therefrom will stand out in the dream-content with particular intensity or, conversely, that the things that are especially vivid and striking in a particular dream can be traced back to such actual sleep sensations. However, my experience has never confirmed this. It is not true that the elements of a dream that spring from actual impressions received during sleep (nervous stimuli) distinguish themselves, in terms of vividness, from other' elements that stem from recollections. So far as determining the intensity of dream-images is concerned, the reality factor counts for nothing.

A further expectation might be that the sensory intensity (vividness) of individual dream-images bears some relationship to the psychical intensity of the corresponding elements in the relevant dream-thoughts. In the latter, intensity coincides with psychical valency; the most intense elements are quite simply the most significant ones, those forming the core of the dream-thoughts. We know, of course, that precisely these elements usually fail, for reasons of censorship, to find a place in the dream-content. But might it not be that their nearest descendants in the dream, representing them, summon up a greater degree of intensity without necessarily forming the centre of the way in which the dream presents itself? However, this expectation too is scotched by a comparison of dream and dream-material. The intensity of the elements in the one has nothing to do with the intensity of the elements in the other; the fact is, between dream-material and dream a complete *'revaluation of all psychical values'* takes place. It is often precisely in a fleeting element of a dream, one hidden behind more powerful images, that one finds the one and only direct descendant of what in the dream-thoughts was overwhelmingly dominant.

The intensity of the elements of a dream proves to be determined in a different fashion – by two factors that are independent of each other. To begin with, it is easy to see that those elements are represented with particular intensity through which the relevant piece of wish-fulfilment finds expression. Then, however, analysis shows us that the most vivid elements of a dream also give rise to the largest number of trains of thought, that the most vivid are at the same time the best determined. The meaning does not change if we express the last (empirically acquired) sentence in the following form: the greatest intensity is shown by those elements of a dream that it took the greatest amount of *compression* to form. We can then expect that both this condition and the other concerning wish-fulfilment can be expressed in a single formula.

The problem I have just been discussing (that of what causes individual elements of a dream to be sometimes more, sometimes less intense or clear) is one I am keen should not be mistaken for another problem, one having to do with the different degrees of clarity of entire dreams or sections of dreams. In the first, clarity is contrasted with fuzziness, in the second with confusion. It is obvious, of course, that in both scales the rising and falling qualities occur alongside each other. A part of a particular dream that appears clear to us usually contains intense elements; an unclear dream is on the contrary made up of low-intensity elements. Yet the problem presented by the scale from apparently clear to unclear-confused is far more complicated than that of the fluctuations in vividness of particular elements of the dream; in fact, the former is not amenable to discussion here for reasons that will be cited later. In individual instances one notes with some surprise that the impression of clarity or lack of clarity that one has of a dream means absolutely nothing so far as the structure of the dream is concerned; it stems from the dream-material as a component of the same. I recall a dream, for example, that seemed to me, when I awoke, so well put together, complete and clear that I resolved, even before I was completely awake, to admit a fresh category of dreams, dreams that were not subject to the mechanism of compression and displacement but might be described as 'fantasies during sleep'. Closer examination revealed that this rare dream exhibited the same cracks and fissures in its structure as any other; so I dropped the category of dream-fantasies.[10] The reduced content of the dream, however, was that I was telling my friend about a difficult and long sought-after theory of bisexuality, and the wish-fulfilling force of dream was responsible for the theory (which incidentally was not spelled out in the dream) striking us as clear and complete. So what I had regarded as a verdict on the finished dream was one piece (in fact, the key piece) of the dream-content. Here it was as if dream-work had spilled over into the first waking thought, giving me as a *verdict* on the dream the piece of the dream-material that it had failed to represent precisely in the dream. I once experienced the perfect pendant to this in connection with a patient who at first utterly refused to recount a dream that formed part of the analysis 'because it was so unclear and confused' and who eventually, amid repeated protests that her account could not be considered reliable, said that several people had appeared in the dream (herself, her husband and her father) and that it had been as if she had not known whether her husband was her father or who in fact her father was or some such thing. The juxtaposition of this dream and what came into her head during the session showed beyond doubt that this was the fairly everyday story of a maidservant who has had to confess to being pregnant and who now hears doubts expressed as to 'who in fact the father (of the child) is'.[11] Here too, in other words, the lack of clarity shown by the dream was part of the material that had triggered the dream. *The form of a dream or of dreaming is with very surprising frequency used to represent hidden content.*

Glosses on what has been dreamed, seemingly innocent remarks in this regard, often serve to disguise what has been dreamed and to do so in the most sophisticated manner – while at the same time giving it away. This is the case, for instance, when a dreamer says, 'Here the dream is *blurred*', and analysis reveals a childhood memory of listening to someone cleaning themselves after defecating. In another case, which merits recounting in greater detail, a young man has a very clear dream reminding him of fantasies of his boyhood years that have remained conscious. One evening, in a resort hotel, he gets the room number wrong and mistakenly enters a room in which an older lady and her two daughters are undressing for bed. He continues, *'Then there are some gaps in the dream, something's missing,* and at the end there was a man in the room who wanted to throw me out, I had to wrestle with him.' He tries in vain to recall the content and intention of the boyhood fantasy to which the dream obviously alludes. Eventually, one realizes that the content he is looking for has already been supplied by what he said about the bits of the dream that are unclear. The 'gaps'[12] are the genital apertures of the women who are going to bed; 'something's missing' describes the principal characteristic of female genitalia. In those young years he harboured a burning curiosity to see female genitalia, and he was still inclined to adhere to the infantile sexual theory that ascribes a male member to the female of the species.

A similar reminiscence by another dreamer assumed very much the same sort of form. He dreams, *'I accompany Miss K. to the Volksgarten Restaurant . . .',* then there is an obscure bit, an interruption . . . , *'then I am in the reception room of a brothel where I can see two or three women, one in vest and stockings.'*

Analysis: Miss K. is the daughter of his former boss – a sister-substitute, as he admits himself. Only rarely did he have the opportunity to talk to her, but there was once a conversation between them in which 'we did as it were acknowledge our sexuality, as much as to say, "I am a man and you are a woman."' The restaurant mentioned was one he had been in only once, in the company of his brother-in-law's sister, a girl towards whom he felt complete indifference. On another occasion he accompanied a party of three women as far as the door of the restaurant. The women were his sister, his sister-in-law and the aforementioned sister of his brother-in-law, all of no interest to him whatsoever but all three of them members of the sister line. A brothel was a place he had visited only seldom – possibly two or three times in his life.

The interpretation, taking as its basis the 'obscure bit', the 'interruption' in the dream, asserted that in his boyish thirst for knowledge he had occasionally (not often) inspected his sister's genitals, she being several years younger than him. A few days later, conscious recollection of the misdeed hinted at in the dream returned to mind.

All dreams dreamed in the same night belong in terms of content to the same whole; their being separated into several fragments and the grouping and number of those fragments are all meaningful and may be regarded as a piece of communication from the latent dream-thoughts. When it comes to interpreting dreams that consist of several major fragments or indeed any dreams belonging to the same night, the possibility must also not be overlooked that these different dreams, occurring one after another, all mean the same thing, giving expression to the same stimuli through a range of dream-material. The earliest of such homologous dreams in time is then often the more distorted, shyer one, the next one bolder and clearer.

The biblical dream that the pharaoh had about the ears of grain and the cows, the one that Joseph interpreted – that was of this kind. There is a fuller account of it in Josephus (*Antiquities of the Jews*, Book II, chapters 5 and 6) than in the Bible.[13] After recounting the first dream, the pharaoh says, 'After this first vision I awoke disturbed and wondered what the thing might mean, but gradually, pondering thus, fell back into sleep. Then I had a second, much stranger dream, which plunged me even further into fear and confusion.' After hearing the dream recounted, Joseph says, 'Your dream, O King, would appear to be twofold, but the two stories have a single meaning.'

Jung, who in his 'On the psychology of rumour' tells how a schoolgirl's concealed erotic dream was understood by her friends without interpretation and taken further in a string of variations, notes in connection with one of these dream-narratives 'that the concluding idea of a long series of dream-images contains exactly what the first image of the series had sought to portray. Censorship shifts the complex as far away as possible by constantly renewing symbolic concealments, displacements, forays into the innocuous, etc.' (*Zentralblatt für Psychoanalyse*, vol. I, 1910, p. 87). Scherner [writing in 1861] showed that he was familiar with this characteristic of dream-representation and described it in connection with his organic-stimuli theory as a separate law:

> Eventually, however, the imagination observes the universally valid law in all dream-formations proceeding from specific nerve stimuli, namely that at the beginning of the dream it depicts only the most remote and freest allusions to the stimulus-object but at the end, where pictorial effusion has run its course, nakedly portrays the stimulus itself or the relevant organ or its function, whereupon the dream, pointing to its own organic cause, comes to an end [. . .].[14]

A neat confirmation of Scherner's law was supplied by Otto Rank in his essay 'A Dream that interprets itself' [1910; 'Ein Traum, der sich selbst deutet']. The dream (dreamed by a young girl) that he recounts there consisted of two separate dreams occurring some time apart in the same night, the second of which ended in a nocturnal orgasm. This wet dream permitted an analysis that was able to go into some detail largely without the contributions of the dreamer, and the wealth of links between the contents of the two dreams made it possible to see that the former dream expressed the same (albeit more shyly represented) as the latter, with the result that the second dream, the wet dream, helped to provide a full explanation of the first. Using this example, Rank quite justifiably discusses the significance of wet dreams for the theory of dreaming generally.

However, it is only rarely, in my experience, that one finds oneself in such a situation – where clarity or confusion in a dream can be translated into certainty or doubt in the dream-material. I shall later have to disclose the hitherto unmentioned factor in dream-formation on the influence of which this scale of qualities of dreams essentially depends.

In some dreams that hold a specific situation and specific scenery for a moment there are interruptions that are described in the following words: 'But then it's as if at the same time it was somewhere else where this and that occurred.' The thing that thus interrupts the main plot of the particular dream, which after a while can be continued, turns out, in the dream-material, to be a kind of subordinate clause, an inserted thought. The condition in the dream-thoughts is represented in the dream through simultaneity (if – when).

What is the meaning of the sensation of inhibited movement that occurs so often in dreams and that comes so close to fear? One wants to walk but cannot move; one wishes to do something and encounters nothing but obstacles. The train is about to start and one cannot reach it; one raises a hand to avenge an insult and the hand refuses to fall, and so on. We came across such sensations in connection with exhibitionist dreams but made no serious attempt to interpret them. The easy but inadequate answer is to say that motor paralysis exists in sleep and makes itself apparent in the said sensation. We might ask, 'Why does one not dream constantly of such inhibited movements?' and we might expect this sensation (which can be evoked whenever we sleep) to serve some sort of representational purpose and to be aroused only by the need for such representation being present in the dream-material.

The not-being-able-to-do-anything does not always occur in dreams as a sensation but also simply as a piece of dream-content. I consider such a case particularly apt to enlighten us as to the significance of this requisite of dream. I shall recount, in an abbreviated form, a dream in which I appear to stand accused of dishonesty.

The location is a blend of a private nursing home and a number of other establishments. An orderly arrives to summon me to an examination. In the dream I am aware that something has gone missing and the examination has been prompted by the suspicion that I have appropriated the lost item. Analysis reveals that the word 'examination' is to be taken in two senses, including medical examination. Aware of my innocence and my position as a consulting physician in this establishment, I calmly accompany the orderly. At a door we are received by another orderly, who says, indicating me, 'You've brought him with you, he's a decent person all right.' Then, unescorted, I enter a large room that has various machines in it and that reminds me of an inferno with its hellish penal assignments. Harnessed to one device is a colleague of mine who would have every reason to note my presence but is not even looking at me. I am then told I can go. However, I am unable to find my hat so cannot go after all.

Obviously the wish-fulfilment element of the dream is that I should be acknowledged to be an honest man and can go; so there must have been all kinds of material present in the dream-thoughts indicating the contrary view. My being permitted to go is the sign of my absolution; so if the end of the dream brings something that prevents me from going, the obvious implication is that because of this feature the suppressed material of the contradiction is able to assert itself. So my not being able to find my hat means, 'You're not an honest man after all.' The not-being-able-to-do-anything of the dream is an *expression of contradiction*, a *'no'*, which means that my earlier assertion that a dream cannot express a 'no' needs correction.[15]

In other dreams, in which the not-being-able-to-do-anything in terms of movement is present not simply as a situation but as a sensation, the same contradiction resulting from the sensation of inhibited movement is more powerfully expressed as a will coming up against a counter-will. So the inhibited-movement sensation represents a *clash of wills*. We shall be hearing later that precisely this motor paralysis in sleep is one of the fundamental conditions affecting the psychical process during dreaming. The impulse transmitted to the motor pathways is in fact none other than the will, and it is the fact that we can be sure of feeling this impulse inhibited during sleep that makes the entire process so very suitable for representing the *will* and the *'no'* opposing it. According to my explanation of fear [*Angst*], it is also easy to understand that the sensation of inhibited will is so close to fear and is so often coupled with it in dream. Fear is a libidinal impulse that proceeds from the unconscious and is inhibited by the preconscious.[16] So wherever, in dream, the sensation of being inhibited is coupled with fear, a kind of willing must be present that was once capable of producing libido – a sexual stimulus, in other words.

What it means when, as often happens in dreams, the verdict 'It's only a dream, after all' is pronounced and what psychical power pronounces that verdict are questions I shall be discussing elsewhere (see Chapter 6, section I]). Here I simply point out in advance that such verdicts are intended to undermine what is dreamed. The interesting and closely associated problem of what is being expressed when a specific part of the dream-content is itself described as having been 'dreamed', the riddle of the 'dream within a dream' – this has been solved by W. Stekel, who analysed a number of persuasive examples in a similar sense. Again, the 'dreamed' element of a dream is meant to be undermined, robbed of its reality; what a person goes on dreaming after waking from the 'dream within a dream', the dream-wish wants to substitute for the expunged reality. So presumably the *'dreamed'* element contains the representation of reality, the true memory, while on the other hand the continuing dream contains the representation of what only the dreamer wishes. Including a certain content in a 'dream within a dream' is thus tantamount to wishing that what is described as a dream in this way had not happened. To put it another way: if dream-work itself inserts a particular event into a dream, it implies the most decisive confirmation of the reality of that event, the strongest possible *approval* of it. Dream-work is using dreaming itself as a form of rejection, thus attesting the conclusion that dreams are wish-fulfilment.

Notes

1. I have since given a full analysis and synthesis of two dreams in 'Bruch-stück einer Hysterie-Analyse' (1905); ['Fragment of an Analysis of a Case of Hysteria', *Standard Edition*, vol. VII, p. 3; a new translation by Shaun Whiteside may be found in the New Penguin Freud series, in *The Psychology of Love*, London 2006]. The analysis carried out by O[tto] Rank, 'Ein Traum, der sich selbst deutet' [1910; 'A dream that interprets itself'] must be recognized as the fullest interpretation of a more extended dream.

2. I learned from a study by K. Abel, 'The counter-meaning of primitive words' (['Der Gegensinn der Urworte'], 1884; see my lecture in *Jahrbuch für psychoanalytische Arbeit*, vol. II, 1910; *Gesammelte Schriften*, vol. X) the astonishing fact, confirmed by other linguistic researchers, that the earliest languages behave very similarly to dream in this respect. Originally they have only one word for the two opposite ends of a series of properties or activities (strongweak, oldyoung, farnear, combine/divide) and only secondarily formulate separate terms to describe the two opposites through slight modifications of the joint primitive word. Abel demonstrates these circumstances very largely in ancient Egyptian, but he also shows clear traces of the same development in Semitic and Indo-Germanic languages.

3. [The reference is to the novel by Alexandre Dumas *fils*, *La dame aux camélias*, published in 1848 (and very successfully dramatized by the author four years later).]

4. Compare what Aristotle said about what makes a good interpreter of dreams (see p. 132, note 2).

5. See also pp. 283 and 292, note 32.

6. If I am in any doubt as to which of the persons appearing in a dream represents my 'I' in disguise, I observe the following rule: the person who, in the dream, is subject to an affect that I, as sleeper, also feel – that is the one behind whom my 'I' is concealed.

7. [The 'paralytic' is Mr M.'s brother (see p. 454).]

8. [*Einem die Kehrseite zeigen*. The expression will have seemed the more 'contemptuous' to Freud for the fact that *Kehrseite*, as well as denoting 'back', also denotes 'backside'.]

9. The same technique of reversing time is sometimes used by a hysterical fit in order to hide its meaning from the onlooker. A hysterical girl, for example, has to act out a little story in a fit, a story she had made up in her unconscious in connection with an encounter on a train. How the man concerned, attracted by the beauty of her foot, addresses her as she is reading and how she then goes with him and experiences a tempestuous love-scene. Her fit begins with a portrayal of that love-scene through involuntary physical movements (with lip-movements for the kissing, arm-folding for the embrace), then she runs into the next room, sits down on a chair, lifts her dress to show her foot, pretends to be reading a book, and addresses me (answers a question). See also something Artemidorus wrote: 'When interpreting dream-narratives, one needs to look at them once from beginning to end, another time from the end, working back towards the beginning [. . .].'

[Artemidorus Daldianus was a second-century soothsayer and author of the *Oneirocritica*, a compilation of dreams and discussion of their interpretation.]

10. I still [1929] do not know whether I was right to do so.

11. Accompanying hysterical symptoms: missed periods and this patient's main malady: enormous disgruntlement.

12. [*Lücken* can also mean 'holes'.]

13. [Genesis 41:1–32; the quotations given here are from Josephus.]

14. [K. A. Scherner, *Das Leben des Traumes* ('Dream-life'), Berlin 1861, p. 166.]

15. In the full analysis, a link to a childhood experience comes out through the following chain of association: 'The Moor has done his duty, he can go' [Schiller]. And then [since the verb *gehen* also means 'to walk'] the riddle, 'How old is the Moor when he does his duty?' 'One, then he can walk.' (Apparently I was brought into the world with such a tangle of thick black hair that my young mother said I must be a Moor.) Being unable to find my hat is something I experience daily (our maid, who is brilliant at putting things away safely, having hidden it), and I have used the experience to mean various things. A rejection of sad thoughts about death was another thing concealed behind this dream-conclusion: 'I have not yet done my duty by a long way; I cannot go yet.' Birth and death as in the dream I had had shortly before this about Goethe and the paralytic (see below [pp. 454ff.]).

16. This proposition no longer holds good in the face of fresh insights.

D *Dream's concern for what can be represented*

Up to now we have been examining how dreams represent relationships between the relevant dream-thoughts, though in the process we have several times returned to the wider subject of what sort of change dream-material as a whole undergoes for the purposes of dream-formation. The thing is, we know that dream-material, largely divested of its relationships, goes through a process of compression,[1] while at the same time shifts of intensity among its elements impose a psychical revaluation on that material. The shifts or displacements we looked at turned out to be replacements of a particular idea by another one that was in some way associated with it, and they were rendered useful so far as compression is concerned in that, in place of two elements, a common mean between them found its way into the relevant dream. There is another kind of displacement that we have not mentioned at all so far. Yet analyses show us that it exists and that it announces itself through an exchange, whereby *linguistic expression is substituted* for the thoughts concerned. On both occasions the displacement occurs along a chain of association, but the same process happens in various psychical spheres, and the outcome of the displacement is in one instance that an element is replaced by another element, in another instance that an element exchanges its wording for a different one.

This second type of displacement occurring in connection with dream-formation is not only of great theoretical interest; it is also particularly apt as regards throwing light on the appearance of fantastical absurdity that dream assumes. As a rule, the shift takes place in the direction of a colourless, abstract expression of the particular dream-thought being replaced by a pictorial, concrete one. The advantage (and hence the purpose of this exchange) is obvious. A thing that is pictorial is *capable of being represented* in dream; it can be slotted into a situation where abstract expression of the thing represented in dream would give rise to the same sorts of problem as, in a newspaper, a political leading article would present to an illustrator. But it is not only representability that can gain from such an exchange; so too can the interests of compression and censorship. If the abstractly expressed, unusable dream-thought is first transformed into pictorial language, the reaction between this new expression and the rest of the dream-material will more readily than previously produce the interactions and identities that dream-work requires and that it will create where they are not present, since in every language concrete terms, because of the way they have evolved, offer more points of contact than conceptual terms. One imagines that a good part of the intermediate work that goes on in connection with dream-formation, seeking to reduce the separate dream-thoughts to the pithiest, most uniform expression possible, proceeds in this way, by appropriate linguistic transformation of the individual thoughts. One thought, the expression of which may perhaps be fixed for other reasons, will have a distributive, selective effect on the others' possibilities of expression, and this may happen from the outset, rather like the way a poet works. If a poem is to rhyme, the second rhyming line is bound by two conditions: it must express the appropriate sense, and that expression must sound the same as the first rhyming line. The best poems are those where one is unaware of the intention to find a rhyme but where both thoughts have from the outset, by mutual induction, selected the linguistic expression that with some small adjustment gives rise to the same sound.

In some cases, exchange of expression serves the process of dream-compression even more directly by arranging for a construction to be used that, being ambiguous, enables more than one dream-thought to find expression. The whole area of punning is thus harnessed in the service of dream-work. We should not be surprised at the part words play in dream-formation. A word, as the nodal point of multiple ideas, constitutes a predestined ambiguity, so to speak, and neuroses (obsessions, phobias) exploit the advantages that words present as regards compression and disguise quite as fearlessly as dream.[2] That dream-distortion also benefits from a shift of expression can easily be shown. It is confusing, is it not, when an ambiguous word replaces two unambiguous ones, and replacing a sober, everyday mode of expression with a pictorial one checks our understanding, particularly since dreams never say whether the elements they convey are to be interpreted literally or metaphorically or whether they should be related directly to the dream-material or through the medium of interpolated idioms. Generally speaking, when it comes to interpreting each individual dream-element, there is some doubt as to whether it:

a) should be taken in the positive or the negative sense (opposition relationship);

b) should be interpreted historically (as reminiscence);

c) or symbolically, or whether

d) evaluation of it should proceed from the wording.

This versatility notwithstanding, the representation of dream-work, which *does not of course set out to be understood*, confronts the translator with no greater problems than, say, those that ancient hieroglyph writers pose for their readers.

I have already given several examples of dream-representations that are held together only by ambiguity of expression ('Her mouth then does open all right' in the injection dream [see above, p. 119]; '[I] cannot go after all' in the last dream cited [see above, p. 350], etc.). I shall now recount a dream in the analysis of which pictorialization of an abstract thought plays a larger role. How this kind of dream-interpretation differs from interpretation using symbolism can still be clearly defined; in symbolic dream-interpretation the key to the symbolization is chosen by the interpreter arbitrarily; in our cases of linguistic disguise, those keys are generally known and laid down by established linguistic practice. If one has at one's disposal the right association on the right occasion, dreams of this kind can even be resolved, wholly or in part, independently of the details supplied by the dreamer.

A lady of my acquaintance dreamed: *She is at the opera. It is a performance of Wagner that has lasted until a quarter to eight in the morning. In the front and rear stalls tables have been set up at which people are eating and drinking. Her cousin, just back from his honeymoon, is seated at one such table with his young wife; next to her an aristocrat, of whom it is said that the young woman quite openly brought him back from the honeymoon, much as one brings a hat back from one's honeymoon. In the middle of the front stalls stands a tall tower with a platform at the top, surrounded by iron railings. High up there is the conductor, with the features of Hans Richter; he walks around constantly behind the railings, perspiring frightfully and from this position conducting the orchestra, which is arranged below him around the base of the tower. She herself is sitting in a box with a lady friend* (someone I know). *Her younger sister wants to hand up to her, from her position in the front stalls, a large lump of coal, on the grounds that my friend, having been quite unaware that it would take so long, would surely be feeling miserably cold by now. (Rather as if the boxes should be heated during this lengthy performance.)*

The dream is pretty nonsensical, though otherwise well 'situated', so to speak. The tower in the middle of the stalls, from the top of which the conductor conducts the orchestra; but above all the lump of coal that her sister is handing up to her! I deliberately refrained from demanding an analysis of this dream; having some knowledge of the dreamer's personal relations, I managed to interpret parts of it on my own. I knew that she had had a great liking for a musician, whose career had been broken off prematurely by mental illness. So I decided to take the tower in the stalls *literally*. What emerged was that the man whom she had wished to see occupy the place of Hans Richter, *towered* above the other members of the orchestra.[3] The tower should be described as a *'composite formation by apposition'*; its substructure represents the stature of the man, while the railings surrounding the top, behind which he paces like a prisoner or like a caged animal (an allusion to the poor man's name),[4] represent his eventual fate. *Narrenturm* is perhaps the word in which both ideas might have met.[5]

Having discovered the dream's mode of representation, I was able to try to use the same key to resolve the second apparent absurdity, the one involving the lump of coal handed up to her by her sister. 'Coal' had to mean 'secret love'.

Kein Feuer, keine Kohle
kann brennen so heiss
als wie heimliche Liebe
von der niemand was weiss.

[No fire, no coal so hotly glows as secret love of which no one knows.]

She herself and her friend have never married; they have been *'left on the shelf'*.[6] The younger sister, who still has a chance of marrying, hands the piece of coal up to her 'on the grounds that my friend [had] been quite unaware *that it would take so long'*. What would take so long the dream does not say; if this were a story, we should say 'the performance'; in the dream, we can look at the sentence as a whole, pronounce it ambiguous, and complete it with 'to find a husband'. The 'secret love' interpretation is then backed up by mention of the cousin, who is sitting in the front stalls with his wife, and by the *open affair* imputed to the latter. Contrasts between secret and open love, between her fire and the young woman's coldness, dominate the dream. On both sides, incidentally, a *'person of high standing'* provides the mean term between the aristocrat and the musician of whom so much is expected.

With the foregoing discussions we have finally discovered a third factor whose contribution towards turning dream-thoughts into dream-content should not be underestimated: a *concern for what can be represented in the characteristic psychical material that dreams use* – in other words, usually in visual images. Among the various lateral associations attached to the essential dream-thoughts, preference goes to the one that permits of visual representation, and dream-work does not shy away from the effort of first (say) recasting obdurate thoughts in a different linguistic form, even if this is a more unusual one, provided only that it makes representation possible, so putting an end to the psychological distress of strangulated thinking. At the same time, however, this pouring of thought-content into a different form can put itself at the service of compression, creating links to another thought, links that would not have existed otherwise. That other thought may perhaps have already altered its original expression for the purpose of rendering itself more accessible.

Herbert Silberer[7] has shown a good way of observing the transformation of thoughts into images that occurs during dream-formation directly and thus studying this one factor of dream-work in isolation. If in a state of fatigue and drowsiness he made himself think hard, it often happened that the thought eluded him and in its place an image appeared to him, which he was then able to see was a substitute for the thought. Silberer refers to this substitute (not entirely suitably) as 'auto-symbolic'. Here are some examples from Silberer's article (to which I shall be returning later [see pp. 519ff.] because of certain properties of the phenomena observed):

> Example 1. I think about my intention of improving a clumsy passage in an essay.
> Symbol: I see myself planing a piece of wood.
> Example 5. I try to recall the purpose of certain metaphysical studies that I currently have in mind to carry out. That purpose, it seems to me, consists in the fact that, in searching for the ground of being, one works one's way through to ever higher forms of awareness or strata of existence.
> Symbol: I am sliding a long knife under a cake as if to remove a slice of it.
> Interpretation: My movement with the knife refers to the 'working one's way through' in question ... The explanation of what produces the symbol is as follows: One of my jobs at table occasionally is to cut up and serve a cake, an operation that I perform with a broad, flexible knife and that requires a certain amount of care. In particular, extracting the cut slice of cake cleanly is associated with certain difficulties; the knife must be slid gently *under* the slice concerned (the slow 'working one's way through' to reach the ground of being). But the image contains even more symbolism. The cake

in the symbol was in fact a Dobos cake – that is to say, one in which the knife had to cut through various *layers* (the strata of consciousness and thought).[8]

Example 9. Pursuing a train of thought, I lose the thread. I try hard to pick it up again but have to acknowledge that the link eludes me completely.

Symbol: A piece of writing where the last few lines are missing.

In view of the part that puns, quotations, songs and proverbs play in the intellectual lives of educated people, it was only to be expected that such disguises should be used with enormous frequency to represent dream-thoughts. What, for example, is the meaning, in dream, of carts filled with different kinds of vegetables? It lies in the notional contrast between 'greens' and 'carrots' [in the German expression *wie Kraut und Rüben durcheinanderliegen*, 'to lie around like greens and carrots'] – that is to say, it denotes disorder. To my surprise, this dream has only been recounted to me once.[9] Only in respect of a few materials has a universally valid dream-symbolism emerged on the basis of allusions and word-substitutions with which everyone is familiar. Much of such symbolism, incidentally, as well as featuring in dreams, is common to psychoneuroses, legends and popular customs.

Indeed, looking at the matter more closely, we have to concede that dream-work is in fact doing nothing original when it indulges in this kind of substitution. To achieve its purpose (which in this case is representability of a kind that will escape censorship), it is simply altering paths it finds already trodden in unconscious thought, preferring transformations of repressed material that, as jokes and allusions, are likewise permitted to become conscious and that fill the fantasies of the neurotic. Here, suddenly, we gain an insight into the dream-interpretations of Scherner, the inner truth of which I have defended elsewhere [see above, pp. 241ff.]. An imaginative preoccupation with one's own body is by no means something that is peculiar to or characterizes dream alone. My analyses have shown me that it is regularly present in the unconscious thinking of the neurotic and that it goes back to sexual curiosity, which for the growing young man or woman focuses not only on the genitals of the other sex but also, of course, on those of his or her own. However, as Scherner and Volkelt so aptly stress, the house is not the sole group of ideas used to symbolize physicality – not in dream and certainly not in the unconscious fantasizing of neurosis. I know of patients who in fact cling to the architectonic symbolism of the body and the genitals (because of course sexual interest goes far beyond the sphere of the external genitals), where piers and columns mean legs (as in the Song of Solomon), where every door suggests one of the bodily apertures ('hole'), every water-pipe the urinary system, and so on. But quite as readily selected as hideaways for sexual imagery are the groups of ideas surrounding plant life or the kitchen;[10] in the former case linguistic usage, the record of imaginative comparisons from the earliest times, has done much groundwork (the king's 'vineyard',[11] the 'seed', the young woman's 'garden' in the Song of Solomon). In apparently innocent allusions to various kitchen tasks, the ugliest and the most intimate details of sexual life can be thought and dreamed, and the symptomatology of hysteria becomes totally opaque if we forget that sexual symbolism finds its best hideaways behind the everyday, the unobtrusive. It makes good sense, sexually, when neurotic children shun the sight of blood and raw meat or vomit over eggs and noodles, when the natural human fear of snakes finds itself, in the neurotic, monstrously enhanced; whenever neurosis masks itself thus it is treading paths that once, in ancient times, all humanity trod and to the existence of which (just beneath the surface) usage, superstition and custom still testify today.

Here is the flower dream, recounted by a female patient of mine, that I announced earlier [see above, pp. 330]. In the account, I put in contrasting type everything that calls for a sexual interpretation. It is a lovely dream, but once it had been interpreted the dreamer said she no longer liked it.

a) Pre-dream: *She goes into the kitchen where the two maids are and scolds them for not being ready 'with that little bit of food', and in the kitchen she sees so many upturned utensils standing to drain, pots and pans piled in heaps.* Later addition: *The two maids go to fetch water, for which they have to step into a river, which comes right into the house or as far as the yard.*[12]

b) Main dream:[13] *She is descending from higher up*[14] *through strange paddocks or fenced areas joined together in a broad checked pattern and forming a lattice-work of small squares.*[15] *She is not actually dressed for scrambling; she is constantly concerned to find somewhere to put her foot, and she is glad that her dress does not get caught up anywhere in the process, that her progress thus remains respectable.*[16] *At the same time she has a* large branch *in her hand*[17] – *more like a tree, actually, thickly covered with* red flowers, *bifurcating and spreading.*[18] *The associated idea is cherry* blossom, *but they also resemble double* camellias, *which of course do not grow on trees. During the descent she has first one, then suddenly two, then one again.*[19] *As she reaches the bottom, most of the lower flowers have already* dropped their petals. *She then, having reached the bottom, sees a manservant* [doing something with] *just such a tree – she almost said, combing it; he was using a* stick to pull at *thick tufts of hair hanging down from it like moss. Other workmen have cut down similar* branches *from a garden and thrown them in the* road, where they *lie around, with the result that* many people take one. *But she asks whether that is all right – simply to take one.*[20] *In the garden stands a young* man (someone she knows by sight, a stranger), *whom she approaches to enquire how such* branches *might be transplanted* into her own garden.[21] *He embraces her, whereupon she resists and asks him what he is thinking of, whether a person may simply embrace her like that. He says there's nothing wrong with that, it's allowed.*[22] *He then announces that he is willing to accompany her into the* other garden *to show her how to do the planting, and he says something to her that she does not fully understand: 'Anyway, I need another three* metres' (later she says: square metres) *'or three fathoms of ground.' It is as if he would be asking something of her in return for his willingness, as if he meant to* seek reimbursement in her garden *or as if he intended to* cheat *some law and have some gain without her incurring a loss. Whether he then really does show her something, she does not know.*

This dream, which I have highlighted because of its symbolic elements, is a so-called 'biographical' dream. Such dreams occur frequently during psychoanalyses but perhaps only rarely outside that context.[23]

I of course have a superfluity of just such material, but recounting it would take us too deeply into a discussion of neurotic conditions. It would all lead to the same conclusion, namely that we do not need to posit any special symbolic mental activity in connection with dream-work but that dream makes use of such symbolizations as already exist ready-made inside unconscious thought, since they satisfy the requirements of dream-formation better because of their representability and usually, too, because they have escaped censorship.

Notes

1. [Here Freud actually uses the word *Kompression*, which suggests that rendering *Verdichtung* by 'compression' (in place of 'condensation'; see p. 318, note 1) is perhaps closer to what Freud meant.]
2. *Der Witz und seine Beziehung zum Unbewussten* [*Jokes and their Relation to the Unconscious*; *Standard Edition*, vol. VIII; a new translation by Joyce Crick appears in the New Penguin Freud: *The Joke and Its Relation to the Unconscious*, London 2002], 1905, and the 'word-bridges' in the solutions of neurotic symptoms.
3. [Freud is indeed being literal. The German word he cites is *turmhoch* – 'tower-high'.]
4. Hugo Wolf [the name conveying the same meaning in English as it does in German].
5. [*Narrenturm* is a made-up word in German, the sense of which can be deduced from *Narrenhaus* or 'madhouse'.]
6. [*Sitzenbleiben*, as well as obviously suggesting 'to remain seated', has various connotations to do with being 'left behind'.]
7. *Jahrbuch von Bleuler-Freud*, I, 1909.
8. [A Dobos cake (the name indicates a Hungarian origin) comprises several slices of sponge alternating with chocolate cream, the whole topped with toasted caramel.]
9. This representation really is one I have never come across again, so I have lost faith in the legitimacy of the interpretation.

10. Abundant evidence in this connection is contained in the three supplementary volumes of Eduard Fuchs's *Illustrierte Sittengeschichte* ['Illustrated history of manners' (1909–12)] (privately printed by A. Langen, Munich).

11. [More graphic in German, where *Weinberg* is literally 'wine-mount'. And in what follows, Freud definitely writes *Samen*, though in the Song of Solomon, while there are 'shoots' and 'fruits', there is no mention of 'seed'. A *Fehlleistung*, perhaps, a 'mis-hit' or (as it is usually termed) a 'Freudian slip'?]

12. For an interpretation of this preliminary dream (which should be understood 'causally'), see above, p. 331ff.

13. Her life-story.

14. High-born origins, a counter-wish to the pre-dream.

15. A composite formation blending two places together: the 'grounds' (as she called them) of her parental home, where she used to play with her brother, object of her later fantasies, and the farm of a wicked uncle, who used to tease her.

16. Counter-wish to a real memory of the uncle's farmyard, where she was in the habit of exposing herself while asleep.

17. As the angel in Annunciation pictures holds a lily-stem.

18. For the explanation of this composite formation, see above, p. 334; innocence, monthly, *La dame aux camélias*.

19. A reference to the plurality of persons serving her fantasies.

20. Whether one may in fact 'pull one down' [*einen herunterreissen*; or, as we might say, 'jerk off'], i.e. masturbate.

21. The branch or bough has long represented the male member (while at the same time containing a very clear allusion to her [the patient's] surname.

22. This (together with what comes next) relates to marital precautions.

23. A similar 'biographical' dream is the one cited as my third example under dream-symbolism [see below, p. 376]; another, the 'Dream that interprets itself' that [Otto] Rank recounts in such detail [see Other Literature]; yet another, which needs to be read 'backwards', the one recounted by [Wilhelm] Stekel [1909], p. 486.

E *Representation by symbols in dream – further typical dreams*

Analysis of the last biographical dream is proof that I spotted symbolism in dream from the outset. However, a full appreciation of its extent and significance is something I attained only gradually, as a result of accumulated experience and under the influence of the works of Wilhelm Stekel,[1] about which this is the appropriate place to say something.

This author, who may have done as much harm to psychoanalysis as good, proposed a large number of unsuspected symbol translations that were initially disbelieved but of which the majority subsequently found confirmation and had to be accepted. Stekel's contribution is not belittled by our commenting that other people's sceptical reserve was not unjustified. Because the examples on which he based his interpretations were often unconvincing, and the method he had employed should be dismissed as scientifically unreliable. Stekel hit upon his symbol-interpretations using intuition, thanks to his unique ability to grasp symbols directly. However, such a skill cannot be assumed to be universal, its capacity has eluded all criticism and its findings thus have no claim to credibility. It is as if one were to base diagnosis of infectious diseases on olfactory impressions received at the patient's bedside, despite the fact that there were undoubtedly some clinicians whose sense of smell, given that in most instances this has atrophied, achieved more than others and who really could diagnose a case of abdominal typhus by smell.

The continuing experience of psychoanalysis has enabled us to discover patients who evinced this kind of direct understanding of dream-symbolism in a quite remarkable way. Often these were *dementia praecox* sufferers, so that for a while there was a tendency to suspect all dreamers with such an understanding of symbols of being so afflicted. However, that is not the case; what we have here is a personal gift or characteristic possessing no apparent pathological significance.

Having once become familiar with the extensive use of symbolism for the representation of sexual material in dreams, one has to wonder whether it is not true that many of those symbols, like the 'grammalogue' of shorthand, have their meaning laid down once and for all, and one is tempted to draw up a new dream-book using the encoding method. In this connection it should be pointed out that such symbolism is not the exclusive property of dream; it also belongs to the unconscious imagination, particularly the popular imagination, and is more fully present in folklore, myths, legends, idioms, sayings and the jokes doing the rounds among a populace than it is in dream. So we should need to range far beyond the task of dream-interpretation if we wished to do justice to the significance of symbols and to discuss the many problems (most of them as yet unsolved) associated with the term symbol.[2] Here we want to confine ourselves to saying that representation through the medium of a symbol is one of the indirect modes of representation, but that all sorts of indications warn us against indiscriminately lumping symbolic representation together with other types of indirect representation without having a clear conceptual understanding of such distinguishing characteristics. In some cases, what the symbol has in common with the actual thing for which it stands is obvious; in others it is hidden, making the choice of symbol appear puzzling. It is precisely these latter cases that must be able to throw light on the ultimate significance of the symbolic relationship; they suggest that it is of a genetic nature. What is today connected symbolically was probably, in primitive times, united by conceptual and linguistic identity.[3] The symbolic relationship appears to be a leftover and marker of previous identity. In which connection, in a number of cases symbolic community can be found to exceed the bounds of linguistic community, as [Gotthilf Heinrich] Schubert observed back in 1814.[4] Some symbols are as old as language-formation itself; others are continually being created in the present (e.g. the Zeppelin airship).

Turning back to dream, it makes use of such symbolism to represent, in disguise, its latent thoughts. Now, among the symbols used in this way there are many that always or almost always set out to denote the same thing. But remember the peculiar plasticity of psychical material. Quite often in dream-content a symbol needs to be interpreted not symbolically but in its actual sense; at other times, a dreamer may give himself the right, from special memory-material, to use everything conceivable as a sexual symbol, including things not generally so used. Where the dreamer is able to choose between several symbols to represent a particular content, he will go for the symbol that also exhibits objective links to his other thought-material – in other words, that permits an individual motivation alongside the one that holds good typically.

If the latest research on dream since Scherner has made acceptance of dream-symbolism impossible to refute (even H[avelock] Ellis acknowledges that our dreams are indubitably filled with symbolism), it must be admitted that the task of interpreting a dream is not only made easier by the existence of symbols in dreams; it is also rendered more difficult. The interpreting technique that pursues ideas occurring to the dreamer spontaneously usually lets us down as regards the symbolic elements of dream-content. Going back to the kind of arbitrary dream-interpretation practised in antiquity (and apparently enjoying a revival in the extravagant interpretations of Stekel) is inadmissible on grounds of scientific rigour. Hence the elements present in a particular dream-content that need to be understood symbolically force us to adopt a combined technique that is on the one hand based on the dreamer's associations and on the other hand supplies what is missing in the interpreter's understanding of symbols. Critical caution in the resolution of symbols and careful study of the same on the basis of particularly transparent examples of dream need to come together if the accusation of arbitrariness in dream-interpretation is to be invalidated. The uncertainties that still attach to our dream-interpreting activities derive partly from our imperfect knowledge (which further study can progressively remedy); but they also, in part, stem precisely from certain properties of dream-symbols. Such symbols are frequently ambiguous; indeed, they may have many meanings, with the result that, as with Chinese writing, only the context makes it possible to get them right every time. Coupled with this multiple ambiguity of symbols, there is the tendency of dreams to allow of multiple interpretations, representing different and often by their very nature highly divergent thought-formations and wish-stimuli.

Having registered these qualifications and objections, I resume: The emperor and empress[5] (king and queen) really do represent the dreamer's parents, a prince or princess the dreamer him- or herself. The same lofty authority as the emperor possesses is also accorded to great men, which is why in many dreams Goethe, for instance, features as a father symbol (Hitschmann). All longitudinally extended objects such as sticks, tree trunks, umbrellas (because of the way they are put up, which calls to mind an erection) as well as all long, sharp weapons such as knives, daggers or pikes are meant to represent the male member. A frequent but somewhat unlikely symbol of the same is the nail-file (because of the friction and the toing and froing, perhaps). Cans, boxes, caskets, cupboards and ovens correspond to the female abdomen, as do caves, ships and all manner of containers. Rooms in dream are usually women,[6] with the description of their various entrances and exits leaving us in no doubt as to this particular interpretation.[7] Interest in whether the room is 'open' or 'closed' is easily understandable in this context. (See also Dora's dream in 'Fragment of an Analysis of a Case of Hysteria'.)[8] The key that unlocks the room does not then need to be specified; the symbolism of lock [*Schloss*, which also means 'castle'] and key is something that Uhland used for a delightfully suggestive word-play in his ballad 'Count Eberstein'.[9] The dream of passing through a suite of rooms is a brothel or harem dream. But as H[anns] Sachs has shown with some fine examples it is used to represent marriage (an 'opposite'). An interesting link with childhood sexual exploration arises when a dreamer dreams of two rooms that used to form one, or when a room in a dwelling that is familiar to the dreamer appears, in dream, as divided into two, or the other way around. In childhood, the female sexual organ (the *Popo* or 'botty') was seen as a single room (the infantile cloacal theory); only later did one learn that this part of the body comprises two separate cavities and apertures. Steps, ladders, stairs and climbing them or descending by them are symbolic representations of the sexual act.[10] Smooth[11] walls on which one climbs, housefronts down which (often in great fear) one lowers oneself – these correspond to upright human bodies; in dream they doubtless echo the small child's memory of clambering up parents and nannies. 'Smooth' walls are men; 'protruberances' from façades are things one often clings to in dream-fear. Tables, set tables and boards are also women, probably through 'oppositeness', which here eliminates the curves of the [female] body. 'Wood', because of its linguistic links, stands for a female 'material' ('Madeira', the name of the island, means 'wood' in Portuguese). Since 'bed and board' constitute marriage, in dream the latter is often substituted for the former and, wherever possible, sexual ideas transposed to those associated with eating. As regards items of clothing, a woman's hat can very often be definitely interpreted as genitalia – male genitalia, that is. So can an overcoat [Man*tel*], though it remains an open question how large a part assonance plays in this symbolic attribution. In men's dreams, the necktie often symbolizes the penis, presumably not only because it is longitudinally extended, hangs down and typifies the male sex but also because a man can choose it at his discretion – a freedom that in respect of the actual object behind the symbol nature withholds.[12] People who employ this symbol in dreams often make a great luxury of ties in life and own whole collections of them. All intricate pieces of machinery and appliances in dream are very likely genitals (usually male), in describing which dream-symbolism turns out to be as indefatigable as joke-work.[13] Quite unmistakably, too, all weapons and tools are used as symbols of the male member: plough, hammer, shotgun, revolver, dagger, sabre, and so on. Similarly, many dream-landscapes (particularly those with bridges or wooded hillsides) are not hard to recognize as genital portrayals. Marcinowski [1911–12] collected a series of examples in which dreamers clarified their dreams by means of drawings intended to represent the landscapes and interiors occurring in them. These drawings make the difference between manifest and latent meaning in dream very clear. Whereas to the innocent eye they seem to reproduce plans, maps and so on, closer examination shows them to be representations of the human body, genitals, etc., and it is only when seen thus that they make the relevant dream comprehensible.[14] Apparently nonsensical neologisms are something else that can be taken as assemblages of components having a sexual significance. Children, too, in dream, frequently signify genitals – and indeed [German-speaking] men and women are in the habit of referring to their sex organs fondly as 'my little one'. Stekel was right to identify 'my little brother' as the penis. Playing with a small child, slapping a small child, etc. are often dream-representations of masturbation. To represent castration symbolically, dream-work makes use of baldness, hair-cutting, losing one's teeth and decapitation. And it signifies a defence against castration when one of the common penis symbols features two or more times in a dream. The appearance of lizards in dream (lizards grow a new tail when they lose the old one) carries the same connotation.[15] Several of the animals used in mythology and folklore as genital symbols also play that role in dream: fish, snail, cat, mouse (because of genital hair), but above all the most important symbol for the male member, the snake. Small animals, vermin, represent small children – the unwanted sibling, for instance; suffering an infestation of vermin is often the same as being pregnant. Mention should be made of a dream-symbol for the male member that is of great current relevance,[16] namely the airship, which both because of its connection with flight and sometimes because of its shape is justly used in this way. Stekel lists a series of other symbols (some yet to be adequately verified) and cites examples of them in evidence. Stekel's writings (notably his book *The Language of Dream* [see Other Literature]) contain the largest collection of symbol solutions, some of which constitute astute guesses that subsequent re-examination has proved correct – for instance, in the section of his book that deals with the symbolism of death. However, the author's deficient critical sense and his tendency to generalize at all costs render some of his other interpretations dubious or inapplicable, so that anyone using these books is urged to do so with care. I shall therefore confine myself to highlighting only a few examples.

According to Stekel, *right and left* in dream should be understood ethically. 'The right-hand way invariably means the way of justice, the left-hand that of crime. The left, for example, may represent homosexuality, incest, perversion, while the right may represent marriage, intercourse with a prostitute – that sort of thing. Always evaluated from the individual moral standpoint of the dreamer' (op. cit., p. 466). *Family members* in general usually, in dream, play the part of genitals (p. 473). Here, so far as this interpretation is concerned, I can only confirm son, daughter and little sister – in other words, wherever the 'little one' writ runs. On the other hand, there are warranted examples of *sisters* as symbols of breasts and of *brothers* as symbols of the larger hemispheres. *Not catching up* with a carriage is something Stekel interprets as regret at an age difference that can never be made good (p. 479). The *luggage* with which a person travels is (he says) the burden of sin by which that person is weighed down (ibid.). However, travel luggage often proves to be an unmistakable symbol for the dreamer's own genitals. The numbers that occur frequently in dreams are something else to which Stekel attributed fixed symbolic meanings; however, those solutions seem neither adequately guaranteed nor universally valid, though in individual instances the interpretation can usually be accepted as probable. The number three, incidentally, is a sure symbol of the male genitals, guaranteed by many authors. One of the generalizations that Stekel puts forward has to do with the ambiguity of genital symbols. 'When was there ever a symbol that (should the imagination even begin to permit it) could not be used as both male and female simultaneously?' The parenthesis, of course, robs this assertion of much of its certainty, because the fact is, the imagination does not always permit it. However, I do not think it superfluous to point out that in my experience Stekel's universal proposition needs to retreat in the face of recognition of a greater degree of diversity. Apart from symbols that stand as often for the male as for the female genital organs, there are some that primarily or almost exclusively denote one of the sexes and others of which only the male or only the female significance is known. The fact is, imagination simply does not permit elongated solid objects to be used as symbols of the female sex organ or cavities (boxes, cartons, cans, and so on) as symbols of the male.

It is true that the tendency of dreams and unconscious fantasies to employ sexual symbols bisexually reveals an archaic trait, since in childhood the fact that the genitals differ is unknown and the same sex organs are attributed to both sexes. However, a person may be misled into a false assumption regarding a bisexual sex symbol if he forgets that in many dreams a universal sexual reversal is implemented, with male being portrayed by female and the other way around. Such dreams, for instance, will give expression to a woman's wish that she would rather be a man.

The genitals can also be represented in dream by other parts of the body, the male member by the hand or the foot, the female genital aperture by the mouth, the ear, even the eye. The secretions of the human body (mucus, tears, urine, sperm) may, in dream, be substituted for one another. On the whole, Stekel's list is correct, but it has been subjected to some legitimate critical qualification by remarks made by R. Reitler (*Internationale Zeitschrift für Psychoanalyse*, I, 1913). In essence, these concern replacement of a significant secretion such as semen by one whose significance is trivial.

These highly incomplete suggestions will have to suffice to encourage others to make more careful anthologies.[17] I attempt a far more detailed account of dream-symbolism in my *Vorlesungen zur Einführung in die Psychoanalyse* (1916–17) [*Introductory Lectures on Psychoanalysis*].[18] I shall now add a small number of examples of the use of such symbols in dreams, the intention being to show how impossible it becomes to interpret a particular dream successfully if one closes one's eyes to dream-symbolism, but also how irrefutably, in many cases, such symbolism imposes itself. At the same time, however, I should like to issue an emphatic warning against overrating the importance of symbols so far as interpreting dreams is concerned – limiting the work of dream-translation to translating symbols, for instance, and abandoning the technique of making use of the dreamer's ideational associations. The twin procedures of interpreting dreams need to complement each other; but practically as well as theoretically the technique just referred to, the technique of attaching decisive importance to what the dreamer says, remains pre-eminent, with the kind of symbol-translation that we practise functioning as an aid.

1 Hats as symbolizing men (male genitals)[19] (Fragment of a dream by a young woman, whose agoraphobia stems from temptation anxiety)

I am walking down a street in summertime, wearing an oddly shaped straw hat, the middle bit of which is bent upwards while the side bits hang down (description hesitant here), *and the way they hang down means that one is lower than the other. I feel happy, sure of my mood, and as I pass a troop of young officers I think to myself, 'You can't hurt me – none of you.'*

She is incapable of producing an idea in association with the hat in the dream, so I tell her, 'The hat is probably a set of male genitals with its raised middle bit and the two side bits hanging down.' The fact that the hat is meant to be a man is perhaps curious, but they do say, '*Unter die Haube kommen*' [literally, 'to come under the cap',[20] as an expression for 'to get married']! I deliberately refrain from interpreting the detail about the two side bits hanging down unequally, although it is just such details that inevitably show the way in terms of pointing to the interpretation. I go on to tell her that if she has a husband with such splendid genitals she need fear nothing from the officers (needs nothing from them, in other words) because normally she is very much held back by her temptation fantasies from going about unprotected and unaccompanied. I had already, on the basis of other material, been able repeatedly to give her this explanation for her anxiety.

But what is really remarkable is how the dreamer behaves after this interpretation. She withdraws the description of the hat and denies ever saying that the two side bits hung down. Too sure of what I had heard to be misled, I insist that she did. She is silent for a while, then finds the courage to ask what it means that one of her husband's testicles hangs lower than the other and whether it is like that with all men. With that, the curious detail of the hat was cleared up and she accepted the whole interpretation.

The hat symbol had long been familiar to me when my patient recounted this dream. From other, less transparent instances I was able, I believed, to infer that hats also sometimes stand for female genitals.[21]

2 *The little one is the sex organ – being run over is a symbol of sexual intercourse (Another dream by the same agoraphobic patient)*

Her mother is sending her little daughter away in order that she must walk on her own. She is then riding with her mother in a train and sees her little one walking straight towards the track, where she will inevitably be run over. The bones can be heard cracking (accompanied by an uncomfortable feeling but no actual dismay). Then she peers out of the carriage window to see whether the parts cannot be seen behind. Then she chides her mother for having let the little one go on her own.

Analysis: The complete dream-interpretation is not easy to give here. The dream is from a cycle of dreams and can only be fully understood in connection with the others. The fact is, it is not easy to obtain the material necessary to prove the symbolism in sufficient isolation. Initially, the patient finds that the train journey needs to be interpreted historically as alluding to a journey away from a mental hospital with whose director she was of course in love. Her mother fetched her from there, the doctor appeared at the station and handed her a farewell bunch of flowers; she was embarrassed that her mother had to witness this tribute. So at this point her mother appears as disturber of her amorous endeavours – a role that had actually fallen to this stern woman during her girlhood years. The next thought to occur to her relates to the sentence, '[. . .] she peers out [. . .] to see whether the parts cannot be seen from behind'.[22] On the surface of the dream one naturally and inevitably thinks of the parts of the little girl who has been run over and crushed. But the thought that occurs to the patient points in quite a different direction. She recalls that once, in the bathroom, she saw her father naked from behind, goes on to speak of the differences between the sexes, and singles out the fact that in men the genitals are still visible from behind, in women not. In this connection she proceeds to make her own interpretation that the little one equals the sex organ and her little one (she has a four-year-old daughter) her own sex organ. She resents her mother for having expected her to live as if she had no sex organ, and she is reunited with that resentment in the dream's introductory sentence: 'Her mother is sending her little daughter away in order that she must walk on her own.' In her imagination, walking down the street on her own means having no husband, no sexual relationship (*coire* = to walk or go together), and this she does not like. According to everything she told me she really had suffered, as a girl, from her mother's jealousy as a result of her father's preference for her.

The deeper interpretation of this dream arises out of another dream, dreamed on the same night, in which she identifies herself with her brother. She really had been something of a tomboy; in fact, she had often been told that she might have been a boy. This identification with her brother makes it particularly clear that 'the little one' signifies the sex organ. His/her mother threatens him/her with castration, which can only be a punishment for playing with the penis; her identifying herself with her brother thus reveals that she too masturbated as a child – which her memory had hitherto retained only with regard to her brother. Knowledge of the male sex organ (a knowledge she later lost) is something that on the evidence of this second dream she must have acquired early on. Moreover, the second dream points to the infantile sexual theory that little girls are made from boys by castration. After I tell her about this childish opinion, it finds instant confirmation in her knowing the story of the boy asking the girl, 'Cut off?' to which the girl replies, 'No, it's always been that way.'

So the sending-away of the little one, the sex organ, in the first dream also relates to the castration threat. Her mother, after all, grumbles that she was not born a boy.

That 'being run over' symbolizes sexual intercourse would not have been obvious from this dream had it not been known about for certain from numerous other sources.

3 The sex organ represented by buildings, stairways, shafts (A dream had by a young man inhibited by his father complex)

He is walking with his father in a place that is undoubtedly the Prater[23] because the Rotunda *can be seen. In front of the Rotunda there is a smaller* vestibule extension *with a* captive balloon *moored to it; the balloon, however, looks a bit limp. His father asks him what this is all for; he is surprised by the sight but explains it to his father. They then enter a* courtyard *in which a large sheet of metal is laid out on the ground. His father is about to* tear off *a large piece of this but first looks around to make sure no one can see. He tells him he need only ask the supervisor, then he can take as much as he wants. From the courtyard a* flight of stairs *leads down to a shaft of which the sides are padded, rather in the manner of a leather armchair. At the end of this shaft there is an elongated platform before a new shaft begins . . .*

Analysis: This dreamer belongs to a type of patient who is not easy to treat; such patients show no resistance to analysis whatsoever up to a certain point, beyond which they are virtually unreachable. He interpreted this dream almost unaided. The Rotunda, he said, represents my genitals, the captive balloon moored before it my penis, the limpness of which is causing me some distress. In greater detail, then, the Rotunda may be translated as his bottom (which children always include in the genitals), the smaller vestibule extension as his scrotum. In the dream, his father asks him what this is all for – that is to say, what are genitals for and how do they work. One is tempted to reverse this state of affairs in such a way that he [the dreamer] is asking the question. No such interrogation of the father having actually taken place, the dream-thought has to be seen as a wish or perhaps understood conditionally: 'If I had asked my father about the facts of life . . .' We shall come across the continuation of this thought elsewhere.

The courtyard in which the metal is laid out should not primarily receive a symbolic reading; it comes from the father's business premises. For reasons of discretion I have substituted 'metal' for the other material in which his father deals, though apart from that I have left the wording of the dream unchanged. The dreamer had gone into his father's business and taken violent exception to the somewhat shady practices on which the profits were partly based. So the continuation of the said dream-thought might well have been this: '(Had I asked him), he would have deceived me the way he does his customers.' As regards the *tearing off* used to represent the father's commercial dishonesty, the dreamer himself supplies the second explanation – namely, that it signifies masturbation. Not only have we long been aware of this (see pp. 362 and 364, note 20); it also fits very well with the way in which the secret of masturbation is expressed by its opposite ('Look, this can be done quite openly'). It further chimes with every expectation that the masturbatory activity is again shifted on to the father, like the asking of the question in the first scene of the dream. The shaft he interprets immediately (with reference to the softly upholstered walls) as a vagina. That climbing down, like (normally) climbing up, seeks to describe vaginal intercourse is something that I contribute on the basis of other findings (see my comments in *Zentralblatt für Psycho-Analyse*, I, 1, 1910; see also p. 414, note 10).

The details (that the first shaft is followed by an elongated platform, then by a new shaft) he interprets himself, in biographical terms. After practising sexual intercourse for a while, he ceased because of inhibitions; he now hopes that with the aid of this course of treatment he will be able to take it up again. However, towards the end the dream becomes less clear, and to the initiate it inevitably appears plausible that as early as the second scene of the dream the influence of another subject comes into play – to which the father's business, his fraudulent conduct, and the first shaft/vagina all allude in such a way that a connection with the dreamer's mother may be assumed.

4 *Male genitals symbolized by persons, female by a landscape*
(A dream by a woman of the people whose husband is a policeman, reported by B. Dattner)

. . . Then someone broke into the flat and she fearfully summoned a policeman. But he, accompanied by two 'rascals', had peaceably entered a church,[24] *to which several steps*[25] *led up; behind the church there was a hill,*[26] *she said, topped by a dense forest.*[27] *The policeman was apparently wearing a helmet, a ring collar and a cloak.*[28] *He had a brown beard. The two travelling scholars, who had gone quietly with the policeman, had pouchlike cloths bound around their loins.*[29] *In front of the church a path led to this hill. The path was overgrown on both sides with grass and brambles, which thickened progressively and by the top of the hill had become a regular forest.*

5 *Children's castration dreams*

a) A boy of three years and five months, clearly uncomfortable about his father's return from military service, wakes up one morning flustered and disturbed, asking over and over again, 'Why was

Daddy carrying his head on a plate? Last night Daddy was carrying his head on a plate.'

b) A student currently suffering from a serious obsessive neurosis recalls that at the age of five he repeatedly had the following dream: He goes to the hairdresser to have his hair cut. A tall, stern-featured woman comes striding up to him and chops his head off. He recognizes the woman as his mother.

6 On urinary symbolism

The drawings printed overleaf are from a picture sequence that Ferenczi came across in a Hungarian comic magazine (*Fidibusz*) and recognized as constituting a useful illustration of dream-theory. O[tto] Rank has already used the page (which is entitled 'The French nursery maid's dream') in his article on 'Layers of symbolism in the waking dream' etc.[30]

Not until the final picture, which shows the maid waking up as a result of the child's crying, do we see that the previous seven pictures portray phases of a dream. The first picture acknowledges the stimulus that is to lead to waking. The boy has expressed a need and asked for the appropriate help. However, for the situation in the bedroom dream substitutes that of a walk. In the second picture she has already stood the child at a street corner, he has begun to urinate – and she can sleep on. But the waking-stimulus persists, indeed grows in intensity; the boy, finding himself ignored, screams louder and louder. The more urgently he demands that his maid wake up and help him, the more powerfully the dream reinforces its assurance that everything is fine and there is no need for her to wake up. In the process it translates the waking-stimulus into symbolic dimensions. The stream of water from the urinating boy becomes more and more ample. In the fourth picture it is already sufficient to float a canoe, then a gondola, a yacht and finally an ocean-going liner! The struggle between the selfish need to sleep and the relentless waking-stimulus is here wittily illustrated by a mischievous artist.

379

7 A staircase dream
(Reported and interpreted by Otto Rank)

'I am grateful to the same colleague who produced the tooth-stimulus dream (cited below, p. 399) for the following, similarly obvious emission dream:

'*"I am leaping down the stairs, chasing after a small girl who has done something or other to me; I want to punish her. At the bottom of the stairs someone (an adult female?) catches the girl for me; I grab hold of her but do not know whether I have struck her, then suddenly I was halfway up the stairs having sexual intercourse with the child (in mid-air, as it were). Actually, it wasn't intercourse, I was simply rubbing my sex organ against her external sex organ, of which I had a very clear view as well as of her head, which was thrown back and to one side. During the sex act I saw hanging above me to the left (also as if in mid-air) two small paintings, landscapes depicting a house amid greenery. At the bottom of the smaller one, in place of the artist's signature, was my own forename, as if the picture were meant as a birthday present for me. Then there was something else hanging in front of the pictures, a note saying that cheaper pictures were also available; (I then see myself very unclearly as if lying in bed up on the landing) and am woken by the feeling of dampness resulting from my having ejaculated."*

'*Analysis*: On the evening of the dream-day, the dreamer had been in a bookseller's shop where, while he waited, he inspected some of the artwork on display, which depicted similar subjects to the dream-paintings. There was one small picture that he had liked particularly, and he stepped closer to look at the painter's name; however, it was completely new to him.

'Later that same evening, in company, he had heard tell of a Bohemian servant-girl, who boasted that her illegitimate child had been "conceived on the stairs". Enquiring about the details of this not exactly everyday occurrence, the dreamer learned that the maid and her suitor had been returning home to her parents' flat, where there would have been no opportunity for sexual intercourse, and that the excited man had performed coitus on the stairs. Hearing this story, the dreamer had made a joking allusion to the malicious expression for adulterating wine: the child, he said, really had "grown on the cellar stairs".

'These are the daytime links that are represented quite insistently in the dream-content and are reproduced by the dreamer spontaneously. With the same ease, however, he produces an ancient piece of childhood recollection that has also found a use in his dream. The stairwell is that of the house in which he had spent most of his boyhood years and where in particular he had made his first conscious acquaintance with sexual problems. He had often played on those stairs, and one of the things he had done was to straddle the banister and slide down, during which he experienced sexual arousal. Now, in dream, he is also hurtling down the stairs with unusual speed, so swiftly that by his own clear account his feet do not touch the individual stairs but, as one says, he finds himself *"flying* down" – or sliding. So far as the childhood recollection is concerned, this first part of the dream seems to represent the moment of sexual arousal. However, in that stairwell and in his parents' flat he had also frequently played boisterous sexual games with the children from adjoining flats, during which he had satisfied himself in much the same way as happened in the dream.

'To anyone who knows, from Freud's researches into sexual symbolism (see *Zentralblatt für Psycho-Analyse*, I, 1910, pp. 2f.) that, in dream, staircases and climbing stairs almost always symbolize coitus, this particular dream becomes wholly transparent. Its driving force (as indeed its effect – seminal emission – demonstrates) is purely libidinal in nature. As the narrator sleeps, sexual arousal (represented in the dream by rushing down the stairs/sliding down the banister) awakes, its sadistic element suggested by the pursuit and subduing of another child that those boisterous sexual games had once involved. This libidinal arousal intensifies to the point of making sexual action (represented in the dream by the dreamer's grasping the child and the child's being transported to a position halfway up the stairs) imperative. Up to this point the dream is couched entirely in sexual symbolism, which would make it utterly obscure to the unversed dream-interpreter. However, this symbolic gratification, which would have ensured the calm of sleep, does not satisfy so overpowering a libidinal arousal. The arousal leads to orgasm, and with that the whole stair-climbing symbolism as representing sexual intercourse is unmasked. If Freud stresses the rhythmic nature of both actions as one of the reasons for the sexual connotation of the staircase symbol, this dream appears to provide especially clear evidence of such a connotation, since by the dreamer's own express account the rhythm of his sex act (a rubbing up and down) had been the mostly clearly pronounced element of his entire dream.

'One further comment about the two pictures, which apart from their actual significance also serve in a symbolic sense as *Weibs-bilder*[31] ["females"], as demonstrated by the simple fact that one of the pictures is large and the other small, just as in the dream-content we have a large woman (an adult) and a small girl. The fact that cheaper *Bilder* are also available leads to the prostitute complex, as on the other hand the dreamer's forename on the small picture and the idea that it is intended for his birthday point to the parent complex (born on the stairs = produced in coitus).

'The unclear final scene in which the dreamer sees himself lying in bed up on the half-landing and senses dampness appears to point beyond infant masturbation even further back into childhood and is probably modelled on similarly pleasurable scenes of bed-wetting.'

8 *A modified staircase dream*

I point out to one of my patients, a severely ill abstinent whose imagination is fixated on his mother and who has dreamed repeatedly of climbing stairs in her company, that moderate masturbation would probably do him less harm than his enforced abstinence. This suggestion brings on the following dream:

His piano-teacher reproaches him for neglecting his piano-playing and not practising the Moscheles Études *and Clementi's* Gradus ad Parnassum.

In this connection, he comments that *gradus* [in Latin] are also stairs and the keyboard itself is a flight of stairs, containing as it does a scale.[32]

There is (one might say) no group of ideas that would baulk at representing sexual facts and desires.

9 A *sense of reality and the representation of repetition*

A man who is now thirty-five recounts a dream he well remembers having when, he claims, he was four years old: *The notary public with whom his father's last will and testament was deposed* (he had lost his father when he was three) *brought two large white butter pears, one of which he was given to eat. The other lay on the living-room windowsill.* He woke up convinced of the reality of what he had dreamed and persistently asked his mother for the second pear; it was lying on the windowsill, he said. His mother laughed.

Analysis: The notary public was a jovial old man whom he thought he remembered actually bringing pears one time. The windowsill was as he saw it in the dream. Nothing else comes to his mind on the subject – except possibly that his mother recently recounted a dream to him. She has two birds perched on her head and wonders when they will fly away; however, they do not fly away, though one flies to her mouth and sucks from it.

The dreamer's failure to produce associated ideas gives us the right to try interpreting the dream by substituting symbols. The two pears (*pommes ou poires*) are the mother's breasts that nourished him; the windowsill is the projection formed by the bosom – like the balconies in dreams about houses (see above, p. 369). His sense of reality upon waking is correct, since his mother really did suckle him (well beyond the usual period, in fact) and he might still have had the breast. The dream should be translated: Mother, give me (show me) the breast again at which I used to drink. The 'used to drink' is represented by the eating of the first pear, the 'again' by the yearning for the second. In dream, *repetition* of an act in time regularly becomes the *numerical increase* of an object.

It is of course extremely striking that symbolism already plays a part in the dreams of a four-year-old, but this is no exception; this is the rule. Dreamers may be said to have access to symbolism *from the very beginning*.

How early a person uses symbolic representation, even outside dream-life, is shown by the following unsolicited recollection of a woman who is now twenty-seven: *She is between three and four years old. Nanny sends her, her brother (eleven months younger than her) and a cousin who is between the two of them in age to the lavatory to do 'number ones' before going out for their walk. As the eldest, she sits on the seat while the other two use pots. She asks her cousin, 'Have you got a* purse, *too?' Walter has a little* sausage; *I have a* purse.' *The cousin replies, 'Yes, I have a purse, too.' Nanny listens with a smile and recounts the conversation to Mummy, who reacts with a sharp rebuke.*

Here let me insert a dream whose delightful symbolism permits interpretation with little help from the dreamer.

10 *'On the question of symbolism in the dreams of healthy people'*[33]

[Robitsek writes:] An objection frequently advanced (most recently by Havelock Ellis)[34] by opponents of psychoanalysis is that dream-symbolism may possibly be a product of the neurotic psyche but is quite invalid as regards the normal one. The fact is, while psychoanalytic research recognizes no distinction of principle but only quantitative distinctions between normal and neurotic mental life, analysis of dreams (in which of course repressed complexes take effect in the same way whether the dreamer is healthy or sick) shows that such mechanisms as symbolism are completely identical in both cases. Indeed, the uninhibited dreams of healthy people often contain a far simpler, more transparent, more typical kind of symbolism than those of neurotics, whose dreams are often (because of the more powerful effect of censorship and the more extensive dream-distortion to which this gives rise) tormented, obscure and difficult to interpret. The dream recounted below will perhaps serve to illustrate this. It was had by a non-neurotic girl of a somewhat prudish, guarded disposition; I discover in the course of conversation that she is engaged to be married but that certain obstacles stand in the way of the marriage – obstacles that are likely to delay it. Spontaneously, she tells me the following dream:

'*I arrange the centre of a table with flowers for a birthday.*'[35] Asked about this, she indicates that in the dream she is as if in her own home (which she currently does not possess) and *feels happy*.

'Popular' symbolism enables me to translate the dream for myself. It expresses her wishes as a bride: the table with the floral centre-piece symbolizes herself and her sex organ; she portrays her wishes for the future as fulfilled in that she is already preoccupied by thoughts of the birth of a child; the wedding, in other words, lies well behind her.

I point out to her that '*the centre of a table*' is an unusual ex-pression, which she concedes, but I cannot, of course, go on asking direct questions here. I was careful to avoid suggesting to her what the symbols mean, simply asking her what occurred to her in connection with the individual parts of the dream. As the analysis proceeded, her restraint gave way to a clear interest in the interpret-ation and to a frankness made possible by the seriousness of the conversation. When I asked her what flowers they had been, she initially answered, '*Expensive flowers; one has to pay for them.*' She went on, '*Lilies of the valley, violets and pinks or carnations.*' I assumed that the word 'lily' appeared in this dream in its popular meaning as a symbol of modesty;[36] she confirmed this assumption when the idea she associated with 'lily' was 'purity'. 'Valley' is a common female dream-symbol; thus the chance conjunction of the two symbols in the English flower name itself becomes a piece of dream-symbolism, used to stress the dreamer's precious virginity ('*Expensive flowers; one has to pay for them*') and to give expression to her expectation that her husband will appreciate her value. As will emerge, the remark *'expensive flowers . . .'* etc. has a different meaning in connection with each of the three flower symbols.

The secret meaning of the ostensibly quite asexual *'violets'* I tried (very boldly, I thought) to explain in terms of an unconscious reference to the French word *viol*. To my astonishment the dreamer produced the association 'violate'. The fact that the words 'violet' and 'violate'[37] happen to be very similar is seized on in the dream to express ('with flowers') the notion of the violence of defloration (the very word uses flower symbolism) and possibly also a masochistic streak on the girl's part. A fine example of the word-bridges over which the paths of the unconscious lead. The *'one has to pay for them'* here denotes the life she must deliver in return for becoming a woman and a mother.

In connection with *'pinks'* (which she goes on to call *'carnations'*), I am struck by how the word relates to everything carnal. However, the idea she associated with it was *'colour'*. She added that *carnations* were the flowers that her fiancé presented her with *often and in large quantities*. At the end of the conversation, she abruptly makes the spontaneous admission that she was not telling me the truth: the word that had come into her head had been not *colour* but *incarnation* – one I had been expecting; in fact, even *colour* had not been far off as an association but had been dictated by the meaning of *carnation* ('flesh-colour') – that is to say, by the complex. This piece of insincerity shows that her resistance was greatest at this point, in line with the fact that the symbolism is at its most transparent here, the struggle between libido and repression at its height in connection with this phallic theme. The remark that these flowers were often given to her by her fiancé, together with the double meaning of the word *carnation*, is a further indication of their phallic significance in the dream. The everyday occasion of flower-giving is used to express the idea of sexual giving and counter-giving: she is making a gift of her virginity and in return expects a rich love-life. Here too the *'expensive flowers; one has to pay for them'* may well possess significance (actual, financial significance, no doubt). So the flower symbolism of this dream contains the virginal-womanly aspect, the masculine symbol and the link with violent defloration. Note that sexual flower symbolism, which in other contexts too is extremely widespread, symbolizes the human sex organs by means of flowers, which are the sex organs of plants; the giving of flowers between lovers may have this unconscious significance generally.

The birthday for which she is preparing in the dream surely signifies the birth of a child. She is identifying with the bridegroom, representing for his benefit how he gets her ready for a birth – that is to say, has intercourse with her. The latent thought might be, 'If I were him I shouldn't wait, I'd deflower the bride without asking her, I'd use violence.' Indeed, the 'violate' also points in this direction. This is how the sadistic libido component, too, finds expression.

At a deeper level, the '*I arrange*' etc. probably has an auto-erotic, infantile significance.

She also has a sense (possible only in dream) of her physical inadequacy; she sees herself as being as flat as a table; all the more stress is laid on the great value of the '*centre*' (elsewhere she calls it '*a centrepiece of flowers*'), namely her virginity. The horizontality of the table, too, probably contributes an element to the symbol. The dream is remarkably concentrated; nothing is superfluous; every word is a symbol.

Later, she contributes a postscript to the dream: '*I decorate the flowers with green crinkled paper*.' She adds that it is '*fancy paper*'[38] with which the ordinary flower-pots are covered. She goes on, '*To hide untidy things, whatever was to be seen, which was not pretty to the eye; there is a gap, a little space in the flowers. The paper looks like velvet or moss*.' Her association with '*decorate*' is (as I had expected) '*decorum*'. The colour green figures prominently; this she associates with '*hope*' – another link to pregnancy. In this part of the dream, it is not identification with the husband that predominates; instead, ideas of shame and frankness come to the fore. She makes herself beautiful for him, and she admits to physical shortcomings of which she is ashamed and that she seeks to correct. The ideas of velvet and moss are a clear indication that we are dealing here with *crines pubis* [pubic hair].

The dream is an expression of thoughts of which the girl's waking mind is scarcely aware; thoughts that are preoccupied by sensuality and her organs; she is 'being prepared for a birthday', i.e. copulated with; her fear of defloration, possibly also of pleasure-oriented suffering, both come out; she admits to herself her physical short-comings, then over-compensates for these by over-estimating the value of her virginity. Her sense of shame excuses the evidence of sensuality on the grounds that the purpose of it is in fact the child. Material considerations (foreign to the lover) also find expression. The affect of the simple dream, namely the feeling of happiness, shows that powerful complexes of emotion have found satisfaction here.

[Freud comments:] Ferenczi has rightly pointed out[39] how easy just such 'dreams by the unsuspecting' make it to guess the meaning of symbols and the significance of dreams.

I insert the following analysis of a dream had by a historical personal-ity of our own time[40] because in it an object that would in any case lend itself to representing the male member is very clearly, in an added qualification, characterized as a phallic symbol. The 'endless extension' of a riding-crop cannot easily signify anything but an erection. This dream also provides a fine example of how serious thoughts, having nothing to do with matters sexual, are brought to portrayal by infantile-sexual material.

11 *A dream of Bismarck's (by Dr Hanns Sachs)*[41]

In his memoirs, Bismarck tells of a letter he wrote to Emperor Wilhelm on 18 December 1881.[42] The letter includes the following passage: 'Your Majesty's communication emboldens me to narrate a dream that I had in the spring of 1863, in the gravest days of fighting from which no human eye could see a viable way out. I dreamed (and first thing in the morning recounted the dream to my wife and other witnesses) that I was riding along a narrow Alpine track with an abyss to the right and cliffs to the left; the track grew narrower, the horse baulked, both turning back and dismounting out of the question for lack of space; grasping my riding-crop in my left hand, I struck the smooth wall of rock and called upon God; the riding-crop grew endlessly in length, the cliff collapsed like a stage-flat and gave way to a broad track with a view of hills and forests, as in Bohemia, Prussian troops with flags, and within me (still in the dream) thoughts of how I might swiftly report this to Your Majesty. The dream came true and I awoke from it pleased and strengthened.'

The action of the dream falls into two sections: in the first part the dreamer gets into difficulties from which in the second part he is miraculously set free. The tricky dilemma in which horse and rider find themselves is an easily recognizable dream-representation of the statesman's critical situation that, as he mulled over his political problems on the evening before the dream, he may have felt to be particularly dire. With the allegorical turn of events that finds itself represented, Bismarck is himself portraying, in the extract from a letter reproduced above, the hopelessness of his current position; so it was thoroughly familiar and apparent to him. Surely, too, we have here a splendid example of Silberer's 'functional phenomenon'. The processes at work in the mind of the dreamer who encounters insurmountable obstacles in connection with every solution that his thoughts explore, but who at the same time cannot tear those thoughts away from worrying about the problems – all this is very aptly conveyed by the rider who can go neither forward nor back. The pride that prevents him from giving up or retreating finds expression in the dream in the words 'both turning back and dismounting out of the question'. In his capacity as an active being in a state of constant endeavour, always concerned for the good of others, it was quite natural for Bismarck to liken himself to a horse. It was something he did on various occasions, as in his famous dictum: 'A valiant horse dies in harness.'[43] Looked at in this way, the words 'the horse baulked' mean simply that in his exhaustion he feels the need to turn away from the troubles of the present – or, to put it another way, he is about to throw off the shackles of the reality principle by means of sleep and dream. The wish-fulfilment that then comes out so strongly in the second part is heralded already by the phrase 'Alpine track'. Bismarck was no doubt already aware that he would be spending his next leave in the Alps (namely in [Bad] Gastein); this dream, by placing him there, freed him at a stroke from all burdensome affairs of state.

In the second part the dreamer's wishes are doubly (undisguisedly and tangibly, but also symbolically) represented as fulfilled. Symbolically, through the disappearance of the inhibiting cliff, in place of which a wide path (the desired way out in its most comfortable form) appears; undisguisedly, because of the sight of advancing Prussian troops. No mystical circumstances need be construed to explain this prophetic vision; Freud's wish-fulfilment theory is quite adequate. Bismarck was already looking longingly, as the best way out of Prussia's internal conflicts, in the direction of a victorious war with Austria. If he now sees Prussian troops in Bohemia (that is to say, in enemy territory), parading their flags, it is because this is how his dream represents the wish as fulfilled – just as Freud postulates. The only significant thing in this particular case is that the dreamer did not stop at wish-fulfilment but was also able to constrain reality. A feature that will inevitably strike any student of the psychoanalytic mode of interpretation is the riding-crop that grows 'endlessly in length'. Riding-crop, cane, lance and suchlike implements are familiar to us as phallic symbols; however, when that riding-crop also possesses the most striking quality of the phallus, namely the ability to extend, there can scarcely be any doubt. Exaggerating the phenomenon by making such extension 'endless' appears to indicate the kind of overcharging that occurs in infancy.[44] The 'grasping' of the riding-crop ['in my left hand'] is a clear allusion to masturbation, in which context one should of course think not of the dreamer's current circumstances but of childish pleasures lying far in the past. Of great value at this point is the interpretation uncovered by Dr Stekel whereby *'left'*, in dream, denotes all that is wrong, forbidden, sinful – as would be most applicable to childhood masturbation practised in defiance of a ban. Between this deepest, infantile stratum and the topmost stratum having to do with the statesman's day-to-day plans there can be shown to be another, median stratum related to both the others. The whole process of miraculous release from a predicament by striking a rock while at the same time calling upon God's help is very reminiscent of a biblical scene – the one where Moses strikes water from the rock for the parched children of Israel.[45] We can confidently assume that Bismarck, who came from a Protestant family that believed in the Bible, knew the passage well. The leader-figure Moses (whom the people he is keen to set free repay with rejection, hatred and ingratitude) was someone with whom Bismarck, in time of war, had no difficulty in comparing himself. So that would back up his current wishes. On the other hand, the passage from the Bible contains certain details that lend themselves readily to use in the masturbation fantasy. Contrary to God's command, Moses does reach for his rod [in the account in the Book of Numbers; see Numbers 20:2–13], and for this transgression the Lord punishes him by telling him that he must die before setting foot in the Promised Land. The forbidden reaching for the rod (in the dream, the unambiguously phallic riding-crop), the production of liquid by striking with it, and the death threat – here we have all the principal elements of childhood masturbation assembled together. It is interesting how the two heterogeneous images (one from the psyche of the brilliant statesman, the other from the promptings of the primitive child-mind) are welded together by means of the biblical account, with the editorial process contriving to erase all embarrassing elements. That 'reaching for the rod' is a forbidden, rebellious action is hinted at only symbolically (by the fact that it is through the left hand that it occurs). In the manifest dream-content, however, the action is accompanied by calling upon God, as if to repudiate very pointedly any notion of its being forbidden or secret. Of God's two assurances to Moses that he will see but not set foot in the land that God has promised to the children of Israel, one is represented very clearly as having been fulfilled (the view of hills and forests), the other (highly embarrassing) one receives no mention. The water has probably fallen victim to the secondary processing[46] that successfully brings this scene into conformity with the previous one; the cliff collapses instead.

We should expect the conclusion of an infantile masturbation fantasy in which the prohibition motive is represented to be that the child wishes the authority figures in his vicinity to hear nothing of what has happened. In the dream, this wish is replaced by its opposite, namely the wish to report the occurrence to the emperor immediately. However, this reversal follows supremely well and quite unobtrusively on the victory fantasy contained in the uppermost stratum of the dream-thoughts and in part of the manifest dream-content. This kind of dream about victory and conquest often masks an erotic conquest wish; individual features of the dream (as, for example, that the invader meets with resistance but that after use of the extending riding-crop a broad path appears) probably pointed in this direction but did not suffice to reveal a specific intellectual and optative trend running right through the dream. What we have here is a prime example of a thoroughly successful piece of dream-distortion. Offensive material is reworked in such a way that nowhere does it stick up through the fabric that is spread over it as a protective cover. As a result, any release of fear could be blocked. This is an ideal instance of successful wish-fulfilment undamaged by censorship, and it becomes understandable that the dreamer awoke from such a dream 'pleased and strengthened'.

[Freud continues:] I close with

12 *A chemist's dream*

had by a young man who was trying to give up his masturbatory habits in exchange for intercourse with women.

Preamble: On the day before the dream he had been explaining to a student about the Grignard reaction, in which magnesium is to be dissolved in absolutely pure ether with iodine acting as a catalyst. Two days earlier, in connection with a similar reaction, there had been an explosion in which a workman had burned his hand.

Dream: I) *He is to make phenyl magnesium bromide, he can see the apparatus with especial clarity, but he has substituted himself for the magnesium. He is now in a strangely vacillating mood, saying over and over to himself, 'It's quite right, it's fine, my feet are already dissolving, my knees are becoming soft.' Then he reaches out and feels his feet, having in the mean time (he does not know how) taken his legs out of the retort, saying to himself again, 'That can't be. – Yes, it can, it was done correctly.' Here he partially wakes up and repeats the dream to himself because he wants to recount it to me. He is really afraid of the dream dissolving, during this period of light sleep he is very upset and repeats constantly, 'Phenyl, phenyl.'*

II) *He is in —ing with his whole family, at half-past eleven he has an appointment to meet that certain lady at Schottentor, but he does not wake up until half-past eleven. He tells himself, 'It's too late now. By the time you're there, it will be half-past twelve.' Next moment he sees the whole family gathered around the table, his mother and the maid with the soup tureen being especially clear. He then says to himself, 'Well, if we're eating already I can't get away.'*

Analysis: There is no doubt that even the first dream is connected with the lady of his rendezvous (the dream occurred in the night before the expected meeting). The student he was instructing is a particularly nasty character; he told him, 'That is not right', because the magnesium was still quite intact, and the student replied as if he could not have cared less, 'So it's not right.' That student must be himself (he is just as indifferent towards his *analysis* as the student towards his *synthesis*), but the 'he' in the dream, who performs the operation, is me. How horrid he must seem with his indifference to the outcome!

On the other hand, he is the person with whom the analysis (synthesis) is being made. It is about the treatment succeeding. The legs in the dream are reminiscent of an impression of the previous evening. At dancing-class he met a lady whom he wishes to conquer; he pressed her to him so hard that one time she cried out. When he ceased the pressure against her legs, he felt her powerful counter-pressure on his lower leg up to above the knee – on the places mentioned in the dream. So in this situation the woman is the magnesium in the retort, which is finally doing what it should. He is feminine towards me as he is virile towards the woman. If things are all right with the lady, things are also all right with the treatment. How he feels and his awareness of his knees suggest masturbation and correspond to his weariness of the previous day. The rendezvous really had been arranged for half-past eleven. His desire to miss it through oversleeping and remain with his domestic sex objects (i.e. with masturbation) corresponds to his resistance.

On the repetition of the name phenyl, he says all these radicals ending in '-yl' have always appealed to him greatly as being very easy to use: benzyl, acetyl and so on. That in itself explains nothing, but when I put to him the radical '*Schlemihl*' he laughs uproariously and tells me that during the summer he read a book by Prévost and in it, in the chapter entitled '*Les exclus de l'amour*' ['Love's outcasts'], there had in fact been talk of '*Schlémiliés*', in connection with a description of which he had said to himself, 'That's me all over.' In fact, it would have been a 'Schlemihlism' if he had missed the rendezvous.[47]

Apparently, sexual dream-symbolism has already received direct experimental corroboration. In 1912, encouraged by H. Swoboda, Dr K. Schrötter generated dreams in deeply hypnotized persons by means of suggestive instructions that established a large part of the dream-content. When the suggestion instructed the person to dream of normal or abnormal sexual intercourse, dream carried out such instructions by replacing sexual material with the symbols familiar to us from psychoanalytical dream-interpretation. For instance, following the suggestion that the hypnotized woman dream about homosexual intercourse with a girlfriend, the girlfriend appeared in the resultant dream carrying a shabby *suitcase* labelled with the words, 'Only for ladies'. Allegedly, the woman dreaming had never been told anything about symbolism in dreams and dream-interpretation. It is a pity that evaluation of this important study was interrupted by the unhappy fact that Dr Schrötter committed suicide shortly afterwards. The only report of his dream experiments is a provisional communication in the *Zentralblatt für Psycho-Analyse*.

G. Roffenstein published similar findings in 1923. However, some experiments conducted by Betlheim and Hartmann seem particularly interesting since they eliminated hypnosis. These authors (*idem*, 'Uber Fehlreactionen bei der Korsakoffchen Psychose' ['Concerning incorrect responses with Korsakoff's psychosis'], in *Archiv für Psychiatrie*, vol. 72, 1924) told patients suffering from the said condition of confusion stories with a blatantly sexual content and observed the distortions that occurred when those stories were reproduced. It emerged that in the process the symbols familiar from dream-interpretation became apparent (climbing stairs, stabbing and shooting as symbols of coitus; knives and cigarettes as penis symbols). Particular value is attached to the appearance of the staircase symbol since, as the authors rightly remark, 'this kind of symbolization would be beyond the reach of a conscious desire to distort'.

Only after a proper appreciation of symbolism in dream can we resume the discussion of *typical dreams* that we broke off at the end of the last chapter. I consider it justified to divide such dreams basically into two classes: those that really do mean the same thing each time and secondly those that, despite having the same or similar content, need to be interpreted in a wide variety of ways. As regards typical dreams of the first kind, I have already dealt in depth with the examination dream.

Because of the similar affective impression, dreams of failing to catch a train merit assimilation with examination dreams. Elucidating them then justifies such assimilation. They are consolation dreams directed at another anxiety stimulus experienced in sleep, namely fear of dying. 'Departing' [*Abreisen*, literally 'journeying away'] is one of the commonest and most easily explained symbols for death. What the dream says in consolation is, 'Don't worry, you won't die (depart)', as the examination dream said soothingly, 'Have no fear; nothing will happen to you this time either.' The difficulty in understanding both types of dream comes from the experience of anxiety being coupled precisely with this expression of consolation.

The meaning of the '*tooth-stimulus dreams*' that I quite often had to analyse in treating my patients escaped me for a long time because to my surprise the interpretation of such dreams regularly came up against excessive resistance.

Eventually, the massive weight of evidence left me in no doubt that in the case of men such dreams are driven quite simply by the masturbatory pleasures of puberty. Let me analyse two 'tooth-stimulus dreams', one of which is at the same time a 'flying dream'. Both were dreamed by the same person, a young man of pronounced (if in practice inhibited) homosexuality.

He is watching a performance of Fidelio *from a seat in the stalls next to L., a person whom he likes and with whom he wishes to become friends. Suddenly he flies obliquely across the stalls to the end, then reaches into his mouth and pulls out two teeth.*

Describing the flight himself, he says it was like being 'thrown' into the air. Since this is a performance of *Fidelio*, one is reminded of the poet's words:

> *Wer ein holdes Weib errungen –*
>
> [Who a loving wife has won him –][48]

However, winning himself even the most loving wife is not among the dreamer's wishes. Another couplet fits his case better:

> *Wem der grosse Wurf gelungen*
> *Eines Freundes Freund zu sein –*
>
> [Who has gained the great good fortune of a friend to be a friend –]

The dream in fact includes this 'great good fortune', but it is more than just wish-fulfilment. It also conceals the embarrassing thought that his previous efforts at attracting friends have so often been unsuccessful, he has been 'thrown out',[49] and his fear that such a fate might be repeated in connection with the young man

397

beside whom he is enjoying a performance of *Fidelio*. And there then ensues what for this sensitive young man is the shameful admission that on one occasion, following rejection by a friend, his longing led him, twice in succession, to masturbate in a state of sensual arousal.

The other dream: *Two university professors* (strangers to him) *are treating him in my stead. One of them does something to his penis; he is afraid of an operation. The other thrusts an iron bar against his mouth in such a way that he loses one or two teeth. He is tied up with four silk scarves.*

The sexual meaning of this dream is scarcely in doubt. The silk scarves correspond to an identification with a homosexual of his acquaintance. The dreamer, who has never performed coitus and never, in reality, sought sexual intercourse with males, imagines such intercourse in terms of the pubertal masturbation that was once familiar to him.

It is my belief that even the many modifications of the typical tooth-stimulus dream (such as, for example, that someone else is pulling the dreamer's tooth) become comprehensible through the same explanation.[50] However, it may seem something of a mystery how what we call a 'tooth stimulus' is able to take on this meaning. Here I draw attention to the very frequent shift from below to above that serves the purposes of sexual repression and by dint of which in hysteria all kinds of sensations and intentions that should occur in and relate to the genitals can at least find realization in alternative, irreproachable parts of the body. The same kind of shift is involved when in the symbolism of unconscious thought the genitals are replaced by the face. Linguistic usage plays the same game by recognizing *Hinterbacken* [literally, 'rear cheeks'; modern usage talks about 'arse cheeks'] as equivalent to facial cheeks [*Backen*] and *Schamlippen* ['labia'; literally, 'pubic lips'] as equivalent to the features that frame the oral fissure. The nose in many allusions is equated with the penis, and the presence of hair in all locations completes the similarity. Only one feature allows no possibility of comparison, namely the teeth, and it is just this clash between coincidence and difference that makes the teeth suitable for the purpose of representation beneath the weight of sexual repression.

I am not trying to pretend that interpreting the tooth-stimulus dream as a masturbation dream (which I have no doubt is correct) has become wholly transparent.[51] I supply as much as I can to explain it and must leave a remnant unresolved. But I must also point to another connection that [German] linguistic usage implies. In our countries there is an indelicate expression for the act of masturbation: *sich einen ausreissen* or *sich einen herunterreissen* [literally, 'to yank one out (for oneself)' or 'to yank one down'].[52] I cannot say where the expressions came from, what kind of 'vision' underlies them, but in the first of the two versions the word 'tooth' would fit very well.

Since in popular superstition dreams of teeth being pulled or falling out are interpreted in terms of the death of a family member, although psychoanalysis can at most only grant them such an interpretation in the parodistic sense alluded to above, at this point I insert a 'tooth-stimulus dream' supplied by Otto Rank:[53]

On the subject of tooth-stimulus dreams, a colleague who for some time now has been taking a livelier interest in problems of dream-interpretation gave me the following report:

'I recently dreamed that I am at the dentist's and he is drilling one of my lower back teeth. He works on it for so long that in the end the tooth is useless. He then grips it with the pliers and pulls it out with a consummate ease that fills me with admiration. He says I should not worry about a thing because that is not even the tooth he is actually treating, and he places it on the table, where the tooth (an upper incisor, it now appears to me) disintegrates into several layers. I get up from the operating-chair, curious, and move closer; I am interested and ask a medical question. The dentist explains to me, while separating the individual pieces of the strikingly white tooth and using an instrument to grind them (pulverize them), that this has to do with puberty and that it is only before puberty that teeth come out so easily; in the case of women, he tells me, the decisive moment in this respect is the birth of a child.*

'I then become aware (while dozing, I believe) that this dream was accompanied by an emission, though I am unable confidently to attribute this to a particular point in the dream; it seems to me most likely that it occurred back when the tooth was being pulled.

'*I go on to dream of an event I no longer recall that ended with my leaving my hat and jacket somewhere (possibly in the dentist's cloakroom) in the hope that these garments would be brought on after me and, dressed only in my greatcoat, hurrying to catch a departing train. I succeeded, too, in jumping on to the rear carriage at the last minute, where I found someone already standing. However, I was no longer able to proceed inside the carriage but had to make the journey in an uncomfortable position, from which I tried to free myself and was eventually successful. We pass through a large tunnel, with two trains passing in the opposite direction as it were through our train, as if this were the tunnel. I am looking into a carriage window as if from outside.*

'Material for an interpretation of this dream is provided by the following events and thoughts of the previous day:

'I.   I have actually been having some dental treatment recently. At the time of the dream I am in constant pain from the lower tooth that is being drilled in the dream and that the dentist does indeed work on for longer than I want him to. On the morning of the dream-day I had again visited the dentist because of the pain and been advised to have another tooth extracted, not the one being treated but in the same jaw, which was probably the one from which the pain emanated. This was a "wisdom tooth" that was just coming through. I had taken the opportunity to test his medical integrity with a related question.

'II.   In the afternoon of the same day I was obliged to apologize to a lady for the filthy mood my toothache had put me in, whereupon she told me she was afraid to have a root extracted, the crown of which had almost completely crumbled away. She thought that extraction was particularly painful and dangerous in the case of eye-teeth, although an acquaintance had told her on the other hand that in the case of upper teeth (and she was talking about an upper tooth) it was easier. The same acquaintance had also informed her that she had once, under anaesthetic, had the wrong tooth pulled – information that had only increased her reluctance to undergo the requisite operation. She then asked me whether "eye-teeth" meant molars or canines and what was known about these. On the one hand I drew her attention to the superstitious element in all these opinions, though without neglecting to emphasize the kernel of truth in many a traditional popular view. She is able to tell me about what in her experience is a very ancient and widely known popular belief, according to which, *when a pregnant woman has toothache, she is carrying a boy*.

'III.   The saying struck me as interesting in the light of what Freud says in his *Die Traumdeutung* (second edition, pp. 193f.) about the typical significance of tooth-stimulus dreams being as a masturbation substitute, because in the popular mind, too, teeth and the male sex organ (boy) are somehow associated. So in the evening of the same day I re-read the relevant passage in *Die Traumdeutung* and found there among other things the following comments, whose influence on my dream is as transparently obvious as the impact of the two experiences described above. Freud writes of the tooth-stimulus dream that "in the case of men such dreams are driven quite simply by the masturbatory pleasures of puberty".[54] He goes on: "It is my belief that even the many modifications of the typical tooth-stimulus dream (such as, for example, that someone else is pulling the dreamer's tooth) become comprehensible through the same explanation. However, it may seem something of a mystery how what we call a 'tooth stimulus' is able to take on this meaning. Here I draw attention to the very frequent *shift from below to above* [in the present dream, too: from the lower jaw to the upper jaw][55] that serves the purposes of sexual repression and by dint of which in hysteria all kinds of sensations and intentions that should occur in and relate to the genitals can at least find realization in alternative, irreproachable parts of the body. [. . .] But I must also point to another connection that [German] linguistic usage implies. In our countries there is an indelicate expression for the act of masturbation: *sich einen ausreissen* or *sich einen herunterreissen* [literally, 'to yank one out (for oneself)" or 'to yank one down'].[56] I was familiar with this expression in early youth as denoting masturbation, and from this point the practised dream-interpreter will have no difficulty in finding the way to the childhood material that possibly underlies this dream. I mention only that the ease with which the tooth in the dream (which after extraction turns into an upper incisor) comes out reminds me of something that happened in my own childhood when I had a loose *upper front tooth* that I *pulled out myself*, easily and painlessly. This occurrence, every detail of which I remember clearly to this day, dates from the same early period as my first conscious attempts at masturbation (covering memory).[57]

'Freud's reference to a communication from C. G. Jung whereby *for women tooth-stimulus dreams have the significance of birth dreams*[58] and the superstition regarding the significance of toothache in women who are pregnant has caused the female meaning of such dreams to be set against the male meaning (puberty). In this connection, I recall a former dream in which, soon after being discharged by a dentist from a course of treatment, I dreamed that the gold crowns I had just had fitted fell out, which because of the considerable expense involved, which I had still not entirely got over, caused me (in the dream) great annoyance. Now, in the light of a certain experience, the dream becomes comprehensible to me as a positive appraisal of the material advantages of masturbation as compared with object-love, which was financially disadvantageous in every way (gold crowns), and I think it was what that lady said about the significance of toothache in pregnant women that reawakened this train of thought in my mind.'

[Rank goes on:] So much for the utterly plausible and, as I believe, also impeccable interpretation supplied by my colleague, to which I have nothing to add except perhaps an indication of the probable meaning of the second part of the dream, which by way of the word-bridges *Zahn-* ['tooth'] (*ziehen-Zug* [literally, 'pull-train'] and *reissen-reisen* [literally, 'yank-travel']) represents the dreamer's evidently problematic transition from masturbation to sexual intercourse (tunnel, through which trains pass in and out in different directions) as well as the risks of the latter (pregnancy; *Überzieher* [= both 'greatcoat' and 'contraceptive sheath']).

Theoretically, on the other hand, the case strikes me as interesting in two ways. First, it proves the connection, discovered by Freud, that ejaculation (in the dream) follows the act of pulling a tooth. So we are forced to see emission, whatever form it takes, as a masturbatory gratification obtained without the aid of mechanical stimuli. Also, in this instance the gratifying emission is not, as it normally is, a response to an object, albeit only an imaginary one, but is objectless, as it were, purely auto-erotic; at most, it reveals a homosexual tinge (dentist).

A second point seems to me worth stressing. The objection suggests itself that a superfluous attempt is made here to impose Freud's view, because in fact the experiences of the previous day are quite adequate on their own to make the contents of the dream comprehensible to us. The visit to the dentist, the conversation with the lady and reading *Die Traumdeutung* furnished a wholly adequate explanation for why the sleeper, made restless by toothache during the night as well, should have produced this dream; even, at a pinch, to get rid of the sleep-destroying pain (by imagining the removal of the painful tooth while at the same time using libido to drown out the dreaded pain sensation). Now, even after making the most extensive concessions in this direction, no one will seriously wish to claim that reading Freud's explanations could have fabricated or even simply activated the connection in the dreamer's mind between tooth-extraction and the act of masturbation unless, as the dreamer himself admits ('yanking one out'), such a connection had long existed. What is far more likely to have awakened that connection, in addition to the conversation with the lady, is revealed by the dreamer's later assertion that, on reading *Die Traumdeutung*, he did not, for understandable reasons, really want to believe in this typical meaning of tooth-stimulus dreams and in fact cherished a wish to know whether this applied in respect of all such dreams. His dream now confirms that, at least so far as he himself is concerned, thus revealing why he had had to doubt the fact. So in this respect too the dream represents the fulfilment of a wish, namely to be convinced of the scope and durability of this Freudian view.

[Freud resumes:] The second group of typical dreams includes those in which one is flying, hovering, falling, swimming and such-like. What do such dreams mean? We cannot say in general terms. As we shall hear, they mean something different in each case; only the material, the sensations they contain, stems from the same source each time.

From the information gleaned from psychoanalyses, it must be concluded that these dreams too reiterate impressions from child-hood, relating specifically to those active games that hold such an extraordinary attraction for children. What uncle has not made a child fly by running through the room with him, arms outstretched, or played falling with him by rocking him on his knees and suddenly sticking one leg out straight or holding him high and suddenly pretending to withdraw all support. Children shriek with delight on such occasions and tirelessly ask for more, especially if there is an element of fright and giddiness involved; then, years later, they recreate the experience in dream except that, in dream, they leave out the hands that held them, with the result that they now swoop and plummet freely. All small children love such games as well as playing on swings and seesaws; everyone knows that. And when, later on, they see gymnastic tricks performed at the circus, memories are refreshed once more. In many boys, hysterical fits consist only of reproductions of such tricks, which they execute with great skill. And it is not unusual for these inherently innocent games to reawaken sexual feelings as well. To use a word that we [German-speakers] draw on frequently to cover all these activities, it is the *Hetzen* [= 'hurrying/harrying', 'rough-and-tumble'] of childhood that dreams of flying, falling, losing one's balance, etc. pick up and repeat, this time with the feelings of pleasure turned to fear. But as every mother knows, in reality children's *Hetzen*, too, quite often ends in strife and tears.

So I have good reason to dismiss the explanation that the state of our cutaneous sensations during sleep, the sense of movement created by our lungs, and so on – that it is these things that evoke dreams of flying and falling. I can see that such feelings are them-selves reproduced from the memories to which dreams relate –

in other words, that they constitute dream-content rather than dream-sources.[59]

This movement-sensation material, which is of the same kind and stems from the same source, is in fact used to represent the widest possible variety of dream-thoughts. These usually pleasurable dreams of flying or hovering call for very different interpretations, particularly in the case of certain persons, but interpretations of a typical nature in the case of others. One of my female patients used very often to dream that she was hovering at a certain height above the street without touching the ground. She was a very small woman and shunned every contamination that mixing with people involves. Her hovering dream fulfilled two wishes for her in that it lifted her feet off the ground and caused her head to penetrate higher regions. In other [female] dreamers, flying dreams had a sense of yearning: 'If I were a birdie' ['*Wenn ich ein Vöglein wär*''], as a popular song of the day put it; yet others became angels at night – for want of being called angels by day. Understandably, given the close association between flying and the idea of the bird [*Vogel*], in men dreams of flying usually have a coarsely sensual meaning [the verb *vögeln* = 'to screw']. We shall also not be surprised to hear that this or that [male] dreamer is invariably very proud of his flying ability.

Dr Paul Federn (Vienna) has temptingly conjectured that many of these flying dreams are erection dreams, since the remarkable phenomenon of erection (a source of unending preoccupation so far as the human imagination is concerned) inevitably comes across as abolishing the force of gravity. (Think of the winged phalluses of antiquity.)

It is worth noting that the sober dream-experimenter Mourly Vold, who is actually disinclined to accept any kind of interpretation, likewise champions the erotic interpretation of flying/hovering dreams in his book *Concerning Dream*.[60] He calls eroticism 'the principal motive of the hovering dream', referring to the powerful feeling of vibration in the body that accompanies such dreams and to the fact that such dreams are frequently coupled with erections or emissions.

Dreams of *falling* are more often characterized by fear. In the case of women they are not at all difficult to interpret because women almost always accept the symbolic use of falling, which describes giving in to erotic temptation. We have yet to exhaust the infantile sources of the falling dream; nearly all children have fallen over at one time or another and afterwards been picked up and fussed over, or, if they fell out of bed at night, been taken into their nursemaid's bed.

People who frequently dream of *swimming* (parting the waves with huge contentment – that sort of thing) are usually former bed-wetters repeating in dream a pleasure from which they long ago learned to abstain. What types of representation swimming dreams easily lend themselves to we shall soon discover from one or the other example.

Interpreting dreams about *fire* justifies a nursery ban on children 'playing with fire' lest they wet their beds at night. The fact is, fire dreams too are based on memories of childhood *enuresis nocturna*. In 'Fragment of an Analysis of a Case of Hysteria (Dora)' (1905),[61] I give the full analysis and synthesis of such a fire dream in connection with the [female] dreamer's medical history and show what stirrings of more mature years this infantile material is used to portray.

It would be possible to go on citing a large number of 'typical' dreams, if by that one understands the fact of the same manifest dream-content recurring frequently in a variety of dreamers. Examples would include dreams of walking through narrow streets, of walking through a whole suite of rooms, dreams of nocturnal burglars (not forgetting the precautionary measures that nervous people take before retiring to bed), dreams of being chased by wild animals (bulls, horses) or of being threatened with knives, daggers, spears (the latter two types of dream characterizing the manifest dream-content of people suffering from anxiety), and so on. A study devoted specifically to such material would be extremely rewarding. Instead, I have two[62] comments to make – neither of which in fact relates solely to typical dreams.

The more time one spends resolving dreams, the more readily one has to accept that most adult dreams deal with sexual material and voice erotic wishes. Only someone who truly analyses dreams, penetrating from the manifest content of the same through to the latent dream-thoughts, can form an opinion about them, never someone who is content simply to record the manifest content (as Näcke, for instance, does in his works on sexual dreams). Let us be clear from the outset that this fact does not in any way surprise us; rather, it accords completely with our principles of dream-elucidation. No other drive has, since childhood, had to undergo so much suppression as the sex drive in its many components;[63] none has left unresolved so many powerful unconscious wishes that now, in the sleeping state, generate dreams. Never, in connection with interpreting dreams, should the importance of sexual complexes be overlooked – but neither, of course, should it be exaggerated to the point of excluding all else.

With many dreams it is possible to establish, on careful interpretation, that they even need to be understood bisexually in that they yield an irrefutable extra layer of interpretation[64] in which homosexual stimuli are realized – that is to say, stimuli opposed to the dreamer's normal sexual activity. However, to claim as Stekel[65] and Adler[66] do that all dreams should be interpreted bisexually is a generalization that seems to me to be as unprovable as it is improbable; it is not one I should care to argue. Above all, I could not simply eliminate the obvious fact that there are many dreams that satisfy other requirements than (in the broadest sense) erotic ones – namely hunger and thirst dreams, comfort/convenience dreams, and so on. Similar assertions (to the effect that 'behind every dream the death proviso may be found' [Stekel] or that every dream reveals 'a progression from the female to the male line' [Adler]) also strike me as going far beyond the permitted bounds of dream-interpretation. The claim that *all dreams call for a sexual interpretation*, against which a tireless polemic is being conducted in the literature, has no place in my *Interpreting Dreams*. In fact, it is nowhere to be found in seven editions of this book, and it stands in tangible contradiction to other things contained therein.

That strikingly *innocuous* dreams all, without exception, embody blatantly erotic desires is something we have put forward already and were able to corroborate with numerous fresh instances.

However, many apparently neutral dreams that present nothing particularly remarkable in any respect lead back, after analysis, to indubitably sexual wish-stimuli of an often surprising kind. Who, for example, prior to the work of interpretation, would suspect a sexual wish in connection with the following dream? The dreamer recounts: *Between two stately palaces, slightly set back, stands a little house behind closed gates. My wife leads me along the short stretch of street to the house; she breaks the door down, whereupon I quickly and easily slip into a gently rising courtyard.*

Of course, anyone with a certain amount of practice in translating dreams will be reminded immediately that penetrating small spaces and opening closed doors are among the most common sexual symbols; such a person will have no difficulty in finding in this dream a representation of an attempt at intercourse from behind (between the two stately buttocks of the female body). The narrow, gently rising passage is of course the vagina; the assistance attributed to the dreamer's wife must be interpreted as meaning that in reality only consideration for his wife had prevented him from making such an attempt; and questioning elicited the information that on the dream-day the dreamer's household had been joined by a young girl whom he found very attractive and who gave him the impression that she would not offer excessive resistance to an approach of that sort. The little house between the two palaces is taken from a memory of the Hradschin in Prague [the famous 'Castle'] and thus refers to the same girl, who came from that city.

If in dealing with male patients I stress the frequent occurrence of the Oedipal dream of having sexual intercourse with one's own mother, I get the answer: 'No, I can't recall such a dream.' Immediately afterwards, however, a recollection of a different, indecipherable, neutral-seeming dream surfaces, a dream that the person concerned has had often, and analysis reveals that this dream has the same content, that it is in fact an Oedipal dream. And believe me: concealed dreams of sexual intercourse with one's mother are many times more frequent than straightforward ones.[67]

There are dreams of landscapes or places in connection with which, in the dream, a certainty ('I've been here before') is highlighted. In dreams, however, this feeling of *déjà vu* has a particular significance. There, the place is always the mother's genital region; indeed, of nowhere else can one claim with such certainty to have 'been here before'. Only once has an obsessional neurotic embarrassed me by recounting a dream in which, so he said, he was visiting a flat where he had already been *on two occasions*. However, that selfsame patient had told me some time before of an event that had taken place in his sixth year, when he had once shared his mother's bed and taken improper advantage of the opportunity to insert a finger in the sleeping woman's sex organ.

A large number of dreams, many of them filled with fear and often having as their content passing through narrow passages or living in water, are based on fantasies about intrauterine life, spending time in the womb, and the experience of being born.[68] Below, I reproduce a dream by a young man who in his imagination took the intrauterine opportunity to eavesdrop on a sex act between his parents.

He is in a deep shaft in which there is a window, as in the Semmering Tunnel. Through this he sees an initially empty landscape, then he builds an image into it – whereupon the image is immediately there, filling the emptiness. The image is of a field deeply churned up by the tool, and the fine air, the idea of thorough, painstaking work that is implicit here, the blue-black clods of earth, together convey a splendid impression. Then he progresses further, sees an educational manual open . . . and wonders why it pays so much attention to the (child's) sexual feelings, in which connection he has to think of me.

A beautiful water-dream had by a [female] patient who was approaching a particular turning-point in her treatment runs as follows:

In her summer holidays on Lake — she plunges into the dark water at the point where the pale moon is reflected in the surface.

Dreams of this kind are birth-dreams; they can be interpreted if the facts related in the manifest dream are turned around – that is to say, if instead of 'plunges into the dark water' we read 'emerges from the water', i.e. is born.[69] The place from which one is born becomes recognizable if one thinks of the mischievous meaning of *la lune* in French. The pale moon is then the white botty from which the child soon works out that it emerged. So what does it mean that the patient wishes, while on holiday, to 'be born'? I ask the dreamer, who replies without hesitation, 'Am I not, as a result of the treatment, sort of *reborn*?' The dream thus becomes an invitation to continue the treatment at her summer house – that is to say, to visit her there; it may also contain a bashful hint at her wishing to become a mother herself.[70]

I take another birth-dream, together with its interpretation, from a study by E[rnest] Jones:

> *She was standing on the seashore, minding a small boy, apparently hers, while he waded in the water. He went out so far that the water covered him and she could only see his head bobbing up and down on the surface. The scene then changed into the packed lobby of a hotel. Her husband left her and she fell into conversation with a stranger.*

The second half of the dream, when analysed, easily revealed itself as representing an escape from her husband and the start of intimate relations with a third person. The first part of the dream was obviously a birth fantasy. In dreams as in mythology, the delivery of a child from the amniotic fluid[71] is usually portrayed as the reverse: the child entering water. Along with many others, the births of Adonis, Osiris, Moses and Bacchus offer well-known instances of this. The way the head bobs up and down in the water immediately puts the dreamer in mind of the sensation of foetal movement with which she had become familiar during her one and only pregnancy. Thinking about the boy entering the water kindled a reverie in which she saw herself pulling him out of the water, taking him into the nursery, washing and dressing him, and eventually taking him home.

So the second half of the dream represents thoughts that concern the going-away related to the first half of the hidden dream-thoughts; the first [second] half of the dream corresponds to the latent content of the second [first] half, the birth fantasy.[72] As well as the aforementioned reversal, other reversals demand a place in that half of the dream. In the first half the child *enters the water* and then his head bobs up and down; in the underlying dream-thoughts the foetal movements occur first and then the child *leaves* the water (a double reversal). In the second half her husband leaves her; in the dream-thoughts she leaves her husband.

Translated [from English to German] by O[tto] Rank.

Another birth-dream, this one recounted by Abraham, was had by a young woman who was about to experience her first delivery. From a point on the floor of the bedroom an underground canal leads straight into the water (birth canal – amniotic fluid). She lifts a trapdoor in the floor, and immediately a creature clad in brownish fur appears, a creature bearing a marked resemblance to a seal. This turns out to be the dreamer's younger brother, towards whom she had always had a maternal relationship.

Rank has shown from a series of dreams that birth-dreams use the same symbolism as urinary-stimulus dreams. In them, the erotic stimulus is portrayed as a urinary stimulus; the layers of meaning in these dreams correspond to a change in the meaning of the symbol since childhood.

At this point we can return to the subject we broke off from on p. 255, namely the part played in dream-formation by organic stimuli such as disturb sleep. Dreams occurring under these influences not only show us quite openly the wish-fulfilment tendency and the comfort/convenience character of the phenomenon but also, very often, show us a completely transparent symbolism, because it is not unusual for a stimulus to lead to awakening, *satisfaction of which had already been sought (vainly) in symbolic disguise in a dream*. This is true of wet dreams as it is true of dreams triggered by the urinary stimulus or by an urgent need to pass a motion. The special character of wet dreams not only allows us to expose directly certain sex symbols that, though already acknowledged as typical, are still highly controversial; it is also able to convince us that many an apparently innocent dream-situation is at the same time simply the symbolic prelude to a coarsely sexual scene – which, however, usually finds itself directly portrayed only in the relatively infrequent wet dream, whereas it quite often turns into an anxiety-dream, which also causes the dreamer to wake up.

The symbolism of *urinary-stimulus dreams* is particularly transparent and has always been so. Even Hippocrates argued that it signified a bladder disturbance when a person dreamed of fountains and springs (H[avelock] Ellis). Scherner studied the very varied nature of urinary-stimulus symbolism and likewise maintained [back in 1861] that 'a quite strong urinary stimulus always includes the sexual sphere and its symbolic images in the stimulus ... The urinary-stimulus dream often represents a sex dream at the same time.'

O[tto] Rank, whose argument in his study of 'Layers of symbolism in the waking dream ...' I have followed here, has made it very likely that a large number of so-called 'urinary-stimulus dreams' are actually caused by sexual arousal that initially seeks satisfaction regressively in the infantile form of urethral eroticism. Particularly instructive in this connection are the instances in which the urinary stimulus thus generated makes the dreamer wake and empty the offending bladder – after which, however, the dream continues none the less, the need now finding expression in undisguisedly erotic imagery.[73]

Entirely analogously, bowel-stimulus dreams reveal the associated symbolism, confirming a connection that is also much in evidence in popular psychology, namely that between *gold* and *excrement*.[74] 'For instance, a woman dreams at a time when she is having medical treatment for a *bowel disorder* of a treasure-hunter burying *treasure* near a small wooden hut that looks like a rural *lavatory*. A second part of the dream has for content how, when her child (a little girl) *soils* herself, she *wipes the child's bottom*.'

Dreams of *'rescues'* belong together with *birth-dreams*. Rescuing, particularly rescuing from water, means the same thing as giving birth, if dreamed by a woman, but means something different if the dreamer is a man.[75]

The robbers, nocturnal burglars and ghosts that people fear before going to bed and that also sometimes haunt sleepers – these all stem from one and the same childhood memory. They are the nocturnal visitors that used to wake the child up to put it on the pot lest it wet the bed or who lifted the covers in order to take careful note of how it held its hands while asleep. Analysing some of these anxiety-dreams has enabled me to identify who the nocturnal visitor was. The robber was invariably the father; ghosts, on the other hand, tend to correspond to female figures in white nightdresses.

Notes

1. W[ilhelm] Stekel, *Die Sprache des Traumes* ['The language of dream'], 1911.

2. See also the works of [Eugen] Bleuler and his Zürich pupils ([Alphonse] Maeder, [Karl] Abraham and the rest) on symbolism, and the non-medical authors to whom they refer (Kleinpaul, etc.). The most appropriate things said on this subject are to be found in the first chapter of the book by O[tto] Rank and H[anns] Sachs, *Die Bedeutung der Psychoanalyse für die Geisteswissenschaften* ['*The Significance of Psychoanalysis for the Mental Sciences*'], 1913. See also E[rnest] Jones, 'Die Theorie der Symbolik', *Internationale Zeitschrift für Psychoanalyse*, V, 1919.

3. This view was to find extraordinary support in a theory put forward by Dr Hans Sperber. In his article 'Über den Einfluss sexueller Momente auf Entstehung und Entwicklung der Sprache' ['Concerning the influence of sexual factors on the emergence and development of language'], in *Imago*, I, 1912, Sperber reckons that the earliest words all denoted sexual objects and then lost this sexual significance by passing to other objects and activities that were likened to the sexual dimension.

4. For instance, a ship [*Schiff*] under way on water appears in the urinary dreams of Hungarian dreamers despite the fact that their language knows nothing of the [German] word *schiffen* as a slang term for 'to piss' (Ferenczi; see also above, p. 379). In the dreams of French people and other Romance-language speakers, the word 'room' serves to represent woman symbolically although such people do not have the German expression '*Frauenzimmer*' [although made up of *Frau* ('woman') and *Zimmer* ('room'), the composite term *Frauenzimmer* is simply an informal word for 'woman'; perhaps 'her indoors' is an analogous English usage].

5. [Until 1918, Austria-Hungary was ruled by an emperor and empress, who were of course familiar figures in Vienna.]

6. [I.e. *Frauenzimmer*; see note 4 above.]

7. 'A patient living in a boarding-house dreams of meeting one of the maids and asking her which number she has; to his surprise, she answers, "14." He did in fact start a relationship with the said girl, visiting her several times in her room. Understandably afraid that the landlady suspected her, on the day before the dream she suggested to him that they meet in one of the empty rooms. In reality, it was that room that was numbered 14, whereas in the dream the woman had that number. Clearer proof of the identification of woman and room can scarcely be imagined' (Ernest Jones, *Internationale Zeitschrift für Psychoanalyse*, II, 1914; see also Artemidorus, *The Symbolism of Dreams*: 'Thus for instance the bedroom stands for the wife, should such a person be present in the house').

8. [Sigmund Freud, 'Bruchstück einer Hysterie-Analyse' (1905) ('Fragment of an Analysis of a Case of Hysteria'), *Standard Edition*, vol. VII, p. 3; for a new translation by Shaun Whiteside in the New Penguin Freud, see Sigmund Freud, *The Psychology of Love*, London 2006.]

9. [Ludwig Uhland (1787–1862), lawyer, politician and poet, is regarded as one of the founders of German literary and philological studies. The 'delightfully suggestive word-play' would take too long to translate here, but the ballad can be found on the internet.]

10. Here I repeat something I have said elsewhere (in 'Die zukünftigen Chancen der psychoanalytischen Therapie' ['The future prospects of psychoanalytic therapy'], *Zentralblatt für Psycho-Analyse*, I, no. 1, 1910; *Standard Edition*, vol. XI, p. 141): Some time ago it became known to me that a psychologist who is not on close terms with us accosted one of our number with the remark that we undoubtedly overestimated the secret sexual significance of dreams. His most frequent dream, he said, was of climbing a flight of stairs – and there was surely nothing sexual about that. Alerted by this objection, we looked out for the occurrence of stairs, steps and ladders in dreams and were soon able to ascertain that stairs (and the like) constitute a definite coitus symbol. It is not difficult to work out on what the comparison rests; in rhythmic stages, coupled with increasing shortness of breath, a person attains a high point, after which that person can quickly, in a few leaps, be back down. The rhythm of coitus is thus reflected in that of climbing stairs [*Stiegesteigen*]. And let us not neglect to draw on linguistic usage, which shows us that the verb *steigen* is very often used to denote sexual activity. We say, 'The man is a *Steiger*'; *nachsteigen* means 'to chase after'. In French, a step is *une marche*, and the French expression *un vieux marcheur* corresponds exactly to our [German] expression *ein alter Steiger*. [In English, the word 'mount' springs to mind, but English usage does not seem to draw the same link as German and French between climbing stairs and coital exertion.]

11. [*Glatt*, which also = 'flat'.]

12. See the drawing by a nineteen-year-old manic reproduced in *Zentralblatt für Psycho-Analyse*, II, p. 675, showing a man with, in place of a *tie*, a snake turning towards a girl. Also in this connection, see the story 'Der Schamhaftiger' ['The bashful man'], in *Anthropophyteia*, VI, p. 334): A woman entered a bathroom where there was a man who hardly had time to don his shirt; deeply embarrassed, he immediately covered his throat with the front of the shirt, saying, 'I do beg your pardon, I'm not wearing a *tie*.'

13. [*Witzarbeit*; on the analogy of *Traumarbeit* ('dream-work'), this is the psychical process involved in making jokes.]

14. See also, in this connection, [Oskar] Pfister's studies of cryptography and picture puzzles [cited below in Other Literature].

15. See also the lizard dream cited above, on pp. 22f.

16. [*Rezent*; see p. 199, note 2.]

17. Despite all the differences between Scherner's view of dream-symbolism and that developed here, I must emphasize that Scherner should be recognized as the true discoverer of symbolism in dream and that the experiences of psychoanalysis have belatedly honoured a book that was deemed fantastical when it was published many years ago (1861).

18. [*Standard Edition*, vols XV–XVI.]

19. From 'Nachträge zur Traumdeutung' ['Supplementary remarks on interpreting dreams'], *Zentralblatt für Psycho-Analyse*, I, nos. 5–6, 1911.

20. ['*Haube*', in Austria, particularly denotes the sort of white cap currently worn by nurses and formerly by wet-nurses and other household servants, though the word can also mean 'bonnet, hood or crest'.]

21. For one such example, see Kirchgraber's piece in *Zentralblatt für Psycho-Analyse*, III, 1912, p. 95. Stekel reports a dream (*Jahrbuch*, vol. I [1909], p. 475) in which a hat with a feather stuck in the middle at an angle symbolized a man – but one who was impotent.

22. [Freud misquotes the dream here, writing in effect 'whether the parts cannot be seen *from* behind' instead of 'whether the parts cannot be seen behind'. This makes sense in the light of what follows, but it does seem to court a charge of 'cooking the evidence'.]

23. [A large park in Vienna.]

24. Or chapel = vagina.

25. Symbol of coitus.

26. *Mons veneris*.

27. *Crines pubis*.

28. Cloaked and hooded demons are apparently, according to one expert, phallic in nature.

29. The two halves of the scrotal sac.

30. Otto Rank, 'Die Symbolschichtung im Wecktraum und ihre Wiederkehr im mythischen Denken' ['Layers of symbolism in the waking dream and its recurrence in mythical thought'], in *Jahrbuch für Psycho-Analyse*, IV, 1912, p. 99.

31. [*Weibsbilder* is a derogatory German term for which I offer 'females' as an approximate translation; it incorporates the word *Bild*, 'picture', which here results in an untranslatable pun.]

32. [As well as *Skala* (the word Freud uses here), a scale in German is also a *Tonleiter* – literally, a 'note-ladder'.]

33. Alfred Robitsek in *Zentralblatt für Psycho-Analyse*, II, 1911, p. 340. [Except for the last two paragraphs, section 10 is an extended quotation from Robitsek's article.]

34. See his *The World of Dreams*, London 1911, p. 168.

35. [Robitsek cites these and the rest of the girl's words in English, appending (as Freud would probably not have done) a German translation.]

36. [The dreamer is speaking English, remember; the large (often white) flower called *Lilie* in German is quite different from *Maiglöckchen* ('Maybells'), the German term for 'lily of the valley'.]

37. [Robitsek adds a parenthesis here: 'English pronunciation distinguishes them only by sounding the last syllable differently.']

38. [Amusingly mistranslated (presumably by Robitsek) as *Phantasiepapier* ('fantasy paper') in the original.]

39. In his article 'Träume von der Ahnungslosen', ['Dreams of naive people'], in *Internationale Zeitschrift für Psychoanalyse*, IV, 1916–17.

40. [Otto von Bismarck, having resigned as German chancellor in 1890, had died in 1898.]

41. [This section, too, consists of an extended quotation.]

42. Otto von Bismarck, *Gedanken und Erinnerungen* ['Thoughts and recollections'], vol. II (*Volksausgabe*), p. 222.

43. ['*Ein wackeres Pferd stirbt in seinen Sielen*'.]

44. [*Infantile Überbesetzung*. In this and the *Mass Psychology* volume of the New Penguin Freud series I draw on an electrical metaphor to translate *Besetzung*, an already existing German word that Freud and his fellow psychoanalysts commandeered to denote the impregnation of an object (an emotion or a person) with psychical energy. *Besetzung* means 'occupation, investment' (though it also has the theatrical connotation of 'casting'); Strachey fabricated his 'cathexis' to take in areas of meaning that no one

English word will cover – evidently on Humpty Dumpty's somewhat corrosive principle of word use: 'When *I* use a word . . . it means just what I choose it to mean . . .']

45. [Exodus 17:1–7.]

46. [See below, Chapter 7, section E.]

47. [English readers may need some elucidation here. The Yiddish word *Schlemihl* (pronounced 'shlay-meal'; a *Pechvogel* or 'unlucky fellow') is not dissimilar in sound to the German pronunciation of the radicals referred to in the previous sentence: *Benzyl, Azetyl usw.* It was used by Adelbert von Chamisso (1781–1838) as the name of the central character of his 1814 story *Peter Schlemihls wundersame Geschichte* (translated into English as *Peter Schlemihl's Remarkable Story*, 1927). The 'Prévost' referred to is French novelist Marcel Prévost (1862–1940).]

48. [This and the following quotation are in fact from Friedrich Schiller's *Ode to Joy*, though the first can also be found in the finale of Act 2 of Beethoven's opera *Fidelio*, where it appears to have been 'borrowed' – possibly by the original librettist Josef Sonnleithner.]

49. [*Hinausgeworfen*, an allusion to the *grosse Wurf* (the 'big throw' – as of dice) referred to in the second *Ode to Joy* quotation.]

50. A tooth being pulled by someone else is usually to be interpreted as castration (like hair being cut by a hairdresser; Stekel). A distinction needs to be drawn between tooth-stimulus dreams and dental dreams in general – as for instance Coriat (*Zentralblatt für Psycho-Analyse*, III, p. 440) recounts.

51. According to C. G. Jung, tooth-stimulus dreams in women have the significance of birth dreams. E[rnest] Jones has provided sound confirmation of this. What such an interpretation has in common with the one advanced here is that in both instances (castration – birth) there is a removal of part of the bodily entity.

52. See also the 'biographical' dream above, p. 362 and p. 364, note 20.

53. [The following twelve paragraphs are quoted from Otto Rank.]

54. [See above, p. 397.]

55. [This parenthesis is added by Otto Rank.]

56. [See above, pp. 398f.]

57. [*Deckerinnerung*; 'screen memory' is the usual translation, but in an age when most screens are used to render things visible (by reflecting them) rather than invisible (by concealing them), perhaps we need a new translation for what Laplanche and Pontalis describe as 'a childhood memory characterized both by its unusual sharpness and by the apparent insignificance of its content', adding: 'The analysis of such memories leads

back to indelible childhood experiences and to unconscious fantasies' (Jean Laplanche and Jean-Bertrand Pontalis, *The Language of Psychoanalysis*, translated by Donald Nicholson-Smith, London 1973). In other words, they 'cover' something.]

58. [See above, note 51.]

59. In the interests of coherence, I repeat here the passage about movement dreams from the last section of Chapter 5 (see above, p. 284).

60. [J. Mourly Vold, *Über den Traum, Collected Works*, vol. III.]

61. [*Standard Edition*, vol. VII, p. 3; *The Psychology of Love*, translated by Shaun Whiteside, London 2006, pp. 56–82.]

62. [Editorial note added to eleventh edition (2003): This 'two' is a leftover from the 1909 and 1911 editions, in which all discussion of 'typical' dreams is brought together in Chapter 5. In later editions, however, these passages were very substantially expanded by the addition of fresh material. In the 1909 edition the 'two comments' fill only some five pages altogether; by 1930 they take up forty-two.]

63. See my *Drei Abhandlungen zur Sexualtheorie*, 1905, sixth edition 1926 [*Three Essays on Sexual Theory, Standard Edition*, vol. VII, p. 125; *The Psychology of Love*, translated by Shaun Whiteside, pp. 111–220].

64. [*Überdeutung*. On the analogy of *Überdeterminierung*, another of Freud's 'über-' combinations, the prefix adds a sense of plurality rather than any suggestion of superiority or excess.]

65. Wilhelm Stekel, *Die Sprache des Traumes* ['The language of dream'], 1911.

66. Alfred Adler, 'Der psychische Hermaphroditismus im Leben und in der Neurose' ['Psychical hermaphroditism in life and neurosis'], in *Fortschritte der Medizin* ['Medical advances'], 16, 1910, and subsequent works in the *Zentralblatt für Psycho-Analyse*, I, 1910–11.

67. I published a typical example of such a concealed Oedipal dream in the first issue of the *Zentralblatt für Psycho-Analyse* (see below [the final paragraph of this note]); another one, complete with a detailed interpretation, was published by O[tto] Rank in the fourth issue. On other concealed Oedipal dreams in which eye symbolism figures prominently, see Rank in *Internationale Zeitschrift für Psychoanalyse*, I, 1913; The same journal has carried articles on 'eye dreams' and eye symbolism by Eder, Ferenczi and Reitler. Blinding, both in the Oedipus myth and elsewhere, represents castration. The ancients, incidentally, were likewise no strangers to the symbolic interpretation of undisguised Oedipal dreams. See this passage from O[tto] Rank in *Jahrbuch* [*der Psychoanalyse*], II, p. 534: 'There is a tradition, for instance, that Julius Caesar once dreamed of having sexual

intercourse with his mother, a dream that the interpreter explained as a good omen for the seizure of the earth (*mother/earth*). We also know of the oracle delivered to the Tarquins whereby mastery of Rome would fall to him among them who first *kissed his mother* (*osculum matri tulerit*), which Brutus understood as a reference to *mother-earth* (*terram osculo contigit, scilicet quod ea communis mater omnium mortalium esset*; Livy, I, LVI).' See also, in this connection, Hippias' dream in Herodotus, VI, 107: 'However, the barbarians were taken by Hippias to Marathon after he had had the following vision in the previous night: Hippias had pictured himself sleeping with his own mother. From this dream he drew the conclusion that he would return home to Athens, rule over the city once again, and die in his homeland an old man.' These myths and interpretations suggest a correct psychological recognition. I have found that persons who are aware of being preferred or singled out by their mothers show, in life, that special self-assurance and that unshakable optimism that not infrequently appear heroic and compel true success.

Typical example of a hidden Oedipal dream:

A man dreams: *He has a secret affair with a lady who intends to marry someone else. He is concerned that the other person may discover the affair, in which case the marriage would come to nothing, and he therefore behaves very tenderly towards the man, cuddling up to him and kissing him.* The facts of the dreamer's life connect with the dream only in one respect. He is conducting a secret affair with a married woman, and an ambiguous remark made by her husband, who is a friend of his, has led him to suspect that the husband may have noticed something. In reality, however, there is something else going on as well, something that the dream avoids mentioning yet is the only thing that provides the key to understanding the dream. The husband's life is under threat from an organic disorder. His wife is prepared for the possibility of his sudden death, and our dreamer consciously concerns himself with his resolve, following the husband's demise, to take the young widow to wife. As a consequence of this external situation, the dreamer finds himself shifted into the constellation of the Oedipal dream; his wish may kill the man in order to gain the woman as his wife; his dream gives expression to that wish in terms of a hypocritical distortion. Instead of her being married to the other man, it has another man in fact wanting to marry her, which matches his own secret intention, and the hostile wishes towards the husband hide behind ostentatious caresses stemming from his own recollection of childhood contacts with his father.

68. [*Geburtsakt*; my dictionary suggests that I translate this word as 'parturition', but I am anxious to avoid any suggestion that Freud is thinking here of the *mother's* experience.]

69. On the mythological significance of water-birth, see [Otto] Rank, 'Der Mythos von der Geburt des Helden' ['The myth of the birth of the hero'], 1909.

70. The significance of fantasies and unconscious thoughts about life in the womb is something I did not learn to appreciate until late on. They contain both the explanation for the curious fear experienced by so many people of being buried alive and the very profound unconscious basis for the belief in life after death, which is simply a projection into the future of this alien-seeming life before birth. *Incidentally, being born is the first experience of fear* [Angsterlebnis], *which makes it a source of and pattern for the fear affect.*

71. [*Fruchtwasser* ('fruit-water') – so much more personal, somehow! Perhaps some of Bruno Bettelheim's antipathy to the 'remoteness' of many English translations of Freud (*Freud and Man's Soul*, 1983) is due to the readiness of the English language to cover up embarrassingly personal medical facts with abstruse terminology; most German medical terms strike the English reader as almost crudely direct.]

72. [This surely makes better sense if we assume, as I have done, that Freud reversed his 'first' and 'second' here.]

73. 'The same symbolic representations as in the infantile sense underlie the vesical [bladder] dream appear in the "living", "still-active" ["*rezent*"; see p. 199, note 2; the inverted commas suggest that perhaps Freud does indeed use the word in a rather special way and that the writer (Rank) is aware of the fact] sense in finely tuned sexual significance: water = urine = sperm = amniotic fluid; *Schiff* ["ship"] = *schiffen* ["to piss"] = follicle/ uterus [*Fruchtbehälter*; literally, "fruit container"] (cupboard); getting wet = enuresis = coitus = pregnancy; swimming = a full bladder = abode of the unborn child; rain = urinate = fertility symbol; taking a trip (*fahren* ["travelling"] = disembarking) = getting out of bed = having sexual intercourse (a slang meaning of *fahren*; honeymoon); urinating = having a sexual emission' (Rank, loc. cit.).

74. Freud, 'Charakter und Analerotik' ['Character and anal eroticism']; Rank, 'Layers of symbolism in the waking dream . . .'; Dattner, *Internationale Zeitschrift für Psychoanalyse*, I, 1913; Reik, *Internationale Zeitschrift*, III, 1915.

75. One such dream may be found in Pfister, 'A case of psychoanalytical pastoral care and soul-saving' ['Ein Fall von psychoanalytische Seelsorge und Seelenheilung'] in *Evangelische Freiheit* ['Evangelical freedom'], 1909.

On the subject of the 'rescuing' symbol, see also my lecture 'Die zukünftigen Chancen der psychoanalytischen Therapie' ['The future prospects of psychoanalytic therapy'; *Standard Edition*, vol. XI, p. 141] and *Beiträge zur Psychologie des Liebeslebens*, I, 'Über einen besonderen Typus der Objectwahl beim Mann' ['Articles on the psychology of the Love Life', I, 'Concerning a special type of object-choice made by men', *Standard Edition*, vol. XI, p. 165]. See also Rank, 'Belege zur Rettungsphantasie' ['Instances of rescue fantasy'] (*Zentralblatt für Psycho-Analyse*, I, 1911, p. 331); Reik, 'Zur Rettungssymbolik' ['Concerning rescue symbolism'] ibid., p. 499); Rank, 'Die "Geburtsrettungsphantasie"' ['The "birth-rescue fantasy"'] in 'Traum and Dichtung' ['Dream and poetry'], *Internationale Zeitschift für Psychoanalyse*, II, 1914.

F *Examples – counting and speaking in dream*

Before I proceed to assign the fourth of the factors controlling dream-formation to its rightful place, I want to extract a number of examples from my dream collection, some of which shed light on how the three factors already familiar to us act in combination, others of which either furnish evidence for claims freely advanced or are such as may make it possible to deduce irrefutable consequences from them. The fact is, in the foregoing description of dream-work I have found it very difficult to prove my findings with examples. Examples for individual propositions only have evidential value in connection with a particular dream-interpretation; wrenched out of context, they lose their beauty, and dream-interpretation, even quite shallow dream-interpretation, quickly becomes so extensive as to cause the thread of discussion that it is meant to help illustrate to become lost. Let this technical motive be my excuse for now citing one after another all sorts of things that are held together only by the fact that they relate to the text of the previous section.

We start with a number of examples of particularly characteristic or unusual modes of representation in dream. One lady's dream runs: *A chambermaid is up a ladder as if to clean windows, and she has a chimpanzee and a gorilla-cat* (later corrected to *an Angora cat*) *with her. She throws the animals at the woman dreaming; the chimpanzee cuddles up to her, which is quite horrible*. This dream achieved its purpose by very simple means in that it took a figure of speech literally and represented it *verbatim*. 'Ape' is an insult, as are animal names generally, and the dream-situation is simply saying *'to hurl insults around'*. This same collection will very soon supply further examples of the use of this simple trick in dream-work.

Another dream goes very similarly: *A woman with a child that has a very obviously misshapen skull; of this child she heard that it had got like that because of the way it lay in the womb. It would be possible, the doctor said, to give the skull a better shape by compression, but that would damage the brain. She thinks, because it is a boy, the damage will be less.* This dream contains a concrete representation of the abstract term 'childhood impressions', which the dreamer heard in the explanations about the treatment.[1]

Dream-work adopts a slightly different course in the following example. The dream contains a recollection of an outing to the Hilmteich, near Graz: *It is dreadful weather outside; a wretched hotel, water dripping down the walls, the beds are damp.* (The latter part of the content is less direct in the dream than I give it.) The dream signifies 'superfluous' [*überflüssig; Fluss* = 'river, flow']. The abstract idea present in the dream-thoughts has initially been rendered rather violently equivocal (replaced by 'overflowing' [*überfliessend*], perhaps, or by 'fluid and superfluous' [*flüssig und überflüssig*]) and then brought to representation by an accumulation of similar impressions. Water outside, water inside on the walls, water as dampness in the beds – all fluid and 'excessively' [*über-*] fluid. That for the purposes of representation in dreams the spelling of words lags behind the sound will hardly come as a surprise to us when rhyme (for instance) is able to permit itself similar liberties. In a rambling dream had by a young girl, recounted and very thoroughly analysed by Rank, we are told that she is walking between fields where she cuts beautiful *ears* [*Ähren*, pronounced *'air*-en'] of barley and corn. Coming the other way is a friend from her youth, whom she is keen to avoid meeting. Analysis reveals that this is about a *Kuss in Ehren* [the last word is also pronounced *'air*-en', and the phrase means, literally, a 'kiss in honour', such as one might bestow to signal 'hello', 'goodbye', 'thank you' and the like; the real point, however, is that *Ehren* rhymes with *Ähren*] (*Jahrbuch*, II, p. 482). The ears of corn, which must not be ripped off but cut, serve as such in this dream, and through being compressed with *honours* and *honouring* they represent a whole series of other thoughts.

On the other hand, in other instances language has made it very easy for dream to represent dream-thoughts, having at its disposal a whole series of words that were originally meant figuratively and concretely but are now used in a colourless, abstract sense. All dream need do is give such words back their earlier, full meaning or undo something of the word's change in meaning. For instance, someone dreams that his brother is in a box [*Kasten*]; in the process of interpretation the box is replaced by a 'cupboard' [*Schrank*], and the dream-thought is now to the effect that the brother should 'economize' [*sich einschränken*] – in the dreamer's stead, in this particular case. Another dreamer climbs a mountain from which he has a quite exceptional *view* [*Aussicht*]. In so doing, he is identifying with a brother who edits a *review* [*Rundschau* = 'look-around, panorama'] dealing with Far Eastern relations.

In a dream in [the Gottfried Keller novel] *Der Grüne Heinrich*[2] a high-spirited horse rolls in the most beautiful oats – each grain of which, however, is 'a sweet almond kernel, a raisin and a new penny [. . .] wrapped up together in red silk and tied with a length of pig's bristle'. The writer (or the dreamer) immediately gives us the interpretation of this dream-representation, for the horse, feeling pleasantly tickled, calls out, '*I'm feeling my oats*'.[3]

Particularly abundant use of dreams involving popular sayings and puns is made (according to [Wilhelm] Henzen) in the Old Norse sagas, where virtually every instance of a dream contains a double meaning or a play on words.

It would be a special study, collecting such modes of representation and arranging them according to the principles underlying them. Many such representations almost deserve to be called witty. What they mean would have remained a mystery, one feels, had the dreamer not personally told us.

1) A man dreams that *he is being asked for a name but cannot think of it*. He himself says this means: *I'd never dream of . . .*

2) A female patient recounts a dream in which *everyone involved was particularly tall*. This, she adds, is meant to convey that I must

be dealing here with an event from my early childhood, for then, of course, all grown-ups seemed so enormously tall to me. Her own person did not figure in this dream-content.

The transfer to childhood is also expressed differently in other dreams by time being translated into space. The persons and scenes concerned are seen as if a long way away, at the end of a long path, something like that, as if one were looking at them through opera glasses held the wrong way around.

3) A man who in waking life tends towards an abstract, somewhat vague way of expressing himself but otherwise possesses a ready wit dreams in certain contexts that *he is walking into a station just as a train is arriving. Then, however, the platform is moved closer to the stationary train* – in an absurd reversal, that is to say, of the true sequence of events. This detail, it turns out, is simply a reminder that something else in the dream-content needs to be reversed. Analysis of this same dream leads to recollections of illustrated books in which men were shown standing on their heads and walking on their hands.

4) The same dreamer tells on another occasion of a brief dream almost reminiscent of the technique of the rebus or picture-puzzle. *His uncle gives him a kiss in the car [Automobil].* He adds the interpretation immediately, which is one I should never have hit upon: *auto-eroticism.* A joke told in the waking state might have run thus.

5) The dreamer *pulls a woman out from behind the bed* [the verb is *vorziehen*]. This means: she has his *preference [er gibt ihr den Vorzug].*

6) The dreamer *is sitting at a table as an officer, opposite the Emperor.* He is *contrasting* himself with his father.

7) The dreamer *is treating another person for a broken bone.* Analysis reveals this break to represent a *broken marriage,* etc.

8) In dream-content, times of day very often represent periods of childhood. To take an example, for one dreamer 5:15 a.m. means the age of five years and three months – the significant moment when a younger brother was born.

9) A different representation of *times of life* in dreams: *A woman is walking with two small girls, who are one and a quarter years apart*. The dreamer can think of no family of her acquaintance for which this is the case. Her interpretation is that both children represent herself and that the dream is reminding her that the two traumatic events of her childhood occurred that far apart (at three and a half and four and three-quarter years).

10) It is not surprising that people undergoing psychoanalytical treatment often dream about it and need to express, in dream, all the thoughts and expectations it arouses. The image chosen for the course of treatment is, as a rule, that of a journey, usually by car, as being a new and complicated type of vehicle;[4] references to the speed of the motor car offer a rich field for patients' ridicule. Should the 'unconscious' as an element of the [patient's] waking thoughts find representation in dream, it has itself very expediently replaced by 'underground' localities that on other occasions (quite unrelated to the analytical treatment) had signified the female abdomen or the womb. *'Below'* in dream very often refers to the *genitals*, while the opposite ('above') refers to face, mouth or breast. In general, 'wild animals' are used by dream-work to symbolize passionate drives, both the dreamer's own and those of other people of whom the dreamer is afraid – so with a very slight shift the actual people who evince those passions. From here it is not a long way to representing the feared father – reminiscent of totemism, this – with savage animals (dogs, wild horses). These wild animals might be said to represent the libido, which is feared by the 'I' and fought with the weapon of repression. The relevant neurosis itself, the 'sick person', is often split off by the dreamer and bodied forth, in dream, as an autonomous being.

11) (H[anns] Sachs:)

> We know from *Interpreting Dreams* that dream-work has various different ways of representing a word or saying in concrete sensory terms. For instance, it can take advantage of the fact that the expression to be represented is ambiguous and, using the double meaning as a 'set of points', incorporate in the manifest dream-content not the first meaning occuring in the dream-thoughts but the second.

This happened in the little dream recounted below – and it happened as a result of skilful use, as representation material, of such still-vivid [*rezent*] impressions of the day as lent themselves to the purpose.

On the dream-day I had had a cold, so I had decided that evening not to get out of bed during the night if at all possible. Apparently the dream simply had me continue the work I had been occupied with that day; I had been pasting newspaper cuttings into a book, taking great care to stick each one in its proper place. The dream went like this:

I am trying hard to paste a cutting in the book; however, it won't fit on the page, which pains me greatly.

I woke up, whereupon I became aware that the pain in the dream was still there as an actual physical pain, which then obliged me to break my resolution. Dream, as the 'guardian of sleep', had faked the fulfilment of my wish to remain in bed by representing the words, 'however, it won't fit on the page'.

[Freud resumes:] Dream-work, in fact, can be said to use all means at its disposal to portray dream-thoughts visually, regardless of whether or not such means seem permissible to the critical faculty of the waking person, and as such it exposes itself to the doubts as well as to the derision of all who have only heard of dream-interpretation and never practised it themselves. Stekel's book *The Language of Dream*[5] is particularly rich in just such examples, but I have avoided taking my evidence from that source because the author's uncritical approach and technical arbitrariness will unsettle even someone not mired in prejudice.

12) From a study by V. Tausk, 'Clothes and colours in the service of dream-representation' ['Kleider und Farben im Dienste der Traumdarstellung'], in *Internationale Zeitschrift für Psycho-analyse*, II, 1914:

a) A. dreams *of seeing his former governess in a black lustre dress* [*Lüsterkleid*] *that fits snugly over the behind.* This means he is saying the woman is *lascivious* [*lüstern*].

b)   C. sees, in dream, a *girl on X Road surrounded by white light and wearing a white blouse.*

On that road, the dreamer exchanged his first kiss with a Miss Weiss ['White'].

c)   Mrs D. dreams *of seeing old Blasel* (an eighty-year-old Viennese actor) *in full armour [in voller Rüstung], lying on the couch. Then he leaps over the table and chairs, drawing a dagger, and as he does so he catches sight of himself in a mirror and waves the dagger around in mid-air as if duelling with an imaginary enemy.*

Interpretation: The dreamer has *a long-standing bladder [Blasen] complaint.* She lies on the couch during analysis, and when she glimpses herself in the mirror she secretly thinks that, her years and her illness notwithstanding, she still looks *very sprightly [sehr rüstig].*

13) The *'great achievement'* in dream.

The male dreamer sees himself *lying in bed as a pregnant woman. He begins to find the condition extremely uncomfortable. He calls out, 'I'd rather . . .'* (in analysis he completes the sentence, after remembering a nurse, *'. . . break stones'). Hanging behind his bed is a map, the lower edge of which is held straight by a strip of wood. He pulls this strip down violently by grabbing it at both ends, whereupon instead of breaking in half crossways it splits into two halves longitudinally. By doing this he has brought relief to himself and also helped the birth.*

Without prompting, he interprets the violent pulling down of the *strip [Leiste]* as a major *achievement [Leistung;* no etymological connection], through which he frees himself from his awkward situation (the treatment) by wrenching himself out of his female guise . . . The absurd detail of the wooden strip not merely breaking but splitting in half lengthways is explained by the dreamer's recalling that duplication combined with destruction contains an allusion to castration. Dream very often represents castration through a defiant wish-opposite involving the presence of two penis symbols. And the 'groin' [another *Leiste*, this one sharing the same etymology as *Leiste* = 'strip'] is of course a part of the body very close to the genitals. The dreamer then summarizes the interpretation as his overcoming the castration threat that had made him dream of being a woman.[6]

14) In an analysis that I am conducting in French I am required to interpret a dream in which I appear as an elephant. Naturally, I have to ask how I come to be so portrayed. '*Vous me trompez,*' the dreamer replies ['You dupe me', but the French word *trompe* also denotes '(elephant's) trunk'].

Dream-work often manages to represent something on the basis of very meagre material (such as proper names, for example) by strained exploitation of very remote connections. In one of my dreams *old Brücke[7] has set me a task. I am making a preparation and am picking something out of it that looks like a screwed-up piece of silver paper* (more of this dream later [see below, pp. 466ff]). The associated idea in this connection (not easy to find) turns out to be '*Stanniol*' [= 'tinfoil'], and I now realize that I mean the name *Stannius*, author of a treatise on the nervous system of fishes that in my young days I held in high esteem. The first scientific task that my teacher set me did indeed relate to the nervous system of a fish – ammocoetes. The latter name was evidently unusable for picture-puzzle purposes.

I very much want at this point to include another dream having a special content – one that is further remarkable as a childhood dream and that finds a very ready explanation through analysis. A lady recounts: 'I can remember as a child repeatedly dreaming that *God has a pointed paper hat on his head*. You see, I very often had such a hat placed on my head at table to prevent me from inspecting the other children's plates to see how much of the particular dish concerned they had been given. I had been told that God knows everything, so the dream means that I know everything too, despite the hat that has been set on my head.'

What dream-work consists of and how it treats its material (the relevant dream-thoughts) can be instructively illustrated in terms of the numbers and calculations that occur in dreams. Moreover, dreamed numbers are regarded by the superstitious as especially significant. So I shall choose a few dreams of this kind from my collection.

1. From a lady's dream just before the end of her treatment:

She wishes to pay for something; her daughter takes 3 florins 65 kreuzer[8] *from her purse; but the lady says, 'What are you doing? It only costs 21 kreuzer.'* This dream-fragment was intelligible to me on the basis of the dreamer's circumstances without further explanation on her part. The lady was a foreigner who had placed her daughter in a Viennese educational establishment and was able to continue to receive treatment from myself for as long as her daughter remained in Vienna. In three weeks the daughter's school year would come to an end – and with it the treatment. On the day preceding the dream the headmistress had suggested to the mother that she might consider leaving the girl in her care for a further year. Subsequently my patient had clearly continued with this idea on her own, working out that in that case she would also be able to prolong the treatment by a year. This is what her dream in fact refers to, since a year comprises 365 days, while the three weeks to the end of the school year equate to twenty-one days (albeit not the same number of treatment hours). The numbers that in the dream-thoughts stand for times are given monetary values in the dream – not without a deeper meaning finding expression in the process, since *'time is money'*.[9] 365 kreuzer in fact equal 3 gulden [florins] 65 kreuzer. The smallness of the sums figuring in the dream is an obvious piece of wish-fulfilment, with wish reducing both the treatment costs and those of a year's schooling.

2. The numbers in another dream lead to more complicated relationships. A young lady who in spite of her youth has been married for some years learns that an almost contemporaneous acquaintance of hers, Elise L., has just become engaged. She then dreams: *She and her husband are sitting in the theatre. One side of the stalls is completely empty. Her husband tells her that Elise L. and her fiancé had also wanted to come. However, they had only been offered poor seats, 3 for 1 florin 50 kreuzer, and these they had been unable to accept. She thinks it would not in fact have been the end of the world.*

Why 1 florin 50 kreuzer; where does the figure come from? From what was actually a trivial [*indifferent*] incident of the previous day. Her sister-in-law had received 150 florins as a gift from *her* husband and had lost no time in getting rid of them by buying a piece of jewellery. Note that 150 florins is a hundred times more than 1 florin 50 kreuzer. What about the 3 associated with the theatre seats? There is only one link here: the fact that the engaged acquaintance is that number of months (*three*) younger than herself. The dream is then resolved by my asking what the dream-feature 'one side of the stalls is completely empty' might mean. This is a straight allusion to a small matter that had given her husband good reason to tease her. She had decided to attend one of the advertised shows of the week and had taken the precaution of buying tickets several days in advance, for which she had had to pay a pre-booking fee. Arriving at the theatre, they found that one side of the auditorium was nearly empty; there had been *no need* for her *to be in such a rush*.

I shall now replace the dream by the dream-thoughts: 'It *made no sense*, getting married so soon; there was *no need* for me *to be in such a rush*. The example of Elise L. shows me that I should still have found a husband. In fact, one *a hundred times* better (husband, riches) if I had only *waited* (in contrast to her sister-in-law's being *in such a rush*). I could have had *three* such husbands for the money (the dowry)!' We begin to realize that in this dream the numbers have undergone a far greater change in terms of their significance and coherence than in the one we were discussing earlier. The transformation work and distortion work of dream have been more extensive here, which we interpret to mean that, before finding representation, these dream-thoughts had to overcome a particularly high degree of resistance within the psyche. Nor should we overlook the fact that this dream contains an element of the absurd, namely that *two* people should occupy *three* seats. We are entering the territory of how to interpret absurdity in dreams [see below, pp. 442ff.] when we point out that this absurd detail of the dream-content is meant to represent the most heavily emphasized of the dream-thoughts, namely that it *made no sense* to get married so soon. The three implicit in an entirely incidental relationship between the persons compared (a three-month age difference) has been cleverly used to produce the non-sense required by dream. Reducing the actual 150 florins to 1 florin 50 kreuzer corresponds to *disparagement* of the husband (or riches) in the dreamer's suppressed thoughts.

3. A further example introduces us to arithmetic in dream, which has brought it so much scorn. A man dreams: *He is sitting next to B . . .* (a member of a family he used to know) *and says: 'It was absurd that you didn't give me Mali.'*[10] Then he asks the girl, 'How old are you, in fact?' Answer: 'I was born in 1882.' 'Ah, so you're twenty-eight.'

The dream having occurred in 1898, the dreamer has clearly got the sum wrong; in fact his poor arithmetic is almost paralytic – unless, that is, there is some other explanation for it. My patient was one of those people who, once they set eyes on a woman, cannot keep their minds off her. For several months his regular successor in my consulting-room was a young lady whom he of course met, after whom he frequently enquired, and towards whom he sought to be thoroughly polite. It was she whose age he put at twenty-eight. That explains the result of his apparent calculation. But 1882 was the year in which he had got married. He had been unable to prevent himself from similarly starting up conversations with the other two female persons whom he met at my place, the two by no means youthful maids who, by turns, opened the door to him. And finding the maids less than forthcoming, he had told himself that they doubtless saw him as a mature, *'settled'* gentleman.

Another counting dream, this one characterized by transparent determination or rather multiple determination [*Überdeterminierung*], I owe (together with its interpretation) to Mr B. Dattner:

> *My landlord, a security employee with the municipal authorities, dreams that he is standing guard in the street, which is wishfulfilment. An inspector approaches him, wearing the numbers 22 and 62 or 26 on his collar. Anyway, there were several twos present.*
> The mere fact of his bisecting the number 2262 in recounting the

dream suggests that the two halves mean different things. The day before, he now recalls, they had been talking at the station about their respective lengths of service. The occasion had been the retirement of an inspector at the age of 62. The dreamer had served only 22 years and needed a further 2 years and 2 months for a 90 per cent pension. In the first place, his dream reflects the fulfilment of a long-held wish to be promoted to the rank of inspector. The superior with 2262 on his collar is himself; he is performing his duties on the beat (another dear wish), and he has served out his 2 years and 2 months and can now, like the 62-year-old inspector, retire from his post on full pension.[11]

Taking these and similar examples (see below) together, we can say: dream-work does no arithmetic at all, either correctly or incorrectly; it simply brings together in the form of a sum numbers that occur in dream-thoughts and can be used as allusions to material that eludes portrayal. In so doing it treats numbers as material to give expression to its intentions – in precisely the same way as it treats all other ideas such as names and speeches, where these are recognizably verbal ideas.

The fact is, dream-work cannot even create speech from scratch. No matter how much speech and counter-speech may occur in dreams that may or may not make sense in themselves, analysis invariably reveals that the dream concerned has simply taken from the dream-thoughts fragments of things actually said or heard and processed them in an extremely high-handed fashion. It has not only wrenched them out of context and broken them up, keeping one bit and discarding another; often, too, it has reassembled them in such a way that an apparently coherent dream-speech comes apart on analysis, falling into three or four pieces. Many times, in connection with this kind of re-use, it will have disregarded the meaning that the words had in the dream-thoughts and coaxed a wholly new meaning from the same wording.[12] On closer inspection one distinguishes (in dream-speech) clearer, compact components from others that serve as binding agent and have probably been added to, as we add missing letters and syllables as we read. Dream-speech thus has the structure of breccia, a rock in which quite large pieces of disparate materials are held together by a hardened mass of intermediate matter.

Strictly speaking, though, this description applies only to the items of spoken material in dream that have something of the sensory character of speech and are described as 'speeches'. The rest, which are not, as it were, experienced as heard or spoken (have no acoustic or motor reinforcement in the relevant dream), are simple thoughts as they occur in our daytime thinking activity and pass into many dreams unaltered. As regards speech-material in dream that is deemed no longer vivid [*indifferent*], reading provides another abundant and not easily traceable source. However, anything in a dream that somehow stands out as speech can be traced back to things actually said or heard by the dreamer.

We have already come across examples of the derivation of such dream-speeches in analysing dreams that were recounted for other purposes. The 'innocuous market dream' on p. 194 is one; in it, the speech, *'That's no longer to be had'*, serves to identify me with the butcher, whilst the function of a fragment of the other speech, *'That's new to me, I shan't have any'*, is precisely to render the dream innocuous. The dreamer had in fact, the day before, rejected some unreasonable demand made by her cook with the words, 'That's new to me. *Behave yourself!'* and had now taken the neutral-sounding [*indifferent klingende*] first part of this speech and incorporated it in her dream in order to use it as an allusion to the second part, which would have fitted extremely well into the fantasy underlying the dream but would also have given that fantasy away.

A similar example to stand for the many that in fact all give the same result:

A large courtyard in which cadavers are being burned. He says, 'I'm off, I can't bear it.' (Not a clear speech.) *Then he meets two butcher-boys and asks, 'That all right, then?' One replies, 'Naa, weren't no good.' As if it had been human flesh.*

The innocuous occasion of this dream is as follows: after supper he and his wife call on the good-hearted but distinctly *unappetizing* neighbours. The hospitable old lady is just having her supper and *forces* him (in jest, between men, a composite word with a sexual meaning is used for the purpose) to eat something. He declines, saying he is no longer hungry. '*Get away with you*, it won't hurt', or words to that effect. So he has to eat, and in her presence he praises what he is given, saying '*Not bad at all.*' Alone again with his wife, he then complains about both the neighbour's insistence and the quality of the food he had eaten. The 'I can't bear it', which in the dream, too, does not figure as actual speech, is a thought relating to the physical charms of the lady who had invited him; translated, it means that he does not exactly yearn for the sight of her.

A more instructive example will be my analysis of a different dream that I recount at this point because of the very clear speech around which it revolves (but that I shall not be explaining until we come to assess affects in dreams [see section H below]). I dreamed very clearly: *I have gone to Brücke's laboratory at night where, following a tap at the door, I admit Professor Fleischl* (the late Professor Fleischl), *who enters with a number of strangers and after a few words sits down at his desk.* A second dream then follows: *My friend Fl. has paid a discreet visit to Vienna in July; I meet him in the street in conversation with my friend P.* (my late friend P.) *and go with them to some place where they sit opposite each other, as if at a small table, with me at the near, narrow end of the table. Fl. is talking about his sister, saying, 'In three-quarters of an hour she was dead', and then something like: 'That's the threshold.' Since P. does not understand him, Fl. turns to me and asks me how much I have told P. about his affairs. Whereupon I, in the grip of remarkable affects, wish to tell Fl. that P. (cannot in fact know anything because he) is not in fact alive. But instead, aware of the mistake myself, I say, 'Non vixit.' I then stare penetratingly at P., who under my gaze becomes pale, blurred, his eyes take on a sickly blue colour – and at length he fades away completely. I am hugely delighted at this, understanding now that Ernst Fleischl, too, was simply a manifestation, a ghost, and finding it entirely possible that such a person exists only so long as one wants it to and that another person's wish can get rid of it.*

This beautiful dream combines so many of the puzzling characteristics of dream-content – criticism during dreaming itself (my being aware of my own mistake in saying '*Non vixit*' instead of '*Non vivit*'), uninhibited frequenting of dead persons (whom the dream itself pronounces deceased), the absurdity of the conclusions reached, coupled with the high degree of satisfaction these afford me – that I 'cannot wait' to disclose the complete solution to the riddle. In reality, though, I am incapable of sacrificing consideration for such cherished persons to my ambition (as in fact I do in the dream). However, any disguise would have ruined what I am well aware is the meaning of the dream. I will therefore content myself – here initially and again later on – with picking out certain elements of the dream for interpretation.

The dream revolves around a scene in which I destroy P. with a look. In the process, his eyes become this amazing, mysterious blue colour, then he fades away. This scene is an unmistakable copy of one I did actually experience. I was a demonstrator at the Institute of Physiology, I was on duty early, and Brücke had found out that on several occasions I had been late arriving at the students' laboratory. So one day he got there punctually at opening time and waited for me. What he said to me was brief and to the point; however, the words were not what mattered. The overwhelming impression came from the terrible blue eyes with which he looked at me and before which I quailed – like P. in the dream, which to my relief jumbled the roles. Anyone who remembers the great master's splendid gaze (which he retained well into old age) and who ever saw him angry will not find it difficult to empathize with the affects experienced by that young sinner.

But for a long time I was unable to trace the '*Non vixit*' of which I had been so critical in the dream until I realized that these two words had possessed such clarity in the dream not as things heard or spoken but as things *seen*. I then knew instantly where they came from. On the pedestal of the Emperor Joseph memorial in Vienna's Hofburg appear the fine words:

Saluti patriae vixit
non *diu sed totus*

[For the good of the fatherland he lived not long but in full][13]

From this inscription I picked out what suited one of the trains of thought in my dream-thoughts, a hostile one to the effect: 'The fellow has nothing to say in the matter, he isn't even alive.' And now I was obliged to recall that the dream had occurred a few days after the unveiling of the Fleischl memorial in the arcade of the university, when I had seen the Brücke memorial again and must (in my unconscious mind) have mused ruefully on the fact that my gifted friend P., a man wholly devoted to science, had through his premature death forfeited his rightful claim to a memorial in this place. So in my dream I erected such a memorial to him: '*Josef*' had been my friend P.'s first name.[14]

According to the rules of dream-interpretation I should still not be justified in replacing the *non vicit* [present tense] that I need with the *non vixit* [past] supplied by my recollection of the Emperor Joseph monument. Another component of the dream-thoughts must have made this possible as a result of its contribution. I now need to pay some attention to the fact that two currents of thought about my friend P. meet in the dream-scene, one hostile and one affectionate, the former on the surface, the latter concealed, both finding representation in the selfsame words: *Non vixit*. Because of his services to science, I set up a memorial to him; but because he is guilty of an evil wish (as finds expression at the end of the dream) I destroy him. The sentence I have crafted here is a strikingly sonorous one; some model must have influenced me in this connection. But where does such a thought-and-counter-thought arrangement occur, this kind of juxtaposition of two conflicting reactions to the same person, both of which claim to be fully justified yet neither of which has any wish to interfere with the other? In one place only, but it is one that makes a deep impression on the reader: in the apologia spoken by Brutus in Shakespeare's *Julius Caesar*: 'As Caesar loved me, I weep for him; as he was fortunate, I rejoice at it; as he was valiant, I honour him; but, as he was ambitious, I slew him . . .' [Act III, scene 2]. Is that not the same sentence-structure, the same intellectual antithesis as in the dream-thoughts that I have uncovered? So I, in the dream, am playing Brutus. If I could just find in the dream-content a further confirmatory trace of this surprising collateral connection! Well, I think it might be this: My friend Fl. is visiting Vienna in *July*. This detail has no foundation in reality. My friend has never, so far as I know, been in Vienna during the month of *July*. But *July* is named after *Julius Caesar*, so it could very well constitute the allusion I am looking for, i.e. to the intermediate thought that I am playing the role of Brutus.[15]

Remarkably, I did in fact once play Brutus. I took the part of Brutus in a [dramatized] performance of 'Brutus und Caesar' from Schiller's *Poems* in front of an audience of children; I was a boy of fourteen, and I played opposite my nephew, who is a year older than myself. He was visiting us from England at the time – which also made him a kind of *ghost*,[15] because here, once more, was the playmate of my earliest childhood. Up until my third birthday we had been inseparable, very fond of each other yet always fighting, and as I have already indicated it was this childhood relationship that governed all my subsequent emotions in dealings with contemporaries. Since that time, my nephew John has been through a great many incarnations, reviving now one, now another aspect of his nature as fixed indelibly in my unconscious memory. Sometimes he must have treated me very badly, and I must have shown courage in the face of my tyrants because in later years I was often told repeatedly about a brief apologia with which I defended myself when taken to task by my father (his grandfather): 'Why are you hitting John?' In the words of a not-yet-two-year-old, the speech ran: 'I hit him 'cos he hit me.' It must have been this childhood scene that changed the *non vivit* into a *non vixit*, because in the language of later childhood 'hit' [*Schlagen*] becomes 'bash' [*Wichsen* – the sound of which is suggestive of the Latin root *vix*-]; dream-work is not above using such connections. What in reality was a quite unjustified hostility towards my friend P. (who was vastly superior to myself and therefore capable of constituting yet another new edition of my former playmate) undoubtedly derives from my complicated childhood relationship to John.

As I say, I shall be returning to this dream [see below, pp. 496ff.].

Notes

1. ['Childhood impressions' = *Kindereindrücke*. The reader should bear in mind that, because of the 'hard-edged' nature of many German words, *Eindrücke* delivers something like the linguistic impact of 'press-ins'.]

2. ['Green Henry' – 'green' because the eponymous hero likes to dress in that colour.]

3. ['*Der Hafer sticht mich.*' Here English and German sayings almost coincide verbally.]

4. We know that Freud added this paragraph in 1919.

5. [Wilhelm Stekel, *Die Sprache des Traumes*, 1911.]

6. *Internationale Zeitschrift für Psychoanalyse*, II, 1914.

7. [Professor Ernst Brücke, head of the Physiological Laboratory of Vienna University, under whom Freud studied.]

8. [The florin (or gulden) and the kreuzer (worth one hundredth of a florin) constituted the currency of Vienna until 1892.]

9. [Freud cites these words in English.]

10. [Or possibly, 'It was absurd that you didn't give me the supplementary premiums' – not that it matters.]

11. For analyses of other number dreams, see Jung, Marcinowski and other authors. Such dreams often posit very complicated mathematical operations – which the dreamer then performs with astonishing ease. See also [Ernest] Jones, 'Über unbewusste Zahlenbehandlung' ('On dealing with figures unconsciously'), in *Zentralblatt für Psycho-Analyse*, II, 1912, pp. 241f.

12. Neurosis behaves in the same way as dream. I know a patient who suffers from hearing arbitrarily and involuntarily (hallucinating) songs or scraps of songs without being able to understand what they mean so far as her mental life is concerned. (She is certainly not paranoiac, by the way.) Analysis then reveals that, having taken certain liberties with the texts of these songs, she has misapplied them. '*Leise, leise, fromme Weise*' ['Softly, softly, in a pious manner'] she unconsciously understands as '*fromme Waise*' [pronounced identically but meaning 'pious orphan'], which describes herself. '*O du selige, o du fröhliche*' ['Oh thou blessed, oh thou blissful] is the beginning of a Christmas carol, but by not going on to the word 'Christ-

mastide' she turns it into a bridal hymn. And she does other similar things.

Incidentally, the same distortion mechanism may occur without hallucination, simply as an associated idea. The reason why one of my patients is haunted by the memory of a poem he had to learn as a boy:

> *Nächtlich am Busento lispeln . . .*

> [By night on the Busento, whispering . . .]

is that his imagination is content with the incomplete line:

> *Nächtlich am Busen . . .*

> [By night at the breast . . .]

Parody is known to have indulged in the same technique. [The humorous weekly] *Fliegender Blätter* once included among illustrations of German 'classics' a scene from Schiller's 1802 ballad 'Siegesfest' ['Victory feast'] with the prematurely truncated caption:

> *Und des frisch erkämpften Weibes*
> *Freut sich der Atrid und strickt*

> [And the fresh-caught female prisoner makes delighted Atrid knit]

The verse continues:

> *Um den Reiz des schönen Leibes*
> *Seine Arme hochbeglückt.*

> [Both his arms in highest rapture round her captivating form.]

13. The actual inscription is:

> *Saluti* publicae *vixit*
> non *diu sed totus.*

As to the motive for my slip in writing *patriae* instead of *publicae*, Wittels [an early Freud biographer] is probably correct in his guess.

14. As a contribution to multiple determination: my excuse for being late

was that, after working long hours in the evening, next morning I had to make the long journey from *Kaiser-Josef*-Strasse ['Emperor Joseph Street'] to Währinger Strasse.

15. Another one is *Cäsar-Kaiser* ['Caesar-Emperor'].

16. [Freud uses the French word *revenant* – literally, someone who 'comes back'.]

G *Absurd dreams – intellectual performance in dream*

In our dream-interpretations hitherto we have so often come across the element of *absurdity* in dream-content that we are loath to put off any longer investigating where it comes from and what it might mean. Remember, the absurdity of dreams was one of the main arguments put forward by those who, rejecting a positive appraisal of dreams, see them as nothing but the meaningless product of a reduced, fragmented level of mental activity.

I begin with a number of examples in which the absurdity of the dream-content is only apparent; on closer examination of the meaning of the dream, it vanishes completely. These are dreams that (by chance, so it would seem initially) deal with dead fathers.

I

The dream of a patient who had lost his father six years earlier:

His father has been in a major accident. He was travelling by night train, there was a derailment, the seats concertinaed, and his head got squashed together sideways. The patient then sees him lying in bed with a wound running vertically above his left eyebrow. He is surprised to find his father has been in an accident (because he is already dead, as he explains when recounting the dream). *The eyes are so clear.*

According to the prevailing view of dreams, on this occasion the dream-content should have been elucidated thus. Initially, as the dreamer is imagining his father's accident, he has forgotten that the old man has been in his grave for years; as he dreams on, this memory revives and makes him wonder, while still dreaming, at his own dream. However, the first thing analysis of the dream shows is that snatching at such explanations serves no purpose. The dreamer had commissioned an artist to make a *bust* of his father, and two days before the dream he went to inspect it. It is the bust that strikes him as *verunglückt*.[1] The sculptor never saw the father; he is working from photographs he has been given. On the day before the dream itself the pious son sent an old servant of the family to the studio to see whether he too reached the same conclusion regarding the marble head, namely that it has come out *too narrow between the temples*. There now follows the memory material that contributed towards the structure of this dream. The father had had a habit, when plagued by business worries or difficulties in the family, of pressing both hands against his temples as if his head was becoming too wide for him and he was trying to compress it. As a child of four our dreamer had been present when a pistol that happened to be loaded had gone off, blackening his father's eyes (*the eyes are so clear*). In the place where the dream showed the father's injury, the living father, whenever he was thoughtful or sad, had displayed a deep vertical furrow. The fact that in the dream this furrow is replaced by a wound points to the second thing that prompted the dream. The dreamer had taken a photograph of his daughter; the plate slipped out of his hand, and when he picked it up there was a crack running like a vertical furrow down the little girl's forehead as far as the eyebrows. At this, he was unable to ward off superstitious premonitions, because the day before his mother died his photographic plate bearing a portrait of her had cracked.

So the absurdity of this dream is simply the result of a careless piece of linguistic expression, refusing to distinguish the bust and the photograph from the person. We all habitually say things like: 'My father to a T, don't you think?' Of course, the appearance of absurdity in this dream could easily have been avoided. Venturing to pass judgement on the basis of a single experience, one might say that, on this occasion, the appearance of absurdity is permitted or deliberate.

II

A second, very similar example from my own dreams (I lost my father in 1896):

My father, after his death, played a political role among the Magyars, uniting them politically, in which connection I see a small, indistinct image: *a crowd of people, as in parliament; one person standing on a chair or possibly two chairs, with other people around him. I recall that on his deathbed he looked a bit like Garibaldi, and I am pleased that this promise did indeed come true.*

That is absurd enough, surely? It was dreamed around the time when the Hungarians had placed themselves in a state of lawlessness through parliamentary *obstruction* and were going through the crisis from which Koloman Széll liberated them. The minor circumstance that the scene observed in the dream comprises such small images is not without significance as regards explaining this element. The usual visual representation of our thoughts in dream results in images that give us the impression of being approximately life-sized; my dream-image, however, reproduces a wood-engraving inserted into the text of an illustrated history of Austria and showing Maria Theresa at the Pressburg parliament in the famous '*Moriamur pro rege nostro*' scene.[2] Like Maria Theresa on that occasion, in the dream my father is surrounded by a crowd of people; he, however, is standing on a chair [*Stuhl*] or possibly two, making him a *Stuhlrichter*.[3] (He *united them politically* – the link being the saying 'We shan't be needing a *judge*'.) His striking deathbed resemblance to Garibaldi really was apparent to all of us standing around. He had a *post-mortem* temperature rise, his cheeks glowed redder and redder . . . involuntarily, we continue: 'Behind him, bathed in insubstantial light, holding us all in thrall, lay our common lot.'[4]

Such a lifting of our thoughts prepared us for the fact that we should soon have to face precisely this 'common lot'. The '*post-mortem*' nature of the temperature rise corresponds to the words '*after his death*' in the dream-content. The most excruciating of his sufferings was the complete intestinal paralysis (*obstruction*) of his final few weeks. This provides a link for all kinds of disrespectful thoughts. A contemporary of mine, who lost his father while still at senior school (on which occasion, deeply affected, I offered him my friendship) once told me scornfully of the pain suffered by a relative of his whose father had died in the street and been brought home, and when the corpse was undressed it was found that at the time of death or just after (*post-mortem*) there had been a *bowel evacuation*. So distressed was the man's daughter that this ugly detail had the inevitable effect of spoiling her memory of her father. Here we have penetrated as far as the wish that this dream incorporates. *After one's death, to stand pure and tall before one's children* – who would not wish for that? What has happened to absurdity in this dream? Its appearance derives purely from the fact that a perfectly admissible saying, in connection with which we are used to ignoring such absurdity as may lurk between its component parts, is reproduced in the dream with total fidelity. Again, the impression cannot be overlooked that the appearance of absurdity is intentional, that it has been evoked deliberately.[5]

The frequency with which, in dream, dead people appear, acting and interacting with us as if they were alive, has caused undue surprise and produced some curious explanations that make our lack of understanding of the dream-world very evident. Yet the explanation of such dreams is extremely obvious. How often do we find ourselves thinking, '*If* my father were still alive, what would he say about this?' That '*if*' is something that a dream can represent only through the present, in a specific situation. For instance, a young man whose grandfather has left him a large legacy dreams on the occasion of a reproach about heavy spending that his grandfather has come back to life and is calling him to account. What we see as rebellion against the dream, namely the objection flowing from our superior knowledge that the man is indeed dead, is in reality the comforting thought that the deceased need no longer have that experience or a sense of relief that he can no longer interfere.

Another type of absurdity occurring in dreams of dead relatives does not express scorn and derision but serves the most extreme rejection, the representation of a repressed thought that one would like to pretend is utterly unthinkable. Dreams of this kind appear soluble only when it is remembered that dream draws no distinction between the wished-for and the real. For instance, a man who had looked after his father when the latter was ill and had suffered terribly from his death dreamed the following nonsensical dream a short while later: *His father was alive again, talking with him as usual; however,* (the remarkable thing was that) *he was in fact dead, just not aware of it.* This dream makes sense if after the words 'he was in fact dead' we insert '*as a result of the dreamer's wish*' and if we change 'just not aware of it' to 'just not aware that the dreamer had this wish'. During the period of looking after his father the son had often wished him dead – that is to say, had what was in fact the compassionate thought: 'Let death finally put an end to this torment. In the son's grief following the father's death even this sympathetic wish became an unconscious reproach, as if by entertaining it he really had helped to shorten the sick man's life. By awakening the earliest childhood stirrings against the father, it became possible for this reproach to find expression as a dream, but precisely because there was such a world of difference between the dream-trigger and the daytime thought the dream had to assume this absurd form. (See also, in this connection, my 'Formulations on the Two Principles of Mental Functioning'.[6])

The fact is, dreams about the dear departed always present dream-interpretation with problems, and these cannot always be resolved successfully. The reason perhaps lies in the particularly pronounced emotional ambivalence dominating the dreamer's relationship with the dead person. It is very common in such dreams for the deceased to be treated initially as if he were living, then for him suddenly to be referred to as dead, but in the continuation of the dream for him to be alive again. The effect of this is confusing. In the end, I guessed that this interchange between death and life is meant to represent the dreamer's *indifference* ('It's the same to me whether he's alive or dead'). That indifference is of course not actual but wished for; it is meant to help deny the dreamer's very intense, often conflicting emotional attitudes and as such becomes the dream-representation of the dreamer's *ambivalence*. For other dreams featuring dead people, the following rule often helped to point the way. If in the dream there is no reminder that the dead person is in fact dead, the dreamer is comparing himself to the dead person, dreaming of his own death, whereas a sudden occurrence in the dream of the surprised realization that 'he's been dead for some time, surely?' is a protest against such commonality and a rejection, by the dreamer, of the significance of death. However, I admit to feeling that dream-interpretation is still a long way from eliciting all the secrets of dreams having this content.

III

In the example I now cite I am able to catch dream-work in the act of deliberately fabricating an absurdity for which the material provides no occasion whatsoever. The example is from the dream prompted by my encounter with Count Thun prior to my holiday trip [see above, pp. 223ff.]: *I am riding in a one-horse carriage and tell the driver to go to a station. 'I can't make the actual railway journey with you,' I say, he having first raised some objection as if I had overtired him. Yet it is as if I had already come some way with him, covering a stretch for which one would normally have taken the train.* For this confused, nonsensical story analysis furnishes the following explanations. During the day I had taken a one-horse carriage that was to drive me to an out-of-the-way street in Dornbach. However, the driver did not know the way and in the manner of those good folk simply kept on driving until I noticed and showed him the way, not without treating him to a few sarcastic remarks in the process. From that coachman a train of thought leads to aristocrats, one of whom I am to meet later. Provisionally, simply the suggestion that to us bourgeois plebs the aristocracy stand out because they have a predilection for the coachman's place; Count Thun, of course, drives the *Austrian* 'coach of state'. The next section of the dream, however, relates to my brother – meaning that I identify him with the coachman of the one-horse carriage.

447

This year I had turned down the idea of our travelling to Italy together ('*I can't make the actual railway journey with you*'), and this refusal was a sort of punishment for his usual complaint to the effect that I *overtire* him on these trips (which finds its way into the dream unchanged) by making unreasonable demands on him in terms of asking him to accept a too-rapid change of location or too much beauty in one day. My brother had come with me to the station that day but had got out at the Westbahnhof suburban-railway stop just before the station to catch a suburban train to Purkersdorf. I had pointed out to him that he could stay with me a while longer by travelling to Purkersdorf not by suburban railway but with the Western Railway. What got into the dream from that was that I had travelled some way *in the carriage – covering a stretch for which one would normally have taken the train*. In actual fact it was the other way around (and as the saying goes, '*The other way around is a journey too*').[7] I had told my brother, 'The journey you make by suburban railway you can also make in my company by taking the Western Railway.' The entire dream-confusion is caused by myself in that, in the dream, I say 'carriage' instead of 'suburban railway' (which incidentally does no harm as regards conflating the coachman with my brother). This gives me, in the dream, something nonsensical, something that explanation seems scarcely capable of disentangling and that comes close to creating a contradiction of an earlier speech of mine ('*I can't make the actual railway journey with you*'). However, since there is absolutely no need for me to confuse suburban railway and one-horse carriage, I must have made up this very puzzling story in the dream deliberately.

Why, though? What we need to find out now is: what does absurdity in dream mean, and for what reasons is it permitted or created? In the foregoing case, the answer to the secret is this. In the dream I need an absurdity and something incomprehensible in connection with 'travelling' because in the dream-thoughts I have a certain opinion that demands to be represented. One evening in the company of the hospitable and witty lady who appears in another scene of the same dream as 'a housekeeper' I had heard two riddles

I was unable to solve. The rest of the company knew them, so with my unsuccessful efforts to find the answer I cut a somewhat ridiculous figure. They involved puns on the [German] words for 'descendants' and 'ancestors'.[8] I believe they went like this:

> *Der Herr befiehlt's,*
> *Der Kutscher tut's.*
> *Ein jeder hat's,*
> *Im Grabe ruht's. (Ancestors)*

[The master commands it, the coachman does it. Everyone has it, it lies in the grave.]

Confusingly, the second riddle has the same two lines as the first:

> *Der Herr befiehlt's,*
> *Der Kutscher tut's.*
> *Nicht jeder hat's,*
> *In der Wiege ruht's. (Descendants)*

[The master commands it, the coachman does it. Not all possess it, it lies in the cradle.]

Now, when I saw Count Thun *drive up* [likewise *vorfahren*] so authoritatively and when I slipped into Figaro's fancy of seeing the merit of high-ups as lying in their having taken the trouble to be born (thus becoming *descendants* [*Nachkommen*]), these two riddles became intermediate thoughts for dream-work purposes. Since aristocrats are easily interchangeable with coachmen and since it used to be the custom, in our part of the world, to address the coachman as *Herr Schwager* [the word now means 'brother-in-law'], compression made it possible to include my brother in the same piece of representation. However, the dream-thought operating in the background here is: *It's nonsense, being proud of one's ancestors. I prefer to be an ancestor, a forebear, myself.* So because of this verdict ('It's nonsense') we have the nonsense of the dream. Now, presumably, the last riddle of this obscure dream-passage is also solved – namely, that I had *travelled* with the coachman *before* [*vorhergefahren* = *vorgefahren*].

A dream, then, is made absurd if one element of the content of the dream-thoughts is the opinion: *'That's nonsense'* – if, in fact, any kind of criticism and mockery motivate one of the dreamer's unconscious trains of thought. Absurdity, in other words, becomes a means whereby dream-work represents contradiction – reversal of a material relationship between dream-thoughts and dream-content, for instance, or exploitation of a feeling of motor inhibition. However, the absurdity of a dream should not be translated by a simple 'no'; it is intended to reflect the arrangement of the dream-thoughts at the same time as deriding or laughing at the contradiction. This is the only purpose for which dream-work comes up with something ridiculous. Here again it turns *a portion of the latent content into a manifest form.*[9]

Actually, we have already come across a convincing example of such a meaning in an absurd dream. The dream (interpreted without analysis) of the Wagner performance that lasts until a quarter to eight in the morning, where the orchestra is conducted from the top of a tower, etc. (see above, p. 357), is clearly trying to say, 'This is an *upside-down* world and a *crazy* society. Anyone deserving doesn't succeed, and anyone who doesn't make a fuss, does' (by which the dreamer means what is happening to her as compared with what is happening to her cousin). Likewise, the fact that the first examples of the absurdity of dreams to present themselves to us were dreams about dead fathers is no coincidence. Here, the conditions for the creation of absurd dreams are present in characteristic guise. The authority that typifies fatherhood drew the child's criticism at an early stage; the strict demands made by its father drove the child to seek relief in keeping a sharp lookout for every sign of weakness on its father's part; however, the piety that, in our way of thinking, surrounds the person of the father, particularly after his death, strengthens the censorship that prevents expressions of such criticism from reaching consciousness.

IV

Another absurd dream about my dead father:

I receive a letter from the municipal council of my native town about payment owed for a stay in hospital in 1851 that I had needed following an accident. I laugh at this, because for one thing I had yet to be born in 1851 and for another my father, to whom it might relate, is already dead. I go to him in the next room, where he is lying in bed, and tell him about it. To my surprise, he recalls that he had, back in 1851, once been drunk and had had to be locked up or taken into protective custody. It was when he worked for the firm of T— 'So you drank, too?' I ask. 'And you got married shortly after that?' I work out that I was in fact born in 1856, which I imagine as coming immediately afterwards.

The way in which this dream positively flaunts its absurdities is something that, after the foregoing remarks, we shall translate simply as indicating a particularly bitter and impassioned polemic in the dream-thoughts. We are all the more astonished, then, to note that in this dream the polemic is conducted openly and my father is described as the person at whom the mockery is addressed. Such openness appears to contradict our assumptions regarding censorship in dream-work. However, one explanation is that in this case my father is only a front man, as it were, while the argument is with another person, who appears in the dream as a result of a single allusion. Where dreams normally deal with rebellion against other people, behind whom one's father is concealed, in this case it is the other way around; my father becomes a front to hide others, and the reason why the dream is able to deal so frankly with his otherwise sacrosanct person is that it also involves the certain knowledge that he is not the one really meant. These circumstances are learned through what occasioned the dream. The fact is, the dream occurred after I had heard that a senior colleague, whose judgement is considered impeccable, was expressing scorn and surprise that a patient of mine should be continuing psychoanalytical work with me *for a fifth year*. The first few sentences of the dream serve in a transparently disguised fashion to indicate that for a while this colleague had undertaken the duties my father was no longer able to perform (*payment owed, a stay in hospital*); and as the friendship between us began to dissolve I found myself experiencing the same conflict of sensibilities as is forced on one by the role and former functions of the father in the event of a disagreement between father and son. The dream-thoughts now defend themselves fiercely against the charge that I am *not making progress fast enough*, which extends from my treatment of this patient to include other things as well. So does he know of anyone who could make it faster? Does he not realize that such conditions are otherwise quite incurable and last a lifetime? What are *four or five years* compared to the span of an entire life, particularly if, during treatment, the patient's existence has been so greatly improved?

In this dream, the stamp of absurdity largely results from the fact that sentences from different areas of the dream-thoughts are placed one after another with no transitional material. For instance, the sentence beginning '*I go to him in the next room*' quits the topic from which the foregoing sentences emerged and faithfully reproduces the circumstances of my telling my father of my high-handed betrothal. It is trying to remind me of the noble selflessness that the old man evinced at the time and to contrast this with the behaviour of someone else, a different person. I note at this point that the reason why the dream is allowed to make fun of my father is that, in the dream-thoughts, he is held up as an example to others in full acknowledgement. It is in the nature of all censorship that, of the things that are banned, a person is more likely to be allowed to say what is not true than the truth. The next sentence (that he recalls *once having been drunk and therefore locked up*) contains nothing else that in reality relates to my father. The person covered by him is none other than the great – Meynert, in whose footsteps I followed with such huge respect and whose conduct towards me, after a brief period of preferential treatment, changed abruptly to undisguised hostility. The dream reminds me of his own announcement that he had once, as a young man, indulged in the habit of *drugging himself with chloroform* and had for that reason had to *withdraw to an institution*; it also puts me in mind of a second experience with him, shortly before his demise. I had had a bitter literary argument with him about male hysteria (which he denied), and when I visited him during his terminal illness and asked how he was feeling he described his condition at some length, closing with the words, 'As you know, I was always a prime case of male hysteria.' To my satisfaction and surprise, he had admitted something he had stubbornly fought against for so long. However, the reason why I am able, in this scene of the dream, to cover Meynert with my father does not lie in my having found an analogy between the two figures; it lies in a brief but wholly adequate representation of a conditional sentence in the dream-thoughts. In full, that sentence runs, 'Yes indeed, if I were second generation, the son of a Professor or Counsellor [*Hofrat*], I should of course have made more rapid progress.' In the dream, I actually make my father a Counsellor and Professor. The most glaring and disturbing absurdity in the dream lies in the treatment of the number of the year, *1851*, which I see as no different from *1856, as if the five-year difference meant nothing at all*. However, that is exactly what is meant to be given expression from the dream-thoughts. *Four or five years* is the period of time during which I enjoyed the support of the colleague I mentioned before, but it is also the time I made my fiancée wait to be married, and by a chance coincidence that the dream-thoughts are happy to exploit it is the time I am now making my most familiar patient wait for a complete cure. '*What are five years?*' the dream-thoughts ask. '*No time at all, so far as I am concerned, not worth bothering about.* I have plenty of time ahead of me, and as the thing you also refused to believe in did eventually come about, I shall make this happen too.' However, the number *51*, separated from the century, is also differently determined (in the opposite sense, in fact); that is why it crops up in the dream several times. Fifty-one is the age when a man appears to be particularly at risk, the age when I have seen colleagues die suddenly, including one who after a prolonged wait had been made professor only days previously.

V

A different absurd dream that plays with numbers:

An acquaintance of mine, Mr M., has been attacked, in an essay, by no less a person than Goethe – with unjustified vehemence, we all think. Mr M. is of course crushed by this article. He complains bitterly about it at a dinner party; however, his admiration for Goethe sustains no damage from this personal experience. I try for my own benefit to throw some light on the temporal circumstances, which seem to me improbable. Goethe died in 1832; since his attack on M. must of necessity have occurred earlier, Mr M. was then a very young man. It strikes me as plausible that he was eighteen. However, I am not sure what year we are in at present, so the whole calculation sinks into obscurity. The attack, incidentally, is contained in Goethe's well-known essay 'Die Natur'.

We shall soon be in possession of the means of justifying the stupidity of this dream. Mr M., whom I met at a dinner party, had recently asked me to examine his brother, who was beginning to display symptoms of *paralytic mental disturbance*. The supposition was correct; during the visit, much to my embarrassment, without the conversation offering any occasion for it, the patient exposed his brother by referring to his *youthful exploits*. I had asked the patient for his date of birth and repeatedly made him make small calculations in order to bring out how his memory was deteriorating – tests in which he in fact acquitted himself very well. I am already aware that in the dream I am behaving like a paralytic. (*I am not sure what year we are in.*) Other material in the dream stems from another still-vivid source. A friend of mine who edits a medical journal had accepted for publication in his magazine an extremely harsh, indeed *'destructive'* review of my [Berlin] friend Fl.'s latest book, the reviewer being *very young* and scarcely competent to judge. Believing I had a right to intervene, I took the editor to task; he greatly regretted accepting the review but refused to promise a remedy. I promptly broke off relations with the journal, stressing in my letter of cancellation that I hoped *our personal relations would not suffer as a result of this business*. The third source of the dream is the account a female patient had just given me of the onset of the mental illness that had attacked her brother, which had caused him to fall into a fit of maniacal rage, shouting, '*Nature, nature!*' The doctors thought the cry came from reading that fine *essay by Goethe* and pointed to the patient having overtaxed himself with his studies of natural philosophy. I preferred to think of the sexual sense in which even the less well-educated among us speak of 'nature', and the fact that the unfortunate fellow went on to mutilate himself in the genital region appeared at least not to prove me wrong. *Eighteen* was the age of the patient when the fit occurred.

If I add that my friend's book, which had come in for such harsh criticism ('One wonders whether the author is crazy or one is crazy oneself,' another critic had written), deals with life's *temporal circumstances* and attributes Goethe's tally of years to a multiple of a biologically significant number, it is plain to see that in the dream I am putting myself in my friend's place. (*I try to throw a little light on the temporal circumstances.*) However, I conduct myself like a paralytic and the dream wallows in absurdity. In other words, the dream-thoughts are saying ironically, 'He's the fool, *of course*, the madman, and you are the geniuses, you know better. But might it perhaps be the other way around?' And that *reversal* is generously represented in the dream-content in that *Goethe* attacked the young man (which is absurd), whereas it would be easy, even today, for someone very young to attack the immortal Goethe, and in that I calculate from the *year of Goethe's death*, whereas I had the paralytic calculate from the *year of his birth*.

But I also promised to show that no dream is prompted by other than egoistical stimuli. That means I must justify the fact that in this dream I make my friend's cause my own and put myself in his place. My critical conviction in the waking state is not equal to the task. However, the story of the eighteen-year-old patient and the different interpretations of his cry of 'Nature!' alludes to the conflict into which I have brought myself vis-à-vis most doctors with my assertion of a sexual aetiology for psychoneuroses. I can tell myself: 'Like your friend, you too will fare similarly with the critics, have to some extent already done so', and now I can substitute a 'we' for the 'he' in the dream-thoughts: 'Yes, you're right, we are a pair of fools.' That *mea res agitur* is something I am forcefully reminded of by mention of the brief, incomparably beautiful essay by *Goethe*, since it was a recitation of that essay in a popular lecture that pushed me, a vacillating school-leaver, into studying the natural sciences.

VI

I still owe an explanation as to why yet another dream (in which my 'I' does not feature) is egoistical. I mentioned a short dream in the last chapter [see above, p. 282] in which Professor M. pronounces the words: '*My son, the myopic* . . .', and I stated that this was simply an introductory dream coming before another in which I do play a role. Here is the missing main dream, which presents us with an absurd, incomprehensible neologism for elucidation:

Because of certain things that have happened in the city of Rome it is necessary to spirit the children away, which is what is done. The scene is then in front of a gateway, a double gateway of the kind built in antiquity (the Porta Romana *in Siena, as I am aware in the dream itself). I am sitting on the edge of a fountain, very depressed, almost weeping. A female (gatekeeper, nun) brings the two boys out and hands them over to their father, who is not me. The elder of the two is clearly my eldest, I cannot see the other one's face; the woman bringing the boys asks him for a farewell kiss. She has a prominent red nose. The boy declines to kiss her but says as, in parting, he shakes her by the hand, 'Auf Geseres' and to us both (or one of us) 'Auf Ungeseres'. I take the latter to indicate a preference.*

This dream is based on a sheaf of ideas stimulated by a play I had seen at the theatre, *The New Ghetto [Das neue Ghetto]*. The Jewish question, concern about the future of children who cannot be given a homeland,[10] concern about how to bring them up in such a way that they can become liberal – all these things are easily recognizable in the relevant dream-thoughts.

'*By the waters of Babylon, there we sat down and wept.*'[11] Siena, like Rome, is famous for its beautiful fountains; for Rome, when I am dreaming (see also above, pp. 209ff.), I need to find some kind of substitute from places I know. Near Siena's *Porta Romana* we saw a large, brightly lit house. We learned that it was the *Manicomio*, the lunatic asylum. A short while before the dream I had heard that a co-religionist[12] had had to give up his laboriously acquired position at a state lunatic asylum.

Our interest is aroused by the spoken words '*Auf Geseres*' where in accordance with the situation recorded in the dream one would inevitably have expected '*Auf Wiedersehen*' ['Till we meet again' – the usual way of saying 'Goodbye' in German] and by its wholly nonsensical counterpart '*Auf Ungeseres*'.

According to information gathered from scriptural scholars, '*Geseres*' is a genuine Hebrew word; a derivative of the verb '*goiser*', it is best rendered as 'enjoined suffering, [a person's] undoing'. As used in slang, it apparently means 'weeping and wailing'. '*Ungeseres*' is my very own neologism and after initially attracting my attention baffles me completely. The little comment at the end of the dream (that '*Ungeseres*' represents something preferable to '*Geseres*') opens the door to associated ideas and hence to understanding. The same relationship exists with regard to caviar; the *unsalted* stuff is more highly prized than the *salted*. Caviar to the general,[13] 'noble passions': this carries a jocular allusion to a member of my household who, since she is younger than myself, will I hope take care of my children's future. It is in line with this that another member of my household, our excellent nanny, is recognizably portrayed in the dream as the gatekeeper (or nun). However, there is still no connecting link between the '*salted–unsalted*' pair and '*Geseres–Ungeseres*'. In '*leavened–unleavened*' [respectively '*gesäuert*' and '*ungesäuert*'] there is such a link; in the rush of their flight from Egypt, the children of Israel had no time to allow their bread dough to ferment, and to this day they eat unleavened bread at Easter-time to commemorate the fact. Here I can also introduce the associated idea that suddenly occurred to me during this portion of the analysis. I recall how in the last days of *Easter* we were strolling, my friend from Berlin and I, through the streets of Breslau,[14] a city that was unfamiliar to us. A little girl asked me the way to a certain street; I had to apologize, telling her I did not know the street, and then, turning to my friend, I said, 'One hopes that in later life the girl will show greater perspicacity in choosing the people she asks to guide her.' Shortly thereafter I spotted a nameplate: 'Dr *Herodes*, consulting hours . . .' I thought, 'Not a paediatrician, one hopes.' My friend, meanwhile, had been treating me to an account of his views on the biological significance of *bilateral symmetry* and had begun one sentence with the words, 'If we had one eye in the middle of our forehead, like the *Cyclops* [*Zyklop*] . . .' This led to the remark made by the professor in the preliminary dream: '*My son, the myopic* [*Myop*] . . .' And I had now been steered to the principal source of '*Geseres*'. Many years ago, when this son of Professor M. (now an independent thinker) was still sitting at a *schooldesk*, he contracted an eye infection that according to the doctor gave cause for concern. So long as it remained *unilateral*, he said, there was nothing to worry about, but if it were to spread to the *other eye* it would be serious. The disease healed in one eye with no harm done; shortly afterwards, however, symptoms did indeed start to appear in the other eye. Horrified, the boy's mother immediately summoned the doctor to the solitude of their country retreat. But the doctor promptly *switched sides*. '*What's all this weeping and wailing?*' ['*Was machen Sie für Geseres?*'] he barked at the mother. 'If it got better on one side, it'll get better on the *other*.' And it did, too.

And now the connection with myself and members of my household. The *schooldesk* at which Professor M.'s son acquired his first pearls of wisdom was given away by the young man's mother and passed into the ownership of my eldest, in whose mouth (in the dream) I place the words of farewell. One of the wishes that can be attached to that attribution is now easily guessed. But the desk is supposed to be constructed in such a way as to protect the child against becoming *short-sighted* and *lopsided* [one-sided]. Hence, in the dream, *myopic* (with the *Cyclops* behind it) and the comments on *bilaterality*. The concern about *one-sidedness* has more than one meaning; it may refer not only to physical one-sidedness but also to one-sided intellectual development. But does not the dream-scene, in its madness, appear to negate just such a concern? After the child has *on the one hand* [*nach der einen Seite hin*] said his farewell, *on the other hand* he calls out the opposite – as if to restore the balance. *The child, as it were, acts in accordance with bilateral symmetry!*

A dream, then, is often most deeply meaningful where it appears to be craziest. All down the ages those with something to say that they could not say without danger have readily donned the fool's cap. The listener for whom the forbidden words were intended tolerated them better if in the process he was able to laugh and flatter himself with the opinion that what was unpleasant clearly had its foolish side. Just as dreams behave in reality, so the prince behaves on stage when he has to resort to playing the fool, which is why we can also say of dreams what Hamlet, suppressing the real circumstances and substituting a jesting incomprehensibility, says of himself:

> I am but mad north-north-west: when the wind is southerly, I know a hawk from a handsaw! [= 'heron-shaw' or simply 'heron']¹⁵

So my solution to the problem of absurdity in dream is to this effect: dream-thoughts are never absurd (at least, not in connection with the dreams of people of sound mind), and dream-work produces absurd dreams and dreams with individual absurd elements when it is presented, in the relevant dream-thoughts, with criticism, mockery and derision for portrayal in its form of expression. I now want to show that dream-work actually amounts to no more than a combination of the said three factors (together with a fourth, yet to be mentioned); I want to show that it does nothing but translate the relevant dream-thoughts in accordance with the four conditions prescribed and that the question of whether the dreaming mind operates with all its intellectual abilities or only some of them is in fact wrongly posed and misses the real point. However, since there are a great many dreams in which judgements are passed, criticisms voiced and facts acknowledged, in which astonishment at a particular element of the dream appears, explanations are ventured and lines of argument put forward – in the light of all this I must counter the objections arising from such circumstances with the aid of selected examples.

My rejoinder is this: *Everything occurring in dreams as an apparent exercise of judgement should not be seen as some sort of intellectual performance on the part of dream-work but belongs to the material of the relevant dream-thoughts and has made its way from there, as a finished object, into the manifest dream-content.* In fact I can go further: even of the opinions that we form *after waking* with regard to a remembered dream and of the feelings that our reproducing the dream evoke in us, much belongs to the latent dream-content and needs to be fitted into any interpretation of the dream.

I) I have already cited a striking instance of this [pp. 345f.]. A patient declines to recount her dream on the grounds that it is *too unclear*. She saw a person in the dream and does not know *whether it was her husband or her father*. A second dream-fragment then ensues in which a 'dung-basket' features. This prompts the following memory. As a young housewife she had once jokingly remarked in the presence of a young relative who often visited the house that her next concern must be to procure a new dung-basket. She was sent one next morning, but it was filled with lilies of the valley. This dream-fragment serves to represent the saying, 'Not grown on my own dungheap.' Pursuing the analysis to its conclusion leads to the discovery that the relevant dream-thoughts deal with the after-effects of a story heard in her younger days of a girl who had fallen pregnant in circumstances where it *was unclear who the actual father was*. In other words, here a dream-account spills over into waking thought and causes one of the elements of the dream-thoughts to be represented by a judgement about the whole dream passed by the waking mind.

II) A similar case: a patient of mine has a dream that strikes him as interesting, because the moment he wakes up he says to himself,

'*I must tell the doctor about that.*' When analysed, the dream provides very clear allusions to an affair that he had begun during treatment and of which he had resolved *to tell me nothing*.[16]

III) A third example from my own experience:

I am walking to the hospital with P. through a district in which there are houses and gardens. I have an idea that I have seen this district before in several previous dreams. I am a bit lost; he shows me a route leading through a particular area to a restaurant (indoor, not outdoor), where I ask for Frau Doni. I am told she lives with three children in a small room at the rear of the building. I proceed in that direction and before I get there encounter an unclear person with my two little girls, whom I then take with me, having first stood with them for a while. A kind of reproach to my wife for leaving them there.

On waking up I experience great *satisfaction*, which I attribute to thinking that I shall now, from analysis of the dream, discover what people mean when they say, '*I've had this dream before.*'[17] However, analysis of the dream teaches me nothing about it, showing me only that the feeling of satisfaction belongs to the latent dream-content and not to a judgement about the dream. It is *satisfaction at the fact that in my marriage I have been given children*. P. is a woman with whom I walked side by side along some of life's way, who then far outstripped me both socially and materially, but whose marriage remained childless. The two triggers of the dream can take the place of proof through full analysis. The previous day I had read in the paper the announcement of the death of a Frau *Dona A—y* (from which I make my *Doni*), who died in *childbirth*; my wife informed me that the deceased had been attended by the same midwife as herself when she bore our two youngest. The name *Dona* had caught my attention because I had recently come across it for the first time in an English novel. The other thing that prompted the dream was the date of the latter occasion; it was the night before the birthday of my eldest son, who appears to have a talent for writing.

IV) I was left with a similar feeling of satisfaction after waking from the absurd dream that my father, after his death, played a political role among the Magyars [see above, p. 444], when it was motivated by continuation of the feeling that had accompanied the final section of the dream: *I recall that on his deathbed he looked a bit like Garibaldi, and I am pleased that it did indeed come true . . . (Then a continuation that I have forgotten.)* I am now, as a result of analysis, able to supply the missing part of this dream. It is the mention of my second son, to whom I gave the forename of a great historical personage who in my boyhood years, particularly after my stay in England, exerted a powerful attraction over me. All through the year preceding the birth I harboured the intention of employing this very name if it was a boy, and it was with great *satisfaction* that I used it to greet the newborn. It is easy to see how the suppressed megalomania of the father transfers itself to the children in his thoughts; indeed, one would like to believe that this is one of the ways in which such suppression of the same as life necessitates does in fact occur. The boy owes his right to be included in the context of this dream to the fact that at the time he suffered the same accident (readily excusable in both the infant and the moribund), namely that of soiling one's linen. See also, in this connection, the *'Stuhlrichter'* allusion and the dream-wish: to stand before one's children *tall and pure* (see above, p. 445).

V) If I am now to select expressions of opinion or judgements that remain within the confines of the dream-state itself and do not persist in the waking state or transfer themselves to the waking state, my task will be made much easier if I am allowed to use dreams that have already been recounted for other purposes. The dream about *Goethe* attacking Mr M. [see above, p. 454] appears to contain numerous acts of judgement. *'I try for my own benefit to throw some light on the temporal circumstances, which seem to me improbable.'* Does that not look like a critical reaction against the nonsense of Goethe allegedly mounting a critical attack on a young man of my acquaintance? *'It strikes me as plausible that he was eighteen.'* That surely sounds like the result of a calculation, albeit a feeble-minded one.' And *'I am not sure what year we are in at present'* would be an instance of doubt or uncertainty in dream.

The fact is, however, I know from having analysed this dream that these acts of judgement, apparently first made in the dream, by their wording admit of a different view, as a result of which they become indispensable for the process of dream-interpretation while at the same time any absurdity is avoided. With the sentence '*I try for my own benefit to throw some light on the temporal circumstances*' I am putting myself in my friend's shoes, so to speak; he really is trying to throw light on the temporal circumstances of life. The sentence thus loses the character of a verdict directed against the nonsense of previous sentences. The interpolation '*which seem to me improbable*' belongs together with the later '*It strikes me as plausible*'. It was with almost the same words that I answered the lady who had told me her brother's medical history: '*In my view, the cry "Nature, nature" is unlikely to have had anything to do with* Goethe: *far more plausible to me is that it had the sexual significance you know of.*' Here, incidentally, a judgement has been made, but not in the dream: in reality – in connection with an occasion recalled and exploited by the relevant dream-thoughts. The dream-content appropriates that judgement like any other fragment of the dream-thoughts.

The number 18, with which the judgement is nonsensically associated in the dream, still preserves the trace of the context from which the real judgement was wrenched. Lastly, the fact that '*I am not sure what year we are in at present*' is simply and solely intended to assert my identification with the paralytic in whose examination this one clue really had arisen.

In connection with analysing the acts of judgement apparently made in dream, it is worth remembering the rule laid down at the outset as regards performing the task of interpretation: the coherence of dream-components established in a dream should be set aside as mere appearance; each element needs to be traced back in its own right. A dream is a conglomerate that for the purposes of investigation should be taken apart and reduced to its original elements. On the other hand, note that in dreams a psychical force finds expression that creates that apparent coherence, subjecting the material acquired by dream-work to *secondary processing*. We have before us here expressions of that force that we shall later acknowledge to be the fourth of the factors involved in dream-formation.

VI) Let me think of other instances of judgement being exercised in dreams I have already recounted. In the absurd dream of the communication from the council [see above, p. 451] I ask, '*And you got married shortly after that?*' I work out that I was in fact born in 1856, which I imagine as coming immediately afterwards. This takes the exact form of a *conclusion*. My father got married in 1851, shortly after the accident; I am the eldest child, born in 1856; that's right, then. We are aware that this conclusion is falsified by wish-fulfilment, knowing as we do that the dream-thoughts are dominated by the words *four or five years, no time at all, counts for nothing*. However, each step of this conclusion, in terms of both content and form, should be seen as having been dictated by a different dream-thought. It is the patient of whose patience my colleague complains who intends to get married as soon as the cure is complete. The manner in which I conduct myself with my father in the dream recalls an *interrogation* or *examination* and hence a university tutor who during the registration period would record full personal particulars: born when? 1856 – *Patre*? At this one gave one's father's first name with a Latin ending, and we students assumed that the tutor drew *conclusions* from the father's forename that the forename of the person registering did not always allow him to draw. So the *drawing of a conclusion* in the dream would simply echo the *drawing of a conclusion* that forms part of the material of the dream-thoughts. This teaches us something new. If a conclusion occurs in the dream-content, it undoubtedly springs from the dream-thoughts; however, it may be contained in the dream-thoughts as a piece of remembered material, or it may tie a series of dream-thoughts together as a logical ribbon. Either way, the conclusion in the dream represents a conclusion from the dream-thoughts.[18]

This would be the place to continue analysing this dream. The tutor's interrogation is followed by my recalling the roll of students at the university (which in my day was written in Latin). Also by my general progress as a student. Again, the *five years* prescribed for studying medicine were not enough for me. I worked on quite happily for several more years, and among my circle of friends I was considered lazy; people doubted whether I would ever be *'finished'*. I then made a *rapid* decision to take my exams and did indeed complete the course – *in spite of the delay*. A further reinforcement of the dream-thoughts, which I defiantly hold up to my critics. 'And even if you refuse to believe it, since I am taking my time; I am in fact nearly finished, I'm approaching a *conclusion*. This has often been the case before.'

The beginning of the same dream contains several sentences in respect of which it cannot easily be denied that they are in the nature of a line of argument. And that line of argument is not even absurd; it might equally well be from waking thought. *I laugh at this* [the letter from the council], *because for one thing I had yet to be born in 1851 and for another my father, to whom it might relate, is already dead.* Both are not only correct in themselves; they also chime completely with the actual lines of argument that I should deploy if such a letter arrived. We know from the previous analysis (see above, p. 451) that this dream sprang from deeply embittered dream-thoughts steeped in scorn; if we are further permitted to assume that the motives for censorship are extremely strong, we shall understand that dream-work has every reason to create a *faultless refutation of a nonsensical and unreasonable demand* after the pattern contained in the dream-thoughts. However, our analysis shows that the dream-work involved here was not in fact given a free hand to rewrite history, as it were, but that material from the dream-thoughts had to be used for the purpose. It is as if an algebraic equation contained not only numbers but a + and a –, a power sign and a radical sign, and someone who transcribed that equation without understanding it took the operative signs together with the numbers into his copy but then muddled them both up. Both arguments can be traced to the ensuing material. It distresses me to think how some of the premises on which I base my psychological resolution of psychoneuroses, once they become known, will draw forth disbelief and ridicule. I must maintain, for example, that impressions from as early as the second year of life, sometimes even from the first, leave a lasting trace in the emotional life of the subsequent invalid and (albeit in many instances distorted and exaggerated by memory) may result in the first and deepest reason for a hysterical symptom. Patients whom I confront with this at a suitable point usually parody the recently acquired explanation by saying that they are willing to search for memories from the period *before they were born*. I expect a similar reception to be given to the discovery of the unsuspected part played by the *fathers* of female patients in their earliest instances of sexual arousal (see the discussion on pp. 271ff.). And yet it is my well-founded conviction that both are true. To back this up, I can think of a number of examples where the father died when the child was very young and subsequent incidents for which there is no other explanation show that the child has in fact unconsciously retained memories of the person who disappeared from his or her life at such an early stage. I know that both my claims are based on *conclusions* whose validity will be contested. So it is a piece of wish-fulfilment if the material of precisely *those conclusions* that I fear will be disputed is used by dream-work to produce *impeccable conclusions*.

VII) In a dream that I only touched on before [see above, p. 429] there is a clear expression, at the beginning, of amazement at the topic occurring.

Old Brücke must have set me some problem; strangely enough this has to do with dissecting my own underpinnings, my pelvis and legs, which I see before me in the dissecting room but without being aware of missing them on my body and without any feeling of horror. Louise N. is standing beside me, working with me. The pelvic girdle has been emptied of its contents, revealing now the view from above, now the view from below, all muddled up. There are thick, flesh-coloured lumps visible (which even in the dream remind me of piles). It was also necessary to pick something out with great care, something that lay over it and looked like tinfoil.[19] Then I was once again in possession of my legs and making an excursion through the city, though (because of weariness) in a carriage. To my astonishment the carriage drove in through a house-door, which opened to allow it to pass along a passage that, having turned a corner, eventually carried on further into the open air.[20] Eventually, I was hiking with an Alpine guide (who carried my

*things) through a shifting landscape. On one stretch (out of consider-
ation for my weary legs) he carried me. The ground was swampy;
we circled it; there were people sitting on the ground, a girl among
them, like Red Indians or gypsies. Previously, I had made progress
over the slippery ground myself, constantly amazed that, after the
dissection, I am able to do this so well. At length we came to a small
wooden hut that terminated in an open window. There the guide
set me down and laid two planks, which stood there ready, on the
windowsill in such a way as to bridge the abyss that needed to be
negotiated from the window. I now felt really anxious about my
legs. Instead of the anticipated crossing, however, I saw two grown
men lying on wooden benches against the walls of the hut and two
children, as it were, sleeping beside them. As if not the planks but
the children were to make the crossing possible. I wake up with
mental fright.*

Anyone who has even once received a proper impression of the
sheer richness of dream-compression will easily be able to imagine
the number of sheets of paper that thorough analysis of this dream
must fill. Fortunately, all I am going to extract in this connection is
an instance of amazement in a dream, as revealed in the interpolation *'strangely enough'*. I look at what triggered the dream. It
was a visit from the same Louise N. who assists me with the problem
in the dream. 'Lend me something to read.' I offer her *She* by Rider
Haggard. 'A *strange* book but full of hidden meaning,' I want
to explain to her; 'the Eternal Feminine, the immortality of our
emotions . . .' She interrupts me at this point: 'I know that already.
Haven't you anything of your own?' 'No, my own immortal works
have not yet been written.' 'So when are they coming out, your
so-called "ultimate explanations" that you say we too will be able
to read?' she asks somewhat provocatively. Here I become aware
that someone else is prompting me through her mouth, and I say
nothing. I think of the effort of will it is costing me to place before
the public even the work on dreams, in which I must expose so
much of my own inner being. 'The best things you can know you
still mayn't tell to boys.'[21] In other words, the dissection carried out
on my own body, which is the problem set me in the dream, is the

self-analysis associated with communicating dreams. Old Brücke rightly comes into this; even in the earliest years of my scientific career it sometimes happened that I kept quiet about a discovery until his vigorous admonitions forced me to publish it. But the further thoughts that develop from my talk with Louise N. reach too deep to become conscious; they are diverted by way of the material that is incidentally stirred up in me by mention of Rider Haggard's *She*. It is to this book and to another by the same author, *Heart of the World*, that the judgement *'strangely enough'* applies, and many elements of the dream are taken from these two fantastical novels. The swampy ground over which one is carried, the abyss to be crossed with the aid of the planks that have been brought along – these come from *She*; the Red Indians, the girl, the wooden hut – these are from *Heart of the World*. In both novels a woman is the guide; both concern dangerous journeys (in *She*, this is a bold venture into the unexplored, indeed virtually untrodden). The weary legs, according to a note I find with the dream, are an actual sensation experienced at the time. No doubt they went with a mood of weariness and the despairing question, 'How far will my legs go on carrying me?' In *She*, the adventure ends with the guide, rather than obtaining immortality for herself and the others, meeting her death in the mysterious central fire. That kind of fear unmistakably stirred in the dream-thoughts. The *wooden hut* is undoubtedly also the *coffin*, i.e. the tomb. However, in representing this most unwelcome of thoughts by a piece of wish-fulfilment, dream-work here delivered its master stroke. You see, I had already been in a tomb, but it was an Etruscan tomb near Orvieto, one that had been emptied of its contents, a narrow chamber with two stone benches along the walls on which the skeletons of two adults had been laid. That is precisely how the interior of the hut in the dream looks, except that the stone has been replaced by wood. The dream seems to be saying, 'If you have to be in the tomb already, let it be the Etruscan tomb', and with this substitution it turns the saddest expectation into a highly desirable one. Unfortunately, as we shall hear, it can only transform the image accompanying the affect into its opposite, not always the affect itself. As a result, I wake up with '*mental fright*', after the idea has forcibly secured representation that children may possibly achieve what their father failed to do – a further allusion to that strange novel in which a person's identity is maintained through a two-thousand-year line of generations.

VIII) In connection with another dream we find not only an expression of surprise at what is experienced in the dream but also, bound up with it, an attempted explanation so striking, so far-fetched and so ingenious that I should have to subject the whole dream to analysis for that reason alone – even if the dream did not possess two further points to attract our interest. On the night of 18–19 July I am travelling on the Southern Railway line and hear an announcement in my sleep: '*Hollthurn, ten minutes.*' *I immediately think of holothurians* [sea-cucumbers] – *a natural history museum – that this is a place where brave men unsuccessfully defended themselves against the superior might of their sovereign. Ah yes, the Counter-Reformation in Austria! As if it was a town in Styria or the Tyrol. Now I can dimly see a small museum in which the remains or acquisitions of these men are kept. I should like to get out but hesitate. There are women with fruit on the platform, squatting on the ground and holding their baskets out invitingly. The reason for my hesitation was not being sure whether we had enough time, and here is the train, still motionless. Suddenly, I am in a different carriage, where leather and seats are so narrow that one is pressing directly against the back rest.*[22] *I am surprised at this,* but of course I may have changed carriages in my sleep. *Several people, including an English brother and sister; a row of books clearly on a shelf on the wall. I can see* The Wealth of Nations *and* Matter and Motion (*by* [James Clerk] *Maxwell*), *thick tomes bound in brown linen. The man asks his sister about a book by Schiller, whether she has forgotten it. The books are sometimes mine, sometimes theirs. I should like to join in the conversation to offer confirmation or support* ... I wake up sweating profusely because all the windows are closed. The train has stopped at Marburg [in Styria].

As I am writing the dream down a fragment occurs to me that was trying to escape memory. *I tell the siblings in connection with*

a certain work, 'It is from . . .', then correct myself: 'It is by . . .'[23]
The man remarks to his sister, 'Now he's got it right.'

The dream begins with the name of the station, which must presumably have failed to wake me completely. I replace that name, which is Marburg, with Hollthurn. That I heard Marburg from the first or possibly a subsequent announcement is proved by the mention, in the dream, of Schiller, who was of course born in Marburg, albeit not the one in Styria.[24] I was in fact travelling first class on this occasion, but it was in extremely unpleasant circumstances. The train was crowded. In the compartment I had come across a lady and gentleman who seemed very distinguished and who lacked the style or did not deem it worth the effort to make any secret of their aversion to the intruder. My polite greeting went unreturned; although the man and the woman were sitting side by side (with their backs to the engine), the woman lost no time, as I looked on, in reserving the window seat opposite her with an umbrella; the door was closed immediately, and pointed remarks were exchanged about the window being opened. No doubt they quickly had me down as a fresh-air fiend. It was a warm night, and the air in the wholly sealed compartment soon became stifling. My travel experience has taught me that such aggressively selfish behaviour is typical of people who have not paid for or have paid only half the value of their tickets. When the conductor arrived and I presented my dearly purchased ticket, the following deliberately opaque and almost threatening remark issued from the lady's lips: 'My husband has authorization.' She was an imposing figure with displeasure etched on her features, and she was not far off the age when a woman's beauty deserts her; her husband said nothing at all but simply sat there, motionless. I tried to sleep. In my dream I wreak hideous vengeance on my unlovely travelling companions; no one would suspect how much abuse lies buried beneath the shreds and scraps of the first half of the dream. This need once assuaged, the second wish asserted itself, namely to switch compartments. The dream switches scene so frequently and without the slightest offence being taken at the change that it would not have been the least bit conspicuous if my memory had immediately replaced my travelling companions by more pleasant ones. Here, however, we have an instance of something or other objecting to the change of scene and thinking it requires explanation. How did I suddenly find myself in a different compartment? I could not recall having made the change. So there was only one explanation: *I must, in my sleep, have alighted from the carriage* – a rare occurrence but one for which the experience of neuropathologists can in fact furnish examples. We know of people who undertake railway journeys in a state of doziness without giving any indication of their abnormal condition until, somewhere along the way, they come to completely and are then astonished at the gap in their memory. In the dream, then, I pronounce just such a case of '*automatisme ambulatoire*' to be mine.

Analysis enables me to offer another solution. The attempted explanation that I find so surprising when I had to attribute it to dream-work is not original but copied from the neurosis of one of my patients. I have already spoken elsewhere [see above, p. 274] about a well-educated and in life soft-hearted man who, shortly after the death of his parents, began to accuse himself of murderous leanings and was now suffering from the precautionary measures he had to take to guard against such inclinations. It was a case of grave obsessions coupled with full retention of insight. At first, strolling in the street was spoiled for him by a compulsion to account personally for where all the passers-by went; if, as he followed someone with his gaze, that individual suddenly disappeared, he would be left with the painful feeling and the mental possibility that he might have despatched them. Among other things there was a Cain fantasy behind this, because 'all men are brothers'. Given the impossibility of living up to this ideal, he stopped going out for walks and spent his life imprisoned within his own four walls. However, even in his room news constantly reached him through the newspaper of murders that had taken place in the outside world, and his conscience tended to suggest to him, in the form of doubts, that he was the wanted assassin. For a while, being sure that he had not left the flat for weeks shielded him from these charges, until one day the possibility occurred to him that he might have *gone out of the house in an unconscious state* and so committed the murder without realizing. From then on he locked the front door and gave the key to the aged housekeeper, insisting that she never let it fall into his hands, even should he ask for it.

Hence, therefore, the attempted explanation (that I had changed carriages in a state of unconsciousness) is taken from the material of the dream-thoughts and put straight into the dream, where it is clearly intended to identify me with the person of that patient. Recollection of him was aroused in me by suggestive association. A few weeks previously I and that man had caught the last night-train. Cured, he was travelling with me to his relatives in the country, who had asked to see me; we had a compartment to ourselves, where we left all the windows open all night long and, for as long as I stayed awake, enjoyed splendid conversation. I was aware that feelings of enmity towards his father in sexual contexts during his childhood had lain at the root of his illness. So by identifying with him I was trying to admit something similar to myself. The second scene of the dream does really dissolve into a spirited fantasy to the effect that the reason why my two elderly travelling companions treated me so coldly is that my coming thwarted their plan to exchange intimacies during the night. The fantasy, however, goes back to an early childhood scene in which the child, probably driven by sexual curiosity, finds its way into the parental bedroom and is banished therefrom by the father's authority.

I consider it superfluous to cite further such instances. They would all merely confirm what we have learned from those already given – namely, that an act of judgement, in a dream, simply repeats an example from the dream-thoughts. It is usually an ill-fitting repetition, thrust into an unsuitable context, but occasionally (as in our last examples) one so skilfully employed as to give an initial impression that perhaps independent mental activity is taking place in the dream. On this basis we might turn our attention to that psychical activity that, while it does not appear to exercise a regular influence on dream-formation, takes care, when it does so, to blend dream elements of different provenance into a consistent, meaningful whole. However, before we do that we feel there is a pressing need to deal with expressions of emotion as they occur in dreams and to compare them with the affects that analysis discovers in the relevant dream-thoughts.

Notes

1. [The word carries two meanings: it echoes the fact that the dreamer's father has been in an accident, and it suggests that the sculptor has failed to capture his likeness.]

2. I have forgotten in which author's work I found mention of a dream in which there were masses of unusually small images, a dream whose source turned out to be one of the engravings of Jacques Callot, which the dreamer had been looking at during the day. Incidentally, those engravings contain an enormous number of very small figures; one series concerns the horrors of the Thirty Years War. [Pressburg = Bratislava, now the capital of Slovakia but then one of the regional seats of the Austro-Hungarian monarchy.]

3. [*Stuhlrichter*: literally, a 'chair judge'; historically, a county court judge in Westphalia; colloquially, the president of a 'kangaroo court'.]

4. [What the mourners recite are Goethe's lines, part of an ode written in honour of his recently deceased friend Schiller:

Und hinter ihm, in wesenlosem Scheine
Lag, was uns alle bändigt, das Gemeine.]

5. [Three things need to be elucidated in connection with this paragraph. If Freud is being ironic in the first sentence, it is relevant to point out that '*Gemein*', as well as denoting 'common', can also denote 'horrid'. Secondly, 'bowel evacuation' is '*Stuhlentlehrung*' – that '*Stuhl*' again! And in the 'saying' '*Nach seinem Tode rein und gross vor seinen Kindern dazustehen*', 'stand . . . before' = 'appear to'; actual standing is of course impossible for a corpse.]

6. ['Formulierungen über die zwei Prinzipien des psychischen Geschehens' (1911); *Standard Edition*, vol. XII, p. 215.]

7. ['*Umgekehrt ist auch gefahren*' is an Austrian saying, of course.]

8. ['*Vorfahren*' and '*Nachkommen*'. Both words carry connotations of time and place, and in the first couplet of each riddle they mean, respectively, 'drive on' and 'keep up'.]

9. Dream-work, in other words, parodies the thought it has marked out as ridiculous by creating something ridiculous in regard to that thought. Heine does something similar when he sets out to poke fun at the poor verse written by the Bavarian king. He does so in lines that are even worse:

> *Herr Ludwig ist ein grosser Poet,*
> *Und singt er, so stürzt Apollo*
> *Vor ihm auf die Knie und bittet und fleht,*
> *'Halt ein, ich werde sonst toll, oh!'*

> [Mr Ludwig is a famous bard, and when he sings, Apollo sinks to his knees
> before him and implores, 'Do stop, or I'll go mad, methinks!'
>
> Heinrich Heine, *Lobgesänge auf König Ludwig*
> [('Hymns of praise to King Ludwig')]

10. [The German word is of course *Vaterland* – literally: 'fatherland'.]

11. [Ps. 137:1. Quotations from the Bible are as rendered in the Revised Standard Version (RSV). A recommended (though less accessible) Jewish English translation of the Jewish scriptures, by Rabbi Avraham J. Rosenberg, is published by the Judaica Press in their Tanach Series.]

12. [The very secular Freud does actually use the word *Glaubensgenosse* here (literally: 'faith-comrade'). Presumably he meant simply a fellow Jew.]

13. [An allusion to *Hamlet*, Act II, scene 2, where 'general' = 'general public' and the phrase means much the same as 'pearls before swine'.]

14. [Now Wrocław in Poland.]

15. [*Hamlet*, Act II, scene 2. Freud notes at this point:] This dream also provides a good example of the generally valid principle that dreams of the same night, though separated in memory, spring from the same thought-material. Incidentally, the dream-situation in which I spirit my children away from the city of Rome is distorted by being retrospectively linked to a similar occurrence from my childhood. The point is that I envy certain relatives who had an opportunity many years back to move their children to a different country.

16. Such a reminder contained in the dream itself or the resolution '*I must tell the doctor about that*' in connection with dreams occurring during psychoanalytical treatment regularly corresponds to a major resistance to confessing the dream and is not infrequently followed by the patient's forgetting the dream.

17. A subject on which a wide-ranging discussion has developed in recent volumes of the *Revue philosophique* ('Paramnesia in dream').

18. These findings correct certain details of my earlier statements about how logical relationships are portrayed (see above, p. 328). Those remarks describe the general behaviour of dream-work but fail to take account of its most delicate, most meticulous achievements.

19. *Stanniol* [in German], an allusion to Stannius, [author of] *Nervensystem der Fische* (see p. 429).

20. The place in my apartment building where residents park their prams [*Kinderwagen* – literally, 'baby carriages']; but otherwise multiply determined.

21. [See above, p. 173.]

22. I myself find this description incomprehensible, but I follow the principle of recording a dream in the words that occur to me when I am writing it down. The words chosen are themselves a part of dream-representation.

23. [Freud quotes himself in English here.]

24. Schiller was born not in a place named Marburg but in Marbach, as every German schoolboy knows – and as I knew myself. It is another of those errors (see also p. 232, note 8) that creep in as a substitute for a deliberate falsification elsewhere and that I tried to explain in my *Psychopathologie des Alltagslebens* [*The Psychopathology of Everyday Life*, of which there is a new translation by Anthea Bell in the New Penguin Freud, London 2002].

H *Affects in dream*

A perceptive comment by Stricker drew our attention to the fact that expressions of emotion in dream do not permit the kind of disparaging dismissal with which we tend to shrug off dream-content on waking: 'If in dream I am afraid of robbers, the robbers may be imaginary but the fear is real', and the same applies when I feel happy in dream. According to the evidence of our senses, an affect experienced in dream is of no lesser quality than one of similar intensity experienced while we are awake; moreover, the affect content of a dream will stake a more vigorous claim to being numbered among real mental experiences than its ideational content. We do not bring this classification into play in the waking state because we have no other way of appreciating an affect psychically than by associating it with a particular ideational content. If affect and ideational content fail to match in terms of type and intensity, our waking judgement becomes confused.

In dreams, people have always been surprised that ideational content does not bring with it the affect influence that in waking thought we should regard as inevitable. Strümpell maintains that, in dream, ideas are stripped of their psychical values. However, in dream there is no lack of the opposite state of affairs as well – namely, that intensive expression of affect occurs in connection with a content that appears to offer no occasion for such release. In dream I may be in an atrocious, risky, appalling situation yet feel neither fear nor aversion; on another occasion I may be horrified by harmless things and delighted by things that are childish.

This riddle of the world of dream vanishes as suddenly and

completely as perhaps no other if we make the transition from manifest dream-content to latent dream-content. Explaining it will not be our business, since it has ceased to exist. Analysis shows us *that ideational content has undergone shifts and substitutions while affect content remains unchanged.* No wonder the ideational content, altered by dream-distortion, no longer matches the affect, which is still the same; but nor should it any longer be a source of surprise that analysis has restored the correct content to its former position.[1]

In a psychical complex that has undergone the influence of resistance censorship, affects are the part least influenced and the only part capable of pointing us in the direction of the proper completion. Even more clearly than in dreams this relationship reveals itself in psychoneurotic conditions. Here, the affect is always right, at least in terms of its quality; its intensity can of course be increased by shifts in neurotic attention. When the hysteric is surprised by the need to have such fear of a minor detail or the obsessive that so keen a reproach can proceed from a trifle, both are making the mistake of assuming that the ideational content (the minor detail or the trifle) constitutes the essence, and they defend themselves in vain by taking that ideational content as the starting-point for their thinking. Psychoanalysis then shows them the right way by, on the contrary, recognizing the affect as legitimate and looking for the idea that goes with it but has been ousted by a replacement. The prerequisite here is that affect-release and ideational content do not form the kind of indissoluble organic entity we tend to treat them as but that both elements can be soldered together in such a way that analysis is able to separate them. Interpreting dreams shows that this is indeed the case.

My first example is one in which analysis explains the apparent absence of affect in connection with an ideational content that ought to compel affect-release.

I

In a desert she sees three lions, one of which is laughing, but she is not afraid of them. Then, however, she must have fled from them after all because she is about to climb a tree but finds her cousin, who is a French teacher, already up there etc.

Analysis supplies the following additional material. The trivial occasion of the dream was supplied by a sentence in her English homework: 'The mane is the *lion's* adornment.' Her father wore that kind of beard; it framed his face like a *mane*. Her English teacher's name is Miss *Lyons*. A friend sent her the ballads of [Carl] *Loewe* ['lion' in English]. So those are the three lions; why should she have any fear of them? She recalls reading a story in which a black man who has been inciting his fellows to revolt is hunted with bloodhounds and climbs up a tree to save himself. Then, very jauntily, come such scraps of memory as the advice about how to catch lions given in [the satirical weekly] *Fliegender Blätter*: 'Take a wilderness and pass it through a sieve; lions will be what you are left with.' Another one is the highly amusing but none too decent story of the humble office worker who, when asked why he did not try harder to ingratiate himself with his boss, replies that he had tried creeping but his immediate superior was *already up there*. All this material becomes comprehensible when one learns that, on the day of the dream, the lady received a visit from her husband's manager. He treated her with extreme courtesy, kissing her hand, and *she was not at all afraid of him*, despite the fact that he was [as they say in German, where we should perhaps say a 'big cheese'] a very *'big animal'* and in the capital of her country was considered a *'social lion'*. That lion, in other words, is like the one in *A Midsummer Night's Dream*, who turns out to be Snug the joiner – as are all dream-lions who do not inspire fear.

II

My second example is taken from the dream [see above, p. 169] of that girl who saw her sister's little boy lying dead in a coffin but without (as I now add) experiencing any trace of pain or grief. Analysis tells us why not. The dream merely disguised her wish to see the man she loved once more; the affect must have been tuned to the wish rather than to its disguise. So there was no occasion for grief.

In some dreams, the affect is still at least connected to the ideational content that has replaced the one that matches it. In others, the loosening-up of the complex is taken further. The affect appears wholly separated from its associated idea and is accommodated elsewhere in the relevant dream, where it fits into the new arrangement of the dream-elements. The situation is then similar to the one we found in connection with acts of judgement in dream. If among the dream-thoughts there is an important conclusion, the relevant dream will itself contain one; however, the conclusion in the dream may be shifted to quite different material. It is not unusual for this shift to take place in accordance with the principle of opposites.

The latter possibility is one I shall illustrate in terms of the following example, a dream I have subjected to the most exhaustive analysis.

III

A castle by the sea, later situated not directly on the sea but on a narrow canal leading to the sea. The governor is a Mr P. I am standing with him in a large, three-windowed drawing room outside which wall-projections rise like battlements. I have been assigned to the garrison as a sort of voluntary naval officer. Being in a state of war, we fear the arrival of enemy warships. Mr P. plans to go away; he is giving me instructions as to what should happen if the thing we fear transpires. His sick wife is in the threatened castle with the children. If the bombardment starts, the great hall is to be evacuated. He is breathing heavily and is about to leave; I hold him back and ask how I am to get news to him if I need to. Thereupon, after saying something further, he immediately falls down dead. No doubt I had been placing an unnecessary strain on him with my questions. After his death, which otherwise makes no impression on me, thoughts about whether the widow will remain in the castle and whether I should report the death to headquarters and as the next in command take over running the castle. I am now standing at the window, surveying the ships going by; they are merchantmen, speeding past over the dark water, some with several chimneys, others with bulging decks (very like the station buildings in the [unreported]² preliminary dream). *Then my brother is standing beside me and we are both looking out of the window at the canal. One ship alarms us and we cry, 'Here comes the warship.' It turns out, however, that it is only the same ships coming back that I know already. At this point a small ship comes along that is strangely truncated, ending in mid-girth; visible on deck are some strange objects resembling cups or pots. We call out with one voice, 'Here's the breakfast-ship.'*

The rapid movement of the ships, the very dark blue of the water, the brown smoke of the chimneys – all these things together convey a tense, gloomy impression.

The places in this dream are drawn from several trips to the *Adriatic* region (Miramare, Duino, Venice, Aquileia). A brief but most enjoyable Easter visit to *Aquileia* with my brother a few weeks before the dream was still fresh in my memory. The *naval war* between America and Spain and, bound up with this, concerns about the fate of my relatives living in America also play a part. Affective influences are prominent at two points in the dream. In one place, an affect that might have been expected fails to materialize; express emphasis is laid on the fact that the governor's death makes no impression on me. Another time, as I think I spot the warship I feel *alarmed* and am aware, in my sleep, of all the sensations of alarm. Affects are accommodated in this well-structured dream in such a way that any striking contradiction is avoided. There is no reason, after all, why I should feel alarm at the death of the governor, whereas it is doubtless fitting that, as the castle's commanding officer, the appearance of the warship should alarm me. What analysis reveals is that Mr P. is simply a substitute for myself (in the dream I am his substitute). I am the governor who suddenly dies. The dream-thoughts have to do with the future of my family after my premature death. No other painful thought is contained in the dream-thoughts. The alarm that in the dream is soldered to the sight of the warship needs to be prised loose from there and affixed here. Conversely, analysis shows that the area of the dream-thoughts from which the warship is taken is packed full of the most delightful reminiscences. It was a year earlier in Venice that we were standing, one magically beautiful day, at the windows of our room on the Riva Schiavoni, looking out over the blue of the lagoon, where there was more movement that day than usual. Some English[3] ships were expected, which were to be given a ceremonial reception, and suddenly my wife called out gaily, like a child, *'Here comes the English warship!'* In the dream these same words alarm me; we see again that spoken words in dream derive from spoken words in life. I shall show in a moment how even the word 'English' in this piece of speech does not escape the relevant dream-work. Here, then, between dream-thoughts and dream-content I am turning happiness into alarm and need only intimate that with this change I am myself giving expression to part of the latent dream-content. However, the example is proof that dream-work is at liberty to unbind the cause of an affect from its attachments in the dream-thoughts and insert it anywhere else in the dream-content.

I seize on this incidental opportunity to subject the 'breakfast-ship' (the appearance of which in the dream so nonsensically concludes a situation that had been recorded quite rationally) to more detailed analysis. Looking at the dream-object more closely, I am struck in hindsight by the fact that it was black and by the fact that its being cropped at its widest point made it look, at this end, very like something that had caught our interest in the museums of Etruscan towns. This was a rectangular tray of black clay with two handles on which stood things like coffee-cups or tea-cups – not entirely dissimilar to one of our modern services for the *breakfast table*. Our enquiries revealed that this was the toilet-set of an Etruscan lady, bearing boxes of make-up and powder; and we remarked in jest that it would not be a bad idea to take such a thing home to the wife. The dream-object, in other words, means – *black toilet-set/outfit*, mourning, and alludes directly to a death. The other end of the dream-object is reminiscent of the *Nachen* (from the root νέχυς, as my linguistically sophisticated friend tells me)[4] in which in prehistoric times corpses were laid and consigned to the sea for burial. This explains why in the dream the ships are coming back.

Silently, on the salvaged vessel, the old man drifts into port.[5]

It is the return voyage after the shipwreck [*Schiffbruch*; literally, 'ship-breaking']; the breakfast-ship is indeed broken, as if right across. But where does the name come from? This is where the 'English' comes in that we had spare in connection with the warships – '*breakfast*'. The '*breaking*' refers to the shipwreck; the '*fasting*' links up with the black toilet-set/outfit.

However, in this 'breakfast-ship' it was only the name that the dream rearranged. The thing existed and puts me in mind of one of the merriest episodes of the last trip. Not trusting the food in Aquileia, we had brought our own from Görz [Gorizia], purchasing a bottle of superb Istrian wine in Aquileia. And while the little post-steamer slowly passed along the delle Mee canal into the desolate stretch of the lagoon below *Grado* we, the only passengers, in the merriest of moods, breakfasted on deck, enjoying the meal as we had seldom enjoyed a breakfast before. So that was the '*breakfast-ship*', and it is precisely behind this reminiscence of the most pleasurable enjoyment of life that my dream conceals the most depressing thoughts about an unknown, sinister future.

The detachment of affects from the bodies of ideas that brought them forth is the most striking thing that happens to them in dream-formation, but it is neither the sole change nor the most important change that they undergo on the way from dream-thoughts to manifest dream. If we compare the affects in the dream-thoughts with those in the dream, one thing becomes clear immediately: wherever there is an affect in the dream, the same affect is also present in the dream-thoughts, but not the other way around. Dreams generally are poorer in affects than the psychical material that they process and from which they spring. When I reconstruct the relevant dream-thoughts, I can see how the most intense mental stimuli regularly struggle to assert themselves therein, usually in conflict with others that are in sharp contradiction. If I then look back at the dream, I not infrequently find it colourless, lacking that more intense emotional tone. Through dream-work, not only the content but also, in many cases, the emotional tone of my thinking has been reduced to the level of the trivial. Dream-work, I might say, has brought about a *suppression of affects*. Take, for instance, the dream of the botanical monograph [first recounted pp. 181ff.]. Its equivalent in thought is an impassioned plea for my freedom to act as I do, to arrange my life in such a way as I and I alone think right. The dream proceeding therefrom sounds unimportant: I have written a monograph, a copy of it lies before me, it has colour plates, dried plants come with each book. The dream resembles the calm of a field of corpses: none of the din of battle is audible any more.

Things can be different, of course: lively expressions of emotion can enter into dream itself. But let us, for the moment, dwell on the undoubted fact that so many dreams appear trivial, whereas one cannot make the dream-thoughts one's own without feeling deeply involved.

The full theoretical explanation for this suppression of affect during dream-work cannot be given here, for it would require us to go most meticulously into the theory of affects and into the mechanics of suppression. Here I want to mention only two thoughts on the subject. Affect-release is something that (for other reasons) I need to see as a centrifugal process directed towards the interior of the body, analogous to the processes of motor and secretory innervation. Just as during sleep the transmission of motor impulses towards the outside world appears to have been halted, so too might the centrifugal arousal of affects be made more difficult during sleep by unconscious thought. That would make the affective stimuli occurring as the dream-thoughts run their course inherently weak stimuli and hence those finding their way into the subsequent dream no stronger. According to this line of thinking, 'suppression of affects' would not be a product of dream-work at all but a consequence of sleep. That may be so, but it cannot possibly account for everything. Another thing we must consider is that every halfway composite dream has also turned out to be a compromise resulting from a conflict of psychical forces. On the one hand, the thoughts constituting the wish have to battle against contradiction by a censoring authority; on the other hand, we have often observed that in unconscious thinking itself each train of thought was yoked together with its contradictory counterpart. Since all those trains of thought are affect-capable, we shall hardly, by and large, be mistaken if we regard affect-suppression as flowing from the inhibition that the opposites exert upon one another and that censorship exerts upon the tendencies it has suppressed. *This would make affect-inhibition the second product of dream-censorship, as dream-distortion was the first.*

I should like at this stage to cite an instance of a dream in which the trivial sensory atmosphere of the dream-content can be explained by the conflictual nature of the dream-thoughts. I need to recount the following brief dream, which every reader will note with disgust.

IV

A hill on which there is a sort of open-air lavatory, a very long bench with a large hole at one end. The entire rear edge is thickly covered with piles of faeces of all sizes and stages of freshness. Behind the bench there is scrubland. I urinate on the bench; a long stream of urine rinses everything clean, the splodges of excrement come off easily and fall down the aperture. A sense that at the end there is still something left.

Why, in dreaming this, did I feel no revulsion?

The reason, as analysis shows, is that this dream was in part brought about by the most pleasant and satisfying thoughts. During the analysis, I think immediately of the *Augean stables* that Hercules cleans. I am that Hercules. The hill and the scrubland are modelled on Aussee,[6] where my children are currently staying. I am the discoverer of the infantile aetiology of neurosis, thus preventing my own children from falling ill. The bench (except for the aperture, of course) faithfully reproduces a piece of furniture given to me by a devoted female patient. It reminds me of the high regard in which my patients hold me. Even the museum of human excrement is in fact capable of a heart-warming interpretation. Although it disgusts me when I am there, in the dream it brings to mind a beautiful country, Italy, where of course all lavatories in small towns look like that. The stream of urine that rinses everything clean is an unmistakable reference to a delusion of grandeur. That is how Gulliver puts out the big fire among the Lilliputians, despite the fact that in doing so he incurs the displeasure of the tiny queen. But Gargantua too, Maître Rabelais' superman, takes his revenge on the people of Paris by riding on Notre-Dame and directing his stream of urine at the city. I had been leafing through Garnier's illustrations to Rabelais before going to sleep the evening before. And, oddly, here is further evidence that the superman is me! The platform of Notre-Dame used to be my favourite place in Paris; every free afternoon I would climb around on the towers of the cathedral among the monsters and gargoyles that hung there. That all the excrement disappears so rapidly in the stream is the motto '*Afflavit et dissipati sunt*', which is the heading I shall one day give to the section on treating hysteria [see also above, pp. 277–8].

And now the real trigger of the dream. It had been a hot summer afternoon; in the evening I had given my lecture on the link between hysteria and perversion, and everything I had contrived to say thoroughly displeased me and seemed to me stripped of all value.

I was weary, I took no pleasure whatsoever in all my hard work and I longed to be far away from this rummaging in human filth, I longed for my children and then for the beauties of Italy. In this mood I left the lecture theatre and went to a café to sit at an outside table and take a modest snack, for my appetite had deserted me. However, one of my listeners accompanied me, asking to be allowed to sit with me as I drank my coffee and struggled with my pastry, and he began to say flattering things to me: how much he had learned from me, and that he now saw everything through different eyes, and that I had cleaned out the *Augean stables* of error and prejudice in neurosis theory – briefly, that I was a very great man. My mood scarcely matched his eulogy; struggling with nausea, I went home early to get away, and before going to bed I leafed through my Rabelais and read a novella by C. F. Meyer, 'The Sufferings of a Boy'.

It was from this material that the dream had sprung. The novella by Meyer contributed the memory of scenes from childhood (see also the dream of Count Thun, final image [first recounted on pp. 223ff.]). The day's mood of disgust and weariness imposed itself on the dream in so far as it was permitted to supply almost all the material for the dream-content. During the night, however, the contrary mood of powerful, even immoderate self-emphasis took hold and swept the other away. The dream-content had to assume a form that enabled the same material to give expression both to the delusion of inferiority and to an overestimate of self. This compromise formation resulted in an ambiguous dream-content but also (as a result of a reciprocal inhibition of opposites) in a rather trivial sensory tone.

According to the wish-fulfilment theory, this dream would not have been made possible had not the opposite notion (suppressed, admittedly, but carrying the emphasis of pleasure) of a delusion of grandeur been added to that of disgust. The fact is, embarrassing things are not meant to be represented in dream. That which embarrasses us in our daytime thoughts can only force its way into a dream if at the same time it lends itself (by the way in which it is couched) to a piece of wish-fulfilment.

There is something else that dream-work can do to affects in dream-thoughts, apart from admitting them or reducing them to nothing. It can *turn them into their opposite*. We have already come across the rule of interpretation whereby each element of a dream can also, so far as interpretation is concerned, represent its opposite just as easily as itself. One never knows in advance whether to take the one or the other; only the context decides. A suspicion of this state of affairs clearly imposed itself on popular consciousness; when it comes to interpreting dreams, dream-books very often proceed on the principle of contrast. This kind of transformation into the opposite is made possible by the deep associative linkage that in our thinking binds the idea of a thing to its opposite. Like every other shift, it serves the purposes of censorship, but it is also often the product of wish-fulfilment, for wish-fulfilment, after all, consists simply in replacing an unlovely object with its opposite. Just like notions of things, then, affects in dream-thoughts can also appear to have been reversed in the relevant dream, and this turning of affects into their opposite is likely, most times, to have been brought about by dream-censorship. After all, in social life too (and social life provides us with the usual analogy for dream-censorship), both *affect-suppression and affect-reversal* primarily serve the object of *disguise*. When I am in conversation with a person with regard to whom I must exercise caution, while I should like to say hostile things it is almost more important that I hide my feelings from that person than that I govern how I word my thoughts. If, addressing him in words that are not impolite, I nevertheless accompany them with a look or gesture of hatred or scorn, the effect I have upon that person is not so very different than if I had thrown my derision in his face mercilessly. So censorship tells me above all to suppress my affects, and if I am a master of disguise I shall feign the opposite affect, smiling when I am angry and simulating affection where I should prefer to lash out.

We are already familiar with an excellent example of this kind of affect-reversal in dream serving the purposes of dream-censorship. In the 'my uncle's beard' dream [first mentioned on p. 151ff.] I feel great affection for my friend R. – whereas and for the reason that

487

the associated dream-thoughts dismiss him as a dunce. It was this instance of affect-reversal that gave us the first indication of the existence of such a thing as dream-censorship. There is no need to assume here either that dream-work creates such a counter-affect entirely from scratch; usually it finds it lying to hand in the material of the dream-thoughts and simply enhances it with the psychical force of the defensive motive until it is able (so far as forming the relevant dream is concerned) to prevail. In the uncle dream to which I have just alluded, the tender counter-affect probably stems from an infantile source (as the continuation of the dream suggests), because for me, given the special nature of my earliest childhood experiences (see also the analysis on p. 438 above), the uncle/nephew relationship became the source of all friendships and all hatreds.

An excellent example of this kind of affect-reversal is found in a dream reported by Ferenczi:

> An elderly gentleman is woken up during the night by his wife, who had become anxious because he was laughing so loudly and unrestrainedly in his sleep. The husband later explained that he had had the following dream: *I was lying in my bed, a man I know entered the room, I tried to turn the light on, couldn't, kept trying – no good. At that my wife got out of bed to help me, but she could do nothing either; then, feeling embarrassed in the man's presence because of her state of undress, she eventually gave up and climbed back into bed; all this was so comical that I had a terrible laughing fit. My wife asked, 'What are you laughing at, what are you laughing at?' but I simply kept on laughing until I woke up.* Next day the gentleman was very depressed and had headaches – 'From all the laughter that had racked me,' he thought.
>
> Looked at analytically, the dream appears less amusing. In the latent dream-thoughts the 'man I know' who enters the room is the image, which he had recalled the previous day, of death as the 'great unknown'. The old gentleman, who suffered from arteriosclerosis, had had occasion, the day before, to think about dying. The unrestrained laughter takes the place of weeping and sobbing at the idea of having to die. It is the light of life that he can no longer turn on.

This sad thought may have linked up with certain recent optimistic but unsuccessful attempts at sexual intercourse, in connection with which even the assistance of his wife in a state of undress had been no good to him; he realized that he had already reached his declining years. Dream-work was able to transform the sad notion of impotence and dying into a comic scene and the sobbing into laughter.[7]

There is a class of dreams that have a special claim to be termed 'hypocritical' and that test the wish-fulfilment theory severely. My attention was drawn to them when at a meeting of the Viennese Psychoanalytical Association [*Wiener Psychoanalytische Vereinigung*] Dr M. Hilferding brought up for discussion an account of a dream related by Rosegger.[8] I reproduce his account.

In the second volume of his *Waldheimat* ['Forest home'], in the story entitled 'Fremd gemacht' ['Fired'; p. 303], Rosegger writes:

I enjoy sound sleep as a rule, yet I've lost many a night's rest; alongside my modest existence as a student and man of letters I have for years been dragging the shadow of a veritable tailor's existence[9] around with me like a spectre, unable to shake it off.

It is not true that during the day I have spent so much time and energy thinking about my past. A fellow with ambition, a real 'angry young man' sprung from the skin of a Philistine, has other things to do. But nor is your likely lad going to devote a great deal of thought to his nightly dreams; only later, once I had got into the habit of reflecting on everything or possibly when the Philistine in me had begun to stir again, did it occur to me to wonder why in my dreams (when I dreamed at all) I was always the tailor's journeyman and as such spent so long working in my master's workshop unpaid. I was very well aware, as I sat beside him sewing and ironing, that I did not really belong there any more, that as a city-dweller I should have been getting on with other things; yet I was always on holiday, I was always out in the sunny open, and that was why I was sitting there, assisting my master. I often felt quite uncomfortable about it, I regretted the loss of time that I might have put to better use.

Occasionally, when something refused to come out exactly according to measurement and cut, I had to take a hiding from my master; yet there was never any question of wages. Often, sitting there in the dark workshop with shoulders hunched, I resolved to give notice and make myself scarce. Once I even did, but my master paid no heed, and next thing I was back sitting beside him, sewing.

What a pleasure it was to wake up after such hours of boredom! So I made up my mind that, if this persistent dream ever presented itself again, I should throw it off vigorously, crying, 'It's just an illusion, I'm lying in bed, trying to sleep . . .' And the very next night, back I was, sitting in the tailor's workshop.

It went on like that for years with eerie regularity. Then, one night, as we were both working, my master and I, at Alpelhofer's (he was the farmer where I had begun my apprenticeship), my master showed himself to be quite exceptionally dissatisfied with my work. 'Scatterbrain!' he grumbled. 'Where are those thoughts of yours? – that's what I'd like to know!' And he gave me a black look. I felt the most sensible thing I could do in the circumstances would be to stand up, tell my master I was only with him as a favour, and walk off. But I didn't do it. I made no objection when my master took on an apprentice and told me to make room for him on the bench. I moved over into the corner and went on sewing. That same day we took on another journeyman, too, a bigot, a Czech who had worked for us nineteen years before, when on one occasion, walking back from the pub, he had fallen into the ditch. When he now tried to sit down, there was no room. I looked enquiringly at my master, who told me, 'You, you're no great shakes at tailoring, *you can go, you're fired.*' Mightily alarmed, I woke up.

The first light of dawn shone in through the clear windows, illuminating my familiar home. I was surrounded by art objects; in my stylish bookcase stood my timeless Homer, my towering Dante, my incomparable Shakespeare, my glorious Goethe – all the great masters, all the immortals. From the next room there came to me the high voices of the children, now awake and playing with their mother. I felt as if I was discovering this idyllic sweetness, this peaceful, poetic, brightly cerebral existence in which I had experienced such tranquil human bliss so often and so deeply – I felt as if I was discovering it all over again. And yet it rankled that I had not anticipated my master's giving me notice but had let him discharge me.

And how curious I find it: since that night when my master 'fired' me I have enjoyed my sleep; I no longer dream of my tailoring days, now long gone, days that were so contented in their undemanding simplicity but cast so long a shadow over my subsequent existence.

In this dream-sequence by a writer who in his younger days had been a tailor's journeyman, it is hard to see wish-fulfilment as the dominant presence. Everything pleasant lies in daytime life, while dream seems to perpetuate the spectral shadow of an unpleasant existence finally overcome. Similar dreams of my own have enabled me to throw some light on such dreams. As a young doctor I worked for a long time in the Chemical Institute without managing to make any progress in the skills required there, and for that reason I never like to think in the waking state of that barren and really rather shameful episode of my education. On the other hand it became a recurring dream for me that I am working in the laboratory, conducting analyses, experiencing various things, and so on; dreams of this kind are uncomfortable in much the same way as examination dreams and are never very clear. As I was interpreting one such dream, my attention was finally drawn to the word *'analysis'*, which offered me the key to understanding. Since then I have indeed become an 'analyst', conducting analyses that are highly acclaimed, albeit *psychoanalyses*. I now understood: if in daytime life I have come to be proud of analyses of this type, even wishing to congratulate myself on the progress I have made, at night dreams hold up to me those other, failed analyses of which I had no reason to be proud; these are the punishment dreams of the upstart, as were those of the tailor's journeyman who had become a celebrated writer. But how does it become possible for a dream to enter into the conflict between the pride of the parvenu and his own self-criticism, side with the latter and take as its content not an impermissible wish-fulfilment but a sensible warning? As I say, this is a difficult question to answer. We can infer that initially an overweening-ambition fantasy formed the basis of the dream; instead, however, its attenuation and humiliation find their way into the dream-content. Remember: there are masochistic tendencies in the life of the mind to which such a reversal can be attributed. I could have no objection to such dreams being called *punishment dreams* and as such distinguished from *wish-fulfilment dreams*. I should not regard it as a qualification of the dream-theory that I have championed hitherto but simply as a linguistic concession to the approach that sees the coincidence of opposites as something strange and exotic. However, closer examination of certain of these dreams reveals another thing. In the vague accompanying details of one of my laboratory dreams I had the precise age that placed me in the darkest and least successful year of my medical career; I still had no job and did not know how I was to earn my living, yet suddenly it was the case that I had a choice between several women as potential marriage partners! In other words, I was young again and so, above all, was the woman who had shared all those difficult years with me. With that, one of the relentlessly gnawing wishes of the ageing man was exposed as the unconscious dream-trigger. The struggle between vanity and self-criticism raging in other psychical strata had indeed determined the dream-content, but only the more deeply rooted youth-wish had made it possible as a dream. One does, after all, sometimes say in the waking state, 'Yes, things are very good today, and times were once hard; but it was lovely then, was it not, and you were still so young!'[10]

Another group of dreams that I have often come across in myself and recognized as hypocritical has as its content a reconciliation with people towards whom amicable relations ceased long ago. Analysis then regularly uncovers an occasion that might require me to set aside the last remains of consideration for these former friends and treat them as strangers or as enemies. The relevant dream, however, takes pleasure in depicting the opposite relationship.

When it comes to assessing dreams recounted by a writer, it can very often be assumed that the writer has excluded from the account details of the dream-content that he found disturbing and deemed

unimportant. His dreams will then pose riddles that precise reproduction of the dream-content would quickly have solved.

O[tto] Rank has further drawn my attention to the fact that in
the Grimms' story of the valiant little tailor or 'Seven with one blow'
a very similar upstart dream is narrated. The tailor, who has become
a hero and the king's son-in-law, has a dream one night when he is
with the princess, his wife, about his trade; her suspicions are
aroused, and the next night she orders armed guards to listen to
the words spoken in the dream and seize the dreamer. But the
tailor, forewarned, is able to change the dream.

A good overview of the complex processes of suppression, sub-
traction and reversal whereby the affects of the dream-thoughts
eventually become those of the dream can be obtained from suitable
syntheses of dreams that have been analysed in full. Here I want to
deal with a few more examples of affect-arousal in dreams that may
show some of the cases discussed as realized.

V

In the dream about the special task set me by old Brücke to dissect
my own pelvic girdle [see above, pp. 466f.], *I note in the dream
itself that the appropriate feeling of horror is missing.* The fact is,
this is wish-fulfilment in more than one sense. The dissection means
the self-analysis that I am completing at the same time by publishing
the dream-book – and that in reality I found so painful that, though
the manuscript lay ready, I put off having it printed for more than
a year. The wish now arises that I should be able to overcome this
feeling of holding back, which is why in the dream I experience no
horror [*Grauen*]. '*Grauen*' in the other sense ['*grau*' = 'grey'] is
something I should be happy to miss; I am already going grey very
quickly, and this *greying* of the hair is at the same time a warning
not to hold back any longer. We know, do we not, that at the end
of the dream the idea comes through that I shall have to leave it to
the children to pursue this difficult journey and reach the goal.

In the two dreams that postpone the expression of satisfaction until the moments immediately after waking [see above, pp. 461f.], that satisfaction is motivated in one instance by the expectation that I shall now experience what it means to feel, 'I've had this dream before', and relates in reality to the birth of the first children, in the other instance by the conviction that what is about to happen 'was foretold by a sign', and that satisfaction is the same as greeted my second son when he was born. Here the affects that dominated the dream-thoughts remain in the dream, but probably no dream proceeds as simply and straightforwardly as that. If we go a little further into both analyses, we learn that this satisfaction, which is not subject to censorship, receives a boost from a source that is threatened with censorship and the affect of which would un-doubtedly arouse opposition if it did not cover itself with a similar, readily admissible satisfaction affect from the permitted source – if it did not, so to speak, insinuate itself behind such an affect. I cannot prove this from the dream-example itself, unfortunately, but an example from a different sphere will make plain what I mean. I posit the following case. Say there is a person close to me whom I detest, so that a lively desire stirs in me to take pleasure when that person encounters some misfortune. However, the moral side of my being refuses to bow to that desire; I dare not say how much I want such a misfortune to occur, and when through no fault of that person it does occur I suppress my satisfaction and force myself to utter words of regret and reflections of sympathy. Everyone will have experienced a similar situation. At this point, however, the detested person, by committing some excess, gets into trouble in a way that is richly deserved; now I am able to give free rein to my satisfaction at the fact that the person has met with the proper punishment, and in this I voice my agreement with many others who lack my bias. However, I am also able to note that my satisfac-tion takes a more intense form than other people's; it has received a boost from the source of my detestation that internal censorship had hitherto prevented from supplying affect but in the altered circumstances is no longer impeded. Such a case applies generally in society, wherever antipathetic persons or members of an unpopular minority invite blame. Their punishment does not then correspond to their fault; rather, their fault is increased by the previously ineffective ill will directed against them. Those inflicting the punishment are undoubtedly committing an injustice here; however, they will be prevented from seeing this by the deep satisfaction with which removal of a long-maintained restraint now fills them. In such cases, while justified in terms of its quality, the affect is not justified in terms of its extent; and self-criticism, pacified in one respect, all too readily neglects to examine the other. The door once thrown open, it is easy for more people to push through than one originally intended to let in.

One conspicuous feature of the neurotic personality (namely that, with neurotics, occasions capable of prompting an affect produce an effect that is qualitatively justified but quantitatively disproportionate) is explained in this way, in so far as it admits of a psychological explanation at all. However, the excess flows from hitherto unconscious, suppressed sources of affect that are able to establish an associative link with the real occasion and for whose affect-release the unobjectionable, authorized source of affect provides the desired pathway. This reminds us that between the suppressed and suppressing agencies of the mind we should not look solely at the relations of reciprocal inhibition. Equal attention should be paid to the cases in which the two agencies produce a pathological effect by working together, each reinforcing the other. Let us now apply these outline remarks about psychical mechanics to understanding how affects are expressed in dream. A satisfaction that reveals itself in a dream and is of course immediately to be found in its place in the relevant dream-thoughts is not always fully explained by that evidence alone. As a rule, one will need to search the dream-thoughts for a second source for it on which censorship exerts pressure and that, under that pressure, generated not satisfaction but the opposite affect; however, as a result of the presence of the first dream-source that second source is enabled to prevent its satisfaction-affect from being repressed and add it, as a reinforcement, to the satisfaction flowing from a different source. Consequently, affects in dream seem to combine a number of tributaries and appear to have multiple determinations in the material of the dream-thoughts; *sources of affect capable of delivering the same affect come together, in dream-work, to give rise to that affect.*[10]

Some insight into these complicated circumstances is provided by analysing the fine dream that revolves around 'Non vixit' (see above, p. 435). In this dream, expressions of affects of different qualities are forced together at two places in the manifest content. Feelings of enmity and embarrassment (in the dream itself I am 'in the grip of remarkable affects') overlap where I eliminate the hostile friend with the two words. At the end of the dream I am immensely happy and pronounce appreciatively on a possibility that on waking I recognized as absurd, namely that some ghosts can be got rid of simply by wishing them away.

I have yet to disclose what prompted this dream. This is something very important and takes us a long way towards understanding the dream. I had been informed by my friend in Berlin (whom I call 'Fl.') that he was about to undergo surgery and that relatives living in Vienna would give me further news of his condition. The first report following the operation was not good, and I was worried. I should have loved to go to him myself, but at the time I was myself suffering from a painful affliction that made my every movement agony. From the dream-thoughts I now learn that I feared for my dear friend's life. I knew that his only sister, whom I never met, had died young after a very short illness. (In the dream: *Fl. is talking about his sister, saying, 'In three-quarters of an hour she was dead.'*) I must have formed the impression that his own constitution was not much more resistant and imagined myself, on receiving far worse news, making the journey at last and arriving too *late*, for which I might reproach myself endlessly.[11] This accusation of arriving too late became the focal point of the dream, but it represented itself in a scene in which the esteemed master of my student years, Brücke, hurls the accusation at me with a terrifying flash of his blue eyes. What caused this diversion of the scene will soon emerge; the scene itself is not something the dream is capable of reproducing as I experienced it. It does give my interlocutor the blue eyes, but it places me in the destructive role – a reversal that is clearly the work of wish-fulfilment. Concern about my friend's life, the reproach that I do not make the journey to see him, my shame (he *paid a discreet visit* to Vienna – to see me), my need to consider myself excused by my indisposition – all these things together make up the storm of emotion that, clearly felt in my sleep, rages in that region of the dream-thoughts.

But there was something else in what gave rise to this dream that had a quite contrary effect on me. When I received the bad news about the first few days after the operation, I was also told not to discuss the whole business with anyone, which I found insulting since it presupposed an unnecessary lack of faith in my silence. I was aware, of course, that this injunction did not come from my friend but constituted a piece of clumsiness or an excess of anxiety on the part of the person who told me, but even so I was deeply pained by the implied accusation because – well, it was not wholly unjustified. Accusations where there is 'nothing in it' famously do not stick; they have no power to upset one. Not in my friend's case, admittedly, but earlier, when I was much younger, having two friends who both, I am honoured to say, called me a friend too, I had unnecessarily disclosed something that one had said about the other. It is the same with the reproaches that were heaped on me on that occasion: I have never forgotten them. One of the two friends between whom I then played the opposite of peacemaker was Professor Fleischl; the other can be replaced by the forename Joseph, which was also that of P., my friend and opponent in the dream.

The charge that I can keep nothing to myself is evinced in the dream by the elements *discreet visit* and Fl.'s question about *how much I have told P. about his affairs*. But it is the intervention of this recollection that shifts the reproach of having come too late from the present into the time when I was living in Brücke's laboratory, and by replacing the second person in the elimination scene of the dream by someone called Joseph I am having this scene represent not only the accusation that I am too late but also the more deeply repressed accusation that I cannot keep a secret. Here the compression and displacement work of dream as well as the motives behind them become strikingly obvious.

However, the small amount of irritation in the present at the injunction to reveal nothing draws reinforcements from sources flowing at a deeper level and so swells to a stream of hostile feelings against people whom in reality I love. The spring supplying reinforcement lies in the world of infancy. I have already said how my warm friendships as well as my hostile relations with contemporaries go back to childhood dealings with a nephew who was a year older than myself; he was stronger than me, I soon learned to defend myself; inseparable, we lived together, loved each other, and occasionally, as older people have recounted, fought each other and – hurled *accusations* at each other. All my friends are in some sense incarnations of this first figure, 'who early on appeared before my troubled gaze';[12] they are *revenants*. My nephew himself came back in our boyhood years, when we acted Caesar and Brutus together. An intimate friend and a hated enemy have always been essential requirements of my emotional life; I have always managed to re-create both for myself, and not infrequently I have come so close to my childhood ideal that friend and foe are combined in the same person – not any longer simultaneously, of course, or alternating a number of times, as may have been the case in my earliest childhood.

I do not wish to pursue, in these pages, how in the circumstances described above a freshly vivid [*rezent*] occasion for affect-generation is able to reach back into childhood in order to have the childhood occasion replace it as regards generating the affect. That is a matter for the psychology of unconscious thought and belongs in the context of a psychological discussion of neuroses. Let us assume, for our dream-interpretation purposes, that a childhood memory presents itself (or is formed by the imagination) having, say, the following content: The two children start to argue over an object (we leave open what object, although the memory or feigned memory is of a quite specific one), with each claiming to have *got there sooner* and consequently to have a prior entitlement; a fight ensues, and might triumphs over right; according to hints supplied in the dream, I may have been conscious of being in the wrong (*aware of the mistake myself*); however, this time I win the fight, I stand my ground, the loser runs to my father (his grandfather), levels an accusation against me, and I defend myself with the famous words, recounted to me by my father, '*I hit him 'cos he hit me*'; so this memory or probably fantasy that springs involuntarily to mind as I analyse the dream (without further guarantee, I do not myself know how) is a central part of the dream-thoughts, drawing together the emotional stirrings at work in the dream-thoughts as the basin of a fountain gathers the streams of water that are fed into it. From here, the dream-thoughts flow along the following channels: It serves you right that you had to admit defeat; why did you want to force me out? I don't need you; I'll easily find someone else to play with, and so on. Then the channels open along which these thoughts flow back into the dream-portrayal. I once had to chide my late friend Joseph with such an '*Ôte-toi que je m'y mette*' [the originally humorous French saying, 'Out of my way!']. He had followed in my footsteps as a research assistant in Brücke's laboratory, but advancement there was a lengthy business. Neither of the two assistants made any progress, and in their youth they became impatient. My friend, who knew his time was limited and whom no ties of intimacy bound to his superior, occasionally voiced his impatience out loud. Since that superior was a very sick man, the wish to have him out of the way (other than in the sense of 'through promotion') was also capable of an offensive secondary interpretation. Naturally, a few years earlier the same desire to move into a newly vacant job had been entertained far more vigorously by myself; wherever in the world rank and promotion exist, the way is open for the suppression of ardent wishes. Even at his sick father's bedside, Shakespeare's Prince Hal cannot resist the temptation of trying on the crown. But my dream, understandably, exacts punishment for this thoughtless wish not from me but from him.[13]

'As he was ambitious, I slew him.' Because he could not wait for the other person to get out of his way, he was himself removed. I had this idea immediately after attending the unveiling, at the university, of the memorial to the other person. So part of the satisfaction I felt in the dream means: 'Just punishment; serves you right.'

At the funeral of that friend, a young man made the inappropriate-seeming remark, 'The speaker made it sound as if, without this one person, the world could not go on.' There stirred in him the rebellion of the truthful person, whose grief is disturbed by exaggeration. However, associated with the speech are the dream-thoughts: 'Actually, no one is irreplaceable; how many have I already seen buried; but I am still alive, I have survived them all, I am standing my ground.' Such a thought, occurring at the moment when I am afraid I shall find my friend has departed this life if I travel to see him, can only lead on to one thing: my being delighted that I have survived someone else, that the one who has died is not *me* but *him*, that I have stood my ground as I did in that imagined childhood scene. This sense of satisfaction, stemming from the infantile world, that I have stood my ground, covers the major part of the affect taken up into the dream. I am delighted to have survived, and I voice this with the naive egoism of the husband-and-wife story: 'If one of us dies, I'm going to live in Paris.' So far as my expectation is concerned, it is equally self-evident that I shall not be the one.

There is no concealing the fact that it takes a great deal of will-power to interpret and recount one's dreams. One has to reveal oneself as the only villain among all the noble souls with whom one shares this life. So I find it quite understandable that *revenants* should exist only for as long as one wants and that they can be removed by wishing them away. So that is what my friend Joseph was punished for. However, the *revenants* are successive incarnations of my childhood friend; so I am satisfied that I have always replaced these people, and even for those whom I am now in the process of losing there will be replacements. No one is irreplaceable.

But why is there no dream-censorship here? Why does dream-censorship not raise the liveliest objection to this train of thought with its naked self-obsession, turning the satisfaction attaching to it to deep displeasure? My view is that it is because other, irreproachable trains of thought about the same individuals also result in satisfaction and their affect offsets the one proceeding from the forbidden infant source. At a different level of thinking, I said to myself on the occasion of that ceremony when the memorial was unveiled, 'I have lost so many dear friends, either through death or through the friendship ending; how nice that those friends have been replaced, that I have gained a new friend who means more to me than the others were able to do, and that now, at an age where one no longer readily forms new friendships, I shall cling to this one for ever.' The satisfaction of having found this replacement for the friends I have lost is something I can incorporate in my dream without a qualm, but behind it the hostile satisfaction from a childhood source slips in too. Infantile affection certainly helps to reinforce the affection I justly feel today; but so has infantile hatred found its way into dream-representation.

However, this dream also contains a clear indication of a different train of thought that may result in satisfaction. Shortly before, following a long wait, my friend had had a little daughter. I know how deeply he had mourned the sister he lost prematurely, and I wrote to tell him that he would transfer to this child the love he felt for his sister; this little girl would finally make him forget his irreplaceable loss.

So this train of thought likewise links back to the intermediate thoughts of the latent dream-content, from which paths diverge in opposite directions: no one is irreplaceable. Look, nothing but *revenants*; every person one has lost returns. And now the associative ties between the conflicting components of the dream-thoughts are drawn tighter by the fortuitous circumstance that my friend's daughter has the same name as the playmate of my own youth, the sister (who was the same age as myself) of my oldest friend and adversary. I heard the name 'Pauline' with *satisfaction* and, as an allusion to this coincidence, in the dream I replaced one Joseph by another Joseph and found it impossible to suppress the same initial sound in the names 'Fleischl' and 'Fl'. From here, a train of thought then runs to naming my own children. I was keen that their names should not be chosen according to the fashion of the day but should be determined in order to commemorate loved individuals. Their names make the children '*revenants*'. And finally, is not having children, for all of us, our only access to *immortality*?

Concerning affects in dreams, let me just add a few comments from a different perspective. In the mind of the sleeper an affective inclination (what we call a mood) may reside as a dominant element and thus help to determine dreaming. That mood may proceed from the experiences and thoughts of the day, it may have somatic sources; in both cases it will be accompanied by appropriate trains of thought. The fact that the ideational content of the dream-thoughts will sometimes primarily determine the affective inclination and sometimes be secondarily aroused by an emotional disposition to be accounted for somatically – that makes no difference so far as dream-formation is concerned. This is governed every time by the limitation that it can only represent what is wish-fulfilment and that it can only derive its psychical driving force from a wish. The mood currently present will receive the same treatment as the sensation currently occurring during sleep (see above, p. 241), which is either ignored or reinterpreted in terms of wish-fulfilment. Embarrassing moods during sleep become driving forces of dreams by arousing vigorous wishes that the relevant dream is intended to fulfil. The material to which they stick is reprocessed and reprocessed until it can be used to express wish-fulfilment. The more intense and the more dominant the element of the embarrassing mood is in the dream-thoughts, the more certain it is that the most powerfully suppressed desires will make use of the opportunity to attain representation, since because of the actual existence of the displeasure that they would otherwise have to manufacture themselves they find the greater part of the work involved in their attaining representation already done, and with these considerations we touch once more on the problem of anxiety-dreams, which will prove to be the borderline case so far as dream-performance is concerned.

Notes

1. If I am not much mistaken, the first dream I was able to detect in my twenty-month-old grandson shows that dream-work had managed to transform its material into wish-fulfilment while the relevant affect imposed

itself unchanged even in sleep. In the night preceding the day when its father was due to go off to war, the child cried out with a great sob, 'Papa, Papa – Bebi' ['Dada, dada – baba']. That can only mean: 'Dada and baba stay together', while the weeping acknowledged the imminent farewell. The child was quite capable, at the time, of giving expression to the concept of separation. '*Fort*' ['gone']; (represented by a peculiarly stressed, long-drawn-out 'oooh') was one of his first words, and several months before this first dream the boy had acted out '*fort*' with all his toys, which went back to an act of will that he had accomplished at an early age – namely, letting his mother 'go'.

2. [These square brackets appear in Freud's original.]

3. [They would have been 'British' ships of course, but '*Englisch*' is often used in German to mean 'British', and it will soon be clear why I have retained Freud's usage here.]

4. [Perhaps Freud's 'linguistically sophisticated friend' meant νέχυς ('corpse'); incidentally, the German word '*Nachen*' should be translated as 'barque' – which of course has a quite different etymology.]

5. [*Still, auf gerettetem Boot, treibt in den Hafen der Greis*. The second line of Schiller's two-line epigram 'Expectation and fulfilment', contrasting the vigour of youth with the passivity of age.]

6. [Spa and popular holiday resort in Steiermark (Styria) in south-central Austria.]

7. [Sandor Ferenczi], *Internationale Zeitschrift für Psychoanalyse*, IV, 1916.

8. [Peter Rosegger (1843–1918), a prolific Austrian poet and novelist (his *Collected Works* run to forty volumes) who sometimes wrote in dialect.]

9. [A life of hand graft for little return may, in German, be referred to as *ein Schneiderleben*.]

10. Since psychoanalysis divided the person into an 'I' and an 'Above-I' [*Mass Psychology and Analysis of the 'I'*, translated by J. A. Underwood in *Mass Psychology and Other Writings* in the New Penguin Freud, London 2004] it is easy to see these punishment dreams as wish-fulfilments of the 'Above-I'.

[All things considered (as I noted in the volume cited above), it seemed best to render these central concepts (the 'I', the 'It' and the 'Above-I') in English but to capitalize them and place them within inverted commas. I realize that repeatedly coming across (for example) 'I' in place of the more usual 'ego' will tend to break the reader's stride in a way that is not strictly relevant to Freud's purpose. However, may I simply ask the reader to bear in mind three rather obvious things:

1) Freud could himself have used Latin words for these concepts; the choice was open to him.

2) The German words he did use are quite ordinary (though of course he does not use them in ordinary ways). Using Latin words makes the concepts seem 'strange' in a way that is perhaps itself irrelevant to Freud's purpose.

3) The 'above' in 'Above-I' does not of course make it 'better' than the 'I'; it merely places it in a certain relationship to the 'I'.]

11. I explain the extraordinarily powerful pleasurable effect of the tendentious joke in a similar way [in *Der Witz und seine Beziehung zum Unbewussten*; *Standard Edition*, vol. VIII; *The Joke and Its Relation to the Unconscious*, translated by Joyce Crick, London 2002].

12. It is this fantasy from the unconscious dream-thoughts that imperiously demands *'non vivit'* in place of *'non vixit'*. 'You came too late: he's no longer alive.' That the manifest situation of the dream is also aimed at *'non vivit'* was indicated on p. 437.

13. [The quotation (from the 'Dedication' of Goethe's *Faust*) is spoken by the author figure as he addresses his own ghosts.]

14. The reader will have been struck by the fact that the name *Joseph* [*Josef*] plays so large a part in my dreams (see the uncle dream [pp. 151ff.]). My 'I' is able to hide behind persons of that name particularly easily because *Joseph* was also the name of the well-known biblical *interpreter of dreams*.

I *Secondary processing*

Finally, let us turn our attention to bringing out the fourth of the factors involved in dream-formation.

Pursuing our study of dream-content in the manner begun above, namely by examining striking events in dream-content in terms of their origin in the relevant dream-thoughts, we find ourselves faced with other elements for which only a wholly new assumption can account. I am thinking of the times when one experiences surprise in a dream, or anger, or reluctance – in reaction to a portion of the dream-content itself. Most such stirrings of criticism in dream are not directed against the dream-content but instead turn out to be borrowed and suitably employed bits of the dream-material, as I have shown using appropriate examples. However, some of those elements do not fit such a derivation; nothing in the dream-material corresponds to them. What, for instance, is the meaning of a critique that occurs not infrequently in dream: 'Never mind: it's only a dream'? This is a genuine critique of the dream-state such as I might exercise in the waking state. Very often, in fact, it is simply the precursor of waking up; even more frequently it will be preceded by an embarrassing feeling that subsides once the dream-state has been noted. However, in occurring while the dream is still going on, the thought 'It's only a dream' means what it is meant to imply on the open stage in the mouth of Offenbach's *la belle Hélène*; it seeks to disparage the importance of what has just been experienced and to enable the person to bear what is to come. It serves to put to sleep a certain agency that would, at a given moment, have had every reason to rise up and prevent the dream (or the scene) from continuing. It is more comfortable, though, to go on sleeping and put up with the dream 'because it's only a dream, is it not?' I can imagine that the disparaging critique 'It's only a dream' is voiced in dream when censorship, which never sleeps entirely, feels caught unawares by the dream it has already allowed to pass. Too late to suppress the dream now, so censorship uses this remark to counter any fear or embarrassment arising therefrom. This is a piece of *esprit d'escalier* on the part of the agency responsible for psychical censorship.

However, this example furnishes us with perfect proof that not everything dream contains comes from the relevant dream-thoughts but that a psychical function indistinguishable from our thinking when awake may contribute towards dream-content. The question now is: does this occur only very exceptionally, or does the psychical agency that normally operates only as censor play a regular part in dream-formation?

We must unhesitatingly plump for the latter. There is no doubt that the censoring agency whose influence we have hitherto acknowledged only in restrictions and omissions in dream-content is also responsible for insertions into and increases in the same. Such insertions are often easily spotted; they are recounted timidly, prefaced by an 'as if', they do not really possess any great degree of animation, and they are always made at points where they can serve to link two pieces of a particular dream-content together, paving the way for some connection between two portions of the dream concerned. They evidently last less long in memory than true derivatives of the relevant dream-material; where dream is forgotten, they are the first things to go, and I have a strong suspicion that our frequent complaint that we dreamed copiously but have forgotten most of it, retaining only fragments [see above, p. 295] – I strongly suspect that this is because precisely these binding ideas vanish so quickly. Full analysis will sometimes identify such insertions by the fact that they lack any corresponding material in the relevant dream-thoughts. However, on more careful examination I have to pronounce this case something of a rarity; as a rule, link ideas can in fact be traced back to material in the dream-thoughts, though neither on the basis of its own valency nor as a result of multiple determination could such material lay claim to inclusion in the actual dream. Only exceptionally does the psychical function involved in dream-formation that we are now considering seem to rise to fresh creation; wherever possible, it uses things it can pick out of the dream-material to suit its purpose.

What marks out and reveals this part of dream-work is its bias, its slant. This function is not dissimilar to the one the poet [Heine] mischievously attributes to the philosopher: with its shreds and patches it stops up the holes in the structure of a particular dream. Thanks to its efforts, that dream loses the appearance of absurdity and incoherence and comes close to the model of a comprehensible experience. However, such efforts are not always crowned with complete success. Some dreams, looked at superficially, may appear quite logical and correct; they start from a realistic situation, take it through changes that avoid contradiction, and bring it (though this happens rarely) to a conclusion that does not disconcert. Such dreams have undergone the most profound processing by a psychical function that resembles waking thought; they appear to make sense, but that sense is in fact utterly remote from the true meaning of the relevant dream. Analysing this, one is persuaded that secondary processing has here dealt very freely with the dream-material, retaining the least of its relations. These are dreams that, so to speak, have already been interpreted once, before we subject them to interpretation in the waking state. In other dreams, this tendentious processing has been only partially successful; wherever coherence appears to prevail, the dream becomes nonsensical or confused, possibly in order to rerun itself and in so doing raise itself to an appearance of comprehensibility. In [yet] other dreams, processing has failed completely, and we find ourselves confronted, as it were helplessly, by a meaningless heap of fractured content.

It is not my wish, as regards this fourth force shaping dreams, which we shall soon see as one we recognize (actually, it is the only one of the four dream-shapers with which we are already familiar from another context) – it is not my wish, I say, peremptorily to deny that this fourth factor has any ability to act creatively, making fresh contributions to dream. But there is no doubt that its influence, like that of the other factors, finds expression primarily in promoting and selecting preformed psychical material in dream-thoughts. There is one case, however, in which its job of throwing up a kind of façade for the particular dream concerned is rendered largely superfluous by the fact that such a thing already exists, waiting to be used. The element of the dream-thoughts that I have in mind is what I usually describe as '*fantasy*'; I shall perhaps avoid misunderstandings if I immediately identify the *day-dream* as the analogous element from waking life.[1] The role of this element in our mental life has not been fully acknowledged and explored by psychiatrists; M. Benedikt has, it seems to me, made a very promising start with this more positive appraisal. The significance of day-dreams has not escaped the unwavering perspicacity of writers; one well-known example is the description that Alphonse Daudet sketches in *Le Nabab* of the day-dreams of one of the secondary characters of his novel. The study of psychoneuroses leads to the surprising discovery that such fantasies or day-dreams are the immediate precursors of hysterical symptoms (or at least of a whole series of them). It is not to the memories themselves that the symptoms of hysteria are attached but to the fantasies built up on the basis of the memories. The frequent occurrence of conscious day-time fantasies helps us to understand these phenomena; however, while some of those fantasies exist consciously, huge numbers of them are unconscious and must remain so because of their content and their provenance from repressed material. More detailed examination of the nature of such day-time fantasies shows us with what justification they have been given the same name as our nocturnal thought-productions: *dreams*. They share a great many characteristics with night-dreams; in fact, studying them might have provided us with our best and most immediate way of understanding their nocturnal counterpart.

Like dreams, they are wish-fulfilments; like dreams, they are largely based on the impressions of childhood experiences; like dreams, they enjoy a certain relaxation of censorship as regards their creations. Looking closely at how they are put together, one

becomes aware of how the wish-motive that operates in their production, seizing the material of which they are constructed, has
jumbled that material up, rearranged it and assembled it to form a
fresh whole. To the childhood recollections to which they hark
back, they stand in something like the same relationship as some of
Rome's baroque palaces stand to the classical ruins whose columns
and dressed stones provided the materials for their reconstruction
in modern forms.

In the 'secondary processing' that we have attributed to our
fourth dream-shaping factor as it moulds dream-content, we find
the same activity as is able, uninhibited by other influences, to find
expression in the creation of day-dreams. We could say straight out,
in fact, that our fourth factor takes the material it is offered and
tries to create *something like a day-dream*. However, where such a
day-dream has already been formed in connection with the dream-
thoughts, this element of dream-work prefers to seize upon it and
seek to give it a place in the dream-content. Some dreams consist
only of the reiteration of a day-time fantasy, one that may have
remained unconscious, an example being the dream of the boy
riding in a war-chariot with the heroes of the Trojan War. In my
Autodidasker dream (see above, p. 313), the second part of the
dream at least is an exact repetition of an intrinsically innocent
day-time fantasy about my dealings with Professor N. Because of
the complicated set of conditions that a dream must satisfy when it
comes into being, it is more common for the pre-existent fantasy to
form only part of the dream or for only part of it to penetrate as far
as the dream-content. On the whole, the fantasy is then treated
like any other component of the latent material; but often, in the
particular dream, it is still recognizable as an entity. My own dreams
often contain bits that stand out by virtue of an impression differing
from the rest. Those bits seem to me to have a certain fluency; they
strike me as more coherent and yet more fleeting than other portions of the same dream; I know that these are unconscious fantasies
that as coherent entities find their way into the dream, but I have
never managed to pin down such a fantasy. Moreover, like all other
components of the dream-thoughts, such fantasies are compressed

and concentrated, overlap one another, etc., though there are transitional instances between, on the one hand, the case where they are permitted to form the dream-content or at least the façade of the dream virtually unchanged, and the opposite case, where they are represented in the dream-content only by one of their elements or by a remote allusion to such an element. Again, as regards the fate of fantasies in the dream-thoughts, it is clearly crucial what advantages they are able to offer in the face of the claims of censorship and the urgent need to compress.

In my choice of examples for dream-interpretation purposes, I have so far as possible avoided dreams in which unconscious fantasies play a substantial part, since introducing this psychical element would have necessitated extensive discussions on the psychology of unconscious thought. However, even in this context I cannot ignore 'fantasy' completely, because often a day-dream will find its way into a night-dream in its entirety and even more frequently it shines clearly through one. I should just like to cite one more dream that appears to consist of two different, contrasting fantasies that even overlap at several points; one fantasy is the surface one, while the other seeks as it were to interpret the first.[2]

The dream (and it is the only one concerning which I have no careful notes) runs something like this: The dreamer (a young bachelor) is sitting in what, strictly speaking, is his local; several people come in to take him away, including one who wants to arrest him. He says to his table companions, 'I'll pay later. I'm coming back.' But they laugh derisively, calling out, 'We've heard that one before, that's what they all say.' One guest calls after him, 'There goes another one.' He is then taken into a cramped bar where he finds a woman holding a child. One of the people escorting him says, 'This is Herr Müller.' A police inspector or some other official leafs through a pile of notes or letters, saying over and over again, 'Müller, Müller, Müller.' Finally, he asks him a question, which he answers in the affirmative. He then looks around for the woman and notices she has grown a large beard.

In this case, the two components are easy to separate. On the surface, this is an *arrest fantasy* and seems to us to be formed by dream-work from scratch. Visible behind it, however, is the material that dream-work has reshaped slightly, namely the *fantasy of marriage*, and the features that may be common to both re-emerge with unusual clarity, as in one of Galton's composite photographs.[3] The promise by the man who used to be a bachelor that he will reoccupy his usual place at the table of regular customers, the incredulity of his fellow regulars, whose long experience has taught them better, the cry of 'There goes another one (into wedlock)' that follows him out – all these features fit easily into the other interpretation. So does the affirmative answer given to the official. The leafing through a pile of papers while saying the same name over and over again corresponds to a minor but easily recognizable feature of the wedding festivities – the recital of the stack of congratulatory telegrams that have arrived, all of course bearing the same name. With the personal appearance of the bride in this dream, the marriage fantasy has even triumphed over the arrest fantasy covering it up. The fact that at the end of the dream the bride displays a beard I was able to explain by an enquiry (there was no analysis in this case). The previous day the dreamer, out walking with a friend who was as anti-marriage as himself, had crossed the road and drawn the friend's attention to a brown-haired beauty coming towards them. The friend, however, had remarked, 'Yes, if only these women did not grow beards with age like their fathers.'

In this dream too there is of course no shortage of elements in connection with which dream-distortion has done a more radical job. The speech 'I'll pay later', for instance, may relate to how it was feared the father-in-law might behave in the matter of the dowry. Clearly all kinds of misgivings are holding the dreamer back from surrendering joyously to the marriage fantasy. One of those misgivings, namely that with marriage one loses one's freedom, is embodied in the transformation into an arrest scene.

Going back to the way dream-work likes to make use of a ready-made fantasy rather than first assembling one from the material of the relevant dream-thoughts, we may, with this insight, have solved one of the most interesting riddles of the dream-phenomenon. On page 38 I recounted Maury's experience of being hit on the back of the neck by a headboard and waking up with an extended dream, a complete novel from the time of the French Revolution. Since the dream is presented as coherent and wholly oriented towards explaining the stimulus that woke the sleeper up (a stimulus of which the sleeper can have had no premonition), the only assumption left seems to be that the whole copious dream must have been put together and have taken place in the brief period of time between the headboard falling on the back of Maury's neck and his enforced awakening as a result of the blow. Reluctant to attribute such rapidity to intellectual work in the waking state, we eventually conceded, as a privileged ability of dream-work, a remarkable speeding up of the course of events.

This conclusion quickly became popular, but more recent authors (Le Lorrain and Egger among them) have vehemently refuted it. In part they doubt the accuracy of Maury's account of his dream; in part they seek to show that the rapidity of our intellectual performance in the waking state is as great as we are able to attribute, undiminished, to dream-performance. The debate has brought up questions of principle that will not, it seems to me, be quickly resolved. However, I have to say that the arguments advanced (by Egger, for example) against Maury's guillotine dream in particular did not entirely convince me. I would suggest the following explanation for the dream: Would it in fact be so unlikely that Maury's dream represents a fantasy that had lain ready in his memory for years and had been aroused (*alluded to* might be better) in the instant of his discerning the stimulus that woke him up? For a start, this gets rid of the whole problem of composing so extensive a story with all its details in the extremely short time that was available to the dreamer in this case; it was already composed. Had the piece of wood hit Maury in the back of the neck while he was awake, there might have been room for the thought, 'That's just as if one were being guillotined.' However, the headboard having hit him while he was asleep, dream-work quickly used the incidence of the stimulus to manufacture a piece of wish-fulfilment, *as if* it were thinking (this is very much meant to be taken figuratively): 'Here is an excellent opportunity to realize the wish-fantasy I formed once upon a time while reading a book.' That the dreamed fiction was of precisely the kind that the young man used to form under powerfully arousing impressions seems to me indisputable. Who would not have felt gripped (particularly a Frenchman who was also a cultural historian) by accounts from the time of the Terror in which the aristocracy, men and women, the flower of the nation, demonstrated how it was possible to die serenely, remaining true, right up until their ghastly demise, to the bright wit and refinement of their way of life? How tempting to imagine oneself in the midst of such a situation as one of the young men who, taking leave of their ladies with a kiss on the hand, mount the steps to the scaffold unafraid! Or, if ambition was the principal motive behind the fantasy, to place oneself in the shoes of one of those powerful individuals who solely by the power of their ideas and by their fiery eloquence dominate a city in which at the time the heart of mankind is beating so convulsively, who despatch thousands to their deaths out of conviction, paving the way for the transformation of Europe, yet who are unsure of their own heads and one day lay them down beneath the blade of the guillotine – in the role of the Girondins, possibly, or of the heroic Danton! That Maury's fantasy was of this ambitious kind appears to be suggested by the retention in memory of the phrase 'accompanied by vast crowds'.

However, there is no need for this fantasy, formed long before, to be rehearsed in its entirety during sleep: it is enough if it is simply 'touched on'. I mean this in the following way. When a couple of bars are struck up and someone says, as in *Don Giovanni*, 'That is from Mozart's *Marriage of Figaro*', all of a sudden a thousand memories well up in me – of which, moments later, not one is capable of rising to consciousness. The keyword serves as a point of penetration, and from that point a whole entity is aroused simultaneously. It need be no different in unconscious thinking. The stimulus to wake up arouses the psychical phase that gives access to the entire guillotine fantasy. However, this is rehearsed not in sleep but only in the memory of the person who has been awakened. Awake, that person recalls the details of the fantasy that in the dream was touched on as an entity. He has no way of being sure that he really is recalling something dreamed. This same explanation (namely, that one is dealing here with ready-made fantasies that the waking stimulus arouses in each case as an entity) can be used for other dreams triggered by a waking stimulus, one example being Napoleon's battle dream of the exploding time bomb [see above, p. 38]. Of the dreams that Justine Tobowolska collected in her 1900 dissertation about apparent duration in dream, the greatest evidential value seems to me to attach to the one Macario (1857) recounts as being had by dramatist Casimir Bonjour.[4] Keen to attend the first performance of a play of his one evening, Bonjour was in fact so weary that, seated in his chair in the wings, he nodded off at the precise moment when the curtain rose. In his sleep he proceeded to run through all five acts of his play, observing all the varied signs of emotion shown by the audience at individual scenes. At the end of the performance he heard, to his great delight, his name being proclaimed to the liveliest applause. Suddenly he woke up. Scarcely believing his eyes or his ears, he noted that the performance had not progressed beyond the first lines of the first scene; he could not have been asleep for more than two minutes at most. It is surely not too bold to assert in connection with this dream that the dreamer's working his way through the five acts of the play and noting the audience reaction at particular points do not necessarily come from a fresh performance during sleep but may reiterate a fantasy in the foregoing sense that the dreamer had woven previously. Tobowolska, together with other authors, highlights as a common feature of dreams with an accelerated sequence of imagined events that they appear particularly coherent, quite unlike other dreams; they also, she points out, tend to be recalled in a much more summary way, rather than in detail. But these would be precisely the characteristics that such ready-made fantasies, touched on by dream-work, would display – though this is a conclusion that the said authors do not draw. I make no claim that all dreams that lead to waking admit of such an explanation, or that the problem of accelerated presentation in dreams can simply be swept away in this fashion.

It is inevitable that we should concern ourselves here about how this secondary processing of dream-content relates to the other factors of dream-work. Could it be, for instance, that the dream-forming factors (the endeavour to compress, the compulsion to evade censorship and a concern for representability in the psychical medium of dream) initially mould the material into a provisional dream-content, which is then, in a subsequent operation, re-arranged until it comes as close as possible to the requirements of a second agency? That is hardly likely. We have to assume instead that, right from the outset, the requirements of that agency consti-tute one of the conditions that dream must meet and that that condition (simultaneously with those of compression, resistance censorship and representability) exerts an inductive, selective effect on the total dream-thought material. However, of the four con-ditions of dream-formation, the one we have acknowledged last is certainly the one whose requirements appear to be least compelling so far as dream is concerned. That this psychical function (which performs what we have termed secondary processing of dream-content) is identical to the workings of our waking thought proceeds with a high degree of probability from the following consideration. Our waking (preconscious) thought reacts to perception material of any kind in precisely the same way as the function at issue here reacts to dream-content. Its nature is to create order in such material, setting up relationships and bringing it within the require-ments of an intelligible context. We tend to overdo this: conjuring tricks ape us in taking their cue from this intellectual habit of ours. In our efforts to assemble in comprehensible fashion sensory impressions received, we often make the most curious mistakes or even falsify the truth of the material we have before us. The evi-dence of this is too generally known to need extensive citation. We gloss over potentially nonsensical printing errors by inadvertently picturing the correct version to ourselves. The editor of a widely read French journal is said to have wagered that he would have the printers insert into every sentence of a lengthy article the words 'from in front' or 'from behind' without a single reader noticing. He won his bet. A comical instance of a false connection struck me some years ago as I was reading a newspaper. After the session of the French Chamber in which Dupuy, by uttering the courageous words, '*La séance continue*',[5] quashed alarm at the explosion of a bomb hurled into the Chamber by anarchists, statements were taken from visitors to the gallery as to their impressions of the attack. Among those visitors were two people from the provinces, one of whom said that, immediately after the end of a speech, he had indeed heard a detonation but had thought it was the custom, in parliament, to let off a gun when someone finished speaking. The other, who had probably listened to several speakers already, took the same view but with the qualification that such shots were fired only after particularly successful speeches.

So it is in fact no other psychical agency than our normal thinking that approaches dream-content with the demand that it must make sense, subjects it to an initial interpretation, and thus occasions complete misunderstanding of the same. As regards interpretation, it remains the rule that no notice whatsoever should be taken of the ostensible coherence of a dream as being of suspect provenance; from the pellucid as well as from the obscure the same path should be retraced to the relevant dream-material.

In the process, however, we notice what the scale of quality of dreams from blurred to clear (see above, p. 343) essentially depends on. Clarity is the quality possessed (in our eyes) by those parts of a dream where secondary processing was able to accomplish something, while confusion characterizes those other parts where this factor failed. Since the confused parts of a dream are often also those less sharply defined, we may conclude that secondary dream-work should also be held partly responsible for the vividness with which individual dream-figments are presented.

Casting around for something with which to compare the definitive shaping of dream as revealed with the help of normal thought, all I can find are those mysterious inscriptions with which [the satirical journal] *Fliegender Blätter* entertained its readers for so long. A sentence, which for the sake of contrast is written half in dialect and implies something as scurrilous as possible, is made to look as if it contains a Latin inscription. Letters of words are torn from their syllabic context and rearranged. Occasionally, a genuine Latin word does result, while in other places we think we are dealing with abbreviations of such words; in yet other places we allow the appearance of weathered portions or lacunae in the inscription to distract us from the meaningless nature of letters standing by themselves. To avoid being taken in by the joke, we need to disregard all the properties of an inscription, concentrate on the letters and without worrying about the arrangement presented assemble them to form words in our mother tongue.

Secondary processing is the factor in dream-work that most authors have commented on and acknowledged as being important. H[avelock] Ellis provides an amusing illustration of this function:

> Sleeping consciousness we may even imagine as saying to itself in effect: Here comes our master, Waking Consciousness, who attaches such mighty importance to reason and logic and so forth. Quick, gather things up, put them in order – any order will do – before he enters to take possession.[6]

That this *modus operandi* is identical with waking thought is brought out particularly clearly by Delacroix:

> *Cette fonction d'interprétation n'est pas particulière au rêve; c'est le même travail de coordination logique que nous faisons sur nos sensations pendant la veille.*

> [This function of interpretation is not peculiar to dream; it is the same task of logical co-ordination that we perform on our sensory impressions in the waking state.][7]

J. Sully takes the same view, as does Tobowolska:

> *Sur ces successions incohérentes d'hallucinations, l'esprit s'efforce de faire le même travail de coordination logique qu'il fait pendant la veille sur les sensations. Il relie entre elles par un lien imaginaire*

toutes ces images décousues et bouche les écarts trop grands qui se trouvaient entre elles.

[Faced with these incoherent series of hallucinations, the mind tries hard to perform the same task of logical co-ordination as it performs during the waking state when faced with sensory impressions. It links all these disconnected images together with an imaginary thread and plugs any excessively wide gaps that existed between them.][8]

Some authors have this task of ordering and interpreting begin while the dream is still going on and continue in the waking state. Paulhan, for example, writes:

Cependant j'ai souvent pensé qu'il pouvait y avoir une certaine déformation, ou plutôt réformation du rêve dans la souvenir [. . .]. La tendance systématisante de l'imagination pourrait fort bien achever après le réveil ce qu'elle a ébauché pendant le sommeil. De la sorte, la rapidité réelle de la pensée serait augmentée en apparence par les perfectionnements dus à l'imagination éveillée.

[I had often thought, however, that there might be some distortion or rather reshaping of the dream in memory [. . .]. The tendency of the imagination to systematize might well complete after waking what it had begun during sleep. Thus the speed of thought, which really is very great, would appear to be increased by the finishing touches added by the waking imagination.][9]

Leroy and Tobowolska:

[. . .] *dans le rêve, au contraire, l'interprétation et la coordination se font non seulement à l'aide des données du rêve, mais encore à l'aide de celles de la veille* [. . .]

[[. . .] in a dream, on the other hand, interpretation and co-ordination are performed not only with the aid of the dictates of dreaming but also with the aid of those of the waking state [. . .].][10]

Inevitably, then, this one factor of dream-formation was exaggerated in terms of its importance, with the result that it was made responsible for the entire performance of creating dreams. This creative process is apparently completed at the moment of waking up, as Goblot and to an even greater extent [Marcel] Foucault assume, both authors crediting waking thought with the ability of forming the relevant dream from the thoughts that crop up in sleep.

Of this view, Leroy and Tobowolska say:

> *On a cru pouvoir placer le rêve au moment du réveil et ils ont attribué à la pensée de la veille la fonction de construire le rêve avec les images présentes dans la pensée du sommeil.*

> [They believed they could locate dreaming at the moment of waking up, and they credited the waking mind with the function of constructing dreams from the images present to the mind in sleep.]

To this positive appraisal of secondary processing I add that of a fresh contribution to dream-work demonstrated by some sensitive observations carried out by H[erbert] Silberer. Silberer, as I have already mentioned (see p. 359), caught the conversion of thoughts into images *in flagrante*, as it were, by forcing himself to perform intellectual operations while tired and half-asleep. In such states the processed thought disappeared from his mind and in its place a vision presented itself that proved to have supplanted what was usually an abstract idea (see the examples on pp. 359f.). During these experiments, what happened was this: the image that cropped up and that was supposed to equate to an element of the dream represented something different from the thought awaiting processing, namely the tiredness itself, the difficulty of undertaking or reluctance to undertake the work involved – in other words, the subjective condition and *modus operandi* of the person making the effort instead of the object of that effort. Silberer called this eventuality (which happened to him very frequently) the *functional* phenomenon as opposed to the (anticipated) *material* phenomenon. He gave an example:

I am lying on my couch one afternoon. I feel extremely sleepy but force myself to cogitate a philosophical problem, namely seeking to compare Kant's and Schopenhauer's views of time. I am unable, because of my drowsy state, to hold up the thought processes of both men side by side, as I should need to do in order to compare them. After several vain attempts, I once again imprint on my mind the Kantian deduction, using all my will-power, and proceed to apply it to the way Schopenhauer poses the problem. I then turn my attention to the latter, but when I try to recall Kant I find that he has disappeared again, and my efforts to bring him back meet with failure. This vain endeavour to retrieve promptly the Kant file that I have mislaid somewhere in my head now suddenly presents itself to me (behind closed eyelids) as in a dream-image, as a visible, three-dimensional symbol: *I am asking a surly secretary for some information; the secretary, bent over a desk, refuses to let my urging stir him. Half straightening up, he gives me an uncooperative, dismissive look.*[11]

Other examples refer to the fluctuation between sleeping and being awake:

Example no. 2. – Conditions: morning, on waking up. Reflecting while still to some extent asleep (dozing) on a dream just had – as it were, dreaming it out [*nach- und austräumend*] – I feel myself approaching wakeful awareness but wish to go on dozing.

Scene: *I am reaching over a stream with one leg but immediately pull it back, seeking to stay on this side.*

Example no. 6. – Same conditions as in example no. 4. (He wishes to stay lying down a little longer without falling asleep.) I wish to surrender to sleep a little longer.

Scene: *I am saying goodbye to someone and arranging to meet him (or her) again soon.*[12]

The 'functional' phenomenon, 'representation of the situational rather than the objectively present', is something that Silberer observed basically in the two states of falling asleep and waking up. Quite understandably, only the latter case is relevant so far as dream-interpretation is concerned. Silberer cites some fine examples to show that the final acts of the manifest content of many dreams, the acts that immediately precede waking, quite simply represent the decision to wake up or the actual process of waking up. Such an intention is served by crossing a threshold ('threshold symbolism'), leaving one room in order to enter another, a departure, a home-coming, parting from a companion, plunging into water, and so on. But I cannot help observing that, in my own dreams as in those of people undergoing analysis with me, I have come across dream-elements relating to threshold symbolism far less frequently than Silberer's comments would lead one to expect.

It is by no means unthinkable or unlikely that such 'threshold symbolism' would also shed light on many elements central to the context of a particular dream – for instance, places where there were fluctuations in the depth of sleep and an inclination to break the dream off. However, solid examples of this happening have yet to be adduced. More often there appears to be an instance of multiple determination; a piece of the dream that draws its material content from the structure of the relevant dream-thoughts is *also* used to represent a situational element in the mental activity involved.

Silberer's very interesting functional phenomenon has through no fault of its discoverer led to a great deal of misuse in that the old tendency towards an abstract, symbolic interpretation of dreams has drawn support from it. Favouring the 'functional category' is taken so far by some writers that they speak of the functional phenomenon wherever intellectual operations or emotional processes feature in the content of dream-thoughts, despite the fact that such material is no more and no less entitled than any other residue of the day to find a place in dream.

We are prepared to acknowledge that Silberer's phenomena represent a second contribution to dream-formation on the part of waking thought, though one that is less consistent and less significant than the first, which we introduced as 'secondary processing'. It has become apparent that part of the attentiveness active by day continues to be applied to dreams during sleep, controlling them, criticizing them and retaining the power to interrupt them. It seemed to us reasonable to see in this mental agency that remains awake the censorship whose task it is to exert so powerfully inhibiting an effect on the way dreams are shaped. What Silberer's observations bring to this is the fact that in certain circumstances a kind of self-observation may be involved here, making its contribution to the relevant dream-content. It will be proper to deal elsewhere with the probable relations of this self-observing agency (which is perhaps particularly obtrusive in the case of the philosophically minded) to endopsychical perception, to attention mania, to conscience and to dream-censorship.[13]

I shall now attempt to sum up these extensive discussions about dream-work. The question that faced us was whether the mind applies all its faculties to dream-formation, deploying them without restriction, or whether it uses only a fraction of those faculties – a fraction inhibited in its performance. Our investigations lead us to reject such a way of posing the question altogether as being inadequate to the circumstances. However, if our answer is to stand on the same ground as the question forces us to occupy, we must accept both opposing views, despite the fact that they apparently cancel each other out. The mind performs two tasks in connection with dream-formation: it produces dream-thoughts, and it turns them into dream-content. Dream-thoughts are formed entirely correctly, drawing on all the psychical energy at our disposal; they belong to thinking that has not become conscious, thinking from which, following a certain conversion process, our conscious thoughts also proceed. No matter how much about them is also worth knowing and poses enigmas, those enigmas have no particular connection with dream and do not merit discussion in the same context as dream-problems.[14] By contrast, the second task (that of transforming unconscious thoughts into dream-content) is peculiar to and characteristic of the life of dreams. The fact is, this dream-work proper departs much further from the model of waking thought than even the most critical belittlers of psychical performance in dream-formation supposed. It is not, say, more careless,

less correct, more forgetful, less complete than waking thought; it is qualitatively quite different from waking thought and therefore not to be compared with it in the first place. It does not think, calculate or judge at all but confines itself to reshaping. It can be described in full if we look at the conditions that its outcome must satisfy. That product (a dream) needs above all to be removed from *censorship*, and to that end dream-work uses a *shifting of psychical intensities* to the point of re-evaluating all psychical values; thoughts are to be reflected solely or primarily in the material of visual or acoustic memory-traces, and from this requirement there arises, so far as dream-work is concerned, a *concern for representability*, which it meets by means of fresh displacements. The (probable) intention is to create greater intensities than are available in the relevant dream-thoughts at night, and it is this that the extensive *compression* undertaken with the components of those dream-thoughts serves to promote. Little consideration is paid to the logical relations of the thought-material; they eventually find concealed representation in *formal* properties of the dreams concerned. Affects associated with dream-thoughts undergo less important changes than their ideational content. Usually, they are suppressed; if preserved, they are detached from the ideas and grouped by similarity. Only a portion of dream-work – namely, reprocessing (of variable extent) by a partially aroused waking mind – in fact fits in with the view that the literature seeks to assert in respect of the entire activity of dream-formation.

Notes

1. *Rêve, petit roman – day-dream, story.* [Freud's elucidatory footnote (the word *Tagtraum* being as yet unfamiliar to German readers) uses the original French and English words.]
2. I analysed a fine example of such a dream, consisting of a number of fantasies laid one on top of another, in 1905 in my 'Bruchstück einer Hysterie-Analyse' ['Fragment of an Analysis of Hysteria (Dora)' in *The Psychology of Love*, translated by Shaun Whiteside, London 2006, p. 56;

Standard Edition, vol. VII, p. 3]. Incidentally, I tended to underrate the importance of such fantasies as regards dream-formation while I was still dealing primarily with my own dreams, day-dreams more usually which are rarely based on discussions and intellectual conflicts. In other people, *total analogy of nocturnal dreaming with day-dreaming* is often much easier to prove. With hysterics, it is often possible to replace a fit by a dream; that makes it easy to satisfy oneself that the day-dream fantasy is the immediate prelude to both psychical formations.

3. [Anthropologist and eugenicist Sir Francis Galton (1822–1911) famously used the technique of superimposing photographic images to highlight certain physical traits.]

4. [Justine] Tobowolska, [*Étude sur les illusions de temps dans les rêves du sommeil normal*, Paris (thesis), 1900], p. 53.

5. ['The session will continue.' French politician Charles-Alexandre Dupuy (1851–1923) was president of the Chamber of Deputies at the time.]

6. [Havelock Ellis, *The World of Dreams*, London 1911, 'Introduction', pp. 10f. Freud in fact supplies this bibliographical reference (as he does many of those that follow) but in a much truncated form, which is why in this fuller version it and the others appear between square brackets.]

7. [Delacroix, 'Note sur la cohérence des rêves', *Rapport et C.R. du 2ème Congrès international de Philosophie*, p. 526.]

8. [Justine Tobowolska, op. cit. (see note 4 above), p. 93.]

9. [Paulhan, 'À propos de l'activité de l'esprit dans le rêve', in *Revue philosophique*, vol. 38, 1894, p. 547.]

10. [B. Leroy and Justine Tobowolska, 'Mécanisme intellectuel du rêve', in *Revue philosophique*, I, vol. 51, 1901, p. 592.]

11. [Herbert Silberer, 'Bericht über eine Methode, gewisse symbolische Halluzinationserscheinungen hervorzurufen und zu beobachten', in *Jahrbuch von Bleuler-Freud*, vol. I, 1909, p. 514.]

12. [*idem*, in *Jahrbuch von Bleuler-Freud*, vol. III, pp. 625, 627.]

13. 'Zur Einführung des Narzissmus' ['On the introduction of narcissism'], in *Jahrbuch der Psychoanalyse*, VI, 1914 [translated into English as 'On Narcissism: an Introduction' in *Standard Edition*, vol. XIV, p. 69, and as 'On the Introduction of Narcissism' in *Beyond the Pleasure Principle and Other Writings*, translated by John Reddick, London 2003].

14. I used to find it extraordinarily difficult to accustom readers to distinguishing between manifest dream-content and latent dream-thoughts. Repeatedly, arguments and objections were drawn from uninterpreted dream, as preserved in memory, while my demand for dream to be interpreted was ignored. Now, since analysts at least have got used to substituting

for the manifest dream its meaning as discovered by analysis, many of them are guilty of making a different mistake, to which they cling just as obstinately. They seek the essence of dream in that latent content, overlooking the fact that latent dream-thoughts and dream-work are different. Dream, basically, is nothing but a special *form* of thinking made possible for us by the conditions of the sleeping state. It is *dream-work* that creates that form, and dream-work alone constitutes the essence of dream, accounting for what makes it special. I say this to do justice to the notorious 'prospective tendency' of dream. That dream should concern itself with seeking solutions for the tasks facing our mental lives is no more remarkable than that our conscious waking life should so concern itself; the only thing dream adds is that this task can also proceed in the preconscious, which we knew already.

7

On the Psychology of Dream-Processes

Among the dreams I have learned from other people's accounts is one that now has a very special claim to our attention. It was told to me by a patient who had herself heard it in a lecture on dream; the original source remains unknown to me. However, its content made such an impression on my patient that she lost no time in 're-dreaming' it – that is to say, repeating elements of it in a dream of her own in order, by such copying, to express her agreement with one specific point.

The preconditions of this exemplary dream are these. For whole days and whole nights a father has kept watch at his sick child's bedside. When the child dies, he retires to an adjacent room to rest but leaves the door open in order to be able to see, from his bedroom, into the one in which the child's body has been laid out, surrounded by tall candles. An old man has been asked to keep vigil and sits beside the body, murmuring prayers. After sleeping for a few hours the father dreams *that the child, now standing by his own bed, takes hold of his arm and whispers reproachfully, 'Father, can't you see I'm burning?'* He wakes up, notices a bright light coming from the next room and rushes in there to find that the old man has dozed off and the wrappings and one arm of the beloved corpse have been scorched by a candle falling on them.

The explanation of this moving dream is quite simple and had indeed, as my patient recounted, been correctly provided by the lecturer. The bright light, entering through the open door, penetrated the sleeper's eye and prompted him to draw the same conclusion as he would have drawn had he been the one keeping vigil

– namely, that a candle had fallen over and started a fire near the body. Possibly, too, the father had taken with him into sleep his concern that the elderly watchman might not be up to the job.

We too find nothing in this interpretation that we should change, except that we claim in addition that the content of the dream must be multiply determined and the child's speech consist of words actually uttered during life and attached to significant occurrences so far as the father was concerned – the complaint 'I'm burning', say, to the child's high temperature at the time of death and the words 'Father, can't you see . . .' to some other unknown but highly emotional situation.

However, having acknowledged the dream as a meaningful sequence of events that fit the context of the psychical process, we may be permitted to express surprise that a dream occurred at all in circumstances where the swiftest possible awakening was called for. We then notice that not even this dream is devoid of wish-fulfilment. In the dream, the dead child behaves like a live one, urging its father itself, coming to his bedside and pulling at his arm, as probably happened in the memory from which dream retrieved the first fragment of the child's speech. For the sake of this wish-fulfilment, the father now prolonged his sleep for a moment. Dream took precedence over reflection in the waking state since it was able to show the child alive once again. Had the father first woken up and then drawn the conclusion that led him into the room where the body lay, he would (as it were) have been shortening the child's life by that brief moment.

There can be no doubting what peculiarity of this little dream it is that holds our interest. Our chief concern thus far has been with what constitutes the secret meaning of dreams, down which path this will be found and how, using what means, dream-work has concealed it. Hitherto, the tasks involved in dream-interpretation have occupied the centre of our field of vision. Now we are faced with a dream that is no trouble to interpret and the sense of which is undisguised, and we realize that this dream still retains the essential characteristics by which a dream differs markedly from our waking thought, activating our need for explanation. Only after eliminating everything to do with the task of interpretation are we able to see how incomplete our psychology of dream still is.

However, before proceeding with our thinking down this new route, let us pause and look back to check whether, in our wanderings up to this point, we have not left something important out of account. Because about one thing we must be clear: the cosy, comfortable stretch of our journey lies behind us. Up to now, if I am not greatly mistaken, all the paths we have trodden have brought us in the direction of enlightenment, explanation, full understanding; from the moment when we decide to delve deeper into the mental processes involved in dreaming, all paths lead into the dark. There is no question of our being able to *elucidate* dream as a psychical process, because explaining something means harking back to what is known and there is currently no body of psychological knowledge to which we might subordinate what can be deduced from the psychological examination of dreams as an explanation of or reason for them. On the contrary, we shall have to posit a series of fresh assumptions that offer tentative conjectures regarding the structure of our mental apparatus and the play of forces active therein, but that we must be careful not to spin out too far beyond the first logical link, since otherwise their value will dissipate and become indeterminable. Even if we make no errors of deduction and take all resultant logical possibilities into account, we face the threat that the probability of our formulating the rudiments incompletely will wholly skew our calculation. Information about the construction and *modus operandi* of the tool that is the mind will not be gained or at least cannot be substantiated from even the most careful investigation of dream or any other *single* function of mind; rather, in pursuing this end it will be necessary to assemble, through comparative study of a whole series of things that the mind does, what emerges as a constant requirement. The psychological assumptions that we have gleaned from analysing dream-processes will thus have to mark time, so to speak, until they are in a position to link up with the findings of other investigations that, each advancing from a different starting-point, seek to penetrate to the heart of the same problem.

A *How dreams get forgotten*

So I want us first to turn our attention to a subject from which an objection derives that we have disregarded up to now but that might in fact undermine our dream-interpretation efforts completely. The reproach has been levelled at us from more than one quarter that we have no actual knowledge of the particular dream we are trying to interpret or rather, more accurately, that we have no guarantee of knowing it as it actually occurred (see also above, pp. 55ff.).

In the first place, what we remember of a dream and exercise our interpretative skills on is garbled by the infidelity of our memory, which seems quite peculiarly incapable of preserving dreams and may possibly, indeed, have lost the most crucial parts of the dream in question. The fact is, we so often have cause to complain, when seeking to examine our dreams, that we dreamed a great deal more and unfortunately only recall the one fragment – with even that recollection appearing strangely indistinct. Secondly, however, there is every indication that our memory provides not only a fragmentary but also an unfaithful, distorted reflection of dream. Just as on the one hand we can doubt whether what we dreamed really was as confused and incoherent as we have it in memory, so on the other hand we may question whether a dream was as coherent as we recount it or whether, in seeking to rehearse it, we replace missing bits or plug gaps created by forgetting with fresh material chosen at random, thus embellishing, polishing and finishing the dream in such a way that any judgement as to its true content becomes impossible. Indeed, in one author (Spitta)[1] we find the suggestion that in fact all such order and coherence as a dream possesses is injected into it only when we try to recall it. There is a danger, therefore, of the very thing whose value we have undertaken to determine being wrested out of our hand.

Up to now, in our dream-interpretations we have ignored such warnings. On the contrary, we have found the tiniest, unlikeliest, least certain elements of dream-content to call for interpretation no less audibly than the relevant dream's plainly evident, clearly defined components. In the dream of Irma's injection [see above, pp. 119ff.] I *quickly* call in Dr M., and we assumed that even this little touch would not have got into the dream unless it could be traced to a separate source. This brought us to the story of the unfortunate patient to whose bedside I '*quickly*' summoned my older colleague. In the apparently absurd dream [see above, pp. 451ff.] in which the difference between fifty-one and fifty-six is treated as a *quantité négligeable* [Freud's original French], the number fifty-one was mentioned several times. Rather than find this self-evident or a matter of no importance, we deduced from it a second train of thought in the latent dream-content leading to the number fifty-one, and when we followed this trail further it led us to fears that put fifty-one years as the upper limit of life – in marked contrast to a prevalent line of thinking that throws around years of life in a boastful, arrogant manner. In the '*Non vixit*' dream [see above, pp. 435ff.], an inconspicuous insertion that I initially overlooked was the passage, '*Since P. does not understand him, Fl. turns to me and asks . . .*' When the interpretation subsequently ran into the ground I went back to those words and, from them, found my way into the childhood fantasy that features in the dream-thoughts as an intermediate junction. This happened through the medium of the poet's lines:

> *Selten habt ihr mich verstanden,*
> Selten auch verstand ich Euch,
> Nur wenn wir im Kot *uns fanden,*
> *So verstanden wir uns gleich!*

[Rarely did you *understand* me; rarely, too, did I understand you. Only when we were both *in the shit* did we understand each other instantly!
From 'Die Heimkehr' ('Homecoming') in Heinrich Heine,
Buch der Lieder]

Every analysis could show examples proving how it is precisely the least striking features of a dream that are indispensable as regards interpreting it and how completion of that task will be delayed if attention is paid to them only belatedly. The same positive appraisal is something to which, when interpreting dreams, we would treat each nuance of the linguistic expression in which a particular dream was presented to us; in fact, presented with non-sensical or inadequate wording as if the attempt to translate the dream into the correct version had failed, we would respect even such defective expression. Briefly, what some writers say is an improvisation cooked up hurriedly in an awkward situation, we treated as a sacred text. This contradiction requires explanation.

The explanation favours ourself without saying that therefore the others are wrong. From the standpoint of our newly acquired understanding of how dreams come about, the contradictions combine perfectly. It is true that we distort dreams when we try to reproduce them; we find reflected there what we have called the secondary and often misleading processing of dreams by the agency of normal thought. However, that distortion is itself simply part of the processing to which dream-thoughts are regularly subject as a result of dream-censorship. The writers have glimpsed or noticed in this the manifestly operating portion of dream-distortion; that scarcely affects us, knowing as we do that a far more substantial distortion operation, less easily comprehensible, has already singled the relevant dream out from the concealed dream-thoughts as its object. The only mistake the writers make is to see the modification that a dream undergoes when we recall it and put it into words as arbitrary, incapable of being broken down further, and therefore likely to mislead us as regards our taking cognizance of the dream. They underrate determinism in the psychical realm. Nothing, there, is arbitrary. It can be shown as a general rule that a second train of thought immediately takes over the task of determining an element that the first has left vague. For instance, I wish to have a number occur to me quite arbitrarily; this is not possible; the number that does come into my mind is clearly and inevitably determined by thoughts within me that may be far removed from my current intention.[2] Nor is there anything arbitrary about the editorial changes that a dream undergoes when the dreamer is awake. They remain associatively linked with the content that they replace, and they help to show us the way to that content, which may itself have replaced a different content.

I make a habit, when analysing dreams with patients, of putting this statement to the following test (which never fails). If at first the account of a patient's dream strikes me as difficult to understand, I ask the patient to repeat it. The repetition rarely uses the same words. However, the places where the wording has changed will enable me to identify the weak points of the dream's disguise; they do the same for me as the embroidered sign on Siegfried's cloak does for Hagen.[3] That is where the work of dream-interpretation can begin. My challenge having alerted the person narrating the dream to the fact that I mean to make particular efforts to resolve it, that person moves swiftly, under the impulse of resistance, to protect the weak points of the dream-disguise by replacing an expression that threatens to give the game away by one that is more remote. In this way my attention is drawn to the expression that has been excised. From the effort invested in preventing resolution of the dream, I can also deduce the care that has gone into weaving the dream's integument.

The writers are less correct in devoting so very much space to the doubt that in our view dream-narration encounters. The fact is, such doubt lacks any intellectual warranty; our memory knows no guarantees whatsoever, yet far more often than can be justified objectively we find ourselves compelled to give credence to its testimony. Doubt about whether or not the dream in question or individual details thereof are being reproduced correctly is again simply a derivative of dream-censorship, of resistance to the possibility of the relevant dream-thoughts forcing their way through to consciousness. Such resistance sometimes amounts to more than simply the shifts and replacements that it has effected; it latches on to what it has let through and calls it doubtful. What makes it easier for us to fail to recognize such doubt is the fact that it is careful never to assail intensive elements of the dream in question but only ones that are feeble and indistinct. We, however, are already aware that between dream-thoughts and the resultant dream a complete reappraisal of all psychical values has taken place; distortion was possible only as a result of withdrawal of value, regularly taking that form and occasionally going no further. If an indistinct element of dream-content has doubt added to it, we are able, following this indicator, to recognize it as a more direct derivative of one of the outlawed dream-thoughts. The situation is like that following a major upheaval in one of the republics of the ancient world or of the Renaissance. The noble, powerful families who had previously been in charge are now banished and all high positions occupied by upstarts; only very impoverished and powerless members or remote dependants of the families that have been overthrown are tolerated in the city henceforth. Even these, though, do not enjoy full civil rights and are monitored mistrustfully. Where in the example there is mistrust, in our case we have doubt. That is why, when I am analysing a dream, I require that the whole gamut of assessments of sureness be shrugged off and that the slightest chance of something of the kind having occurred in the dream be treated as utter certainty. Unless a person resolves, when a dream-element is being pursued, to renounce any such making of allowances, that person's analysis will progress no further. Belittling the element in question has the psychical effect, so far as the analysand is concerned, of preventing any of the involuntary ideas behind that element from occurring to him as associations. Such an effect is not actually self-evident; it would not be absurd for someone to say, 'Whether this or that was present in the dream I'm not sure; but the following does occur to me in this connection.' No one ever does say that, and it is precisely this effect of doubt, as something disturbing the process of analysis, that unmasks it as a derivative and tool of psychical resistance. Psychoanalysis is right to be mistrustful. One of its rules is: *Whatever interferes with continuation of the work constitutes a resistance.*[4]

Another thing that remains unfathomable until we invoke the power of psychical censorship to explain it is how dreams get forgotten. The sense that one has dreamed a great deal in a particular night and retained only a little may in a series of cases bear a different significance – perhaps that dream-work has proceeded perceptibly throughout the night and left only one brief dream behind. Otherwise, there can be no doubt but that, after waking, one forgets more and more of what one dreamed. Often one forgets it despite painstaking efforts not to. But what I think is that, just as we tend to exaggerate the extent of such forgetting, so we also exaggerate the forfeiture of knowledge of a dream that we connect with its being incomplete. Everything that such forgetting has cost in terms of dream-content can often be recovered by analysis; at any rate, it is possible in a great many instances to start from a single surviving fragment and recover not the dream itself (that does not matter) but the dream-thoughts. One needs to expend more vigilance and will-power during analysis; that's all, but it does show that a degree of hostile intent was involved in [the patient's] forgetting the dream.[5]

Convincing proof of the tendentious nature of forgetting dreams and the way it serves resistance[6] is something that, in connection with analyses, one gains from acknowledging a preliminary stage in forgetting. It quite often happens that, in the middle of interpreting a dream, a part that had been omitted crops up, having previously been deemed forgotten. Such a dream-fragment, wrested from oblivion, in fact turns out every time to be the most important part; lying on the shortest path to a resolution of the dream, it was most exposed to resistance. The specimen dreams that I have sprinkled throughout this study include one in which I must insert a piece of dream-content subsequently in this way. This is a travel dream [see above, p. 469f.] that takes revenge on two not very pleasant travelling companions and that, because of its partly very coarse content, I left virtually uninterpreted. The omitted portion runs, *I say of a Schiller title, 'It is from . . .' But then, spotting my own mistake,*

correct myself, 'It is by . . .' Whereupon the man remarks to his
sister, 'He's got it right now, you see.'[7]

Self-correction in dream, which many writers have found so
marvellous, is probably not worth bothering about. I prefer, when
discussing speech-error in dream, to cite an example from my own
memory. I was nineteen, visiting Britain for the first time, and I
spent a day on the shore of the Irish Sea. I naturally revelled in the
catch of sea creatures left behind by the tide, and I was just examining a starfish (the dream in question begins with *Hollthurn-*
Holothurien)[8] when a charming little girl came up to me and asked,
'*Is it a starfish? Is it alive?*' I replied, '*Yes, he is alive*', but then,
ashamed of my mistake, I repeated the sentence correctly. In place
of the speech-error that I committed on that occasion, this dream
now offers another, to which a German-speaker is equally vulner-
able. '*Das Buch is von Schiller*' needs to be translated using not
'from . . .' but 'by . . .'. It should come as no surprise to us, after all
we have heard about the intentions of dream-work and its ruthlessness in its choice of means, that dream-work effects this replacement since [the English preposition] 'from', sounding as it does
very like [the German adjective] *fromm* [= religious, god-fearing],
makes a splendid piece of compression possible. But what does my
innocent memory from the beach imply in the context of this
dream? It illustrates, using as innocuous an example as possible, a
misuse on my part of *gender*; I am introducing the *gender word*
'he' where it does not belong. This is in fact one of the keys to
solving the dream. Anyone who has heard the derivation of the
book-title *Matter and Motion* (*Moliére in* [his play] Le *Malade-*
Imaginaire: La matière est-elle laudable? – a motion of the bowels)[9]
will easily be able to supply what is missing.

I, by the way, am able to furnish proof that the forgetting of
dream is largely a resistance operation – proof in the form of a
demonstratio ad oculos. A patient tells me that he had a dream but
has completely forgotten it; the dream is then deemed not to have
occurred. We continue working; I come up against some resistance;
I elucidate something for the patient, helping him, by offering
encouraging words and applying pressure, to come to terms with

some disagreeable thought; and hardly has this been achieved than he exclaims, 'Now I remember my dream!' The same resistance as disturbed his analysis that day had caused him to forget the dream. By overcoming the resistance, I promoted recall of the dream.

Similarly, a patient who has reached a certain stage of the work [of analysis] can recall a dream that occurred three, four or more days earlier and had remained in oblivion until that moment.[10]

Psychoanalytical experience has given us further proof that forgetting dreams has far more to do with resistance than with any difference of nature between the waking and sleeping states, as the writers suppose. It quite frequently happens to me as it happens to other analysts and patients receiving psychoanalytical treatment that, roused from sleep by a dream, as we like to say, we proceed immediately, in full possession of our intellectual capacities, to interpret that dream. On many such occasions I made no movement until I was in possession of a complete understanding of the dream, yet still it might happen that, after waking up, I had forgotten the work of interpretation as utterly as I had forgotten the dream-content, despite being aware that I had had a dream and had interpreted it. It was much more common for the dream to have dragged the outcome of the work of interpretation with it into oblivion than for the activity of my intellect to have succeeded in retaining the dream in memory. However, there is not the psychical gulf between the work of interpretation and waking thought by which the writers seek exclusively to explain dream-forgetting. In challenging my explanation on the grounds that dream-forgetting is simply a special case of amnesia regarding what he calls 'dissociated states', Morton Prince maintains that the impossibility of extending my explanation of this special amnesia to other types of amnesia also renders it worthless as regards its immediate purpose. He further reminds the reader that in all his descriptions of such 'dissociated states' he has never attempted to find the dynamic explanation of such phenomena. Had he done so, he would inevitably have discovered that repression (or the resistance to which it gives rise) is just as much the cause of such dissociations as of the amnesia to which their psychical content is subject.

Dreams (as an experience I had while working on this manuscript showed me) are no more forgotten than other mental acts; in fact, their hold on memory likewise puts them entirely on a par with other mental functions. The experience was this. In my notes I had recorded a great many of my own dreams that at the time, for whatever reason, I was able to interpret only very incompletely or not at all. With some of them I made a second attempt, one or two years later, to interpret them with a view to giving myself material to illustrate my claims. In every instance the attempt was successful; I might even say, in fact, that the work of interpretation proceeded more easily after so lengthy an interval than it had done while the dreams were still fresh experiences, and I should like to put forward as one possible explanation for this that I have since overcome certain resistances in my inner life that were troubling me at the time. In connection with such retrospective interpretations, I compared the then results in terms of dream-thoughts with today's usually much more varied crop and found the former turning up unchanged among the latter. I promptly countered my astonishment at this by reflecting that I have in fact long been in the habit, with my patients, of getting them to interpret dreams from bygone years (which they occasionally tell me about) as if they had been dreams from the previous night, using the same method and meeting with the same success. In discussing anxiety-dreams [later in this chapter] I shall recount two instances of such belated dream-interpretation. When I first tried this, I was guided by a legitimate expectation that here too dream would simply behave like a neurotic symptom. The fact is, if I am treating a psychoneurotic (a hysteric, say) by means of psychoanalysis, I need to throw light on the earliest, long since overcome symptoms of the patient's condition just as much as on those still existing today, which are what brought the patient to me, and I find the first task simply easier to perform than the one that is now urgent. As early as 1895, in *Studien über Hysterie*,[11] I was able to explain an initial hysterical fit that a woman over forty had had in her fifteenth year.[12]

Somewhat loosely connected with this, let me put forward at this point something that I need to say about interpreting dreams and

537

that may possibly give some guidance to any reader wishing to verify my contentions by working on his own dreams.

No one should expect the interpretation of his dreams to fall into his lap effortlessly. Simply perceiving endoptic phenomena and other sensations that are usually removed from attention takes practice, although no psychical motive militates against this group of perceptions. It is very much more difficult to pick up 'involuntary ideas'. Anyone seeking to do this will have to fill himself with the expectations that have been aroused in this treatise and, following the rules laid down herein, will be at pains, during the operation, to suppress in himself any criticism, any bias – in short, any kind of emotional or intellectual prejudice. He will be mindful of the motto that [French physiologist] Claude Bernard prescribed for the experimenter in the physiological laboratory: *'Travailler comme une bête'* ['Work like an animal'] – that is to say, with the same tenacity but also with the same indifference to the outcome. However, anyone following this advice will no longer find the task difficult. Nor does interpreting a dream always proceed in one go; often one feels one has reached the limit of one's ability after tracing a chain of associations; the dream has no more to say to one that day; in which case it will be a good idea to break off and return to the task another time. Then a different piece of the dream-content will attract one's attention, giving access to a fresh stratum of dream-thoughts. 'Fractionated' dream-interpretation, we might call it.

The hardest thing is to persuade the novice dream-interpreter to recognize the fact that his task is not in fact complete once he has his hands on a comprehensive interpretation of the dream in question, one that is meaningful, coherent and provides information about every element of the dream-content. There may be another interpretation as well, a super-interpretation of the same dream, which had eluded him. It is far from easy to gain an idea of the wealth of unconscious trains of thought struggling for expression in our minds or to credit the skill with which dream-work devises multiple forms of expression – each time, as it were, hitting seven flies with one blow, like the tailor in the story [by the Brothers Grimm]. The reader will always be inclined to accuse the author [of the dream] of deploying overmuch ingenuity, but anyone acquiring personal experience of the matter will soon learn better.

On the other hand I cannot agree with the claim, first put forward by H[erbert] Silberer, that all dreams (or even simply many dreams, certain groups of dreams) require two different interpretations – which even stand in a fixed relationship to each other. One of those interpretations, which Silberer calls the *psychoanalytical* interpretation, gives the dream an arbitrary meaning usually having to do with childhood sexuality; the other, more significant interpretation, which he terms *anagogic* ['mystical', 'spiritual'], shows the more serious, often profound thoughts that dream-work has adopted as material. Silberer does not prove this claim by recounting a series of dreams that he has analysed in both directions. My objection must be that such a state of affairs does not exist. Most dreams do not require multiple interpretation and are above all incapable of an anagogic interpretation. The influence of a tendency seeking to obscure the fundamental circumstances of dream-formation and divert attention away from its rootedness in drives is as unmistakable in connection with Silberer's theory as it is in connection with other theoretical endeavours of recent years. In certain instances I was able to confirm what Silberer says; analysis then showed me that dream-work had found itself faced with the problem of taking a series of highly abstract thoughts from waking life, thoughts such as were incapable of direct representation, and turning them into a dream. It tried to solve this problem by appropriating different thought-material that stood in a looser, often to be termed *'allegorical'* relationship to those abstract thoughts and was therefore less difficult to represent. The abstract interpretation of a dream that has come about in this way is provided by the dreamer instantly; the correct interpretation of the appropriated material needs to be sought with the familiar technical means.

To the question whether every dream can be successfully interpreted, the answer must be 'No'. Remember, one embarks on the task of dream-interpretation with the psychical forces responsible for distorting the dream ranged against one. So it becomes a question of the balance of forces, whether one is capable (with one's

intellectual interests, one's will-power, one's psychological knowledge and one's skill at dream-interpretation) of showing the forces
of internal resistance who is master. To some extent this is always
possible – sufficiently, at least, to form the conviction that a dream
is a meaningful entity and usually, too, to gain some inkling of what
that meaning is. On many occasions a dream following immediately
will enable one to be sure of the interpretation first assumed and
to take it further. A whole series of dreams stretching over weeks
or months will often be based on common ground and will therefore
need to be subsumed within the same interpretive context. Often,
in connection with a succession of dreams, it becomes evident how
one dream will centre on what in the next is only hinted at on the
periphery, and *vice versa*, with the result that both dreams also
complement each other when it comes to interpreting them. I have
already cited examples to show how the various dreams of one and
the same night ought always to be treated by the dream-interpreter
as a single whole [see above, pp. 347f.].

In the best-interpreted dreams, one often needs to leave a particular passage obscure, having become aware, during the work of
interpretation, that a knot of dream-thoughts rises there that refuses
to unravel but in fact made no further contribution to the dream-
content. This then is the hub of the dream, the place where it squats
on the unacknowledged. The vast majority of the dream-thoughts
that one comes across must of course remain unresolved and seep
away in all directions into the web-like entanglement of the world
of our thoughts. From a spot on this intricate web that is denser
than the rest, the dream-wish then arises like a fungus from its
mycelium.

Let us return to the circumstances surrounding the fact of dreams
being forgotten. You see, we failed to draw one important conclusion here. If waking life demonstrates an unmistakable determination to forget the dream formed during the previous night, either
as a whole, immediately after waking, or piece by piece over the
course of the ensuing day, and if we as the chief participants
recognize this forgetting process as the mental resistance to dream
that already did its bit in the night against the dream being dreamed,

the obvious question is: what was it actually that, in the teeth of such resistance, made dream-formation possible at all? Let us look at the most glaring case in which waking life eliminates the night's dream as if it had never occurred. Taking into account the play of psychical forces, we have to say that the dream would never have come about in the first place if resistance had ruled by night as it does by day. Our conclusion is that, during the night-time, resistance forfeited some of its power; we know that it was not removed altogether because we have shown the part it plays in dream-formation in the guise of dream-distortion. However, the possibility urges itself upon us that at night it was less powerful, and that this diminished resistance enabled dream-formation to occur, making it easy for us to understand that, restored to full power on the dreamer's awakening, it promptly gets rid of what, in its weakened state, it had been obliged to allow. Descriptive psychology teaches us, indeed, that the chief requirement of dream-formation is that the mind should be asleep; we might now add: *the sleeping state makes dream-formation possible by reducing endopsychical censorship.*

It is tempting for us, certainly, to see this conclusion as being the only one possible from the circumstances of dream-forgetting, and to go on to draw further conclusions from it with regard to the energy-relations between the sleeping and waking states. However, for the present we intend to refrain from doing so. When we have gone a little deeper into the psychology of dreams, we shall learn that what enables dream-formation to take place can in fact be imagined otherwise. Resistance to dream-thoughts becoming conscious can perhaps also be circumvented without its undergoing any inherent diminution. It is also plausible that both factors favouring dream-formation (diminution of resistance *and* its circumvention) are made possible simultaneously by the sleeping state. Here we shall break off this discussion – to resume it in a short while.

There is a different series of objections to our method of interpreting dreams, and these we must now address. The fact is, the way we proceed is that we set aside all other purposive ideas[13] dominating reflection, direct our attention at a single dream-element and note subsequently what involuntary thoughts drop into our mind in that connection. We then pass to another component of the dream-content, do the same thing there, and without worrying about the direction in which the thoughts are taking us let them carry us along – indeed, as the saying goes, carry us away. Yet we do so in the confident expectation that, quite without willing it, we shall come across the dream-thoughts that gave rise to this particular dream. Critics, on the other hand, will advance something like the following objection. They will say that there is nothing wonderful about starting out from an individual element of a dream and getting somewhere or other. Every idea is capable of leading, by association, to something else; the only surprise is that by following such an aimless, arbitrary train of thought one should stumble across (of all things) the relevant dream-thoughts. Probably [the critics will go on to say] this is self-delusion; one follows the chain of association from an individual element until one finds that, for some reason, it breaks off; if one then takes up a second element, it is only natural that the original complete freedom of association will now be somewhat restricted. With the earlier chain of ideas still fresh in one's memory, one will therefore, while analysing the second idea represented in the dream, more readily encounter individual associations that have something in common with associations from the first chain. One will then become convinced that one has discovered an idea forming a junction between two dream-elements. Since one usually allows oneself every freedom in the context of association of ideas, ruling out only such transitions from one idea to another as take effect in normal thinking, it will not, ultimately, be difficult to take a series of 'intermediate thoughts' and concoct something one then calls 'dream-thoughts', passing these off (without any guarantee, since they are known in no other way) as the psychical equivalent of the relevant dream. However, this is all arbitrary, an apparently ingenious exploitation of chance, and anyone undertaking this pointless endeavour can, using this method, start from any dream and come up with any interpretation he chooses.

When such objections actually are levelled at us, we are able, in our defence, to appeal to the impression left by our dream-interpretations, to the surprising links to other dream-elements that emerge during our pursuit of individual ideas and to the unlikelihood of something that so perfectly covers and accounts for a particular dream as one of our dream-interpretations being obtainable in any other way than by our tracing back previously formed psychical links. We might also enlist as further justification the fact that the procedure involved in interpreting dreams is exactly the same as that used to clear up hysterical symptoms, where the correctness of the procedure is guaranteed by the appearance and disappearance of the symptoms in their place – in other words, where exegesis of the text is supported by the illustrations included. However, we have no reason to side-step the problem of how, by following an arbitrarily, aimlessly unfolding chain of ideas, it is possible to reach a pre-existent purposive idea since, while this is not a problem we can solve, it is one we are able to eliminate completely.

The fact is, it is demonstrably untrue that we are committing ourselves to an aimless procession of ideas when, as in the task of interpreting dreams, we abandon reflective thought and allow involuntary ideas to rise to the surface. It can be shown that we are invariably able to dispense only with the purposive ideas that are known to us and that, as soon as these cease to apply, unknown (we say imprecisely 'unconscious') purposive ideas come into play that then control the course of development of such involuntary ideas as spring to mind. Thought that is innocent of purposive ideas can never be produced by our personally exerting influence on our mental life; nor do I know in what states of psychical breakdown it is produced otherwise.[14] Psychiatrists have here been far too quick to abandon the solidity of psychical structure. I know that an unregulated sequence of thoughts devoid of purposive ideas no more occurs in the context of hysteria and paranoia than in connection with the formation or dissolution of dreams. In connection with endogenic psychical maladies it may not occur at all; according to an intellectually stimulating conjecture put forward by Leuret, even the deliriums of the confused make sense and become incomprehensible to us only as a result of omissions. I became similarly convinced where I had an opportunity to make such observations. Deliriums are the work of a kind of censorship that no longer troubles to hide its prevalence; instead of lending its influence to a revision that is no longer offensive, such censorship ruthlessly strikes out everything it objects to, with the result that what is left loses its coherence. Such censorship proceeds very much like Russian newspaper censorship at the border, which simply sprinkles foreign journals with black lines before delivering them into the hands of the readers to be protected.

Free play of ideas in accordance with random association may possibly occur in connection with destructive organic brain processes; what in connection with psychoneuroses is regarded as such is invariably explicable in terms of the influence of censorship on a train of thought that purposive ideas that had remained hidden now thrust into the foreground.[15] It has been deemed an unmistakable sign of association that is free of purposive ideas if the ideas (or images) that crop up appear bound together by ties of so-called 'superficial association' (assonance, verbal ambiguity, temporal coincidence without an internal sense-connection) – that is to say, by all the connections we allow ourselves to exploit when making a joke or a play on words. This characteristic is true of the thought-connections that lead us from elements of the dream-content to the intermediate thoughts and from there to the true dream-thoughts; in many dream-analyses we came across instances of this that we inevitably found disconcerting. No link was too loose, no joke too reprehensible to be permitted to throw a bridge from one thought to another. Yet the proper understanding of such leniency is not hard to find. *Each time a psychical element is joined to another by an offensive, superficial association, there is also a correct, more profound link between the two that is subject to the resistance of censorship.*

Pressure of censorship, not removal of purposive ideas, is the right reason for the prevalence of superficial associations. Superficial associations replace deep ones in representation when censorship renders these normal connecting routes unviable. It is as if a general obstacle to traffic (a flood, for instance) in mountainous country had rendered the broad main roads impassable; communications are then maintained over difficult, steep footpaths normally used only by hunters.

It is possible to distinguish two cases here that are in essence one and the same. Either censorship is directed purely against the connection between two thoughts that, separated from each other, are unobjectionable. The two thoughts then enter consciousness one after the other; their connectedness remains hidden; instead, a superficial link between them occurs to us that we should not have thought of otherwise and that generally starts in a different corner of the ideational complex from the one from which the suppressed but essential connection proceeds. Or, on the other hand, both thoughts are inherently subject to censorship because of their content; in which case both appear not in their correct form but in a modified, replacement form, and the two replacement thoughts are chosen in such a way as to reflect, through a superficial association, the essential connection between the thoughts they replace. *Under pressure of censorship a shift has taken place here in both instances from a normal, serious association to a superficial, ostensibly absurd one.*

Knowing about such shifts, we have no qualms, when interpreting dreams, about placing implicit faith even in superficial associations.[16]

Of these two propositions – that when conscious purposive ideas are abandoned, dominion over the development of ideas passes to hidden purposive ideas, and that superficial associations are simply a displacement substitute for deeper associations that have been suppressed – psychoanalysis makes very extensive use in connection with neuroses; indeed, it elevates them to the status of cornerstones of its technique. When I instruct a patient to abandon all reflective activity and then tell me whatever pops into his or her head, I cling to the assumption that he or she will not be able to abandon the purposive ideas behind the treatment, and I feel justified in concluding that the most innocent (apparently), most arbitrary (apparently) things I am told will be connected with that patient's condition. Another purposive idea, of which the patient suspects nothing, is that of my own person. It follows that a full appreciation and thoroughgoing proof of both propositions form part of the description of psychoanalytical technique as a therapeutic method. Here we have reached one of the connecting points at which we deliberately drop the subject of dream-interpretation.[17]

One thing only is correct, one objection remains; it is that there is no need for us to locate all the idea-associations of the work of interpretation in nocturnal dream-work as well. The fact is, as we interpret a dream in the waking state we are creating a path that leads back from dream-elements to dream-thoughts. Dream-work did the reverse, and it is most unlikely that these paths going the other way are practicable. Rather, it transpires that by day, using new thought-connections, we sink shafts that meet the intermediate thoughts and the dream-thoughts now in one place, now in another. We are able to see how the fresh thought-material of the new day slips into the ranks of our interpretation – and probably, too, obliges the increased resistance that has come in since the nocturnal hours to make fresh, extended detours. However, the number or type of collaterals that we thus develop during the day is of no psychological significance whatsoever, provided only that they show us the way to the dream-thoughts we are looking for.

Notes

1. In [Marcel] Foucault and Tannery, too.
2. See [my] *Psychopathologie des Alltagslebens*, first edition 1901 and 1904, eleventh edition 1929. [*The Psychopathology of Everyday Life* in *Standard Edition*, vol. VI; a new translation by Anthea Bell has appeared with the same title in the New Penguin Freud series, London 2002.]
3. [In the *Nibelungenlied*.]
4. The principle so peremptorily advanced here ('whatever interferes with continuation of the work constitutes a resistance') might easily be misunderstood. It has the importance only of a technical rule, of course – a reminder for the analyst. This is not to deny that during an analysis various things may occur that cannot be blamed on the intention of the person being analysed. The patient's father may die without the patient having killed

him; war may even break out, bringing the analysis to an end. However, behind the obviously exaggerated nature of the principle lies a new and valuable sense. Even if the event 'interfering with continuation of the work' is real and independent of the patient, often only the patient is responsible for just how disruptive it is allowed to be, and resistance betrays its unmistakable presence in the eager, excessive way in which such an opportunity is exploited.

5. As an example of the importance of doubt and uncertainty in dreaming, coupled with a shrinking of dream-content to a single element, the following dream, taken from my *Vorlesungen zur Einführung in die Psycho-analyse* [*Introductory Lectures on Psychoanalysis* [1916–17; *Standard Edition*, vols XV and XVI], was successfully analysed a short time after being dreamed:

'A sceptical patient has an extended dream in which certain persons tell her about my book on "Jokes" [Der Witz und seine Beziehung zum Unbewussten (1905), translated into English as Jokes and their Relation to the Unconscious, Standard Edition, vol. VIII; The Joke and Its Relation to the Unconscious, translated by Joyce Crick, London 2002], praising it highly. Then something is said about a "channel", possibly there is mention of a different book in which the word channel occurs or something else to do with a channel . . . she doesn't know . . . it's very unclear.

'You will tend to believe, will you not, that the element "channel" is trying to evade interpretation, being itself so indeterminate. You are right about the supposed difficulty, but the reason for the difficulty is not because it is unclear; rather, it is unclear for another reason – the same reason that also makes it difficult to interpret. The dreamer forms no association with "channel"; nor, of course, can I say anything myself. Some time later (the next day, actually) she tells me that something has come into her mind that *may* be connected. This too is a joke she heard someone tell. On a boat between Dover and Calais, a well-known writer is in conversation with an Englishman, who in a certain context quotes [in French, Napoleon's dictum:] *"Du sublime au ridicule il n'y a qu'un pas"* ["From the sublime to the ridiculous is but a step"]. The writer replies, *"Oui, le pas de Calais"*, meaning that he finds France sublime and England ridiculous. Now, the "Pas de Calais" is in fact a channel, the English Channel [or rather part of it, namely the Strait of Dover]. Do I think this association has anything to do with the dream?' "I certainly do," I tell her; "it does indeed supply the answer to the mysterious dream-element. Or do you mean to question whether the quip already existed prior to the dream, providing the unconscious background to the 'channel' element; are you saying it was added subsequently?" The fact is, the association testifies to the scepticism that, in her, hides behind obtrusive expressions of admiration, and resistance is probably the reason for them both – not only for the fact that the association occurred to her so tardily but also for the way the corresponding dream-element turned out to be so indistinct. Look at the relationship of the dream-element to its unconscious background. It is like a fragment of that unconscious, a sort of allusion thereto; isolation has made it utterly mysterious.'

6. As regards the intention behind any kind of forgetting, see also my short article 'Über den psychischen Mechanismus der Vergesslichkeit' ['On the psychical mechanism of forgetfulness'] in *Monatsschrift für Psychiatrie und Neurologie* (1898) (which later became the first chapter of my *Psychopathologie des Alltagslebens*, op. cit. [see note 1 above]).

7. Such corrections of usage in foreign languages occur not infrequently in dreams but are usually attributed to foreigners themselves. Maury (p. 143) once dreamed while learning English that he informed someone of his visit the previous day in the words, '*I called* for *you yesterday.*' The other person correctly [Freud, of course, is discussing this point in German, though he does give the spoken comments in the original] replied, 'That's: "*I called on you yesterday.*"'

8. [*Hollthurn* appears to be Freud's own invention; *Holothurie* are in fact sea-cucumbers. But see also the original account of the dream on p. 469.]

9. [Freud's typically dense reference assumes that his readers will know that *Matter and Motion* is the title of Scottish physicist James Clerk Maxwell's best-known work and that the joke in the Molière quotation is that the '*matière*' in question here is as defined in the English phrase that follows the French.]

10. E[rnest] Jones describes the analogous case (which happens often) where during analysis of a dream a second dream from the same night is recalled that had previously been forgotten – indeed, not even suspected.

11. [Sigmund Freud and Joseph Breuer, *Studien über Hysterie* (1895); *Studies on Hysteria, Standard Edition*, vol. II; a new translation by Nicola Luckhurst is available in the New Penguin Freud, *Studies in Hysteria*, London 2004.]

12. Dreams that occurred in the earliest years of childhood and have quite often been preserved in memory for decades in all their original sensory freshness almost invariably assume huge importance as regards understanding the development and neuroses of the dreamer. Analysing them shields the doctor against errors and uncertainties that might confuse him theoretically as well.

13. [*Zielvorstellungen*; the normal English translation would be 'objectives',

but Freud used the term *Zielvorstellung* in a rather special way 'to account for what directs the flow of thoughts, as much conscious as preconscious and unconscious ones' (Jean Laplanche and Jean-Bertrand Pontalis, *The Language of Psychoanalysis*, 1973, translated from the French by Donald Nicholson-Smith; reprinted London 1988, p. 373). To mark this special usage, I retain the rendition 'purposive idea' – 'idea' (*Vorstellung*) being itself a technical term of philosophy and psychology for 'that which one represents to oneself, that which forms the concrete content of an act of thought' (ibid., p. 200).]

14. Only subsequently was it brought to my attention that E[duard] von Hartmann puts forward the same view on this psychologically important point: 'While discussing the role of the unconscious in artistic creation in *Philosophy of the Unconscious* (1869, vol. I, sec. B, ch. V) Edward von Hartmann states the law of association of ideas steered by unconscious objectives in clear terms, though without being aware of the law's scope. He is concerned to prove that every combination of sensory ideas, when not left to pure chance but intended to lead to a specific goal, requires the help of the unconscious, and that conscious interest in a specific association of ideas acts as a spur to the unconscious to find, among the countless possible ideas, the one that is most appropriate. "It is the unconscious that chooses in accordance with the purposes of interest: and that is true in respect of *association of ideas in connection with abstract thinking, whether as sensory imagination or artistic combination, or in connection with the ingenious "fall-in"* [Einfall, the 'first thing you think of']. So restricting association of ideas to the idea that evokes or is evoked in the sense of pure associative psychology is not sustainable. Such a restriction would be "truly justified only if conditions in human life obtain in which a person is free not only of any conscious purpose but also of the dominance or influence of every unconscious interest, every mood. This, however, is a state that hardly ever obtains, because even *if a person appears to leave his sequence of ideas entirely to chance or if he gives himself over wholly to the involuntary dreams of fantasy, nevertheless different principal interests, dominant feelings and moods will prevail at one time than at another, and these will invariably influence any association of ideas"* (*Philosophie des Unbewussten*, eleventh edition, vol. I, p. 246). In semi-unconscious dreams, only those ideas ever appear that correspond to the current (unconscious) chief interest (loc. cit.). Highlighting the influence of feelings and moods on free association of ideas makes the methodological procedure of psychoanalysis appear thoroughly justified, even from the standpoint of Hartmann's psychology' (N. E. Pohorilles in *Internationale Zeitschrift für ärztliche Psycho-*

analyse, I, 1913, pp. 605f.). [Carl] Du Prel concludes from the fact that a name we have trouble remembering often suddenly comes back to us for no apparent reason that there exists an unconscious yet nevertheless goal-directed type of thinking, the results of which then enter consciousness (see his *Die Philosophie der Mystik*, Leipzig 1885, p. 107).

15. See also the brilliant confirmation of this statement supplied by C. G. Jung in his analyses of *dementia praecox* patients (*Zur Psychologie der Dementia Praecox* ['The psychology of dementia praecox'], 1907).

16. The same considerations also apply, of course, where the superficial associations in the dream-content are exposed – as, for instance, in the two dreams recounted by Maury (see above, p. 70: *pèlerinage – Pelletier – pelle; kilomètre – kilogramme – Gilolo – lobelia – Lopez – lotto*). I know from my work with neurotics what type of reminiscence likes to represent itself in this way. It is the leafing through encyclopedias (dictionaries generally) with which at the time of pubertal curiosity most people satisfied their need for enlightenment regarding the riddles of sex.

17. The propositions advanced here, which at the time sounded highly improbable, subsequently met with experimental corroboration and were put to use by the 'diagnostic associative studies' carried out by Jung and his pupils.

B *Regression*

Now, though, having defended ourselves against the objections or at least shown where our weapons of defence lie, we cannot further postpone embarking upon the psychological investigations for which we have been so long prepared. Let us summarize the chief findings of our study so far. Dream[1] is a psychical act bearing its full weight; what drives it in each case is a wish seeking fulfilment; the fact that it is unrecognizable as a wish, together with its many special characteristics and absurdities, stems from the influence of the psychical censorship it underwent during formation; in addition to the compulsion to escape such censorship, its formation was also influenced by a compulsion to compress psychical material, a concern for representability in sensory images and a concern (though this is not invariably present) that the resultant dream should present a rational, intelligible exterior. Each of these propositions leads on to psychological postulates and conjectures; the reciprocal relationship between the wish motive and the four conditions, plus the ways in which these relate to one another, all require investigation; dream needs to be set in the context of the life of mind.

We placed a dream at the head of this chapter [see above, p. 526] to remind ourselves of the riddle that has yet to be solved. Interpreting this dream of the burning child presented us with no problems, although the interpretation was not, in our sense, given in full. We wondered why, in this instance, the person had dreamed at all, rather than waking up, and we recognized that among the dreamer's motives was the wish to picture the child alive. Further discussion will show us that another wish is involved here as well.

Initially, then, it is for the sake of wish-fulfilment that the thought-process in sleep is transformed into a dream.

Reversing this, one is left with only one characteristic that distinguishes the two types of psychical event from each other. The dream-thought would have run like this: I see a light coming from the room where the body is lying; a candle may have fallen over, and the child is on fire! The resultant dream reflects the outcome of this piece of ratiocination unaltered but represented in a situation that can be grasped currently and sensorily as a waking experience. However, this is the most universal, most conspicuous psychological characteristic of dreaming; a thought (usually what is wished) is objectivized in a dream, represented as a scene, or (as we think) experienced.

But how is one to explain this typical feature of dream-work or (to put it more modestly) place that feature in the context of psychical processes?

On closer examination, of course, one notices that in the form in which this dream manifests itself two characteristics that are virtually independent of each other are markedly in evidence. One is presentation as a current situation, omitting the 'may' [have fallen over, etc.]; the other is translation of thought into visual images and speech.

The transformation that dream-thoughts undergo in that the expectation expressed therein is set in the here and now may not, particularly in the case of this dream, appear very obvious. That has to do with the special (actually, subsidiary) role of wish-fulfilment in this dream. Let us take a different dream, one in which the dream-wish is not separate from the continuation of waking thought in sleep – the dream of Irma's injection, for instance [see above, p. 119.]. Here the dream-thought attaining representation is in the optative mood: 'If only Otto were to blame for Irma's illness!' The dream suppresses the optative mood and substitutes a simple present tense: 'Yes, Otto is to blame for Irma's illness.' So this is the first of the changes that even a distortion-free dream makes to the dream-thoughts. We shall not dwell at length on this first peculiarity of dream. We account for it in terms of conscious fantasy, day-dream – which treats its imaginative content in the same way. When Daudet's Monsieur Joyeuse,[2] strolling unemployed through the streets of Paris while his daughters inevitably think he has a job and is sitting in some office, dreams of the events that are to bring him patronage and help him to acquire a position, he likewise uses the present tense. In other words, dream uses the present tense in the same way and with the same right as day-dream. The present is the tense in which wishes are represented as fulfilled.

The second characteristic, however, is peculiar to dream alone – as opposed to day-dream; this is the fact that the ideational content is not thought but transformed into sensory images that the dreamer believes in and feels he is experiencing. Let us add immediately that not all dreams show this transformation from ideation to sensory image; some dreams consist only of thoughts while still, incontrovertibly, partaking of the essence of dreams. My 'Autodidasker – the day-time fantasy with Professor N.' dream [see above, p. 313] is one such, incorporating scarcely more sensory elements than if I had thought up its contents by day. There are also, in every dream of any length, elements that have not made the change into the sensory dimension, elements that are simply thought or known in the fashion that is familiar to us from the waking state. Moreover, let us remind ourselves at this point that this kind of transformation of ideas into sensory images does not feature in dreams only but also in hallucination, in the visions that, for instance, appear spontaneously in health or as symptoms of psychoneuroses. In short, the relationship we are looking at here is not exclusive in any direction; the fact remains that this feature of dream, where it appears, seems to us the most remarkable, so that we cannot imagine dream-life without it. However, understanding it will require far more extensive discussion.

Among all the comments on the theory of dreaming to be found in the literature, I should like to single out one as worth taking up. The great G. T. Fechner, in connection with certain discussions of dream in his book [*Elemente der*] *Psychophysik* [second edition, 1889] (Part 2, p. 520; translated into English as *Elements of Psychophysics*), conjectures that *the scene of dreams is different from that of the waking ideational life*. No other assumption makes it possible to grasp the peculiar features of dream-life.

The notion that is thus made available to us is that of a *psychical locality*. Let us leave entirely aside the fact that the mental apparatus we are dealing with here is also known to us as an anatomical preparation [i.e. as something prepared for dissection]; let us also scrupulously avoid the temptation to define this locality in any anatomical way. Staying on purely psychical ground, we propose only to respond to the challenge of imagining the instrument that serves mental performance as a compound microscope, say, or a photographic appliance – that sort of thing. Psychical locality then corresponds to a point inside such a piece of apparatus at which one of the early stages of the image comes about. In the case of the microscope and telescope, of course, these are to some extent virtual locations at which no tangible component of the apparatus is situated. I see no need to apologize for the imperfections of this and all similar images. The sole purpose of such similes is to support an experiment designed to help us understand the complexity of psychical performance by in fact dissecting it, as it were, isolating what each bit does, and attributing that function to an individual component of the apparatus. No one, so far as I am aware, has yet attempted to ascertain the composition of the mental instrument by dismantling it in this way. Nor, it seems to me, can any harm come of the method. My view is that we may give free rein to conjecture, provided only that in the process we keep a cool head and do not mistake the scaffolding for the building. And since we need nothing else to serve as imaginative aids towards an initial approach to an unknown object, we shall seize, for the time being, on the rawest, most tangible assumptions in preference to all others.

So, then, we picture the mental apparatus as a composite instrument, the parts of which we shall call *agencies* or, for the sake of clarity, *systems*. We then form the expectation that those systems may stand in a constant spatial orientation in relation to one another, much as the different lens systems of the telescope are in line. Strictly speaking, we need not assume a true spatial arrangement of the psychical systems. All we require is for a fixed sequence to be established by having the systems, in connection with certain psychical processes, visited by a stimulus in a specific temporal order. That order may differ in connection with other psychical processes; we want to leave such a possibility open. From now on we shall call the components of the apparatus 'ψ-systems' for short.[3]

The first thing that strikes us is that this apparatus made up of ψ-systems has a direction. All our psychical activity proceeds from (internal or external) stimuli and culminates in innervations. Consequently, we ascribe to the apparatus a sensory end and a motor end; at the sensory end is a system that receives perceptions, while at the motor end another system opens the floodgates of motility. The psychical process generally runs from the perception end [*p*] to the motility end [*m*]. So the most general diagram of the psychical apparatus would look like this:

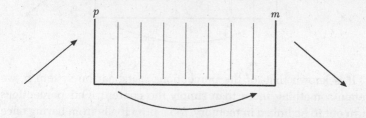

But this is simply the fulfilment of the (to us) familiar old demand that the psychical apparatus must be constructed like a reflex apparatus. The reflex process remains the pattern for all psychical performance as well.

We now have reason to allow an initial differentiation to enter the picture at the sensory end. Of the perceptions that reach us, there remains in our psychical apparatus a trace – let us call it a '*memory-trace*'. The function that relates to that trace is one that we of course call 'memory'.[4] If we are serious about our plan to link psychical processes with systems, the memory-trace has to consist in permanent changes to the elements of the systems. But there are obvious difficulties, as has been pointed out elsewhere, in expecting one and the same system faithfully to preserve changes to its elements and at the same time remain constantly fresh and receptive in the face of new occasions for change. According to the principle governing our experiment, we shall have to assign these two performances to different systems. We make the assumption that a system right at the front of the apparatus receives the perceptual stimuli but retains nothing of them (in other words, has no memory) and that behind lies a second system that converts the momentary arousal of the first into permanent traces. Our psychical apparatus, expressed as a diagram, would then look like this (*me* = memory-trace):

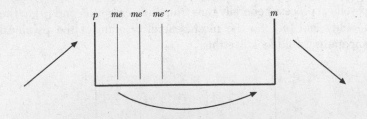

It is known that, of the perceptions that bear on system *p*, we retain something more than simply the content. Our perceptions turn out to be linked in memory, too – principally from having once coincided in time. We call this the fact of *association*. Clearly, if the *p* system has no memory at all, it is incapable of retaining the traces for association; the individual *p* elements would be intolerably hindered in their function if a residue of an earlier connection were to assert itself against a fresh perception. So we must assume that memory-systems form the basis of association instead. In which case the fact of association consists in the sensory arousal tending (as a result of reductions of resistance and creation of pathways on the part of one of the *me* elements) to spread more readily to a second *me* element than to a third.

On closer examination, it becomes necessary to assume not one but a number of such *me* elements in which the same arousal, propagated through the *p* elements, becomes fixed in different ways. The first of those *me* systems will in any case have the association fixed in it as a consequence of simultaneity; in those lying at a greater remove, the same arousal material will be arranged in accordance with other types of coincidence – so that those subsequent systems would represent relations of similarity, say, or the like. It would be pointless, of course, trying to indicate the psychical significance of such a system in words. Its nature would lie in the intensity of its relations with elements of the raw material of memory – that is to say (if we wish to adumbrate a profounder theory), in the gradations of resistance as regards guidance in the direction of such elements.

A comment of a general nature, which may indicate something important, ought to be inserted here. The p system, which has no capacity for preserving changes, no memory (to put it another way), supplies our consciousness with the whole enormous range of sensual qualities. Conversely, our memories (including those stamped most deeply within us) are essentially unconscious. They can be made conscious; however, there is no doubt that in the unconscious state they exert their full effect. What we call our character is based, is it not, on the memory-traces of our impressions, and the fact is that precisely those impressions that influenced us most powerfully, namely those of our earliest youth, are impressions that hardly ever become conscious. But if memories do become conscious again they exhibit no sensory quality or only a very slight one in comparison with the perceptions. If it could be confirmed *that memory and quality are mutually exclusive as regards awareness of ψ-systems*, a most promising insight would open up into the conditions of neurone arousal.[5]

What we have assumed hitherto (regarding the composition of the psychical apparatus at the sensory end) takes no account of dream and the psychological explanations that can be inferred from dream. However, as regards identifying a different portion of the apparatus dream will become our source of evidence. We saw how it became impossible for us to explain dream-formation unless we ventured to posit two psychical agencies, one of which subjects the actions of the other to a critique of which the result is exclusion from consciousness.

The criticizing agency, we concluded, is more closely related to consciousness than the one criticized. It stands between the latter and consciousness like a protective screen. We also found grounds for identifying the criticizing agency with what guides our waking life and makes decisions about our arbitrary, conscious behaviour. If we now, in obedience to our assumptions, replace those agencies with systems, in consequence of this last-mentioned recognition the criticizing system is moved along to the motor end. Let us now register the two systems in our diagram, using the names we have given them to express their relationship to consciousness [*unc* = unconscious; *prec* = preconscious]:

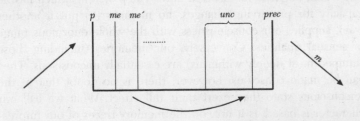

The last of the systems at the motor end we call the preconscious – to indicate that the arousal processes in it are able to reach consciousness without further delay, should certain conditions be fulfilled, including attainment of a certain degree of intensity, a certain deployment of the function we must call attention – that sort of thing. At the same time it is the system that holds the key to voluntary motility. The system behind it we call the *unconscious* because it has no access to consciousness *except through the preconscious*, in passing through which its arousal process must submit to changes.[6]

In which of these systems are we to locate the impulse to dream-formation? For simplicity's sake, in the *unc* system. Granted, we shall be hearing in subsequent discussions that this is not entirely correct, that dream-formation has to hook on to dream-thoughts that belong to the *prec* system. But we shall also, elsewhere (when we come to deal with the dream-wish), learn that the driving force behind dream is provided by the *unc*, and because of this last factor we shall be assuming that the unconscious system is the starting-point of dream-formation. This dream-arousal will then, like any other thought-formation, endeavour to continue itself in the *prec* and from there gain access to consciousness.

Experience teaches us that, during the day, this path leading through the preconscious to consciousness is barred to dream-thoughts by resistance censorship. In the night they find their way through to consciousness, but the questions arise: how do they do so and as a result of what change? If this were made possible for dream-thoughts by a reduced watchfulness on the part of the resistance that patrols the frontier between the unconscious and the preconscious, we should have dreams that were clothed in the material of our ideas – ideas lacking in the hallucinatory character that now interests us.

In other words, this kind of enfeebled censorship between the two systems *unc* and *prec* can account only for such dream-formations as [my] *Autodidasker* [see above, p. 313.] but not dreams like that of the *burning child* [see above, pp. 526f.], which we posed as a problem at the outset of these investigations.

What happens in a hallucinatory dream is something we can only describe by saying: arousal takes a *retrograde* path; it goes backwards. Instead of propagating itself towards the motor end of the apparatus it does so in the direction of the sensory end, eventually reaching the system of perceptions. If we call the direction in which the psychical process emerges from the unconscious in the waking state *progredient*, we can say of dream that it possesses a *regredient* character.[7]

Now, this *regression* is surely one of the most important psychological characteristics of the dream-process; however, we should not forget that it is not unique to dreaming. Deliberate remembering and other partial processes of normal thought likewise correspond to a harking back within the psychical apparatus from some complicated imaginative act to the raw material of the memory-traces underlying it. In the waking state, such harking back never goes beyond remembered images; it is incapable of bringing about a hallucinatory revival of the images of perception. Why is this different in dream? When we were talking about the compression work performed in dream, we could not avoid making the assumption that, as a result of dream-work, the degrees of intensity attaching to ideas are transferred in full from one to the next. Probably it is this change in the customary psychical process that makes it possible to energize the p system to full sensory vividness in the reverse direction, starting from thoughts.

I hope we are a long way from harbouring any illusions as to the possible implications of such discussions. All we have done is to give a name to a phenomenon that cannot be explained. We call it 'regression' when, in a dream, an idea turns back into the sensory image from which at some time it proceeded. But even this step calls for justification. Why bestow a name when doing so teaches us nothing new? What I think is this: the name 'regression' does serve some purpose by linking a fact of which we are aware to the schema of the mental apparatus as conceived directionally. However, this is the first time it has been worthwhile drawing up such a schema. The fact is, another peculiarity of dream-formation now becomes comprehensible to us without further consideration, merely with the aid of the schema. If we look upon the dream-process as a regression within what we have taken to be the apparatus of mind, the empirically established fact that, in connection with dream-work, all the thought-relationships of the dream-thoughts become lost or find only laborious expression becomes easily explicable. According to our schema, such thought-relationships are contained not in the first *me* systems but in others lying further on, and it is inevitable, given this regression towards the images of perception, that they lose some of the force of their expression. *During regression, the structure of dream-thoughts is broken down into its raw material.*

But by what change is regression, impossible by day, made possible? Here we shall have to make do with conjectures. We must, presumably, be dealing with changes in the energy-charges[8] held by the different systems, as a result of which they become more or less open to the passage of an arousal stimulus; however, in every such apparatus the same effect as regards the passage of an arousal stimulus could be brought about by more than one kind of change in this connection. One thinks immediately, of course, of the sleeping state and of alterations of charge that it occasions at the sensory end of the apparatus. By day there is a constant stream flowing from the ψ-system of the p end towards motility; at night this ceases and could no longer constitute an obstacle to a stream of arousal flowing in the opposite direction. This would be the 'exclusion from the outside world' that in the theorizing of certain authors ostensibly sheds light on the psychological character of dreams (see also above, pp. 63f.). However, in explaining regression in dream one would have to take account of those other regressions that arise in morbid waking states. In connection with these forms, of course, the information just provided is no use. Regression occurs in spite of an uninterrupted sensory current flowing in a progredient direction.

As regards the hallucinations of hysteria and paranoia and the visions of mentally normal people, the explanation I can supply is that they do indeed correspond to regressions – in other words, they are thoughts transformed into images – and that the only thoughts to undergo this transformation are ones that are closely associated with memories that have been suppressed or have remained unconscious. For example, one of my youngest hysterics, a twelve-year-old boy, is prevented from going to sleep by *'green faces with red eyes'*, which horrify him. The source of this manifestation is the suppressed but once conscious memory of a boy whom he used often to see four years back and who, in his eyes, presented a warning image of many bad habits of childhood, including that of masturbation, arising out of which he now levels a belated reproach against himself. His mummy had remarked at the time that the badly brought-up youngster had a *greenish* complexion and *red* (meaning *red-rimmed*) eyes. Hence the nightmare, which was in fact simply intended to remind him of another of mummy's predictions – namely, that such youths become imbecilic, learn nothing at school and die prematurely. Our little patient is making part of the prophecy come true (he is doing badly at school) and, as listening to his involuntary associations of ideas reveals, he is dreadfully afraid of the [last] part.[9] In a short time, incidentally, treatment has produced the successful result that he is now sleeping, he is losing his anxiety and he has completed the school year with an excellent report.

Here I can add the resolving of a vision that a forty-year-old hysteric recounted to me from her healthy days. One morning she opens her eyes to find her brother in the room, although her brother, to her knowledge, is in the lunatic asylum. Her small son is asleep in bed beside her. To prevent the child from *taking fright* and *having convulsions* at seeing his *uncle*, she draws the *quilt* over him, whereupon the figure disappears. The vision is a reworking of one of the woman's childhood memories, which while itself conscious was very closely related to all the unconscious material deep inside her. Her nanny had told her that her mother, who had died very early on (she herself had been only eighteen months old at the time), had suffered from epileptic or hysterical fits – ever since her brother (my patient's *uncle*) had given her a fright by appearing to her as a ghost with a *quilt* over his head. The vision contains the same elements as the memory: her brother's appearance, the quilt, the fright and its effect. However, those elements are assigned to fresh contexts and transferred to different persons. The obvious motive of the vision, the thought that it has replaced, is the concern that her young son, who so resembled his uncle physically, might share the same fate.

Both examples cited here are not wholly unconnected with the sleeping state and may therefore be ill-suited to the evidential role in which I am casting them. So I refer to my analysis of a hallucinating paranoiac[10] and to the findings of my as yet unpublished studies into the psychology of psychoneuroses to confirm that in such cases of regredient thought-transformation the influence of a memory (usually a childhood memory) that has been suppressed or remains unconscious ought not to be overlooked. Such a memory, as it were, draws the thought associated with it (but prevented by censorship from finding expression) into regression as into the form of representation in which it is itself psychically present. Here I may be permitted to cite as a finding of studies of hysteria that childhood scenes (be they memories or fantasies), when successfully rendered conscious, are regarded as hallucinatory, only shedding this character when recounted. It is also known that, even in people who are not normally visual in terms of the way they remember things, the earliest childhood memories retain the character of sensory vividness until late in life.

If we now remember what role is allocated, in dream-thoughts, to infant experiences or the fantasies based thereon, how often fragments of the same reappear in dream-content, how dream-wishes themselves are frequently derived from them, we shall not reject the possibility (as regards dream as well) that the transformation of thoughts into visual images may be in part a consequence of the *attraction* that the visually represented memory seeking revival exerts upon the thoughts that, cut off from consciousness, are fighting to find expression. Understood thus, dream might also be described as *a replacement of the infantile scene, altered as a result of being transferred on to the still-vivid/recent.*[11] The infantile scene cannot bring about its own renewal; it must be content to return in the form of dream.

The reference to the almost exemplary significance of infantile scenes (or their repetitions in fantasy) so far as dream-content is concerned renders one of the assumptions made by Scherner and his followers regarding internal sources of stimulation superfluous. Scherner assumes a condition of 'visual stimulus', of internal arousal in the organ of sight, when dreams exhibit particularly vivid visual elements or a particular wealth of such elements. Without needing to rebut this assumption, we may content ourselves with (say) positing such a state of arousal simply for the psychical perceptual system of the organ of sight, albeit asserting that that state of arousal is a revival, created by memory, of what at the time was a current visual stimulus. I cannot, from my own experience, come up with a good example of that kind of influence being exerted by an infantile arousal; my dreams are altogether less rich in sensory elements than I have to assume other people's are; but in the most beautiful, most lifelike dreams of recent years I have no difficulty in tracing the hallucinatory clarity of the dream-content to sensory qualities of still-vivid impressions recently received.[12] On pp. 479f. I mentioned a dream in which the deep blue colour of the water, the brown colour of the smoke from the ships' chimneys, and the darker brown and red of the buildings I could see made a deep impression on me. If any dream asks to be interpreted in terms of visual stimuli, this one does. And what had placed my visual organ in this state of arousal? A still-vivid impression that linked up with a series of earlier impressions. The colours I saw were originally those of the building-blocks with which on the day preceding my dream the children had erected a splendid edifice for me to admire. There was that same dark red on the big blocks, the blue and brown on the small ones. These impressions were joined by colour impressions from the last Italian trip: the beautiful blue of the Isonzo and the lagoon and the brown of karst. The lovely colours of the dream were simply a repetition of those seen in memory.

Let us sum up what we have learned about the peculiar habit dreams have of recasting their ideational content in sensual images. True, we have not explained this characteristic of dream in the sense of tracing it back to known laws of psychology, but we have singled it out as indicating unknown circumstances and described it as *'regredient'*. We said that, wherever it occurs, such regression is doubtless an effect of the resistance that seeks to prevent thought from breaking through to consciousness by the usual route as well as of the simultaneous attraction that sensorily powerful and currently available memories exert on it.[13] In the case of dreams, regression is possibly made easier by the progredient daily flow from the sense organs ceasing, with what is a contributory factor in connection with other forms of regression needing to be made up for by a strengthening of the remaining regression motives. Let us not forget, either, that in pathological cases of regression, as in dream, the process of energy transfer may well be different than in regressions in normal mental life since it enables full hallucinatory charging of perceptual systems. What in our analysis of dream-work we described as a 'concern for representability' probably has to do with the *selective attraction* of the visually remembered scenes touched on by the relevant dream-thoughts.

On the subject of regression, one other thing we want to say is that it plays just as important a role in the theory of neurotic symptom-formation as in that of dream. Here we distinguish a threefold type of regression: *a)* a *topical*[14] aspect in terms of the ψ-system schema developed above; *b)* a *temporal* aspect in that it has to do with harking back to older psychical formations; and *c)* a *formal* aspect, where primitive modes of expression and representation replace the usual ones. However, all three types of regression are basically one and the same and in most cases occur together, because the older in time is also the more primitive in form and in psychical topography closer to the perception end.

Nor can we leave the subject of regression in dream without voicing an impression that has already forced itself upon us repeatedly and that following a deeper study of psychoneuroses will return even more strongly. This is that dreaming as a whole is a piece of regression to the dreamer's earliest circumstances, a resuscitation of the dreamer's childhood and of the drive-stimuli that had been predominant and the modes of expression that had been available at the time. Behind this individual childhood we are then promised a glimpse into phylogenetic childhood, into the development of the human race, of which that of the individual is in fact an abbreviated replay shaped by the accidents of life. We sense how right Fr[iedrich] Nietzsche was when he wrote that in dream 'an ancient piece of humanity continues to make itself felt that is now scarcely reachable by a direct route', and we are led to expect that analysing dreams will give us knowledge of man's archaic inheritance, what is innate in man's mind. Dream and neurosis have apparently preserved for us more of the antiquities of mind than we could have suspected; psychoanalysis can thus lay claim to an honoured place among the sciences endeavouring to reconstruct the earliest, most shadowy phases of the dawn of mankind.

Quite possibly, we shall ourselves find this initial portion of our psychological evaluation of dreams not particularly satisfactory. Let us console ourselves with the thought that we are having of necessity to build out into the dark. If we are not completely mistaken in our assumptions, we must now, approaching the target from a different

565

point, end up in approximately the same area – where we shall then perhaps find ourselves better able to cope.

Notes

1. [May I remind the reader that a choice has been made here – namely, to translate *'der Traum'* by one of the two alternatives that cover its meaning in English, the general rather than the particular (see my Translator's Preface) – and that, as with most choices, the rejected alternative does not cease to exist; it remains present by implication?]

2. [In the novel *Le Nabab*, already referred to above, on p. 306.]

3. [The Greek letter ψ is pronounced 'psi'; it was common, for example, for members of the psychoanalytical community to refer (among themselves) to psychoanalysis as 'ψA'.]

4. [This must inevitably sound rather clumsy in English. The reader should be asked to bear in mind that, in German, two different words are used for 'memory' here: *Erinnerung*, in what is usually rendered in English as 'memory-trace' (*Erinnerungsspur*), and *Gedächtnis*, of which 'memory' is the usual English rendition (though sometimes 'remembrance' is more appropriate). Etymologically, *Erinnerung* implies movement (literally: 'internalization') while *Gedächtnis* has a whiff of reverence about it.]

5. I later came to believe that consciousness in fact emerges *in place of* the memory-trace. (See most recently my *Notiz über den 'Wunderblock'*, 1925 ['A Note upon the "Mystic Writing-Pad"'; *Standard Edition*, vol. XIX, p. 227; and in *The Penguin Freud Reader*, New Penguin Freud, London 2006].)

6. Further development of this linear diagram will have to take account of the assumption that the system following *prec* is the one to which we must ascribe consciousness – meaning that $p = c$ [consciousness].

7. The first hint of this regressive factor comes in the work of Albertus Magnus. The *'imaginatio'*, he says, constructs a dream out of the preserved images of manifest objects. The process takes place in reverse, compared with the waking state (quoted by Diepgen, p. 14). And [Thomas] Hobbes says (in *Leviathan*, [English publication:] 1651): 'In sum, our dreams are the reverse of our waking imaginations, the motion, when we are awake, beginning at one end, and when we dream at another' (quoted by H[avelock] Ellis, p. 112).

[*'Progrediente'* and *'regrediente'* are unusual German words; they were presumably chosen by Freud to indicate that his *'Regression'* possesses an exclusively directional quality – that is to say, one that carries no connotation of 'better' or 'worse'.]

8. [*'Energiebesetzungen'*. Freud's use of the word *'Besetzung'*, with its military ('occupation') and theatrical ('casting') connotations, famously led Strachey to commit the cardinal sin of translation: he *invented* something (in this instance, the Greek-based word *cathexis*) to convey what he felt to be Freud's meaning. Since 'cathexis' means nothing to anyone not steeped in psychoanalysis (in the 'English' language) or rejoicing in what used to be called a classical education, I prefer to render the 'occupation/casting' connotations by the notion of a 'charge' (of an electrical nature, say). For a full explanation of Freud's use of the term *Besetzung*, see Laplanche and Pontalis, *The Language of Psychoanalysis*, London 1973, pp. 62–5.]

9. [Freud's text refers to 'the second part'; I have assumed the boy was particularly afraid of suffering an early death.]

10. 'Weitere Bemerkungen über die Abwehr-Neuropsychosen' ['Further Remarks on the Neuro-psychoses of Defence'], in *Neurologisches Zentral-blatt*, 1896, no. 10 [*Standard Edition*, vol. III, p. 159].

11. [See p. 199, note 2.]

12. [See p. 199, note 2.]

13. In an account of the theory of repression we should need to state that a thought becomes repressed as a result of the combined action of two factors bearing upon it. On the one hand it is rejected (by the censorship of *c*); on the other it is attracted (by the *unc*) – rather as one reaches the summit of the Great Pyramid. (See also my essay 'Die Verdrängung' [1915; 'Repression', in *Standard Edition*, vol. XIV, p. 143].)

14. [In the medical sense of 'localized'.]

C *Concerning wish-fulfilment*

The dream of the burning child introduced at the beginning of this chapter [see above, p. 526] gives us a welcome opportunity to acknowledge problems confronting the theory of wish-fulfilment. We all, surely, will have found it a disconcerting experience to be told that dream is simply wish-fulfilment – one reason being of course the contradiction posed by the anxiety-dream. The early elucidations provided by analysis taught us that, concealed behind dream, lie meaning and psychical value, but we should certainly not have expected that meaning to be so unambiguously defined. According to the correct if meagre definition supplied by Aristotle, dream constitutes the continuation of thought in the sleeping state – that is to say, when the dreamer is asleep. But if by day our thinking accomplishes so wide a variety of psychical acts (judgements, conclusions, rebuttals, expectations, intentions and so on), why should it be obliged to confine itself at night purely to generating wishes? Are there not in fact many dreams that turn a different kind of psychical act into dream-form (a worry, for instance), and is not the said example, the particularly transparent dream had by the boy's father, just such a one? From the glow that falls into his eyes even while he is asleep, he draws the worried conclusion that a candle may have fallen over and set the body alight; that conclusion he transforms into a dream by couching it in a meaningful situation and placing it in the present tense. What is the role of wish-fulfilment here, and are we, as a result, somehow underestimating the superior power of thought, whether continuing from the waking state or stimulated by the new sensory impression?

All this is true, and it compels us to look more closely at the part played by wish-fulfilment in dream and the significance of waking thoughts continuing in sleep.

This very phenomenon (wish-fulfilment) has already caused us to divide dreams into two groups. We found some dreams that frankly presented themselves as wish-fulfilment, while in others the wish-fulfilment element was unrecognizable – indeed, was often obscured by every means available. In the latter, we recognized the workings of dream-censorship. Undistorted wish-dreams we found mainly in children; *brief*, quite candid wish-dreams also *seem* (and I stress the reservation) to occur in adults.

Now, we can ask whence the wish comes each time that finds realization in a dream. But to what antithesis or to what diversity does that 'whence' apply? I believe it has to do with the antithesis between a daytime life that has become conscious and a psychical activity that remains unconscious and can only attract attention at night. I then find a threefold possibility for where a wish comes from. It may 1) have been triggered by day and not found satisfaction because of external circumstances, in which case it removes the need for an acknowledged, unfulfilled wish during the night; 2) it may have cropped up during the day but been rejected, removing the need for us to find an unfulfilled but suppressed wish; 3) it may have nothing to do with daytime life and be one of those wishes that emerge from suppression and come to life in us only at night. Taking our schema of the psychical apparatus, we localize a wish of the first kind in the *prec* system; as regards a wish of the second type, we assume that it has been pushed back from the *prec* system to the *unc* system and is preserved (if at all) only there; regarding the third type of wish-stirring, it is our belief that this is quite incapable of going beyond the *unc* system. The question is, do wishes from these different sources have the same value for dream, the same power to stimulate a dream?

A survey of the dreams at our disposal for answering this question first bids us add a fourth source of dream-wishes: current wish-stimuli arising during the night (feeling thirsty, for instance, or needing sex). Secondly, it becomes probable, in our eyes, that where the dream-wish comes from makes no difference to its ability to stimulate a dream. I remember the little girl's dream that continued the voyage interrupted during the day and the other children's dreams cited in the same context; they are explained by an unfulfilled but not suppressed daytime wish. Plenty of examples can be shown of a wish suppressed during the day venting itself in dream; I could add a very simple one here. A lady somewhat given to mockery, whose younger friend has become engaged, when asked by acquaintances during the day whether she knows the fiancé and what she thinks of him, eulogizes the young man unreservedly, keeping her real opinion to herself, for she would have liked to have told the truth: *'He's a very ordinary sort of person.'* That night she dreams the same question is being addressed to her, and she replies with the formula: *'When reordering, quote number only'*. Finally, the results of numerous analyses have taught us that in all dreams suffering distortion the wish arises from the unconscious and is beyond perception during the day. For the time being, then, it would seem that, so far as forming dreams is concerned, all wishes are of equal value and have the same power.

I cannot prove at this point that it does not in fact work that way, but I am much inclined to assume that dream-wishes are more strictly determined. You see, children's dreams leave us in no doubt that a wish not fulfilled during the day can trigger a dream. But let us not forget that this is a child's wish, a wish-stimulus of the strength peculiar to the infantile sphere. I doubt very much whether a wish not fulfilled during the day is sufficient, in an adult, to create a dream. It strikes me as far more likely that, as control over our drives through intellectual activity advances, we increasingly renounce forming or preserving wishes as intense as those a child knows, deeming such behaviour fruitless. Individual differences may assert themselves here, of course; one person may retain the infantile type of mental processes longer than another – as indeed such differences also exist in relation to the weakening of the originally clear vision. In general, however, I believe that, in the adult, a wish that the day has left unfilled is not sufficient to create a dream. I readily concede that the wish-stimulus stemming from the conscious mind will help to trigger dream, but that is probably all. Dream would not arise if the preconscious wish failed to find reinforcement elsewhere.

And that 'elsewhere' is the unconscious. *The way I see it, the conscious wish only becomes a dream-trigger when it succeeds in arousing an unconscious wish to the same effect, from which it receives reinforcement.* To my mind such unconscious wishes, according to hints supplied by the psychoanalysis of neuroses, are perpetually active, ready at any time to find expression where opportunity offers, to form an alliance with a stimulus from the conscious, and to transfer its greater intensity to the lesser intensity of the other.[1] Inevitably, it then looks as if only the conscious wish finds realization in the resultant dream; however, a small yet striking oddity in the structure of that dream acts like a signpost, putting us on the track of the powerful assistant from the unconscious realm. Such perpetually active, as it were immortal wishes of our unconscious, recalling the legendary Titans on whom since ancient times the great mountain masses had rested that had once been rolled down on them by the victorious gods and that still, from time to time, quaked from the twitching of their limbs – such repressed wishes, I maintain, are themselves of infantile origin, as psychological research into neuroses teaches us. So I should like to strike out the principle enunciated earlier about the origin of the dream-wish being of no importance and replace it by another, which runs: *the wish represented in a dream must be an infantile wish.* It stems in adults from the *unc*; in children, where no separation of and censorship between *prec* and *unc* exist as yet, or where they are only gradually coming into being, it is an unfulfilled, unrepressed wish from waking life. It is a view that cannot be universally proven, I know; but I contend that it can be demonstrated frequently, even where it had not been suspected, and that it cannot be generally refuted.

So I let the wish-stimuli left over from conscious waking life retreat into the background as regards dream-formation. I assign them no other role than, for example, I do to the material of current sensations during sleep as regards the relevant dream-content (see also pp. 249ff.). It is in keeping with the line laid down for me by this train of thought if I now consider the other psychical stimuli that are left over from daytime life and that are not wishes. We may succeed in bringing the energy-charges of our waking thoughts to a provisional halt when we decide to go to sleep. Anyone who can do that well is a good sleeper; the first Napoleon is said to have been a model of the breed. But we do not always succeed, nor is our success complete every time. Unsolved problems, tormenting worries, sheer weight of impressions keep us thinking even during sleep and maintain mental processes in the system we have called the preconscious. When we come to classify these thought-stimuli continuing in sleep, we are able to divide them into the following groups: 1) what was left unfinished during the day because of a random cessation of activity; 2) what was not dealt with, left unresolved, as a result of a waning of intellectual vigour on our part; 3) what was rejected during the day and suppressed. In addition, there is another powerful group: 4) what the work of the preconscious has activated in our *unc* during the day. And lastly we can add a further group: 5) the day's indifferent impressions that were not dealt with for that reason.

The psychical intensities introduced into the sleeping state by these residues of the life of the day, notably from the unresolved group, should not be underestimated. These arousals will certainly strive to find expression during the night-time, too, and with equal certainty we may assume that the sleeping state will render impossible the usual continuation of the arousal process in the preconscious and its conclusion by becoming conscious. As long as we are still capable of becoming conscious of our thought-processes in the usual manner, even at night, we are not in fact asleep. What kind of change the sleeping state evokes in the *prec* system, I cannot say;[2] but the place to look for the psychological characteristics of sleep undoubtedly lies in the changing degrees of charge carried by precisely the system that also controls access to the motility paralysed in sleep. By contrast, I know of no reason from the psychology of dream bidding us assume that sleep changes anything in the circumstances of the *unc* system at other than a secondary level. So nocturnal arousal in the *prec* has no alternative but to use the route taken by wish-triggers from the *unc*; it must seek reinforcement from the *unc* and follow the detours of unconscious arousals. But how do the day's preconscious residues relate to dream? There is no doubt that plenty of them find their way into dreams, using dream-content to impose themselves on consciousness even at night; in fact, they sometimes dominate dream-content, forcing it to continue the work of the day; it is also certain that the day's residues can equally well possess any other character, just as much as that of wishes; but it is highly instructive in this connection as well as absolutely crucial as regards the wish-fulfilment theory to see what condition they must abide by in order to find entry into a dream.

Let us look back at one of our earlier dream specimens – the one, for example, that has my friend Otto present with indications of Basedow's disease (p. 282). That day I had formed a concern on the basis of Otto's appearance, and like everything to do with that person it lay close to my heart. It followed me, presumably, into sleep. I expect I wanted to discover what he might be lacking in. During the night my worry found expression in a dream, as recounted, the content of which firstly made no sense and secondly corresponded to no wish-fulfilment. However, I started to explore where the disproportionate expression of the concern I had felt during the day came from, and through analysis I found a connection in that I identified him with a Baron L. but myself with Professor R. As to why I had had to choose these particular replacements for my daytime thought, only one explanation was possible. At the level of *unc* I must always have been ready to identify with Professor R., since through that identification one of the immortal wishes of childhood was fulfilled – namely, the megalomaniac wish. Mean thoughts directed against my friend, which by day would certainly have been rejected, had taken the opportunity to slip in and find representation at the same time, but so too had the day's worry found a sort of expression in the dream-content, using substitution. The daytime thought (which was not in fact a wish but on the contrary a concern) had somehow to attach itself to an infantile wish that was now unconscious and suppressed, which then caused a badly knocked-about version of it to 'emerge' into consciousness.

The more dominant the worry, the more forced might be the association to be established; between the substance of the wish and that of the worry there need be no connection of any kind, and indeed in our example there was none.

It may possibly be useful to tackle the same question again in the form of an investigation into how dreams behave when offered, in the relevant dream-thoughts, materials that run directly counter to wish-fulfilment: legitimate worries, painful considerations, embarrassing insights – that sort of thing. The variety of possible outcomes can be subdivided as follows. A) Dream-work contrives to replace all embarrassing ideas by their opposites and to suppress the associated unpleasant affects. This then produces a dream of pure gratification, a tangible 'wish-fulfilment' where there is apparently no more to discuss. B) The embarrassing ideas find their way, more or less changed but still quite recognizable, into the manifest dream-content. This is the eventuality that raises doubts about the wish-theory of dream and requires further investigation. Such dreams having an embarrassing content may either be experienced as indifferent, or they may bring with them all the embarrassing affect that appears justified by their ideational content, or they may even generate fear and make the dreamer wake up.

Analysis then shows that even these aversion dreams are wish-fulfilments. An unconscious, repressed wish, fulfilment of which could not be experienced by the dreamer's 'I' as anything other than embarrassing, has taken advantage of the opportunity offered to it by the fact that the day's embarrassing residues have retained their charge, using it to lend them its support and thereby make them capable of being dreamed. However, whereas in the first case, A, the unconscious wish coincided with the conscious one, in case B the gulf between the unconscious and the conscious (the repressed and the 'I') is exposed, creating the situation set out in the fairytale of the three wishes that the fairy grants the couple (see below, p. 603, note 5). Satisfaction at having the repressed wish fulfilled may be so great that it balances out the embarrassing affects associated with the day's residues; the dream is then indifferent/neutral in terms of its emotional tone although on the one hand it is the fulfilment of a wish and on the other of a fear. Or it may transpire that the sleeping 'I' takes an even greater emotional interest in the process of dream-formation, that it reacts with violent indignation to the satisfaction of the suppressed wish that has now come about, and itself terminates the dream in an atmosphere of anxiety. So it is not hard to recognize that aversion dreams and anxiety-dreams are, in terms of the theory, just as much wish-fulfilments as plain satisfaction dreams.

Aversion dreams can also be *'punishment dreams'*. Admittedly, by accepting them as part of dream-theory one is in a sense adding something new. What they fulfil is likewise an unconscious wish – the wish that the dreamer should be punished for a repressed, forbidden wish-stirring. To that extent dreams meet the requirement put forward here that the driving force behind dream-formation would have to be contributed by a wish belonging to the unconscious. However, more delicate psychological dissection reveals the difference from other wish-dreams. In the group B cases the unconscious, dream-forming wish belonged to the repressed; with punishment dreams it is likewise an unconscious wish but one we must attribute not to the repressed but to the 'I'. In other words, punishment dreams point to the possibility of an even deeper involvement of the 'I' in dream-formation. In fact, the whole machinery of dream-formation becomes far more transparent if for the antithesis of 'conscious' and 'unconscious' we substitute that of the 'I' and the 'repressed'. This cannot happen without regard to the processes involved in psychoneurosis, which is why it has not been implemented in this book. I simply point out that punishment dreams are not generally linked to the condition of embarrassing day's residues. They tend instead to emerge most readily in contrary circumstances, where the day's residues are thoughts of a satisfying nature but that express forbidden satisfactions. Of those thoughts, nothing finds its way into the manifest dream but their direct opposite, much as was the case in the dreams of group A. So the essential character of punishment dreams would remain that, in them, it is not the unconscious wish from the repressed (the *unc* system) that forms the dream but the punishment wish reacting against it – a wish that belongs to the 'I', even if it is unconscious (i.e. preconscious).[3]

I want to clarify some of the things I have said here in terms of a dream of my own, particularly the way in which dream-work deals with a day's residue consisting of embarrassing expectations:

> *Unclear beginning. I tell my wife I have news for her, something very special. She takes fright and refuses to listen. I promise her, on the contrary, something that will make her very happy, and I start to tell her that the officer corps has sent our son a sum of money (5,000 crowns?) . . . something about recognition . . . distribution . . . As I am explaining, I have gone with her into a small room, a sort of larder, in order to fetch something. All of a sudden, I see my son appear, he is not in uniform but rather in a tight-fitting sports outfit (like a seal?) with a little cap. He climbs up on to a basket standing beside a cupboard as if to place something on top of the cupboard. I call out to him; no reply. It looks to me as if his face or forehead is bandaged, he is putting something in his mouth, stuffing something into himself. His hair, too, has a grey gleam. I think, 'Could it be that he's so exhausted? And has he got false teeth?' Before I can call out to him again I wake up, unafraid but with my heart pounding. The clock on my bedside table shows half past two.*

Again, it is impossible for me to provide a full analysis. I shall confine myself to highlighting certain crucial points. The dream had been occasioned by a torment of expectations during the day; once again there had been no news for more than a week of the young man fighting at the front. It is easy to see why a belief finds expression in the dream-content to the effect that he is wounded or has fallen. At the beginning of the dream one notes the vigorous endeavour to replace painful thoughts by their opposite: I have some really good news, something about a money transfer, recognition, distribution. (The amount stems from a welcome event in the medical practice so is an attempt to divert attention from the subject altogether.) But the endeavour fails. The boy's mother suspects something dreadful and refuses to listen to me. Besides, the disguises are too thin; the connection with what is supposed to be suppressed shines through everywhere. If our son has fallen, his comrades will be sending his belongings back to us; I shall have to distribute his estate among his siblings and others; recognition is something frequently granted to an officer who has suffered a 'hero's death'. My dream, in other words, sets out to give direct expression to what at first it tried to deny – with, in addition, the wish-fulfilling tendency drawing attention to itself through distortions. (The change of place in the dream is no doubt to be understood in terms of Silberer's threshold symbolism [see above, p. 521].) We have no idea, of course, what lends it the necessary driving force. But our son appears not as someone 'falling' but as someone 'climbing'. He used to be a keen mountaineer, you see. He is not in uniform but in a sports outfit, which means that the casualty we currently fear has been replaced by an earlier, sporting one suffered when he fell during a skiing tour and broke his thigh. But the way he is dressed, making him look like a seal, is immediately reminiscent of a younger person, our funny little grandson; the grey hair recalls the boy's father, our son-in-law, on whom the war has taken its toll. What is that supposed to mean? But enough of his appearance; the place (a larder), the cupboard from which he wants to take something down (put something up in the dream) – these are clear allusions to an accident I had myself some time in my second year. I climbed up on a stool in the larder to get at something good that lay on top of a cupboard or on a table. The stool tipped over, the edge catching me behind my lower jaw. I could have lost all my teeth. A reprimand accompanies the process: 'Serves you right', like a hostile stirring directed against the brave warrior. Pursuing the analysis further then enables me to identify the secret stirring that might find satisfaction in the dreaded accident to my son. It is envy of youth, which the older man believes he has thoroughly smothered in his life, and there is no mistaking how the very strength of the painful emotion experienced when such an accident really does occur will seek out, to give itself some relief, this kind of repressed wish-fulfilment.

I can now clearly describe what unconscious wishes mean so far as dream is concerned. I am prepared to concede that there is an entire class of dreams the *stimulus* for which comes primarily or even exclusively from what is left over from the life of the day, and I reckon that even my wish to become *professor extraordinarius* at last could have let me sleep in peace that night, had not the worry I had felt about my friend's health during the day been still active. Yet that worry would not of itself have produced a dream; the *driving force* required by dream had to be provided by a wish; it was a matter of some concern to acquire such a wish as driving force for the dream. Let me couch this in a metaphor. It is entirely possible for a daytime thought to play the part of *entrepreneur* for a dream; however, the entrepreneur, the person who is said to have the idea and the impetus to put it into action, can do nothing without capital; he needs a *capitalist* to cover the expense, and that capitalist, who contributes the psychical expenditure for the relevant dream, is always, without exception, *a wish from the unconscious*.

At other times the capitalist is himself the entrepreneur; in fact, for dream this is the more usual case. Through the work of the day an unconscious wish has been stimulated, and this now gives rise to a dream. For all other possible variations on the business relationship used as an example here, what happens in dream also constitutes a parallel: the entrepreneur can himself make a small contribution to capital; a number of entrepreneurs can turn to the one capitalist; a number of capitalists can jointly provide what the entrepreneurs require. Some dreams, for instance, are supported by more than one dream-wish, and so on; such variations are easily overlooked and are of no further interest to us here. What these discussions regarding dream-wishes still lack is something we shall not be able to supply until later.

The *tertium comparationis* of the metaphors employed here, the quantity made freely available in a measured amount, can be used in an even more refined manner to throw light on dream-structure. In most dreams it is possible to identify a centre furnished with especial sensory intensity, as set out on p. 321. This, as a rule, is the direct representation of the relevant wish-fulfilment, because if we reverse the displacements of dream-work we find the psychical intensity of the elements in the dream-thoughts replaced by the sensory intensity of the elements in the dream-content. The elements close to the relevant wish-fulfilment often have nothing to do with the meaning thereof but turn out to be derivatives of painful thoughts running counter to the wish. However, as a result of the often artificially manufactured connection with the central element they have received so much intensity as to have become capable of being represented. Thus the representational power of the relevant wish-fulfilment diffuses through a certain sphere of coherence, within which all elements, even those possessing least means of their own, are raised to the level of representation. In dreams having several wishes driving them, it is easy to demarcate the individual spheres of wish-fulfilment from one another and often, too, to see the gaps in the relevant dream as border zones.

Even if the foregoing remarks limit the significance of the day's residues so far as dream is concerned, it is worth paying a certain amount of attention to those residues none the less. They must, after all, constitute a necessary ingredient of dream-formation if experience is able to surprise us with the fact that every dream reveals, as part of its content, a connection with a still-vivid [*rezent*] daytime impression, often of the most trivial nature. We failed to grasp the need for this addition to dream-blending previously (see pp. 191f.). The fact is, it only arises if one stresses the role of the unconscious wish and then turns to the psychology of neuroses for information. From this source one learns that the unconscious idea is not, as such, remotely capable of entering the preconscious, and that it is only able to exert any influence there by associating itself with an innocuous idea that already belongs to the preconscious, transferring its intensity to that idea, and having that idea cover it. This is the phenomenon of *transference*, which carries with it the explanation of many striking events in the mental lives of neurotics. Transference can leave the idea taken from the pre-conscious (which thereby achieves undeservedly great intensity) unchanged, or it may itself impose a change on it through the content of the idea doing the transferring. I hope I may be forgiven my liking for metaphors from everyday life, but I am tempted to say that the situation of the repressed idea is not unlike that which, in our country, faces the American dentist who may not practise unless he uses a qualified doctor of medicine as a 'front man' to cover himself in the eyes of the law. And just as it is not exactly the busiest doctors who form such alliances with the dental technician, in the psychical realm, too, the ideas chosen to cover a repressed one are not those preconscious or conscious ideas that have attracted enough of the attention operating in the preconscious on their own account. For preference, the unconscious ensnares with its connections those impressions and ideas of the preconscious that have either remained beyond consideration as being indifferent or from which such consideration is withdrawn again immediately as a result of rejection. It is a well-known principle of the theory of association, invariably confirmed by experience, that ideas that have formed a very profound connection in one direction behave as it were dismissively towards entire groups of fresh connections; I once attempted to base a theory of hysterical paralyses on this principle.

If we assume that the same need for transference on the basis of repressed ideas as analysis of neuroses teaches us also asserts itself in dream, two of the riddles of dream are explained at a stroke – namely, that each dream-analysis shows evidence of a still-vivid [*rezent*] impression having been woven in, and that that still-vivid impression is often of the most trivial kind. We would add something we have already learned elsewhere, which is that the reason why these still-vivid, indifferent elements so often find their way into dream-content as substitutes for the oldest by far of the relevant dream-thoughts is that at the same time they have least to fear from resistance censorship. However, whereas freedom from censorship only explains to us the preference for trivial elements, the constancy of still-vivid [*rezent*] elements points in the direction of the compulsion towards transference. Both groups of impressions meet the demand of the repressed for material that is still association-free – the indifferent, because they have given no occasion for extensive connections, the still-vivid because there has not yet been time to form such connections.

So we see that the day's residues, to which we may now ascribe such indifferent impressions, not only borrow something from the *unc* when they make a contribution towards dream-formation, namely the driving force that the repressed wish has at its disposal; they also offer the unconscious something indispensable, which is the requisite attachment to transference. If at this stage we wished to penetrate deeper into the processes of the mind, we should need to focus more on the interplay of arousals between the preconscious and the unconscious; the study of psychoneuroses may well urge us in that direction, but dream offers no clue.

Just one further comment on the day's residues. There is no doubt that they are the true disturbers of sleep, not dream; in fact, dream is concerned to protect sleep. We shall be returning to this later.

Hitherto we have been looking at the phenomenon of the dream-wish, deriving it from the *unc* region and dissecting its relationship to the day's residues, which may themselves be wishes or psychical stirrings of some other kind or simply still-vivid [*rezent*] impressions. In so doing we have made room for the claims that can be advanced in favour of the dream-forming significance of waking thought in all its diversity. In fact, it is not impossible that, on the basis of such thinking, we should throw light even on those extreme cases in which dream, by continuing the work of daytime, brings a task not resolved in the waking state to a happy conclusion. The only thing is, we lack a suitable example by analysing which we might discover the infantile or repressed wish-source that, when drawn upon, so effectively reinforced the efforts of preconscious activity. However, we have not come so much as a step closer to solving our problem: why, in sleep, does the unconscious have nothing to offer except the driving force behind an act of wish-fulfilment? Answering this question must throw some light on the psychical nature of wishing; let our diagrammatic representation of the psychical apparatus help to supply it.

We do not doubt that that apparatus too has reached its present state of perfection only after a lengthy process of development. Let us try to rewind that process, as it were, to an earlier stage of the mind's capacity. Assumptions made on other grounds inform us that the apparatus initially strove to keep itself as dull [*reizlos*; in this context, literally 'stimulus-free'] as possible; this is why as first constituted it assumed the pattern of a reflex apparatus, which enabled it, the instant a sensory stimulus reached it from outside, to direct the stimulus immediately along motor pathways. However, the stresses of life spoil the simplicity of this function; because of them, the apparatus is prompted to develop further. The first way in which the stresses of life impinge upon it is in the form of the major bodily needs. The arousal triggered by an inner need will seek an outlet in motility that can be described as an 'inner transformation' or 'expression of emotional agitation'. The hungry child will scream helplessly or flail its arms and legs. The situation remains unchanged, however, since the arousal proceeding from the inner need corresponds not to a momentary impulse but to a continuous force. It can only change when by some means or other (in the child's case, by someone else helping) a *satisfaction experience* is felt, removing the inner stimulus. An essential component of that experience is the appearance of a certain perception (in our example: being fed), recollection of which henceforth remains associated with the memory-trace of arousal of the need. As soon as that need reappears, thanks to the association a psychical stirring will arise that seeks to recharge the memory of that perception and recall the perception itself – in fact, to put it another way, it aims to restore the situation of the first satisfaction. Such a stirring we call a wish; reappearance of the perception is the fulfilment of that wish, and when arousal of the need invests such a perception with a full charge, that is the shortest way to such wish-fulfilment. There is nothing to prevent us from positing a primitive state of the psychical apparatus in which this path is actually followed – in other words, wishing turns into hallucination. So this initial psychical activity aims at an *identity of perception*, namely at repeating the perception associated with satisfaction of the need.

Some bitter experience must have changed this primitive thinking activity into a more useful, secondary kind. Producing identity of perception along the short, regredient channel within the apparatus does not, elsewhere, have the effect associated with charging the same perception from outside. Satisfaction does not ensue; the need persists. To give the inner charge the same value as the outer one, that charge would have to be maintained continually, as does actually happen in hallucinatory psychoses and hunger fantasies, where psychical performance is concerned only to *keep hold of* the object wished for. To achieve a more useful expenditure of psychical force, it becomes necessary to halt total regression before it goes beyond the remembered image, and to do so in such a way that it is able, starting from that image, to seek out ways that eventually lead to producing the desired identity on the basis of the outside world.[4] This inhibition, together with subsequent diversion of the arousal, becomes the responsibility of a second system that controls voluntary motility – that is to say, to the performance of which the use of motility for previously remembered ends first becomes attached. However, all the complicated intellectual activity that unfolds from the re-membered image to the production of identity of perception by the external world simply constitutes *a roundabout way to wish-fulfilment* that experience has made necessary.[5] Thinking, after all, is simply a substitute for hallucinatory wishing, and if dream is wish-fulfilment, this in fact becomes self-evident, since nothing but a wish is capable of prompting our mental apparatus into action. Dream, which fulfils its wishes along short, regredient paths, has simply preserved for us a sample of the primary mode of operating (since abandoned as inefficient) of the psychical apparatus. What once dominated the waking state, at a time when psychical life was still young and inept, is now, it seems, exiled to the life of night – rather as we rediscover in the nursery the bow and arrow, the primitive weapons of adult mankind, since laid aside. *Dreaming is a piece of the mental life of childhood, which has now been superseded.* In psychoses, such modes of operation of the psychical apparatus, nor-mally suppressed in the waking state, forcibly reassert themselves, exposing their inability to satisfy our needs in relation to the outside world.[6]

The unconscious wish-stirrings clearly strive to assert themselves by day as well, and the fact of transference and also psychoses both teach us that they would like, by taking the path through the system of the preconscious, to penetrate to consciousness and to a control over motility. In the censorship between *unc* and *prec* that dream virtually obliges us to assume, we have therefore to recognize and pay tribute to the guardian of our intellectual health. But surely it is carelessness on the part of this watchman that he becomes less active in the night-time, allowing the suppressed stirrings of the *unc* to find expression and thus making hallucinatory regression possible once more? I think not, for when the critical watchman retires to rest (we have proof that he does not in fact sleep deeply) he also closes the door to motility. No matter what stirrings from the otherwise restrained *unc* now cavort on the stage, they may be allowed to do so; they remain harmless, being in no position to set in motion the motor apparatus that can alone influence (because alter) the outside world. The sleeping state guarantees the safety of the stronghold to be guarded. A less innocuous situation results when the shift in forces is produced not by any nocturnal diminution of the force expended by critical censorship but by a pathological weakening of the same or by a pathological strengthening of the stirrings of the unconscious while the preconscious is still charged up and the door to motility is still open. Then the watchman is overpowered and the stirrings of the unconscious conquer the *prec*, from where they control what we say and do, or they wrest to themselves hallucinatory regression and steer the apparatus not intended for them by virtue of the attraction that our perceptions exert over the distribution of our psychical energy. We call this condition psychosis.

Here we find ourselves well on the way towards extending the psychological scaffolding that we left after inserting the two systems *unc* and *prec*. However, we still need to linger awhile over appraising wish as the sole psychical driving force behind dream. We have accepted the explanation that the reason why dream is invariably wish-fulfilment is that it is a function of the *unc* system, which has no other operational goal than wish-fulfilment and has at its disposal no other forces than those of wish-stirrings. If we are now determined to insist, even for one moment longer, that interpreting dreams gives us the right to make such far-reaching psychological speculations, it is incumbent upon us to show that, by those speculations, we are fitting dream into a context that can also include other psychical formations. If an *unc* system (or something that, for the purposes of our discussions, resembles it) does in fact exist, dream cannot be its sole expression; each dream may constitute an act of wish-fulfilment, but there must be other forms of abnormal wish-fulfilment than dream. And the theory of all psychoneurotic symptoms does indeed culminate in the one principle: *that they too must be understood as wish-fulfilments of the unconscious.*[7] As explained by ourselves, dream is simply the first link in what for the psychiatrist is a highly significant chain, understanding which means solving the purely psychological portion of the psychiatrist's task.[8] However, from other links in this chain of wish-fulfilments (from hysterical symptoms, for instance) I know of one essential characteristic that I fail to find in dream. The fact is, I have learned from the investigations frequently alluded to in the course of this study that, for a hysterical symptom to be formed, both currents of our mental life have to come together and meet. A symptom is not simply the expression of an unconscious wish that has been realized; it must be joined by a wish from the preconscious that finds fulfilment in the same symptom. In other words, the symptom must be determined *at least* twice: once each by the two conflicting systems. Further multiple determination is (as with dreams) potentially unlimited. Determination that does not spring from the *unc* is always, so far as I can see, a train of thought reacting against the unconscious wish – self-punishment, for example. In very general terms, then, I can say that *a hysterical symptom only comes into being where two conflicting wish-fulfilments, each springing from a different psychical system, are able to come together in a single expression.* (See, in this connection, my most recent formulations on the origin of hysterical symptoms in my 1908 essay 'Hysterische Phantasien und ihre Beziehung zur Bisexualität'.)[9] Examples would be of little use here since only complete uncovering of the degree of complication involved would carry conviction. So I simply make the assertion, offering an example only because of its vividness, not for its evidential value. A female patient's hysterical vomiting turned out on the one hand to fulfil an unconscious fantasy from the time of puberty – namely, the wish to be permanently pregnant and have countless children, to which was subsequently added: by as many men as possible. This unrestrained wish had evoked a powerful defence reaction. However, since as a consequence of such vomiting the patient might forfeit so much of her beauty and voluptuousness as no longer to find any favour with men, the symptom also fitted in with the punitive train of thought and, accepted by both sides, was able to become reality. It is the same way of acceding to a wish-fulfilment as the Parthian queen chose to adopt towards the triumvir Crassus; believing that he had undertaken the campaign because of a craving for gold, she arranged to have molten gold poured down the throat of his corpse, saying, 'Here you are – this is what you wanted!' So far, all we know about dream is that it expresses a wish-fulfilment on the part of the unconscious; apparently, the dominant preconscious system ensures that such wish-fulfilment is granted after first imposing certain distortions upon it. Nor is one really in any position to establish general proof of a train of thought running counter to the dream-wish and, like its counterpart, finding realization in the relevant dream. Only occasionally, when analysing dreams, have we come across reaction-creations – one instance being the affection felt for my friend R. in the uncle dream (see pp. 153ff.). However, the ingredient from the preconscious that is missing here we are able to find elsewhere. A dream may give expression, after all kinds of distortions, to a wish from the *unc*, whereas the dominant system, having withdrawn to the *wish to sleep*, realizes that wish by doing what it can to alter the levels of charge within the psychical apparatus, ultimately holding on to it throughout the period of sleep.[10]

This wish to sleep (to which the preconscious clings) has the general effect of making dream-formation easier. Think of the dream in which the glow coming from the room where the body lay led the father to deduce that the body might have caught fire [see above, pp. 526ff.]. Among the psychical forces prompting the dreaming father to draw this conclusion (rather than let the glow wake him up), we singled out the wish that, for that moment, prolongs the life of the child pictured in the dream. Other wishes springing from the repressed no doubt escape our attention, because we are unable to analyse this dream. However, as a second driving force behind the dream we can probably assume the father's need for sleep; just as the dream prolongs the child's life for a moment, so too is the father's sleep prolonged. 'Let the dream go on,' runs this motivation, 'otherwise I shall have to wake up.' And as with this dream, so with all other dreams the wish to sleep lends support to the unconscious wish. We talked on pp. 137f. about dreams that clearly present themselves as comfort/convenience dreams. Actually, all dreams could claim to be called that. In the case of those wake-up dreams that process the external sensory stimulus in such a way as to make it compatible with sleep continuing, weaving that stimulus into a dream in order to wrest from it the demands it might impose as a reminder of the outside world, here the effectiveness of the wish to sleep on is most easily recognized. But the same thing must similarly contribute towards letting in all other dreams that are only capable of jolting the sleeping state like an alarm clock from inside. What the *prec* tells consciousness in many instances when a dream drives it too hard ('Don't fret, go on sleeping, it's only a dream') altogether describes the way our dominant mental activity behaves (if only implicitly) towards dreaming. I have to conclude *that the whole time we are sleeping we are as confidently aware that we are dreaming as we are that we are asleep*. It is essential that we treat with disparagement the objection that our consciousness is never directed towards the one kind of awareness and towards the other only on specific occasions – when censorship feels it has been taken by surprise, as it were. On the other hand, there are people who very obviously cling, at night, to the knowledge that they are asleep and dreaming – and who appear, therefore, to be possessed of a conscious ability to direct their dream-life. For example, if such a dreamer is dissatisfied with the turn a dream is taking, he will break it off (without waking) and begin the dream again, making it take a different turn, much as a popular playwright will, if asked, give his drama a happier ending.

Or another time he may think, while sleeping, if a dream has placed him in a sexually arousing situation, 'I don't want to go on dreaming this and spend myself in a nocturnal emission, I'd rather save it for a real situation.'

The Marquis d'Hervey (cited in Vaschide [1911], p. 139) claimed to have acquired such power over his dreams that he could speed up their unfolding at will and send them off in any direction he liked. In his case, the wish to sleep seems to have granted space to a different preconscious wish – namely, the wish to observe his own dreams and take delight in them. Sleep is as reconcilable with such a wish-intention as it is with a reservation as condition of waking up (the wet-nurse's sleep). Also, in all people an interest in dreaming is known to increase substantially the number of dreams remembered on waking.

Discussing other observations of imparting direction to dreams, Ferenczi says, 'Dream will work on the thoughts currently preoccupying mental life from all sides, dropping one dream-image when the wish-fulfilment involved threatens to fail, trying a different kind of solution, until eventually it succeeds in creating a compromise wish-fulfilment that satisfies both agencies of the life of the mind.'

Notes

1. They share this indestructible character with all other truly unconscious mental acts (that is to say, such as belong only to the *unc* system). These are paths carved out once and for all, channels that never clog up and that will repeatedly guide the arousal process to exhaust itself, as often as the unconscious stimulus charges them up again. To employ a simile, there is no other sort of destruction for them than for the shades of the Odyssean underworld, which awake to new life the moment they drink blood. Processes that depend on the preconscious system are destructible in quite a different sense. That difference forms the basis of the psychotherapy of neuroses.

2. I attempted a further foray into understanding the circumstances of the sleeping state and the conditions of hallucination in my essay 'Metapsychol-

ogische Ergänzung zur Traumlehre' ['A Metapsychological Supplement to the Theory of Dreams', *Internationale Zeitschrift für die Psychoanalyse*, IV, 1916/18; *Standard Edition*, vol. XIV, p. 219].

3. This is the place to insert what psychoanalysis subsequently recognized as the 'Above-I' [otherwise known in English as the 'superego'; see note 10 on p. 503].

4. In other words, employing a 'reality test' is deemed necessary.

5. Of wish-fulfilment in dream, Le Lorrain rightly boasts: '*Sans fatigue sérieuse, sans être obligé de recourir à cette lutte opiniâtre et longue qui use et corrode les jouissances poursuivies*' ['With no serious trouble, without having to resort to that stubborn, extended struggle that wears down and eats away at the enjoyment sought'].

6. I took this train of thought further elsewhere (in 'Formulierungen über die zwei Prinzipien des psychischen Geschehens' [1911; 'Formulations on the Two Principles of Mental Functioning', in *Standard Edition*, vol. XII, p. 215; and as 'Formulations on the two Principles of Psychic Functioning' in *The Unconscious*, translated by Graham Frankland, London 2005]), describing the 'two principles' as the pleasure principle and the reality principle.

7. To be more precise: part of the symptom constitutes unconscious wish-fulfilment, another part a reaction thereto.

8. Hughlings Jackson had said: 'Find out all about dreams and you will have found out all about insanity.'

9. ['Hysterical Phantasies and their Relation to Bisexuality'; *Standard Edition*, vol. IX, p. 157, and with the same title in *Studies in Hysteria*, translated by Nicola Luckhurst, London 2004.]

10. I have borrowed these ideas from the sleep theory of Liébeault, the man who has revived hypnotic research in our time (*Le sommeil provoqué et les états analogues*, Paris, 1889).

D When a dream wakes one up – the function of dream – the anxiety-dream[1]

Now that we know the preconscious is tuned, at night, to the wish to sleep, we can take our understanding of the dream-process further. But first let us summarize what we have found out about that dream-process so far. We are saying that, from the work of the waking mind, certain day's residues are left over from which the charge of energy could not be fully withdrawn. Alternatively, through the work of the waking mind during the day one of the unconscious wishes has been activated. Or, both things occur together – we have already discussed the kind of diversity that is possible here. Either during the course of the day or only with the onset of sleep the unconscious wish, having fought its way through to the day's residues, effects transference to them. The result is a wish that has transferred itself to still-vivid [rezent] material, or the suppressed wish that is still vivid has given itself new life by drawing additional strength from the unconscious. That wish is now keen to take the normal path of thought-processes through the *prec* (the natural home, indeed, of one of its components) and thus reach consciousness. However, it encounters censorship, which here persists and by which it is now influenced. This is where it assumes the distorted form for which its transference to something still vivid prepared the ground. Up to this point, it is on the way to becoming almost an obsession, a delusion, that sort of thing – in other words, an idea that has become reinforced as a result of transference and that censorship has distorted in its expression. Now, though, the fact that the preconscious is asleep blocks any further advance; probably the system has protected itself against invasion by reducing its arousals. So the dream-process takes the path of regression that the unique nature of the sleeping state has just opened up. In this, it is responding to the attraction exerted on it by memory groups, some of which are themselves present merely as visual charges,[2] not as a translation into the signs of the subsequent systems. On the way to regression it acquires representability. Compression we shall deal with later. The dream-process has now completed the second leg of its convoluted course. The first (progredient) leg spun itself from unconscious scenes or fantasies to the preconscious; the second reaches from the frontier of censorship back towards the perceptions. But if the dream-process has become perception content, it has as it were bypassed the obstacle posed for it in the *prec* by censorship and the sleeping state. It succeeds in drawing attention to itself and entering the purview of consciousness. The fact is, consciousness, which to us denotes a sense organ for grasping psychical qualities, is in the waking state capable of being aroused from two locations. From the periphery of the entire apparatus, the system of perception, first of all; and secondly, from the pleasure and aversion triggers that turn out to be almost the sole psychical quality associated with energy conversions inside the apparatus. All other processes in ψ-systems (including those in the *prec*) lack any kind of psychical quality and therefore do not form an object of consciousness in so far as they do not supply it with a perception of pleasure or aversion. We shall have to make up our minds to accept that *these releases of pleasure and aversion automatically regulate the way in which charging processes unfold*. Subsequently, however, it turned out to be necessary, in order to make more delicate functions possible, to make the unfolding of ideas less dependent on signs of aversion. To this end, the *prec* system required qualities of its own that might attract consciousness, and these it very probably received by linking the preconscious processes to a system that is not without qualities – namely, the memory system of language signs. As a consequence of the qualities of this system, consciousness, which was previously only a sense organ for the perceptions, now also becomes a sense organ for part of our thought-processes. There are two sensory surfaces, so to speak – one turned towards perception, the other towards preconscious thought-processes.

I have to assume that the onset of sleep renders the sensory surface of consciousness facing the *prec* far less arousable than the one that is directed at the *p* systems. The fact is, abandoning interest in nocturnal thought-processes also serves a purpose. Nothing is to happen in terms of thinking; the *prec* wants to sleep. However, once dream has become perception it is able, because of the qualities it has now acquired, to arouse consciousness. This sensory arousal performs what is in fact its function; it directs part of the energy-charge available in the *prec* as attention to what is doing the arousing. It must be conceded, then, that dream invariably *wakes* [in the sense of 'arouses'] in that it activates part of the dormant power of the *prec*. It then undergoes, at the hands of that power, the kind of influence that we have described as secondary processing with regard to coherence and comprehensibility. In other words, dream is treated by that power like any other piece of perception; it is subjected to the same expectations, so far as its material allows. And in so far as there is a question of a direction of unfolding in connection with this third leg of the dream-process, that direction is once again progredient.

To prevent misunderstandings, a word about the temporal properties of these dream-processes is in order. A very attractive train of thought proposed by Goblot [1896], clearly inspired by Maury's guillotine dream [see above, pp. 38, 512], seeks to demonstrate that dream takes up no other time than the transitional period between sleeping and waking. Waking up is not instantaneous, and it is during this interval that dreams occur. People say that the final image of a particular dream was so powerful as to force them awake. In reality, the only reason why it was so powerful was because, at the moment of dreaming it, the dreamer was already so close to waking. '*Un rêve c'est un réveil qui commence*' ['A dream is the beginning of waking up'].[3]

Dugas [1897] has already drawn attention to the fact that Goblot would need to eliminate much reality if he is to give his thesis general validity. There are also dreams that do not wake one up –

including some in which one dreams one is dreaming. From what we know of dream-work, we cannot possibly concede that these extend only over the period of waking. On the contrary, it inevitably strikes us that the first leg of dream-work is accomplished during the day – under the dominion, still, of the preconscious. The second leg (amendment by censorship, the attraction of unconscious scenes, penetration through to perception) goes on all night, and to that extent we are probably always right when we say that we feel we dreamed the whole night through, even if we cannot say what we dreamed. However, I do not believe there is any need for us to assume that dream-processes really do adhere, right up to the moment of entering consciousness, to the chronological order described: first [we say] the transferred wish is there, then distortion by censorship occurs, this is followed by the directional switch of regression, and so on. We had to establish such a sequence while describing it; in fact, it is probably much more a question of a simultaneous trying of this avenue and that, a surging of arousal first one way, then the other, until eventually, as a result of the most appropriate accumulation of these things, one grouping in particular achieves permanence. I would even, after certain personal experiences, be inclined to believe that dream-work frequently needs more than a day and a night to deliver its result – whereupon the extraordinary skill involved in constructing a dream sheds all its miraculous qualities. Even a concern for comprehensibility as a perceptual event is able in my view to take effect before a particular dream attracts consciousness. From this point on, though, the process speeds up, because the dream now gets the same treatment as any other perception. It is like a firework, which takes hours to prepare but is let off in a moment.

As a result of dream-work, the dream-process now either attains enough intensity to attract consciousness to itself and awaken the preconscious, regardless of the duration and depth of sleep; or its intensity is insufficient to do so and it must remain in readiness until, just prior to the moment of waking, it is met by a more mobile attention. Most dreams seem to operate with comparatively low levels of psychical intensity, since they wait for the moment of waking. But this also explains why we usually perceive something we have dreamed when we are wrenched abruptly from a deep sleep. Here our first glance, as when we wake spontaneously, is for the perceptual substance created by dream-work, our second for that which is given from outside.

However, greater theoretical interest attaches to the dreams that are able to wake a person up in mid-sleep. Remembering the efficiency so much in evidence elsewhere, one wonders why a dream (an unconscious wish) should be given the power to disturb sleep, which is the fulfilment of a preconscious wish. The reason must presumably lie in energy relations that we fail to understand. If we did understand them, we should probably find that giving the dream free rein, as it were, and expending a certain detached attention on it represent a saving of energy in case the unconscious should need to be kept within bounds at night as much as during the day. Experience shows that dreaming, even where it interrupts sleep several times in a night, is still compatible with sleeping. One wakes for an instant and immediately goes back to sleep. It is as if, in one's sleep, one shoos away a fly; one wakes up *ad hoc*. If one goes back to sleep, the interruption is no more. Fulfilling the sleep wish, as familiar examples of such phenomena as nursing sleep show us, is quite compatible with maintaining a certain expenditure of attention in a specific direction.

At this point, however, an objection deserves a hearing that is based on a better understanding of unconscious processes. We have described even unconscious wishes as being constantly alive. Even so [we say], in the daytime they lack the power to make themselves perceptible. But when the sleeping state supervenes and the unconscious wish has shown itself powerful enough to form a dream and use it to rouse the preconscious, why does that power peter out once the dream has been noted? Surely the dream ought continually to renew itself, just like the bothersome fly that, however many times we drive it away, always likes to return? By what right have we claimed that dream does away with sleep-disturbances?

It is quite true that unconscious wishes remain constantly alive. They represent avenues that are always viable, whenever a quantum of arousal makes use of them. In fact, a very prominent feature of unconscious processes is that they remain indestructible. In the unconscious, nothing can be brought to an end, nothing is ever gone or forgotten. The strongest impression of this comes from the study of neuroses, notably hysteria. The unconscious avenue of thought that leads to discharge in a fit can immediately be re-accessed, just as soon as sufficient arousal has built up. The hurt that occurred thirty years ago, once it has gained access to the unconscious well-springs of affect, will never lose its freshness throughout that period. Each time the memory of it is touched upon, it revives and shows itself charged with arousal, which then finds motor discharge in a fit. This is precisely where psychotherapy needs to intervene. The task of psychotherapy is to settle unconscious processes and consign them to oblivion. The fact is, what we tend to take for granted and explain as a primary influence of [the passage of] time on mental memory-residues, the fading of memories and the weakening of affects prompted by impressions that have lost their vividness, are in reality secondary changes brought about by hard work. It is the preconscious that does that work, *and psychotherapy can take no other line than to bring the* unc *under the control of the* prec.

For the individual unconscious arousal process, then, there are two possible outcomes. Either it is left to its own devices, in which case it will eventually break through somewhere and, this once, give its arousal an outlet in motility, or it comes under the influence of the preconscious and its arousal is *bound* by it rather than *released*. *In the dream-process, however, it is the latter that occurs*. The charge that dream-become-perception receives from the *prec*, having been directed thither through the arousal of consciousness, binds the unconscious arousal of the particular dream and neutralizes it as a potential disturbance. If the dreamer wakes up for a moment, he really has shooed away the fly that threatened to disturb his sleep. We may now have a sense that it really was more efficient and less costly to let the unconscious wish have its head, so to speak (opening up the avenue of regression for it to go down, enabling it to form a dream, and then binding and dealing with that dream by means of a small outlay of preconscious effort), than it was to keep the unconscious reined in for the whole period of sleep as well. It was only to be expected, after all, that dream, even though not originally a purposeful process, should in the interplay of forces that is mental life have usurped a function. We can see what that function is. It took on the task of bringing the arousal of the *unc*, once set free, back under the control of the preconscious; this it does by drawing off the arousal of the *unc*, offering it a safety-valve, and at the same time, in return for a small outlay of waking activity, securing the sleep of the preconscious. It thus puts itself forward as a compromise, exactly like the other psychical formations of the same order, serving both systems simultaneously by fulfilling both wishes, in so far as they are mutually compatible. A glance at Robert's 'elimination theory', which we mentioned on p. 92, will show that in the main matter (determining the function of dream) we must concede that that author was right, although we differ from him over the conditions for and appreciation of the dream-process.[4]

The qualification '*in so far as they* [both wishes] *are mutually compatible*' hints at the possible cases in which the function of dream meets with failure. The dream-process is initially admitted as wish-fulfilment of the unconscious; if this attempted wish-fulfilment so shakes the preconscious as permanently to disturb its calm, dream has violated the compromise, no longer fulfilling the other part of its task. It is then instantly broken off and replaced by full awakening. Actually, here again it is not the fault of dream if, normally the guardian of sleep, it has to figure as its destroyer, nor need this bias us against dream's usefulness. This is not the only instance in the organism of a normally useful facility losing its usefulness and becoming disruptive as soon as the circumstances of its emergence are slightly altered, in which case the disruption at least serves a new purpose in that, by pointing out the change, it awakens the organism's regulatory mechanism against it. I am thinking, of course, of the anxiety-dream, and lest I give the impression that I am dodging this piece of evidence against the wish-fulfilment theory whenever I encounter it, let me try to throw fresh light on the anxiety-dream, at least by suggestion.

For us, there has long been no contradiction in the fact that a psychical process generating anxiety may nevertheless constitute wish-fulfilment. We have learned how to explain the occurrence to ourselves in this way: the wish belongs to one system, namely the *unc*, whereas the *prec* system has rejected that wish and suppressed it.[5] Subjugation of the *unc* by the *prec* is not complete, even in a person enjoying full psychical health; the degree of such subjugation is the measure of our psychical normality. Neurotic symptoms indicate to us that the two systems are in conflict; they are the compromise outcome of that conflict, bringing it to a provisional end. On the one hand they provide the *unc* with a way out through which to discharge its arousal, they are its emergency exit, while on the other hand they make it possible for the *prec* to control the *unc* to some extent. It is instructive, for example, to consider the significance of a hysterical phobia or what we call 'place-anxiety' [*Platzangst*; agoraphobia]. A neurotic, say, is incapable of crossing the street unaccompanied, which we rightly cite as a 'symptom'. Now neutralize the symptom by forcing that neurotic to perform something of which he feels incapable. The result is an anxiety attack, and indeed an anxiety attack on the street often causes agoraphobia to be produced. This teaches us that the symptom had been constituted in order to prevent anxiety from breaking out; the phobia is set before anxiety like a border fortress.

Our discussion can be taken no further unless we look into the role of affects in connection with these processes, which is only imperfectly possible here. Let us, therefore, posit the principle that the chief reason why suppression of the *unc* is necessary is that the unfolding of ideas in the *unc*, if left to itself, would develop an affect that originally had the character of pleasure but now, since the process of *repression*, is of the nature of aversion. Suppression has the aim but also the effect of preventing such aversion from developing. Suppression extends to the ideational content of the *unc* because it is from the ideational content that aversion might spring. Underlying this is a quite specific assumption regarding the nature of affect-development. It is seen as a motor or secretory function, the innervation key to which lies in the ideas of the *unc*.

As a result of the control exercised by the *prec*, those ideas are choked off, as it were; they are inhibited as regards emitting the affect-developing impulses. The danger, if charging by the *prec* should dry up, is thus of the unconscious arousals giving rise to the kind of affect that (as a result of the repression that has taken place earlier) can only be experienced as aversion or anxiety.

This danger is unleashed by the dream-process being given its head. The conditions for its realization are that repressions have occurred and that the suppressed wish-stimuli are capable of becoming strong enough. In other words, they stand entirely outside the psychological framework of dream-formation. But for the fact that, because of this one factor of the freeing of the *unc* during sleep, our subject is connected with that of how anxiety develops, I might avoid discussing the anxiety-dream and spare myself, at this point, all the obscurities that come with it.

The theory of the anxiety-dream belongs, as I have already stated repeatedly, to the psychology of neuroses. It is no longer any concern of ours, once we have shown where it touches upon the subject of the dream-process. I can do only one thing more. Having claimed that neurotic anxiety stems from sexual sources, I can subject anxiety-dreams to analysis in order to demonstrate the sexual material in their dream-thoughts.

For good reasons I have decided against using here any of the examples that neurotic patients supply me with in such profusion, giving preference to anxiety-dreams had by young people.

I myself have not had any proper anxiety-dreams for decades now. I remember one (from when I was six or seven) of which I did an interpretation some thirty years later. It was extremely vivid and showed me *my dear mother with a curiously calm look on her face, as if she was asleep, being carried into the room by two (or three) people with birds' beaks and laid upon the bed.* I woke up weeping and screaming and disturbed my parents' sleep. The (curiously draped) elongated figures with the birds' beaks I had taken from the illustrations in the *Philippson* Bible;[6] I believe they were sparrowhawk-headed gods from an Egyptian tomb-relief. But analysis also supplied the memory of an ill-mannered janitor's son who used to play with us children on the grass in front of the house – and whose name, I am inclined to think, was *Philipp*. I have the further impression that it was from this boy that I first heard the vulgar word that denotes sexual intercourse;[7] the educated simply substitute a Latin-based word (*coitieren*), but the vulgar version is quite clearly indicated by the choice of the sparrowhawk heads. I must have guessed the sexual connotation of the word from the expression on my worldly-wise teacher's face. My mother's facial expression in the dream was copied from that of my grandfather, whom I had seen in a coma, snoring, a few days prior to his death. So the interpretation of the secondary processing in my dream must have been: my *mother* is dying. The *tomb*-relief also confirms that. In my anxiety I woke up and would not desist until I had roused my parents. I can remember suddenly calming down when I set eyes on my mother, as if I had needed the reassurance: she's not dead, then. However, this secondary interpretation of the dream took place under the influence (already) of an anxiety previously engendered. I was not anxious because I had dreamed my mother was dying; rather, my preconscious processing interpreted the dream in that way because I was already a prey to anxiety. That anxiety can in fact be traced, through the medium of repression, to an obscure, obviously sexual yearning that had found appropriate expression in the visual content of the dream.

A twenty-seven-year-old man who had been seriously ill for the previous year dreamed repeatedly between the ages of eleven and thirteen, with deep anxiety, *that a man with a hatchet is after him; he wants to run but is somehow paralysed and cannot move*. This is an excellent example of a very common anxiety-dream that is beyond suspicion of being sexual. During analysis, the first thing this dreamer digs up is a story his uncle used to tell at a later period about being attacked in the street one night by a suspicious-looking individual, and he himself concludes from this association that at the time of the dream he may have heard of a similar experience. As to the weapon, he recalls having once, around that time, injured his hand with a *hatchet* while chopping wood. He then abruptly starts talking about his relationship with his younger brother, whom he was in the habit of ill-treating and knocking over; he particularly recalls one occasion when, having hit his brother on the head with a boot, making him bleed, he heard his mother say, 'I'm worried [*Ich habe Angst*] he's going to kill him one of these days.' While he appears to be thus stuck on the subject of *violence*, a memory suddenly comes back to him from when he was eight. His parents, returning home late, went to bed while he was pretending to be asleep. He then heard panting and other sounds that struck him as frightening, and he was able to make out the positions of the two of them in bed. His further thoughts reveal that he had drawn an analogy between his parents' relationship and his own relationship with his younger brother. He put what his parents were involved in under the heading of *violence* and *rough-house*. Evidence for this view, so far as he was concerned, was provided by the fact that he had often noticed *blood in his mother's bed*.

That sexual intercourse between adults strikes children who become aware of it as frightening and sparks anxiety within them is a matter, I venture to say, of everyday experience. For such anxiety I have put forward the explanation that what is at issue here is sexual arousal that is not dealt with by an understanding of it, and that probably another reason why it encounters rejection is because one's parents are involved in it, which is why it turns into anxiety. At an even earlier period in a child's life, sexual stirrings for the parent of the opposite sex do not yet meet with repression and express themselves freely, as we have seen (on p. 272).

I would have no hesitation in applying the same explanation to the nocturnal anxiety attacks accompanied by hallucinations (the phenomenon known as *pavor nocturnus*) that are so frequently suffered by children. Here too there can be no question of anything but poorly understood, repudiated sexual stirrings, in the recording of which a temporal periodicity will also probably emerge, since an increase in sexual libido can be engendered quite as much by random arousing impressions as by spontaneous developmental processes occurring in successive phases.

I lack the requisite observational material to carry this explanation through.[8] On the other hand, paediatricians appear to lack the standpoint that would alone supply an understanding of the whole series of phenomena both from the somatic side and from the psychical side. As a comical instance of how closely the blinkers of medical mythology enable one to approach and pass by such cases without understanding them, let me cite the case I came across in Debacker's 1881 thesis on *pavor nocturnus* (p. 66).

A thirteen-year-old boy of feeble health started to become anxious and dreamy; his sleep became increasingly restless, and almost once a week he was woken up by a powerful attack of anxiety with hallucinations. His recollection of those dreams was always very clear. He could recount, for example, that the *devil* had screamed at him, 'This time we've got you, this time we've got you', after which there was a smell of pitch and sulphur, while fire scorched his skin. He then started up from this dream and was unable to cry out at first until his voice became free and he was heard to say clearly, 'No, no, not me, I've haven't done anything', or another time, 'Please don't, I'll never do it again.' On a number of occasions he also said, 'Albert didn't do it.' He subsequently avoided getting undressed 'because the fire only came over him when he was undressed'. In the midst of these devil dreams, which were putting his health at risk, he was packed off to the country where, over the course of eighteen months, he recovered; afterwards, aged fifteen, he confessed on one occasion, 'I didn't dare own up, but I constantly felt a tingling sensation and arousals in my *privates*;[9] in the end it got on my nerves so much that several times I thought of throwing myself out of the dormitory window.'[10]

It is really not difficult to guess 1) that in earlier years the boy had masturbated, probably denied it, and been threatened with grave punishments for his bad habit (his admission: 'I'll never do it again'; his lie: 'Albert didn't do it'); 2) that with the onset of puberty the temptation to masturbate revived in the tickling feeling in the genitals; but 3) that a repression struggle now broke out in him that suppressed the libido, converting it into anxiety, and that anxiety subsequently took the punishments formerly threatened upon itself.

However, let us listen to our author's rather different conclusions (p. 69):

It emerges from this observation that 1) the effect of puberty on a boy of weakened health may induce a state of great weakness, possibly resulting in *very substantial cerebral anaemia*.[11]

2) That cerebral anaemia produces a character change, demono-manic hallucinations and very violent nocturnal (possibly also diurnal) anxiety states.

3) The demonomania and the boy's self-reproaches go back to the influence of a religious upbringing, which had affected him as a child.

4) All symptoms vanished as a result of an extended stay in the country with physical exercise and a return of strength after puberty had run its course.

5) Possibly we may attribute to heredity and to the father's old syphilis a predisposing influence towards the emergence of the cerebral condition in the child.

And finally: 'We have filed this observation under the heading of apyretic deliria of inanition, because we ascribe this particular condition to cerebral ischaemia.'[12]

Notes

1. [A reminder to the reader that the German word *Angst*, which in Freudian contexts is normally translated as 'anxiety', covers a broader range of meaning (from mild worry to naked fear) than its English counterpart.]
2. [*visuelle Besetzungen*.]
3. [Quoted in French (without a translation) in the original.]
4. Is this the sole function we can attribute to dream? I know of no other. A[lphonse] Maeder [1912] has tried to enlist other, 'secondary' functions for dream. He starts out from the correct observation that many dreams contain attempts to resolve conflicts that are in fact subsequently implemented; in other words, they act like early rehearsals for waking operations. He therefore draws a parallel between dreaming and the play of animals and children, which is to be seen as an early exercise of inborn instincts [*Instinkte*; Freud's *Trieben* I translate as 'drives'] and a preparation for later serious activity, and he posited a *fonction ludique* ['play function'] for

dreaming. Shortly before Maeder, Alf[red] Adler had also highlighted the 'forward-looking' function of dream. (In an analysis published by myself in 1905, a dream that asked to be seen as an intention was repeated every night until it was executed.)

A moment's reflection will inevitably show us that this 'secondary' function of dream merits no recognition in the context of a dream-interpretation. Thinking ahead, forming intentions, working out possible solutions that may subsequently find implementation in waking life – these and much else are things performed by the unconscious and preconscious intellect, things that continue in the sleeping state as 'day's residue' and may then come together with an unconscious wish (see p. 579) to form a dream. So the forward-looking function of dream is much more a function of preconscious waking thought, the outcome of which may be revealed to us by our analysing dreams or indeed other phenomena. Having for so long had dreams coincide with their manifest content, we must also now guard against confusing them with their latent dream-thoughts.

5. [Added by Freud to the fifth edition:] 'A second, much more important and far-reaching factor that the layman likewise overlooks is the following. A wish-fulfilment would undoubtedly give pleasure, but the question is, to whom? To the person who has the wish, of course. However, we know that the dreamer stands in a very special relationship to his wishes. He rejects them, censors them – in a word, dislikes them. So having them fulfilled can give him no pleasure, only the opposite. Experience then shows that that opposite, for reasons yet to be explained, appears in the form of anxiety. So in his relationship to his dream-wishes, the dreamer can be likened only to a summation of two persons who are nevertheless linked by a powerful common bond. Rather than commenting any further, let me tell you a well-known story in which you will find the same relationships echoed: A good fairy promises a poor man and his wife that their first three wishes will come true. Overjoyed, they resolve to choose those three wishes with care. The woman, however, allows the smell of the sausages being fried next door to distract her into wishing that she had a couple of sausages herself. And in an instant, there they are; the first wish has come true. Livid, the husband bitterly voices a wish that the sausages should fetch up dangling from the end of his wife's nose. This duly happens, and the sausages are not to be budged from their new location; the second wish has now been fulfilled, but it was the husband's wish; for the wife, its fulfilment was far from pleasant. The rest of the story you know. Both of them, husband and wife, being basically one, the third wish has to be that the sausages should cease to be attached to the woman's nose. We might

use the story several other times in different contexts; here let it simply serve to illustrate the possibility that one person's wish-fulfilment may lead to another's displeasure, if the two do not agree.' ([Freud] *Vorlesungen zur Einführung in die Psychoanalyse* [1916–17; *Introductory Lectures on Psychoanalysis, Standard Edition*, vols XV–XVI]).

6. [A new translation of the Jewish bible by Ludwig Philippson began to appear in 1839. A later edition of it contained illustrations by Gustave Doré.]

7. [The verb that for some reason achieved this status is *vögeln*; all the English reader needs to know is that *Vogel* = 'bird'.]

8. Such material has since been supplied in great profusion by the psycho-analytical literature.

9. My emphasis; but surely unmistakable.

10. [Quoted in French in the original: *'Je n'osais pas l'avouer, mais j'éprouvais continuellement des picotements et des surexcitations aux* parties; *à la fin, cela m'énervait tant que plusieurs fois, j'ai pensé me jeter par la fenêtre du dortoir.'*]

11. My emphasis.

12. [Quoted in French in the original: *'Nous avons fait entrer cette observation dans le cadre des délires apyrétiques d'inanition, car c'est à l'ischémie cérébrale que nous rattachons cet état particulier.'*]

E *Primary and secondary processes –*
repression

In seeking to penetrate more deeply into the psychology of dream-processes, I have taken on a hard task. It is also one to which my descriptive skills are barely adequate. Conveying the simultaneity of so intricate a coherence by means of consecutive presentation while appearing, each time I advance a view, to do so without preconception is something that, in the long run, exceeds my ability. Indeed, I am paying for my inability, in portraying the psychology of dream in these pages, to trace the historical development of my insights. The standpoints for discussing dream were set out for me by previous studies in the psychology of neuroses, to which I have no wish to allude here but repeatedly must allude. The fact is, I prefer to approach the matter the other way around, starting from dream and going on to make the connection with the psychology of neuroses. I am aware of the problems this causes the reader, yet I see no way of avoiding them.

Frustrated by this state of affairs, I am pleased to dwell for a moment on another viewpoint that seems to me to enhance the value of my efforts. I found a subject that was dominated by the sharpest contradictions in the views of the writers involved, as the introduction to my first chapter shows. After our discussion of the problems of dream, most such contradictions have been accommodated. Only two of the views expressed – namely, that dream is meaningless and that it is a somatic process – did we need to contradict decisively ourselves; otherwise we have been able to admit all mutually contradictory opinions at some point in the complicated picture and to demonstrate that they uncovered something correct. That dream continues the ideas and interests of waking life has been universally confirmed by the discovery of hidden *dream-thoughts*. These concern themselves solely with what strikes us as important and is of enormous interest to us. Dream never bothers with little things. Yet we have also admitted the opposite: that dream picks up the trivial refuse of the day, and that it cannot take hold of a major daytime interest until that interest has to some extent escaped the work of the waking mind. We found this to be true of the *dream-content* that gives expression to the relevant dream-thoughts in a way that is altered by distortion. The dream-process, we said, will for reasons dictated by the mechanics of association more easily take hold of fresh or trivial ideational material that has not yet been tarnished by waking mental activity, and for reasons of censorship it will transfer psychical intensity from what is significant but at the same time offensive to what is indifferent. The hypermnesia of dream and its access to childhood material have for us become key elements; in our dream-theory we assign the role of indispensable driving force for dream-formation to a wish stemming from the infantile realm. It never, of course, occurred to us to doubt the experimentally verified significance of external sensory stimuli during sleep, but we placed such material in the same relationship to the dream-wish as the thought-residues left over from day-work. That dream will interpret an objective sensory stimulus in the manner of an illusion is not something we need dispute; however, we supply the motive for such an interpretation (left unspecified by the authors of the literature). That interpretation is to the effect that the perceived object becomes harmless so far as disturbing sleep is concerned and can be used for the purposes of wish-fulfilment. As for the subjective state of arousal of the sense organs during sleep that Trumbull Ladd [1892] appears to have demonstrated, while not accepting this as a separate dream-source we are able to account for it in terms of regredient revival of the memories operating behind dreams. The internal organic sensations that people like to take as a central point of dream-explanations also, in our view, retain a role, albeit a more modest one. Sensations of falling, floating, being hemmed in – all these provide us with constantly available material that dream-work uses whenever necessary to give expression to dream-thoughts.

That the dream-process is a rapid, momentary one strikes us as correct with regard to perception by consciousness of the dream-content portrayed; as far as the previous legs of the dream-process are concerned, we find a slow, undulating progress to be more plausible. As to the riddle of the superabundant dream-content squeezed into the briefest moment, we were able to contribute that this is a case of drawing upon ready-made figments of psychical life. That dreams are distorted and mutilated by memory we found to be correct though not an obstacle, this being simply the final, manifest part of a distortion process that has been going on since the onset of dream-formation. In the bitter and apparently irreconcilable dispute as to whether the life of mind sleeps at night or enjoys all the capacities it enjoys by day, we were able to agree to some extent with both sides but not entirely with either. In dream-thoughts, we found proof of a highly complicated intellectual function operating with virtually all the resources of the mental apparatus; yet there is no denying that those dream-thoughts emerged by day, and it is essential to assume that the life of mind does have a sleeping state. As a result, even the theory of partial sleep was positively entertained; however, it was not in the collapse of mental coherence that we found the defining characteristic of the sleeping state but in the way in which the psychical system that controls the day becomes focused on the wish to sleep. In our view, too, a turning-away from the outside world remains significant; it helps, even if it is not the only factor, to make the regression of dream-representation possible. That a relinquishment of voluntary control over the development of ideation takes place is incontrovertible; however, this does not make psychical life aimless since, as we have heard, as soon as deliberate objectives are abandoned involuntary ones gain control. A loose associative linkage in dream is something we have not simply accepted; we credit its dominance with far greater scope than could have been suspected. However, we found that it is only an enforced substitute for a different form of associative linkage – one that is both correct and meaningful.

Granted, we too dubbed dream absurd; but examples showed us how clever dream is being when it pretends to be absurd. As to the functions attributed to dream, there is no conflict between us. That dream relieves the mind like a valve and that, as Robert [1886] puts it, all sorts of harmful stuff is rendered harmless by being represented in a dream, not only accords precisely with our theory of dual wish-fulfilment through dream; it is even, for us, in terms of its wording, more intelligible than in Robert. The free, assured progress of mind in the interplay of its capacities is echoed in our thinking by having dreams given their head by preconscious activity. The 'return to the embryonic standpoint of mental life in dream' and Havelock Ellis's comment about 'an archaic world of vast emotions and imperfect thoughts' seem to us happy anticipations of our own remarks to the effect that *primitive* modes of operation, which are suppressed by day, play a part in dream-formation; Sully's assertion to the effect that 'dream brings back the personalities that we developed successively at earlier stages, our old way of looking at things, impulses and modes of reaction that controlled us long ago' is one we have been able to adopt unreservedly; with us as with Delage [1891] the 'suppressed' becomes the driving force behind dreaming.

The role that Scherner [1861] attributes to dream-imagination as well as Scherner's own interpretations have received our full recognition, but we had as it were to locate them elsewhere in the problem. It is not dream that forms imagination; rather, in the formation of dream-thoughts, unconscious imaginative activity plays the greatest part. We remain indebted to Scherner for pointing out the source of dream-thoughts; however, almost all the things he attributes to dream-work should in fact be ascribed to the operation of the unconscious as active during the day, which yields the stimuli for dreams no less than those for neurotic symptoms. We have had to separate dream-work from that operation as being something quite different and very much more delimited. Finally, far from abandoning the connection between dream and mental disturbance, we place it on firmer ground.

In other words, held together by what is new in our dream-theory as by a higher entity, we find the most disparate and the most contradictory findings of the authors of the literature fitting into our edifice, some of them used in a different way but only a few of them rejected altogether. However, our structure too is incomplete. As well as the many uncertainties that we have drawn down upon ourselves with our attempt to penetrate the darkness of psychology, a fresh contradiction appears to oppress us. While on the one hand we have dream-thoughts emerge from completely normal intellectual work, on the other hand we have uncovered a range of quite abnormal thought-processes among dream-thoughts (and from there getting into dream-content) that we then repeat in connection with interpreting the dream concerned. Everything we call 'dream-work' seems to us to be so far removed from the processes we are told are correct that the harshest verdicts of the authors of the literature about the inferior psychical performance of dreaming inevitably strike us as reasonable.

In this predicament, it is possibly only by penetrating deeper that we shall shed light and find help. Let me single out one of the situations that lead to dream-formation.

We have learned that a dream replaces a number of thoughts stemming from daytime life and fitting together with perfect logic. That is why we can have no doubt that such thoughts spring from our normal intellectual life. All the qualities that we prize in our trains of thought, the things that characterize them as complicated functions of a high order, we find reflected in dream-thoughts. However, nothing obliges us to assume that that intellectual work has been performed during sleep, which would badly skew the idea of the psychical sleeping state that we have entertained hitherto. Rather, those chains of thought may well stem from the day, have continued, unnoticed by consciousness, from the moment of their conception, and with the advent of sleep find themselves complete. If we are to deduce anything from this state of affairs, it is at most evidence *that the most complicated intellectual feats can be accomplished without the cooperation of consciousness,* as we should in any case inevitably learn from any psychoanalysis of a hysteric or of a person afflicted with obsessions. Such dream-thoughts are certainly not inherently incapable of becoming conscious; if during the day they have not entered our consciousness, there may be various reasons for this. Becoming conscious depends upon application of a specific psychical function, namely attention, only a specific quantity of which is apparently expended, a quantity that it has been possible to divert from the train of thought concerned by means of other objectives. Another way in which such trains of thought can be kept from consciousness is this. We know from our conscious thinking that in expending attention we are pursuing a particular course. If that course brings us to an idea that does not bear criticism, we break off; we cease the investment [*Besetzung*] of attention. It now appears that the train of thought begun and abandoned is able to resume its course without further attention being paid to it, provided that it does not at any point achieve a particularly high degree of intensity such as compels attention. So an initial, perhaps consciously effected decision to reject something as incorrect or unusable for the current purpose of ratiocination may cause a thought-process to continue unnoticed by consciousness until the thinker falls asleep.

Let us recapitulate: we call such a train of thought 'preconscious', we deem it to be wholly correct and we consider that it may just as well be one that has been simply ignored as one that has been broken off and suppressed. And let us state quite frankly how it is that we picture the course of ideation. We believe that when a purposive idea is conceived it pushes a certain quantity of arousal (called by us 'charging energy' [*Besetzungsenergie*]) along the associative path chosen by that purposive idea. A train of thought that has been 'ignored' has not received such a charge; one that has been 'suppressed' or 'rejected' has had such a charge withdrawn; both are left to their own arousals. In certain circumstances the purposive train of thought [one that is 'charged' with an objective] will be capable of attracting the attention of consciousness, in which case it will receive, through this agency, what we might call a *'double charge'* [*Überbesetzung*]. We shall need to set out our assumptions regarding what consciousness is and does at a slightly later stage.

A train of thought stimulated in the preconscious in this way may spontaneously fade away, or it may be preserved. The way we picture the former outcome is that its energy diffuses in all associative directions radiating from itself, placing the entire chain of thought in a state of arousal that lasts for a while but then subsides in that the arousal seeking relief is transformed into a state of quietly holding a charge. Where this first outcome occurs, the process is of no further significance for dream-formation. However, there lurk in our preconscious other purposive ideas stemming from unconscious, perpetually active wishes. These can seize upon the arousal in the group of thoughts that has been left to its own devices, establish a connection between that group and the unconscious wish, and *transfer* the energy inherent in the unconscious wish to that group; from this point on, the neglected or suppressed train of thought is able to remain in existence, although it does not, as a result of that reinforcement, receive any claim to become conscious. We can say that a formerly preconscious train of thought has been *drawn into the unconscious*.

Other situations in which dreams might form are that the preconscious train of thought was connected with the unconscious wish from the outset and for that reason met with rejection by the dominant purposive idea, or that an unconscious wish, activated for other reasons (somatic, for example), spontaneously seeks transference to psychical residues not invested with a charge by the *prec*. All three cases converge and eventually meet in a single result, which is that a train of thought arises in the preconscious that, vacated by its preconscious charge, finds itself invested with a fresh charge by the unconscious wish.

From here on the train of thought undergoes a series of transformations that we no longer regard as normal psychical processes and that produce a result that we find disconcerting, namely a psychopathological formation. We shall now highlight those processes and arrange them.

1) The intensities of individual ideas become capable, in their entirety, of disgorging themselves and pass from one idea to another

in such a way that some ideas emerge that are equipped with enormous intensity. Because this process is repeated a number of times, the intensity of a whole train of thought can eventually collect in a single ideational element. This is the phenomenon of *compression* or *intensification* with which we have become familiar as part of dream-work.[1] It is chiefly to blame for the disconcerting impression conveyed by dream, because we know of nothing like it from the normal life of mind as available to consciousness. Here too we have ideas that possess enormous psychical importance as nodal points or end-results of entire chains of thought, but that valency[2] does not manifest itself in any *obvious* character so far as internal perception is concerned; hence what the idea represents does not in any way become more intense. In the compression process, all psychical coherence is converted into the *intensity* of the ideational content. It is like when in a book I have a word to which I attach exceptional value as regards the understanding of the text printed spaced out[3] or in bold. In speaking, I would enunciate the same word loudly and slowly, giving it great emphasis. The former analogy leads straight to an example borrowed from dream-work (*trimethylamine* in the dream of Irma's injection [see above, pp. 119ff.]). Art historians point out to us that the most ancient historical sculptures follow a similar principle in that they express the rank of the people portrayed by the size of the image. The king is shown twice or three times the size of his retainers or of the enemy he has overcome. An image from the Roman period will use more refined means to the same end. It will place the figure of the *imperator* in the middle, drawn up to his full height; it will take especial care over depicting his form, placing his enemies at his feet, but it will no longer make him look like a giant among midgets. Incidentally, having the subordinate bow before his or her superior in our society today echoes this ancient principle of representation.

The path that the compressions of dream follow is dictated on the one hand by the right preconscious relations of the dream-thoughts and on the other by the attraction of visual recollections in the unconscious. The outcome of the work of compression achieves the intensities required to break through in the direction of the systems of perception.

2) Again as a result of these intensities being freely transferable and as an aid to compression, *intermediate ideas* are formed – compromises, so to speak (there are many examples of this). Similarly, something unheard of in the normal course of ideas, where it is mainly a question of selecting and retaining the 'right' ideational element. On the other hand, mixed and compromise formations occur with extraordinary frequency when we try to find linguistic expression for preconscious thoughts; such formations are referred to as various types of 'slip of the tongue'.

3) The ideas that transfer their intensities to one another are *very loosely interrelated* and are linked together by such types of association as our thinking spurns and makes available for use only to comic effect. In particular, assonance and literal associations are granted the same status as the rest.

4) Mutually contradictory thoughts, instead of trying to cancel each other out, co-exist side by side, often *as if there was no contradiction*; they join together to form compression products, or they form compromises that we should never forgive ourselves for thinking but in our actions often countenance.

Such would be some of the most striking abnormal processes to which once rationally constituted dream-thoughts are subjected in the course of dream-work. Recognizably, their chief characteristic is that supreme importance is attached to making the energy with which objects are charged fluid and *capable of being drained off*; the content and original meaning of the psychical elements to which those charges adhere become of secondary importance. One might even suppose that compression and compromise-formation occur only in the service of regression, where it is a question of turning thoughts into images. However, analysis (and to an even greater extent, synthesis) of dreams that lack regression to images (the dream I call '*Autodidasker* – conversation with Professor N.', for instance [see above, pp. 313ff.]) yields the same processes of distortion and compression as the rest.

So we cannot close our minds to the insight that two utterly different psychical processes are involved in dream-formation: one creates perfectly correct dream-thoughts that have the same value as normal thinking; the other deals with those thoughts in a highly disconcerting, incorrect manner. We identified the latter in Chapter 6 as dream-work proper. What can we now say about the derivation of this latter psychical process?

We should not be able to supply an answer here had we not penetrated some way into the psychology of neuroses, and in particular of hysteria. What in fact we learn from this is that the same incorrect psychical processes (together with others we have not specified) control the production of hysterical symptoms. In hysteria, too, we first find a series of thoughts that are quite correct and entirely equal in value to our conscious thoughts but of the existence of which in this form we can learn nothing, reconstructing it as we do only subsequently. When they have somewhere found their way through to our perception, we see from analysing the symptom formed that these normal thoughts have undergone abnormal treatment and *have been transposed into the symptom by means of compression and compromise-formation, via superficial associations, through covering up their contradictions, possibly, in the end, by way of regression*. Given the complete identity between the distinguishing features of dream-work and those of the psychical activity that finds expression in psychoneurotic symptoms, we shall feel justified in transferring to the phenomenon of dream conclusions that hysteria has forced upon us.

From hysteria theory we adopt the principle *that the only time this kind of abnormal psychical processing of a normal train of thought occurs is when it is used to give expression to an unconscious wish stemming from infancy and currently in repression*. It is for the sake of this principle that we have constructed the theory of dream on the assumption that the driving dream-wish invariably stems from the unconscious, which as we have ourselves admitted cannot be universally proved – though it cannot be disproved, either. But to enable us to say what '*repression*' is (and we have made much of the label) we need to extend part of our psychological scaffolding.

We had become engrossed in the fiction of a primitive psychical apparatus, the operation of which is governed by the endeavour to avoid any accumulation of arousal and to keep itself so far as possible free thereof. That was why it was constructed on the model of a reflex apparatus; motility (in the first place, the path to an internal change in the body) was the discharge route available to it. We then discussed the psychical consequences of a satisfaction-experience and were able, at that point, to introduce the second assumption, which is that any accumulation of arousal (by what means need not trouble us here) is experienced as aversion and sets the apparatus in operation in order to re-occasion the satisfactory outcome whereby a reduction of arousal conferred pleasure. This kind of tendency in the apparatus, proceeding from aversion and aiming at pleasure, we call a wish; we stated that nothing but a wish is capable of activating the apparatus, and the course that the arousal takes within it is governed automatically by the perceptions of pleasure and aversion. The first wishing was probably a hallucinatory charging of the memory of a satisfaction. However, that hallucination, if not sustained until exhaustion, turned out to be incapable of causing the need to cease – that is to say, of occasioning the pleasure associated with the satisfaction.

Consequently, a second operation (or, as we put it, the operation of a second system) became necessary, an operation that, rather than permit the memory-charge to push through to perception and thence commit the psychical forces, instead leads the arousal proceeding from the need-stimulus around a detour that at length, through the medium of voluntary motility, changes the outside world in such a way that actual perception of the satisfaction-object is able to occur. We have already traced the schema of the psychical apparatus up to this point; the two systems are the embryo of what we insert in the fully developed apparatus as *unc* and *prec*.

Being able to change the outside world appropriately by means of motility calls for the accumulation of a large quantity of experiences in the memory-systems and a very varied definition of the connections evoked by various purposive ideas in that memory-material. We now move on in our assumptions. The often tentative activity of the second system, emitting charges and withdrawing them again, calls on the one hand for all memory-material to be freely available; on the other hand, it would constitute superfluous outlay if that activity were to direct large amounts of charge down individual thought-paths that were then going to flow away to no purpose, reducing the amount needed to change the outside world. So for efficiency's sake I postulate that the second system does manage to preserve a large proportion of the energy-charges in a state of calm, using only a small amount for displacement purposes. How such processes work I have no idea; anyone inclined to take these ideas seriously would need to locate the physical analogies and find a way to give visual expression to the movement process in neurone stimulation. I simply record the notion that the activity of the first ψ-system is directed at *free evacuation of quantities of arousal*, and that the second system, through the charges issuing from it, leads to an *inhibition* of such evacuation, a transformation into a steady charge-content, probably at a higher level. So I assume that the course taken by the arousal is coupled with quite different mechanical circumstances under the control of the second system than under that of the first. If the second system has finished its experimental thought-work, it also terminates the inhibition and congestion of arousals and allows them to flow away to motility.

An interesting chain of reasoning emerges if we focus on how this inhibition on evacuation by the second system relates to regulation by means of the aversion principle. Let us look at the opposite of the primary satisfaction-experience, the *external fright-experience*. Say a perceptual stimulus acts on the primitive apparatus that gives rise to a sensation of pain. As a result, uncoordinated motor expressions will ensue until one of them withdraws the apparatus from the relevant perception and at the same time from the pain, and if the perception reappears that motor expression will immediately be repeated (as escape, for example) until the perception has disappeared again. But here there will be no residual proneness to recharge the perception of the pain-source through hallucination or in some other way. Rather, in the primary apparatus a proneness will persist to drop the painful memory-image again whenever something or other revives it, because the fact is, having its arousal overflow on to perception would give rise (more precisely, will start to give rise) to aversion. This turning away from memory, which is simply a repetition of the former flight from perception, is also facilitated by the fact that, unlike a perception, a memory does not possess sufficient quality to arouse consciousness and thus attract a fresh charge. This effortlessly and regularly occurring turning away of the psychical process from the memory of what was once painful gives us the pattern and first example of *psychical repression*. It is widely known how much of this turning away from the painful, this 'hiding-one's-head-in-the-sand', remains in evidence in the normal mental life of the adult.

Because of this aversion principle, the first ψ-system is therefore quite incapable of drawing something unpleasant into the context of thought. The system can do nothing but wish. If this continued to be the case, the ratiocination of the second system would be hampered, needing as it does to have at its disposal all the memories deposited in experience. There are now two possible ways forward: either the work of the second system frees itself completely from the aversion principle and pursues its course without bothering about memory-aversion; or it is able to charge the aversion memory in such a way as to avoid releasing the aversion. We can reject the first possibility because the aversion principle also shows itself to be the regulator for the course taken by arousal in the second system; that leaves us with the second, which is that this system charges a memory in such a way that evacuation from it is blocked – even the type of evacuation (comparable to a motor innervation) that develops aversion. So the hypothesis that charging by the second system at the same time constitutes an obstacle to the evacuation of arousal is one we are led to from two starting-points: from taking account of the aversion principle and from the principle of the smallest innervation outlay. But let us emphasize (and this is the key to the repression theory) *that the second system is only able to impart a charge to an idea when it is in a position to inhibit the aversion development flowing therefrom*. What (we maintain) eludes this inhibition, for instance, would also remain inaccessible to the second system and according to the aversion principle would immediately be abandoned. However, inhibition of aversion need not be complete; a beginning of the same has to be admitted, because it indicates to the second system the nature of the recollection and perhaps its unsuitability for the purpose that thought is looking for.

The psychical process that only the first system will admit I shall call the *primary process*; the one that emerges under the inhibition of the second I refer to as the *secondary process*. There is another point by which I am able to demonstrate why [to what end] the second system needs to correct the primary process. The primary process endeavours to discharge arousal in order to produce a *perceptual identity*[4] with the quantity of arousal thus accumulated; the secondary process has abandoned this intention and chosen the other instead – that of attaining a *thought identity*. All thinking is simply a roundabout way of getting from the satisfaction-memory adopted as purposive idea to the identical charging of the same memory, which is to be regained by way of motor experiences. Thinking must interest itself in the connecting paths between ideas without allowing the intensities of those ideas to lead it astray. It is clear, however, that compressions of ideas as well as intermediate and compromise formations represent obstacles to the attainment of that identity objective; by inserting one idea in place of the other, they distract from the path that would have led on from the former. So such processes are scrupulously avoided in secondary thinking. And it is not hard to see that the aversion principle, which otherwise supplies the thinking process with the most important clues, also places difficulties in the way of that process as regards pursuing identity of thought. So the tendency of thinking must be towards increasingly freeing itself from regulation by the aversion principle alone and reducing affect-development by thought-work to the minimum that can still be used as a signal. This refinement of performance is to be achieved by the addition of a fresh charge of attention as imparted by consciousness. We know, however, that even in normal mental life this is seldom completely successful; our thinking always remains open to falsification through the intervention of the aversion principle.

But this is not what constitutes the loophole in the functional efficiency of our mental apparatus, as a result of which it becomes possible for thoughts presenting themselves as products of secondary thought-work to fall victim to the primary psychical process, with which form of words we can now describe the work leading to dream and to the symptoms of hysteria. That inadequacy arises out of the coming together of two factors from our developmental history, one of which belongs entirely to the mental apparatus and has crucially influenced the relationship between the two systems, the other of which asserts itself in varying amounts and introduces driving forces of organic origin into mental life. Both stem from the childhood years and are an expression of the change that our mental and physical organism has undergone since infancy.

My labelling of one of these psychical processes in the mental apparatus as *primary* was dictated not only by their relative rank and effectiveness; I was probably also giving temporal circumstances a say in the choice of name. Granted, a psychical apparatus possessing only the primary process does not exist, so far as we are aware, and to that extent is a theoretical fiction; but this much is fact – namely, that the primary processes are there from the outset, whereas it is only gradually, over the years, that the secondary processes develop, inhibiting and overlaying the primary processes and possibly not gaining full control over them until a person reaches the prime of life. The result of this delayed advent of the secondary processes is that the core of our being, consisting of unconscious wish-stirrings, remains incomprehensible to and cannot be inhibited by the preconscious, the role of which is once and for all confined to directing wish-stirrings stemming from the unconscious down the most suitable route. For all subsequent mental efforts, these unconscious wishes constitute a compulsion with which they must comply – which they may endeavour to divert, say, and direct towards higher goals. Also, a large area of memory-material remains inaccessible to preconscious charging in consequence of this delay.

Now, among these wish-stirrings stemming from infancy and incapable of being destroyed or inhibited there are some whose fulfilments have entered into a contradictory relationship with regard to the purposive ideas of secondary thinking. Fulfilling such wishes would no longer evoke a pleasurable affect but one of aversion, *and it is precisely this change of affect that constitutes the essence of what we term 'repression'*. By what route and driven by what forces such a change is able to take place – that is the whole problem of repression (which we only need touch on here). All we need emphasize is that such an affect-transformation does occur in the course of development (one only has to think of the first appearance of disgust, of which the child originally knows nothing) and that it is linked to the activity of the secondary system. The memories out of which the unconscious wish brings forth the affect-release have never been accessible by the *prec*; that is why their affect-release cannot be inhibited. Precisely because of that affect-development, these ideas can now also not be accessed from the direction of the preconscious thinking to which they have transferred their optative power. The aversion principle comes into effect instead and causes the *prec* to turn away from these transference thoughts. These are left to their own devices, 'repressed', and as a result the presence of a childhood store of memories that are kept from the *prec* from the outset becomes a precondition of repression.

In the most favourable instance, the development of aversion comes to an end and the charge of energy is withdrawn from the transference thoughts in the *prec*, and this result characterizes the intervention of the aversion principle as effective. Things are different, however, when the repressed unconscious wish undergoes an organic reinforcement that it is able to lend to its transference thoughts, putting them in a position where they can attempt to break through with their arousal, even if they have been abandoned by the charge of energy formerly present in the *prec*. Two things then ensue: a defensive struggle in that the *prec* strengthens the opposition to the repressed thoughts (counter-charging) and subsequently a breakthrough by the transference thoughts, vehicle of the unconscious wish, in some form of compromise through symptom-formation. However, from the moment when the repressed thoughts receive a powerful charge from the unconscious wish-arousal but on the other hand lose one from the preconscious, they are subject to the primary psychical process, aiming purely at motor discharge or, if the way is free, at hallucinatory animation of the desired perceptual identity. Earlier, we found by empirical means that the incorrect processes described unfold only with thoughts that are in repression. We now comprehend a further piece of the context. In the psychical apparatus, these incorrect processes are the *primary* ones; they crop up wherever ideas, having lost their preconscious charge of energy, are left to their own devices and are able to fill themselves with the uninhibited energy, striving for evacuation, that flows from the unconscious. One or two other observations lend additional support to the view that these so-called 'incorrect' processes are not really falsifications of normal circumstances, i.e, thinking mistakes, but the working methods of the psychical apparatus when freed from an inhibition. We see, then, that the passage from preconscious arousal to motility occurs by the same processes and that associating preconscious ideas with words readily exhibits the same shifts and mix-ups that we attribute to inattention. Finally, evidence of the additional work that becomes necessary in connection with inhibiting these primary modes of occurrence may possibly arise from the fact that we achieve a *comic* effect, a surplus needing *laughter* to discharge it, *when we allow these modes of occurrence of thinking to penetrate as far as consciousness*.

The theory of psychoneuroses states with absolute certainty that it can only be sexual wish-stirrings from infancy that undergo repression (affect-transformation) in the developmental periods of childhood, that are then capable of being renewed in subsequent development periods (whether because of the sexual constitution, which of course emerges from the original bisexuality, whether in consequence of unfavourable influences of the sexual life), and that thus provide the driving forces behind all neurotic symptom-formation. Only by introducing these sexual forces can the loopholes still in evidence in the theory of repression be closed. I want to leave open the question of whether the claim of the sexual and infantile can also be asserted in respect of dream-theory; I leave this incomplete here, having already gone a step beyond what can be proved by assuming that all dream-wishes stem from the unconscious.[5] Nor do I intend to investigate further what constitutes the difference in the play of psychical forces in dream-formation and in the formation of hysterical symptoms; the fact is, we lack precise knowledge of one of the terms of such a comparison. But there is another point to which I do attach great value, and I acknowledge in advance that it is only because of this point that I have included here all the discussions about the two psychical systems, how they work, and the business of repression. The question now, do you see, is not whether I have understood the psychological connections we are talking about here in an approximately correct fashion or, as is quite possible with such difficult matters, got them wrong or picked up only some of them. However the interpretation of psychical censorship, the correct and abnormal editing of dream-content – however these things may change, it remains the case that such processes play a part in dream-formation and that in essence they exhibit the greatest similarity to processes already known about in connection with the formation of hysterical symptoms. Dream, though, is not a pathological phenomenon; it does not presuppose any disturbance of psychical equilibrium; it leaves behind it no enfeeblement of performance potential. The objection that my dreams and those of my neurotic patients bear no relation to the dreams of healthy people can surely be dismissed out of hand. So when we draw inferences from the phenomena as to the forces that drive them, we are recognizing that the psychical mechanism that neurosis exploits has not been created from scratch by a chronic disturbance affecting mental life but lies to hand in the normal make-up of the mental apparatus. The two psychical systems, the transitional censorship going on between them, the inhibition and overlaying of one activity by the other, how both relate to consciousness (or what a more accurate interpretation of actual circumstances may yield in their stead) – all these things belong to the normal make-up of our mental instrument, and dream shows us one of the ways leading to an understanding of that instrument's structure. If we are prepared to be content with a minimum of fully secured additional knowledge, we shall say that dream proves to us *that in normal people, too, what has been suppressed continues to exist and remains capable of psychical performance*. Dream is itself one of the expressions of that suppressed material. Theory tells us that all dreams are so; tangible experience tells us that they are so at least in a great many cases, which are the ones that demonstrate the outstanding features of dream-life with especial clarity. That which has been suppressed in the mind, which in waking life was prevented from coming out by *the contrary settlement of contradictions* [*die gegensätzliche Erledigung der Widersprüche*] and cut off from internal perception, finds at night, under the dominion of compromise formations, ways and means of forging a path to consciousness.

> *Flectere si nequeo superos, acheronta movebo.*
>
> [If I can't bend those above, I'll stir the lower regions.]

But interpreting dreams is the via regia, *the royal road to knowledge of the unconscious in the life of the mind.*

Tracing the way dreams are analysed gives us a certain amount of insight into the composition of this most marvellous and most mysterious of instruments – only a certain amount, admittedly, but a start has been made to making further progress in dissecting that instrument from the standpoint of other (we should term them 'pathological') formations. Because illness (at least what is rightly called 'functional illness') does not presuppose destruction of that apparatus, the production of fresh splits within it, it is to be explained *dynamically* in terms of a strengthening and weakening of the components of the play of forces by which so many effects are covered up during normal functioning. One might show elsewhere how the fact that the apparatus is composed of both agencies permits a refinement of even its normal functioning that would have been beyond the reach of one of them in isolation.[6]

Notes

1. [The words Freud uses here are respectively '*Kompression*' and '*Verdichtung*'. See Chapter 6, section A and in particular p. 318, note 1.]
2. [*Wertigkeit*.]
3. [T h i s is a German printing convention for indicating emphasis; Freud uses it a lot, but in this edition we have used *italics*.]
4. ['*Wahrnehmungsidentität*', although in at least one edition (G. B. Fischer, 1961) the word is *Wahrnehmungsintensität* – a simple editorial mistake, apparently.]
5. Here as elsewhere there are gaps in the treatment of the subject that I have left deliberately, since filling them would on the one hand take too long and on the other hand involve drawing support from material unconnected with dream. For instance, I have avoided saying whether I associate something different with the word 'suppressed' [*unterdrückt*] than with the word 'repressed' [*verdrängt*]. The only thing that should have become clear is that the latter lays more stress on the fact of its belonging to the unconscious than does the former. I have not gone into the obvious problem of why dream-thoughts suffer distortion through censorship even where they renounce progredient advance to consciousness and opt instead for the path of regression – and I have made other such omissions. My chief concerns were to give an impression of the problems to which further classification of dream-work leads and to touch on the other topics that this encounters along the way. I did not always find it easy to decide at which point to break off the pursuit.

My failing to deal exhaustively with the role of the sexual imagination as regards dream and my having avoided interpreting dreams with a clearly sexual content stem from a special motivation that may not chime with the reader's expectations. It is of course quite alien to my personal views and to the professional opinions that I hold in neuropathology to regard the sexual life as an object of shame with which neither the doctor nor the scientific researcher should be concerned. I also find absurd the moral indignation that moved the [German] translator of Artemidorus of Daldis in the 'Symbolism of Dreams' to deprive his readers of all knowledge of the chapter contained therein that deals with sexual dreams. My sole criterion was that in elucidating sexual dreams I should have to delve deeply into the as yet unexplained problems of perversion and bisexuality, so I decided to save this material for a different context.

6. Dream is not the only phenomenon that psychopathology makes it possible to justify in terms of psychology. In a small and as yet incomplete series of articles in *Monatsschrift für Psychiatrie und Neurologie* ('Über den psychischen Mechanismus der Vergesslichkeit' ['On the psychical mechanism of forgetfulness'], 1898, and 'Über Deckerinnerungen' ['On screen memories'], 1899) I tried to interpret a number of everyday psychical manifestations as supporting the same finding. These and other articles on forgetting, promising, making mistakes, etc. have since been collected together and published as *Psychopathologie des Alltagslebens* (1904) [a new English translation of *The Psychopathology of Everyday Life* by Anthea Bell appeared in the New Penguin Freud series in 2002].

F *The unconscious and consciousness –*
reality

On closer examination, it is the continued existence not of two systems near the motor end of the apparatus but of *two different processes* or *types of evacuation of arousal* that the psychological discussions of the preceding section suggested we posit. Never mind: we must always be prepared to drop back-up notions once we feel able to replace them with something else that comes closer to the reality we are looking for. Let us now attempt to correct certain views that could have led to misunderstandings so long as we were looking at the two systems in the crudest, most immediate way as two localities within the mental apparatus – views that have left their mark on the terms 'repressed' and 'break through'. To put it a different way, when we say that an unconscious thought strives for translation into the preconscious in order then to 'break through' into consciousness, we do not mean that a second thought needs to be formed in a different place, a sort of transcription, alongside which the original continues to exist; similarly, from the phrase 'breaking through to consciousness' we are keen to expunge any notion of a change of location. When we say that a preconscious thought is repressed and then taken up by the unconscious, such images, borrowed from the imaginative realm of the struggle over a piece of territory, might tempt us to assume that one arrangement in one psychical locality really is dissolved and replaced by a fresh arrangement in a different locality. For such similes, let us substitute something that seems to correspond better to what is actually going on, and say that a charge of psychical energy is laid upon a particular arrangement or withdrawn from it in such a way that the psychical entity comes under or is removed from the control of a particular agency. Again there is a replacement, but this time we are replacing a topical way of seeing things by a dynamic way; it is not the psychical entity that seems to us to be the moving part but its innervation.[1]

Nevertheless, I regard it as useful and justifiable to continue to cultivate the three-dimensional idea of the two systems. We shall avoid any abuse of this style of presentation if we bear in mind that ideas, thoughts and psychical constructs in general should never be localized in organic elements of the nervous system but rather *between them*, so to speak, where resistances and the carving of channels form the corresponding correlate. Everything capable of becoming an object of our inner perception is *virtual*, like the image resulting from the passage of light rays through a telescope. But the systems involved, which themselves have nothing psychical about them and never become accessible to our psychical perception, are things we are entitled to assume, as we are the lenses of the telescope that produce the image. Extending the analogy, the censorship that occurs between two systems would correspond to the refraction that accompanies passage into another medium.

Up to now we have been practising psychology on our own terms; it is time we took a look at the doctrines that dominate present-day psychology, examining how they relate to our propositions. The question of the unconscious in psychology is in the powerful words of Theodor Lipps[2] not so much a psychological question as the question of psychology. As long as psychology continued to deal with this question by means of the verbal explanation that the 'psychical' was in fact the 'conscious' and that to speak of 'unconscious psychical processes' was a tangible contradiction, any psychological evaluation of the observations of abnormal mental circumstances that a doctor was able to make was quite impossible. Only then do the physician and the philosopher meet when they both acknowledge unconscious psychical processes to be 'the appropriate, legitimate expression for an established fact'. The physician cannot but reject the statement, 'consciousness is of the essence of the psychical', with a shrug, possibly assuming, if his respect for the utterances of philosophers is still sufficiently great, that they are not talking about the same thing, not pursuing the same branch of knowledge. Because even a single sympathetic study of the mental life of a neurotic, just one analysis of a dream, must force upon him the unshakeable conviction that the most intricate, most correct thought-processes (to which no one would wish to deny the name of psychical processes) may occur without stirring a person's consciousness.[3] Granted, the physician receives no knowledge of such unconscious processes until they have exerted an effect upon consciousness such as can be communicated or observed. However, that consciousness effect may display a psychical character diverging widely from the unconscious process, with the result that inner perception cannot possibly recognize one as replacing the other. The physician must defend his right to forge a path, by means of a *process of deduction*, from the consciousness effect to the unconscious psychical process; somewhere along that path he will learn that the consciousness effect is only a remote psychical reflection of the unconscious process and that the latter has not become conscious as such – also that it has existed and taken effect without in any way betraying itself to consciousness.

This retreat from overrating the property of consciousness becomes the essential prerequisite for any true understanding of the way in which the psychical proceeds. As Lipps says, the unconscious has to be accepted as the foundation of all psychical life. The unconscious is the larger circle that includes the smaller circle of the conscious. Everything conscious has an unconscious preliminary stage, whereas the unconscious is able to remain at that stage and still lay claim to the full value of a psychical function. The unconscious is in fact the real psychical, *as unknown to us in terms of its inner nature as the reality of the outside world and as incompletely rendered to us by the data of consciousness as the outside world is rendered by the information supplied by our sense organs.*

If the old antithesis between conscious life and dream-life is undermined by inserting the unconscious psychical in its rightful place, this gets rid of a series of dream-problems that deeply preoccupied earlier writers. Many functions that, when performed in dream, occasioned great amazement are now no longer to be attributed to dreaming but to unconscious thought, which is also active by day. If a particular dream appears to play with a symbolizing portrayal of the body, as described by Scherner, we know that this is the work of certain unconscious fantasies that are probably responses to sexual stirrings and that come out not only in dreams but also in hysterical phobias and other symptoms. If a dream continues and completes daytime operations and even brings to light valuable ideas, we need only strip away the dream-disguise as being a product of dream-work and a mark of the assistance of dark powers in the depths of the mind (see the devil in Tartini's sonata dream).[4] Intellectual function itself [in dream] falls to the same mental forces as in the daytime accomplish all such functions. Very likely, too, we tend hugely to overrate the conscious nature of intellectual and artistic production. The fact is, we know from what we have been told by a number of highly productive people such as Goethe and Helmholz that the essence and originality of their creations came to them as sudden notions, entering their perception almost ready-made. There is nothing strange about conscious activity lending a hand in other instances, where all intellectual forces were being exerted. But it is the much-abused privilege of conscious activity that it is allowed to blind us to all other types of activity wherever it is involved.

It is scarcely worth the effort of erecting the historical importance of dreams into a separate subject. Where, for instance, a chieftain was persuaded by a dream to embark upon a bold enterprise that, in succeeding, changed the course of history, a fresh problem arises only in so far as dream as a phenomenon is set against other, more familiar mental forces as a kind of foreign power; the problem disappears if dream is seen as a *form of expression* for stirrings that, having met with resistance during the day, are able at night to draw reinforcement from deep-seated sources of arousal.[5] However, the respect that ancient peoples accorded to dream is an act of homage (based on correct psychological premonition) to what is untamed and indestructible in the human mind, the *demonic* element that furnishes the dream-wish and that we find again in our unconscious.

I say deliberately '*in our unconscious*' because what we call by that name is not the same as the philosophers' unconscious, nor is it the same as the unconscious in Lipps. There the word is meant simply to denote the opposite of the conscious; that as well as conscious processes there are also unconscious psychical processes is the hotly disputed, vigorously defended discovery. In Lipps we hear of the further proposition that everything psychical is present unconsciously, some of it also consciously. But it is not to prove *that* proposition that we bring in the phenomena of dream and of the formation of hysterical symptoms; observation of normal, everyday existence is all that is needed to put that well beyond doubt. The new thing that analysing psychopathological formations (and certainly the first part of such analysis, namely dreams) teaches us is that the unconscious (the psychical, that is to say) occurs as a function of two separate systems and does so even in normal mental life. So there are *two different unconsciouses*, which we do not yet find psychologists distinguishing. Both are unconscious in terms of psychology; in ours, however, one of them, which we call *unc*,[6] is also *incapable of consciousness*, whereas we call the other one *prec* because its arousals, admittedly also after certain rules have been adhered to, possibly only after surviving fresh censorship but in any case without regard to the *unc* system, are capable of reaching consciousness. The fact that the arousals, in order to reach consciousness, have to pass through an unalterable sequence, a chain of agencies that is revealed to us by their changing under censorship, helped us to posit an analogy drawn from the three-dimensional world. We described how the two systems relate to each other and to consciousness by saying that the *prec* system forms as it were a screen or protective partition between the *unc* system and consciousness. The *prec* system (we are saying) not only blocks access to consciousness; it also controls access to voluntary motility and is able to send out a mobile charge of energy, part of which is familiar to us as attention.[7]

We must also keep our distance from the *outer* and *inner consciousness* distinction that has become so popular in the recent literature dealing with psychoneuroses, since this in particular appears to stress that the psychical and the conscious are the same thing.

What role is left, in our account, for the once all-powerful consciousness, the faculty covering and concealing all others? Simply that of *a sense organ for perceiving psychical qualities*. According to the basic idea behind our schematic venture, the only way we can understand the perception of consciousness is as the special function of a separate system, for which the abbreviation c suggests itself. In terms of its mechanical characteristics, we think of that system as resembling the perceptive systems p – that is to say, as being excitable by qualities and incapable of retaining the trace of changes, i.e. having no memory. The psychical apparatus that is turned towards the outside world with the sense organ of the p systems is itself an outside world so far as the c sense organ is concerned, the teleological justification of which rests on that relationship. Here again, we come up against the principle of the chain of agencies that seems to control the structure of the apparatus. Arousal material flows towards the c sense organ from two directions – from the p system, arousal of which (prompted by qualities) probably undergoes fresh processing before becoming conscious sensation, and from the interior of the apparatus itself, the quantitative processes of which are experienced as a series of qualities of pleasure and aversion when they have arrived at certain changes.

Those philosophers who became aware that correct and highly composed thought-formations are possible even without consciousness making any contribution were then faced with the problem of finding something [anything] for consciousness to do; it seemed to them to be a superfluous reflection of the finished psychical process. Drawing an analogy between our c system and the systems of perception whisks this embarrassment away from us. We see that the consequence of perception by our organs of sense is to prompt a charging of attention towards the paths along which the incoming sensory arousal spreads; qualitative arousal of the p system serves the mobile quantity in the psychical apparatus as a regulator of the way it runs its course. We can lay claim to the same function for the overlapping sense organ of the c system. In perceiving fresh qualities, that organ makes a fresh contribution towards steering and suitably distributing mobile quantities of energizing charge. Through perceiving pleasure and aversion, it influences the course of the energizing charges within the otherwise unconscious psychical apparatus, operating as this does through quantitative shifts. Probably, the aversion principle regulates the shifts of charge automatically at first: but it may very well be that consciousness of these qualities adds a second, more delicate regulation that can even oppose the first and that perfects the efficiency of the apparatus by enabling it, in contrast to its original predisposition, to charge with energy and subject to processing even things associated with the release of aversion. The psychology of neuroses teaches us that such regulation as a result of quality arousal of the sense organs is destined to play a major role in the functional activity of the apparatus. The automatic dominance of the primary aversion principle and the associated reduction of efficiency are broken by these delicate regulatory operations – which are themselves, in turn, automatisms. We learn that repression (which, from having originally served some purpose, turns into a damaging abandonment of inhibition and mental control) takes effect so much more readily on memories than on perceptions because in the case of the former the increase in energetic charging resulting from arousal of the psychical sense organs is inevitably absent. If a thought that must be repulsed on the one hand does not become conscious because it suffers repression, on other occasions it may be repressed simply because there are other reasons why it is withheld from the perception of consciousness. These are signs that therapy uses to undo repressions once they have been effected.

The value of the supplementary charge of energy resulting from the regulating influence of the c sense organ on mobile quantity is in teleological terms demonstrated by nothing so well as by the creation of a fresh series of qualities and hence of a fresh regulation that gives mankind its prerogative over the animals. The fact is, thought-processes are in essence quality-free, save for the pleasure and aversion arousals that accompany them and that indeed ought, as potential disturbers of thought, to be kept within bounds. To lend them a quality, in the individual they are associated with the verbal memories whose qualitative residues suffice to attract the attention of consciousness to themselves and from consciousness bestow upon thought a fresh mobile charge.

The only way to glimpse the full diversity of the problems of consciousness is by dividing up the spectrum of hysterical thought-processes. This gives one the impression that the transition from preconscious to consciousness energy-charging is associated with a kind of censorship not unlike that between *unc* and *prec*. This censorship, too, starts only at a certain quantitative level; less intensive thought-formations escape it. All potential cases of withholding from consciousness and of getting through to the same with limitations are brought together within the framework of psychoneurotic phenomena; they all point towards the deep, reciprocal link between censorship and consciousness. Let me conclude these psychological discussions by reporting two such occurrences.

One of last year's consultations introduced me to a bright, apparently uninhibited young girl. The way she presents herself is somewhat disconcerting; where a woman's get-up is usually full of life down to the last fold, she will have one stocking hanging down and two buttons of her blouse undone. Complaining of pains in a leg, she spontaneously exposes a calf. Her chief complaint, however, I give in her own words: she has a sensation in her body as if something *were poking into it*, something that *moves to and fro* and makes her *tremble* right through. Sometimes while this is happening her body goes almost *rigid*. At this point my colleague (also present) gives me a look; to him the complaint is quite clear. Both of us find it curious that the patient's mother has no thoughts in connection with what is going on; she must, after all, repeatedly have found herself in the situation her child is describing. The girl herself has no idea of the significance of her words, otherwise they would never have passed her lips. Here we have an instance of censorship being so successfully blotted out that a fantasy that usually remains in the preconscious is as if innocently admitted to consciousness in the guise of a medical complaint.

Another example: I begin a course of psychoanalysis with a four-teen-year-old boy suffering from a convulsive tic, hysterical vomit-ing, headaches and the like by assuring him that after closing his eyes he will see images or think of ideas that he should tell me about. He replies in images. The last impression received before coming to me revives in his memory visually. He had been playing a board game with his uncle and now sees the board in front of him. He talks about various positions that are either favourable or un-favourable, moves that are not permitted. Then he sees a dagger lying on the board, an object that his father owns but that his imagination places on the board. Then there is a sickle lying on the board, then a scythe is added, and now the image of an old peasant appears, using the scythe to mow the grass in front of the remote house in which he grew up. In a few days I came to understand this succession of images. Unpleasant family circumstances had upset the lad. A harsh father with a violent temper who lived in a state of conflict with his mother, using threats as an aid to upbringing; the father's divorcing his delicate, tender mother; his father's remarriage, when one day he brought home a young woman as the new mummy. It was in the days immediately following that the fourteen-year-old boy's illness had broken out. What had assembled those images into com-prehensible allusions was suppressed rage against his father. A reminiscence from mythology had provided the material. The sickle is the one that Zeus used to castrate his own father; the scythe and the image of the peasant reflect Chronos, the brutal old man who eats his children and on whom Zeus wreaks such unchildlike ven-geance. The father's marriage was an opportunity to return the reproaches and threats that the child had once heard from him on account of the child's having *played* (the board game) with its genitals; the forbidden moves; the dagger, which can be used to kill. These are long-repressed memories and their derivatives (which remain unconscious); via byways made available to them they sneak into consciousness as *ostensibly meaningless* images.

So I am inclined to look for the theoretical value of a study of dream in the contributions it can make to psychological knowledge and in the way it leads on to an understanding of psychoneuroses.

Who can even suspect what importance a thorough acquaintance with the structure and performance of the mental apparatus may yet attain, when the present state of our knowledge already allows us to exert a beneficial therapeutic influence on the basically curable forms of psychoneuroses? And what of the practical value of such a study, I hear you ask, as regards understanding how the mind works and uncovering the hidden characteristics of the individual? Don't the unconscious stirrings that dream reveals have the value of actual powers in the life of mind? Is the ethical importance of suppressed desires to be deemed so slight when, just as they create dreams, they may one day create something else?

These are questions I do not feel entitled to answer. My thinking has not pursued this aspect of the dream-problem. I simply feel that the Roman emperor was quite wrong who had a subject hanged for having dreamed that he had assassinated the *imperator*. The emperor's first concern should have been to find out what the dream meant; very probably this was not the same as what the dream displayed. And even if a dream that ran otherwise did have that subversive, crown-toppling significance, there would be grounds none the less for remembering Plato's dictum: the virtuous man is content to dream of what the wicked man actually does. I also believe that dreams are best given their head. Whether unconscious wishes in fact have *reality*, I cannot say. They must of course be denied any transitional, intermediate thoughts. With unconscious wishes, reduced to their last and truest expression, before one, one must no doubt say that *psychical reality* is a separate form of existence, not to be confused with *material* reality. There then seems no justification for people refusing to accept responsibility for the immorality of their dreams. By appreciating how the mental apparatus functions and understanding the relationship between the conscious and the unconscious, we can usually make the ethically offensive side of our dream and fantasy life disappear.

'What dream tells us about relations to the present (reality), let us then also seek in consciousness, and let us not be surprised if the monster that we saw under the magnifying glass of analysis turns out to be a tiny infusorium' (H[anns] Sachs).

For the practical necessity of judging a person's character, action and a basic attitude finding conscious expression are generally enough. Action above all merits a place in the front rank because many impulses that have made their way through to consciousness are annulled by actual powers of mental life before they can culminate in action; in fact, often the reason why they meet with no psychical obstacle in their path is that the unconscious is confident they will be blocked in some other way. Certainly, it is still instructive to explore the much-turned soil from which our virtues proudly sprout. The complexity of a human character, in constant movement in all directions, very rarely allows of resolution in terms of a simple alternative, as our superannuated moral theory would like to see happen.

And the value of dream as regards knowing the future? That, of course, is quite out of the question. Better to say: as regards knowing the past. For it is from the past that dream springs – in every sense. Granted, even the age-old belief that dreams show us the future is not wholly without truth-content. By showing us a wish as having been fulfilled, dream does in fact lead us into the future; however, the future that the dreamer takes as present is moulded by the indestructible wish into a mirror of that past.

Notes

1. This view underwent some development and change in consequence of the recognition that the essential nature of a preconscious idea lies in its being associated with residual verbal ideas ('Das Unbewusste', 1915 ['The Unconscious'; *Standard Edition*, vol. XIV, p. 161; *The Unconscious*, translated by Graham Frankland, London 2005]).

2. Theodor Lipps, 'Der Begriff des Unbewussten in der Psychologie' ['The concept of the unconscious in psychology'], lecture to the Third International Congress for Psychology in Munich, 1897.

3. I am delighted to be able to cite an author whose study of dreams has led him to the same conclusion regarding the relationship between conscious and unconscious activity.

Carl Du Prel [1885] says: 'The question of what mind is obviously calls for a prior investigation into whether consciousness and mind are identical. Precisely this prior question is in fact denied by dream, which shows that the concept of mind exceeds that of consciousness, rather as the attraction exercised by a star extends further than its light' (*Die Philosophie der Mystik* ['The philosophy of mysticism'], p. 47).

'It is a truth that cannot be over-emphasized that consciousness and mind are not concepts having the same reach' (ibid., p. 306).

4. [The reference is to Italian violinist/composer Giuseppe Tartini (1692–1770), whose sonata *The Devil's Trill* was inspired by a dream.]

5. See in this connection the Σά Τύρος dream recounted above (p. 134, note 5) that Alexander the Great had at the siege of Tyre.

6. [A reminder: *unc* = unconscious; *prec* = preconscious; *c* = consciousness; *p* = perception.]

7. See also, in this connection, my 'Bemerkungen über den Begriff des Unbewussten in der Psychoanalyse' ['A Note on the Unconscious in Psychoanalysis'], in *Proceedings of the Society for Psychical Research*, vol. XXVI [published in English in 1912], in which the descriptive, dynamic and systematic meanings of the highly ambiguous term 'unconscious' are distinguished from one another.

Other Literature

[This bibliography accompanies the latest German edition of Die Traum-deutung *(with the exception of one entry – Volkelt, 1875 – to which Freud refers repeatedly but which was omitted from the original version), so it presumably represents the literature as it was known to Freud. As such it is of mainly historical interest, of course; many up-to-date bibliographies of works associated with this book are available today. Where an author and (for the reader's convenience) date are cited in the text of the present edition, they refer to this bibliography; where a date is not given in the text, it is because the bibliography contains a number of publications by the author concerned and there is nothing to indicate which one is being referred to.]*

A Up until publication of the first edition (1900)

Achmetis, F. Serim, *Oneirocriticae*, Nik. Rigaltius, Paris, 1603

Alberti, Michael, *Diss. de insomniorum influxi in sanitatem et morbos*, Resp. Titius Halae M., 1744

Alix, 'Les rêves', *Rev. Scientif.*, third series, vol. VI (no. 32 in the collection), third year, second sem., Nov. 1883, pp. 554–61

— 'Étude du rêve', *Mém. de l'acad. de sc. etc. de Toulouse*, Toulouse, 1889, ninth series, vol. 1, pp. 283–326

Almoli, Salomo, *Pithrôn Chalômôth*, Solkiev, 1848

Apomasaris . . . auss griecher Sprache ins Latein bracht durch Lewenklaw jetzt und . . . verteutschet (dream-book), Wittemberg

Aristotle, *On dreams*, translated [into German] by Bender
— *On prophesying by dreams*

Artemidorus of Daldis, *Symbolism of dreams*, translated [into German] by Friedr. S. Krauß, Vienna, 1881

— 'Erotic dreams and their symbolism', translated [into German] by Dr Hans Licht, *Anthropophyteia*, vol. IX, pp. 316–28

Artigues, 'Essai sur la valeur séméiologique du rêve', thesis, Paris, 1884

Bacci, Domenico, *Sui sogni e sul sonnombulismo, pensieri fisiologico-metafisici*, Venice, 1857

Ball, *La morphinomanie, les rêves prolongés*, Paris, 1885

Benezé, Émil, *Das Traummotiv in der mittelhochdeutschen Dichtung bis 1250 und in alten deutschen Volksliedern*, Halle, 1897 (Benezé, 'Sagengesch. und lit.-hist. Unters.', '1. Das Traummotiv')

Benini, V., 'La memoria e la durata dei sogni', *Rivista italiana di filosofia*, March–April 1898

— 'Nel moneto dei sogni', *Il Pensiero nuovo*, April 1898

Binz, C., *Über den Traum*, Bonn, 1878

Birkmaier, Hieron, *Licht im Finsterniß der nächtlichen Gesichte und Träume*, Nuremberg, 1715

Bisland, E., 'Dreams and their mysteries', *N. Am. Rev.*, 1896, 152, pp. 716–26

Börner, J., *Das Alpdrücken, seine Begründung und Verhütung*, Würzburg, 1855

Bradley, J. H., 'On the failure of movement in dream', *Mind*, July 1894

Brander, R., *Der Schlaf und das Traumleben*, Leipzig, 1884

Bouché-Leclercq, *Histoire de la divination dans l'antiquité* (vol. 1), Paris, 1879

Bremer, L., 'Traum und Krankheit', *New York med. Monatschr.*, 1893, V, 281–6

Büchsenschütz, B., *Traum und Traumdeutung im Altertum*, Berlin, 1868

Burdach, *Die Physiologie als Erfahrungswissenschaft*, vol. 3, 1830

Bussola, Serafino, 'De somniis' (diss.), Ticini Reg, 1834

Caetani-Lovatelli, 'I sogni e l'ipnotismo nel mondo antico', *Nuova Antol.*, 1 December 1889

Calkins, Mary Whiton, 'Statistics of dreams', *Amer. J. of Psychology*, V, 1893

Cane, Francis E., 'The physiology of dreams', *The Lancet*, December 1889

Cardanus, Hieron, *Synesiorum somniorum, omnis generis insomnia explicantes libri IV*, Basileae, 1562 (second edition in *Opera omnia Cardani*, vol. V, pp. 593–727, Lugduni, 1603)

Cariero, Alessandro, *De somniis deque divinatione per somnia*, Patavii, 1575

Carpenter, 'Dreaming', in *Cyclop. of anat. and phys.*, IV, p. 687

Chabaneix, [*Physiologie cérébrale:*] *le subconscient chez les artistes, les savants, et les écrivains*, Paris, 1897

Chaslin, Ph., 'Du rôle du rêve dans l'évolution du délire', thesis, Paris, 1887

Clavière, 'La rapidité de la pensée dans le rêve', *Revue philosophique* XLIII, 1897

Coutts, G. A., 'Night-terrors', *Americ. J. of Med. Sc.*, 1896

D. L., 'À propos de l'appréciation du temps dans le rêve', *Rev. philos.*, vol. 40, 1895, pp. 69–72

Dagonet, 'Du rêve et du délire alcoolique', *Ann. méd-psychol.*, 1889, série 7, t. X, p. 193

Dandolo, G., *La coscienza nel sonno*, Padua, 1889

Davidson, Wolf, *Versuch über den Schlaf*, second edition, Berlin, 1799

Debacker, '[Des hallucinations et] terreurs nocturnes chez les enfants', thesis, Paris, 1881

Dechambre, 'Cauchemar', *Dict. encycl. de sc. méd.*, [1880]

Delage, Yves, 'Une théorie du rêve', *Revue scientifique*, 11 July 1891

Delboeuf, J., *Le sommeil et les rêves*, Paris, 1885

Dietrich, Joh. Dav., 'An ea, quae hominibus in somno et somnio accidunt, iisdem possint imputari?', *resp. Gava Vitembergae*, 1726

Dochmasa, A. M., *Dreams and their significance as forebodings of disease*, Kazan, 1890

Dreher, E., 'Sinneswahrnehmung und Traumbild', *Reichs-med. Anzeiger*, Leipzig, 1890, XV

Ducosté, M., *Les songes d'attaques épileptiques*, 1889

Dugas, 'Le souvenir du rêve', *Revue philosophique*, XLIV, 1897

— 'Le sommeil et la cérébration inconsciente durant le sommeil', *Revue philosophique*, XLIII, 1897

Du Prel, Carl, 'Oneirokritikon; der Traum vom Standpunkte des transcend. Idealismus', *Deutsche Vierteljahrschrift*, issue II, Stuttgart, 1869

— *Psychologie der Lyrik*, Leipzig, 1880

— *Die Philosophie der Mystik*, Leipzig, 1885

— 'Künstliche Träume', *Monatsschrift 'Sphinx'*, July 1889

Egger, V., 'Le sommeil et la certitude, le sommeil et la mémoire', *La Critique philos.*, May 1888, I, pp. 341–50

— 'La durée apparente des rêves', *Revue philosophique*, July 1895

— 'Le souvenir dans le rêve', *Revue philosophique*, XLVI, 1898

Ellis, Havelock, 'On dreaming of the dead', *Psychological Review*, II, no. 5, September 1895

— 'The stuff that dreams are made of', *Appleton's Popular Science Monthly*, April 1899

— 'A note on hypnagogic paramnesia', *Mind*, April 1897

Erdmann, J. E., *Psychologische Briefe*, sixth edition, Leipzig, 1848

— *Ernste Spiele (XII: Das Träumen)*, lectures, third edition, Berlin, 1875

Erk, Vinz von, *Über den Unterschied von Traum und Wachen*, Prague, 1874

Escande de Messières, 'Les rêves chez les hystériques', *Th. méd.*, Bordeaux, 1895

Faure, 'Étude sur les rêves morbides. Rêves persistants', *Arch. génér. de méd.*, 1876, vol. 1, p. 550

Fechner, G. Th., *Elemente der Psychophysik*, second edition [Leipzig], 1889 [first edition, Leipzig, 1860]

Fenizia, 'L'azione suggestiva delle cause esterne nei sogni', *Arch. per l'Anthrop.*, XXVI

Féré, Ch., 'A contribution to the pathology of dreams and of hysterical paralysis', *Brain*, January 1887

— 'Les rêves d'accès chez les épileptiques', *La méd. mod.*, 8 December 1897

Fichte, I. H., *Psychologie. Die Lehre vom bewußten Geiste des Menschen*, Part I, Leipzig, 1864

Fischer, Joh., 'Ad artis veterum onirocriticae historiam symbola', dissertation, Jena, 1899

Florentin, V., 'Das Traumleben. Plauderei', *Die alte und die neue Welt*, 1899, thirty-third year, p. 725

Fornaschon, H., 'Geschichte eines Traums als Beitrag der Transcendentalpsychologie', *Psychische Studien*, 1897, pp. 274–81

Freiligrath, dream-book (in the Buchner biography)

Frensberg, 'Schlaf und Traum', *Samml. gemeinverst. wiss. Vortr. Virchow-Holtzendorf*, series XX, issue 466, Berlin, 1885

Frerichs, Joh. H., *Der Mensch: Traum, Herz, Verstand*, second edition, Norden, 1878

Galen, *On prophesy in dream*

Gießler, C. M., *Beiträge zur Phänomenologie des Traumlebens*, Halle, 1888

— *Aus den Teifen des Traumlebens*, Halle, 1890

— *Die physiologischen Beziehungen der Traumvorgänge*, Halle, 1896

Girgensohn, L., *Der Traum, psychol.-physiol. Versuch*, S. A., 1845

Gleichen-Rußwurm, A. von, 'Traum in der Dichtung', *Nat.-Ztg.*, 1899, nos. 553–9

Gley, E., 'Appréciation du temps pendant la sommeil', *L'Intermédiaire des Biologistes*, 20 March 1898, no. 10, p. 228

Goblot, 'Sur le souvenir des rêves', *Revue philosophique*, XLII, 1896

Gomperz, Th., 'Traumdeutung und Zauberei', lecture, Vienna, 1866

Gorton, D. A., 'Psychology of the unconscious', *Amer. Med. Times*, 1896, XXIV, 33, 37

Gould, *Dreams, Sleep, and Consciousness*, Open Court, 1899

Grabener, Gottl. Chr., 'Ex antiquitate iudaica de menûdim bachalôm sive excommunicatis per insomnia exerc.', *resp. Klebius*, Vitembergae, 1710

Graffunder, *Traum und Traumdeutung*, 1894

Greenwood, *Imagination in dreams and their study*, London, 1894

Griesinger, *Pathologie und Therapie der psychischen Krankheiten*, third edition, 1871

Grot, Nicolaus, 'Dreams, an object of scientific analysis' (Russian), Kiev, 1878

Guardia, J. M., 'La personnalité dans les rêves', *Rev. philos.*, Paris, 1892, XXXIV, 225–58

Gutfeldt, J., 'Ein Traum', *Psych. Studien*, 1899, pp. 491–4

Haffner, P., 'Schlafen und Träumen', 1887, *Frankfurter zeitgemäße Broschüren*, vol. 5, issue 10

Hallam, Fl., and Sarah Weed, 'A study of dream consciousness', *Amer. J. of Psychology*, VII, no. 3, April 1896, pp. 405–11.

Hampe, Th., 'Über Hans Sachsens Traumgedichte', *Zeitschrift für den deutschen Unterricht*, tenth year, 1896, pp. 616f.

Heerwagen, 'Statist. Untersuch. über Träume u. Schlaf', *Philos. Stud.*, V, 1889, p. 301

Hennings, Justus Chr., *Von [den] Träumen und Nachtwandlern*, Weimar, 1784

Henzen, Wilh., 'Über die Träumen in der altnord. Sagaliteratur', dissertation, Leipzig, 1890

d'Hervey, *Les rêves et les moyens de les diriger*, Paris, 1867 (anon.)

Hildebrandt, F. W., *Der Traum und seiner Verwertung für's Leben*, Leipzig, 1875

Hiller, G., 'Traum. Ein Kapitel zu den zwölf Nächten', *Leipz. Tagbl. und Anz.*, 1899, no. 657, first Beil

Hippocrates, book about dreams (*Collected Works* translated [into German] by Dr Robert Fuchs, Munich, 1895–1900, vol. I, pp. 361–9

Hitschmann, F., 'Über das Traumleben der Blinden', *Zeitschr. f. Psychol.*, VII, 5–6, 1894

Ideler, '[Über] die Entstehung des Wahnsinns aus den Träumen', *Charité Annalen*, 1853, vol. III

Jastrow, 'The dreams of the blind', *New Princetown Rev.*, New York, January 1888

Jean, Paul, 'Blicke in die Traumwelt', *Museum* (1813) II (*Works* [ed. Hempel], 44, pp. 128–52)

— 'Über Wahl- und Halbträume', ibid., pp. 142f.

— 'Wahrheit aus seinem Leben', 2, pp. 106–26

Jensen, Julius, *Träumen und Denken*, Berlin, 1871 (Samml. gemeinverst. wiss. Vortr. Virchow-Holtzendorf, series VI, issue 134)

Jessen, *Versuch einer wissenschaftlichen Begründung der Psychologie*, Berlin, 1855

Jodl, *Lehrbuch der Psychologie*, Stuttgart, 1896 (third edition 1908)

Kant, I., *Anthropologie in pragmatische Hinsicht* (Kirchmann edition), Leipzig, 1880

Kingsford, A. B., *Dreams and dream-stories* (ed. Maitland), second edition, London, 1888

Kloepfel, F., 'Träumerei und Traum. Allerlei aus unserem Traumleben', *Universum*, 1899, fifteenth year, columns 2469–84, 2607–22

Kramar, Oldrich, *O spànku a snu.*, Prager Akad. Gymn., 1882

Krasnicki, E. von, 'Karls IV. Wahntraum', *Psych. Studien*, 1897, p. 697

Krauß, A., 'Der Sinn im Wahnsinn', *Allgemeine Zeitschrift für Psychiatrie*, XV and XVI, 1858–59

Kucera, Ed., 'Aus dem Traumleben', *Mähr.-Weißkirchen Gymn.*, 1895

Ladd, 'Contribution to the psychology of visual dreams', *Mind*, April 1892

Laistner, Ludw., *Das Rätsel der Sphinx*, 2 vols, Berlin, 1889

Landau, M., 'Aus dem Traumleben', *Münchner Neueste Nachrichten*, 9 January 1892

Lasègue, 'Le délire alcoolique n'est pas un délire, mais un rêve', *Arch. gén. de méd.*, 1881 (reprinted in *Études méd.*, vol. II, pp. 203–27, Paris, seventh series, vol. VI, pp. 513–36, 1884)

Laupts, 'Le fonctionnement cérébral pendant le rêve et pendant le sommeil hypnotique', *Annales méd.-psychol.*, 1895

Leidesdorf, M., *Das Traumleben*, Vienna, 1880 ('Alma Mater' Collection)

Le Lorrain, 'La durée du temps dans les rêves', *Rev. philos.*, vol. 38, 1894, pp. 275–9

— 'Le rêve', *Revue philosophique*, July 1895.

Lélut, 'Mémoire sur le sommeil, les songes et le somnambulisme', *Ann. méd.-psych.*, 1852, vol. IV

Lemoine, *Du sommeil au point de vue physiologique et psychologique*, Paris, 1855

Lerche, Math. Fr., 'Das Traumleben und seiner Bedeutung', *Gymn. Progr.*, Komotau, 1883–4

Liberali, Francesco, 'Dei sogni', dissertation, Padua, 1834

Liébeault, A., *Le sommeil provoqué et les états analogues*, Paris, 1889

— 'À travers les états passifs, le sommeil et les rêves', *Rev. de l'hypnoth. etc.*, Paris, 1893, 4, VIII, 41, 65, 106

Lipps, Th., *Grundtatsachen des Seelenlebens*, Bonn, 1883

Luksch, L., *Wunderbare Traumerfüllung als Inhalt des wirklichen Lebens*, Leipzig, 1894

Macario, 'Du sommeil, des rêves et du somnambulisme dans l'état de santé et dans l'état de maladie', 1857

— 'Des rêves considérés sous le rapport physiologique et pathologique', *Ann. méd.-psychol.*, 1846, vol. VIII

— 'Des rêves morbides', *Gaz. méd. de Paris*, 1889, no. 8

MacFarlane, A. W., 'Dreaming', *Edinb. Med. J.*, 1890, t. 36

Maine de Biran, *Nouvelles considérations sur le sommeil, les songes, et le somnambulisme*, Éditions Cousin, 1792

Manaceine, Marie de, *Le sommeil, tiers de notre vie*, Paris, 1896

— *Sleep; its physiology, pathology and psychology*, London, 1897

Maudsley, *The pathology of mind*, 1879

Maury, A., 'Analogies des phénomènes du rêve et de l'aliénation mentale', *Annales méd.-psych.*, 1853, V, VI

— 'De certains faits observés dans les rêves', *Ann. méd-psychol.*, 1857, vol. III.

— *Le sommeil et les rêves*, Paris, 1878

Meisel (pseud.), *Natürlich-göttliche und teuflische Träume*, Sieghartstein, 1783

Melinaud, 'Dream and reality', *Pop. Sc. Mo.*, vol. LIV [1898], pp. 96–103

Melzentin, C., 'Über wissenschaftliche Traumdeutung', *Die Gegenwart*, 1899, no. 50

Mentz, Rich., *Die Träume in den altfranzösischen Karls- und Artus-Epen*, Marburg, 1888

Monroe, W. S., 'A study of taste-dreams', *Am. J. of Psychol.*, January 1899

Moreau de la Sarthe, 'Rêve' article in *Dict. des sc. méd.*, vol. 48, Paris, 1820

Moreau, J., 'De l'identité de l'état de rêve et de folie', *Annales méd.-psych.*, 1855, p. 261

Morselli, A., 'Dei sogni nei genii', *La Cultura*, 1899

Motet, 'Cauchemar', *Dict. de méd. et de chir. pratiques*

Murray, J. C., 'Do we ever dream of tasting?', *Proc. of the Americ. Psychol.* [Ass.], 1894, 20

Nagele, Anton, 'Der Traum in der epischen Dichtung', Marburg secondary modern school [*Realschule*] programme, 1889

Nelson, J., 'A study of dreams', *Amer. J. of Psychology*, I, 1888

Newbold, W. R., 'Subconscious reasoning', *Proc. Soc. Ps. Res.*, 1896, XII, 11–20

— 'Über Traumleistungen', *Psychol. Rev.*, March 1896, p. 132

Passavanti, Jac., *Libro dei sogni*, published by Bibl. diamante, Rome, 1891

Paulhan, *L'activité mentale et les éléments de l'esprit*, Paris, 1889

— 'À propos de l'activité de l'esprit dans le rêve', *Rev. philos.*, vol. 38, 1894, pp. 546–8

Pfaff, E. R., *Das Traumleben und seine Deutung nach den Principien der Araber, Perser, Griechen, Indier und Ägypter*, Leipzig, 1868

Pichon, *Contribution à l'étude des délires oniriques ou délires de rêve*, thesis, Bordeaux, 1896

Pick, A., 'Über pathologische Träumerei und ihre Beziehungen zur Hysterie', *Jahrbuch für Psychiatrie*, 1896

Pilcz, 'Über eine gewisse Gesetzmässigkeit in den Träumen', self-review in *Monatsschrift für Psychologie und Neurologie*, March 1899

Prévost, 'Quelques observations psychologiques sur le sommeil', *Bibl. univ. des sc., belles lettres et arts*, 1834, vol. I, 'Littérature', pp. 225–48

Purkinje, 'Wachen, Schlaf, Traum und verwandte Zustände', article in *Wagners Handwörterbuch der Psychologie*, 1846

Radestock, P., *Schlaf und Traum*, Leipzig, 1879

Ramm, Konrad, *Diss. pertractans somnia*, Vienna, 1889

Régis, 'Les rêves Bordeaux', *La Gironde (Variétés)*, 31 May 1890

— 'Les hallucinations oniriques [ou du sommeil] des dégénérés mystiques', *C. R. du Congrès des méd. aliénistes etc.*, fifth session, 1894, Paris, 1895, p. 260

'Rêves et l'hypnotisme', *Le Monde*, 25 August 1890

Richard, Jérome, *La théorie des songes*, Paris, 1766

Richardson, B. W., 'The physiology of dreams', *The Asclep.*, London, 1892, IX, 129, 160

Richier, 'Onéirologie ou dissertation sur les songes considérés dans l'état de maladie', thesis, Paris, 1816

Robert, W., *Der Traum als Naturnotwendigkeit erklärt*, Hamburg, 1886

Robinson, L., 'What dreams are made of', *N. Americ. Rev.*, New York, 1893, CLVII, 687–97

Rousset, 'Contribution à l'étude du cauchemar', thesis, Paris, 1876

Roux, J., 'Les rêves et les délires oniriques', *Province méd.*, 1898, p. 212

Ryff, Walther Herm., *Traumbüchlein*, Straßburg, 1554

Sante de Sanctis, *Emozione e sogni*, 1896

— 'I sogni nei delinquenti', *Arch. di psichiatr. e antrop. criminale*, Turin, 1896, XVII, 488–98

— *I sogni e il sonno nell'isterismo e nella epilessia*, Rome, 1896

— 'Les maladies mentales et les rêves', 1897 [taken from *Annales de la société de medicine de Gand* [Ghent].

— 'Sui rapporti d'identità, di somiglianza, di analogia e di equivalenza fra sogno e pazzia', *Rivista quindicinale di Psicologia, Psichiatria, Neuropatologia*, 15 November 1897

— 'I sogni dei neuropatici e dei pazzi', *Arch. di psichiatr. e antrop. crim.*, 1898, issue 4 (with further references)

— 'Psychoses et rêves', *Rapport au Congrès de neurol. et d'hypnologie de Bruxelles*, 1898, Comtes rendus, issue 1, p. 137

— *I sogni*, Turin, 1899 (translated [into German] by O. Schmidt, Halle, 1901)

Santel, Anton, *Poskus raz kladbe nekterih pomentjivih prikazni spanja in sanj*, grammar school [*Gymnasium*] programme, Görz [Gorizia], 1874

Sarlo, F. de, 'I sogni', *Saggio psicologico*, Naples, 1887

Sch., Fr., 'Etwas über Träume', *Psych. Studien*, 1897, 686–94

Scherner, K. A., *Das Leben des Traumes*, Berlin, 1861

Schleich, K. L., 'Schlaf und Traum', *Die Zukunft*, 1899, vol. 29, 14–27, 54–65

Schleiermacher, Fr., *Psychologie*, published by L. George, Berlin, 1862

Scholz, Fr., *Schlaf und Traum*, Leipzig, 1887

Schopenhauer, 'Versuch über das Geistersehen und was damit zusammenhängt', *Parerga und Paralipomena*, vol. I, 1851

Schubert, Gotthilf Heinrich [von], *Die Symbolik des Traumes*, Bamberg, 1814

Schwartzkopff, P., *Das Leben im Traum. Eine Studie*, Leipzig, 1887

'Science of dreams', *The Lyceum*, Dublin, October 1890, p. 28

Siebeck, H., *Das Traumleben der Seele*, 1877 (Virchow-Holtzendorf Collection, no. 279)

Simon, [P.] M., *Le monde des rêves*, Paris, 1888 (Bibliothèque scientifique contemporaine)

Spitta, H., *Die Schlaf- und Traumzustände der menschlichen Seele*, second edition, Freiburg im Breisgau, 1892 [Tübingen, 1882]

Stevenson, R. L., 'A chapter on dreams', in *Across the plain*, 1892

Stricker, *Studien über das Bewußtsein*, Vienna, 1879

— *Studien über die Assoziation der Vorstellungen*, Vienna, 1883

Strümpell, L., *Die Natur und Entstehung der Träume*, Leipzig, 1877

Stryk, M. von, 'Der Traum und die Wirklichkeit (nach C. Mélinand)', *Baltische Monatsschrift*, Riga, 1899, pp. 189–210

Stumpf, E. J. G., *Der Traum und seine Deutung*, Leipzig, 1899

Sully, J., 'Étude sur les rêves', *Rev. scientif.*, 1882, p. 385

— 'Les illusions des sens et de l'esprit', *Bibl. scientif. internat.*, vol. 62, Paris (German: 'Die Illusionen, eine psychol. Unters.', Leipzig, 1884)

— *Human mind*, London, 1892

— 'The dreams as a revelation', *Fortnightly Rev.*, March 1893
— 'Laws of dream fancy', *Cornhill Mag.*, vol. L, p. 540
— 'Dreams' article in *Encyclop. Brit.*, ninth edition

Summers, T. O., 'The physiology of dreaming', *Saint-Louis, clin.* 1895, VIII, 401–6.

Surbled, *Le rêve*, second edition, 1898
— 'Origine des rêves', *Rev. de quest. scient.*, 1895

Synesius, *Oneiromantik* (German by Krauß), Vienna, 1888

Tannery, M. P., 'Sur l'activité de l'esprit dans le rêve', *Rev. philos.*, nineteenth year, XXXVIII, pp. 630–34, 1894
— 'Sur les rêves des mathématiciens', *Rev. philos.*, 1898, I, p. 639
— 'Sur la paramnésie dans les rêves', *Rev. philos.*, 1898
— 'Sur la mémoire dans le rêve', *Revue philosophique*, XLV, 1898

Thiéry, A., 'Aristote et Psychologie physiologique du rêve', *Rev. nev. scol.*, 1896, III, 260–71

Thomayer, S., 'Sur la signification de quelques rêves', *Rev. neurol.*, no. 4, 1897
— 'A contribution to the pathology of dreams' (in Czech), Polyclinic of the Czech University in Prague, 1897

Tissié, Ph., 'Les rêves; rêves pathogènes et thérapeutiques; rêves photographiés', *Journ. de méd. de Bordeaux*, 1896, XXXVI
— *Les rêves, physiologie et pathologie*, 1898 (Bibliothèque de philosophie contemporaine) [Paris]

Titchener, 'Taste dreams', *Amer. J. of Psychology*, VI, 1895

Tonnini, 'Suggestione e sogni', *Arch. di psichiatr. antrop. crim.*, VIII, 1887

Tonsor, J. Heinrich, 'Disp. de vigilia, somno et somniis', *prop. Lucas*, Marpurgi, 1627

'Traum' article in *Allgemeine Enzyklopädie der Wissenschaft und Künste von Ersch und Gruber*

Tuke, Hack, 'Dreaming' in *Dict. of Psycholog. Med.*, 1892

Ullrich, M. W., *Der Schlaf und das Traumleben, Geisteskraft and Geistesschwäche*, third edition, Berlin, 1896

Unger, F., *Die Magie des Traumes als Unsterblichkeitsbeweis*, with a Foreword by C. du Prel, 'Okkultismus und Sozialismus', second edition, Münster, 1898

'Utility of dreams', *Edit. J. Comp. Neurol.*, Granville, 1893, III, 17–34

Vaschide, 'Recherches experim. sur les rêves', *Comptes rendus de l'acad. des sciences*, 17 July 1899

Vespa, B., 'I signi nei neuro- e psicopatici', *Bull. Soc. Lancisiana*, Rome, 1897

Vignoli, 'Von den Träumen, Illusionen und Halluzinationen', *Internationale wissenschaftliche Bibliothek*, vol. 47

Vischer, F. Th., 'Studien über den Traum', *Beilage z. allg. Ztg.*, 1876, nos. 105–7

Vold, J. Mourly, 'Einige Experimente über Gesichtsbilder im Traume', *Dritter internationaler Kongreß für Psychologie*, Munich, 1897, *Zeitschr. für Psychologie und Physiologie der Sinnesorgane*, XIII, 66–74

— *Expériences sur les rêves et en particulier sur ceux d'origine musculaire et optique*, Christiania, 1896 (review in *Revue philosophique*, XLII, 1896)

[Volkelt, J., *Die Traum-Phantasie*, Stuttgart, 1875]

Vykoukal, F. V., 'Concerning dreams and dream-interpretations' (in Czech), Prague, 1898

Wedel, R., 'Untersuchungen ausländischer Gelehrter über gew. Traumphänomene', *Beiträge zur Grenzwissenschaft*, 1899, pp. 24–77

Weed, [S.] and Hallam, F., 'A study of dream consciousness', *Americ. J. of Psychol.*, VII, no. 3, April 1896, pp. 405–11

Wehr, Hans, 'Das Unbewußte im menschlichen Denken', secondary modern upper school [*Oberrealschule*] programme in Klagenfurt, 1887

Weil, Alex, *La philosophie du rêve*, Paris

Wendt, K., 'Kriemhilds Traum', dissertation, Rostock, 1858

Weygandt, W., *Entstehung der Träume*, Leipzig, 1893

Wilks, S., 'On the nature of dreams', *Med. Mag. Lond.*, 1893–94, II, 597–606

Williams, H. S., 'The dream state and its psychic correlatives', *Americ. J. of Insanity*, 1891–92, vol. 48, 445–57

Woodworth, 'Note on the rapidity of dreams', *Psychol. Review*, IV, 1897, no. 5

Wundt, *Grundzüge der physiologischen Psychologie*, vol. 2, second edition, 1880

X, 'Ce qu'on peut rêver en cinq secondes', *Rev. sc.*, third series, I, XII, 30 October 1886

Zucarrelli, 'Pollutions nocturnes et épilepsie', *Bull. de la Soc. de méd., ment. de Belgique*, March 1895

B From the literature since 1900 [though the latest work cited dates from 1919]

Abraham, Karl, 'Traum und Mythos. Eine Studie zur Völkerpsychologie', *Schriften zur angew. Seelenkunde*, issue 4, Vienna and Leipzig, 1909
— 'Über hysterische Traumzustände', *Jahrbuch f. psychoanalyt. und psychopathol. Forschungen*, vol. II, 1910
— 'Sollen wir die Pat. ihre Träume aufschreiben lassen?', *Intern. Zeitschr. für ärztl. Ps.-A.*, I, 1913, p. 194
— 'Zur narzißtischen Bewertung der Exkretionsvorgänge im Traum und Neurose', *Internat. Zeitschr. f. Ps.-A.*, VI, 64

Adler, Alfred, 'Zwei Träume einer Prostituierten', *Zeitschrift f. Sexualwissenschaft*, 1908, no. 2
— 'Ein erlogener Traum', *Zentralbl. f. Psychoanalyse*, first year, 1910, issue 3
— 'Traum und Traumdeutung', ibid., III, 1912–13, p. 174

Amram, Nathan, *Sepher pithrôn chalômôth*, Jerusalem, 1901

Bianchieri, F., 'I sogni dei bambini di cinque anni', *Riv. di psicol.*, 8, 325–30

Betlheim and Hartmann, 'Über Fehlreaktionen [des Gedächtnisses] bei der Korsakoffschen Psychose', *Arch. f. Psychiatrie*, vol. 72, 1924

Bleuler, E., 'Die Psychoanalyse Freuds', *Jahrb. f. psychoanalyt. u. psychopatholog. Forschungen*, vol. II, 1910
— 'Träume mit auf der Hand liegender Deutung', *Münch. Med. Woch.*, sixtieth year, no. 47, 11 November 1913

Bloch, Ernst, 'Beitrag zu den Träumen nach Coitus interruptus', *Zentralbl. für Ps.-A.*, II, 1911–12, p. 276

Brewster, E. T., 'Dreams and forgetting. New discoveries in dream psychology', *McClure's Magazine*, October 1912

Brill, A. A., 'Dreams and their relation to the neurosis', *New York Medical Journ.*, 23 April 1910
— *Psychoanalysis, its theory and practical application*, Philadelphia and New York, 1912
— 'Hysterical dreamy states', *New York Med. Journ.*, 25 May 1912
— 'Artificial dreams and lying', *Journ. of Abn. Psych.*, vol. IX, p. 321
— 'Fairy tales as a determinant of dreams and neurotic symptoms', *New York Med. Journ.*, 21 March 1914

Brown, W., 'Freud's theory of dreams', *The Lancet*, 19 and 26 April 1913

Bruce, A. H., 'The marvels of dream analysis', *McClure's Magaz.*, November 1912

Burckhard, Max, 'Ein modernes Traumbuch', *Die Zeit*, 1900, nos. 275, 276

Busemann, A., 'Traumleben der Schulkinder', *Zeitschr. f. päd. Psychol.*, tenth year, 1909, 294–301

— 'Psychol. d. kindl. Traumerlebnisse', *Zeitschr. f. päd. Psychol.*, 1910, XI, p. 320

Claparède, E., 'Esquisse d'une théorie biologique du sommeil', *Arch. de Psychol.*, vol. IV, nos. 15–16, February–March 1905

— 'Rêve utile', *Arch. de Psychol.*, 9, 1910, 148

Coriat, I., 'Zwei sexual-symbolische Beispiele von Zahnarzt-Träumen', *Zentralbl. f. Ps.-A.*, III, 1913, p. 440

— 'Träume von Kahlwerden', *Int. Zeitschr. f. Ps.-A.*, II, p. 460

— *The meaning of dreams*, London (Heinemann; 'Mind and Health' series)

Delacroix, 'Sur la structure logique du rêve', *Rev. métaphys.*, November 1904

— 'Note sur la cohérence des rêves', *Rapp. et C. R. du 2. Congrès intern. de Philos.*, 556–60

Delage, 'La nature des images hynagogiques et le rôle des lueurs entoptiques dans le rêve', *Bull. de l'Instit. général psychol.*, 1903, pp. 235–47

Doglia, S., and Bianchieri, F., 'I sogni dei bambini di tre anni. L'inizio dell'attività onirica', *Contributi psicol.*, 1 [1910–11], 9

Eder, M. D., 'Freud's theory of dreams', *Transactions of the Psycho-Medic. Soc.*, London, vol. III, Part 3, 1912

— 'Augenträume', *Internat. Zeitschr. f. ärztl. Ps.-A.*, I, 1913, p. 157

Eeden, Frederik van, 'A study of dreams', *Proceedings of the Society for Psych. Research*, Part LXVII, vol. XXVI

Ellis, H., 'The logic of dreams', *Contemp. Rev.*, 98, 1910, 353–9

— 'The symbolism of dreams', *The Popular Science Monthly*, July 1910

— 'Symbolismen in den Träumen', *Zeitschr. f. Psychotherapie*, III, 1911, pp. 29–46

— *The World of Dreams*, London, 1911 (German translation by H. Kurella, Würzburg, 1911)

— 'The relation of erotic dreams to vesical dreams', *Journ. of abn. Psychol.*, VIII, 3, August–September 1913

Federn, Paul, 'Ein Fall von pavor nocturnus mit subjektiven Lichterscheinungen', *Internat. Zeitschr. f. ärztl. Ps.-A.*, I, 1913, issue 6

— 'Über zwei typische Traumsensationen', *Jahrb. f. Ps.-A.*, VI [1914], p. 89

— 'Zur Frage des Hemmungstraumes', *Internat. Zeitschr. f. Ps.-A.*, VI, p. 73

Ferenczi, S., 'Die psychologische Analyse der Träume', *Psychiatrisch-Neurologische Wochenschrift*, twelfth year, nos. 11–13, June 1910 (translated into English with the title 'The psychological analysis of dreams', in *The American Journal of Psychology*, April 1910)

— 'Symbolische Darstellung des Lust- und Realitätsprinzips im Ödipus-Mythos', *Imago*, I, 1912, p. 276

— 'Über lenkbare Träume', *Zentralbl. f. Ps.-A.*, II, 1911–12, p. 31

— 'Vergessen eines Symptoms und seine Aufklärung im Traume', *Internat. Zeitschr. f. Ps.-A.*, II, p. 384

— 'Affektvertauschung im Traume', *Internat. Zeitschr. f. Ps.-A.*, IV, p. 112

— 'Träume der Ahnungslosen', *Internat. Zeitschr. f. Ps.-A.*, IV, p. 208

— 'Pollution ohne orgastischen Traum und Orgasmus im Traum ohne Pollution', *Internat. Zeitschr. f. Ps.-A.*, IV, p. 187

Flournoy, 'Quelques rêves au sujet de la signification symbolique de l'eau et du feu', *Internat. Zeitschr. f. Ps.-A.*, VI, p. 328

Förster, M., 'Das lat.-altengl. Traumbuch', *Arch. f. d. Stud. d. n. Spr. und Lit.*, vol. 120, pp. 43ff., vol. 125, pp. 39–70, vol. 127, pp. 1ff.

— 'Mittelenglische Traumbücher', *Herrings Archiv*, 1911

Foucault, Marcel, *Le rêve. Études et observations*, Paris, 1906 (Bibl. de Philosophie contemporaine)

Friedjung, J. K., 'Traum eines sechsjährigen Mädchens', *Internat. Zeitschr. f. ärztl. Ps.-A.*, I, 1913, p. 71

Frink, H. W., 'Dreams and their analysis in relation to psychotherapy', *Med. Record*, 27 May 1911

— 'On Freud's theory of dreams', *Americ. Med.*, Burlington, New York, VI, pp. 652–61

— 'Dream and neurosis', *Interstate Med. Journ.*, 1915

Gincburg, Mira, 'Mitteilung von Kindheitsträumen mit spezielle Bedeutung', *Int. Zeitschr. f. ärztl. Ps.-A.*, I, 1913, p. 79

Gottschalk, 'Le rêve. D'après les idées du prof. Freud', *Archives de Neurol.*, 1912, no. 4

Gregory, J. C., 'Dreams as a by-product of waking activity', *Westm. Rev.*, London, 1911, vol. 175, pp. 561–7

Harnik, J., 'Gelungene Auslegung eines Traumes', *Zentralbl. f. Ps.-A.*, II, 1911–12, p. 417

Hitschmann, Ed., *Freuds Neurosenlehre. Nach ihrem gegenwärtigen Stande zusammenfassend dargestellt*, Vienna and Leipzig, 1911, second edition, 1913 (chapter V, 'Der Traum'). (English translation by C. R. Payne, New York, 1912)

— 'Ein Fall von Symbolik für Ungläubige', *Zentralbl. f. Ps.-A.*, I, 1910–11, p. 235

— 'Beiträge zur Sexualsymbolik des Traumes', ibid., p. 561

— 'Weitere Mitt. von Kindheitsträumen mit spez. Bedeutung', *Intern. Zeitschr. f. ärztl. Ps.-A.*, I, 1913, p. 476

— 'Goethe als Vatersymbol in Träumen', ibid., issue 6

— 'Über Träume Gottfried Kellers', *Internat. Zeitschr. f. Ps.-A.*, II, p. 41

— 'Weitere Mitteilung von Kindheitsträumen mit spezieller Bedeutung', *Internat. Zeitschr. f. Ps.-A.*, II, p. 31

— 'Über eine im Traum angekündigte Reminiszenz an ein sexuelles Jugenderlebnis', *Internat. Zeitschr. f. Ps.-A.*, V, p. 205

Hug-Hellmuth, H. von, 'Analyse eines Traumes eines 5½järigen Knaben', *Zentralbl. f. Ps.-A.*, II, 1911–12, pp. 122–7

— 'Kinderträume', *Internat. Zeitschr. f. ärztl. Ps.-A.*, I, 1913, p. 470

— 'Aus dem Seelenleben des Kindes', *Schr. z. angew. Seelenk.*, ed. Freud, issue 15, Vienna and Leipzig, 1913

— 'Ein Traum, der sich selber deutet', *Internat. Zeitschr. f. Ps.-A.*, III, p. 33

Iwaya, S., 'Dream-interpretation in Japan', *Far East*, 1902, p. 302

Jones, E., 'On the nightmare', *Americ. J. of Insanity*, January 1910

— 'The Oedipus-complex as an explanation of Hamlet's mystery: A study in motive', *American Journ. of Psychology*, January 1910, pp. 72–113 (German translation, 'Das Problem des Hamlet und der Ödipus-Komplex', *Schriften zur angew. Seelenkunde*, issue 10, 1912)

— 'Freud's theory of dreams', *American Journal of Psychology*, April 1910

— 'Remarks on Dr M. Prince's article: The mechanism and interp. of dreams', *Journ. of abn. Psychol.*, 1910–11, pp. 328–36

— 'Some instances of the influence of dreams on waking life', *The Journal of abnormal Psychology*, April–May 1911

— 'The relationship between dreams and psychoneurotic symptoms', *Americ. J. of Insanity*, vol. 68, no. 1, July 1911

— 'A forgotten dream', *J. of abn. Psychol.*, April–May 1912

— *Papers on Psycho-Analysis*, London, 1912

— 'Der Alptraum in seiner Beziehung zu gewissen Formen des mittelalterl. Aberglaubens', *Schriften z. angew. Seelenk.*, ed. Freud, issue 14, Leipzig and Vienna, 1912

— 'Die Theorie der Symbolik', *Internat. Zeitschr. f. Ps.-A.*, V [1919], p. 244

Jung, C. G., 'L'analyse des rêves', *L'Année psychologique*, vol. XV

— 'Assoziation, Traum und hysterische Symptom. Diagnostischer Assoziationsstudien', *Beiträge zur experimentellen Psychopathologie*, ed. Doz. C. G. Jung, vol. II, Leipzig, 1910 (no. VIII, pp. 31–66)

— 'Ein Beitrag zur Psychologie des Gerüchtes', *Zentralbl. für Psychoanalyse*, first year, 1910, issue 3

— 'Ein Beitrag zur Kenntnis des Zahlentraumes', ibid., 1910–11, pp. 567–72

— 'Morton Prince's *The Mechanism and Interpretation of Dreams*: Eine kritische Besprechung', *Jahrb. f. ps.-a.u. psychopathol. Forsch.*, III, 1911

Karpinska, L. [von], 'Ein Beitrag zur Analyse "sinnloser" Worte im Traume', *Internat. Zeitschr. f. Ps.-A.*, II [1914], p. 164

Kazodowsky, A., 'Zusammenhang von Träumen und Wahnvorstellungen', *Neurolog. Cbl.*, 1901, pp. 440–47, 508–14

Kostyleff, 'Freud et le problème des rêves', *Rev. philos.*, vol. 72, July–December 1911, pp. 491–522

Kraepelin, E., 'Über Sprachstörungen im Traume', *Psychol. Arbeiten*, 5, Leipzig, 1907

Lauer, Ch., 'Das Wesen des Traumes in der Beurteilung der talmudischen und rabbinischen Literatur', *Intern. Zeitschr. f. ärztl. Ps.-A.*, I, 1913, issue 5

Lehmann, *Aberglaube und Zauberei von den ältesten Zeiten bis in die Gegenwart* (German by Petersen), second enlarged edition, Stuttgart, 1908

Leroy, B., 'A propos de quelques rêves symboliques', *Journ. de psychol. Norm. et pathol.*, 5, 1908, pp. 358–65

— and Tobowolska, J., 'Mécanisme intellectuel du rêve', *Rev. philos.*, 1901, I, vol. 51, pp. 570–93

Löwinger, *Der Traum in der jüdischen Literatur*, Leipzig, 1908 ('Mitteilungen zur jüd. Volkskunde', tenth year, issues 1 and 2)

Maeder, Alphonse, 'Essai d'interprétation de quelques rêves', *Archives de Psychol.*, vol. VI, no. 24, April 1907

— 'Die Symbolik in den Legenden, Märchen, Gebräuchen and Träumen', *Psychiatrisch-Neurolog. Wochenschr.*, tenth year, 1908

— 'Zur Entstehung der Symbolik im Traum, in der Dementia praecox etc.', *Zentralblatt f. Ps.-A.*, I, 1910–11, pp. 383–9

— 'Über die Funktion des Traumes', *Jahrb. f. psychoanalyt. Forsch.*, IV, 1912

— 'Über das Traumproblem', ibid., V, 1913, p. 647

— 'Zur Frage der teleologischen Traumfunktion', ibid., p. 453

Marcinowski, J., 'Gezeichnete Träume', *Zentralbl. f. Ps.-A.*, II, 1911–12, pp. 490–518

— 'Drei Romane in Zahlen', ibid., pp. 619–38

Mitchell, A., *About dreaming, laughing and blushing*, London, 1905

Miura, K., '[Über] Japanische Traumdeuterei', *Mitt. d. deutsch. Ges. f. Natur- u. Völkerk. Ostasiens*, X, 291–306

Näcke, P., 'Über sexuelle Träume', *H. Groß' Archiv*, 1903, p. 307

— 'Der Traum als feinste Reagens f. d. Art d. sexuellen Empfindens', *Monatsschrift f. Krim.-Psychol.*, 1905

— 'Kontrastträume und spez. sexuelle Kontrastträume', *H. Groß' Archiv*, vol. 24, 1907, pp. 1–19

— 'Beiträge zu den sexuellen Träumen', *H. Groß' Archiv*, 29, 363ff.

— 'Die diagnostische und prognostische Brauchbarkeit der sex. Träume', *Ärztl. Sachv.-Ztg.*, 1911, no. 2

Negelein, J. von, *Der Traumschlüssel des Yaggaddeva*, Gießen, 1912 ('Relig. Gesch. Vers.', XI, 4)

Pachantoni, D., 'Der Traum als Ursprung von Wahnideen bei Alkohol-deliranten', *Zentralbl. f. Nervenheilk.*, thirty-second year, 1909, p. 796

Pear, T. H., 'The analysis of some personal dreams, with special reference to Freud's interpretation. Meeting at the British Assoc. for the Advancement of Science, Birmingham, 16–17 September 1913', *British Journ. of Psychol.*, VI, 3/4, February 1914

Pfister, Oskar, 'Wahnvorstellung und Schülerselbstmord. Auf Grund einer Traumanalyse beleuchtet', *Schweiz. Blätter für. Schulgesundheitspflege*, 1909, no. 1

— 'Kryptolalie, Kryptographie und unbewußtes Vexierbild bei Normalen', *Jahrb. f. ps.-a. Forsch.*, V, 1, 1913

Pötzl, Otto, 'Experimentell erregte Traumbilder in ihren Beziehungen zum indirekten Sehen', *Zeitschr. f. d. ges. Neurol. und Psych.*, vol. 37, 1917

Prince, Morton, 'The mechanism and interpretation of dreams', *The Journal of abnorm. Psych.*, October–November 1910

— 'The mechanism and interpr. of dreams; a reply to Dr Jones', *Journ. of abn. Psychol.*, 1910–11, pp. 337–53

Putnam, J. J., 'Aus der Analyse zweier Treppen-Träume', *Zentralbl. f. Ps.-A.*, II, 1911–12, p. 264

— 'Ein charakteristischer Kindertraum', ibid., p. 328

— 'Dream interpretation and the theory of psychoanalysis', *Journ. of abnorm. Psych.*, IX, no. 1, p. 36

Raalte, F. van, 'Kinderdroomen', *Het Kind*, 1912, Jan.

Rank, Otto, 'Der mythos von der Geburt des Helden', *Schr. z. angew. Seelenkunde*, issue 5, Vienna and Leipzig, 1909

— 'Beispiel eines verkappten Ödipustraumes', *Zentralblatt für Psychoanalyse*, first year, 1911

— 'Zum Thema der Zahnreizträume', ibid.

— 'Das Verlieren als Symptomhandlung. Zugleich ein Beitrag zum Verständnis der Beziehungen des Traumlebens zu den Fehlleistungen des Alltagslebens', ibid.

— 'Ein Traum, der sich selbst deutet', *Jahrbuch für psychoanalyt. und psychopathol. Forschungen*, vol. II, 1910

— 'Ein Beitrag zum Narzißmus', ibid., vol. III, 1911

— 'Fehlleistung und Traum', *Zentralbl. f. Ps.-A.*, II, 1911–12, p. 266

— 'Aktuelle Sexualregungen als Traumanlässe', ibid., pp. 596–602

— 'Die Symbolschichtung im Wecktraum und ihre Wiederkehr im mythischen Denken', *Jahrb. f. Ps.-A.*, IV, 1912

— *Das Inzestmotiv in Dichtung und Sage. Grundzüge einer Psychologie des dichterischen Schaffens*, Vienna and Leipzig, 1912

— 'Die Nacktheit in Sage und Dichtung. Eine ps.-a. Studie', *Imago*, II, 1912

— 'Eine noch nicht beschriebene Form des Ödipus-Traumes', *Intern. Zeitschr. f. ärztl. Ps.-A.*, I, 1913, p. 151

— 'Fehlhandlung und Traum', *Internat. Zeitschr. f. Ps.-A.*, III, p. 158

— 'Die Geburtsrettungsphantasie in Traum und Dichtung', *Internat. Zeitschr. f. Ps.-A.*, II, p. 43

— 'Ein gedichteter Traum', *Internat. Zeitschr. f. Ps.-A.*, III, p. 231

Rank, O. and Sachs, H., *Die Bedeutung der Psychoanalyse für die Geisteswissenschaften, Grenzfr. d. Nerven- und Seelenlebens* (ed. Löwenfeld), issue 93, Wiesbaden, 1913

Reik, Th., 'Zwei Träume Flauberts', *Zentralbl. f. Ps.-A.*, III, 1912–13, p. 223

— 'Kriemhilds Traum', ibid., II, p. 416

— 'Beruf und Traumsymbolik', ibid., p. 531

— 'Der Nacktheitstraum eines Forschungsreisenden', *Internat. Zeitschr. f. Ps.-A.*, II, p. 463

— 'Gotthilf Schuberts "Symbolik des Traumes"', *Internat. Zeitschr. f. Ps.-A.*, III, p. 295

— 'Völkerpsychologische Parallelen zum Traumsymbol des Mantels', *Internat. Zeitschr. f. Ps.-A.*, VI, p. 310

— 'Zum Thema: Traum und Traumwandeln', *Internat. Zeitschr. f. Ps.-A.*, VI, p. 311

Robitsek, Alfred, 'Die Analyse von Egmonts Traum', *Jahrb. für psychoanalyt. und psychopathol. Forschungen*, vol. II, 1910

— 'Die Stiege, Leiter, als sexuelles Symbol in der Antike', *Zentralbl. f. Ps.-A.*, I, 1910–11, p. 586

— 'Zur Frage der Symbolik in den Träumen Gesunder', ibid., II [1912], p. 340

Roheim, G., 'Die Urszene im Traume', *Internat. Zeitschr. f. Ps.-A.*, VI, p. 337

Sachs, Hanns, 'Zur Darstellungstechnik des Traumes', *Zentralbl. f. Ps.-A.*, I, 1910–11

— 'Ein Fall intensiver Traumentstellung', ibid., p. 588

— 'Traumdeutung und Menschenkenntnis', *Jahrb. f. Ps.-A.*, III, 1912, p. 568

— 'Ein Traum Bismarcks', *Intern. Zeitschr. f. ärztl. Ps.-A.*, I, 1913, issue 1

— 'Traumdarstellungen analer Weckreize', ibid., p. 489

— 'Das Zimmer als Traumdarstellung des Weibes', *Internat. Zeitschr. f. Ps.-A.*, II, p. 35.

— 'Ein absurder Traum', *Internat. Zeitschr. f. Ps.-A.*, III, p. 35

Sadger, J., 'Über das Unbewußte und die Träume bei Hebbel', *Imago*, June 1913

Schrötter, Karl, 'Experimentelle Träume', *Zentralbl. f. Ps.-A.*, 1912, p. 638

Schwarz, F., 'Traum und Traumdeutung nach "Abdalgani an Nabulusi"', *Zeitschr. d. deutsch. morgenl. Ges.*, vol. 67, 1913, issue III, pp. 473–93

Secker, F., 'Chines. Ansichten über den Traum', *Neue metaph. Rdschr.*, vol. 17, 1909–10, p. 101

Silberer, Herbert, 'Bericht über eine Methode, gewisse symbolische Halluzinationserscheinungen hervorzurufen und zu beobachten', *Jahrb.*, vol. I, 1909

— 'Phantasie und Mythos', ibid., vol. II, 1910

— 'Symbolik des Erwachens und Schwellensymbolik überh.', ibid., vol. III, 1912

— 'Über die Symbolbildung', ibid.

— 'Zur Symbolbildung', ibid., vol. IV, 1912

— 'Spermatozoenträume', ibid.

— 'Zur Frage der Spermatozoenträume', ibid.

Spielrein, S., 'Traum von "Pater Freudenreich"', *Intern. Zeitschr. f. ärztl. Ps.-A.*, I, 1913, p. 484

Spitteler, Karl, 'Mein frühesten Erlebnisse. I. Hilflos und sprachlos. Die Träume des Kindes', *Südd. Monatsh.*, October 1913

Stärke, August, 'Ein Traum, der das Gegenteil einer Wuncherfüllung zu verwirklichen schien, zugleich ein Beispiel eines Traumes, der von einem anderen Traum gedeutet wird', *Zentralbl. f. Ps.-A.*, II, 1911–12, p. 86

— 'Traumbeispiele', *Internat. Zeitschr. f. Ps.-A.*, II, p. 381

Stärke, Johann, 'Neue Traumexperimente in Zusammenhang mit älteren und neueren Traumtheorien', *Jahrb. f. Ps.-A.*, V, 1913, p. 233

Stegmann, Marg., 'Darstellung epileptischer Anfälle im Traum', *Intern. Zeitschr. f. ärztl. Ps.-A.*, I, 1913

— 'Ein Vexiertraum', ibid., p. 486

Stekel, Wilhelm, 'Beiträge zur Traumdeutung', *Jahrbuch für psychoanalytische und psychopatholog. Forschungen*, vol. I, 1909

— *Nervöse Angstzustände und ihre Behandlung*, Vienna–Berlin, 1908, second edition, 1912

— *Die Sprache des Traumes. Eine Darstellung der Symbolik und Deutung des Traumes in ihren Beziehungen zur kranken und gesunden Seele für Ärzte und Psychologen*, Wiesbaden, 1911

— *Die Träume der Dichter*, Wiesbaden, 1912

— 'Eine prophetischer Nummerntraum', *Zentralbl. f. Ps.-A.*, II, 1911–12, pp. 128–30

— 'Fortschritte der Traumdeutung', *Zentralbl. f. Ps.-A.*, III, 1912–13, pp. 154, 426

— 'Darstellung der Neurose im Traum', ibid., p. 26

Swoboda, Hermann, *Die Perioden des menschlichen Organismus*, Vienna and Leipzig, 1904

Tausk, V., 'Zur Psychologie der Kindersexualität', *Intern. Zeitschr. f. ärztl. Ps.-A.*, I, 1913, p. 444

— 'Zwei homosexuelle Träume', *Internat. Zeitschr. f. Ps.-A.*, II, p. 36

— 'Ein Zahlentraum', *Internat. Zeitschr. f. Ps.-A.*, II, p. 39

Tfinkdji, Joseph, Abbé, 'Essai sur les songes et l'art de les interpréter (onirocritie) en Mésopotamie', *Anthropos*, VIII, 2/3, March–June 1913

Tobowolska, Justine, 'Étude sur les illusions de temps dans les rêves du sommeil normal', thesis, Paris, 1900

Vaschide, N., *Le sommeil et les rêves*, Paris, 1911 (Bibl. de Philos. scient., 66), with bibliography of the same author's many other works on dream and sleep.

— and Piéron, *La psychol. du rêve au point de vue medical*, Paris, 1902

Vold, J. Mourly, *Über den Traum. Experimentell-psychologische Untersuchungen* (ed. O. Klemm), vol. I, Leipzig, 1910 (vol. II, 1912)

Weiss, Edoardo, 'Totemmaterial im Traume', *Internat. Zeitschrift. f. Ps.-A.*, II, p. 159

Weiss, Karl, 'Ein Pollutionstraum', *Internat. Zeitschrift f. Ps.-A.*, VI, p. 343

Weygandt, W., 'Beitr. z. Psychologie des Traumes', *Philos. Studien*, vol. 20, 1902, pp. 456–86

Wiggam, A., 'A contribution to the data of dream psychology', *Pedagogical Seminary*, June 1909

Winterstein, Alfr. von, 'Zum Thema: "Lenkbare Träume"', *Zentralbl. f. Ps.-A.*, II, 1911–12, p. 290

Wulff, M., 'Ein interessanter Zusammenhang von Traum, Symbolhandlung und Krankheitssymptom', *Internat. Zeitschr. f. ärztl. Ps.-A.*, I, 1913, issue 6